MANAGEMENT

HOUGHTON MIFFLIN COMPANY

Boston   Toronto

Dallas   Geneva, Illinois   Palo Alto   Princeton, New Jersey

**FIFTH
EDITION**

..............MANAGEMENT

Robert Kreitner

Arizona State University

Dedicated with lots of love to the three wonderful ladies of my life: Margaret, Mom Kreitner, and Mom Sova.

Photo Credits

Cover photograph of the Maine Maritime Academy, Winton Scott Architects; Photographed by Brian Vanden Brink.

Part 1 opener: p. 2, Houston Industries Incorporated/Bryan Smothers Photography. **Chapter 1:** p. 8, Courtesy of Merrill Lynch & Co., Inc.; p. 15 John Madere; p. 20, Diamond Shamrock, Inc.; p. 27, *FORTUNE,* "© 1990 The Time Inc. Magazine Company. All rights reserved." **Chapter 2:** *Photo credits continue on page C1*

Senior Sponsoring Editor: Patrick F. Boles
Senior Development Editor: Paula Kmetz
Project Editor: Susan Westendorf
Design Coordinator: Patricia Mahtani
Production Coordinator: Renée Le Verrier/Jean E. Levitt
Senior Manufacturing Coordinator: Priscilla J. Bailey
Marketing Manager: Mary Jo Conrad/Diane L. McOscar

Printed in the U.S.A.

Library of Congress Catalog Card Number 91-71978

ISBN: 0-395-47290-3

BCDEFGHI-D-98765432

Contents

2

3

4

PART TWO
Planning and Decision Making 139

5

7

10

• •

11

· ·

14

· ·

15

Managing Change and Conflict   485

18

• •

PART SIX

Expanding Horizons in Management 625

19

Preface

Today's managers face immense and exciting challenges. A global economy, increased work force diversity, and calls for more ethical conduct promise to keep things interesting. As trustees of society's precious human, material, and financial resources, today's and tomorrow's managers hold the key to a better world. A solid grounding in management is essential to successfully guiding large or small, profit or not-for-profit organizations through these rapidly-changing times. *Management,* Fifth Edition, represents an important first step toward managerial success. It is a comprehensive, up-to-date, and highly readable introduction to management theory, research, and practice. This fifth edition is the culmination of my twenty years in the management classroom; its style and content have been shaped by interaction with hundreds upon hundreds of students, instructors, and reviewers. Organized according to a time-tested functional/process framework, *Management,* Fifth Edition, integrates classical and modern concepts with a rich array of real-world examples and cases.

Structural Changes

A tighter topical integration has been achieved with the following changes. Social responsibility and ethics are given up-front treatment in Chapter 4, to serve as a vital context for the entire book. Personal values are now discussed as ethical anchors in Chapter 4. The discussion of organizational cultures has been moved forward to Chapter 8. Quality control circles and self-managed teams are discussed in conjunction with participative management in Chapter 12. Group dynamics and teamwork are now covered together in Chapter 13. Conflict and change are now discussed in the same chapter, Chapter 15. Included in Chapter 18 is expanded discussion of quality control. Theory Z has been moved to the discussion of comparative management in Chapter 19. Small business management, entrepreneurship, and public-sector management are given special treatment in Appendix A. Career and stress management have been moved to Appendix B.

A Fresh New Design

A stimulating photo/art program and a disciplined design make the material in this edition more visual, accessible, and interesting. Color photographs of managers in action and organizational life visually extend important concepts and techniques described in the text. To make the book come alive for the reader, photo captions provide necessary detail about real-name people in real-name organizations. Four types of boxed features provide instructive and interesting coverage of topics important to today's managers. They include The World of Management, Managers in Action, Management Ethics, and Insights & Issues.

Many New Topics

Based on feedback from instructors and students who used the previous edition, and reflecting the latest trends in management, many new topics have been added. Among them are learning about management from the "school of hard knocks," managing diversity, sixteen ethical issues for modern managers, ethics training, speed as a strategic competitive advantage, behavioral/perceptual decision traps, organizational values, the shape of tomorrow's organizations, a critique of employee testing techniques, ten principles for dealing with AIDS in the workplace, a contingency model for selecting communication media, discussion of the Malcolm Baldrige National Quality Award, goal setting as a motivational tool, pros and cons of ten different employee compensation plans, self-managed teams, cross-functional teams, team effectiveness criteria, expanded treatment of trust, a new list of influence tactics from recent research, Vroom/Yetton/Jago's updated decision model of leadership, transformational leadership, Nadler/Tushman's new typology of organizational change, seven-stage model for individual reaction to change, concurrent control, performance pyramid for strategic control, executive reality checks, waste reduction, activity-based costing, up-to-date discussion of personal computers and computer networks, executive information systems, concurrent quality control, multimedia and tablet computers, five characteristics of service operations, defining and improving service quality, five service quality criteria, global corporations, high- and low-context cultures, cross-cultural differences in time/interpersonal space/agreements/language/and religion, an international contingency model of leadership, entrepreneurship, seven basic career strategies, and ergonomics and stress.

To make room for this wide variety of new topics, outdated material and unnecessary wording were studiously identified and eliminated. The net result is an efficient and very up-to-date introduction to the field of management.

An International Management Thrust

A burgeoning global economy and the need for today's and tomorrow's managers to think in international terms have elevated international management to a new level of importance within the field. *Management,* Fifth Edition, meets the demand for comprehensive coverage of international topics with an up-to-date chapter on international management (Chapter 19) and seventeen interesting boxed features titled The World of Management. International examples can be found throughout the text. More than one-third of the chapter-opening and chapter-closing cases have international themes. Countries and regions featured in the international boxes, in-text examples, and cases include Canada, Hungary, Japan, Great Britain, Scotland, Soviet Union, Poland, Asia, Sweden, Brazil, Australia, Mexico, Persian Gulf, France, and Switzerland.

A Management Ethics Thrust

Business, religious, and community leaders alike have called for more ethical conduct in the managerial ranks. Accordingly, business ethics is given close attention in Chapter 4. Comprehensive treatment of ethics is achieved by weaving boxed features, titled Management Ethics, into the text. Tough ethical issues are addressed, such as environmental degradation, white-collar crime, business as a religion, employee selection trickery, sexist communication, executive pay, organizational politics, expressing anger, Pentagon waste, electronic supervision, and kickbacks and bribery.

A Managing Diversity Thrust

Chapter 3 details how dramatically work force demographics will change between now and the year 2000. An older, increasingly female, and more racially, ethnically, and culturally diverse work force has moved the topic of managing diversity to the front burner. Managing diversity is defined and framed in Chapter 3. The relationship between affirmative action and managing diversity is discussed in Chapter 10. The opening case for Chapter 10, Managing Diversity Fits at Levi Strauss, is an inspiring example of what can be done by a determined company that values the rich diversity of its employees and customers. Techniques for motivating a diverse work force are discussed in Chapter 12. Women, minority, and physically-challenged managerial role models can be found throughout the book to underscore the fact that management is for everyone and anyone who is willing to accept the challenge.

New Cases

All but a few of the cases at the beginning and end of each chapter are new to this edition. The cases were researched and written exclusively for *Management,* Fifth Edition, thus ensuring a tight conceptual linkage to the textual discussion. Among the large and small, domestic and foreign, profit and not-for-profit, and manufacturing and service organizations featured in the cases are the following: General Electric, Mrs. Fields, Levi Strauss, Hyatt, Asea Brown Boveri, Chicago Lyric Opera, Volvo, Microsoft, Lincoln Electric, McDonald's, Apple, American

Express, British Petroleum, W.L. Gore, Southwest Airlines, the Body Shop, Marriott, General Motors, Hershey, SAS, Disney, and Boeing.

Video Skill Builders

Following each of the first five parts is a unique video instruction tool, called Video Skill Builders. Through an exclusive arrangement with a major training film producer, Salenger Films, Inc., five relevant management training videos have been made available for adopters of this text. A topical outline, and discussion questions in each Video Skill Builder ensure an instructive fit between the videos and the textual material. The idea is to give readers an alternative mode of instruction for key topics: lessons from Hawthorne on managing people, creativity, listening, leadership, and total quality control. Emphasis in this video series is clearly on skill development and "how to do it."

Complete Coverage of AACSB Topics

Though concepts have been expanded, relocated, or refined according to new directions in the discipline, the fifth edition continues to offer major treatment of the following AACSB-recommended topics:

- International management.
- Social responsibility and business ethics.
- Strategic management, with special emphasis on implementation and speed.
- Teams and teamwork.
- The changing environment of management—social, political-legal, economic, and technological dimensions.
- Management history.
- Service organizations and service quality.
- Operations management, productivity, and total quality control.
- Staffing and human resource management.
- Organizational cultures.
- Change and conflict.
- Leadership and communication.

Successful Pedagogical Structure

As with the previous edition, pedagogical features of the main text, along with a set of complete, instructive accompanying ancillaries, make *Management,* Fifth Edition, a complete and valuable teaching/learning tool—one that will satisfy the needs of both students and professors. This is demonstrated by the following:

- Chapter objectives at the beginning of each chapter focus the reader's attention on key concepts.
- Chapter objectives are repeated at appropriate locations, in the text margin, to pace the reader's progress.
- Key terms are emphasized in bold, where first defined, repeated in marginal notes, and listed at the close of each chapter to reinforce important terminology and concepts.
- Clear, comprehensive chapter summaries refresh the reader's memory of important material.
- Cases at the beginning and end of each chapter provide a real-world context for handling management problems.
- Numerous in-text exercises hold the reader's interest and provide opportunities for self-evaluation.
- Ten discussion questions following each chapter enhance understanding by helping the reader personalize the textual material.
- Video Skill Builders at the end of Parts I through V foster experiential learning by providing how-to-do-it instruction on key managerial skills.
- An end-of-text glossary (with chapter annotations) of all key terms provides a handy reference for the study of management.
- A comprehensive study guide by Kreitner and Sova provides additional review and reinforcement of all topics covered in the text. Each chapter in the study guide includes a review of chapter objectives, a chapter summary, and terms to understand. A chapter self-quiz of true/false, multiple-choice, matching, sentence completion, and discussion questions follows, with complete answers at the end of the study guide.
- A computerized management game called *Manager: A Simulation,* Second Edition, prepared by Dr. Jerald R. Smith, University of Louisville, offers students the chance to act as managers themselves; the game simulates a business environment in which student management teams produce and market a product. Players make various management decisions and learn from the positive or negative outcomes.

Acknowledgements

Literally hundreds of people, including colleagues, students, and relatives, have contributed in countless ways to the five editions of this book. For me, this project has been a dream come true; it is amazing where life's journey leads when you have a clear goal, the support of many good people, and a bone-deep belief in the concept of continuous improvement. Whether critical or reinforcing, everyone's suggestions and recommendations have been helpful and greatly appreciated. While it is impossible to acknowledge every contributor here, some key people need to be identified and sincerely thanked. I particularly appreciate the help and thoughtful comments of my colleague and good friend Professor Angelo Kinicki. The Management 301 team at Arizona State University—John Lea, Angelo Kinicki, and George Bohlander—have been very supportive of my work through the years; I thank them for that as well as for their dedication to good teaching. Other colleagues in the Department of Management at ASU deserve thanks for responding so cheerfully and helpfully when I charged into their offices time and again over the years seeking ideas, materials, citations, and moral support. I am grateful for the cornerstone reviews of earlier editions by Professors Jack L. Mendleson and Angelo Kinicki. Sincere thanks also to Maria Muto for her outstanding and creative work on the Instructor's Resource Manual and to my brother, Clint Kreitner, President, Reading Rehabilitation Hospital, for his wise observations from the managerial firing line.

Warmest thanks are also extended to the following colleagues who have provided valuable input for this edition by serving as content advisers or manuscript reviewers:

Steve Bradley
Austin Community College

Irvin Mason
Herkimer County Community
College

John Hall
University of Florida

Raymond Alie
Western Michigan University

Roger Lee
Salt Lake Community College

Deborah Dwyer
University of Toledo

David Chown
Mankato State University

Jane Shuping
Western Piedmont Community
College

Allen H. Pike
Ferrum College

Clyde A. Painter
Ohio Northern University

Gary Ernst
North Central College

Marie Burkhead
University of Southwest Louisiana

Thomas Duda
S.U.N.Y. Canton Tech College

Eva Beer Aronson
Interboro Institute

Molly Burke
Rosary College

George M. Coggins
High Point College

R.B. Barton Jr.
Murray State University

John T. Samaras
Central State University

Linda Hatton
University of Wisconsin—Oshkosh

Debra Miller
Ashland Community College

John Valentine
Kean College of New Jersey

Darlene Orlov
New York University

Ellen Frank
Southern Connecticut State
University

Seymour Barcun
St. Frances College

Benjamin Abramowitz
University of Central Florida

Gus Petrides
Borough of Manhattan Community
College

Stanley Welaish
Kean College of New Jersey

Kathryn Severance
Viterbo College

Lynn J. Richardson
Fort Lewis College

Stephen L. Allen
Northeast Missouri State University

Jacqueline Stow
McMurry University

Bob Bowles
Cecils College

Richard A. Davis
Rosary College

G. David Sivak
Westmoreland County Community
College

Robert W. Risteen
Ohio University—Chillicothe

Glenn M. Blair
Baldwin-Wallace College

Ty Westergaard
Lincoln University

Cathy Jensen
University of Nebraska—Lincoln

C.L. Scott III
Indiana University NW—Gary

Richard A. Wells
Aiken Technical College

Mick Stahler
Stautzenberger College

Joe F. Walenciak
John Brown University

Velta Kelly
University of Cincinnati

J. Stephen Phillips
Ohio University—Chillicothe

Margo Underwood
Brunswick College

Douglas R. Anderson
Ashland University

Andrew J. Batchelor
Ohio University—Chillicothe

Tim Donahue
Sioux Falls College

Roger Best
Louisiana College

John Nagy
Cleary College

Gerald D. Biby
Sioux Falls College

Dorothy Wallace
Chowan College

Roger C. Schoenfeldt
Murray State University

Bob Lower
Minot State University

Wendell J. Roye
Franklin Pierce College

Ann McClure
Ft. Hays State University

Charles Lee
Baldwin-Wallace College

Elaine Adams Casmus
Chowan College

Ralph Roberts
University of West Florida

Sue Granger
Jacksonville State University

Timothy Wiedman
Ohio University—Lancaster

Phyllis Goodman
College of DuPage

Jerome Hufnagel
Horry Georgetown Tech Ed Center

Mary Khalili
Oklahoma City University

Jacque Foust
University of Wisconsin—River Falls

Brian R. Hinrichs
Illinois Wesleyan University

Teshome Abebe
University of Southern Colorado

James L. Mann
Ashland Community College

Peggy Miller
Ohio University—Athens

Janice Feldbauer
Macomb Community College

Thomas Daymont
Temple University—Philadelphia

Fredric L. Mayerson
CUNY—Kingsboro Community
College

Herbert S. Parker
Kean College of New Jersey

My working relationship with Houghton Mifflin Company over the years has been productive and enjoyable. Many Houghton Mifflin Company people have contributed enormously to this project. I would like to offer a hearty thank you to everyone by acknowledging the following key contributors: Dennis Albrecht, David Barton, Patrick Boles, Tom Clarke, Bernice Colt, Mary Jo Conrad, Mary Dalton Hoffman, Joanne Dauksewicz, Nader Darehshori, Nancy Doherty-Schmitt, Liz Hacking, Julie Hogenboom, Ed Kelly, Paula Kmetz, Jean Levitt, Diane McOscar, Pat Murphree, and Susan Westendorf. Other key contributors who deserve special recognition and thanks are Brock Dethier, Janet Theurer, Catherine Johnson, and Melody English.

The discussion of mentoring in Chapter 14 is dedicated once again with respect and appreciation to Coach Don Watchorn and Professor Fred Luthans, two mentors who headed me in constructive directions when I dearly needed it. To Margaret, my best friend and hiking buddy, thanks for being with me *every* step of the way. Oh yes, I also want to thank my cat Amaranth who faithfully sits atop my computer and supervises my every move.

Finally, I would like to thank the thousands of introductory management students I have had the pleasure of working with through the years for teaching me a great deal about tomorrow's managers. Best wishes for a rewarding career in management.

R.K.

MANAGEMENT

PART I

The Management Challenge

Part I provides a background for what lies ahead by defining the management process, reviewing management history, exploring the changing environment of management, and discussing management's broader social and ethical responsibilities. In Chapter 1, the term *management* is formally defined and the practice of management is discussed from different perspectives. A formula for managerial success is provided for those who wish to set their sights on a career in management in large or small businesses or the public sector. Chapter 2 amounts to a brief history of management thought. Modern-day management concepts and approaches make more sense when one appreciates how they have evolved through the years. Because management is not practiced in a vacuum, attention turns in Chapter 3 to the social, political-legal, economic, and technological environments of management. Those who anticipate and prepare for inevitable environmental changes will tend to be the more successful managers. Chapter 4 defines corporate social responsibility and outlines alternative strategies for dealing with it. The topic of business ethics is discussed relative to personal values, and ways to encourage ethical conduct are explored.

1

The Nature of
Management

● ● ● ● ● ● ● ● ● ● ● ● ● ●

*The only choice for an
institution is between
management and
mismanagement. . . .
Whether it is being
done right or not will
determine largely
whether the enterprise
will survive and
prosper or decline
and ultimately fail.*

PETER F. DRUCKER

CHAPTER OBJECTIVES

When you finish studying this chapter, you should
be able to

● Define the term *management* and explain the
managerial significance of the terms *effectiveness* and *efficiency*.

● Contrast the functional and role approaches to
explaining what managers do.

● Summarize the ten facts of managerial life.

● Explain the basic formula for managerial success ($S = A \times M \times O$).

● Explain how managers learn to manage.

● Describe the United States' dual productivity
problem.

● ●

GE Tries to Light Up Eastern Europe

When the Berlin Wall came down in 1990 and revolutions transformed Eastern Europe, thousands of American companies began looking for profitable business ventures in this newly opened territory. General Electric, which had actually begun the search for an Eastern European subsidiary in 1987, was one of the first to commit to a major investment on the other side of what used to be the "Iron Curtain": GE paid $150 million for a controlling interest in Hungary's Tungsram Company. Thus began an experiment that will reveal to the rest of the world how well American capital and management techniques can transform one of the relics of communism.

The transformation will not be easy. GE, the world's second-largest light bulb maker, after Philips, certainly knows Tungsram's business—light bulbs. But many conditions in the Hungarian company would seem alien to any American manager. Some of Tungsram's factories date back to the turn of the century. The company still keeps track of its accounts with pencil and paper and employs 150 people just to stuff cash into 17,000 pay envelopes each month. Years of being a state-run industry led the company and its employees to adopt strange habits. Some workers lined cartons of bulbs with rocks so they could be paid extra for the volume they shipped. In addition, the company's warehouses were packed with unsold, and in some cases unsalable, products shipped there because company executives got bonuses for moving the goods along. Perhaps most appalling from an American manager's point

of view, Tungsram's 18,000 workers regularly produced about one-seventh as much as their American counterparts.

To deal with such unique problems, GE needed someone both familiar with Hungarian culture and schooled in American management techniques and the company's philosophy. It found the perfect chief executive in George Varga. He had been working for GE for 28 years after fleeing his native Hungary as a college student in 1956 and earning an economics degree from Stanford. To assist in his mammoth undertaking, Varga passed over the kind of cocky, arrogant young managers for which GE is known. Instead, he chose veterans he thought would be sensitive to the particular needs of a company trying to achieve a "cultural marriage."

The new managers had to work on many fronts at once. They had to explain to Hungarian engineers what profit is and why the company was interested in it. When they discovered that one of Tungsram's assembly lines was breaking one outdoor light for every six that it produced, they had to search GE's American plants to find a production engineer who had worked—years ago—on the machines Tungsram was using. (They found one in Cleveland.) And, of course, they had to start pouring capital into Tungsram to upgrade its equipment.

The trickiest part of the company's transformation has been dealing with the Hungarian labor force. One reason American companies are so eager to set up operations in Eastern Europe is that the cost of labor there is so low. Hungarian workers typically earn only about one-tenth as much as their American counterparts. Labor, which eats up about one-half of every dollar spent producing bulbs in the United States, accounts for only about one-quarter of the cost of making a Hungarian light bulb. However, although Hungarian workers aren't used to making much money, they are also not used to losing their jobs. Fear of such losses under the new American leadership quickly eroded morale in some Tungsram factories.

Even though American managers assigned to trim costs in an American factory often look first at cutting the labor force, GE's Tungsram managers are moving cautiously. They hoped to reduce the work force by about 2,000 during the first year, simply through attrition and early retirement. After that, the going will become more difficult. Tungsram's union is already asking for a 30 percent pay raise in return for higher productivity, and the company is anxious not to alienate workers by appearing insensitive to their need for job security. GE's managers are looking to cut other costs—particularly those associated with materials—to make Tungsram's factories more efficient. And they hope they can quickly convince Hungarian workers—unlike many American workers who treat the idea with skepticism—that what's good for the company (like increased worker productivity) is also good for the workers.

General Electric's head start over many of its American rivals in Eastern Europe does not mean that it can afford to spend years tinkering with its Hungarian experiment. The big market for Tungsram's products is Western Europe, where GE has commanded only a 3 percent market share. Other companies are moving just as aggressively to grab a share of the European market. In fact, one reason GE is focusing on Europe is that Philips, a Dutch company that is the world's largest light producer, recently bought Poland's leading light bulb maker and has even taken bites out of GE's American market share.

Every company with a stake in Europe must plan for the changes that will surely follow the elimination of the European Community's trade barriers in 1992. This major step toward the formation of a truly global economy will undoubtedly change many of the trading relationships in Europe and give large, established companies an edge. Some observers think GE should prepare for these changes by concentrating on what Tungsram has always done well— selling low-cost light bulbs. GE, however, has other ideas. Tungsram already makes headlamps good enough to be used by Mercedes and BMW, and GE hopes through investments in equipment and advertising to concentrate on the more modern, high-tech end of the light bulb market. Whatever the results of GE's experiment, other American companies will be watching closely to see what they can learn about how to export American capitalism successfully to Eastern Europe.

In our increasingly complex and rapidly changing world, intelligent management is needed more than ever before. Many difficult and worrisome problems have emerged in recent years, and they will not go away by themselves. Modern managers face a wide variety of pressures and challenges. Adequately informed and competent managers must help us move ahead by seeing our problems as opportunities, not obstacles. Exciting and progressive things can happen when managers turn obstacles into constructive and socially responsible opportunities. Careless mismanagement, however, can lead to unthinkable consequences. The

U.S. space program, for example, has demonstrated that effective management and tragic mismanagement are two sides of the same thin coin.

Neil Armstrong's walk on the moon on July 20, 1969, a dramatic testimony to effective management, demonstrated that systematically managed technology and resources can extend our reach to unbelievable limits. The 500,000-mile round trip of *Apollo 11* required eighty-eight major steps, and the failure of even a single step could have destroyed the mission or cost the lives of the crew. The mission was successful. As the largest peacetime program ever undertaken, it amounted to an incredible investment of talent and money. Construction of the *Apollo* rockets, spacecraft, and support equipment required the efforts of 20,000 industrial contractors and a total of 400,000 people. The final price tag for the *Mercury, Gemini,* and *Apollo* programs was over $25 billion.[1] Reviewing the success of his *Apollo* executive group, made up of the chief executive officers of the U.S. industrial firms that contributed to America's moon-landing effort, Dr. George Mueller saw "no black magic in what they did—only determined management."[2]

Unfortunately, *Apollo 11* proved to be a hard act to follow. On January 28, 1986, onlookers were horrified as the space shuttle *Challenger* exploded moments after liftoff, killing all seven crew members. Subsequent investigation uncovered more than just a mechanical problem:

> *Within days the mechanical problem was located: a joint on one of* Challenger's *two solid rocket boosters had failed. But the root cause of the tragedy ran deeper. A presidential commission, headed by former Secretary of State William Rogers, discovered NASA [National Aeronautics and Space Administration] itself was deeply flawed. Far from representing the best of American know-how, the twelve-member commission found, NASA had become a bureaucracy that had lost its way. Before the first shuttle was launched, the agency had known of the fatal seal problem but had buried it under a blizzard of paper while permitting schedule-conscious managers to keep the orbiters flying. In retrospect, it began to seem, the* Challenger *tragedy was all but inevitable.*[3]

Since the *Challenger* disaster, NASA has become the brunt of criticism and jokes as it stumbles from one misadventure to another. In one such instance, amid a flurry of scrubbed launches, NASA put the $1.5 billion Hubble space telescope into orbit in 1990, only later realizing that the telescope was out of focus because a final end-to-end quality check was deemed too costly to justify.[4]

How could NASA go from a maker of magic to a fumbling bureaucracy in a few short years? The subject matter of this book—management versus mismanagement—suggests many possible explanations.

Effective management is the key to a better world, but mismanagement squanders our resources and jeopardizes our well-being. Every manager, regardless of level or scope of responsibility, is either part of the solution or part of the problem. Management or mismanagement—the choice is yours. A basic knowledge of management theory, research, and practice will help prepare you for productive and gainful employment in a highly organized world in which virtually everything is managed.

Merrill Lynch, a well-known investment firm, consistently ranks number one in its field. When other Wall Street firms were wracked with scandal and bankruptcies, Merrill Lynch's reputation for high ethical standards remained intact. These outcomes are not due to luck; they grew from a tradition of strong management that emphasizes technical ability, teamwork, ethics, trust, and rewards for results.

● ● ● ● ● ● ● ● ● ● ● ● ● ● ● ● ●
Define the term *management* and explain the managerial significance of the terms *effectiveness* and *efficiency*.

management the process of working with and through others to achieve organizational objectives in a changing environment

Management Defined

We now need to define management, in order to highlight the importance, relevance, and necessity of studying it. **Management** is the process of working with and through others to achieve organizational objectives in a changing environment. Central to this process is the effective and efficient use of limited resources.

Five components of this definition require closer examination: (1) working with and through others, (2) achieving organizational objectives, (3) balancing effectiveness and efficiency, (4) making the most of limited resources, and (5) coping with a changing environment (see Figure 1.1).

Working with and Through Others

Management is, above all else, a social process. Many collective purposes bring individuals together—building cars, providing emergency health care, publishing books, and on and on. But in all cases, managers are responsible for getting things done by working with and through others.

Aspiring managers who do not interact well with others hamper their careers, as a study of twenty successful managers and twenty-one "derailed" managers demonstrated. In this study, managers were considered to be derailed if they did not live up to their peers' and superiors' initially high expectations. In contrast to their successful colleagues, the derailed managers were found to have been

1. Insensitive to others. They had an abrasive, intimidating, bullying style.

2. Cold, aloof, and arrogant.

3. Guilty of a betrayal of trust (by not accomplishing stated intentions).
4. Overly ambitious. They tended to think of the next job and to play politics.
5. Having specific performance problems with the business.
6. Overmanaging. They were unable to delegate or build a team.
7. Unable to staff effectively.
8. Unable to think strategically.
9. Unable to adapt to a boss with a different style.
10. Overdependent on an advocate or mentor.[5]

Significantly, all but two of these shortcomings, numbers 5 and 8, are directly related to working effectively with and through others. People—whether superiors, peers, or subordinates—can make or break your career in management.

Achieving Organizational Objectives

An objective is a target to be strived for and, one hopes, attained. Like individuals, organizations are usually more successful when their activities are guided by challenging, yet achievable, objectives. From an individual perspective, scheduling a course load becomes more systematic and efficient when a student sets an objective, such as graduating with a specific degree by a given date.

FIGURE 1.1 • Key Aspects of the Management Process

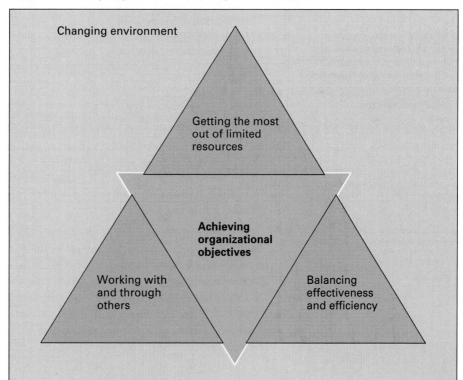

Although personal objectives are typically within the reach of individual effort, organizational objectives or goals always require collective action. Consider for a moment how Motorola has built its reputation for world-class product quality.

The corporate goal is to achieve a quality standard by 1992 equivalent to what the statisticians and industrial engineers call Six Sigma, which means six standard deviations from a statistical performance average. In plain English, Six Sigma translates into 3.4 defects per million opportunities, or production that is 99.99966 percent defect free.[6]

Mobilizing Motorola's employees and resources around this incredible objective was an enormous task. New equipment had to be purchased and installed, work practices had to be updated, and people had to be extensively retrained. Such complex collective action necessitates systematic management, and organizational objectives give purpose and direction to the management process. Organizational objectives also serve later as measuring sticks for performance. Without organizational objectives, the management process, like a trip without a specific destination, would be aimless and wasteful.

Balancing Effectiveness and Efficiency

effectiveness a central element in the process of management that entails achieving a stated organizational objective

efficiency a central element in the process of management that balances the amount of resources used to achieve an objective against what was actually accomplished

Distinguishing between effectiveness and efficiency is much more than an exercise in semantics. The relationship between these two terms is important, and it presents managers with a never-ending dilemma. **Effectiveness** entails achieving a stated objective. Swinging a sledgehammer against the wall, for example, would be an effective way to kill a bothersome fly. But given the reality of limited resources, effectiveness alone is not enough. **Efficiency** enters the picture when the resources required to achieve an objective are weighed against what was actually accomplished. The more favorable the ratio of benefits to costs, the greater the efficiency. Although a sledgehammer is an effective tool for killing flies, it is highly inefficient when the wasted effort and smashed walls are taken into consideration. A fly swatter is both an effective and an efficient tool for killing a single housefly.

Managers are responsible for balancing effectiveness and efficiency (see Figure 1.2). Too much emphasis in either direction leads to mismanagement. On the one hand, managers must be effective, and those who are too stingy with resources will not get the job done. An example of such imbalance occurred when H.J. Heinz's Ore-Ida Division overreacted to corporate cost-cutting goals. *Business Week* reported the impact on Tater Tots, now the leader in the frozen fried potato market:

When Tater Tots sales fell in the period from 1985 to 1987, managers first blamed changing eating habits in the U.S. But further study revealed startling news: Cost-cutting had led plant managers to step up line speeds and change storage and cooking methods. Over a decade, the moves had changed Tater Tots. Their once-chunky insides had turned to mashed potato. The outside had lost its light and crispy coating. "We were pressing so hard on cost that we were affecting quality," says Gerald D. Herrick, president of Ore-Ida Foods Inc. "It's pretty embarrassing."[7]

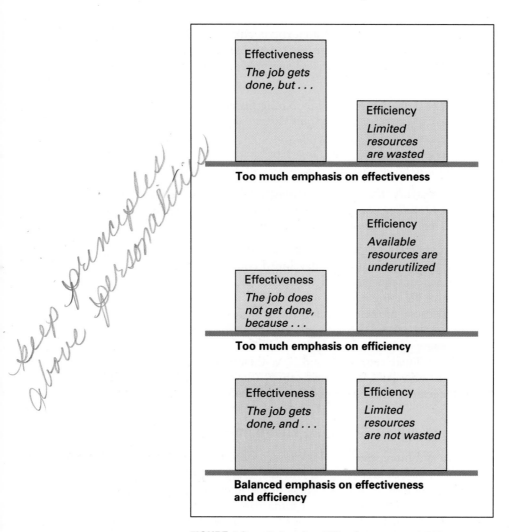

FIGURE 1.2 • Balancing Effectiveness and Efficiency

On the other hand, managers need to be efficient by containing costs as much as possible and conserving limited resources. Managers who waste resources may get the job done, but they risk bankruptcy in the process. A balance between effectiveness and efficiency is the key to competitiveness today.

Making the Most of Limited Resources

We live in a world of scarcity. Those who are concerned with such matters worry not only about running out of nonrenewable energy and material resources but also about the lopsided use of those resources. The United States, for example, with less than 5 percent of the world's population is currently consuming about 25 percent of the world's annual oil production and generating 17 percent of the greenhouse gases linked to global warming.[8]

Although experts and nonexperts alike may quibble over exactly how long it will take to exhaust our nonrenewable resources or come up with exotic, new technological alternatives, one bold fact remains. Our planet is becoming increasingly crowded.

The earth's population is soaring faster than at any time in history:
- *Up 3 people every second.*
- *Up 10,800 people every hour.*
- *Up 250,000 every day.*
- *Up 91 million every year....*

Currently, the world's population is estimated at 5.3 billion. That is up 842 million since 1980. Growth during the 1990s is projected at nearly 1 billion, which is like adding an entire China to the world's population.[9]

Approximately 84 percent of the world's population in the year 2025 will live in relatively poor and less developed countries.[10] Developed and industrialized nations, consequently, will experience increasing pressure to divide the limited resource pie more equitably.

Because of their common focus on resources, economics and management are closely related. Economics is the study of how limited resources are distributed among alternative uses. In productive organizations, managers are the trustees of limited resources, and it is their job to see that the basic factors of production—land, labor, and capital—are used efficiently as well as effectively. Management could be called "applied economics."

Coping with a Changing Environment

More and more, the world is characterized by rapid change. Managers face the difficult task of preparing for and adapting to change rather than being passively swept along by it. An awareness of the major sources of change is an excellent starting point for today's and tomorrow's managers. Chapter 3 presents a detailed view of important changes in management's social, political/legal, economic, and technological environments. At this point, it is instructive to identify three overarching sources of change for today's managers: globalization, environmentalism, and ethics. In its own distinctive way, each promises to significantly reshape the practice of management in the years to come.

Globalization.   Figuratively speaking, the globe is shrinking in almost every conceivable way. Transportation, communication, and economic networks have tied the peoples of the world together as never before. Companies are having to become global players to survive. Business opportunities show little regard for international borders these days. Accordingly, today's model manager is one who is comfortable transacting business in multiple languages and cultures. For example, here is a capsule résumé of an executive recruiter working in Europe:

Erik Slingerland, 34, [is] a Dutchman with a law degree from the University of Zurich and an MBA degree from the University of Virginia. He was hired from Swiss pharmaceuticals company Ciba-Geigy—where he worked as a controller in Brazil and Switzerland. Slingerland speaks French, German, English, and Portuguese, as well as Dutch.[11]

The Greening of McDonald's?

In the last few years, many Americans have become more conscious of how they contribute to the destruction of our environment and particularly to the immense amount of garbage our country produces every year. The average American generates 3.5 pounds of garbage each day, twice as much as the average European. In an attempt to cut down on this waste, many Americans now recycle everything from plastic milk containers to old motor oil, and they have begun putting pressure on businesses—including their favorite fast-food establishments—to become equally conscious of the environment.

McDonald's, which took in more than $17 billion from hungry customers last year, may not be exactly a leader in the environmental movement, but it has begun responding to public pressure and finding ways to make fast food less wasteful. Its successes show that creative thinking can discover endless ways to cut waste. The company now saves 68 million pounds of packaging materials each year by pumping its soft drink syrup directly from trucks to restaurant tanks rather than shipping the syrup in cardboard containers, as it used to do. It buys some $60 million worth of recycled paper for such items as napkins and carry-out trays, and many of its restaurants provide custom-

ers with separate receptacles for recyclable materials. And in 1990, McDonald's announced a new program, McRecycle USA, which ensures that one-quarter of the $400 million the company spends yearly to build and remodel stores will be spent on recycled goods, including roofing material and playground equipment.

Environmentalists felt they'd won a major battle with McDonald's when in 1990 the company finally decided to give up its polystyrene "clamshell" boxes. The company had insisted that the material was not environmentally harmful and could be recycled, but after experts from the Environmental Defense Fund worked with the company to cut waste, top McDonald's management evidently had a change of heart. Ironically, however, one of the substitutes for the polystyrene, made of layers of paper, is not recyclable. As many other companies have discovered, today's ethical environmental solution may be tomorrow's headache.

Sources: Sharon Begley, "The Supply-Side Theory of Garbage," *Newsweek* (November 27, 1989): 76; Martha T. Moore, "Environment, Health on Front Burner," *USA Today* (April 18, 1990): 1B, 2B; Martha T. Moore, "McDonald's to Build on Recyclables," *USA Today* (April 18, 1990): 1B; "One Big McBow to Environmentalism," *Newsweek* (November 12, 1990): 59.

Amazing? Yes. Unusual? No. There is a rapidly growing army of global managers, and you can become a member of it through diligent effort and a clear sense of purpose. Chapter 19 is devoted to the topic of international management. "The World of Management" boxed features in each chapter of this text are intended to broaden your awareness of international management.

Environmentalism. Environmental issues such as deforestation, global warming, depletion of the ozone layer, toxic waste, and pollution of land, air, and water are no longer strictly the domain of campus radicals. Mainstream politicians and managers around the world have picked up the environmental banner. The so-called green movement has spawned successful political parties in Europe and is gaining a foothold in North America and elsewhere. Managers are challenged to develop creative ways to make a profit without unduly harming the environment in the process (see Management Ethics). Some companies, such as 3M, as we will see in Chapter 3, are leading the way. Indeed, cleaning up the environment promises to generate whole new classes of jobs and robust profits in the future.[12] The debate over jobs versus the environment has been rendered obsolete by the need for both a healthy economy *and* a healthy environment.

An Ethical Reawakening. Managers are under strong pressure from the public, elected officials, and respected managers to behave better. This pressure has resulted from years of headlines about illegal campaign contributions, price fixing, insider trading, selling unsafe products, and other unethical practices. Traditional values such as honesty are being reemphasized in managerial decision making and conduct. This conclusion is supported by the results of a recent nationwide survey of executives who were asked to rank the desired characteristics of superior leaders. The number one choice was *honest* (87 percent).[13] Because of closer public scrutiny, ethical questions can no longer be shoved aside as irrelevant. The topic of managerial ethics is covered in depth in Chapter 4 and explored in the "Management Ethics" boxes distributed throughout the text.

Considering the variety of these sources of change in the environment, managers are challenged to keep abreast of them and adjust and adapt as necessary.

What Do Managers Do?

- Contrast the functional and role approaches to explaining what managers do.

managerial functions general administrative duties that need to be carried out in virtually all productive organizations to achieve desired outcomes

managerial roles specific categories of managerial behavior

Although nearly all aspects of modern life are touched at least indirectly by the work of managers, many people do not really understand what the management process involves. Management is much more, for example, than the familiar activity of telling employees what to do. Management is a complex and dynamic mixture of systematic techniques and common sense. As with any complex process, the key to learning about management lies in dividing it into readily understood subprocesses. Currently, there are two different approaches to dividing the management process for study and discussion. One approach, dating back to the early part of this century, is to identify managerial functions. A second, more recent approach focuses on managerial roles.

Managerial functions are general administrative duties that need to be carried out in virtually all productive organizations. **Managerial roles** are specific categories of managerial behavior. A British management scholar recently clarified this distinction by pointing out that managerial functions involve "desired outcomes." Those outcomes are achieved through the performance of managerial roles (actual behavior).[14] Stated another way, roles are the *means* and functions are the *ends* of the manager's job. We shall examine both approaches more closely and then have a frank discussion of some managerial facts of life.

Managerial Functions

For most of this century, the most popular approach to describing what managers do has been the functional view. It has been popular because it characterizes the management process as a sequence of rational and logical steps. Henri Fayol, a French industrialist turned writer, became the father of the functional approach in 1916 when he identified five managerial functions: planning, organizing, command, coordination, and control.[15] Fayol claimed that these five functions were the common denominators of all managerial jobs, whatever the purpose of the

Packages destined for the Indianapolis hub were being incorrectly routed to the Memphis superhub. These four managers created a communication and education campaign that raised the package "capture rate" from 30 percent to over 90 percent in nine months. Managerial teamwork can be an integral ingredient for success.

organization. Over the years Fayol's original list of managerial functions has been updated and expanded by management scholars. This book, even though it is based on more than just Fayol's approach, is organized around eight different managerial functions: planning, decision making, organizing, staffing, communicating, motivating, leading, and controlling (see Figure 1.3). A brief overview of these eight managerial functions will describe what managers do and will preview what lies ahead in this text.

Planning.   Commonly referred to as the primary management function, planning is the formulation of future courses of action. Plans and the objectives on which they are based give purpose and direction to the organization, its subunits, and contributing individuals.

Decision Making.   Managers choose among alternative courses of action when they make decisions. Making intelligent and ethical decisions in today's complex world is a major management challenge.

Organizing.   Structural considerations such as the chain of command, division of labor, and assignment of responsibility are part of the organizing function. Careful organizing helps ensure the efficient use of human resources.

Staffing.   Organizations are only as good as the people in them. Staffing consists of recruiting, training, and developing people who can contribute to the organized effort.

Communicating.   Today's managers are responsible for communicating to their employees the technical knowledge, instructions, rules, and information required to get the job done. Recognizing that communication is a two-way process, managers should be responsive to feedback and upward communication.

FIGURE 1.3 • Identifiable Functions in the Management Process

Motivating. An important aspect of management today is motivating individuals to pursue collective objectives by satisfying needs and meeting expectations with meaningful work and valued rewards.

Leading. Managers become inspiring leaders by serving as role models and adapting their management style to the demands of the situation. The idea of visionary leadership is popular today.

Controlling. When managers compare desired results with actual results and take the necessary corrective action, they are keeping things on track through the control function. Deviations from past plans should be considered when formulating new plans.

Managerial Roles

During the 1970s, a reseacher named Henry Mintzberg criticized the traditional functional approach as unrealistic. From his firsthand observation of managers and similar studies conducted by others, he concluded that functions "tell us little about what managers actually do. At best they indicate some vague objectives managers have when they work."[16] Because of the long-standing popularity of the traditional functional perspective, Mintzberg's work has stirred a degree of controversy in management circles.

Those who agree with Mintzberg believe that the functional approach portrays the management process as far more systematic and rational and less complex than it really is. Even the most casual observation reveals that managers do

Category	Role	Nature of Role
Interpersonal roles	1. Figurehead	As a symbol of legal authority, performing certain ceremonial duties (e.g., signing documents and receiving visitors)
	2. Leader	Motivating subordinates to get the job done properly
	3. Liaison	Serving as a link in a horizontal (as well as vertical) chain of communication
Informational roles	4. Nerve center	Serving as a focal point for nonroutine information; receiving all types of information
	5. Disseminator	Transmitting selected information to subordinates
	6. Spokesperson	Transmitting selected information to outsiders
Decisional roles	7. Entrepreneur	Designing and initiating changes within the organization
	8. Disturbance handler	Taking corrective action in nonroutine situations
	9. Resource allocator	Deciding exactly who should get what resources
	10. Negotiator	Participating in negotiating sessions with other parties (e. g., vendors and unions) to make sure the organization's interests are adequately represented

FIGURE 1.4 ● Mintzberg's Managerial Roles

Source: Adapted from Henry Mintzberg, "Managerial Work: Analysis from Observation," *Management Science,* 18 (October 1971): B97–B110.

not plan on Monday, organize on Tuesday, coordinate on Wednesday, and so on, as the functional approach might lead one to believe. Moreover, according to the Mintzberg view, the average manager is not the reflective planner and precise "orchestra leader" that the functional approach suggests. Mintzberg characterizes the typical manager as follows: "The manager is overburdened with obligations; yet he cannot easily delegate his tasks. As a result, he is driven to overwork and is forced to do many tasks superficially. Brevity, fragmentation, and verbal communication characterize his work."[17]

Mintzberg and his followers have suggested that a more fruitful way of studying what managers do is to focus on the key roles they play. Using a method called "structured observation," which entailed recording the activities and correspondence of five top-level executives, Mintzberg isolated ten roles he believes are common to all managers.[18] These roles (see Figure 1.4) have been grouped into three major categories: interpersonal, informational, and decisional roles.

Interpersonal Roles. Because of their formal authority and superior status, managers engage in a good deal of interpersonal contact, especially with subordinates and peers. The three interpersonal roles that managers play are those of figurehead, leader, and liaison.

Informational Roles. Every manager is a clearinghouse for information relating to the task at hand. Informational roles are important because information is the lifeblood of organizations. Typical roles include acting as nerve center, disseminator, and spokesperson.

Decisional Roles. In their decisional roles, managers balance competing interests and make choices. Through decisional roles, strategies are formulated and put into action. Four decisional roles are those of entrepreneur, disturbance handler, resource allocator, and negotiator.

Merging Functions and Roles

Both the functional approach and the role approach to explaining management are valuable to the student of management. Managerial functions are a useful categorization of a manager's tasks. It is important for future managers to realize that planning and staffing, for example, require different techniques and perspectives. The role approach is valuable because it injects needed realism, emphasizing that the practice of management is less rational and systematic than the functional approach implies. This text merges the functional and role approaches by explaining how the important roles are played within each functional category.

Some Managerial Facts of Life (With No Sugar Coating)

Make no mistake about it, managing is a tough and demanding job today. The hours are long and, at first anyway, the pay may not be generous. Nevertheless, managing can be a very rewarding occupation for those who develop their skills and persist, as John F. Akers, the chief executive officer of IBM, found out. Akers joined the giant computer firm in 1960 as a sales trainee, at a salary of $6,500. Today he earns over $700,000 a year and has collected more than $2.4 million in cash and stock bonuses.[19] On his way to the top, Akers held sixteen different positions, fourteen of them as a manager. Overnight sensations are rare in the managerial ranks of large organizations.

A Hectic Pace. Mintzberg is right. The typical manager's day follows a hectic schedule, with lots of brief and mostly verbal interactions. Interruptions and fragmentation are the norm. Extended quiet periods for contemplation simply don't exist. An observational study by the Center for Creative Leadership gives a realistic picture of managerial life (see Table 1.1). An even quicker pace is in store for future managers.

> ● ● ● ● ● ● ● ● ● ● ● ● ● ● ● ● ●
> Summarize the ten facts
> of managerial life.

Managers Lose Their Right to Do Many Things. Mention the word *manager,* and the average person will probably respond with terms like *power, privilege, authority, good pay,* and so on. Although many managers eventually do enjoy

TABLE 1.1 ● Ten Facts of Managerial Life (from direct observation and diaries)

1. **Managers work long hours.** The number of hours worked tends to increase as one climbs the managerial ladder.

2. **Managers are busy.** The typical manager's day is made up of hundreds of brief incidents or episodes. Activity rates tend to decrease as rank increases.

3. **A manager's work is fragmented; episodes are brief.** Given managers' high activity level, they have little time to devote to any single activity. Interruptions and discontinuity are the rule.

4. **The manager's job is varied.** Managers engage in a variety of activities (paperwork, phone calls, scheduled and unscheduled meetings, and inspection tours/visits), interact with a variety of people, and deal with a variety of content areas.

5. **Managers are "homebodies."** Managers spend most of their time pursuing activities within their own organizations. As managerial rank increases, managers spend proportionately more time outside their work areas and organizations.

6. **The manager's work is primarily oral.** Managers at all levels spend the majority of their time communicating verbally (by personal contact or telephone).

7. **Managers use a lot of contacts.** Consistent with their high level of verbal communication, managers continually exchange information with superiors, peers, subordinates, and outsiders on an ongoing basis.

8. **Managers are not reflective planners.** The typical manager is too busy to find uninterrupted blocks of time for reflective planning.

9. **Information is the basic ingredient of the manager's work.** Managers spend most of their time obtaining, interpreting, and giving information.

10. **Managers don't know how they spend their time.** Managers consistently overestimate the time they spend on production, reading and writing, phone calls, thinking, and calculating and consistently underestimate the time spent on meetings and informal discussions.

Source: Adapted from Morgan W. McCall, Jr., Ann M. Morrison, and Robert L. Hannan, *Studies of Managerial Work: Results and Methods* (Greensboro, N.C.: Center for Creative Leadership, 1978), Technical Report No. 9, pp. 6–18. Used by permission of the authors.

some or all of these good things, they pay a significant price for stepping to the front of the administrative parade. According to one management expert, when you accept a supervisory or managerial position you lose your right to

- Lose your temper.
- Be one of the gang.
- Bring your personal problems to work.
- Vent your frustrations and express all your opinions at work.
- Resist change.
- Pass the buck on tough assignments.
- Get even with your adversaries.
- Play favorites.
- Put your self-interests first.

- Ask others to do what you wouldn't do.
- Expect to be immediately recognized and rewarded for doing a good job.[20]

We tell you this not to scare you away from what could be a financially and emotionally rewarding career, but rather to present a realistic picture so you can choose intelligently. Management is not for everyone—it is not for the timid, the ego-maniac, or the lazy. Management requires clear-headed individuals who can envision something better and turn it into reality by working with and through others.

What Does It Take to Become a Successful Manager?

● ● ● ● ● ● ● ● ● ● ● ● ● ● ● ● ● ●
Explain the basic formula for managerial success (S = A × M × O).

Successful managers come from a wide variety of backgrounds and possess an equally wide variety of traits and skills. No sure-fire formula exists for getting to the top of the managerial ladder, but there are at least three general preconditions for achieving lasting success as a manager: ability (A), motivation to manage (M), and opportunity (O). Together, they constitute a basic formula for managerial success (S): $S = A \times M \times O$. Notice that success depends on a balanced combination of ability, motivation to manage, and opportunity. A total absence of one factor can cancel out strength in the other two. (Hence, the use of multiplication rather than addition signs.) For example, high ability and motivation are useless without opportunity.

It takes hard work to become a top executive. For Roger Hemminghaus, the CEO of petroleum refiner and marketer Diamond Shamrock, it even takes a touch of humility. About six times a year he puts on a retail clerk's outfit and waits on customers at a Diamond Shamrock service station convenience store in Denver, Colorado. Hemminghaus's grass-roots management style keeps him in touch with the needs of customers and employees alike. It also underscores the company's commitment to outstanding customer service.

Ability

As used here, the term **managerial ability** is the demonstrated capacity to achieve organizational objectives both effectively and efficiently. Actually, today's successful manager needs a whole package of conceptual, technical, and interpersonal abilities. According to recent work by the American Assembly of Collegiate Schools of Business (AACSB), an accrediting agency, business school graduates should be able to demonstrate certain skills and personal characteristics. AACSB's package of skills and characteristics can help everyone better understand the term *ability to manage*. They include

1. Leadership.
2. Oral communication and presentation skills.
3. Written communication.
4. Planning and organizing.
5. Information gathering and problem analysis.
6. Decision making.
7. Delegation and control.
8. Self-objectivity (being aware of one's strengths and limitations).
9. Disposition to lead (a willingness and desire to lead others in new directions).[21]

Motivation to Manage

Inspiring stories about handicapped persons and adventurers who succeed despite seemingly insurmountable odds are often summed up in one word: *desire*. The same force drives successful managers. All the ability in the world will not help a future manager succeed if he or she does not possess a persistent desire to move ahead. Frederick W. Smith, the founder of Federal Express Corporation, the original nationwide overnight delivery specialist, is a prime example of what desire can do for one's managerial career:

> *In 1965, writing a paper for an economics course at Yale University, Smith proposed a new kind of freight service. . . . Smith's professor pointed out the futility of the idea, given the regulatory climate and the hostility of the huge, entrenched airlines. He awarded Smith a C for his efforts.*[22]

Six years later, Smith's Federal Express Corporation was well on its way to becoming the multibillion-dollar company that promises to be at our service for guaranteed overnight deliveries.

Until the mid-1960s, this kind of desire was an intangible trait that could be measured only subjectively. Then a management researcher named John B. Miner developed a psychometric instrument to measure objectively an individual's **motivation to manage**. Miner's test, in effect, measures one's desire to be a manager.

The Seven Dimensions of Motivation to Manage. Miner's measure of motivation to manage is anchored to the following seven dimensions:

1. Favorable attitude toward those in positions of authority, such as superiors.
2. Desire to engage in games or sports competition with peers.
3. Desire to engage in occupational or work-related competition with peers.
4. Desire to assert oneself and take charge.
5. Desire to exercise power and authority over others.
6. Desire to behave in a distinctive way, which includes standing out from the crowd.
7. Sense of responsibility in carrying out the routine duties associated with managerial work.[23]

The higher the individual scores on each trait, the greater is the motivation to manage. (Although the complete instrument is not given here, you can probably gauge your own motivation to manage as low, moderate, or high.) Miner's research indicates that this concept can accurately predict how fast and how far one will move up the hierarchy (see Managers in Action).

Motivation to Manage Among Business Students. Miner and his colleagues went on to track motivation-to-manage scores for business students at two major U.S. universities over a 20-year period and came to some interesting conclusions.[24] First, although the steady decline of motivation to manage during the 1960s and early 1970s had stopped, students' motivation to manage still was very low. Generally speaking, students continued to show a distaste for authority, competitiveness, assertiveness, and routine managerial duties. Miner believed this situation foreshadowed a shortage of managerial talent over the coming years. A second conclusion was that female students no longer lagged behind their male counterparts in motivation to manage.

A more recent five-year study of 115 master of business administration (MBA) students from a large eastern U.S. university yielded some interesting and provocative results. Students with high motivation-to-manage scores tended to have higher salaries after graduation than those with low motivation to manage. However, in direct contrast to Miner's second finding, female MBA students had significantly lower motivation-to-manage scores than did their male counterparts.[25] More research is needed to clarify regional and cross-cultural differences in male and female motivation to manage.

Opportunity

Talented and highly motivated potential managers, like seeds, need fertile ground to foster their growth. The opportunity for managerial growth has two requirements: obtaining a suitable managerial job, and finding a supportive climate once on the job.

The situation looks good for landing a managerial job. As indicated in Figure 1.5, the demand for managerial talent in both the public and private sectors has been steadily rising recently in the United States. But, according to the U.S. Bureau of Labor Statistics, opportunities for managers between now and the year 2000 will vary, depending on the sector of the economy:

Ann M. Busquet's Motivation to Manage Could Help Her Become the CEO of American Express

If anyone is on the CEO [chief executive officer] track, Busquet is. She is the most senior woman executive in the card division at American Express, and she has the requisite line-management and international experience in abundance. But expertise isn't enough. There are lots of people with expertise and talent. "You also need ambition, style, and motivation," she says. "You need drive."

Good timing doesn't hurt either. In 1978, when she received an MBA from Columbia University, Wall Street investment banks were recruiting women for the first time—ever. In spite of the fact that her class was approximately 50 percent women, Busquet found herself in a seller's market. "I picked American Express," she says. . . .

As a fast-tracker, she was encouraged to move around, and she took full advantage of the opportunity. She has hit all the major divisions in TRS (Travel-Related Services) and has left her mark at each stop. Working with the American Express card's hotel customers, for example, she developed the company's Assured Reservations Program. "It

was my first thing," she says. "It was very intense and extremely successful."

Then came the pièce de résistance for any manager: development of a major new product. In 1986, she was given the chance to create the marketing plan for the company's first revolving-credit card—Optima. After the product was successfully launched, her boss was promoted, and Busquet became head of the whole division. Most of her experience has been in marketing—"a good place to be at Amex," she says—but at Optima she is filling in a crucial slot in her résumé: line management. She is responsible for marketing, strategic planning, and credit policy. . . .

Busquet shrugs off the difficulties of being a woman in a corporation: "I don't know what it is to be a man, so how can I tell?" Will there ever be a CEO slot on her résumé? "Probably not." But she isn't giving up. "I would like to be the first," she says. "Absolutely."

Source: Excerpted from Mary Billard, "Women on the Verge of Being CEO," *Business Month,* 135 (April 1990): 32–33.

For example, managers and administrators should experience faster than average growth in retail trade and in the services industry division, especially business services. In contrast, those working in government [and manufacturing] are likely to face average or slower than average growth.[26]

In regard to the second requirement, finding a supportive climate once on the job, a potential manager must periodically reassess any job to see if it is meeting his or her expectations. If not, a change may be in order. In short, tomorrow's managers need to start thinking today about how they can best work out their own $S = A \times M \times O$ formula.

Learning to Manage

Students of management are left with one overriding question: "How do I acquire the ability to manage?" This question has stimulated a good deal of debate among those interested in management education. What is the key, theory or

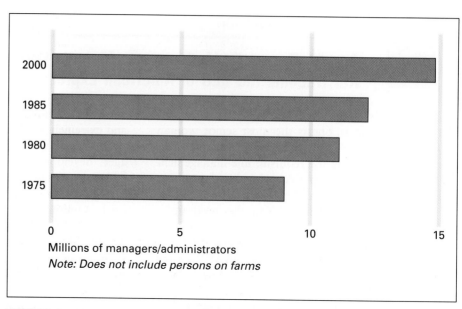

FIGURE 1.5 • Managers/Administrators in the U.S. Labor Force

Sources: Data for 1975–1980 from U.S. Bureau of the Census, *Statistical Abstract of the United States: 1983,* p. 417; data for 1985 from U.S. Bureau of the Census, *Statistical Abstract of the United States: 1987,* p. 385. Projected data for 2000 from U.S. Bureau of Labor Statistics, *Occupational Outlook Handbook,* 1990–1991 Ed., p. 11.

practice? Some contend that future managers need a solid background in management theory acquired through formal education. Others argue that managing, like learning to ride a bicycle, can be learned only by actually doing it.[27] We can leapfrog this debate by looking at how managers learn to manage, understanding how students learn about management, and considering how you can blend the two processes to your best advantage.

How Do Managers Learn to Manage?

●●●●●●●●●●●●●●●●●
Explain how managers
learn to manage.

We have an answer to this simple but intriguing question, thanks to the Honeywell study, which was conducted by a team of management development specialists employed by Honeywell.[28] In a survey, they asked 3,600 Honeywell managers: "How did you learn to manage?" Ten percent of the respondents were then interviewed for additional insights. Successful Honeywell managers reportedly acquired 50 percent of their management knowledge from job assignments (see Figure 1.6). The remaining 50 percent of what they knew about management reportedly came from relationships, including bosses, mentors, and coworkers (30 percent), and formal training and education (20 percent).

Fully half of what the Honeywell managers knew about managing came from the so-called school of hard knocks. To that extent, at least, learning to manage is indeed like learning to ride a bike. You get on, you fall off and skin your knee, you get back on a bit smarter, and so on, until you're able to wobble down the road. But, in the minds of aspiring managers, this scenario raises the question of what classes are held in the school of hard knocks. A second study,

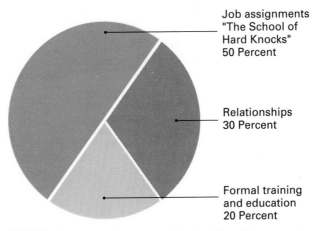

FIGURE 1.6 • The Honeywell Study: How Managers Learn to Manage

Source: Data from Ron Zemke, "The Honeywell Studies: How Managers Learn to Manage," *Training,* 22 (August 1985): 46–51.

this one of British managers, recently provided an answer. It turns out that the following are considered *hard knocks* by managers:

- Making a big mistake.
- Being overstretched by a difficult assignment.
- Feeling threatened.
- Being stuck in an impasse or dilemma.
- Suffering an injustice at work.
- Losing out to someone else.
- Being personally attacked.[29]

These situations are traumatic enough to motivate managers to learn how to avoid repeating the same mistakes.

How Can Future Managers Learn to Manage?

As indicated in Figure 1.7, students can learn to manage by integrating theory and practice. Theory can help you to systematically analyze, interpret, and internalize the managerial significance of practical experience. Although formal training and education contributed only 20 percent to the Honeywell managers' knowledge, it nonetheless represents a needed conceptual foundation. Returning to our bicycle example, a cross-country trip on a high-tech bike requires more than the mere ability to ride a bike. It requires a sound foundation of knowledge about bicycle maintenance and repair, weather and road conditions, and road safety. So, too, new managers who have a good idea of what lies ahead can go farther and faster with fewer foolish mistakes. The school of hard knocks is inevitable. But you can foresee and avoid at least some of the knocks.

Ideally, an individual acquires theoretical knowledge and practical experience at the same time, perhaps through work-study programs or internships. Usually, though, full-time students get a lot of theory and little practice. This

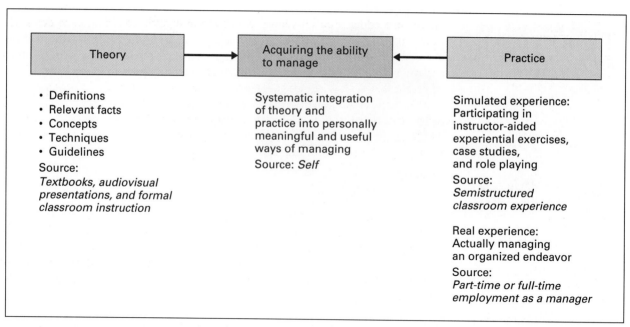

FIGURE 1.7 • Acquiring the Ability to Manage by Merging Theory and Practice

is when simulated and real experience become important. If you are a serious management student, you will put your newly acquired theories into practice wherever and whenever possible (for example, in organized sports; positions of leadership in fraternities, sororities, or clubs; and part-time and summer jobs). What really matters is your personal integration of theory and practice.

Productivity Improvement: A Central Challenge

What do the following situations have in common?

- *Aircraft Manufacturing.* At the beginning of 1989, it took McDonnell Douglas Corporation's employees 160 days to assemble one MD-80 jetliner. By the end of that year, it took only 100 days.[30]
- *Steel Industry.* Between 1982 and 1991, major steel producers in the United States reduced the man-hours required to make a ton of steel from 9.7 hours to 5.3 hours.[31]
- *Air Conditioner Manufacturing.* Carrier Corporation reduced the time it takes to make key parts for its air conditioning units from 10 minutes to 45 seconds by installing an automated manufacturing system.[32]
- *Lumber Industry.* Sawmill blades made of advanced metal alloys that are half as thick as traditional blades have made a big difference at Georgia-Pacific Corporation. "Because the thinner blades take a smaller bite out of the logs, wood that used to wind up as sawdust on the floor can now be converted into 800 railcars of Georgia-Pacific products every year."[33]

When it comes to improving productivity and speeding up the entire development and production process, Toyota is a relentless and respected competitor. The Japanese automaker's subcompact, Tercel, is a good case in point. Toyota's competitors around the globe spend up to $1,600 more per vehicle when manufacturing comparable automobiles. Higher costs mean lower profits for Toyota's competitors. Competing with Toyota is like trying to hit a rapidly moving target.

• • • • • • • • • • • • • • • • • •
Describe the United States' dual productivity problem.

All the preceding situations have two common ingredients. First, each deals with productivity, a central challenge for managers in all types of organizations. Managers are being asked to get more mileage out of all resources: human, financial, and material. Second, in spite of sluggish productivity growth in the United States in recent years, these examples represent signs of progress. But economywide, world-class competitiveness is still a long way off. Managers need to tackle the productivity improvement challenge aggressively and creatively. In this section, we examine America's recent productivity growth record, define organizational productivity, and briefly highlight Japan's approach.

Disappointing Productivity Growth in the United States

After increasing at a steady rate of 2.5 percent per year during the 1950s and 1960s, U.S. productivity growth began to slip. Between 1978 and 1989, the country's nonfarm productivity growth averaged a disappointing 1 percent.[34] Because Japan's productivity grew at about a 6 percent annual rate during the same period, with Germany and France not far behind, a U.S. productivity crisis has been proclaimed and widely discussed.[35]

A Personal Perspective.   A quick glance at these figures might lead the casual observer to ask: "Why get excited about one percentage point?" In a nutshell, there is a direct link between the economy's productivity and your standard of living. In point of fact, as productivity growth stalled at 1 percent during the last decade, real wages (wages adjusted for inflation) remained flat.[36] Princeton economist Alan S. Blinder offered the following perspective:

> The difference between 1% and 2% productivity growth may not sound like much. But when compounded over a long period of time, it is. At 2% annual growth, real wages double every 35 years; in a century, the standard of living increases more than sevenfold. But at 1 percent productivity growth, it takes 70 years for real wages to double, and the standard of living less than triples in a century. Clearly, restoring U.S. productivity growth to its historic 2% norm would be a monumental achievement.[37]

A Dual Productivity Problem.   Importantly, the U.S. productivity growth picture is not all gloom and doom. A somewhat different picture emerges when aggregate figures are broken into manufacturing and nonmanufacturing/service sectors. Productivity in the United States has been either fair or poor in recent years, depending on the sector of the economy one examines (see Figure 1.8). Consequently, America has *two* productivity problems. First, overall productivity growth has not kept pace with that of leading industrialized nations. Second, productivity of the service sector, by far the largest sector of the U.S. economy with 70 percent of the jobs, is barely growing.[38] Both fronts deserve management's closest attention.

Defining Organizational Productivity

National productivity indexes such as those just mentioned are a helpful barometer of economic health, but to the average manager, organizational productivity

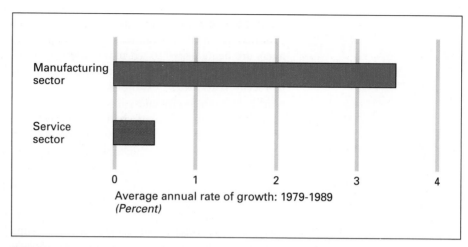

FIGURE 1.8 • U.S. Service Sector Productivity Growth Rate

Source: Data from Gene Koretz, "Productivity in Services Is Not a Problem Abroad," *Business Week* (May 22, 1989): 28.

is more relevant. Whatever the level of analysis, you can measure productivity. From an organizational standpoint, one expert on productivity offered the following introduction to the concept:

> *Many think of productivity as being a measure of labor, usually expressed as output per hour. Actually it is a much broader concept than that. Productivity is any output-to-input ratio. For the firm as a whole, outputs include all goods and services produced during a given time. Inputs include all resources consumed to produce those outputs. Labor is one of the input resources but so too are capital, material, and energy. Virtually all of the resources used by the firm fall into one of these four categories. . . .*
>
> *Total firm productivity is defined as follows:*
>
> $$Productivity = \frac{output}{input} = \frac{goods\ and\ services\ produced}{labor,\ capital,\ materials,\ and\ energy}[39]$$

organizational productivity
the ratio of an organization's total output to total input, adjusted for inflation, for a specified period of time

Formally defined, **organizational productivity** is the ratio of an organization's total output to total input, adjusted for inflation, for a specified period of time. (See Table 1.2 for some illustrative productivity measurements, within an organizational context.)

The Japanese Model: More with Less

Despite a recent slowing in its productivity growth rate, Japan's average annual rate of productivity growth is still well ahead of that of other industrialized nations. Japan's success can be attributed in large part to its highly efficient and productive use of limited resources. In effect, Japan has demonstrated to the rest of the world that it is possible to do more with less. Japan's situation was recently summed up as follows:

TABLE 1.2 • Sample Productivity Measurements for Today's Organizations

	$\dfrac{\textit{Output}}{\textit{Input}}$
Individual performer	
Warehouse handler	$\dfrac{\text{Pounds placed in storage without damage}}{\text{Handler hours} + \text{hours of forklift use}}$
Salesperson	$\dfrac{\text{New accounts opened and retained}}{\text{Salesperson salary} + \text{travel costs}}$
Secretary	$\dfrac{\text{Number of letters typed without error}}{\text{Secretarial hours} + \text{cost of word processor/day}}$
Machine performer	
Grinding machine	$\dfrac{\text{Number of units ground to specific tolerance daily}}{\text{Cost of machine/day} + \text{electric costs to run}}$
Unit performance	
Accounting department	$\dfrac{\text{Number of timely, accurate reports}}{\text{Accountant time} + \text{computer costs}}$
Cereal maker	$\dfrac{\text{Pounds of salable cereal product made}}{\text{Cost of grain} + \text{labor cost} + \text{processing cost}}$
Organizational performance	
Retail sporting goods	$\dfrac{\text{Sales dollars (adjusted for inflation)}}{\text{Cost of production} + \text{cost of sales activities}}$
Health club	$\dfrac{\text{Number of memberships gained or lost}}{\text{Cost of marketing efforts}}$

Source: Robert O. Brinkerhoff and Dennis E. Dressler, *Productivity Measurement: A Guide for Managers and Evaluators,* pp. 84–85, copyright © 1990 by Robert O. Brinkerhoff and Dennis E. Dressler. Reprinted by permission of Sage Publications, Inc.

> *Japan has a population approximately half that of the United States, living in a territorial area roughly equivalent to the state of California. Moreover, the Japanese have practically no natural resources. Their conditions of life force them to function in a "continuing survival mode." And they know that their existence as an economic power depends on their remaining permanently in this state.*[40]

Those who say that Japan's competitive edge can be traced to lower wage rates and lax occupational safety and pollution control laws would have been right several years ago, but not today. Moreover, costly real estate, expensive imported raw materials, an antiquated distribution system, and crowded highways make the cost of doing business in Japan very high.[41] According to the authors of the best-selling book, *The Art of Japanese Management,* "a major reason for the superiority of the Japanese is their managerial skill."[42]

Although Japan's culture and Western cultures differ a great deal, the West can learn a lot from the Japanese success story of doing more with less. The key

Management's Global Agenda for the 1990s, According to GE's Jack Welch

The pace of change in the nineties will make the eighties look like a picnic—a walk in the park. Competition will be relentless. The bar of excellence in everything we do will be raised every day.

The pace of change will be felt in several areas. Globalization is now no longer an objective but an imperative, as markets open and geographic barriers become increasingly blurred and even irrelevant. Corporate alliances, whether joint ventures or acquisitions, will increasingly be driven by competitive pressures and strategies rather than financial structuring. Technological innovation and the translation of that innovation into marketplace advantage will be accelerating ever faster. And in the coming decade, we're going to see increasing demands for sensitivity to the environment. Only a total commitment of everyone in the company can provide the level of responsibility that will be acceptable to governments, employees, and customers.

Simply doing more of what worked in the eighties—the restructuring, the delayering, the mechanical, top-down measures that we took—will be too incremental. More than that, it will be too slow. The winners of the nineties will be those who can develop a culture that allows them to move faster, communicate more clearly, and involve everyone in a focused effort to serve ever more demanding customers.

To move toward that winning culture we've got to create what we call a "boundaryless" company. We no longer have the time to climb over barriers between functions like engineering and marketing, or between people—hourly, salaried, management, and the like. Geographic barriers must evaporate. The lines between the company and its vendors and customers must be blurred into a fluid process with no other objective than satisfying the customer and winning in the marketplace.

If we are to get the reflexes and speed we need, we've got to simplify and delegate more—simply trust more. We need to drive self-confidence deep into the organization. A company can't distribute self-confidence, but it can foster it by removing layers and giving people a chance to win. We have to undo a 100-year-old concept and convince our managers that their role is not to control people and stay "on top" of things, but rather to guide, energize, and excite.

Source: Stratford P. Sherman, "John F. Welch Jr.: We've Got to Simplify and Delegate More," *Fortune,* 121 (March 26, 1990): 30. © The Time Inc. Magazine Company. All rights reserved.

is to adapt, not to blindly imitate or mimic, Japanese management techniques, several of which are covered in this text. Robert Lutz, president of Chrysler Motors, knows what has to be done to compete internationally:

We have no room to maneuver. We can't spend our way to profit, we can't sell our way to profit, we can't fight our way to profit. The only way to get from here to there is to do more, and get more, with less.[43]

Meeting the Challenge

More than anyone else, today's and tomorrow's managers will have to meet the challenge of improving productivity. John F. Welch Jr., the widely respected chief executive officer of General Electric, has framed management's complex agenda for the 1990s (see The World of Management). Accordingly, the balance of this book is intended to help you successfully meet the global productivity challenge.

Summary

Management is an important area of study from both a personal and a broader perspective. On the personal side, knowledge of management is a useful steppingstone to a good job in our highly organized world. From a more global perspective, Neil Armstrong's walk on the moon and the *Challenger* disaster symbolize the extremes of effective management and gross mismanagement.

Formally defined, *management* is the process of working with and through others to achieve organizational objectives in a changing environment. Central to this process is the effective and efficient use of limited resources. An inability to work with people, not a lack of technical skills, is the main reason some managers fail to reach their full potential. A manager is *effective* if he or she reaches a stated objective and *efficient* if limited resources are not wasted in the process. Three overarching sources of change affecting the way management is practiced today are globalization, environmentalism, and an ethical reawakening.

Two ways to answer the question "What do managers do?" are the functional approach and role approach. *Managerial functions* relate to the desired outcomes of managerial action, whereas *managerial roles* categorize managers' actual behavior. This text is organized around eight managerial functions: planning, decision making, organizing, staffing, communicating, motivating, leading, and controlling. Having criticized the functional approach for making management appear to be more orderly than it really is, Henry Mintzberg concluded from his observation of managers that management is best explained in terms of roles. Three managerial role categories, according to Mintzberg, are interpersonal, informational, and decisional.

The basic formula for managerial success is $S = A \times M \times O$ (managerial success = ability × motivation to manage × opportunity). *Managerial ability* results when theory and practice are systematically integrated. John Miner identified seven dimensions of *motivation to manage* that predict how far and how fast managers move up through the ranks. A 20-year study of motivation to manage in college business students indicated that, although the decline in motivation to manage has stopped, it still remains very low. Miner has predicted a shortage in managerial talent for the next fifteen years. Because the number of managers and administrators in the U.S. labor force is projected to increase from 12.2 million in 1985 to 14.8 million by the year 2000, there are many opportunities to manage.

Honeywell researchers found that managers learned 50 percent of what they know about managing from job assignments (or the school of hard knocks). The remaining 50 percent of their management knowledge came from relationships (30 percent) and formal training and education (20 percent). A good foundation in management theory can give management students a running start and help them avoid foolish mistakes.

The United States has a dual productivity problem. Overall productivity growth lags behind international levels, and service-sector productivity growth has nearly stalled. There is much room for improvement if the United States is to match Japan's record of productivity growth. Managers should translate the productivity problem into organizational terms. *Organizational productivity* is the ratio of total output to total input, adjusted for inflation, for a specific period of time. Japan, with the world's highest rate of productivity growth, is an example of how to do more with less. A basic aim of this text is to help today's and tomorrow's managers successfully meet the challenge of improving productivity.

Terms to Understand

management
effectiveness
efficiency
managerial functions

managerial roles
managerial ability
motivation to manage
organizational productivity

Questions for Discussion

1. Drawing on your own experience, can you recall any specific examples of effective management and mismanagement?
2. In your opinion, what is the single most important aspect of the definition of management? Why?
3. Think of a person or operation you have seen recently that did not achieve a workable balance between effectiveness and efficiency. What could have been done to balance the two?
4. What evidence of the three major sources of change—globalization, environmentalism, and ethical reawakening—have you seen lately?
5. Which of Mintzberg's ten managerial roles do you think you are best equipped to play? Explain.
6. Which factor—ability, motivation to manage, or opportunity—should be most heavily weighted in the basic formula for managerial success?
7. Now that you are familiar with Miner's seven dimensions of motivation to manage, how would you rate yourself? Do you feel that this is a valid predictor of your chances to succeed as a manager?
8. Are you at all surprised by the results of the Honeywell study of how managers learn to manage?
9. Why are managers and economists so concerned about low service-sector productivity growth in the United States?
10. What can an individual manager do to meet the challenge to improve productivity?

Back to the Opening Case

Now that you have read Chapter 1, you should be able to answer the following questions about the General Electric–Tungsram case:

1. What role does the balance between effectiveness and efficiency play in this case?
2. Which managerial functions are evident in this case? Cite specific evidence.
3. Which of Mintzberg's managerial roles (see Figure 1.4) does George Varga need to perform most skillfully if he is to successfully transform Tungsram?
4. Respond to a manager who has offered this opinion: "Tungsram has three problems—productivity, productivity, and productivity!"

Through the Looking Glass—A Manager in Action

Among the activities at the Center for Creative Leadership in Greensboro, North Carolina, is a simulation called Looking Glass, Inc. "The design of the simulation," says the Center, "recreates accurately the demanding, fast-paced, complex world of a large organization. By studying the behavior of managers participating in Looking Glass, researchers here hope to answer questions about the relationships between managers and organization." Not long ago the Center sent a member of its Newsletter staff to participate in a simulation session and report. She had the role of plant manager, Commercial Glass Division. Here . . . [are some excerpts from] her story.

It was 8:00, fully one hour before the day would begin and the switchboard would open. The morning mail had yet to be delivered. Still, my in-basket was already overloaded with memos. I began to read quickly, voraciously, knowing these few moments were precious. Once the day actually began, interruption would follow interruption. The incessant ringing of the phone and the inevitable meetings would preclude reflection and concentrated reading.

As usual, my in-basket was a potpourri of problems and issues that required my attention. Some were serious—a possible shortage of soda ash, an ingredient critical to my glass manufacturing operation; a letter from the EPA [Environmental Protection Agency] threatening to shut down my plant if the emissions from the stacks could not be cleaned up; other problems with equipment and personnel. There were also the seemingly less consequential issues—the invitation to brunch at the V.P.'s home; the request from the local Rotary Club for a speaker at their next meeting, which had been routed to me by my boss, the director of manufacturing for the Commercial Glass Division. Since I am ambitious and eager to get ahead, I knew that my responses to these invitations were almost as important to my career as my decisions on the soda ash and emission problems.

I was beginning to feel a little less overwhelmed by 8:45. I had at least glanced at all the memos. I had begun to establish priorities and to think about how to attack the most pressing problems. Then the quiet ended.

I heard the voices of my boss and the other plant manager in Commercial Glass. . . . I decided to get a cup of coffee and get into the conversation.

"Just the person I wanted to see," my boss said to me as I approached the coffee machine. "We're having a division meeting at 9:30. I'll want to discuss union, EPA, sales figures for the quarter, and the production problems in your plant."

I groaned inwardly. Another meeting, and I really needed to get on the soda ash thing. I smiled. . . . My stomach began the familiar tightening. Sales figures, I thought anxiously. They were pretty grim last quarter. Of course, if you're running at 105 percent of capacity, how are you going to sell more? . . . I got on the phone and called my purchasing man. Yes, he knew about the pending soda ash problem. What did I want him to do? I resisted the urge to tell him irritably that I was paying him to be on top of things and to give me suggestions. He was new in the job, and although I prefer to manage people who need virtually no training or supervision, you sometimes have to suit your management style to the situation. I explained what I felt should be done. . . .

9:20. The meeting was ten minutes away and I wasn't prepared. But the phone was ringing insistently and my secretary was away. As I answered, my stomach tightened another notch. It was the quality control manager. Something about the new packing suggested by R&D [research and development] and 200,000 bulb casings that had been shattered. Just what we needed when we were running at capacity. I promised to get back after talking to R&D. Good thing I had to go to the meeting. I didn't need to meet R&D people now. Here I was fighting for renovation dollars, and money was being poured down the tubes to finance their pie-in-the-sky ideas.

I grabbed my notes and memos and dashed to the meeting, my phone jangling behind me.

The meeting seemed interminable. Lots of talk. Not many decisions. My mind kept wandering back to the soda ash [and emission problems]. Then we were talking about sales. I winced when my plant's dismal record was paraded. There were good reasons why we couldn't sell more, although it would take too long to explain them. Fighting back my frustration, I promised to do better. . . .

I returned to my desk. There were four phone messages and five more memos. . . . The phone rang. A plant manager in the Advanced Products Division was requesting a meeting at 1:00 to discuss tactics for a performance appraisal task force we'd been appointed to. Since I was supposed to chair the committee, I agreed reluctantly to a meeting over lunch. . . .

Fatigued with the pressures, I pushed aside the bigger problems, hoping to get a sense of accomplishment by dealing with some smaller ones. I dashed off memos saying "yes" to the brunch and the Rotary Club appearance, approved a raise for my plant engineer, and dictated a note to Legal about the EPA predicament.

Then I concentrated on my notes for the luncheon meeting. I made two calls to get information. One source couldn't give me what I needed, and the other's line was busy.

Before I was ready, it was time to meet and eat. My stomach had registered the full shock of a frenetic, demanding, often frustrating Monday morning in the Looking Glass.

For Discussion

1. What managerial functions has the manager performed? Cite specific evidence for each function identified.

2. How well do you think Mintzberg's managerial roles approach explains what has taken place in this case? What particular roles can you identify?

3. Do you think the manager in this case is a good manager? Explain your answer, citing evidence from the case.

4. If you were the manager in this case, what would you have done differently? Why?

References

Opening Quotation. Peter F. Drucker, *People and Performance: The Best of Drucker on Management* (New York: Harper & Row, 1977), p. 8.

Opening Case. Jonathan B. Levine, "GE Carves Out a Road East," *Business Week* (July 30, 1990): 32–33; Shawn Tully, "GE in Hungary: Let There Be Light," *Fortune* (October 22, 1990):137–142; Murray Weidenbaum, "Changes in Europe Will Challenge U.S. Competitiveness," *The Christian Science Monitor* (December 19, 1989): 8.

Closing Case. Diana Hawes, "Through the Looking Glass—A Manager in Action," *Across the Board,* 17 (October 1980): 57–59. Reprinted by permission of The Conference Board and The Center for Creative Leadership.

1. John Noble Wilford, *We Reach the Moon* (New York: Norton, 1971), p. 19.
2. Evert Clark, "The Moon Program's Business Brain Trust," *Nation's Business,* 58 (May 1970): 36.

3. Ed Magnuson, "Fixing NASA," *Time* (June 9, 1986): 14. See also Malcolm McConnell, *Challenger: A Major Malfunction* (New York: Doubleday, 1987); Kenneth A. Kovach and Barry Render, "NASA Managers and *Challenger:* A Profile and Possible Explanation," *Personnel,* 64 (April 1987): 40–44.

4. See Marshall Ingwerson, "Hubble Trouble and Shuttle Fuel Leaks Raise NASA Questions," *The Christian Science Monitor* (July 5, 1990): 7; and William Booth, "Investigating a Billion-Dollar Blunder," *The Washington Post National Weekly Edition* (July 16–22, 1990): 32.

5. Morgan W. McCall, Jr., and Michael M. Lombardo, "What Makes a Top Executive?" *Psychology Today,* 17 (February 1983): 28.

6. William Wiggenhorn, "Motorola U: When Training Becomes an Education," *Harvard Business Review,* 68 (July–August 1990): 74.

7. Gregory L. Miles, "Heinz Ain't Broke, But It's Doing a Lot of Fixing," *Business Week* (December 11, 1989): 85.

8. Data from Robert P. Hey, "White House, Congress Spar Over Energy Policy," *The Christian Science Monitor* (September 14, 1990): 1–2; and Barbara Vobejda, "The Overpopulation Scare Has Gotten Lost in the Crowd," *The Washington Post National Weekly Edition* (July 9–15, 1990): 31.

9. John Dillin, "Birth Control Lags, Report Warns," *The Christian Science Monitor* (February 26, 1990): 8. Also see David C. Walters, "UN Population Report: Opening Volley for '90s," *The Christian Science Monitor* (May 15, 1990): 4.

10. Data from "One Billion More People in the 1990s," *The Christian Science Monitor* (October 26, 1990): 8.

11. Shawn Tully, "The Hunt for the Global Manager," *Fortune* (May 21, 1990): 143.

12. See, for example, Minda Zetlin. "The Greening of Corporate America," *Management Review,* 79 (June 1990): 10–17.

13. Data from James M. Kouzes and Barry Z. Posner, "The Credibility Factor: What Followers Expect from Their Leaders," *Management Review,* 79 (January 1990): 29–33.

14. Further discussion may be found in Colin P. Hales, "What Do Managers Do? A Critical Review of the Evidence," *Journal of Management Studies,* 23 (January 1986): 88–115. Also see Allen I. Kraut, Patricia R. Pedigo, D. Douglas McKenna, and Marvin D. Dunnette, "The Role of the Manager: What's Really Important in Different Management Jobs," *The Academy of Management Executive,* 3 (November 1989): 286–293.

15. See Henri Fayol, *General and Industrial Management,* trans. Constance Storrs (London: Isaac Pitman & Sons, 1949).

16. Henry Mintzberg, "The Manager's Job: Folklore and Fact," *Harvard Business Review,* 53 (July–August 1975): 49.

17. Ibid., p. 54.

18. See Henry Mintzberg, "Managerial Work: Analysis from Observation," *Management Science,* 18 (October 1971): B97–B110.

19. Data from John A. Byrne, "Be Nice to Everybody," *Forbes* (November 5, 1984): 244–246 and "The Corporate Elite," *Business Week,* Special Issue (October 19, 1990): 154.

20. Adapted from Earnest R. Archer, "Things You Lose the Right to Do When You Become a Manager," *Supervisory Management,* 35 (July 1990): 8–9.

21. Excerpted and adapted from Robert Albanese, "Competency-Based Management Education," *Journal of Management Development,* 8, No. 2 (1989): 69.

22. Eugene Linden, "Frederick W. Smith of Federal Express: He Didn't Get There Overnight," *Inc.* (April 1984): 89.

23. More detailed accounts of Miner's motivation to manage research may be found in John B. Miner, *The Human Constraint: The Coming Shortage of Managerial Talent* (Washington, D.C.: Bureau of National Affairs, 1974), pp. 6–7; John B. Miner and Norman R. Smith, "Decline and Stabilization of Managerial Motivation over a 20-Year Period," *Journal of Applied Psychology,* 67 (June 1982): 297–305.

24. Miner and Smith, "Decline and Stabilization," 1982.

25. See Kathryn M. Bartol and David C. Martin, "Managerial Motivation Among MBA Students: A Longitudinal Assessment," *Journal of Occupational Psychology,* 60 (March 1987): 1–12.

26. Shelley J. Davis, "The 1990–91 Job Outlook in Brief," *Occupational Outlook Quarterly* (Spring 1990): 11.

27. Critical appraisals of management education can be found in Robert J. Samuelson, "What Good Are B-Schools?" *Newsweek* (May 14, 1990): 49; and John A. Byrne, "Is Research in the Ivory Tower 'Fuzzy, Irrelevant, Pretentious'?" *Business Week* (October 29, 1990): 62–63, 66.

28. See Ron Zemke, "The Honeywell Studies: How Managers Learn to Manage," *Training,* 22 (August 1985): 46–51.

29. Adapted from Robin Snell, "Graduating from the School of Hard Knocks?" *Journal of Management Development,* 8, No. 5 (1989), 23–30.

30. See James E. Ellis, "At McDonnell Douglas, Plenty of Work But Little Profit," *Business Week* (May 14, 1990): 36.

31. Data from Gregory L. Miles, "Cancel the Funeral—Steel Is on the Mend," *Business Week* (October 5, 1987): 74–76; Michael Schroeder, "Why Steel Is Still Bent Out of Shape," *Business Week* (July 1, 1991): 27–28.

32. See Todd Vogel, "Can Carrier Corp. Turn Up the Juice?" *Business Week* (September 3, 1990): 78–79, 82.

33. G. David Wallace, "America's Leanest and Meanest," *Business Week* (October 5, 1987): 78.

34. Data from *Perspectives 90* (Houston: American Productivity & Quality Center, 1990), pp. 2–3.

35. For example, see Gene Koretz, "The Surge in Factory Productivity Looks Like History Now . . . ," *Business Week* (October 8, 1990): 24.

36. Based on *Perspectives 90,* p. 6.

37. Alan S. Blinder, "Want to Boost Productivity? Try Giving Workers a Say," *Business Week* (April 17, 1989): 10.

38. Dynamics of service-sector productivity are discussed in Michael J. Mandel, "There's a Silver Lining In the Service Sector," *Business Week* (March 4, 1991): 60–61.

39. William A. Ruch, "Productivity Measurement," *Arizona Business* (February 1981): 20.

40. Reed M. Powell, "A Point of View: Doing More with Less—A Key Concept for the 90s," *National Productivity Review,* 9 (Winter 1989/90): 1–2.

41. See Robert Neff, "Can Japan Cope?" *Business Week* (April 23, 1990): 46–49.

42. See Richard Tanner Pascale and Anthony G. Athos. *The Art of Japanese Management* (New York: Warner Books, 1981), p. 24.

43. Alex Taylor III, "Why U.S. Carmakers are Losing Ground," *Fortune* (October 23, 1989): 116.

2

The Evolution of Management Thought

In the renewing society the historian consults the past in the service of the present and the future.

JOHN W. GARDNER

CHAPTER OBJECTIVES

When you finish studying this chapter, you should be able to

- Identify two key assumptions supporting the universal process approach and briefly describe Henri Fayol's contribution.

- Discuss Frederick W. Taylor's approach to improving the practice of industrial management.

- Describe the aim of the human relations movement and explain the circumstances in which it arose.

- Explain the significance of applying open-system thinking to management.

- Explain the practical significance of adopting a contingency perspective.

- Identify and explain the nature of at least four of Peters' and Waterman's eight attributes of excellence.

You Can Call Me Yuki!

The dark oak paneling and deep, luxuriant carpeting in his hushed Los Angeles office promised little more than another buttoned-down corporate big shot. But as soon as I got through the door, Yukiyasu Togo sprang out of his chair, slapped me on the back, pressed two different business cards into my palm—one with his portrait on it—and said, "You can call me Yuki."

Togo, who seemed to be powered by a small nuclear reactor, is the president and CEO of Toyota Motor Sales, USA, Inc. (TMS), which is selling more cars in America than any other Japanese manufacturer and is poised to overtake Chrysler as America's third-largest automaker. (Chrysler is being crunched on two sides: Toyota in sales, Honda in production.) He was wearing sporty aviator-frame glasses and a sleek, gray double-breasted suit with a stylish red and green tie. He looked more like a movie mogul than a corporate executive. "My slogan is 'Sell like hell,' " he said in flawless Hollywoodese. And he has since 1961 been selling Toyotas like hell wherever Toyota wanted them sold. "When they have a problem," says a Japanese acquaintance, "they send in Togo."

The litany of his stunts is legendary. Bangkok, Thailand, 1971: Anti-Japanese sentiment was rampant, Japanese offices were being vandalized, unions were on strike, Togo spoke little Thai. His solution? He shaved his head, entered a Buddhist monastery, and spent two weeks begging barefoot in the streets. "It was an incredible and humbling experience," he said. "But business improved."

Ottawa, Canada, 1976: Togo was president of Toyota Canada. Sales were lousy, his English was mangled. He went house-to-house selling cars, a common practice in Japan. After knocking on 100 doors, some of which were slammed so hard that snow fell on his head, he sold seven cars. "Maybe I was crazy," he said, "but I got to know the Canadians. Our business improved."

America, 1983 to present: Togo barnstormed around the country "feeling the vibrations," began starring in a monthly video letter to his salesmen, and targeted blacks and Hispanics for special philanthropic—and sales—attention. Business has improved. While overall sales of domestically produced cars have slumped about 2 percent, Toyota's are up 45 percent over last year (partly due to the new Kentucky plant—its first in the U.S.—which opened in 1988).

"There's no magic formula for our success," Togo said. "The difference between America's Big Three and Toyota is that their top executives never visit the front line. My office is where my shoes are. Communication is so important." Togo noted, for instance, that he has never seen the GM managers who work with Toyota at their joint-venture NUMMI plant in California update their production line with sales information. "We do," he said, "because we feel everyone likes feedback." . . .

Since 1973 TMS has operated with two distinct hierarchies under its corporate umbrella. In one pyramid, Americans report only to Americans and deal with day-to-day operations. In the other, Japanese advance along a separate track, as if they were in

Japan, and act as an "interface" with head-quarters and their Japanese colleagues at other plants. "The Americans are like a pitcher and catcher, the Japanese are like the second and third basemen," said Togo, "and I am the coach. There is constant communication among all the players, and the system works very well." (So well, in fact, Nissan is now emulating it.)

But one must wonder whether or not the Americans on "Team Toyota" are playing in the same league as their Japanese counterparts. For the Americans, TMS is the whole ball game; for most Japanese, it's only one stop on an international road trip that will eventually take them back to Japan and into senior positions. . . .

"In Kentucky, we have the newest Toyota plant in the world," Togo said. "American workers are superb if properly guided, and the cars we produce are as good—or better—than those in Japan."

Togo's flamboyance is not something he picked up in America; he brought it with him. He and his wife, Misako, raced Toyotas on the international rally circuit until 1955. He also loves to fly. Early this year, he took the company's newest airplane on a round-the-world test drive in just six days. "A lot of Japanese call me an American," he beamed. "I'm delighted. I prefer being called American to Japanese. I've been abroad for 20 years, and I like going native. In fact, my wife and I might retire here."

• • • • • • • • • • • • • • • • • • The history of management and of management theory can be a fruitful study. Management historians believe that a better knowledge of the past will lead to a more productive future. They contend that students of management who fail to understand the evolution of management thought are destined to repeat past mistakes. Moreover, historians and managers alike believe that one needs to know where management has been if one is to understand where it is going. For example, while participating in a Harvard Business School round-table discussion on the value of management history, a top-level business executive summarized:

> It is always hard to communicate any sort of abstract idea to someone else, let alone get any acceptance of it. But when there is some agreement on the factual or historical background of that idea, the possibilities for general agreement expand enormously.[1]

Historians draw a distinction between history and historical perspective. According to one management scholar:

> Historical perspective is the study of a subject in light of its earliest phases and subsequent evolution. Historical perspective differs from history in that the object of historical perspective is to sharpen one's vision of the present, not the past.[2]

This chapter qualifies as a historical perspective because it is part historical fact and part modern-day interpretation. Various approaches in the evolution of management thought are discussed relative to the lessons each can teach today's managers. The term *evolution* is appropriate here because management theory has developed in bits and pieces through the years. Moreover, pioneering contributors to management theory and practice have come from around the globe (see Figure 2.1). A historical perspective puts these pieces together.

The Practice and Study of Management

The systematic study of management is relatively new. As an area of academic study, management is essentially a product of the twentieth century. Only three universities—Pennsylvania, Chicago, and California—offered business management courses before 1900.[3]

But the actual practice of management has been around for thousands of years. The pyramids of Egypt, for example, stand as tangible evidence of the ancient world's ability to manage. It took more than 100,000 individuals twenty years to construct the great pyramid of Cheops. This remarkable achievement was the result of systematically managed effort. Although the Egyptians' management techniques were crude by modern standards, many problems they faced are still around today. They, like today's managers, had to make plans, obtain and mobilize human and material resources, coordinate interdependent jobs, keep records, report their progress, and take corrective action as needed.

An Information Explosion

Since the building of the pyramids, entire civilizations have come and gone. In one form or another, management was practiced in each. Sadly, during those thousands of years of management experience, one modern element was missing: a systematically recorded body of management knowledge. In early cultures management was something one learned by word of mouth and trial and error not something one studied in school, read about in textbooks, theorized about, experimented with, or wrote about.

Thanks to modern print and electronic media, the collective genius of thousands of management theorists and practitioners has been compressed into a veritable mountain of textbooks, journals, research monographs, microfilms, movies, audio and video tapes, and computer tapes and disks. Never before have present and future managers had so much relevant information at their fingertips, often as close as the nearest library. As an indication of what is available, a 1990 study identified 54 journals dealing with just the behavioral side of management.[4] There are many, many others (see Table 2.1). In fact, so much information on management theory and practice exists today that it is difficult, if not impossible, to keep abreast of all of it.

An Interdisciplinary Field

A principal cause of the information explosion in management theory is its interdisciplinary nature. Scholars from several fields—including psychology, sociology, cultural anthropology, mathematics, philosophy, statistics, political science, economics, logistics, computer science, history, and various fields of engineering—have, at one time or another, been interested in management. In addition, administrators in business, government, church, health care, and education all have drawn from and contributed to the study of management. Each group of scholars and practitioners has interpreted and reformulated management according to its own perspective. With each new perspective have come new questions and assumptions, new research techniques, different technical jargon, and new conceptual frameworks.

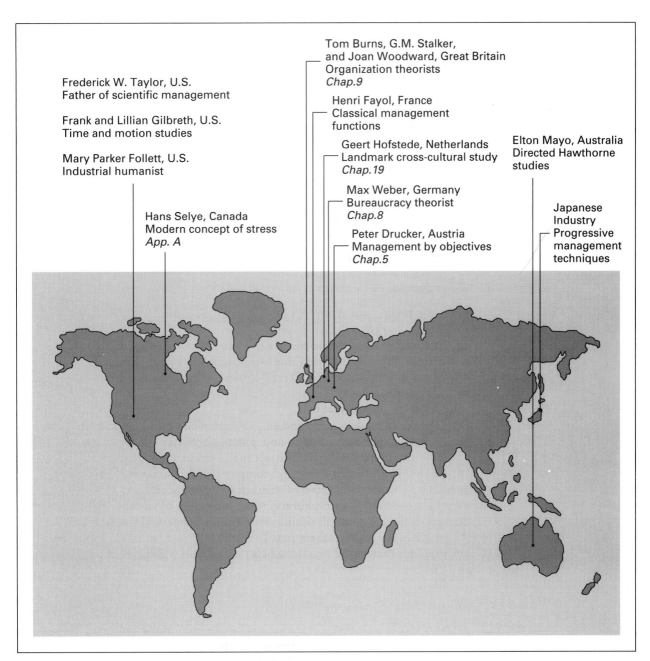

FIGURE 2.1 ● Management Is a Global Affair: Selected Contributors to Management Theory

No Universally Accepted Theory of Management

We can safely state that no single theory of management is universally accepted today.[5] To help put different theories in perspective, we shall discuss five conventional approaches and one modern unconventional perspective. The five conventional approaches are (1) the universal process approach, (2) the operational

TABLE 2.1 ● Where to Read About Management: Selected Periodicals

General Periodicals
Business Week
Business Month
Canadian Business
Forbes
Fortune
Industry Week
International Management (Europe)
Nation's Business
The Wall Street Journal

Scholarly Journals (with a practical orientation)
Academy of Management Executive
Business Horizons
California Management Review
Harvard Business Review
Journal of Business Ethics
National Productivity Review
Organizational Dynamics
Public Administration Review

Academic Journals (with a research orientation)
Academy of Management Journal
Academy of Management Review
Administrative Science Quarterly
Columbia Journal of World Business
Human Relations
Journal of Applied Psychology
Journal of Management

Practitioner Journals (general audience)
HR Magazine (formerly *Personnel Administrator*)
Management Review
Personnel Journal
Supervision
Training

Practitioner Journals (special interest)
Black Enterprise
Datamation (computer applications)
Executive Female
Hispanic Business
Inc. (small business)
Nonprofit World (not-for-profit organizations)
Public Management (public sector)
Purchasing
Technology Review (new technology)

approach, (3) the behavioral approach, (4) the systems approach, and (5) the contingency approach. The unconventional perspective centers on "attributes of excellence," as discussed in the best-selling book *In Search of Excellence* (see Figure 2.2). Understanding these general approaches to the theory and practice of management can help you appreciate how management has evolved, where it is today, and where it appears to be headed.

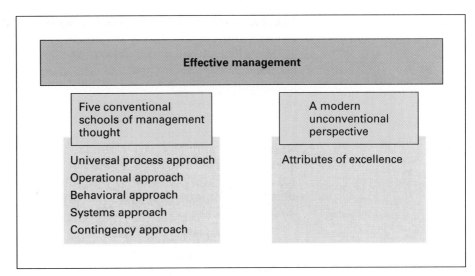

FIGURE 2.2 ● Evolution of Management Thought in the Twentieth Century

The Universal Process Approach

universal process approach
assumes all organizations require the same rational management process

The universal process approach is the oldest and one of the most popular approaches to management thought. It is also known as the universalist or functional approach. According to the **universal process approach,** the administration of all organizations, public or private or large or small, requires the same rational process. The universalist approach is based on two main assumptions. First, although the purpose of organizations may vary (for example, business, government, education, or religion), a core management process remains the same across all organizations. Successful managers, therefore, are interchangeable among organizations of differing purpose. Second, the universal management process can be reduced to a set of separate functions and related principles. Early universal process writers emphasized the specialization of labor (who does what), the chain of command (who reports to whom), and authority (who is ultimately responsible for getting things done).

Henri Fayol's Universal Management Process

In 1916, at the age of seventy-five, Henri Fayol published his now classic book *Administration Industrielle et Générale,* though it did not become widely known in Britain and America until an English translation became available in 1949.[6] Despite its belated appearance in the English-speaking world and despite its having to compete with enthusiastic scientific management and human relations movements in the United States, Fayol's work has left a permanent mark on twentieth-century management thinking.

Fayol was first an engineer and later a successful administrator in a large French mining and metallurgical concern, which is perhaps why he did not resort to theory in his pioneering management book. Rather, Fayol was a manager who attempted to translate his broad administrative experience into practical guidelines for the successful management of all types of organizations.

As we mentioned in the previous chapter, Fayol believed that the manager's job could be divided into five functions, or areas, of managerial responsibility—planning, organizing, command, coordination, and control—which are essential to managerial success. (Some educators refer to them as the POC[3] functions.) His fourteen universal principles of management, as listed in Table 2.2, were intended to show managers how to carry out their functional duties. Fayol's functions and principles have withstood the test of time because of their widespread applicability. In spite of years of reformulation, rewording, expansion, and revision, Fayol's original management functions can still be found in nearly all management texts. In fact, after an extensive review of studies of managerial work, a pair of management scholars drew the following conclusion:

> *The classical functions still represent the most useful way of conceptualizing the manager's job, especially for management education, and perhaps this is why it is still the most favored description of managerial work in current management textbooks. The classical functions provide clear and discrete methods of classifying the thousands of different activities that managers carry out and the techniques they use in terms of the functions they perform for the achievement of organizational goals.[7]*

Lessons from the Universal Process Approach

Fayol's main contribution to management thought was to show how the complex management process can be separated into interdependent areas of responsibility, or functions. Fayol's contention that management is a continuous process beginning with planning and ending with controlling also remains popular today. Contemporary adaptations of Fayol's functions offer students of management a useful framework for analyzing the management process. But as we mentioned in Chapter 1, this sort of rigid functional approach has been criticized for creating the impression that the management process is more rational and orderly than it really is. Fayol's functions, therefore, form a skeleton that needs to be fleshed out with concepts, techniques, and situational refinements from more modern approaches. The functional approach is useful because it specifies what managers *should* do, but the other approaches help explain *why* and *how*.

The Operational Approach

operational approach
production-oriented field of management dedicated to improving efficiency and cutting waste

The term **operational approach** is a convenient description of the production-oriented area of management dedicated to improving efficiency and cutting waste. Since the turn of the century, it has had a number of labels, including scientific management, management science, operations research, production management, and operations management. Underlying this somewhat confusing evolution of terms has been a consistent purpose: to make person-machine systems work as efficiently as possible. Throughout its historical development, the operational approach has been technically and quantitatively oriented.

TABLE 2.2 ● Fayol's Fourteen Universal Principles of Management

1. **Division of work.** Specialization of labor is necessary for organizational success.
2. **Authority.** The right to give orders must accompany responsibility.
3. **Discipline.** Obedience and respect help an organization run smoothly.
4. **Unity of command.** Each employee should receive orders from only one superior.
5. **Unity of direction.** The efforts of everyone in the organization should be co-ordinated and focused in the same direction.
6. **Subordination of individual interests to the general interest.** Resolving the tug of war between personal and organizational interests in favor of the organization is one of management's greatest difficulties.
7. **Remuneration.** Employees should be paid fairly in accordance with their contribution.
8. **Centralization.** The relationship between centralization and decentralization is a matter of proportion; the optimum balance must be found for each organization.
9. **Scalar chain.** Subordinates should observe the formal chain of command unless expressly authorized by their respective superiors to communicate with each other.
10. **Order.** Both material things and people should be in their proper places.
11. **Equity.** Fairness that results from a combination of kindliness and justice will lead to devoted and loyal service.
12. **Stability and tenure of personnel.** People need time to learn their jobs.
13. **Initiative.** One of the greatest satisfactions is formulating and carrying out a plan.
14. **Esprit de corps.** Harmonious effort among individuals is the key to organizational success.

Source: Adapted from Henri Fayol, *General and Industrial Management,* trans. Constance Storrs (London: Isaac Pitman & Sons, 1949). Copyright 1949 by Lake Publishing Company. Reprinted by permission.

Frederick W. Taylor's Scientific Management

••••••••••••••••••
Discuss Frederick W. Taylor's approach to improving the practice of industrial management.

Born in 1856, the son of a Philadelphia lawyer, Frederick Winslow Taylor was the epitome of the self-made man. Because a temporary problem with his eyes kept him from attending Harvard University, Taylor went to work as a common laborer in a small Philadelphia machine shop. In just four years he picked up the trades of pattern maker and machinist.[8] Later, Taylor went to work at Midvale Steel Works, in Philadelphia, where he quickly moved up through the ranks while studying at night for a mechanical engineering degree. As a manager at Midvale, Taylor was appalled at industry's unsystematic practices. He observed little if any cooperation between the managers and the laborers. Inefficiency and waste were rampant. Output restriction among groups of workers, which Taylor called "systematic soldiering," was widespread. Ill-equipped and inadequately trained workers were typically left on their own to determine how to do their jobs. Hence, the father of scientific management committed himself to the relentless pursuit of "finding a better way."[9] Taylor sought nothing less than what he termed a "mental revolution" in the practice of industrial management.

scientific management developing performance standards on the basis of systematic observation and experimentation

According to an early definition, scientific management is "that kind of management which *conducts* a business or affairs by *standards* established by facts or truths gained through *systematic* observation, experiment, or reasoning."[10] The word *experiment* deserves special emphasis because it was Taylor's trademark. While working at Midvale and later at Bethlehem Steel, Taylor started the scientific management movement in industry in four areas: standardization, time and task study, systematic selection and training, and pay incentives.

Standardization. By closely studying metal-cutting operations, Taylor collected extensive data on the optimum cutting-tool speeds and the rates at which stock should be fed into the machines for each job. The resulting standards were then posted for quick reference by the machine operators. He also systematically cataloged and stored the expensive cutting tools that usually were carelessly thrown aside when a job was completed. Operators could go to the carefully arranged tool room, check out the right tool for the job at hand, and check it back in when finished. Taylor's approach caused productivity to jump and costs to fall.

procedures

Frederick W. Taylor, 1856–1915

Time and Task Study. According to the traditional rule-of-thumb approach, there was no "science of shoveling." But after thousands of observations and stopwatch recordings, Taylor detected a serious flaw in the way various materials were being shoveled—each laborer brought his own shovel to work. Taylor knew the company was losing, not saving, money when a laborer used the same shovel for both heavy and light materials. A shovel load of iron ore weighed about thirty pounds, according to Taylor's calculations, whereas a shovel load of rice coal weighed only four pounds. Systematic experimentation revealed that a shovel load of twenty-one pounds was optimum (permitted the greatest movement of material in a day). Taylor significantly increased productivity by having workers use specially sized and shaped shovels provided by the company—large shovels for the lighter materials and smaller ones for heavier work.

Systematic Selection and Training. Although primitive by modern standards, Taylor's experiments with pig iron handling clearly reveal the intent of this phase of scientific management. The task was to lift a ninety-two-pound block of iron (in the steel trade, a "pig"), carry it up an incline (a distance of about thirty-six feet), and drop it into an open railroad car. Taylor observed that on the average, a pig iron handler moved about twelve and a half tons in a ten-hour day of constant effort. After careful study, Taylor found that if he selected the strongest men and instructed them in the proper techniques of lifting and carrying the pigs of iron, he could get each man to load forty-seven tons in a ten-hour day. Surprisingly, this nearly fourfold increase in output was achieved by having the pig iron handlers spend only 43 percent of their time actually hauling iron. The other 57 percent was spent either walking back empty-handed or sitting down. Taylor reported that the laborers liked the new arrangement because they were less fatigued and took home 60 percent more pay.

Pay Incentives. According to Taylor, "What the workmen want from their employers beyond anything else is high wages."[11] This "economic man" assumption led Taylor to believe that piece rates were important to improved productivity. Under traditional piece-rate plans, an individual received a fixed amount of

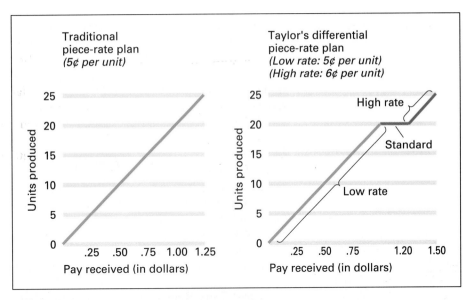

FIGURE 2.3 • Taylor's Differential Piece-Rate Plan

money for each unit of output. Thus, the greater the output, the greater the pay. In his determination to find a better way, Taylor attempted to improve the traditional piece-rate scheme with his differential piece-rate plan.

Figure 2.3 illustrates the added incentive effect of Taylor's differential plan. (The amounts are typical rates of pay in Taylor's time.) Under the traditional plan, a worker would receive a fixed amount (for example, 5 cents) for each unit produced. Seventy-five cents would be received for producing fifteen units and $1.00 for twenty units. In contrast, Taylor's plan required that a time study be carried out to determine the company's idea of a fair day's work. Two piece rates were then put into effect. A low rate would be paid if the worker finished the day below the company's standard, and a high rate when the day's output met or exceeded the standard. As the lines in Figure 2.3 indicate, a hard worker who produced twenty-five units would earn $1.25 under the traditional plan and $1.50 under Taylor's plan.

Taylor's Followers

Among the many who followed in Taylor's footsteps, Frank and Lillian Gilbreth and Henry L. Gantt stand out.

Frank and Lillian Gilbreth. Inspired by Taylor's time studies and motivated by a desire to expand human potential, the Gilbreths turned motion study into an exact science. In so doing, they pioneered the use of motion pictures for studying and streamlining work motions. They paved the way for modern work simplification by cataloging seventeen different hand motions, such as "grasp" and "hold." These they called "therbligs" (actually the name *Gilbreth* spelled backward with the *t* and *h* reversed). Some of their success stories include:

> In laying brick, the motions used in laying a single brick were reduced from eighteen to five—with an increase in output, from one hundred and

Lillian M. Gilbreth,
1878–1972

Frank B. Gilbreth,
1868–1924

twenty bricks an hour to three hundred and fifty an hour, and with a reduction in the resulting fatigue. In folding cotton cloth, twenty to thirty motions were reduced to ten or twelve, with the result that instead of one hundred and fifty dozen pieces of cloth, four hundred dozen were folded, with no added fatigue.[12]

Frank and Lillian Gilbreth were so dedicated to the idea of finding the one best way to do every job that two of their twelve children wrote *Cheaper by the Dozen,* a humorous recollection of scientific management and motion study applied to the Gilbreth household.[13]

Henry L. Gantt. Gantt, a schoolteacher by training, contributed to scientific management by refining production control and cost control techniques. As illustrated in Chapter 5, variations of Gantt's work-scheduling charts are still in use today. He also humanized Taylor's differential piece-rate system by combining a guaranteed day rate (minimum wage) with an above-standard bonus. Gantt was ahead of his time in emphasizing the importance of the human factor and in urging management to concentrate on service rather than profits.[14]

Operations Management

Even though portions of operations management can be traced to Taylor's scientific management, operations management is essentially a product of the post–World War II era. Operations management, like scientific management, aims at promoting efficiency through systematic observation and experimentation. However, operations management (sometimes called production/operations management) tends to be broader in scope and application than scientific management

Henry L. Gantt, 1861–1919

was. Whereas scientific management was limited largely to hand labor and machine shops, operations management specialists apply their expertise to all types of production and service operations, such as the purchase and storage of materials, energy use, product and service design, work flow, safety, quality control, and data processing. Thus, **operations management** is defined as the process of transforming raw materials, technology, and human talent into useful goods and services.[15] Operations managers could be called the front line troops in the war on low productivity growth. Chapter 18 examines this area in detail.

operations management the process of transforming material and human resources into useful goods and services

Lessons from the Operational Approach

Scientific management often appears rather unscientific to those who live in a world of miracle drugs, manned moon landings, industrial robots, and laser technology. *Systematic management* might be a more accurate label. Within the context of haphazard, turn-of-the-century industrial practices, however, scientific management was indeed revolutionary. Heading the list of its lasting contributions is a much-needed emphasis on promoting production efficiency and combating waste. Today, dedication to finding a better way is more important than ever in view of uneven productivity growth and diminishing resources.

Nevertheless, Taylor and the early scientific management proponents have been roundly criticized for viewing workers as unidimensional economic beings interested only in more money. These critics fear that scientific management techniques have dehumanized people by making them act like mindless machines. Not all would agree. According to one respected management scholar who feels that Taylor's work is widely misunderstood and unfairly criticized, Taylor actually improved working conditions by reducing fatigue and redesigning machines to fit people. A systematic analysis of Taylor's contributions led this same management scholar to conclude: "Taylor's track record is remarkable. The point is not, as is often claimed, that he was 'right in the context of his time' but is now outdated, but that *most of his insights are still valid today.*"[16] (See Management Ethics.)

Behavioral management theorists have been critical of the tendency of some operations management specialists to translate everything, including human behavior, into numbers. They argue that people are too multidimensional and unpredictable to have their behavior reduced to abstract models and simplistic mathematical assumptions.

The Behavioral Approach

Like the other approaches to management, the behavioral approach has evolved gradually over many years. Advocates of the behavioral approach to management point out that people deserve to be the central focus of organized activity. They believe that successful management depends largely on a manager's ability to understand and work with people who have a variety of backgrounds, needs, perceptions, and aspirations. The progress of this humanistic approach from the human relations movement to modern organizational behavior has greatly influenced management theory and practice.

Stopwatch Management at UPS

To many workers, the scene looks like a nightmare: everywhere the UPS package deliverer goes, a supervisor follows with a stopwatch, calculating the time it takes her to walk to a customer's door (is she keeping to the standard three-feet-per-second pace?), noting whether she knocks immediately, as she is supposed to, or wastes precious seconds searching for the doorbell. To get the packages to the drivers, sorters must handle 1,124 packages an hour, making a mistake less than once every two hours, and loaders are expected to fill the delivery vans at the rate of at least 500 packages per hour. Engineers have even beveled delivery truck seats to get drivers out the door faster.

Advocates of scientific management are particularly fond of United Parcel Service and point out that it is the nation's largest and most profitable transportation company. The entire company is run on stopwatches, an approach that began in the 1920s when the company's founder, James E. Casey, hired time study engineers to help make his business 30 percent more efficient. And, though UPS's approach may seem inhumane, it has earned the company a consistently high corporate reputation and a low employee turnover rate.

Employees stay partly because of UPS's wages, which can be 30 percent higher than those at nonunion rival Federal Express, and partly because of what one UPS board member calls "managerial socialism." UPS workers earn substantial pieces of the company, and many like the feeling of being an integral part of a team that's working hard and doing a good job. Because the company seldom hires outside executives, drivers can often work their way up to supervisory and management levels, and many retire as millionaires.

Casey declared that he wanted the company to be "owned by its managers and managed by its owners," and in fact most UPS stock is held by 15,000 managers and supervisors. People who work for the company for any length of time therefore get the feeling of being driven not by a faceless, impersonal organization but by themselves. So what may seem like a dinosaur of scientific management continues to succeed in part because the company has a unique human relations approach. Maintaining the balance is tricky, but so far UPS has succeeded.

Sources: Aaron Bernstein, "A Game of Chicken Between the Teamsters and UPS," *Business Week* (August 6, 1990): 32; Kenneth Labich, "Big Changes at Big Brown," *Fortune* (January 18, 1988): 56–64; Daniel Machalaba, "Up to Speed: United Parcel Service Gets Deliveries Done by Driving Its Workers," *The Wall Street Journal* (April 22, 1986): 1; Todd Vogel, "Hello, I Must Be Going: On the Road with UPS," *Business Week* (June 4, 1990): 82.

The Human Relations Movement

human relations movement
an effort to make managers more sensitive to their employees' needs

The **human relations movement** was a concerted effort among theorists and practitioners to make managers more sensitive to employee needs. It came into being as a result of special circumstances that occurred during the first half of this century. As illustrated in Figure 2.4, the human relations movement may be compared to the top of a pyramid. Just as the top of a pyramid must be supported, so too the human relations movement was supported by three very different historic influences: (1) the threat of unionization, (2) the Hawthorne studies, and (3) the philosophy of industrial humanism.

Threat of Unionization. To understand why the human relations movement evolved, one needs first to appreciate its sociopolitical background. From the late 1800s to the 1920s, American industry grew by leaps and bounds as it attempted

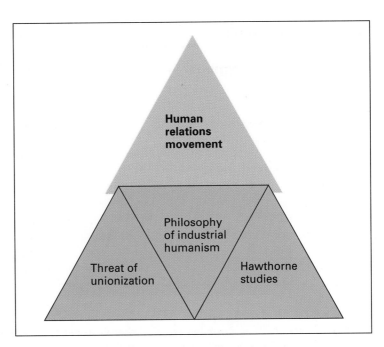

FIGURE 2.4 ● The Human Relations Movement Pyramid

● ● ● ● ● ● ● ● ● ● ● ● ● ● ● ●
Describe the general aim
of the human relations
movement and explain
the circumstances in
which it arose.

to satisfy the many demands of a rapidly growing population. Cheap immigrant labor was readily available, and there was a seller's market for finished goods. Then came the Great Depression in the 1930s, and millions stood in bread lines instead of pay lines. Many held business somehow responsible for the depression, and public sympathy swung from management to labor. Congress consequently began to pass prolabor legislation. When the Wagner Act was passed in 1935, thus legalizing union-management collective bargaining, management began searching for ways to stem the tide of all-out unionization. Early human relations theory proposed an enticing answer: satisfied employees would be less inclined to join unions. Business managers subsequently began adopting morale-boosting human relations techniques as a union-avoidance tactic.

The Hawthorne Studies.   As the sociopolitical climate changed, a second development in industry took place. Behavioral scientists from prestigious universities began to conduct on-the-job behavior studies. Instead of studying tools and techniques in the scientific management tradition, they focused on people. Practical behavioral research such as the famous Hawthorne studies stirred management's interest in the psychological and sociological dynamics of the workplace.

The Hawthorne studies began in 1924 in a Western Electric plant near Chicago as a small-scale scientific management study of the relationship between light intensity and productivity. Curiously, the performance of a select group of employees tended to improve no matter how the physical surroundings were manipulated. Even when the lights were dimmed to moonlight intensity, productivity continued to climb! Scientific management doctrine could not account for what was taking place, and so a team of behavioral science researchers headed by Elton Mayo was brought in from Harvard to conduct a more rigorous study.

Elton Mayo, 1880–1949

By 1932, when the Hawthorne studies ended, over twenty thousand employees had participated in one way or another. After extensive interviewing of the subjects it became clear to researchers that productivity was much less affected by changes in work conditions than by the attitudes of the workers themselves. Specifically, relationships between members of a work group and between workers and their supervisors were found to be more significant. Though the experiments and the theories that evolved from them are criticized today for flawed methodology and statistical inaccuracies, the Hawthorne studies can be credited with turning management theorists away from the simplistic "economic man" model to a more humanistic and realistic view, the "social man" model.[17]

The Philosophy of Industrial Humanism. Although unionization prompted a search for new management techniques and the Hawthorne studies demonstrated that people were important to productivity, a philosophy of human relations was needed to provide a convincing rationale for treating employees better. Elton Mayo, Mary Parker Follett, and Douglas McGregor, although from very different backgrounds, offered just such a philosphy.

Born in Australia, Elton Mayo was a Harvard professor specializing in psychology and sociology when he took over the Hawthorne studies. His 1933 book, *The Human Problems of an Industrial Civilization,* inspired by what he had learned at Hawthorne, cautioned managers that emotional factors were a more important determinant of productive efficiency than physical and logical factors were. Claiming that employees create their own unofficial yet powerful workplace culture complete with norms and sanctions, Mayo urged managers to provide work that fostered personal and subjective satisfaction. He called for a new social order designed to stimulate individual cooperation.

Mary Parker Follett's experience as a management consultant and her background in law, political science, and philosophy produced her strong conviction that managers should be aware that each employee is a complex collection of emotions, beliefs, attitudes, and habits. To get employees to work harder, she

Mary Parker Follett, 1868–1933

Douglas McGregor,
1906–1964

Theory Y McGregor's optimistic assumptions about working people

organizational behavior a modern approach seeking to discover the causes of work behavior and develop better management techniques

believed, managers had to recognize the individual's motivating desires. Accordingly, Follett urged managers to motivate performance rather than to simply demand it. Cooperation, a spirit of unity, and self-control were seen as the keys to both productivity and a democratic way of life.[18] Historians credit Follett, who died in 1933, with being decades ahead of her time in terms of behavioral and systems management theory.[19]

A third philosophical rallying point for industrial humanism was provided by an American scholar named Douglas McGregor. In his 1960 classic, *The Human Side of Enterprise*, McGregor outlined a set of highly optimistic assumptions about human nature. McGregor viewed the typical employee as an energetic and creative individual who could achieve great things if given the opportunity. He labeled the set of assumptions for this optimistic perspective **Theory Y**. McGregor's Theory Y assumptions are listed in Table 2.3, along with what he called the traditional Theory X assumptions. These two sets of assumptions about human nature enabled McGregor to contrast the modern or enlightened view he recommended (Theory Y) with the prevailing traditional view (Theory X), which he criticized for being pessimistic, stifling, and outdated. Because of its relative recency (compared with Mayo's and Follett's work), its catchy labels, and its intuitive appeal, McGregor's Theory X/Y philosophy has left an indelible mark on modern management thinking. Some historians have credited McGregor with launching the field of organizational behavior.

Organizational Behavior

Organizational behavior is a modern approach to management that attempts to determine the causes of human work behavior and translate the results into effective management techniques. As such, it has a strong research orientation. Organizational behaviorists have borrowed an assortment of theories and research techniques from all of the behavioral sciences and applied them to people

TABLE 2.3 ● McGregor's Theories X and Y

Theory X: *Some traditional assumptions about people*	Theory Y: *Some modern assumptions about people*
1. Most people dislike work, and they will avoid it when they can.	1. Work is a natural activity, like play or rest.
2. Most people must be coerced and threatened with punishment before they will work. They require close direction.	2. People are capable of self-direction and self-control if they are committed to objectives.
3. Most people prefer to be directed. They avoid responsibility and have little ambition. They are interested only in security.	3. People will become committed to organizational objectives if they are rewarded for doing so.
	4. The average person can learn to both accept and seek responsibility.
	5. Many people in the general population have imagination, ingenuity, and creativity.

at work in modern organizations. The result is an interdisciplinary field in which psychology predominates. In spite of its relatively new and developing state, organizational behavior has had a significant impact on modern management thought by helping to explain why employees behave as they do. Because human relations has evolved into a practical how-to-do-it discipline for supervisors, organizational behavior amounts to a scientific extension of human relations. Many organizational behavior findings will be examined in Part IV of this text.

Lessons from the Behavioral Approach

Above all else, the behavioral approach makes it clear to present and future managers that *people* are the key to productivity. According to advocates of the behavioral approach, technology, work rules, and standards do not guarantee good job performance. Instead, success depends on motivated and skilled individuals who are committed to organizational objectives. Only a manager's sensitivity to individual concerns can foster the cooperation necessary for high productivity (see Managers in Action).

On the negative side, traditional human relations doctrine has been criticized as vague and simplistic. According to these critics, relatively primitive on-the-job behavioral research does not justify such broad conclusions. For instance, critics do not believe that supportive supervision and good human relations will lead automatically to higher morale and hence to better job performance. Also, recent analyses of the Hawthorne studies, using modern statistical techniques, have generated debate about the validity of the original conclusions.[20]

Fortunately, organizational behavior, as a scientific extension of human relations, promises to fill some of the gaps left by the human relationists while at the same time retaining an emphasis on people. Today, organizational behaviorists are trying to piece together the multiple determinants of effective job performance in various work situations and across cultures.

The Systems Approach

system a collection of parts that operate interdependently to achieve a common purpose

A **system** is a collection of parts that operates interdependently to achieve a common purpose. Working from this definition, the systems approach represents a marked departure from the past; in fact, it requires a completely different style of thinking.

Universal process, scientific management, and human relations theorists studied management by taking things apart. They assumed the whole is equal to the sum of its parts and can be explained in terms of its parts. Systems theorists, in contrast, study management by putting things together and assume that the whole is greater than the sum of its parts. The difference is analytic versus synthetic thinking. According to one management systems expert, "Analytic thinking is, so to speak, outside-in thinking; synthetic thinking is inside-out. Neither negates the value of the other, but by synthetic thinking we can gain understanding that we cannot obtain through analysis, particularly of collective phenomena."[21]

Systems theorists recommend synthetic thinking because management is not practiced in a vacuum. Managers affect, and are in turn affected by, many organi-

Tough Times Require Caring Managers

Team building is key to navigating a downturn. Consider Tom Tyrrell, president of American Steel & Wire Co., which just four years ago was a mothballed unit of USX Corp. One month after the company was resurrected as an independent steelmaker, workers at its only raw steel supplier started a six-month strike. Before the strike was over, American Steel turned back $25 million in orders. But rather than lay off his workers, Mr. Tyrrell put them to work maintaining machinery.

It wasn't all good will. Mr. Tyrrell used job security to build a loyal, productive work force. Today American Steel & Wire is among the lowest-cost, highest-quality wire and rod fabricators in the nation—and sales have quintupled since 1986.

A manager "can't be somebody walking around and giving orders," says Mr. Tyrrell, a 45-year-old executive who jogs to reduce stress. "He's more of a quarterback. He'll jump in and help out."

To build his team, Mr. Tyrrell insists that all employees from top to bottom receive the same vacations, profit sharing and health benefits. Foremen have been outlawed on the shop floor; instead employees are encouraged to find their own ways to cut costs. Yet lavish after-hours parties haven't been eliminated. In fact, Mr. Tyrrell contends that in tough times, employees need social get-togethers more than ever to overcome anxiety and build camaraderie. . . .

One "appreciation dinner" gala featuring an international menu cost $25,000, but it was worth "10 times" the price, he says. And he plans to do it again despite the current slowdown.

If business sours further in coming months, he adds, everyone will be affected equally. Instead of layoffs, employees—including himself—will work a salary-reduced four-day week.

Source: Excerpted from Joan E. Rigdon, "Team Builders Shine in Perilous Waters," Reprinted by permission of *The Wall Street Journal,* © 1990 Dow Jones & Company Inc. All rights reserved worldwide.

zational and environmental variables. Systems thinking has presented the field of management with an enormous challenge: to identify all relevant parts of organized activity and to discover how they interact. Two management writers predicted that systems thinking offers "a basis for understanding organizations and their problems which may one day produce a revolution in organizations comparable to the one brought about by Taylor with scientific management."[22]

Chester I. Barnard's Early Systems Perspective

In one sense, Chester I. Barnard followed in the footsteps of Henri Fayol. Like Fayol, Barnard established a new approach to management on the basis of his experience as a top-level manager. But the former president of New Jersey Bell Telephone's approach differed from Fayol's. Rather than isolating specific management functions and principles, Barnard devised a more abstract systems approach. In his 1938 classic, *The Functions of the Executive,* Barnard characterized all organizations as cooperative systems: "A cooperative system is a complex of physical, biological, personal, and social components which are in a specific systematic relationship by reason of the cooperation of two or more persons for at least one definite end."[23]

According to Barnard, willingness to serve, common purpose, and communication are the principal elements in an organization (or cooperative system).[24]

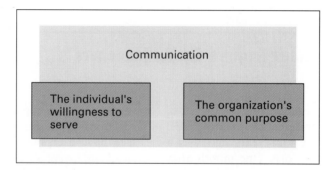

FIGURE 2.5 • Barnard's Cooperative System

He felt that an organization did not exist if these three elements were not present and working interdependently. As illustrated in Figure 2.5, Barnard viewed communication as an energizing force that bridges the natural gap between the individual's willingness to serve and the organization's common purpose.

Barnard's systems perspective has encouraged management and organization theorists to study organizations as complex and dynamic wholes instead of piece by piece. Barnard opened a promising door in the evolution of management thought.

General Systems Theory

general systems theory an area of study based on the assumption that everything is part of a larger, interdependent arrangement

General systems theory is an interdisciplinary area of study based on the assumption that everything is part of a larger, interdependent arrangement. According to Ludwig von Bertalanffy, a biologist and the founder of general systems theory, "In order to understand an organized whole we must know both the parts and the relations between them."[25] This interdisciplinary perspective was eagerly adopted by Barnard's followers because it categorized levels of systems and distinguished between closed and open systems.

Levels of Systems. Envisioning the world as a collection of systems was only the first step for general systems theorists. One of the more important recent steps has been the identification of hierarchies of systems, ranging from very specific systems to general ones. Identifying systems at various levels has helped translate abstract general systems theory into more concrete terms. A hierarchy of systems relevant to management is the seven-level scheme of living systems shown in Figure 2.6. Notice that each system is a subsystem of the one above it.

Closed Versus Open Systems. In addition to identifying hierarchies of systems, general systems theorists have distinguished between closed and open systems. A **closed system** is a self-sufficient entity, whereas an **open system** depends on the surrounding environment for survival. In reality, these two kinds of systems cannot be completely separated from each other. The key to classifying a system as relatively closed or relatively open is to determine the amount of interaction between the system and its environment. A battery-powered digital watch, for example, is a relatively closed system; after the battery is in place, it runs without help from the outside environment. In contrast, a solar-powered clock is a rela-

closed system a self-sufficient entity

open system something that depends on its surrounding environment for survival

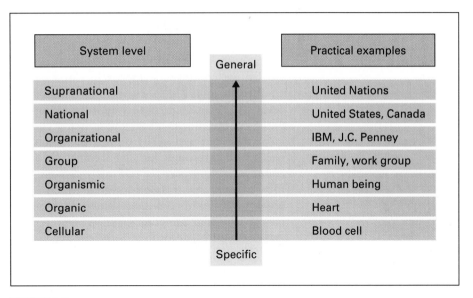

FIGURE 2.6 • Levels of Living Systems

●●●●●●●●●●●●●●●●●
Explain the significance
of applying open-system
thinking to management.

tively open system; it cannot operate without a continual supply of outside energy. The human body is a highly open system because life depends on the body's ability to import oxygen and energy and to export waste. In other words, the human body is highly dependent on the environment for survival.

Along the same lines, general systems theorists tell us that all organizations are open systems because organizational survival depends on interaction with the surrounding environment. Just as "no man is an island," no organization or organizational subsystem is an island, according to this approach.

Lessons from the Systems Approach

Because of the influence of the systems approach, managers now have a greater appreciation for the importance of seeing the whole picture. Open-systems thinking does not permit the manager to become preoccupied with one aspect of organizational management while ignoring other internal and external realities. The manager of a business, for instance, must consider resource availability, technological developments, and market trends when producing and selling a product or service. Another positive aspect of the systems approach is that it tries to integrate various management theories. Although quite different in emphasis, both operations management and organizational behavior have been strongly influenced by systems thinking.

There are critics of the systems approach, of course. Some management scholars see systems thinking as long on intellectual appeal and catchy terminology and short on verifiable facts and practical advice. Even two staunch advocates of a management systems perspective are wary: "Recognizing that the social organization is a contrived system cautions us against making an exact analogy between it and physical and biological systems."[26] At the present time, the systems approach is an instructive way of thinking about managing modern organizations rather than a collection of final answers.[27]

The Contingency Approach

A comparatively new line of thinking among management theorists has been labeled the contingency approach. Contingency management advocates are attempting to take a step away from universally applicable principles of management and toward situational appropriateness. In the words of Fred Luthans, a noted contingency management writer, "The traditional approaches to management were not necessarily wrong, but today they are no longer adequate. The needed breakthrough for management theory and practice can be found in a contingency approach."[28] Formally defined, the **contingency approach** is an effort to determine through research which managerial practices and techniques are appropriate in specific situations. Imagine using Taylor's approach with a college-educated computer engineer! Different situations require different managerial responses, according to the contingency approach.

Generally, the term *contingency* refers to the choice of an alternative course of action. For example, a host may have a contingency plan to move his party indoors if it rains. His subsequent actions are said to be contingent (or dependent) on the weather. In a management context, contingency has become synonymous with situational management. As one contingency theorist put it, "The effectiveness of a given management pattern is contingent upon multitudinous factors and their interrelationship in a particular situation."[29] This means the application of various management tools and techniques must be appropriate to the particular situation because each situation presents to the manager its own problems. A contingency approach is applicable in intercultural dealings in which customs and habits cannot be taken for granted (see The World of Management).

In real-life management, the success of any given technique is dictated by the situation. For example, researchers have found that rigidly structured organizations with many layers of management function best when environmental conditions are relatively stable. Unstable surroundings dictate a more flexible and streamlined organization that can adapt quickly to change. Consequently, traditional principles of management that call for rigidly structured organizations, regardless of the situation, have come into question.

contingency approach research effort to determine which managerial practices and techniques are appropriate in specific situations

Contingency Characteristics

Some management scholars are attracted to contingency thinking because it is a workable compromise between the systems approach and what can be called a purely situational perspective. Figure 2.7 illustrates this relationship. The systems approach is often criticized for being too general and abstract, although the purely situational view, which assumes that every real-life situation requires a distinctly different approach, has been called hopelessly specific. Contingency advocates have tried to take advantage of common denominators without getting trapped into simplistic generalization. Three characteristics of the contingency approach are (1) an open-system perspective, (2) a practical research orientation, and (3) a multivariate approach.

An Open-System Perspective. Open-system thinking is fundamental to the contingency view. Contingency theorists are not satisfied with focusing on just

Test Your Knowledge of International Business Etiquette

Note: Some of the following items have more than one correct answer. Respond and then check your responses against the correct answers below.

1. During business meetings, use first names in:
   a. Great Britain, because everyone is oh so chummy.
   b. Australia, because informality is the rule.
   c. China, because the first name is the surname.
   d. Japan, because the last names are easy to mispronounce.

2. In China, offer expensive gifts to your hosts:
   a. Every time they ask for one.
   b. When you need help getting out of the country.
   c. Never—if they can't reciprocate, they'll lose face.

3. When doing business in Japan, never:
   a. Touch someone (other than handshakes).
   b. Leave your chopsticks in the rice.
   c. Take people to pricier restaurants than they took you to.

   d. All of the above.

4. In some countries, colors are key. Which is true?
   a. For Koreans, writing a person's name in red signifies death.
   b. In China and Japan, gifts wrapped in white or black should only be presented at funerals.
   c. Purple suits in Great Britain represent lack of taste.

5. Which of these choices are obscene gestures?
   a. The okay sign in Brazil.
   b. A hearty slap on the back in Switzerland.
   c. Doing anything with the left hand in Saudi Arabia.
   d. Thumb between second and third finger in Japan.

Answers: 1. b, c; 2. c; 3. d; 4. a, b; 5. a, c, d.

Source: Reprinted with permission, *Business Month*, May 1990. Copyright © 1990, by Goldhirsh Group, Inc., 38 Commercial Wharf, Boston, MA 02110.

the internal workings of organizations. They see the need to understand how organizational subsystems combine to interact with outside social, political, and economic systems.

A Practical Research Orientation. Practical research is that which ultimately leads to more effective on-the-job management. Contingency researchers attempt to translate their findings into tools and situational refinements for more effective management.

A Multivariate Approach. Traditional closed-system thinking prompted a search for simple one-to-one causal relationships. This approach is called bivariate analysis. For example, the traditional human relations assumption that higher morale leads automatically to higher productivity was the result of bivariate analysis. Only one variable, morale, was seen as the sole direct cause of changes in a second variable, productivity. Subsequent multivariate analysis has shown that many variables, including the employee's personality, the nature of the task, rewards, and job and life satisfaction, collectively account for variations in productivity. **Multivariate analysis** is a research technique used to determine how a

multivariate analysis research technique used to determine how a combination of variables interacts to cause a particular outcome

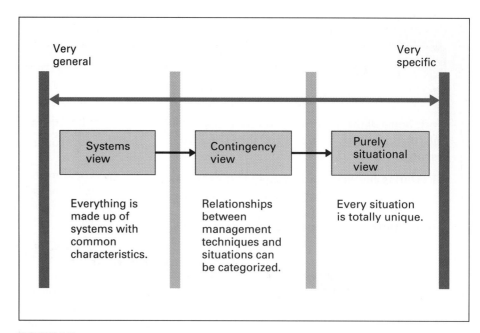

FIGURE 2.7 • The Contingency View: A Compromise

combination of variables interacts to cause a particular outcome. For example, if an employee's personality is authoritarian, the task highly structured, and the individual highly satisfied with his or her life and job, then analysis might show that productivity could be expected to be high. Contingency management theorists strive to carry out practical and relevant multivariate analyses.

Lessons from the Contingency Approach

●●●●●●●●●●●●●●●●●
Explain the practical significance of adopting a contingency perspective.

Although still not fully developed, the contingency approach is a helpful addition to management thought because it emphasizes situational appropriateness. People, organizations, and problems are too complex to justify rigid adherence to universal principles of management. Too, contingency thinking is a practical extension of the systems approach. Assuming that systems thinking is a unifying, synthetic force in management thought, the contingency approach promises to add practical direction.

The contingency approach, like each of the other conventional approaches, has its share of critics. One has criticized contingency theory for creating the impression that the organization is a captive of its environment.[30] If such were strictly the case, attempts to manage the organization would be in vain. In actual fact, organizations are subject to a combination of environmental forces and management practices.

Whether the contingency management theorists have bitten off more than they can chew remains to be seen. At present they appear to be headed in a constructive direction. But it is good to keep in mind that the contingency approach is a promising step rather than the end of the evolution of conventional management thought.

Attributes of Excellence: A Modern Unconventional Perspective

Thomas J. Peters

Robert H. Waterman, Jr.

●●●●●●●●●●●●●●●●
Identify and explain the nature of at least four of Peters' and Waterman's eight attributes of excellence.

In 1982, Thomas J. Peters and Robert H. Waterman, Jr., a pair of management consultants, wrote a book that took the management world by storm. It topped the nonfiction best-seller lists for months, was translated into several foreign languages, and later appeared in paperback. By late 1987, an astonishing five million copies had been sold worldwide.[31] *In Search of Excellence* attempted to explain what makes America's best-run companies successful. Many respected corporate executives hailed Peters' and Waterman's book as the remedy for America's productivity problems. Certain management scholars, however, called the book simplistic and accused the authors of pandering to management's desire for a quick fix. If for no reason other than its widespread acceptance in the management community, *In Search of Excellence* deserves discussion in any historical perspective of management thought.[32]

Peters' and Waterman's approach to management was unconventional for three reasons. First, they attacked conventional management theory and practice for being too conservative, rationalistic, analytical, unemotional, inflexible, negative, and preoccupied with bigness. Second, they replaced conventional management terminology (such as planning, management by objectives, and control) with catch phrases gleaned from successful managers (for example, "Do it, fix it, try it" and "management by wandering around"). Third, they made their key points with stories and anecdotes rather than with objective, quantified data and facts. All this added up to a challenge to take a fresh new look at management. In this section we explore that challenge by discussing the eight attributes of excellence uncovered by Peters and Waterman. Subsequent interpretations of their approach are also examined.

Eight Attributes of Excellence

Peters and Waterman employed a combination of subjective and objective criteria to identify sixty-two of the best-managed companies in the United States. Among the final subsample of thirty-six "excellent" companies that boasted twenty-year records of innovation and profitability were such familiar names as Boeing, Caterpillar, Delta Airlines, Eastman Kodak, IBM, Johnson & Johnson, McDonald's, and 3M. Extensive interviews were conducted at half of these firms and less extensive interviewing took place at the rest.[33] After analyzing the results of their interviews, Peters and Waterman isolated the eight attributes of excellence summarized in Table 2.4. It is important to note that "not all eight attributes were present or conspicuous to the same degree in all of the excellent companies we studied. But in every case at least a preponderance of the eight was clearly visible, quite distinctive."[34]

A Critical Appraisal of the Excellence Approach

Critics have taken Peters and Waterman to task for giving managers more questions than answers, ignoring the contingency approach to management, and

TABLE 2.4 ● Peters' and Waterman's Eight Attributes of Excellence

Attributes of excellence	Key indicators
1. A bias for action	Small scale, easily managed experiments to build knowledge, interest, and commitment.
	Managers stay visible and personally involved in all areas through active, informal communication and spontaneous MBWA ("management by wandering around").
2. Close to the customer	Customer satisfaction is practically an obsession. Input from customers is sought throughout the design/production/marketing cycle.
3. Autonomy and entrepreneurship	Risk taking is encouraged; failure is tolerated. Innovators are encouraged to "champion" their pet projects to see them through to completion.
	Flexible structure permits the formation of "skunk works" (small teams of zealous innovators working on a special project).
	Lots of creative "swings" are encouraged to ensure some "home runs" (successful products).
4. Productivity through people	Individuals are treated with respect and dignity. Enthusiasm, trust, and a family feeling are fostered.
	People are encouraged to have fun while getting something meaningful accomplished.
	Work units are kept small and humane.
5. Hands-on, value-driven	A clear company philosophy is disseminated and followed.
	Personal values are discussed openly, not buried.
	The organization's belief system is reinforced through frequently shared stories, myths, and legends.
	Leaders are positive role models; not "Do-as-I-say, not-as-I-do" authority figures.
6. Stick to the knitting	Management sticks to the business it knows best. Emphasis is on internal growth, not mergers.
7. Simple form, lean staff	Authority is decentralized as much as possible. Headquarters staffs are kept small; talent is pushed out to the field.
8. Simultaneous loose-tight properties	Tight overall strategic and financial control is counterbalanced by decentralized authority, autonomy, and opportunities for creativity.

Source: Adaptation based on eight attributes from *In Search of Excellence: Lessons from America's Best-Run Companies* by Thomas J. Peters and Robert H. Waterman, Jr. Copyright © 1982 by Thomas J. Peters and Robert H. Waterman, Jr. Reprinted by permission of HarperCollins Publishers.

relying too heavily on unsupported generalizations. They also criticize them for taking an overly narrow viewpoint of organizational success. According to one skeptical management consultant:

> *The authors fail to position management effectiveness among the several nonmanagement variables that are also important to sustained corporate*

excellence. Technology, finances, government policy, raw materials, and others must be acknowledged, if only to forestall unreasonable expectations of and for management.[35]

In fact, after reviewing research evidence that fourteen of Peters' and Waterman's "excellent" companies had fallen on hard times by 1984, *Business Week* observed:

One major lesson from all this is that the excellent companies of today will not necessarily be the excellent companies of tomorrow. But the more important lesson is that good management requires much more than following any one set of rules. In Search of Excellence was a response to an era when management put too much emphasis on number-crunching. But companies can also get into trouble by overemphasizing Peters' and Waterman's principles.[36]

Recent research has reinforced the foregoing criticisms of the excellence approach. Unlike Peters and Waterman, Michael Hitt and Duane Ireland conducted a *comparative* analysis of "excellent" companies and industry norms. Companies that satisfied all of Peters' and Waterman's excellent criteria turned out to be no more effective than a random sample of *Fortune* 1000 companies.[37] This outcome prompted Hitt and Ireland to offer five tips for avoiding what they termed "the quick-fix mentality" (see Table 2.5).

Lessons from the Excellence Approach

Certainly more than anything else, Peters and Waterman did a good job of reminding managers to pay closer attention to *basics* such as customers, employees, and new ideas. While reviewing their findings, they noted:

The project showed, more clearly than could have been hoped for, that the excellent companies were, above all, brilliant on the basics. Tools

TABLE 2.5 ● How to Avoid the Quick-Fix Mentality in Management

Our research suggests that practicing managers should embrace appealing ideas when appropriate, but anticipate that solutions typically are far more complex than the type suggested by Peters' and Waterman's search for excellence. To avoid the quick-fix mentality, managers should:

1. Remain current with literature in the field, particularly with journals that translate research into practice.

2. Ensure that concepts applied are based on science or, at least, on some form of rigorous documentation, rather than purely on advocacy.

3. Be willing to examine and implement new concepts, but first do so using pilot tests with small units.

4. Be skeptical when simple solutions are offered; analyze them thoroughly.

5. Constantly anticipate the effects of current actions and events on future results.

Source: Michael A. Hitt and R. Duane Ireland, "Peters and Waterman Revisited: The Unended Quest for Excellence," *Academy of Management Executive*, Vol. 2, No. 2, May 1987, p. 96. Reprinted by permission.

didn't substitute for thinking. Intellect didn't overpower wisdom. Analysis didn't impede action. Rather, these companies worked hard to keep things simple in a complex world. They persisted. They insisted on top quality. They fawned on their customers. They listened to their employees and treated them like adults. They allowed their innovative product or service "champions" long tethers. They allowed some chaos in return for quick action and regular experimentation.[38]

Although discussion of these basics may strike some as a tedious review of the obvious, it is precisely neglect of the basics that keeps many organizations and individuals from achieving excellence.

Despite Peters' and Waterman's subjective research methodology, they deserve credit for reminding managers of the importance of on-the-job experimentation. All the planning in the world cannot teach the practical lessons that one can learn by experimentally rearranging things and observing the results, trying an improved approach, observing, and so on.

A concluding comment is in order to help put the foregoing historical overview into proper perspective. The theoretical tidiness of this chapter, although providing a useful conceptual framework for students of management, generally does not carry over to the practice of management. As the excellence approach makes clear, managers are, first and foremost, pragmatists. They use whatever works. Instead of faithfully adhering to a given school of management thought, successful managers tend to use a "mixed bag" approach. This chapter is a good starting point for you to begin building your own personally relevant and useful approach to management by blending theory, the experience and advice of others, and your own experience.

Summary

Management thought has evolved in bits and pieces over the years. The systematic study of management is largely a product of the twentieth century, however. Management is an interdisciplinary and international field of study that has experienced an information explosion in recent years. Five conventional approaches to management are (1) the universal process approach, (2) the operational approach, (3) the behavioral approach, (4) the systems approach, and (5) the contingency approach. A modern unconventional approach centers on Peters' and Waterman's attributes of corporate excellence.

Henri Fayol's universal process approach assumes that all organizations, regardless of purpose or size, require the same management process. Furthermore, it assumes that this rational process can be reduced to separate functions and principles of management. The universal process approach, the oldest of the various approaches, is still popular today.

Dedicated to promoting production efficiency and reducing waste, the operational approach has evolved from scientific management to operations management. Frederick W. Taylor, the father of scientific management, and his followers revolutionized industrial management through the use of standardization, time and motion study, selection and training, and pay incentives. Largely a product of the post–World War II era, operations management has broadened the scientific pursuit of efficiency to include all productive organizations. Operations management is concerned with the transformation of materials, human talent and skills, and technology into marketable goods and services.

Management has turned to the human factor in the human relations movement and organizational behavior. Emerging from such influences as unionization, the Hawthorne studies, and the philosophy of industrial humanism, the human relations movement began as a concerted effort to make employees' needs a high management priority. Today, organizational behavior tries to identify the multiple determinants of job performance.

Advocates of the systems approach recommend that modern organizations be viewed as open systems. Open systems depend on the outside environment for survival, whereas closed systems do not. Chester I. Barnard stirred early interest in systems thinking in 1938 by suggesting that organizations are cooperative systems energized by communication. General systems theory, an interdisciplinary field based on the assumption that everything is systematically related, has identified a hierarchy of systems and has differentiated between closed and open systems.

A comparatively new approach to management thought is the contingency approach, which stresses situational appropriateness rather than universal principles. The contingency approach is characterized by an open-system perspective, a practical research orientation, and a multivariate approach to research. Contingency thinking is a practical extension of more abstract systems thinking.

In Search of Excellence, Peters' and Waterman's best-selling book, challenged managers to take a fresh, unconventional look at managing. They isolated eight attributes of excellence after studying many of the best-managed and most successful companies in America. Generally, the excellent companies were found to be relatively decentralized and value-driven organizations dedicated to humane treatment of employees, innovation, experimentation, and customer satisfaction. Critics of the excellence approach caution managers to avoid the quick-fix mentality, in which organizational problems and solutions are oversimplified.

Terms to Understand

Universal process approach	System
Operational approach	General systems theory
Scientific management	Closed system
Operations management	Open system
Human relations movement	Contingency approach
Theory Y	Multivariate analysis
Organizational behavior	

Questions for Discussion

1. Why be concerned with management history?
2. Referring to this book's table of contents, what evidence of Fayol's five functions can you find?

3. In your opinion, which of Fayol's fourteen principles of management are still generally valid? Explain.

4. How did scientific management change industrial management?

5. How did the Gilbreths and Gantt extend Taylor's work?

6. Why could the human relations movement be called a significant turning point in management history? How did McGregor help focus needed attention on the "human factor"?

7. Why is an open-system perspective valuable to managers?

8. Cite your own examples of relatively closed and relatively open systems. How can you tell the difference?

9. What important lesson does the contingency approach teach managers?

10. Which of the attributes of excellence listed in Table 2.4 could end up hurting a company if taken to the extreme?

Back to the Opening Case

Now that you have read Chapter 2, you should be able to answer the following questions about the Toyota case:

1. To which school of management thought does Yukiyasu Togo most closely adhere? Explain.

2. What would Chester I. Barnard have to say about Toyota's approach to management?

3. Is it a good idea to have two separate hierarchies in the company? Present your arguments pro or con.

4. What attributes of excellence can you detect in this case?

5. Would you like to work for Yukiyasu Togo? Explain why or why not.

CLOSING CASE

A Curious Search for Excellence at AT&T

January 1, 1984, was a landmark day for American Telephone & Telegraph (AT&T). On that day the federal government's order to divest its twenty-two regional Bell telephone companies took effect. "Ma Bell" ceased to exist as the giant regulated monopoly that had touched the lives of generations of Americans. In fact, the Court even prohibited AT&T from using the famous bell symbol. As an unregulated company, AT&T was free to compete with IBM and other computer and telecommunications companies for pieces of huge information processing and transmitting markets. Critical observers said that AT&T's service-oriented corporate culture would make it difficult, if not impossible, to muster the marketing know-how needed to compete successfully with companies such as IBM. Others were skeptical about AT&T's stated intention to speed up its new product development process. AT&T's top management, meanwhile, was busy reorganizing and putting aggressive go-getters in key positions. What follows is the story of one manager who was brought in to turn AT&T around.

A Golden Opportunity

AT&T Information Systems was created in January 1983 to market information processing equipment. Two major subunits were formed. After the divestiture, General Business Systems (GBS) would be responsible for selling a high volume of small systems. Large accounts were to be handled by the 12,000-person National Business Systems unit. A forty-three-year-old manager, William F. Buehler, was appointed vice president and head of the 3,000-person GBS unit. According to observers, he was given a "free hand" by his boss to shake the old ways. Buehler's sixteen-hour days convinced everyone right from the start that he was serious about pumping some zest into the AT&T bureaucracy.

An Unconventional Approach

A self-proclaimed charismatic leader who reportedly likes the limelight and tends to dominate conversations, Buehler made one thing perfectly clear to his people: he wanted results. But he was willing to do whatever was needed to help them get those results. In a style that was totally out of character with the old Ma Bell way of doing things, Buehler implemented lessons he had learned from two readings of Peters' and Waterman's best seller, *In Search of Excellence*. Through conversations and internal documents he echoed Peters' and Waterman's advice: "bias for action," "keep it simple," "reward results, not process," and "the customer is king." He did a lot of MBWA (management by wandering around), visiting all of his unit's twenty-seven branches across the country. Instead of relying on formal presentations to get across *his way* of doing things, he freely crossed once-sacred hierarchical lines to reach his people more informally. In one instance, Buehler reportedly chatted with

billing personnel in New Jersey while they all lunched on submarine sandwiches. Most branch personnel had never even met an AT&T vice president before.

Not that Buehler was a softy. He established tough sales quotas, making sure that those who met them were handsomely rewarded and those who failed were driven out. To take advantage of peer pressure, he posted sales results for all to see. It took a while for his way to catch on, and his unit's sales initially trailed those of the National Business Systems unit. Other AT&T units appeared to enjoy his apparent failure. At this critical juncture his boss, the man responsible for bringing Buehler in from Pacific Telephone Company, left AT&T.

During Buehler's first year, over one-third of his sales force either quit, were transferred, or were fired. However, the remaining salespeople responded favorably to his willingness to streamline bureaucratic forms (for example, reducing four-page standard contracts to one page) and to eliminate what he believed to be useless memos, meetings, and planning manuals. In addition, he made decisions much more quickly than formerly had been the case. Buehler's unconventional action-oriented approach eventually caught on and salespeople began exceeding their quotas and enjoying the healthy commissions (the highest in AT&T's history) he had established.

A Surprise Ending

One would naturally expect Buehler was destined to become a "crown prince" at AT&T. Unfortunately, such was not to be the case. Barely a year after taking his new position, Buehler was pushed aside into what *The Wall Street Journal* termed "an obscure planning position," though he retained his vice president title. Insiders reported that Buehler's unique style of leadership had ruffled the feathers of top management. Observers were left to ponder if AT&T was thereby stifling the sort of flexibility and competitiveness needed to take on IBM.

For Discussion

1. What aspects of Buehler's approach would Frederick W. Taylor have endorsed?

2. Why do you suppose Buehler was pushed aside? (*Note:* The discussion of organizational cultures in Chapter 8 should give you some hints.)

3. What lessons in excellence had Buehler apparently learned from *In Search of Excellence*?

4. Was Buehler's quest for excellence at AT&T doomed from the start? Explain.

References

Opening Quotation. John W. Gardner, *Self-Renewal: The Individual and the Innovative Society* (New York: Harper & Row, 1964), Chap. 11.

Opening Case. Excerpted from Bill Powell, "Japan's Bosses in America," *Business Month* (August 1990): 38–39, 42.

Closing Case. For additional information on American Telephone and Telegraph (AT&T), see Frank Barbetta, "AT&T Info Sys. Reassigns Small Business User Execs," *Electronic News,* 29 (October 10, 1983): 1, 4; W. Brooke Tunstall, "Cultural Transition at AT&T," *Sloan Management Review,* 25 (Fall 1983): 15–26; Monica Langley, "AT&T Manager Finds His Efforts to Galvanize Sales Meet Resistance," *The Wall Street Journal* (December 16, 1983): 1, 16; Geoff Lewis, "Computer Marketing: AT&T Keeps Banging Its Head," *Business Week* (May 19, 1986): 94; John J. Keller, "A Leaner AT&T Could Cost Thousands of Jobs," *Business Week* (September 15, 1986): 50; Diana Henriques, "Don't Cry for Ma Bell," *Barron's* (March 23, 1987): 8–9, 67; Kathleen K. Wiegner, "Some Modest Proposals," *Forbes* (April 20, 1987): 38, 40.

1. Alonzo L. McDonald, as quoted in Alan M. Kantrow, ed., "Why History Matters to Managers," *Harvard Business Review,* 64 (January–February 1986): 82.

2. Barbara S. Lawrence, "Historical Perspective: Using the Past to Study the Present," *Academy of Management Review,* 9 (April 1984): 307.

3. For a discussion in this area, see "How Business Schools Began," *Business Week* (October 19, 1963): 114–116.

4. See Marian M. Extejt and Jonathan E. Smith, "The Behavioral Sciences and Management: An Evaluation of Relevant Journals," *Journal of Management,* 16 (September 1990): 539–551.

5. An interesting call for the reintegration of management theory may be found in Max S. Wortman, Jr., "Reintegrating and Reconceptualizing Management: A Challenge for the Future," *Review of Business and Economic Research,* 18 (Spring 1983): 1–8.

6. See Henri Fayol, *General and Industrial Management,* trans. Constance Storrs (London: Isaac Pitman & Sons, 1949). An interesting review by Nancy M. Carter of Fayol's book can be found in Allen C. Bluedorn, ed., "Special Book Review Section on the Classics of Management," *Academy of Management Review,* 11 (April 1986): 454–456.

7. Stephen J. Carroll and Dennis J. Gillen, "Are the Classical Management Functions Useful in Describing Managerial Work?" *Academy of Management Review,* 12 (January 1987): 48.

8. Frank B. Copely, *Frederick W. Taylor: Father of Scientific Management* (New York: Harper & Brothers, 1923), I: 3.

9. For expanded treatment, see *Frederick W. Taylor, The Principles of Scientific Management* (New York: Harper & Brothers, 1911). A good retrospective review of Taylor's classic writings may be found in Allen C. Bluedorn, ed., "Special Book Review Section on the Classics of Management," *Academy of Management Review,* 11 (April 1986): 443–447.

10. George D. Babcock, *The Taylor System in Franklin Management,* 2nd ed. (New York: Engineering Magazine Company, 1917), p. 31.

11. Frederick W. Taylor, *Shop Management* (New York: Harper & Brothers, 1911), p. 22.

12. Frank G. Gilbreth and Lillian M. Gilbreth, *Applied Motion Study* (New York: Sturgis & Walton, 1917), p. 42. A retrospective review of the Gilbreths' writings, by Daniel J. Brass, can be found in Allen C. Bluedorn, ed., "Special Book Review Section on the Classics of Management," *Academy of Management Review,* 11 (April 1986): 448–451.

13. See Frank B. Gilbreth, Jr. and Ernestine Gilbreth Carey, *Cheaper by the Dozen* (New York: Thomas Y. Crowell, 1948).

14. For detailed coverage of Gantt's contributions, see H. L. Gantt, *Work, Wages, and Profits,* 2nd ed. (New York: Engineering Magazine Company, 1913). An interesting update on Gantt's

contributions can be found in Peter B. Peterson, "Training and Development: The Views of Henry L. Gantt (1861–1919)," *SAM Advanced Management Journal,* 52 (Winter 1987): 20–23.

15. See Donald W. Fogarty, Thomas R. Hoffman, and Peter W. Stonebraker, *Production and Operations Management* (Cincinnati: South-Western Publishing Co., 1989), pp. 7–8.

16. Edwin A. Locke, "The Ideas of Frederick W. Taylor: An Evaluation," *Academy of Management Review,* 7 (January 1982): 22–23.

17. The Hawthorne studies are discussed in detail in F. J. Roethlisberger and William J. Dickson, *Management and the Worker* (Cambridge, Mass.: Harvard University Press, 1939). Dennis W. Organ's review of this classic book, in which he criticizes the usual textbook treatment of it, can be found in Allen C. Bluedorn, ed., "Special Book Review Section on the Classics of Management," *Academy of Management Review,* 11 (April 1986): 459–463.

18. See Henry C. Metcalf and L. Urwick, *Dynamic Administration: The Collected Papers of Mary Parker Follett* (New York: Harper & Brothers, 1942); Mary Parker Follett, *Freedom and Coordination* (London: Management Publications Trust, 1949). A review by Diane L. Ferry of *Dynamic Administration* can be found in Allen C. Bluedorn, ed., "Special Book Review Section on the Classics of Management," *Academy of Management Review,* 11 (April 1986): 451–454.

19. See L. D. Parker, "Control in Organizational Life: The Contribution of Mary Parker Follett," *Academy of Management Review,* 9 (October 1984): 736–745; and Albie M. Davis, "An Interview with Mary Parker Follett," *Negotiation Journal,* 5 (July 1989): 223–225.

20. For a statistical interpretation of the Hawthorne studies, see Richard Herbert Franke and James D. Kaul, "The Hawthorne Experiments: First Statistical Interpretation," *American Sociological Review,* 43 (October 1978): 623–643. Also see Stephen R. G. Jones, "Worker Interdependence and Output: The Hawthorne Studies Reevaluated," *American Sociological Review,* 55 (April 1990): 176–190.

21. Russell L. Ackoff, "Science in the Systems Age: Beyond IE, OR, and MS," *Operations Research,* 21 (May–June 1973): 664.

22. Charles J. Coleman and David D. Palmer, "Organizational Application of System Theory," *Business Horizons,* 16 (December 1973): 77.

23. Chester I. Barnard, *The Functions of the Executive* (Cambridge, Mass.: Harvard University Press, 1938), p. 65.

24. Ibid., p. 82. A retrospective review, by Thomas L. Keon, of Barnard's *The Functions of the Executive* can be found in Allen C. Bluedorn, ed., "Special Book Review Section on the Classics of Management," *Academy of Management Review,* 11 (April 1986): 456–459.

25. Ludwig von Bertalanffy, "The History and Status of General Systems Theory," *Academy of Management Journal,* 15 (December 1972): 411.

26. Fremont E. Kast and James E. Rosenzweig, *Organization and Management: A Systems Approach,* 4th ed. (New York: McGraw-Hill, 1985), p. 108.

27. For example, see Joseph A. Maciariello, Jeffrey W. Burke, and Donald Tilley, "Improving American Competitiveness: A Management Systems Perspective," *The Academy of Management Executive,* 3 (November 1989): 294–303.

28. Fred Luthans, *Introduction to Management: A Contingency Approach* (New York: McGraw-Hill, 1976), p. 28. Also see Henry L. Tosi, Jr., and John W. Slocum, Jr., "Contingency Theory: Some Suggested Directions," *Journal of Management,* 10 (Spring 1984), pp. 9–26.

29. Y. K. Shetty, "Contingency Management: Current Perspective for Managing Organizations," *Management International Review,* 14, No. 6 (1974): 27.

30. See Joseph W. McGuire, "Management Theory: Retreat to the Academy," *Business Horizons,* 25 (July–August 1982): 37.

31. Data from John A. Byrne, "How the Best Get Better," *Business Week* (September 14, 1987): 98–99.

32. *Business Week* recently listed *In Search of Excellence* among ten indispensable business books. See John A. Byrne, "A Classic Business Bookshelf," *Business Week* (March 5, 1990): 10, 12.

33. Information about the sample in this study may be found in Thomas J. Peters and Robert H. Waterman, Jr., *In Search of Excellence* (New York: Harper & Row, 1982), pp. 19–26.

34. Ibid., pp. 16–17.

35. Daniel T. Carroll, "A Disappointing Search for Excellence," *Harvard Business Review,* 61 (November–December 1983): 88.

36. "Who's Excellent Now?" *Business Week* (November 5, 1984), pp. 76–78.

37. See Michael A. Hitt and R. Duane Ireland, "Peters and Waterman Revisited: The Unended Quest for Excellence," *The Academy of Management Executive,* 1 (May 1987): 91–98.

38. Peters and Waterman, *In Search of Excellence,* p. 13.

3

The Changing Environment of Management

CHAPTER OBJECTIVES

When you finish studying this chapter, you should be able to

- Identify and briefly highlight the thrust of the nine "change drivers" that indicate the general shape of things to come.

- Summarize the demographics of the new workforce.

- Define the term *managing diversity* and explain why it is particularly important today.

- Discuss how the changing political-legal environment is affecting the practice of management.

- Discuss why business cycles, the global economy, and resource management are vital economic considerations for modern managers.

- Describe the three-step innovation process and define the term *intrapreneur*.

Innovation: 3M Company's Eleventh Commandment

At Minnesota Mining & Manufacturing (3M) Company, innovation has been a driving force since it began as a small sandpaper manufacturing operation in 1902. Widely known among consumers for its Scotch-brand tapes, the St. Paul, Minnesota, company today enjoys a reputation as a superbly managed organization. Employee and community relations at 3M have been called exemplary. The company consistently garners top-ten honors in *Fortune* magazine's annual list of America's Most Admired Companies. Among 3M's more than 60,000 products are some exotic offerings, including a suntan lotion that washes off only with soap and water, a surgical stapler, a chemical that makes grass grow more slowly, a hearing aid for the totally deaf, an artificial hip, and a heart-lung machine.

A basic strategy at 3M involves finding and filling cracks in a wide variety of markets rather than trying to dominate individual markets. Approximately 200 new products are launched each year. Despite the widely recognized Scotch brand, most of 3M's sales come from industrial and commercial products. Among those products are coating and bonding materials, X-ray film, photocopiers, and traffic lights. Historically, 3M has competed on the basis of quality and innovative function rather than on the basis of low prices.

An Organization of Entrepreneurs

Preferring to develop its own executives, 3M typically hires engineers right out of midwestern or southern universities. For example, Allen F. Jacobson, an Omaha, Nebraska, native with a chemical engineering degree from Iowa State University, had thirty-nine years with the company when he was appointed chief executive officer in 1986. Because of a desire to be self-sufficient, both upper-managerial talent and new ideas come strictly from within the company. In fact, 3M budgets about 6.5 percent of annual sales for research and development, twice the rate of its U.S. competitors.

Turnover among executives is practically nonexistent. 3M has a powerful incentive for innovators who might be tempted to leave and start their own company. Those who have a great new product idea that turns out to be profitable have a chance to manage it as if it were their own business. Eventually, when several new products are spun off from the original good idea, a separate division may be formed. Accordingly, 3M now has more than forty divisions, each treated essentially as an autonomous profit center with production, marketing, and finance responsibilities.

Pushing Innovation

Top management sets the stage for innovation with a unique carrot-and-stick approach. According to *Fortune:*

Jacobson believes that top managers go astray if they try to impose too much of their own thinking. Says he: "You've got to sponsor your people's ideas. You've got to help them along." At 3M researchers are encouraged to spend 15 percent of their time pursuing projects that will pay off only far down the road. But that carrot hides a stick: Jacobson also insists that 25 percent of each division's annual sales come from products developed in the prior five years.[1]

The "25 percent new product rule" ensures that each 3M researcher keeps one eye on the practical marketability of new ideas. Half of 3M's new products are developed in response to specific customer needs, and half come from basic research. A workable blend of innovation and marketing is important at 3M because the company is constantly in search of a product for a market or a market for a product.

Innovative ideas are nurtured at 3M in a number of ways. First and foremost, even the most far-fetched ideas are given a chance to prove themselves. "Thou shalt not kill a new product idea" is the often-voiced Eleventh Commandment at 3M. In addition, highly sought after innovation awards are granted. "Golden Step" awards are given for products that reach $2 million in sales and achieve a profit within three years of introduction. 3M's annual in-house trade show provides an opportunity for the 115 research centers to show off their latest and greatest ideas. Like participants at any other fair, 3M researchers promote their ideas for three days at attractive display booths. At this unique trade show, however, the customers are not outsiders, but other 3M researchers. Lots of good ideas come from such cross-fertilization. The Carlton Award, named for a former 3M president, is given to top inno-vators as the company's version of the No-bel Prize.

Art Fry, inventor of the yellow Post-it note pads found in most offices today, was honored with a Carlton Award. As the story goes, "Fry found it annoying when the bookmarks fell out of his hymnal at his church in North St. Paul, Minnesota. It would be better, he thought, if he could put in a piece of paper that would adhere to the pages yet be removable to mark other pages."[2] After nearly a year of experiment-ing with various combinations of semiadhe-sives and paper and promoting interest among his colleagues, Fry had a product he thought would sell. And indeed it has, in a rainbow of colors and a variety of sizes. The familiar Post-it notes that peel off without a trace now are a giant commercial success in the highly competitive office supply business.

Things Sometimes Go Wrong

Not all of 3M's promising ideas make it to the marketplace. For example, 3M's innova-tive answer to Johnson & Johnson's highly successful Band-Aid had to be dropped be-cause a cost-competitive manufacturing process could not be developed. Some critics also fault 3M for being slow to take more advantage of consumer markets, thus getting stuck for a time in slow-growth industrial markets. Meanwhile, however, 3M continues to be a leader in what it does best, inno-vation.

● ● ● ● ● ● ● ● ● ● ● ● ● ● ● ●

transience Toffler's term for an accelerating rate of change

Through its emphasis on innovation, 3M provides a good example of how one company handles the ramifications of change in modern society. In his often-quoted books *Future Shock* and *Power Shift,* Alvin Toffler maintains that we are experiencing an unusual form of change today. He applies the term **transience** to the accelerating rate of change that hurls ideas, places, relationships, and technologies at us at an ever faster pace. Using Toffler's language, those who are unprepared to face accelerating change will suffer *future shock,* a disoriented inability to cope.[3]

Managers, by the very nature of their work, often experience a great deal of transience and are prime candidates for future shock. As an example of how

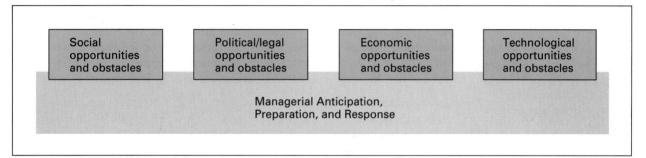

FIGURE 3.1 ● Managing in a Complex and Changing World

fast and dramatically things can change for today's managers, consider what happened to Exxon. Following its highly publicized 1989 Alaskan oil spill, Exxon tumbled from number 6 on *Fortune* magazine's Most Admired Companies list in 1989 to number 110 in 1990.[4] How can managers prepare for an uncertain future? How can they avoid future shock?

The key is for managers to anticipate significant environmental trends and changes and prepare accordingly. Modern managers must keep an ear to the ground, so to speak, for the early warning signs that often precede important changes. These signs can be detected by alert managers who carefully collect, sort out, and interpret reliable and relevant information about events in the outside world. Anticipating change is foresighted and helps managers avoid future shock. Merely reacting to change is hindsighted and thrives on wishful thinking and blind faith in the status quo.

Ignoring the impact of general environmental factors on management makes about as much sense as ignoring the effects of weather and road conditions on high-speed driving. As illustrated in Figure 3.1, the general environment of management includes social, political-legal, economic, and technological dimensions. Changes in each area present managers with unique opportunities and obstacles that will shape not only the organization's strategic direction but also the course of daily operations. The purpose of this chapter, then, is to identify some early warning signs of important sources of change in the general environment of management.

Change Drivers: The General Shape of Things to Come

Each new decade brings a flurry of predictions about what lies ahead. Toffler ushered in the 1970s with *Future Shock* and his prediction of accelerating change.[5] The 1980s brought John Naisbitt's *Megatrends,* with its predictions of an information society, a world economy, the decentralization of power, and greater complexity.[6] With the dawning of the 1990s, yet another round of predictions is at hand.[7] One editorialist, for example, summed up the 1990s as the "Three E" decade. "That stands for *economy, environment,* and *ethics.*"[8] An

Identify and briefly highlight the thrust of the
nine "change drivers"
that indicate the general
shape of things to come.

expanded list of predictions for the 1990s has been offered by forty-four experts representing many different disciplines and professions. They identified one hundred different trends reshaping American society and boiled them down to nine *change drivers*.[9] As a departure point for this chapter, let us sketch an outline for what lies ahead by considering each of the nine change drivers.

1. *A Maturing Population.* As the post–W.W. II baby-boom generation reaches middle age, our preoccupation with youth is giving way to greater sophistication, realism, and responsibility. College education is no longer just for the young. Attempts will be made to reverse the trend toward early retirement.

2. *Society as a Diverse Mosaic.* Growing minority and immigrant populations will contribute to increased ethnic diversity. A multicultural and multilingual workforce will evolve. Products and services will be customized to accommodate individual tastes. Women will move into more executive positions. Political special interest groups will proliferate.

3. *Shifting Societal Roles.* Boundaries between the private (business) and public (government) sectors will blur as social problems such as educational reform are tackled by business leaders. All sorts of government services, from garbage collection to prison administration, will be subcontracted to profit-making firms.

4. *An Information-based Economy.* The marriage of computers and telecommunications technology is making information a key strategic resource. More accessible information will alter traditional patterns of work and leisure and will raise troubling privacy issues. Education will become a top priority as the need for technically skilled workers grows.

5. *Globalization.* As mentioned in Chapter 1, the world is shrinking in all major respects. People, goods, capital, and information are moving around the globe as never before. Foreign ownership of productive assets will increase in the United States and elsewhere. America's dominant role in global economics will diminish somewhat as Japan's and Europe's influence increases. Relationships between "have" and "have-not" nations will be strained as the world population grows and resources diminish.

6. *Emphasis on Quality of Life.* Concerns about personal health and the health of the natural environment will move to the top of the national agenda. Public policy and business practices will be reshaped accordingly. With one out of five American children now growing up in poverty[10] and nearly 32 million Americans presently unable to afford health insurance, questions about social justice are being raised.[11] Toxic waste, quality day care for children and elderly adults, and occupational health risks will get increasing attention.

7. *A Restructured Economy.* Global competition and new technologies are forcing large organizations to become leaner, more flexible, and more responsive to rapidly changing circumstances. Small businesses will continue to mushroom. The service sector will continue to grow. Whole new industries will emerge while others will move to low-wage countries. Comprehensive retraining will get the attention it deserves in a robust and rapidly changing economy.

8. *A Redefinition of Home and Family.* Traditional family chores such as child care, house cleaning, laundry, and meal preparation are increasingly being handled by paid outsiders. The traditional "Leave it to Beaver" family (breadwinning father, housewife/mother, and two children) has given way to a diverse collection of households—single-person homes, childless couples, unmarried couples, single parents, and dual-income families. Thanks to modern information technology, more people will be able to shop, bank, and work in the comfort of their own homes.

9. *Renewed Social Activism.* The phrase "think globally, act locally" will take on new meaning as people tackle tough local problems such as family violence, drug abuse, homelessness, crime, AIDS, and pollution. Business leaders will be called upon to respond ethically, creatively, and generously to community problems. Coalitions will unite former adversaries (such as developers and environmentalists) in cooperative problem solving. Non-profit (volunteer) organizations will grow in importance as they supplement overburdened government agencies in providing social services.

These nine change drivers promise to significantly reshape our world, both for better and for worse. Whether one likes or dislikes them is another matter. Progressive managers must heed them as early warning signals of change in their social, political-legal, economic, and technological environments.

The Social Environment

• • • • • • • • • • • • • • • •
Summarize the demographics of the new workforce.

According to sociologists, society is the product of a constant struggle between the forces of stability and change. Cooperation promotes stability, whereas conflict and competition upset the status quo. The net result is an ever-changing society.[12] Keeping this perspective in mind, we shall discuss four important dimensions of the social environment: demographics, work attitudes, inequalities, and managing diversity. Each presents managers with unique challenges.

Demographics of the New Workforce

demographics statistical profiles of population changes

Demographics—statistical profiles of population size, density, location, and shifts—are a valuable planning tool for managers. Foresighted managers who study demographics can make appropriate adjustments in their staffing and marketing plans. Selected demographic shifts reshaping the U.S. workforce are presented in Figure 3.2. (Other countries have their own demographic trends.) The projections in Figure 3.2 are not "blue sky" numbers. They are based on people already born, more than two-thirds of whom are presently working.[13]

Good and Bad News. In short, the U.S. workforce is getting older, more diverse, and increasingly female. The average age of American workers in the year 2000 will be 39, up from 35 in 1982.[14] Aging of the workforce can be traced to a combination of demographic trends. The baby-boom generation will continue to significantly inflate the 35-to-54 age group during the 1990s. Meanwhile, the 16-to-24 and 25-to-34 age groups will shrink proportionately. Partly because of

When the topic of second languages comes up, most of us automatically think of learning a foreign language. But what about learning sign language to communicate with a hearing-impaired co-worker? Growing up deaf, Bell Atlantic's Brenda Loving learned the importance of a positive attitude and a supportive company. As a volunteer career counselor and corporate role model at the School for the Deaf and Blind in Hampton, Virginia, Loving knows that deaf youngsters often worry about being left behind in the hearing world of work.

the trend toward early retirement and despite higher legal limits for mandatory retirement, the 55-and-over group will barely increase. This changing age mix in the workforce holds both good and bad news for managers. The good news has been summed up as follows by the U.S. Bureau of Labor Statistics:

> *Because workers in their mid-30s to mid-50s usually have substantial work experience and tend to be more stable and reliable than younger workers, this could result in improved productivity and a greater pool of experienced applicants from which employers may choose.*[15]

Now the bad news. Companies employing entry-level workers will experience a labor shortage due to the projected shrinkage of the 16-to-24 age group during the 1990s. Worse yet, the *quality* of available entry-level workers will continue to slip because of deficient reading, writing, and basic math skills. According to *Business Week,*

> *The problem is compounded by a widening mismatch between the skills workers have and the skills employers need. Many jobs in fast-growing service industries require more education than traditional jobs in shrinking blue-collar industries. But schools aren't keeping up with this change. Even worse, more than half a million students [29 percent] drop out of high school every year, and an additional 700,000 who graduate are barely able to read their own diplomas.*[16]

This trend, if allowed to continue, could saddle the U.S. economy with 20 million virtually unemployable young adults by the year 2000.[17] Colleges and the military services will be similarly squeezed. It is no accident that we increasingly find senior citizens waiting on us at the local McDonald's. Through its "McMaster's" program, the company is grooming a new pool of job applicants (and customers) in anticipation of a reduction in its traditional labor and customer base. Not to

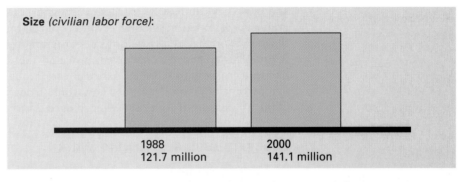

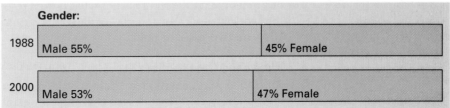

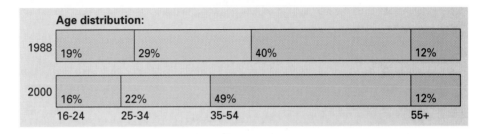

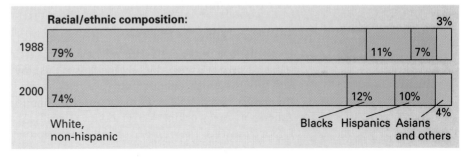

FIGURE 3.2 • The Changing U.S. Workforce: 1988–2000

Sources: Data from U.S. Bureau of Labor Statistics, *Occupational Outlook Handbook,* 1990–1991 edition, pp. 8–12, and *Monthly Labor Review* (November 1989): 9–10, 67.

be outdone, Burger King's new CEO is "redesigning the chain's kitchens with more automated cooking and service operations to compensate for a declining pool of teen labor."[18]

Nobody Home. Managers in small and large businesses as well as in government agencies keep their eyes on demographic projections for more than staffing purposes. They also gauge who their next customers and clients will probably be, and how they can best be reached. Foresight, not hindsight, is required if demographics are to aid marketing. Avon Products, for example, failed to anticipate the impact on their door-to-door sales program of more women in the workforce. Because fewer and fewer women answered the doorbell, Avon representatives had to learn how to sell their personal care products in the workplace. Twenty-five percent of Avon's revenues now come from workplace sales.[19] By the year 2000, 80 percent of American women aged 25 to 54 will be in the labor force.[20]

Changing Attitudes Toward Work

Paul Valéry, a turn-of-the-century French poet, once observed, "The trouble with our times is that the future is not what it used to be." These words aptly describe the work attitudes of today's employees. Organizational loyalty and the work ethic are two cases in point.

Weakened Organizational Loyalty. William H. Whyte's 1956 classic, *The Organization Man*, envisioned a future of large organizations populated by blindly loyal employees. Whyte feared that these "organization men" would lose their sense of self to the organization. According to one observer, precisely the opposite occurred during the 1980s:

> *One major factor weakening corporate loyalty was the dramatic surge in corporate takeovers, leveraged buyouts, "downsizings," and restructuring during the 1980s. These have led to reductions-in-force, indefinite layoffs, early retirements—various names for the millions of people who lost jobs. Many employees have concluded that if their company has no loyalty to them, they deserve no loyalty in return.[21]*

Whyte's organization man (or woman) is the exception to the rule today.

The Work Ethic Is Not Dead. Regarding the work ethic, former President Nixon fretted in the early 1970s that America's celebrated work ethic was being replaced by a welfare ethic. By the late 1980s, the work ethic seemed to be alive and well, as absenteeism among U.S. employees dipped to an all-time low and the number of people working more than one job reached a twenty-year high. Americans are working longer hours as well. According to the U.S. Bureau of Labor Statistics, the number of full-time employees working 49 or more hours per week jumped from 18 to 24 percent between 1980 and 1990.[22] Again, the future of work attitudes has not turned out as predicted.

A New Social Contract between Employer and Employee. Between World War II and the 1970s there was an implicit cultural agreement, a social contract, in the United States between employers and employees: "Be loyal to the company and the company will take care of you until retirement." However, as mentioned above, an era of layoffs and cutbacks has helped shape a new social contract in the workplace, framed in these terms:

> *Survival and success now require organizations to change, shift gears, innovate constantly. This means that any contract that binds them to past conditions—for materials, supplies, parts, capital, distribution, energy or human resources—is dangerous.*

The new contracts have to acknowledge shared interests, shared benefits from the agreement, a commitment to change and innovation, and a "fair exchange" on the part of both parties. What this means is that employment will be increasingly short term, that it will be driven more by individual contracts, that it will be project oriented.[23]

new social contract assumption that employer-employee relationship will be a shorter-term one based on convenience, rather than for life

Thus, the **new social contract** is not based on the notion of lifetime employment with a single employer but rather on shorter-term relationships of convenience. Mikki DelRio, a middle manager at AT&T, put it more bluntly: "Whether you work for AT&T, IBM, or a smaller company, there are no guarantees anymore."[24]

Nagging Inequalities in the Workplace

Can America achieve full and lasting international competitiveness if a large proportion of its workforce suffers nagging inequalities? (See Figure 3.3.) Probably not. Unfortunately, women, minorities, and part-timers often encounter barriers in the workplace. Let us open our discussion by focusing on women, because their plight is shared by all minorities to varying degrees.

Under the Glass Ceiling. As a large and influential minority, women are demanding and getting a greater share of workplace rewards and opportunities. According to U.S. government figures, women held nearly 45 percent of all jobs in the executive, administrative, and managerial category in 1988.[25] But the financial gap is still sizable. In 1988, American women working full time earned on the average only 66 percent of what men earned, up from 61 percent in 1978.[26] Despite this modest improvement, the pay gap between men and women remains large; women presently account for two-thirds of all workers earning minimum wage or less.[27] Moreover, women still bump up against the so-called glass ceiling when trying to reach the top of the managerial ladder. "The **glass ceiling** is a concept popularized in the 1980s to describe a barrier so subtle that it is transparent, yet so strong that it prevents women and minorities from moving up in the management hierarchy."[28] In fact, only two *Fortune* 1000 companies have a female chief executive officer.[29] Why is there a glass ceiling? In a recent survey of 241 chief executive officers, 81 percent of those who acknowledged the glass ceiling laid the blame on *preconceptions* and *stereotyping*.[30]

glass ceiling the transparent but strong barrier keeping women and minorities from moving up the management ladder

Another force is also at work here, siphoning off some of the best female executive talent part way up the corporate ladder. Many women are leaving the corporate ranks to start their own businesses. Indeed, women are starting businesses at more than twice the rate of men and are projected to own half of America's businesses by the year 2000.[31]

Continuing Pressure for Equal Opportunity. Persistent inequality between whites and blacks is underscored by the fact that unemployment among blacks has been more than twice that for whites in recent years. Women, blacks, Hispanics, Native Americans, the physically challenged, and other minorities who are overrepresented in either low-level, low-paying jobs or the unemployment line can be expected to press harder to become full partners in the world of work. Equal employment opportunity (EEO) and affirmative action are discussed in Chapter 10.

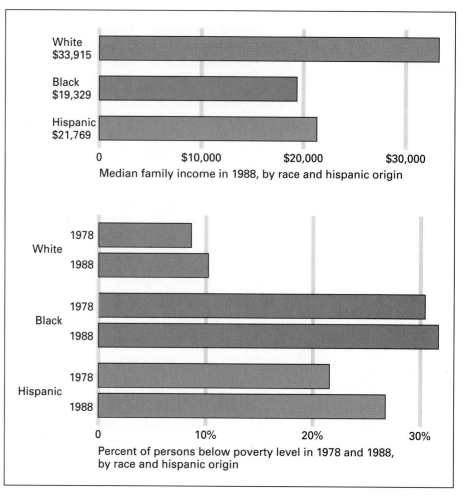

FIGURE 3.3 • Statistics of Inequality in the United States

Source: U.S. Department of Commerce, Bureau of the Census, *Statistical Abstract of the United States,* 1990, pp. 451, 458.

Part-timer Promises and Problems. Driven largely by economic necessity, 25 percent of the U.S. labor force is now made up of **contingent workers.** This category includes a diverse array of part-timers, temporary workers, and self-employed persons. It is growing at a much faster rate than the overall workforce. "Their common denominator is that they do not have a long-term implicit contract with their ultimate employers, the purchasers of the labor and services they provide."[32] Employers are relying more on part-timers for two basic reasons. First, because they are paid at lower rates and do not receive benefits, part-timers are much less costly to employ than full-time employees. Second, as a flexible workforce, they can be let go when times are bad, without the usual repercussions of a general layoff.

On the down side, research indicates that part-time employees tend to have more negative work attitudes than their full-time coworkers. In addition, part-timers express less organizational loyalty and quit more readily than full-timers.[33]

contingent workers part-timers and other employees who do not have a long-term implicit contract with their ultimate employers

Also, critics warn of the risk of creating a permanent underclass of employees. In point of fact, "nearly 80 percent of full-time year-round employees enjoy employer-sponsored health insurance, compared with less than 30 percent of part-timers."[34] Part-time employees also come up seriously short on unemployment and retirement coverage. The plight of part-timers promises to become a major social and political issue in the years to come.

Managing Diversity

managing diversity process of helping all employees, including women and minorities, reach their full potential

Progressive organizations are taking steps to more fully utilize America's increasingly diverse workforce. One highly publicized approach is called simply managing diversity. **Managing diversity** is the process of creating an organizational culture that enables all employees, including women and minorities, to realize their full potential.[35] It builds upon equal employment opportunity and affirmative action programs. EEO and affirmative action are necessary to get more women and minorities into the workplace, but now comprehensive managing-diversity programs are needed to weave them into the fabric of the organization. Also, managing diversity programs embrace white males who have sometimes felt slighted or ignored by EEO and affirmative action programs. Every employee is important in today's diverse workplace, according to this new perspective. The driving motivation behind diversity programs is partly ethical and partly practical (for an example, see Management Ethics).

• • • • • • • • • • • • • • • •

Define the term *managing diversity* and explain why it is particularly important today.

Slow Response. A recent study of U.S. companies criticized American business for responding too slowly and unimaginatively to the new diverse workforce. For example, only 29 percent of the firms said they were training their managers to value and manage diversity.[36] This number is expected to climb sharply during the 1990s.

Promising Beginnings. Among the diversity programs in use today are

- Teaching English as a second language,
- Creating mentor programs (an experienced employee coaches and sponsors a newcomer),
- Providing immigration assistance,
- Fostering the development of support groups for minorities,
- Training minorities for managerial positions,
- Training managers to value and skillfully manage diversity, and
- Actively recruiting minorities.[37]

The scope of managing diversity is limited only by management's depth of commitment and imagination. For example, a supervisor learns sign language to communicate with a hearing-impaired employee. Or a married male manager attends a diversity workshop and becomes aware of the difficulties of being a single working mother. Perhaps a young manager's age bias is blunted after reading a research report documenting that older employees tend to be absent less often and have lower accident rates than younger ones.[38] Maybe a hotel chain executive is stirred to action after reading about Marriott Corporation's Hire-the-Handicapped program.[39]

Social Implications for Management

From these social trends we can infer some future impacts on the practice of management. A reduced supply of qualified entry-level employees will force work organizations to provide more remedial education (basic reading, writing, and math skills). Additionally, companies will become more deeply involved in funding and helping to reform the entire education system.

MANAGEMENT ETHICS

Why Managing Diversity Makes Sense at Corning

Corning characterizes its 1970s affirmative action program as a form of legal compliance. The law dictated affirmative action and morality required it, so the company did its best to hire minorities and women.

The ensuing cycle was classic: recruitment, confidence, disappointment, embarrassment, crisis, more recruitment. Talented women and blacks joined the company only to plateau or resign. Few reached upper management levels, and no one could say exactly why.

Then James R. Houghton took over as CEO in 1983 and made the diverse workforce one of Corning's three top priorities, alongside Total Quality and a higher return on equity. His logic was twofold:

First of all, the company had higher attrition rates for minorities and women than for white males, which meant that investments in training and development were being wasted. Second, he believed that the Corning workforce should more closely mirror the Corning customer base.

In order to break the cycle of recruitment and subsequent frustration, the company established two quality improvement teams headed by senior executives, one for black progress and one for women's progress. Mandatory awareness training was introduced for some 7,000 salaried employees—a day and a half for gender awareness, two-and-a-half days for racial awareness. One goal of the training is to identify unconscious company values that work against minorities and women. For example, a number of awareness groups reached the conclusion that working late had so much symbolic value that managers tended to look more at the quantity than at the quality of time spent on the job, with negative effects on employees with dependent-care responsibilities.

The company also made an effort to improve communications by printing stories and articles about the diverse workforce in its in-house newspaper and by publicizing employee success stories that emphasize diversity. It worked hard to identify and publicize promotion criteria. Career planning systems were introduced for all employees.

With regard to recruitment, Corning set up a nationwide scholarship program that provides renewable grants of $5,000 per year of college in exchange for a summer of paid work at some Corning installation. A majority of program participants have come to work for Corning full-time after graduation, and very few have left the company so far, though the program has been in place only four years.

The company expanded its summer intern program, with an emphasis on minorities and women, and established formal recruiting contacts with campus groups like the Society of Women Engineers and the National Black MBA Association.

Corning sees its efforts to manage diversity not only as a social and moral issue but also as a question of efficiency and competitiveness. In the words of Mr. Houghton, "It simply makes good business sense."

Source: Reprinted by permission of *Harvard Business Review.* An exhibit from "From Affirmative Action to Affirming Diversity" by R. Roosevelt Thomas, Jr., March–April 1990. Copyright © 1990 by the President and Fellows of Harvard College; all rights reserved.

Giant corporations that only a few years ago gave money solely to universities suddenly are pouring hundreds of millions into K–12 education. Volunteers and cash are gushing out of the business community and into a vast array of projects: parenting and nutrition classes for pregnant mothers, dropout-prevention programs, college scholarships, management training for school principals, advanced training for teachers, mentors for students, field trips, satellite schools near corporate offices—the list is long and growing longer.

IBM alone spent more than $20 million on K–12 projects in 1989 and has committed at least $52 million over the next five years.[40]

An aging workforce will challenge management to discard age stereotypes and creatively retrain older employees whose job skills are obsolete.

More women in the workforce will put additional pressures on management to erase gender differences in status and pay. Women working outside the home will demand more flexible and accommodating work arrangements, including job sharing, flexible work schedules, child and elder-parent day care, parental leaves, and support groups at work. Progressive companies such as Avon, CBS, Dayton-Hudson, and US West already provide such programs.[41] Blacks and other ethnic minorities, motivated by persistent economic inequalities, will press management to follow the spirit as well as the letter of existing equal employment opportunity laws.

The Political-Legal Environment

In its broadest terms, *politics* is the art (or science) of public influence and control. Laws are an outcome of the political process that differentiate good and bad conduct. An orderly political process is necessary because modern society is the product of an evolving consensus among diverse individuals and groups, often with conflicting interests and objectives. Although the list of special interest groups is long and still growing, not everyone can have his or her own way. The political system tries to balance competing interests in a generally acceptable manner.

Ideally, elected officials pass laws that, when enforced, control individual and collective conduct for the general good. Unfortunately, as we all know, variables such as hollow campaign promises, illegal campaign financing, and voter apathy throw sand into a democracy's political gears. Managers, as both citizens and caretakers of socially, politically, and economically powerful organizations, have a large stake in the political-legal environment. Two key pressure points for managers in this area are the politicization of management and increased personal legal accountability.

> ●●●●●●●●●●●●●●●●
> Discuss how the changing political-legal environment is affecting the practice of management.

The Politicization of Management

Prepared or not and willing or not, today's managers often find themselves embroiled in issues with clearly political overtones. Consider, for example, the predicament of Domino's Pizza Inc. founder, Thomas S. Monaghan, in 1989:

Consumer groups and state safety officials want to halt the company's thirty-minute delivery guarantee because of dozens of serious accidents involving Domino's drivers. And the National Organization for Women urged a Domino's boycott because of Monaghan's financial support of abortion opponents.[42]

This sort of political pressure has spurred the growth of a practice called *issues management*.

issues management ongoing process of identifying, evaluating, and responding to important social and political issues

Issues Management.   **Issues management** (IM) is defined as the ongoing organizational process of identifying, evaluating, and responding to relevant and important social and political issues. According to a pair of experts on the subject:

The purpose of IM is twofold. First, it attempts to minimize "surprises" which accompany social and political change by serving as an early warning system for potential environmental threats and opportunities. IM analyzes the past development of an issue and assesses its importance for the firm. Second, IM attempts to prompt more systematic and effective responses to particular issues by serving as a coordinating and integrating force within the corporation. Once the issue has been analyzed, IM constructs alternative responses to deal with competing internal and external demands.[43]

IM is not an exact science. It has been carried out in various ways in the name of strategic planning, public relations, community affairs, and corporate communications, among others. IM's main contribution to good management is its emphasis on systematic preparedness for social and political action. With this background in mind, let us turn our attention to three general political responses and four specific political strategies.

General Political Responses.   The three general political responses available to management can be plotted on a continuum, as illustrated in Figure 3.4. Managers who are politically inactive occupy the middle neutral zone and have a "wait and see" attitude. But few managers today can afford the luxury of a neutral political stance. Those on the extreme left of the continuum are politically active in defending the status quo. In contrast, politically active managers on the right end of the continuum try to identify and respond to emerging public wishes.

In recent years, more and more business managers have noticeably swung from being reactive to proactive. Why? In short, they view prompt action as a way to avoid additional governmental regulation. A recent move by 3M Company is illustrative.

Minnesota Mining & Manufacturing is going beyond the call of duty and government deadlines. For example, new federal regulations require replacement or improvement by 1998 of underground storage tanks for liquids and gases. The company decided to comply by 1992 instead, and to have all tanks worldwide in compliance. Cost: more than $80 million. "Regulations are about to overwhelm us," says Robert Bringer, 3M staff vice president for environmental engineering and pollution control. "The only way we see to deal with that is to reduce the number of materials we emit that trigger regulation."[44]

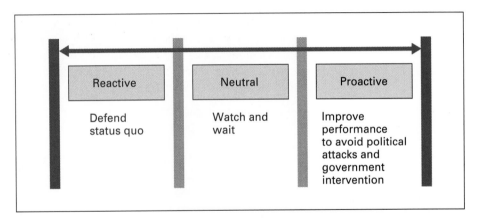

FIGURE 3.4 • Management's Political Response Continuum

Specific Political Strategies. Whether acting reactively or proactively, managers can employ four major political strategies.[45]

1. *Campaign Financing.* Although federal law prohibits U.S. corporations from backing a specific candidate or party with the firm's name, funds, or free labor, a legal alternative is available. Corporations can form political action committees (PACs) to solicit volunteer contributions from employees biannually for the support of preferred candidates and parties. Importantly, PACs are registered with the Federal Election Commission and are required to keep detailed and accurate records of receipts and expenditures. Some criticize corporate PACs for having too great an influence over federal politics. But legislators are reluctant to tamper with a funding mechanism that tends to favor those already in office.[46]

2. *Lobbying.* Historically, lobbying has been management's most popular and successful political strategy. Secret and informal meetings between hired representatives and key legislators in smoke-filled rooms have largely been replaced by a more forthright approach. Today, formal presentations by well-prepared company representatives are the preferred approach to lobbying for political support. According to a 1990 *Business Week*/Harris Poll of Capitol Hill staff, the U.S. banking industry was the most effective lobbier of Congress.[47]

3. *Coalition Building.* In a political environment of countless special interest groups, managers are finding that coalitions built around common rallying points are required for political impact. For example, an unlikely coalition of disenchanted blue-collar workers and conservative business leaders suppressed their differences long enough to help elect Ronald Reagan in 1980 and re-elect him in 1984.

4. *Indirect Lobbying.* Having learned a lesson from unions, business managers now appreciate the value of grassroots lobbying. Members of legislative bodies tend to be more responsive to the desires of their constituents than to those of individuals who vote in other districts. Employee and consumer letter-writing campaigns have proved effective. But care needs to

During the days of high finance in the 1980s, Michael R. Milken was the toast of Wall Street for having developed the concept of junk bonds. These low-quality, high-paying instruments fueled many of the mergers, takeovers, and buyouts that reshaped the American industrial landscape. Unfortunately for Milken, who broke a number of securities laws, the dream ended abruptly in 1990 with a ten-year jail sentence and $600 million in fines.

advocacy advertising promoting a point of view along with a product or service

be taken. U.S. Congress, for example, is inundated with 300 million mailings a year. Only personal letters, properly addressed to a specific legislator, tend to get read. "Post cards are not read or even counted—they are weighed. Preprinted letters are viewed with suspicion."[48] **Advocacy advertising,** the controversial practice of promoting a point of view along with a product or service, is another form of indirect lobbying that has grown in popularity in recent years.[49]

Increased Personal Legal Accountability

Recent changes in the political and legal climate have made it increasingly difficult for managers to take refuge in the bureaucratic shadows when a law has been broken. Managers who make illegal decisions stand a good chance of being held personally accountable in a court of law. For example, consider the following facts.

In 1984, after an employee at a Chicago-area company died of cyanide poisoning, Illinois state prosecutors indicted the firm's five top managers for murder (three were subsequently convicted and given twenty-five-year jail sentences).[50] For the period 1988–1990, *Fortune* tallied the following scorecard for criminals in the savings and loan industry: 446 indictments; 331 convictions; more than 165 sentenced to an average of three and one-half years in prison.[51] In late 1990, Wall Street's junk-bond king, Michael R. Milken, was given a ten-year prison sentence after pleading guilty to securities and tax violations.

The Brits Get Tough on White-Collar Crime

It was a trial worthy of, well, the Guinness Book of World Records. It lasted six months, involved more than 60 witnesses and marked Britain's first major conviction associated with the merger mania of the '80s. When it was over, Ernest Saunders, the former chief executive of brewing conglomerate Guinness PLC, was sentenced to a remarkably stiff five-year jail term in connection with the 1986 takeover of The Distillers Co., a Scotch-whisky and gin maker. The sentence marked a departure from Britain's business-as-usual approach to white-collar crime. "Until now, nobody here was making a political career out of fighting white-collar crime," says Dr. Michael Levi, director of criminological studies at the University of Wales. "The typical British reaction was to say, 'Don't rock the boat'."

It was an American—confessed stock manipulator Ivan Boesky—who finally rocked Guinness's boat. Tips from Boesky reportedly helped authorities convict Saunders and three other financiers of illegally propping up Guinness's stock price. Saunders, a former Nestlé executive who once came under fire for marketing powdered infant formula to Third World countries, had maintained his innocence. In the end, it was he who uttered the most telling comment about the sentence's deterrent effect. "Do you think that I would have risked all this if I thought I would go to jail?"

Milken also paid $600 million in criminal and civil penalties and was banned from the securities business for life.[52] Milken's employer, Drexel Burnham Lambert Inc., went bankrupt. This disturbing chapter in American business history shows a clear pattern of managers being held *personally responsible* for the illegal actions of their companies. The trend is spreading to other countries as well (see The World of Management).

Political-Legal Implications for Management

Managers will continue to be forced into becoming more politically astute, whether they like it or not. Support appears to be growing for the idea that managers can and should try to shape the political climate in which they operate. And the vigilant media and a wary public can be expected to keep a close eye on the form and substance of managerial politics to ensure that the public interest is served. Managers who abuse their political power and/or engage in criminal conduct while at work will increasingly be held personally accountable.

On the legal side, managers are attempting to curb the skyrocketing costs of litigation. U.S. businesses spend over $20 billion annually on court-related legal fees.[53] One promising approach is the legal audit. A **legal audit** reviews all aspects of a firm's operations to pinpoint possible liabilities and other legal problems."[54] For example, a company's job application forms need to be carefully screened by the human resources department to eliminate any questions that could trigger a discriminatory hiring lawsuit. Another approach, called **alternative dispute resolution** (ADR), strives to curb courtroom costs by settling disagreements out of court through techniques such as arbitration and mediation.

legal audit review of all operations to pinpoint possible legal liabilities or problems

alternative dispute resolution avoiding courtroom battles by settling disputes with less costly methods including arbitration and mediation

The modern ADR phenomenon has led to much greater use of older methods such as arbitration and mediation, as well as the creation of many new methods such as mini-trial, summary jury trial, private judging, neutral evaluation, and regulatory negotiation. Variations and hybrids of these techniques are also commonly found today.[55]

As a technical point, a third-party arbitrator makes a binding decision whereas a mediator helps the parties reach their own agreement.

The Economic Environment

These are turbulent times for national and world economics. Supposedly tried and true fiscal and monetary policies have been revamped as the global economy has proved increasingly unpredictable. Conservatives, who believe the competitive marketplace should be the final arbiter of who gets what, recommend less government interference. Liberals, who blame the marketplace for all sorts of ills including poverty and environmental destruction, suggest various government interventions ranging from equal employment opportunity to protective tariffs. As stated in Chapter 1, there is a close relationship between economics and management. Economics is the study of how scarce resources are used to create wealth and how that wealth is distributed. Managers, as trustees of our resource-consuming productive organizations, perform an essentially economic function.

Three aspects of the economic environment of management deserving special consideration are business cycles, the global economy, and resource management.

> Discuss why business cycles, the global economy, and resource management are vital economic considerations for modern managers.

Coping with Business Cycles

business cycle the up and down movement of an economy's ability to generate wealth

The **business cycle** is the up and down movement of an economy's ability to generate wealth; it has a predictable structure but variable timing. Historical economic data from industrialized economies show a clear pattern of alternating expansions and recessions. In between have been peaks and troughs of varying magnitude and duration. According to economist Paul Samuelson, the four phases are like the changing seasons: "Each phase passes into the next. Each is characterized by different economic conditions: for example, during expansion we find that employment, production, prices, money, wages, interest rates, and profits are usually rising, with the reverse true in recession."[56]

Cycle-sensitive Decisions.   Important decisions depend on the ebb and flow of the business cycle (see Figure 3.5). These decisions include ordering inventory, borrowing funds, increasing staff, and spending capital for land, equipment, and energy. Decision making in preparation for a recession is especially difficult. Costs need to be cut, but not so deeply or in such places as to jeopardize the organization's mission or reputation. Delta Air Lines' experience is instructive:

> *In the last slump, Delta Air Lines tried to save money by serving pretzels rather than peanuts. Passengers hated it. One told a stewardess, "You're so cheap, you won't even spring for peanuts." It also sent the wrong signal to flight attendants, who assumed the airline was more interested in costs than service.[57]*

James G. Kaiser exemplifies today's global manager. As senior vice president of Corning's $200-million-a-year technical products division, Kaiser directly oversees Corning's interests in Latin America and the Far East. His approach is to let local managers run their own operations while he orchestrates strategy and pricing. Kaiser's division is leading the way in Corning's widely-imitated "Total Quality" program.

Delta, proud of its strong reputation for service, won't make that mistake again. Managers attempt to make the right decisions at the right time by responding appropriately to valid economic forecasts.

Benefiting from Economic Forecasts. *Timing* is everything when it comes to making good cycle-sensitive decisions. Just as a baseball batter needs to start swinging before the ball reaches home plate, managers need to make appropriate cutbacks prior to the onset of a recession. Failure to do so, in the face of decreasing sales, leads to bloated inventories and idle productive resources—both costly situations. On the other hand, managers cannot afford to get caught short during a period of rapid expansion. Prices and wages rise sharply when everyone is purchasing inventories and hiring at the same time. The trick is to stay slightly ahead of the pack. This is where accurate economic forecasts are a necessity.

In view of the fact that economists generally failed to predict the timing and severity of the 1981–1982 recession, the worst since the Great Depression, and prematurely predicted the end of the 1982–1990 expansion, economic forecasting has come under fire lately.[58] One wit chided economic forecasters by claiming they have predicted eight out of the last four recessions! How can managers get some value from the hundreds of economic forecasts they encounter each year?

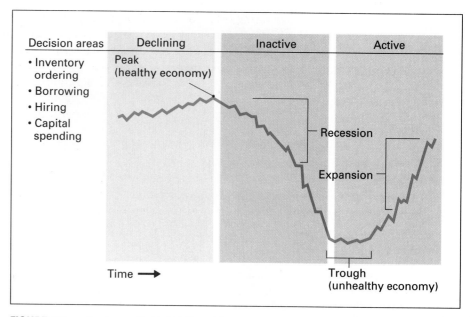

FIGURE 3.5 • Business Cycles Affect Managerial Decisions

A pair of respected forecasting experts recommends a *consensus approach.*[59] They urge managers to survey a wide variety of economic forecasts, taking the forecasters' track records into consideration, and to look for a consensus or average opinion. Cycle-sensitive decisions can then be made accordingly, and slavish adherence to a single forecast avoided. One sure formula for failure is naively to assume that the future will simply be a replication of the past. In spite of their imperfection, professional economic forecasts are better than no forecasts at all. One economist puts it this way: "Forecasters are very useful, in fact indispensable, because they give you plausible scenarios to help you think about the future in an organized way."[60]

The Challenge of a Global Economy

Globalization was one of the change drivers we discussed earlier. Evidence of global trade is all around us in the form of Japanese cars, French perfumes, German beers, and Italian shoes. Twenty-six cents out of every dollar Americans spend on consumer goods goes for imports.[61] Deeper analysis, however, reveals a more profound change. According to John Naisbitt's and Patricia Aburdene's book *Megatrends 2000,* "The new global economy cannot be understood if it is thought to be merely more and more trade among 160 countries; it must be viewed as the world moving from trade among countries to a single economy. One economy. One marketplace."[62] The resulting economic interdependency is exceedingly complex. Global alliances are being formed by the thousands as companies jockey for profitable combinations of costs and markets. As a case in point, Sweden's Volvo and Japan's Mitsubishi Motors plan to jointly manufacture automobiles near the Dutch city of Amsterdam.[63] The Swedes and Japanese want to get their foot in the door of the European Community as it moves toward economic unity by the end of 1992.

Troubling Questions. Although proponents of economic globalization promise a wider variety of less expensive goods, U.S. economists and government officials are troubled by a huge trade deficit (more imports than exports) and the loss of world leadership in key markets. Consider, for example, the production of computers. In 1979, 94 percent of the computers sold in the United States were also made in the United States. By 1989, only 66 percent were U.S. made. Significantly, the United States remains a world leader in other important markets, including computer software, aerospace, and medical instruments.[64] Now that economic globalization is well under way, the key question is: Where do we go from here?

Is Protectionism the Answer? Do you run for cover or stand and compete? This question is the crux of the argument between protectionists and advocates of free trade.[65] Fearing further loss of market share and jobs, businesses that do not export or import and organized labor are calling for trade barriers. Import quotas, protective tariffs, and other trade restrictions are one way of dealing with increased foreign competition. Unfortunately, experience shows that this sort of **protectionism** can backfire if trade wars break out. There are other problems as well.

An unanticipated response to protectionism has been the rapid growth of so-called *transplants*. Made-in-America Toyotas are rolling off the assembly line in Kentucky, as are Hondas in Ohio, and Mazdas in Michigan. An estimated 2,380,000 Japanese cars and trucks will be manufactured in the United States by 1995, up from a mere 1,500 units in 1982. "The irony is that the Japanese were forced to set up shop in the United States because of import restrictions agreed upon in the early 1980s."[66] A Honda car made in America is not an import, and thus not subject to import quotas or tariffs. Are these foreign-owned and operated factories employing American workers a plus or minus for the U.S. economy? They are turning out to be a *mixed blessing* (see Insights & Issues).

Protectionism is also an expensive luxury for end consumers. According to the Institute for International Economics, based in Washington, D.C., import restrictions such as tariffs and quotas cost American consumers $56 billion in 1984. Moreover, the Institute calculated what it cost American consumers to save jobs in various industries. To do this, the direct cost of import curbs was added to the higher cost of domestic goods resulting from the controls. It cost consumers $42,000 to save a single job in the textile industry, $105,000 to save a job in the automobile industry, and $1 million to keep a job in the specialty steel industry from going overseas.[67]

As an alternative to protectionism, experts recommend that the United States stand its ground and compete. They reason that only by facing the rigors of stiff foreign competition will U.S. companies and employees generate the hard work and innovation needed to compete successfully in a global economy. Inevitably, the focus shifts once again to the need for greater productivity.

Stretching Limited Energy and Material Resources

Energy and material resources are vital factors of production. Thus, managers can boost productivity by getting more mileage out of those resources. Thanks to costly Middle East oil-supply shocks during the 1970s and again in 1990, managers and people in general today tend to be more energy-conscious. Indeed,

protectionism fending off foreign competition with import quotas, tariffs, and other trade restrictions

Foreign Transplants Are a Mixed Blessing for the U.S. Economy

A major question mark hangs over all those foreign-owned U.S. plants. Depending on the sort of work that gets done under their roofs, they either sap or support U.S. competitiveness. Some are mere assembly operations offering only "screwdriver" jobs to Americans; the more skilled jobs and the R&D [research and development] are back in Osaka or Paris. Japanese owners of American plants, in particular, have tended to keep R&D and the production of their most advanced products and key components at home. Says Robert Hayes, who teaches manufacturing at the Harvard business school: "Because of their culture, they resist moving away from the motherland."

In a recent issue of the *Harvard Business Review,* Todd Hixon and Ranch Kimball of the Boston Consulting Group describe four stages of foreign involvement in U.S. manufacturing. These range from assembly to "fully integrated business operations" embracing design as well as production. Only at the last stage, say Hixon and Kimball, do foreign investors truly enhance American competitiveness. Among the few examples they find are the U.S. consumer electronics operations of Philips of the Netherlands and Honda's burgeoning U.S. plants.

Honda, the most Americanized of the Japanese auto "transplants," has a production engineering department and builds drive trains here. By 1992, says Honda, the local content of its American cars will reach 75%. A study by Brookings Institution economist Robert Lawrence, conducted for an organization of foreign auto-makers and importers, says the transplants could significantly pare the trade deficit. By 1992 it could be as much as $15 billion lower than it would be if the cars made in these plants were imported. There's only one catch, as basic as Capitalism 101. Though transplants may pay U.S. taxes, hire U.S. workers, use U.S. parts, and even help swell the total of U.S. exports, the profits belong to foreign owners. For that reason they don't deliver quite as big a bang for the U.S. economy

Source: Excerpted from Edmund Faltermayer, "Is 'Made in the U.S.A.' Fading Away?" *Fortune,* September 24, 1990, pp. 63, 65. © 1990 The Time Inc. Magazine Company. All rights reserved.

the United States logged a 21 percent jump in energy efficiency between 1973 and 1987.[68] Still, Japan and some Western European countries are twice as energy efficient as the United States.[69] Rapid population growth makes it imperative that, through intelligent use, we stretch not only our energy resources, but all earthly resources. This section focuses on the need for an enlightened global perspective on resources and a strategy for managing resources more efficiently.

A Global Perspective. We may find news stories about air and water pollution, overflowing garbage dumps, hazardous wastes, the greenhouse effect, and nonstop famine-relief efforts very depressing, but they are necessary constant reminders that resource management is a global affair with personal implications. NASA administrator James C. Fletcher describes the earth as "a spacecraft in a deadly vacuum, with a life-support system as precious as is an astronaut's backpack." Because our tampering with this delicate balance is causing large-scale problems, Fletcher says it's time to investigate the effects of our actions on spacecraft earth.[70] We need more answers from researchers about the dynamic interaction among resource use, environmental impacts, and quality of life. In the meantime, every manager must use limited resources more efficiently and responsibly.

A Strategy for Managing Resources More Efficiently. Rather than getting caught up in the self-defeating argument of exactly which nonrenewable resources—oil, coal, natural gas, uranium, or strategic minerals—will run out and precisely when, it is far more productive to concentrate on how to make the most of what remains. Experts on the subject have identified two strategies: (1) conservation and deprivation and (2) conservation and innovation.[71] The latter route, conservation and innovation, is desirable if the economy is to regain its productive vitality and to grow. Conservation deserves to be a key part of any resource strategy because "seven times more energy has been gotten from conservation in the United States over the past decade than from new sources."[72]

For the innovation portion of the conservation and innovation strategy, the following steps are recommended:

- *Increased Emphasis on Recycling.* Solid waste should be viewed as a valuable resource, not as trash to be discarded. It takes less than 10 percent as much energy to recycle aluminum, for example, as it does to produce new aluminum from bauxite. America recycles about 31 percent of its aluminum annually. For Sweden, the figure is a world-leading 80 to 85 percent.[73] In general, experts claim that about 25 percent of the 220 million tons of waste the United States produces each year could be recycled in waste-to-energy incinerators. The ash produced would be as little as 6 percent of the volume of the original raw garbage, greatly saving landfill space.[74] Plastics recycling is on the verge of major breakthroughs. *Remanufacturing,* the process of restoring worn-out products to working condition, saves energy and materials.[75]

- *Increased Use of Alternative Sources of Energy and Materials.* Renewable energy sources, including solar, geothermal, wind, hydroelectric, ocean thermal energy conversion, and hydrogen energy, can supplement fossil fuels and nuclear energy.[76] Laser beams channeled through glass strands called fiberoptic cables are already replacing cumbersome and costly metal telecommunications cables. New microcrystalline iron alloys and space-age plastics are replacing more scarce and costly metals.

- *Product Redesign.* Resource efficiency experts say the best way to stretch limited material and energy resources and reduce waste is to design products with those goals in mind. An exciting new approach being pioneered by Germany's BMW and Volkswagen is "design for disassembly." The result: vehicles with quick-release fasteners and coded reusable parts that will be easy to take apart for recycling.[77] But longer-lasting and reusable products will not be embraced quickly by a "throwaway society" until basic attitudes toward limited resources are brought into line with reality.

Economic Implications for Management

Economic realities such as business cycles, an increasingly global economy, and periodic resource shortages must prompt innovative responses from managers. Managers can use the growing number of economic forecasting software packages on their personal computers to fine-tune forecasts to their specific industry or organization. Progressive managers will view increasing foreign competition positively and take it as a challenge to design, produce, and market products and services more innovatively. Some productivity improvements have already been achieved by replacing the traditional adversarial relationship between labor and management with more cooperative and participative programs. Energy audits and sophisticated energy management programs can help management bridge the gap between the present age of nonrenewable energy and the future age of renewable energy.[78]

The Technological Environment

Technology is a term that ignites passionate debates in many circles these days. Some blame technology for environmental destruction and cultural fragmentation. Others view technology as the key to economic and social progress. No doubt there are important messages in both extremes. See Table 3.1 for a listing of the top technological breakthroughs of the last quarter-century.

technology all the tools and ideas available for extending the natural physical and mental reach of humankind

For our purposes, **technology** is defined as all the tools and ideas available for extending the natural physical and mental reach of humankind. A central theme in technology is the practical application of new ideas, a theme that is clarified by the following distinction between science and technology: "Science is the quest for more or less abstract knowledge, whereas technology is the application of organized knowledge to help solve problems in our society."[79] Three aspects of technology with important implications for managers are the innovation process, intrapreneurship, and technological displacement.

●●●●●●●●●●●●●●●●●

Describe the three-step innovation process and define the term *intrapreneur.*

The Innovation Process

innovation process the systematic development and practical application of a new idea

Technology comes into being through the **innovation process**, defined as the systematic development and practical application of a new idea. A great deal of time-consuming work is necessary to develop a new idea into a marketable product or service. And many otherwise good ideas do not become technologically

TABLE 3.1 ● Top Ten Technological Breakthroughs

According to the National Academy of Engineering, the top ten technological advances for the past twenty-five years were:
1. The moon landing
2. Application satellites (weather and communication satellites)
3. Microprocessors (so-called computers on a chip)
4. Computer-aided design and manufacturing
5. The CAT scan (computer imaging for medical diagnosis)
6. Advanced composite materials
7. The jumbo jet
8. Lasers (applications include CD players, computer printers, telecommunications, and surgery)
9. Fiberoptics
10. Genetic engineering

Source: Adapted from *The National Academy of Engineers.*

In a hurry? If you're in France you can catch the TGV (*train à grande vitesse*). These high-tech, high-speed trains can zip you from city to city at an average speed of 168 m.p.h. France's growing TGV system is billed as a key link in Europe's 21st century transportation system. Since TGVs began operation in 1981, 140 million passengers have been transported without a major accident. This record so impressed the Texas high-speed rail authority that it selected the French TGV system for its proposed San Antonio-Houston-Dallas super train route, slated for completion in 1998.

feasible, let alone marketable and profitable. A better understanding of the innovation process can help improve management's chances of turning new ideas into profitable goods and services.

A Three-Step Process. The innovation process has three steps (see Figure 3.6). First is the conceptualization step, when a new idea occurs to someone. Development of a working prototype is the second step, called **product technology.** This involves actually creating a product that will work as intended. The third and final step is developing a production process to create a profitable quantity-quality-price relationship. This third step is labeled **production technology.** Successful innovation depends on the right combination of new ideas, product technology, and production technology. A missing or deficient step can ruin the innovation process.

product technology second stage of innovation process involving the creation of a working prototype

production technology third stage of innovation process involving the development of a profitable production process

Innovation Lag. The time it takes for a new idea to be translated into satisfied demand is called **innovation lag.** The longer the innovation lag, the longer society must wait to benefit from a new idea. For example, the heart pacemaker was conceived in 1928 but not put into general use until 1960—a thirty-two-year

innovation lag time it takes for a new idea to be translated into satisfied demand

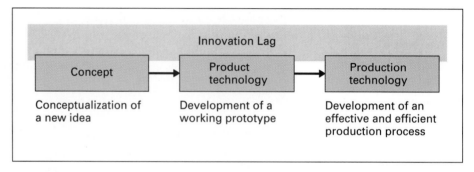

FIGURE 3.6 • The Three-step Innovation Process

innovation lag. The innovation lags for hybrid corn and the video tape recorder were twenty-five years and six years, respectively.[80] Over the years, the trend has been toward shorter innovation lags. Today, the average lag is an estimated twelve years.[81] Shorter innovation lags are possible, but the price tag can be staggering in the world of high tech. Intel, for example, had to invest four years and an estimated $300 million to develop its 80486 microprocessor. The 80486 packs the equivalent of one million transistors onto a silicon wafer the size of a thumbtack. It reportedly can crunch numbers as fast as a mainframe computer.[82]

Shortening Innovation Lag. Reducing innovation lags should be a high-priority goal for modern managers. John Young, chief executive officer of Hewlett-Packard (H-P), has made shorter innovation lags a strategic goal for the computer and scientific instrument company. "Today on average H-P needs three to five years to develop and launch a product, and an additional eighteen to twenty-four months to recoup the cost of development. Young wants to cut that in half by 2000."[83] This is a particularly important goal, considering that H-P generates 50 percent of its annual sales from products developed within the prior three years!

Another step in the right direction is a practice called concurrent engineering. Also referred to as parallel design, **concurrent engineering** is a team approach to product design. This approach lets research, design, production, finance, and marketing specialists have a direct say in the product design process from the very beginning.[84] This contrasts with the traditional, and much slower, practice of having a product move serially from research to design, from design to manufacturing, and so on down the line toward the marketplace. The time to hear about possible marketing problems is while a product is still in the conceptualization stage, not after it has become a warehouse full of unsold goods.

concurrent engineering team approach to product design involving specialists from all functional areas including research, production, and marketing

Promoting Innovation through Intrapreneurship

When we hear someone called an entrepreneur, we generally think of a creative individual who has risked everything while starting his or her own business. Indeed, entrepreneurs are a vital innovative force in the economy. A lesser known but no less important type of entrepreneur is the so-called intrapreneur.

Gifford Pinchot, author of the 1985 book *Intrapreneuring*, defines an **intrapreneur** as an employee who takes personal "hands-on responsibility" for pushing any type of innovative idea, product, or process through the organization.

intrapreneur an employee who takes personal responsibility for pushing an innovative idea through a large organization

Pinchot calls intrapreneurs "dreamers who do." But unlike traditional entrepreneurs, who tend to leave the organizational confines to pursue their dreams, intrepreneurs strive for innovation *within* existing organizations. Intrapreneurs tend to have a higher need for security than entrepreneurs, who strike out on their own. They pay a price for being employees rather than owners. Pinchot explains:

> Corporate entrepreneurs [or intrapreneurs], despite prior successes, have no capital of their own to start other ventures. Officially, they must begin from zero by persuading management that their new ideas are promising. Unlike successful independent entrepreneurs, they are not free to guide their next ventures by their own intuitive judgments; they still have to justify every move.[85]

Art Fry, introduced in this chapter's opening case as the inventor of the 3M Post-it note, is the classic intrapreneur. If today's large companies are to achieve a competitive edge through innovation, they need to foster a supportive climate for intrapreneurs like Fry. According to experts on the subject, an organization can foster intrapreneurship if it

- Focuses on results and teamwork.
- Rewards innovation and risk-taking.
- Tolerates and learns from mistakes.
- Remains flexible and change-oriented.[86]

Our discussions of creativity, participative management, and organizational cultures in later chapters contain ideas about how to encourage intrapreneurship of all types.

Facing the Problem of Technological Displacement

Today's offices and factories are becoming increasingly automated, thanks to what some call the new industrial revolution. Relatively high energy and labor costs and computer and robot technology ensure that the pace of change will accelerate. With networked computers at their fingertips, managers can expedite inventory control, correspondence, accounting transactions, and budget reviews, along with dozens of other applications, all at the touch of a few buttons. Managers in automated offices can compose, edit, send, and file letters and memos in minutes at their own computerized workstations without having to rely on traditional clerical support. Meanwhile, the so-called factory of the future is taking shape. Computer-aided design, computer-aided manufacturing, and robots are allowing traditionally labor-intensive jobs to be automated.

technological displacement occurs when people lose their jobs to machines

Automation carries with it the dilemma of what to do about those who lose their jobs to machines, a problem called **technological displacement**. An estimated 45 percent of all office and factory jobs could be reshaped (with many eliminated altogether) by the year 2000.[87] Consequently, job security, automation, advance notice of plant closings,[88] and retraining have become key collective bargaining issues for unions. Retraining deserves to be a high priority for both government and business because it amounts to the recycling of human resources.

Technological Implications for Management

In an age of increased global competition for technology leadership, pressure on managers to provide the innovative goods and services society demands will remain high. Managers who view employee creativity as a vital resource to be nurtured will have a competitive edge. But regardless of how prepared managers are, the new industrial revolution, with its sweeping automation of offices and factories, is already here. New approaches to hiring, training, and retraining employees will have to be developed as "smart" machines alter most jobs and eliminate others.

Summary

Since the world of most managers is characterized by transience, or accelerating change, they are potential victims of future shock. They can avoid it by preparing for, rather than passively responding to, changes in the social, political-legal, economic, and technological environment. The nine "change drivers" are helpful early warning signs of impending changes.

Society is best described as the result of a constant tug of war between the forces of stability and change. Important aspects of the social environment of management are demographic shifts, changing attitudes toward work, persistent inequalities, and managing diversity. Demographically, the new workforce of the 1990s is older, more diverse, and increasingly female. Lower quantity and quality of entry-level workers is a growing problem. Older workers, who generally have a good work record, deserve a second look. Contrary to the opinion of some social observers, the work ethic is not dead in America. A new social contract between employers and employees is taking shape because the tradition of lifetime employment with a single organization is giving way to shorter-term relationships of convenience.

The persistence of opportunity and income inequalities (and the so-called glass ceiling) among women and minorities is a strong stimulus for change. With part-timers playing a greater role in the U.S. workforce, there is genuine concern about creating a disadvantaged underclass of employees. Managing-diversity programs attempt to go a step beyond equal employment opportunity. The new goal is to tap *every* employee's *full* potential in today's diverse workforce.

Because of government regulations and sociopolitical demands from a growing list of special interest groups, managers are becoming increasingly politicized. More and more believe that if they are going to be affected by political forces, they should be more active politically. Some organizations rely on issues management to systematically identify, evaluate, and respond to important social and political issues. Managers can respond politically in three ways: by being reactive, neutral, or proactive. Four political strategies that managers have found useful for pursuing active or reactive political goals are campaign financing, lobbying, coalition building, and indirect lobbying. In a number of recent court cases managers have been held personally accountable for the misdeeds of their organizations. Alternative dispute resolution tactics such as arbitration and mediation can help trim management's huge litigation bill.

Managers can make timely decisions about inventory, borrowing, hiring, and capital spending during somewhat unpredictable business cycles by taking a consensus approach to economic forecasts. Business is urged to compete actively and creatively in the emerging global economy instead of passively calling for protectionist trade restrictions. Because more efficient resource use means greater productivity, a general strategy of conservation and innovation is recommended to stretch the supply of minerals, energy, and other limited resources. Increased recycling, greater use of alternative materials and sources of energy, and product redesign can help stretch limited resources.

In management's technological environment, innovation lag and technological displacement are special concerns. Including conceptualization, product technology, and production technology, a healthy innovation process is vital to technological development. Innovation lags must be shortened. An organizational climate that fosters intrapreneurship can help. The new industrial revolution promises to reshape the world of work through automation. Many jobs once done by human workers in the office and on the assembly line are now performed by computers and robots. Managers and society are challenged to take advantage of today's technological innovations, while dealing fairly with those who are put out of work by the "smart machines."

Terms to Understand

Transience
Demographics
New social contract (between employer and employee)
Glass ceiling
Contingent workers
Managing diversity
Issues management
Advocacy advertising
Legal audit
Alternative dispute resolution

Business cycle
Protectionism
Technology
Innovation process
Product technology
Production technology
Innovation lag
Concurrent engineering
Intrapreneur
Technological displacement

Questions for Discussion

1. What evidence of transience can you detect in your life? Have you ever been the victim of future shock? Explain.

2. In your opinion, which of the nine change drivers will have the greatest impact on management? Why?

3. Why are demographic shifts relevant to management?

4. What is your attitude toward work, in terms of your aspirations and expectations? How does it fit in with the new social contract between employer and employee?

5. Why is managing diversity important today and what major barriers are organizational diversity programs likely to encounter?

6. Why are today's managers having to polish their political skills?

7. What is happening to managers' legal accountability? What is your opinion of this trend?

8. What evidence do you see in your own community of management doing either a good or bad job of managing resources conservatively and innovatively?

9. Using your imagination and drawing on your personal experience, how do you think management can shorten innovation lags?

10. Why is the effective management of intrapreneurs a particularly difficult challenge for managers?

Back to the Opening Case

Now that you have read Chapter 3, you should be able to answer the following questions about the 3M Company case:

1. Why is 3M a very innovative company?

2. What does 3M do to ensure that all three steps of the innovation process take place?

3. Regarding 3M's answer to the Band-Aid, where did the three-step innovation process go wrong? Why is this a particularly serious problem for a firm that thrives on new ideas?

4. In your opinion, what is 3M's most powerful tool for encouraging innovation? Why?

CLOSING CASE

Room for Intrapreneurs at Hyatt

Back in the 1960s, when Hyatt was a young, quickly expanding chain of hotels, a new, well-educated employee with good motivation could look forward to rapid advancement and the chance to manage a hotel within as little as three years. But now that Hyatt's expansion has slowed and the company's hierarchy is top-heavy with aging baby-boomer managers, a good management prospect may have to wait eight years or more to run even a small Hyatt hotel. Keeping such employees happy, loyal, and motivated has become a major challenge for Hyatt. And, like many other organizations, Hyatt finds one of its solutions in intrapreneurship.

Traditionally, many of America's best business minds have been fascinated with starting something new, creating something. How can a big organization like Hyatt keep such people from being lured away by the prospect of starting their own companies? Hyatt's answer is to find ways to let their people exercise their creativity and keep their loyalty too.

John Allegretti, for instance, was a switchboard operator and assistant housekeeping manager for two years at a Chicago Hyatt. He wanted to be a hotel manager, but he was getting tired of waiting for positions to open up above him. He began pursuing his other interest—helping the environment—by sending résumés to waste-recycling companies. A Hyatt vice president who recognized Allegretti's motivation and interest asked him to work on reducing waste at the 2,000-room hotel. Allegretti's success at this project convinced the company to set up and let him run a new waste-consulting company, International ReCycleCo. The company soon won twenty-four clients in eight states, in addition to several large Hyatts. Now everyone is happy.

In such cases, Hyatt typically gives the intrapreneur the capital to get the business started but retains ultimate control. It gave James E. Jones, Hyatt's director of sales development, $780,000 to start a business to offer the kind of catering and entertainment services Hyatt often hired professional party planners to provide. Although Jones was no whiz at drawing up his first business plan, Hyatt recognized the value of his contacts in professional sports and encouraged him to rewrite the plan. Within a year, Regency Productions by Hyatt had won contracts to manage corporate hospitality tents at the 1991 Superbowl and to handle catering at the 1991 U.S. Open golf tournament.

Such intrapreneurial ventures are in some ways a logical extension of Hyatt's management policy, which has always sought consistency, not uniformity, among its hotels. The Hyatt Corporation is still privately held by the Pritzker family of Chicago, but individual hotels are often designed, built, operated, and at least partially owned by local investor groups. Mirroring Hyatt's own decentralized management approach, these local owners frequently give their employees a good deal of autonomy.

Not all such employee ventures are successful, of course, but Hyatt accepts the risk of failures in order to encourage future attempts. The recent tales of two Hyatt restaurants demonstrate the point. Assistant food and beverage manager Michael O. Smith opened Hyttops at the Hyatt Regency in New Orleans as a sports bar, counting on the hotel's proximity to the Superdome to bring in business and figuring that another typical hotel restaurant couldn't hope to compete with New Orleans' famous eateries. With donated sports paraphernalia and the patronage of sports stars, the bar quickly became a success. In suburban Chicago, meanwhile, a Hyatt manager opened a club and disco without company approval, naming them after himself. Company executives were embarrassed to discover a new disco so close to headquarters, but Hyatt let the manager stay on. Evidently the company figured that if it wanted prospective intrapreneurs to take the first step, it couldn't punish employees for stepping too far.

For Discussion

1. Considering the risks, why does Hyatt bother creating a supportive climate for intrapreneurs?

2. How can the intrapreneur program help the innovation process at Hyatt?

3. Would you have retained (or demoted or fired) the Hyatt manager who opened the club and disco in suburban Chicago without company approval? Explain your rationale. What are the implications of your decision for intrapreneurism at Hyatt?

References

Opening Quotation. Laurence J. Peter, *Peter's Quotations* (New York: Bantam, 1977), p. 387.

Opening Case. For additional information on 3M, see Thomas J. Peters and Robert H. Waterman, Jr., *In Search of Excellence* (New York: HarperCollins, 1982), pp. 224–234; Robert Levering, Milton Moskowitz, and Michael Katz, *The 100 Best Companies to Work for in America* (Reading, Mass.: Addison-Wesley, 1984), pp. 221–224; Patrick Houston, "How Jake Jacobson Is Lighting a Fire

Under 3M," *Business Week* (July 21, 1986): 106–107; Art Fry, "The Post-It Note: An Intrapreneurial Success," *SAM Advanced Management Journal,* 52 (Summer 1987): 4–9; Brian Dumaine, "Ability to Innovate," *Fortune* (January 29, 1990): 43, 46.

Closing Case. James E. Ellis, "Feeling Stuck at Hyatt? Create a New Business," *Business Week* (December 10, 1990): 195; Rick Lyke, "Hyttops Turns Vacant Space into Bar Bucks," *Hotel & Motel Management* (June 25, 1990): 37–38; Ron Zemke, *The Service Edge* (New York: New American Library, 1989), pp. 129–131.

1. Dumaine, *"Ability to Innovate,"* p. 43.

2. Levering, Moskowitz, and Katz, *The 100 Best Companies,* p. 221.

3. See Alvin Toffler, *Power Shift* (New York: Bantam, 1990), p. xix.

4. Data from Sarah Smith, "America's Most Admired Corporations," *Fortune* (January 29, 1990): 58.

5. See Alvin Toffler, *Future Shock* (New York: Bantam, 1970).

6. John Naisbitt, *Megatrends* (New York: Warner Books, 1982), p. 8.

7. For example, see John Naisbitt and Patricia Aburdene, *Megatrends 2000* (New York: William Morrow, 1990).

8. Rushworth M. Kidder, "The Three E's of the 1990s," *The Christian Science Monitor* (March 19, 1990): 12.

9. The following is adapted from "Nine Forces Reshaping America," *The Futurist,* 24 (July–August 1990): 9–16.

10. Data from Aaron Bernstein, "America's Income Gap: The Closer You Look, The Worse it Gets," *Business Week* (April 17, 1989): 78–79.

11. Data from Spencer Rich, "The Working Poor: Lost in a Health Care No-Man's Land," *The Washington Post National Weekly Edition* (June 18–24, 1990): 7.

12. Based on D. Stanley Eitzen, *Social Structure and Social Problems in America* (Boston: Allyn & Bacon, 1974), pp. 12–14.

13. See Lynn R. Offermann and Marilyn K. Gowing, "Organizations of the Future: Changes and Challenges," *American Psychologist,* 45 (February 1990): 95–108.

14. See Martha I. Finney, "Planning Today for the Future's Changing Shape," *Personnel Administrator,* 34 (January 1989): 44–45.

15. U.S. Bureau of Labor Statistics, *Occupational Outlook Handbook: 1990–91 Edition* (Washington, D.C.: 1991), p. 9.

16. Aaron Bernstein, "Help Wanted," *Business Week* (August 10, 1987): 48–49.

17. Data from Louis S. Richman, "The Coming World Labor Shortage," *Fortune* (April 9, 1990): 70–77. Also see William B. Johnston, "Global Work Force 2000: The New World Labor Market," *Harvard Business Review,* 69 (March–April 1991): 115–127.

18. Gail DeGeorge, "Can Barry Gibbons Put the Sizzle Back in Burger King?" *Business Week* (October 22, 1990): 61.

19. See Kate Ballen, "Get Ready for Shopping at Work," *Fortune* (February 15, 1988): 95, 98. The marketing implications of an aging population are discussed in Anne B. Fisher, "What Consumers Want in the 1990s," *Fortune* (January 29, 1990): 108–112.

20. See *Occupational Outlook Handbook: 1990–91 Edition.* Also see Scott Pendleton, "Rise of Women Jobholders Slows," *The Christian Science Monitor* (November 23, 1990): 8.

21. David R. Francis, "How to Revive Corporate Loyalty," *The Christian Science Monitor* (November 2, 1990): 8.

22. Data from George J. Church, "The Work Ethic Lives!" *Time* (September 7, 1987): 40–42; and Haidee Allerton, "Workaholism: Fact or Fiction?" *Training & Development Journal,* 45 (January 1991): 74, 76.

23. Jeffrey J. Hallett, "Worklife in America: Changing Times," *Personnel Administrator,* 32 (April 1987), 21. For more extensive discussion, see Jeffrey J. Hallett, "Worklife Visions," *Personnel Administrator,* 32 (May 1987), 56–65.

24. John A. Byrne, "Caught in the Middle," *Business Week* (September 12, 1988): 88.

25. Data from U.S. Department of Commerce, Bureau of the Census, *Statistical Abstract of the United States: 1990,* p. 389.

26. Data from "Youth, College Narrow Pay Gap a Bit for Women," *The Wall Street Journal* (November 17, 1989): B1.

27. See Elizabeth Ehrlich, "9 to 5, and Then Some: More Women Are Moonlighting," *Business Week* (August 25, 1986): 41.

28. Ann M. Morrison and Mary Ann Von Glinow, "Women and Minorities in Management," *American Psychologist,* 45 (February 1990), 200. (Emphasis added.)

29. They are Marion Sandler, Golden West Financial Corp. and Linda Wachner, Warnaco Group Inc. See Mary Billard, "Women on the Verge," *Business Month* (April 1990): 26–47.

30. Data from Jaclyn Fierman, "Why Women Still Don't Hit the Top," *Fortune* (July 30, 1990): 40–62.

31. Data from "New Economic Realities: The Rise of Women Entrepreneurs," *A Report of the Committee on Small Business, House of Representatives,* June 28, 1988 (Washington, D.C.: U.S. Government Printing Office, 1988), p. iii.

32. Gene Koretz, "Taking Stock of the Flexible Work Force," *Business Week* (July 24, 1989): 12. Also see John Ross, "Effective Ways to Hire Contingent Personnel," *HRMagazine,* 36 (February 1991): 52–54.

33. These research results drawn from Robert P. Vecchio, "Demographic and Attitudinal Differences Between Part-time and Full-time Employees," *Journal of Occupational Behaviour,* 5 (July 1984): 213–218.

34. Koretz, "Taking Stock of the Flexible Work Force." Also see David Greising, "Temp Agencies are Praying the Slump is Just Temporary," *Business Week* (December 11, 1989): 62.

35. For good background information, see R. Roosevelt Thomas, Jr., "From Affirmative Action to Affirming Diversity," *Harvard Business Review,* 68 (March–April 1990), 107–117; and Beverly Geber, "Managing Diversity," *Training,* 27 (July 1990): 23–30.

36. Data from Sheryl Hilliard Tucker and Kevin D. Thompson, "Will Diversity = Opportunity + Advancement for Blacks?" *Black Enterprise,* 21 (November 1990): 50–60. Also see Cindy Skrzycki, "For Most Employers, Seeing is Ignoring," *The Washington Post National Weekly Edition* (April 9–15, 1990): 22.

37. Adapted from Tucker and Thompson, "Will Diversity = Opportunity + Advancement for Blacks?"

38. Research support can be found in Joseph J. Martocchio, "Age-Related Differences in Employee Absenteeism: A Meta-Analysis," *Psychology and Aging,* 4 (December 1989): 409–414. Also see Walter Kiechel III, "How to Manage Older Workers," *Fortune* (November 5, 1990): 183–186.

39. Pros and cons of this program are reviewed in Charles Burgess and Guangli Zhu, "Should All Mentally Challenged People Work?" *Personnel* 67 (January 1990): 20–22.

40. Jack Gordon, "Can Business Save the Schools?" *Training,* 27 (August 1990): 20. Also see Joan C. Szabo, "Learning at Work," *Nation's Business,* 78 (February 1990): 27–28.

41. See Walecia Konrad, "Welcome to the Women-Friendly Company," *Business Week* (August 6, 1990): 48–55.

42. Wendy Zellner, "Why the Pizza King May Abdicate the Throne," *Business Week* (September 25, 1989): 46.

43. Steven L. Wartick and Robert E. Rude, "Issues Management: Corporate Fad or Corporate Function?" *California Management Review,* 29 (Fall 1986): 124–140.

44. David Kirkpatrick, "Environmentalism: The New Crusade," *Fortune* (February 12, 1990): 47.

45. Drawn from S. Prakash Sethi, "Serving the Public Interest: Corporate Political Action for the 1980s," *Management Review,* 70 (March 1981): 8–11.

46. See Charles R. Babcock, "Setting Himself Up As an Example—or a Sacrifice," *The Washington Post National Weekly Edition* (May 28–June 3, 1990): 15; and Douglas Harbrecht and Paula Dwyer, "How to Get the Hill Humming Again," *Business Week* (April 16, 1990): 62–63.

47. See "How Insiders Rate the Capitol Hill Crowd," *Business Week* (April 16, 1990): 58–59.

48. Robert E. Norton, "Can Business Win in Washington?" *Fortune* (December 3, 1990): 76.

49. An instructive historical perspective of advocacy advertising may be found in Roland Marchand, "The Fitful Career of Advocacy Advertising: Political Protection, Client Cultivation, and Corporate Morale," *California Management Review,* 29 (Winter 1987): 128–156.

50. For details, see Jonathan Tasini, "The Clamor to Make Punishment Fit the Corporate Crime," *Business Week* (February 10, 1986): 73. A related case is discussed in Jonathan Tasini, "A Death at Work Can Put the Boss in Jail," *Business Week* (March 2, 1987): 37–38.

51. For details on offenders, see Alan Farnham, "The S&L Felons," *Fortune* (November 5, 1990): 90–108.

52. See Michele Galen, " 'Guilty, Your Honor,' " *Business Week* (May 7, 1990): 33–34; and Larry Reibstein, "Throwing the Book at Milken," *Newsweek* (December 3, 1990): 42.

53. Data from John R. Allison, "Five Ways to Keep Disputes Out of Court," *Harvard Business Review,* 68 (January–February 1990): 166–177.

54. Marianne M. Jennings and Frank Shipper, *Avoiding and Surviving Lawsuits* (San Francisco: Jossey-Bass, 1989), p. 118. Also see David Silverstein, "The Litigation Audit: Preventive Legal Maintenance for Management," *Business Horizons*, 31 (November–December 1988): 34–42.

55. John R. Allison, "Easing the Pain of Legal Disputes: The Evolution and Future of Reform," *Business Horizons*, 33 (September–October 1990): 15. Also see Richard H. Weise, "The ADR Program at Motorola," *Negotiation Journal*, 5 (October 1989): 381–394.

56. Paul A. Samuelson, *Economics*, 10th ed. (New York: McGraw-Hill, 1976): 253.

57. Brian Dumaine, "How to Manage in a Recession," *Fortune* (November 5, 1990): 60.

58. For example, see Annetta Miller, "Laying Odds on a Recession: How the Game is Played," *Newsweek* (February 12, 1990): 43.

59. For an informative discussion of the value of economic forecasting, see Peter L. Bernstein and Theodore H. Silbert, "Are Economic Forecasters Worth Listening To?" *Harvard Business Review*, 62 (September–October 1984): 32–40.

60. Lawrence S. Davidson, "Knowing the Unknowable," *Business Horizons*, 32 (September–October 1989): 7.

61. Data from James C. Cooper, "Rising Interest Rates Will Keep Demand on a Short Leash," *Business Week* (May 30, 1988): 23.

62. John Naisbitt and Patricia Aburdene, *Megatrends 2000* (New York: William Morrow, 1990), p. 21. Also see the Special Report articles on the global economy in *Business Week* (December 17, 1990): 60–93.

63. See Jonathan Kapstein, "Mitsubishi Is Taking a Back Road into Europe," *Business Week* (November 19, 1990): 64.

64. Data from Edmund Faltermayer, "Is 'Made in U.S.A.' Fading Away?" *Fortune* (September 24, 1990): 62–73.

65. Instructive material on protectionism can be found in Michael McFadden, "Protectionism Can't Protect Jobs," *Fortune* (May 11, 1987): 121–128; Marc Levinson, "Asking for Protection Is Asking for Trouble," *Harvard Business Review*, 65 (July–August 1987): 42–47; Karen Pennar, "The Gospel of Free Trade is Losing Apostles," *Business Week* (February 27, 1989): 89; and Annetta Miller, "What Is 'Managed Trade'—And Will It Work?" *Newsweek* (March 5, 1990): 26.

66. Alex Taylor III, "Japan's New U.S. Car Strategy," *Fortune* (September 10, 1990): 65.

67. Data from Karen Pennar, "Protectionism: Making It Pay for Itself," *Business Week* (April 7, 1986): 24.

68. Data from Robert C. Cowen, "Good News Challenges U.S. to Save More Energy," *The Christian Science Monitor* (November 1, 1990): 12.

69. See Donald C. Bacon, "A New Energy Crisis?" *Nation's Business* (February 1990): 20–26.

70. See Robert C. Cowen, "Spaceship Earth: Mankind as a Force of Nature," *The Christian Science Monitor* (March 31, 1987): 16–17.

71. For example, see Newt Gingrich, "Innovation or Deprivation," *The Futurist*, 15 (August 1981): 31–37.

72. Brad Knickerbocker, "Sustainability," *The Christian Science Monitor* (October 16, 1990): 13.

73. Data from Stratford P. Sherman, "Trashing a $150 Billion Business," *Fortune* (August 28, 1989): 90–98; and Shawn Tully, "What the 'Greens' Mean for Business," *Fortune* (October 23, 1989): 159–164.

74. Data from Terri Thompson and Mimi Bluestone, "Garbage: It Isn't the Other Guy's Problem Anymore," *Business Week* (May 25, 1987): 150–151, 154.

75. For more on remanufacturing, see Robert T. Lund, "Remanufacturing," *Technology Review*, 87 (February–March 1984): 18–27.

76. See Peter Hoffmann, "The Fuel of the Future is Making a Comeback," *Business Week* (November 28, 1988): 130–131; and Sharon Begley, "Alternative Energy: Time to Get Serious," *Newsweek* (August 20, 1990): 40.

77. Good background discussion can be found in Paul A. Eisenstein, "Designers Take on 'Green' Concerns; Recyclable Plastics Seen as Priority," *The Christian Science Monitor* (November 29, 1990): 9.

78. See Peter Nulty, "The Beginning of the End for Oil," *Fortune* (September 10, 1990): 35–40.

79. Jerome B. Wiesner, "Technology and Innovation," in *Technological Innovation and Society*, ed. Dean Morse and Aaron W. Warner (New York: Columbia University Press, 1966), p. 11.

80. See Robert C. Dean, Jr., "The Temporal Mismatch—Innovation's Pace vs Management's Time Horizon," *Research Management*, 17 (May 1974): 12–15.

81. Data from Gene Bylinsky, "Technology in the Year 2000," *Fortune* (July 18, 1988): 92–98.

82. For more, see Richard Brandt and Otis Port, "Intel: The Next Revolution," *Business Week* (September 26, 1988): 74–80.

83. Gene Bylinsky, "Turning R&D Into Real Products," *Fortune* (July 2, 1990): 73. Also see Keith Pavitt, "What We Know about the Strategic Management of Technology," *California Management Review,* 32 (Spring 1990): 17–26.

84. For instructive material, see Jeremy Main, "Manufacturing the Right Way," *Fortune* (May 21, 1990): 54–64; Otis Port, "A Smarter Way to Manufacture," *Business Week* (April 30, 1990): 110–117; and William J. Spencer, "Research to Product: A Major U.S. Challenge," *California Management Review,* 32 (Winter 1990): 45–53.

85. See Gifford Pinchot III, *Intrapreneuring* (New York: Harper & Row, 1985), p. xvii.

86. Vince Luchsinger and D. Ray Bagby, "Entrepreneurship and Intrapreneurship: Behaviors, Comparisons, and Contrasts," *SAM Advanced Management Journal,* 52 (Summer 1987): 12. (*Note:* also see related articles on intrapreneurship in same issue.)

87. Data from "Changing 45 Million Jobs," *Business Week* (August 3, 1981): 62.

88. See Angelo Kinicki, Jeffrey Bracker, Robert Kreitner, Chris Lockwood, and David Lemak, "Socially Responsible Plant Closings," *Personnel Administrator,* 32 (June 1987): 116–128.

4

Management's Social and Ethical Responsibilities

We live in a complex, challenging world that is unfriendly to quick fixes. . . . business can make it a better world through sound thinking and sound acting.

MARK PASTIN

CHAPTER OBJECTIVES

When you finish studying this chapter, you should be able to

- Define corporate social responsibility and summarize the arguments for and against it.
- Identify and describe the four social responsibility strategies.
- Explain the role of enlightened self-interest in social responsibility.
- Summarize the two practical lessons from business ethics research.
- Distinguish between instrumental and terminal values and explain their relationship to business ethics.
- Discuss what management can do to improve business ethics.

A Convicted Inside Trader Tells His Story

Dennis Levine made history. The disclosure of his misdeeds exposed those of Ivan Boesky, his illicit partner, and Boesky in turn led the government to Michael Milken and Drexel Burnham Lambert. The stocks Levine bought and sold through offshore bank accounts were mainly of target companies in soon-to-be-announced mergers. According to the Securities and Exchange Commission, he made his largest single insider-trading profit on securities of Nabisco Brands. The SEC alleges that he bought 150,000 Nabisco shares some three weeks before the company announced merger talks with R.J. Reynolds in 1985. When the stock's price rose, Levine sold for a $2.7 million profit.

Here Levine tells his inside story, a personal odyssey to the heights of Wall Street and down to its criminal depths. Boesky and others involved in these felonies differ with aspects of Levine's story, but they are not telling their tales. A notable success as an investment banker on Wall Street, Levine was undone by ambition so intense it drove him over the line. Thereafter he found himself in a quagmire of deceit and betrayal.

I have had four years to reflect on the events leading up to my arrest. Part of that time—15 months and two days—I spent in Lewisburg federal prison camp in Pennsylvania. Getting your comeuppance is painful, and I have tried to take it on the chin. Unfortunately, my family also had to endure the trauma of humiliation, disgrace, and loss of privacy—and they did nothing to deserve it.

I will regret my mistakes forever. I blame only myself for my actions and accept full responsibility for what I have done. No one led me down the garden path. I've gained an abiding respect for the fairness of our system of justice: For the hard work and creativity I brought to my investment banking career, I was well rewarded. When I broke the law, I was punished. The system works.

People always ask, "Why would somebody who's making over $1 million a year start trading on inside information?" That's the wrong question. Here's what I thought at the time, misguided as I was: When I started trading on nonpublic information in 1978, I wasn't making a million. I was a 25-year-old trainee at Citibank with a $19,000 annual salary. I was wet behind the ears, impatient, burning with ambition. In those days people didn't think about insider trading the way they do now: You'd call it "a hot stock tip." The first U.S. criminal prosecution for insider trading wasn't until around that time, and it was not highly publicized. In the early years I regarded the practice as just a way to make some fast money. Of course I soon realized what I was doing was wrong, but I rationalized it as harmless. I told myself that the frequent run-ups in target-company stock prices before merger announcements proved others were doing it too.

Eventually insider trading became an addiction for me. It was just so easy. In seven years I built $39,750 into $11.5 million, and all it took was a 20-second phone call to my offshore bank a couple of times a month—maybe 200 calls total. My account was growing at 125 percent a year, compounded.

Believe me, I felt a rush when I would check the price of one of my stocks on the office Quotron and learn I'd just made several hundred thousand dollars. I was confident that the elaborate veils of secrecy I had created—plus overseas bank-privacy laws—would protect me.

And Wall Street was crazy in those days. These were the 1980s, remember, the decade of excess, greed, and materialism. I became a go-go guy, consumed by the high-pressure, ultracompetitive world of investment banking. I was helping my clients make tens and even hundreds of millions of dollars. I served as the lead banker on Perelman's nearly $2 billion takeover of Revlon, four months of work that enabled Drexel to earn $60 million in fees. The exposure to such deals, the pursuit of larger and larger transactions, and the numbing effect of 60- to 100-hour workweeks helped erode my values and distort my judgment. In this unbelievable world of billions and billions of dollars, the millions I made by trading on nonpublic information seemed almost insignificant.

At the root of my compulsive trading was an inability to set limits. Perhaps it's worth noting that my legitimate success stemmed from the same root. My ambition was so strong it went beyond rationality, and I gradually lost sight of what constitutes ethical behavior. At each new level of success I set higher goals, imprisoning myself in a cycle from which I saw no escape. When I became a senior vice president, I wanted to be a managing director, and when I became a managing director, I wanted to be a client. If I was making $100,000 a year, I thought, *I can make $200,000.* And if I made $1 million, *I can make $3 million.* And so it went.

Competitive jealousy is normal in business. Everybody wants to make more than the guy down the hall. It is the same in investment banking, but the numbers have more zeroes. Only a small percentage of the people these firms hire at the entry level of associate go on to make partner, and as the pyramid narrows, the competition grows ever more intense. By the time I made partner at Drexel, I was out of control.

• • • • • • • • • • • • • • • • • **A**s the social, political, economic, and technological environments of management have changed, the practice of management itself has changed. This is especially true for managers in the private business sector, as we will see in the case of The Body Shop International at the end of this chapter. Today, more than ever, it is far less acceptable for someone in business to stand before the public and declare that his or her only job is to make as much profit as possible. The public is wary of the abuse of power and the betrayal of trust, and business managers—indeed, managers of all types of organizations—are expected to make a wide variety of economic and social contributions. Demands on business that would have been considered patently unreasonable just twenty years ago have become normal today. The purpose of this chapter is to examine management's social and ethical responsibilities.

Social Responsibility: Definition and Perspectives

When John D. Rockefeller was at the zenith of his power as the founder of Standard Oil Company, he handed out dimes to rows of eager children who

Small businessman Wally Grigo's sportswear store in New Haven, CT, is on the front lines of the marketing war between the likes of Reebok, Nike, L.A. Gear, and Converse as they battle for shares of the lucrative inner-city market for high-priced sneakers. In some inner cities, dealing drugs pays for the sneakers, some costing up to $140. To Grigo, making money from the proceeds of the drug business is bad business.

lined the street. Rockefeller did this on the advice of a public relations expert who believed the dime campaign would counteract his widespread reputation as a monopolist who had ruthlessly eliminated his competitors in the oil industry. The dime campaign was not a complete success, however, because Standard Oil was broken up under the Sherman Antitrust Act of 1890. Conceivably, Rockefeller believed he was fulfilling some sort of social responsibility by passing out dimes to hungry children. Since Rockefeller's time, the concept of social responsibility has grown and matured to the point where many of today's companies are intimately involved in social programs that have no direct connection with the bottom line. These programs include everything from support of the arts and urban renewal to environmental protection. But, like all aspects of management, social responsibility needs to be carried out in an effective and efficient manner.

What Does Social Responsibility Involve?

Social responsibility, as defined in this section, is a relatively new concern of the business community. To a large extent, it is a product of the 1960s. The following describes the historical backdrop for modern corporate social responsibility:

> *The Eisenhower era of the 1950s was, by and large, an era of good feeling between business and the American public.*
> *But beginning in the 1960s, an adverse tide of public opinion began to rise against business. A more affluent, better-educated, more critical public began to question the value of ever-increasing production, the resulting*

pollution and environmental decay, and the defective products and services being produced; and they began to protest the public's seeming inability to influence the behavior of the business system. Frustration over the Vietnam War added fuel to the fires of discontent. Suddenly consumerism, stockholderism, racial equalitarianism, antimilitarism, environmentalism, and feminism became forces to be reckoned with by corporate management.[1]

● ● ● ● ● ● ● ● ● ● ● ● ● ●
Define corporate social responsibility and summarize the arguments for and against it.

corporate social responsibility idea that business has social obligations above and beyond making a profit

Events during the 1970s, such as Watergate and corporate bribery scandals, only reinforced the public's demand for greater social responsibility in the business sector. By the time the political pendulum in the United States swung toward a more probusiness administration in the 1980s with the election of Ronald Reagan, the notion of corporate social responsibility had become firmly rooted. However, a wide-ranging disagreement remains over the exact nature and scope of management's social responsibilities.

Voluntary Action. One expert defined **corporate social responsibility** as "the notion that corporations have an obligation to constituent groups in society other than stockholders and beyond that prescribed by law or union contract."[2] A central feature of this definition is that an action must be *voluntary* to qualify as a socially responsible action. For example, Monsanto, the fourth largest chemical company in the United States, took unprecedented steps in 1985 to address the fears of people living near its chemical plants. At the time, *Business Week* noted that Monsanto "surprised critics by announcing a voluntary right-to-know program designed to distribute information about possible hazards and precautions to residents near its 53 plants."[3] By 1989, Monsanto had set a voluntary corporate goal of reducing its air pollution emissions to zero.[4] According to our definition and the ten commandments listed in Table 4.1, Monsanto's actions were socially responsible because they were (1) anticipatory and (2) carried out voluntarily without government coercion.

When lawsuits must be initiated or court orders issued before a company will respond to societal needs, that company is not being socially responsible. A prime example of this type of foot-dragging behavior was the manner in which Beech-Nut Nutrition Corporation, a subsidiary of Switzerland's Nestlé, responded to charges that it had adulterated its supposedly 100 percent apple juice for babies between 1981 and 1983.

Federal and state officials later charged that Beech-Nut's strategy— executed very effectively—was to avoid publicity and stall their investigations until it could unload its $3.5 million inventory of tainted apple juice products. "They played a cat-and-mouse game with us," says one investigator. When the FDA [U.S. Food and Drug Administration] would identify a specific apple juice lot as tainted, Beech-Nut would quickly destroy it before the FDA could seize it, an act that could have created negative publicity.[5]

In 1988, two top Beech-Nut officials who had pleaded guilty to 215 felony charges were sentenced to a year and a day in jail and fined $100,000 apiece.[6] Endless court battles and reluctant compliance do not exemplify corporate social responsibility; neither does the use of hollow public relations ploys in lieu of meaningful action.[7]

TABLE 4.1 • Ten Commandments of Corporate Social Responsibility

> I. Thou Shall Take Corrective Action Before it is Required.
> II. Thou Shall Work with Affected Constituents to Resolve Mutual Problems.
> III. Thou Shall Work to Establish Industrywide Standards and Self-Regulation.
> IV. Thou Shall Publicly Admit Your Mistakes.
> V. Thou Shall Get Involved in Appropriate Social Programs.
> VI. Thou Shall Help Correct Environmental Problems.
> VII. Thou Shall Monitor the Changing Social Environment.
> VIII. Thou Shall Establish and Enforce a Corporate Code of Conduct.
> IX. Thou Shall Take Needed Public Stands on Social Issues.
> X. Thou Shall Strive to Make Profits on an Ongoing Basis.

Source: Excerpted from Larry D. Alexander and William F. Matthews, "The Ten Commandments of Corporate Social Responsibility," *Business and Society Review,* 50 (Summer 1984): 62–66.

An Emphasis on Means, Not Ends. Another key feature of this definition of corporate social responsibility is its emphasis on means rather than ends:

> *Corporate behavior should not, in most cases, be judged by the decisions actually reached, but by the process by which they were reached. Broadly stated, corporations need to analyze the social consequences of their decisions before they make them and take steps to minimize the social costs of these decisions when appropriate. The appropriate demand to be made of those who govern large corporations is that they incorporate into their decision-making process means by which broader social concerns are given full consideration. This is corporate social responsibility as a means, not as a set of ends.*[8]

Unfortunately, social consequences are too often shortchanged in the heat of competitive battle.

What Is the Role of Business in Society?

Much of the disagreement over what social responsibility involves can be traced to a fundamental debate about the exact purpose of a business. Is a business an economic entity responsible only for making a profit for its stockholders? Or is it a socioeconomic entity obligated to make both economic and social contributions to society?[9] Depending on one's perspective, social responsibility can be interpreted either way.

The Classical Economic Model. The classical economic model can be traced to the eighteenth century, when businesses were owned largely by entrepreneurs or owner-managers. Competition was vigorous among small operations, and short-run profits were the sole concern of these early entrepreneurs. Of course, the key to attaining short-run profits was to provide society with needed goods and services. According to Adam Smith, father of the classical economic model, an "invisible hand" promoted the public welfare. Smith believed the efforts of competing entrepreneurs had a natural tendency to promote the public interest when each tried to maximize short-run profits. In other words, Smith believed the public interest was served by individuals pursuing their own self-interests.

This model has survived into modern times. Nobel Prize-winning economist Milton Friedman has no doubts about the role of business in society: "Few trends could so thoroughly undermine the very foundations of our free society as the acceptance by corporate officials of a social responsibility other than to make as much money for their stockholders as possible."[10] Thus, according to the classical economic model of business, short-run profitability and social responsibility are the same thing.

The Socioeconomic Model.   Reflecting society's broader expectations for business (for example, safe and meaningful jobs, clean air and water, charitable donations, safe products), many think the time has come to revamp what they believe to be an obsolete, classical economic model. Oligopolistic industries such as autos, rubber, and brewing, in which a handful of corporate giants dominate the market, are cited as evidence that the classical economic model is outdated. In its place its opponents propose a socioeconomic model, in which business is seen as one subsystem among many in a highly interdependent society.

Advocates of the socioeconomic model point out that many groups in society besides stockholders have a stake in corporate affairs. Creditors, current and retired employees, customers, suppliers, competitors, all levels of government, the community, and society in general have expectations, often conflicting, for management. Some companies go so far as to conduct a **stakeholder audit**.[11] This growing practice involves systematically identifying all parties that could possibly be impacted by the company's performance (for an example, see Figure 4.1). According to the socioeconomic view, business has an obligation to respond to the needs of all stakeholders while pursuing a profit.[12]

stakeholder audit identifying all parties possibly impacted by the organization

Arguments For and Against Corporate Social Responsibility

As one might suspect, the debate about the role of business has spawned many specific arguments both for and against corporate social responsibility.[13] A sample of four major arguments on each side reveals the principal issues.

Arguments For.   Convinced that a business should be more than simply a profit machine, proponents of social responsibility have offered these arguments:

1. *Business Is Unavoidably Involved in Social Issues.*   As social activists like to say, business is either part of the solution or part of the problem. There is no denying that private business shares responsibility for such societal problems as unemployment, inflation, and pollution. Like everyone else, corporate citizens must balance their rights and responsibilities.

2. *Business Has the Resources to Tackle Today's Complex Societal Problems.*   With its rich stock of technical, financial, and managerial resources, the private business sector can play a decisive role in solving society's more troublesome problems. After all, without society's support, business could not have built its resource base in the first place.

3. *A Better Society Means a Better Environment for Doing Business.*   Business can enhance its long-run profitability by making an investment in society today. Today's problems can turn into tomorrow's profits.

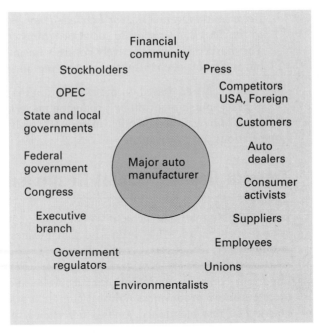

FIGURE 4.1 • A Sample Stakeholder Audit for an Automobile Company

Source: Nancy C. Roberts and Paula J. King, "The Stakeholder Audit Goes Public," Reprinted by permission of publisher, from *Organizational Dynamics,* Winter 1989, © 1989. American Management Association, New York. All rights reserved.

4. *Corporate Social Action Will Prevent Government Intervention.* As evidenced by waves of antitrust, equal employment opportunity, and pollution-control legislation, government will force business to do what it fails to do voluntarily.

Arguments like the above four give business a broad socioeconomic agenda.

Arguments Against. Remaining faithful to the classical economic model, opponents of corporate social responsibility rely on the first two arguments below. The third and fourth arguments have been voiced by those who think business is already too big and powerful.

1. *Profit Maximization Ensures the Efficient Use of Society's Resources.* By buying goods and services, consumers collectively dictate where assets should be deployed. Social expenditures amount to theft of stockholders' equity.

2. *As an Economic Institution, Business Lacks the Ability to Pursue Social Goals.* Gross inefficiencies can be expected if managers are forced to divert their attention from their pursuit of economic goals.

3. *Business Already Has Enough Power.* Considering that business exercises powerful influence over where and how we work and live, what we buy, and what we value, more concentration of social power in the hands of business is undesirable. In fact, in a 1989 *Business Week*/Harris Poll of 1,247 American adults, 69 percent agreed with the statement "Business has gained too much power over too many aspects of American life."[14]

4. *Because Managers Are Not Elected, They Are Not Directly Accountable to the People.*   Corporate social programs can easily become misguided. The market system effectively controls business's economic performance but is a poor mechanism for controlling business's social performance.

These arguments are based on the assumption that business should stick to what it does best—pursuing profit by producing marketable goods and services. Social goals should be handled by other institutions such as the family, school, religious organizations, or government.

Toward Greater Social Responsibility

iron law of responsibility
those who do not use power in a socially responsible way will eventually lose it

Is it inevitable that management will assume greater social responsibility? Some scholars believe so. It has been said that business is bound by an **iron law of responsibility,** which states that "in the long run, those who do not use power in a way that society considers responsible will tend to lose it."[15] This is an important concept, considering that cynicism about business runs deep today, despite a more probusiness political climate worldwide. In the *Business Week/ Harris Poll* just mentioned, only 3 percent of the respondents gave American corporations an "excellent" performance rating. Fifty-six percent rated them "pretty good" and 32 percent "only fair."[16] The demand for business to act more responsibly is clear. If this challenge is not met voluntarily, government reform legislation will probably force business to meet it. In this section we look at four alternative social responsibility strategies and some contrasting expressions of corporate social responsibility.

● ● ● ● ● ● ● ● ● ● ● ● ●
Identify and describe the four social responsibility strategies.

Social Responsibility Strategies

Similar to management's political response continuum, discussed in Chapter 3, is its social responsibility continuum (see Figure 4.2), marked by four strategies: reaction, defense, accommodation, and proaction.[17] Each involves a distinctly different approach to demands for greater social responsibility.

FIGURE 4.2 • A Continuum of Social Responsibility Strategies

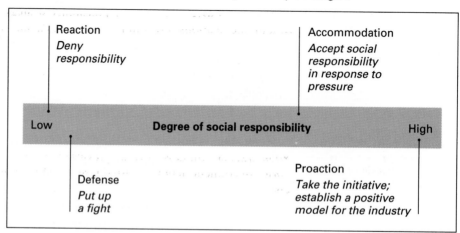

Grandma, what big teeth you have! Perhaps that's what these two Syracuse, NY, youngsters said when exploring the gaping mouth of a live-action dinosaur model. Little did they know at the time that the sophisticated and costly Dinomania exhibit came to their city because of a grant from Fleet/Norstar, a banking company doing business in New York and New England. Fleet/Norstar's expression of enlightened self-interest is good both for the community and for the company.

reactive social responsibility strategy denying responsibility and resisting change

Reaction. A business that follows a reactive social responsibility strategy will deny responsibility while striving to maintain the status quo. For example, in recent years, the tobacco industry has continued to deny any connection between cigarette smoking and cancer. Moreover, it responded to the smoking ban on airplanes with a multimillion-dollar smokers' rights campaign.[18]

defensive social responsibility strategy resisting additional responsibilities with legal and public relations tactics

Defense. A defensive social responsibility strategy uses legal maneuvering and/or a public relations (PR) campaign to avoid assuming additional responsibilities. During the cleanup of the Exxon *Valdez* oil spill, for example, Alaska's governor was quoted as saying: "Exxon's gone out of its way to minimize the effects of the spill, by understating the numbers of animals killed and miles of beaches affected."[19] Exxon denied the charge of engaging in a PR battle.

accommodative social responsibility strategy assuming additional responsibilities in response to pressure

Accommodation. The organization must be pressured into assuming additional responsibilities when it follows an accommodative social responsibility strategy. Some outside stimulus, such as pressure from a special-interest group or threatened government action, is usually required to trigger an accommodative strategy. A prime example is Pfizer's response to mounting evidence that its heart valves, implanted in 56,000 people, were faulty. Through early 1990, 389 recipients of the Bjork-Shiley heart valve had experienced valve failures, and 248 had died. Only after a Pfizer subsidiary was sued and pressured by a consumer advocate group did the company reluctantly agree to notify all valve recipients of possible deadly malfunctions.[20]

Proaction. A proactive social responsibility strategy involves formulating a program that serves as a model for the industry. Proaction means aggressively taking the initiative. Du Pont has provided an inspiring example:

> *E.I. Du Pont de Nemours & Co. is starting a program to buy back used Freon and other chlorofluorocarbons (CFCs) from hundreds of thousands of customers who use the gas to chill refrigerators and air conditioning units.*
>
> *Du Pont's actions . . . [have] important implications for the environment. In the past, large users of CFCs such as supermarkets or office buildings have vented the gas or liquid into the atmosphere. CFCs are now known to harm the ozone layer, a section of Earth's atmosphere that screens out harmful sun rays.*
>
> *Instead, Du Pont, which produces half the CFCs used in the United States, is offering to buy the used product, including that made by its competitors. In addition, Du Pont will supply the vessels to hold the used CFCs and will pay all the freight costs.*[21]

Such creative and trend-setting action qualifies as proactive social responsibility.

Corporate social responsibility proponents would like to see proactive strategies become management's preferred response in both good times and bad. The manner in which Johnson & Johnson's former chief executive officer responded when one of the firm's most successful products became a murder weapon is an excellent case in point (see Management Ethics).

Who Benefits from Corporate Social Responsibility?

Is social responsibility like the old theory of home medicine, "It has to taste bad to be good"? In other words, does social responsibility have to be a hardship for the organization? Those who answer yes believe that social responsibility should be motivated by altruism, an unselfish devotion to the interests of others. This implies that businesses that are not socially responsible are motivated strictly by self-interest. In short-run economic terms, Beech-Nut's cover-up saved it millions of dollars, whereas Johnson & Johnson's actions with Tylenol cost it millions of dollars. On the basis of these facts alone, one would be hard pressed to say that social responsibility pays. In fact, research on the relationship between corporate social responsibility and financial performance has been inconclusive.[22] In other words, socially responsible companies are not significantly more or less profitable than socially irresponsible companies.

Enlightened Self-interest. Enlightened self-interest, the realization that business ultimately helps itself by helping to solve societal problems, involves a balancing of short-run costs and long-run benefits. Advocates of enlightened self-interest contend that social responsibility expenditures are motivated by profit. Research into **corporate philanthropy,** the charitable donation of company resources ($5 billion in 1989),[23] supports this contention. After analyzing Internal

Johnson & Johnson's Proactive Response to the Tylenol Disaster

Few managers of corporate crises have survived an episode of the perfect crime—unsolved murder—in which their product was the murder weapon and their customers the innocent victims. Indeed, James Burke of Johnson & Johnson may be the first CEO ever to have confronted such a horror—twice. He managed it so well that he not only restored Tylenol, his company's single most important profitmaker, to preeminence, but he also enhanced the company's fine reputation in the process. During his tenure Burke also took J&J's earnings and stock prices to new highs. . . .

The company was sailing along serenely when the deadly squall hit in 1982. Among its thousands of products, J&J had a world champion in Tylenol, which at the time had a remarkable 35 percent share of the $1 billion analgesic market and accounted for an estimated 15 percent to 20 percent of the company's earnings. Smart marketing and J&J's prestige explained the success, since Tylenol's only active ingredient is a compound that any pharmaceutical company can make.

Burke was having coffee with the company's president when the bad news broke: Cyanide-laced Tylenol capsules caused, in the final count, seven deaths in the Chicago area. Burke ordered a recall of 31 million bottles of Tylenol and decided to stand by the Tylenol trademark (which

industry analysts were insisting could not survive). But he believes his most important decision in those wild days was "to go to the public directly." He looked concerned and candid on *Donahue* and *60 Minutes,* making the latter appearance over the strong protestations of a colleague, who stormed out of Burke's office, slammed the door, and knocked a favorite painting off the wall.

After the second episode four years later, when a New York woman died of cyanide poisoning, Burke ended the production of Tylenol capsules. Since then J&J has been marketing the product only in pills and caplets, compressed elongated ovals easy to swallow and hard to invade.

Tylenol's share of market dropped from 35 percent to 7 percent after the Chicago murders, and took a second steep slide after the New York death. But despite new competition, Tylenol has climbed back to a 35 percent share—and now the market has doubled to $2 billion. Further, the whole experience enhanced J&J's reputation as a socially responsible corporation. Says Burke: "Every relationship that works is based on trust, and you don't develop trust without moral behavior."

Source: Excerpted from Walter Guzzardi, "The National Business Hall of Fame," *Fortune* (March 12, 1990): 120. © 1990 The Time Inc. Magazine Company. All rights reserved.

---

corporate philanthropy charitable donation of company resources

Revenue Service statistics for firms in thirty-six industries, researchers concluded that corporate giving is a form of *profit-motivated advertising.* They went on to observe that "it would seem ill-advised to use philanthropy data to measure altruistic responses of corporations."[24] This profit-motivated advertising thesis was further supported by a study of 130 large manufacturing firms in the United States. Companies that had committed significant crimes but donated a good deal of money had better social responsibility ratings than companies that had committed no crimes and donated very little money.[25] As demonstrated by public utility (Wisconsin Energy) executive Charles McNeer's following statement, enlightened self-interest can benefit both business itself and society in general.

> *"You need to promote the economic health of the community. Not only the investment health, but also the social and cultural health. You can't get people to live in a community unless they have the cultural things they desire."*[26]

An Array of Benefits for the Organization. In addition to the advertising effect, other possible long-run benefits for the socially responsible organization include:

- Tax-free incentives to employees (such as buying orchestra tickets and giving them to deserving employees).
- Retention of talented managers by satisfying their altruistic motives.
- Help in recruiting talented and socially conscious personnel.
- Swaying public opinion against government intervention.
- Improved community living standards for employees.
- Attracting socially conscious investors.
- A nontaxable benefit for employees in which company funds are donated to their favorite causes. Many companies match employees' contributions to their college alma maters, for example.

Social responsibility can be a "win-win" proposition; both society and the socially responsible organization can benefit in the long run.

The Future of Corporate Social Responsibility

As pointed out repeatedly in this text, the success of organizational programs and changes hinges on top management support. Proactive social responsibility is no exception. As shown in Figure 4.3, a recent survey found strong support among present and future executives for the concept of corporate social responsibility.[27] Businesses are becoming socially involved in many creative ways, as

FIGURE 4.3 • Present and Future Executives Support the Concept of Corporate Social Responsibility

Source: Data from Mark N. Vamos and Christopher Power, "A Kinder, Gentler Generation of Executives?" *Business Week* (April 23, 1990): 86–87.

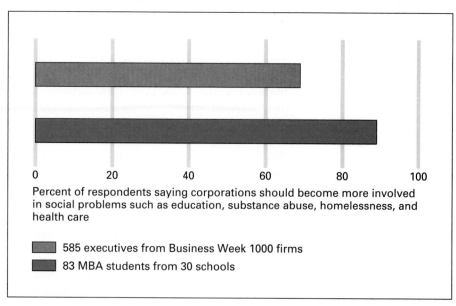

Percent of respondents saying corporations should become more involved in social problems such as education, substance abuse, homelessness, and health care

- 585 executives from Business Week 1000 firms
- 83 MBA students from 30 schools

Ben Cohen and Jerry Greenfield want to run a profitable and ethical business that makes a delicious product, is a fun place to work, and is generous to the community. They have apparently achieved their dream by turning a modest investment and lots of energy into Ben & Jerry's Homemade, Inc. Ice cream lovers crave their products and the firm gives an unusually high percentage of pretax profits to charity. Employees at Ben & Jerry's enjoy many unique touches, such as diaper-changing tables in the company's women's and men's restrooms.

exemplified by Ben & Jerry's, where opportunity is limited only by management's imagination and desire to make the world a better place in which to live, work, and do business (see Managers in Action).

The Ethical Dimension of Management

Highly publicized accounts of corporate misconduct in recent years have led to widespread cynicism about business ethics. For instance, government officials found evidence of fraud in 60 percent of the failed savings and loan (S&L) institutions. The S&L debacle could end up costing every American household about $5,000 ($500 billion total).[28] Some say that "business ethics" is an oxymoron—an absurd contradiction in terms, like "jumbo shrimp." Fortunately, the subject of ethics is receiving serious attention in management circles these days.

ethics study of moral obligation involving right versus wrong

Ethics is the study of moral obligation involving the distinction between right and wrong. *Business ethics*, sometimes referred to as management ethics or organizational ethics, narrows the frame of reference to productive organizations.[29] But, as a pair of ethics experts recently noted, business ethics is not a simple matter:

> *Just being a good person and, in your own way, having sound personal ethics may not be sufficient to handle the ethical issues that arise in a*

Socially Responsible Nuts

Ben Cohen and Jerry Greenfield's success is a classic story of American entrepreneurship. The two boyhood friends learned their business through taking a correspondence course and started it with $12,000 and an old gas station. Within a decade, they were selling millions of dollars worth of their product—gourmet ice cream. But Ben and Jerry are hardly typical businesspeople, and they have used their success to do a lot more than make a profit. Rather than allow their millions to lure them away from their socially conscious 1960s philosophy, they have tried to ensure that every aspect of their business helps the world, not just their bottom line.

Ben & Jerry's commitment to socially responsible business practices begins with the ingredients the company buys. In 1990 it ordered 100 tons of Brazil nuts for its new Rain Forest Crunch ice cream. The nuts grow wild in the rain forest of the Amazon and are gathered and processed in the remote Brazilian town of Xapuri. Environmentalists hope that if the Brazil nuts can become profitable enough, land owners will let the forests stand rather than destroy them to make cattle ranches.

Regardless of where the company gets its ingredients, it contributes 7.5 percent of pretax profits to philanthropy and 1 percent to lobbying to convert the defense budget to more peaceful uses. Its proactive socially responsible policies also extend to the way its 330 employees relate to each other in the company's Burlington, Vermont, headquarters. Worried that company expansion would drive the fun out of the business, Ben established a "Joy Committee" that immediately changed its name to "Joy Gang" and recommended that the company hire a masseur and sponsor a "Barry Manilow Appreciation Day." Not only does the company offer excellent employee benefits (including free counseling to employees' families for any reason) but the founders also put their money where their beliefs are by establishing a rule that no employee can make more than five times as much as the lowest-paid worker.

By proving that a company can make the world a better place while earning handsome profits, Ben & Jerry's has set a new standard for corporate social responsibility. No doubt the founders hope that other companies will copy their ethical business practices as eagerly as they try to copy their successful ice cream flavors.

Sources: Jerry Adler, "Calories of the Rain Forest," *Newsweek* (December 3, 1990): 61; "Brazil's Tropical-Forest Murder Trial," *Newsweek* (December 17, 1990): 38; Jim Castelli, "Finding the Right Fit," *HRMagazine* (September 1990): 38–41; Milton Moskowitz, "Company Performance Roundup," *Business and Society Review* (Spring 1990): 63.

business organization. Many people who have limited business experience suddenly find themselves making decisions about product quality, advertising, pricing, hiring practices, and pollution control. The values they learned from family, church, and school may not provide specific guidelines for these complex business decisions. For example, is a particular advertisement deceptive? Should a gift to a customer be considered a bribe, or is it a special promotional incentive? . . . Many business ethics decisions are close calls. Years of experience in a particular industry may be required to know what is acceptable.[30]

With this realistic context in mind, we turn to a discussion of business ethics research, personal values, ethical issues, and steps that management can take to foster ethical business behavior.

Practical Lessons from Business Ethics Research

●●●●●●●●●●●●●●●●

Summarize the two
practical lessons from
business ethics research.

Empirical research is always welcome in a socially relevant and important area such as business ethics.[31] It permits us to go beyond mere intuition and speculation to determine more precisely who, what, and why. On-the-job research of business ethics has revealed two troublesome ethical areas for managers: (1) pressure from above and (2) discomfort with ambiguity.

Pressure from Above.   A number of studies have uncovered the problem of perceived pressure for results. As discussed later in Chapter 13, pressure from superiors can lead to blind conformity. For example, after surveying 1,227 *Harvard Business Review* readers, researchers noted that "respondents frequently complained of superiors' pressure to support incorrect viewpoints, sign false documents, overlook superiors' wrongdoing, and do business with superiors' friends."[32] A study of public-sector managers led another researcher to conclude that "some managers feel so much pressure to achieve results that they need to compromise their integrity."[33] Younger employees (aged 21–40), in a recent study, reported more pressure to act unethically than did their older coworkers (aged 41–70).[34] By being aware of this problem of pressure from above, managers can (1) consciously avoid putting undue pressure on others and (2) prepare to deal with excessive organizational pressure.

Problems experienced by Eastern Air Lines are an excellent case in point. In late 1990, when the ailing airline, still operating under bankruptcy protection, was indicted on sixty counts of safety and maintenance violations, disgruntled employees were not surprised. "At JFK Airport in New York, Mike O'Connell, president of the JFK machinists local, said the favorite line of Eastern managers in the hangars was, 'We're not in the business of fixing airplanes. We're here to fly people.' "[35] Such pressure for results can cause otherwise good and decent employees to take ethical shortcuts.

Ambiguous Situations.   Surveys of purchasing managers and field sales personnel have uncovered discomfort with ambiguous situations in which there are no clear-cut ethical guidelines. One result of this kind of research is the following statement: "A striking aspect of the responses to the questionnaire is the degree to which the purchasing managers desire a stated policy."[36] In other words, those who often face ethically ambiguous situations want formal guidelines to help sort things out. (Take a moment now to complete the exercise in Table 4.2.) Ethical codes, discussed later, can satisfy this need for guidelines.

A Call for Action.   Corporate misconduct and the foregoing research findings underscore the importance of the following call to action. It comes from Thomas R. Horton, president and chief executive officer of the American Management Association:

> *In my view, this tide can be turned only by deliberate and conscious actions of management at all levels. Each manager needs to understand his or her own personal code of ethics: what is fair; what is right; what is wrong? Where is the ethical line that I draw, the line beyond which I shall not go? And where is the line beyond which I shall not allow my organization to go?*[37]

Horton's call is *personal*. His words suggest each of us can begin the process of improving business ethics by looking in a mirror.

A survey of 2,856 college students from twenty-eight schools across the United States revealed that female students were more concerned about business

TABLE 4.2 • An Ethics Test

Many situations in day-to-day business are not simple right-or-wrong questions, but rather fall into a gray area. To demonstrate the perplexing array of moral dilemmas faced by twentieth-century Americans, here is a "non-scientific" test for slippage . . . Don't expect to score high. That is not the purpose. But give it a try, and see how you stack up.

Put your value system to the test in the following situations:

Scoring Card: **Strongly Agree = SA**   **Disagree   = D**
                      Agree   = A   **Strongly Disagree = SD**

	SA	A	D	SD
1. Employees should not be expected to inform on their peers for wrong doings.	___	___	___	___
2. There are times when a manager must overlook contract and safety violations in order to get on with the job.	___	___	___	___
3. It is not always possible to keep accurate expense account records; therefore, it is sometimes necessary to give approximate figures.	___	___	___	___
4. There are times when it is necessary to withhold embarrassing information from one's superior.	___	___	___	___
5. We should do what our managers suggest, though we may have doubts about its being the right thing to do.	___	___	___	___
6. It is sometimes necessary to conduct personal business on company time.	___	___	___	___
7. Sometimes it is good psychology to set goals somewhat above normal if it will help to obtain a greater effort from the sales force.	___	___	___	___
8. I would quote a "hopeful" shipping date in order to get the order.	___	___	___	___
9. It is proper to use the company WATS [long-distance telephone] line for personal calls as long as it's not in company use.	___	___	___	___
10. Management must be goal-oriented; therefore, the end usually justifies the means.	___	___	___	___
11. If it takes heavy entertainment and twisting a bit of company policy to win a large contract, I would authorize it.	___	___	___	___
12. Exceptions to company policy and procedures are a way of life.	___	___	___	___
13. Inventory controls should be designed to report "underages" rather than "overages" in goods received. [The ethical issue here is the same as that faced by someone who receives too much change from a store cashier.]	___	___	___	___
14. Occasional use of the company's copier for personal or community activities is acceptable.	___	___	___	___
15. Taking home company property (pencils, paper, tape, etc.) for personal use is an accepted fringe benefit.	___	___	___	___

Score Key: (0) for Strongly Disagree (1) for Disagree (2) for Agree (3) for Strongly Agree

If your score is:

0	**Prepare for canonization**	11–15	**Good ethical values**	36–44	**Slipping fast**
1– 5	**Bishop material**	16–25	**Average ethical values**	45	**Leave valuables with warden**
6–10	**High ethical values**	26–35	**Need moral development**		

Source: "Is Your (Ethical) Slippage Showing?" by Lowell G. Rein, copyright September 1980. Reprinted with the permission of *Personnel Journal*, Costa Mesa, California; all rights reserved.

ethics than were their male counterparts.[38] In view of the proportional growth in female managers in recent years, this finding might foretell a needed boost for business ethics. Managers—women or men—who have a well-developed value system are better equipped to confront tough ethical questions.[39]

Personal Values as Ethical Anchors

Values are too often ignored in discussions of management. This oversight is serious because personal values play a pivotal role in managerial decision making and ethics.[40] Contemporary social observers complain that many managers have turned their backs on ethical values such as honesty. But others, including management consultant Michael Blondell, detect a change in the wind: "I think we're going back to basic, fundamental values—issues of trust, respect, dignity, commitment, integrity, and accountability. The world is crying out for these things to become more important."[41] Defined broadly, **values** are abstract ideals that shape an individual's thinking and behavior.[42] Let us explore two different types of values that act as anchors for our ethical beliefs and conduct. In the course of our discussion, we will briefly review three sources of value conflict.

values abstract ideals that shape one's thinking and behavior

Instrumental and Terminal Values. Each manager, indeed each person, values various means and ends in life. Recognizing this means-ends distinction, behavioral scientists have identified two basic types of values. An **instrumental value** is an enduring belief that a certain way of behaving is appropriate in all situations. For example, the time-honored saying, "Honesty is the best policy," represents an instrumental value. A person who truly values honesty will probably behave in an honest manner. A **terminal value**, in contrast, is an enduring belief that a certain end-state of existence is worth striving for and attaining.[43] Whereas one person may strive for eternal salvation, another may strive for social recognition and admiration. Instrumental values (modes of behavior) help achieve terminal values (desired end-states).

instrumental value enduring belief in a certain way of behaving

terminal value enduring belief in the attainment of a certain end-state

● ● ● ● ● ● ● ● ● ● ● ● ● ● ● ●
Distinguish between instrumental and terminal values and explain their relationship to business ethics.

Because a person can hold a number of different instrumental and terminal values in various combinations, individual value systems are somewhat like fingerprints: each of us has a unique set. No wonder managers who face the same ethical dilemma often differ in their interpretations and in their acts.

Identifying Your Own Values. To help you discover your own set of values, refer to the Rokeach value survey in Table 4.3. Take a few moments now to complete this survey. (As a reliability check between your intentions and your actual behavior, have a close friend or spouse evaluate you later with the Rokeach survey.)

If your results surprise you, it is probably because we tend to take our basic values for granted. We seldom stop to arrange them consciously according to priority. For the sake of comparison, compare your top five instrumental and terminal values with the value profiles uncovered in a survey of 220 eastern U.S. managers. On average, those managers ranked their instrumental values as follows: (1) honest, (2) responsible, (3) capable, (4) ambitious, and (5) independent. The most common terminal value rankings were (1) self-respect, (2) family security, (3) freedom, (4) a sense of accomplishment, and (5) happiness.[44] These managerial value profiles are offered for purposes of comparison only; they are not necessarily an index of desirable or undesirable priorities.

Value Conflict. One of the principal benefits of knowing our values is to see whether there are any serious conflicts among the values in each category or among the values in the two different categories. Three potentially destructive types of value conflict are intrapersonal, individual-organizational, and intercultural.

TABLE 4.3 • The Rokeach Value Survey

Instructions: Study the two lists of values presented below. Then rank the instrumental values in order of importance to you (1 = most important, 18 = least important). Do the same with the list of terminal values.

Instrumental values	*Terminal values*
Rank	**Rank**
____ Ambitious (hard-working, aspiring)	____ A comfortable life (a prosperous life)
____ Broadminded (open-minded)	____ An exciting life (a stimulating, active life)
____ Capable (competent, effective)	____ A sense of accomplishment (lasting contribution)
____ Cheerful (lighthearted, joyful)	____ A world at peace (free of war and conflict)
____ Clean (neat, tidy)	____ A world of beauty (beauty of nature and the arts)
____ Courageous (standing up for your beliefs)	____ Equality (brotherhood, equal opportunity for all)
____ Forgiving (willing to pardon others)	____ Family security (taking care of loved ones)
____ Helpful (working for the welfare of others)	____ Freedom (independence, free choice)
____ Honest (sincere, truthful)	____ Happiness (contentedness)
____ Imaginative (daring, creative)	____ Inner harmony (freedom from inner conflict)
____ Independent (self-sufficient)	____ Mature love (sexual and spiritual intimacy)
____ Intellectual (intelligent, reflective)	____ National security (protection from attack)
____ Logical (consistent, rational)	____ Pleasure (an enjoyable, leisurely life)
____ Loving (affectionate, tender)	____ Salvation (saved, eternal life)
____ Obedient (dutiful, respectful)	____ Self-respect (self-esteem)
____ Polite (courteous, well-mannered)	____ Social recognition (respect, admiration)
____ Responsible (dependable, reliable)	____ True friendship (close companionship)
____ Self-controlled (restrained, self-disciplined)	____ Wisdom (a mature understanding of life)

Source: Copyright, 1967, by Milton Rokeach, and reproduced by permission of Halgren Tests, 873 Persimmon Avenue, Sunnyvale, CA 94087.

- *Intrapersonal Value Conflict.* Some value conflicts arise in the individual. For instance, some people experience a serious conflict between the instrumental values of ambition and honesty. For hard-driving, extremely ambitious people, honesty sometimes takes a back seat. Dennis Levine's experience, as chronicled in the Chapter Opening Case, is a prime example. For others, the conflict is between the terminal values of accomplishment and pleasure, particularly with regard to going to work. Someone who works hard to make a lasting contribution at the office may find little time for family, friends, or recreation. Finally, some managers find that their high-priority instrumental values will not help them achieve their terminal values. For instance, imagine the frustration of a manager who values responsibility (an instrumental value) while at the same time yearning for freedom (terminal value).

- *Individual-Organizational Value Conflict.* Another type of value conflict occurs when an individual's values clash with those prompted by the organization's culture. The classic conflict here is between the individual's desire for independence and the organization's insistence on obedience. Personal values may clash with those encouraged by the organization in other ways, too. A noncompetitive person who sees nothing pleasurable about physical exercise would have a difficult time at PepsiCo, Inc., where the organizational culture has been described as follows:

  Like Marines, Pepsi executives are expected to be physically fit as well as mentally alert: Pepsi employs four physical-fitness instructors at its headquarters, and a former executive says it is an unwritten rule that to get ahead in the company a manager must stay in shape. The company encourages one-on-one sports as well as interdepartmental competition in such games as soccer and basketball. . . . In such a culture, less competitive managers are deliberately weeded out.[45]

  Of course, judging the wisdom of PepsiCo's approach depends on one's own value system.

- *Intercultural Value Conflict.* Although subtle differences in values among people with the same cultural background are evident, some characteristic patterns do exist. For example, the profiles of the 220 U.S. managers discussed above are characteristic of American managers. When managers from significantly different cultures interact, their contrasting value systems contain the seeds of conflict (see The World of Management). American managers, with values shaped by a culture that emphasizes personal freedom, independence, and self-respect, are too often seen as selfish and insensitive by people from Europe and Asia. Managers from those regions tend to place more emphasis on instrumental values such as self-control, obedience, and being helpful. As discussed in Chapter 19, cross-cultural sensitivity is essential in today's global economy. An important first step in that direction is an awareness of and sensitivity to the value systems of people from other cultures.

When addressing specific ethical issues, managers need to consider each individual's personal values.

American Women Find a Glass Ceiling in Corporate Japan

After nearly a decade with a large Japanese firm that deals in trade and finance, [an American woman, who chooses to be anonymous] thought she had built up a store of trust. Now she is thinking of leaving. She says her firm, which she doesn't want to name, has not learned how to manage American women. Still, she doesn't want to discourage others: "Come work for a Japanese company if you're looking for an interesting experience, but don't stay too long."

The company transferred her from the United States to Japan several years ago, on the theory that the move would help her understand the company better. It did. Her experience at headquarters has convinced her that the firm doesn't know what it wants from its foreign staff, that opportunity is severely limited, and that she would be better off elsewhere.

Although she is fluent in Japanese and says she "tried not to make waves," cultural clashes often arose. Says she: "The attitude of too many Japanese is that we understand you but you'll never understand us. They're almost smug about that." One male colleague launched into a long exposi-

tion on what he perceived to be a basic difference between the two cultures: the fact that Japanese women wore panties under their pantyhose while American women did not. When she pointed out that most American women actually did wear underwear, he wouldn't be swayed. "He was convinced," she says. "That was the end of the debate. And I'm thinking, 'I can't believe that we're having this discussion.' "

Her fellow workers in Tokyo, who generally do not have the option of leaving the firm as she does, are not sympathetic to her complaints. Says she: "They say, 'Look, we had our dreams too. You're expecting too much.' " She says that while she's been given many opportunities with the company, she has reached a glass ceiling that limits how high non-Japanese can go. "Japanese think of themselves as the managers and Americans as support staff," she says. "I don't ever expect to have Japanese working under me."

Source: Excerpted from Susan Moffat, "Should You Work for the Japanese?" *Fortune* (December 3, 1990): 112, 116. © The Time Inc. Magazine Company. All rights reserved.

Ethical Issues in Today's Organizations

The Ethics Resource Center in Washington, D.C., surveyed 711 U.S. corporations and asked them to identify today's ethical problem areas. The sixteen most troublesome ethical problems,[46] from most to least severe, turned out to be:

1. Drug and alcohol abuse.
2. Employee theft.
3. Conflicts of interest.
4. Quality control.
5. Misuse of proprietary information.
6. Abuse of expense accounts.
7. Plant closings and layoffs.
8. Misuse of company assets.
9. Environmental pollution.
10. Methods of gathering competitors' information.
11. Inaccuracy of books and records.

12. Receiving excessive gifts and entertainment.

13. False or misleading advertising.

14. Giving excessive gifts and entertainment.

15. Kickbacks.

16. Insider trading.

What can managers do about these problems? Let us examine some ways to encourage ethical conduct.

Encouraging Ethical Conduct

Simply telling managers and other employees to be good will not work. Both research evidence and practical experience tell us that words must be supported by action. Four specific ways to encourage ethical conduct within the organization are ethics training, ethical advocates, ethical codes, and whistle-blowing.

Ethics Training

amoral managers neither moral nor immoral, but ethically lazy

Managers lacking ethical awareness have been labeled *amoral* by ethics researcher Archie B. Carroll. **Amoral managers are neither moral nor immoral, but indifferent to the ethical implications of their actions.** Carroll contends that managers in this category far outnumber moral or immoral managers.[47] If his contention is correct, there is a great need for ethics training, a need that too often is not adequately met. According to annual industrial surveys by *Training* magazine, the use of ethical training programs is growing but still relatively small. For companies with more than 100 employees, comparative figures for 1988 and 1990 were 20 percent and 37 percent, respectively.[48]

Some say ethics training is a waste of time because ethical lessons are easily shoved aside in the heat of competition.[49] Hard evidence that ethics training actually improves behavior is also lacking. Nonetheless, carefully designed and administered ethics training courses can make a positive contribution. Key features of effective ethics training programs include the following:

- Top management support.
- Open discussion of realistic ethical cases or scenarios.
- A clear focus on ethical issues specific to the organization.
- Integration of ethical themes into all training.
- A mechanism for anonymously reporting ethical violations. (General Dynamics has had good luck with telephone hot lines.)
- An organizational climate that rewards ethical conduct.[50]

Ethical Advocates

ethical advocate ethics specialist who plays a role in top-management decision making

An **ethical advocate** is a business ethics specialist who sits as a full-fledged member of the board of directors and acts as the board's social conscience.[51] This person may also be asked to sit in on top management decision deliberations.

Why wait until graduation to plow something back into the community? There is a trend toward social responsibility and ethical conduct beginning in school. Maria Anastas was one of 250 Tulane University law students to volunteer their time to an innovative clemency release program for older Louisiana state prison inmates. Anastas invested fifty hours in preparing a case for twelve-year-inmate Albert Vierling. Vierling praised the Tulane program and Anastas for giving him something he had lost, hope.

The idea is to assign someone the specific role of critical questioner (see Table 4.4 for recommended questions). Problems with groupthink and blind conformity, discussed in Chapter 13, are less likely when an ethical advocate tests management's thinking about ethical implications during the decision-making process.

Codes of Ethics

Recent experience has shown codes of ethics to be a step in the right direction, but not a cure-all.[52] To encourage ethical conduct, formal codes of ethics for organization members must satisfy two requirements. First, they should refer to specific practices such as kickbacks, payoffs, receiving gifts, record falsification, and misleading claims about products. For example, Xerox Corporation's fifteen-page ethical code says: "We're honest with our customers. No deals, no bribes, no secrets, no fooling around with prices. A kickback in any form kicks anybody out. Anybody."[53] General platitudes about good business practice or professional conduct are ineffective—they do not provide specific guidance and they offer too many tempting loopholes.

The second requirement for an organizational code of ethics is that it be firmly supported by top management and equitably enforced through the reward-and-punishment system.[54] Selective or uneven enforcement is the quickest way to kill the effectiveness of an ethical code.

Whistle-blowing

Detailed ethical codes help managers deal swiftly and effectively with subordinate misconduct. But what should a manager do when a superior or an entire organization is engaged in misconduct? Yielding to the realities of organizational politics, many managers simply turn their backs or claim they were "just following orders." (Nazi war criminals who based their defense at the Nuremberg trials on the argument that they were following orders ended up with ropes around their necks.) Managers with leadership and/or political skills may attempt to work within the organizational system for positive change.[55] Still others will take the boldest step of all, whistle-blowing. **Whistle-blowing is the practice of reporting perceived unethical practices to outsiders such as the press, government agencies, or public interest groups.**[56]

whistle-blowing reporting perceived unethical organizational practices to outside authorities

Not surprisingly, whistle-blowing is a highly controversial topic among managers, many of whom believe that whistle-blowing erodes their authority and decision-making prerogatives. Because loyalty to the organization is a cherished value in many quarters, whistle-blowing is criticized as the epitome of disloyalty. Consumer advocate Ralph Nader disagrees: "The willingness and ability of insiders to blow the whistle is the last line of defense ordinary citizens have against the denial of their rights and the destruction of their interests by secretive and powerful institutions."[57]

Whistle-blowing generally means putting one's job and/or career on the line, even though the federal government and many states have passed whistle-blower protection acts.[58] Two Ashland Oil managers who blew the whistle on illegal foreign payments by company officials found this out when they were first treated as outcasts and then fired. Eventually, they won a wrongful discharge lawsuit against Ashland, which agreed to a $25 million settlement.[59]

TABLE 4.4 • Twelve Questions for Examining the Ethics of a Business Decision

1. Have you defined the problem accurately?
2. How would you define the problem if you stood on the other side of the fence?
3. How did this situation occur in the first place?
4. To whom and to what do you give your loyalty as a person and as a member of the corporation?
5. What is your intention in making this decision?
6. How does this intention compare with the probable results?
7. Whom could your decision or action injure?
8. Can you discuss the problem with the affected parties before you make your decision?
9. Are you confident that your position will be as valid over a long period of time as it seems now?
10. Could you disclose without qualm your decision or action to your boss, your CEO, the board of directors, your family, society as a whole?
11. What is the symbolic potential of your action if understood? If misunderstood?
12. Under what conditions would you allow exceptions to your stand?

Source: Reprinted by permission of the *Harvard Business Review.* Exhibit from "Ethics Without the Sermon," by Laura L. Nash (November–December 1981). Copyright © 1981 by the President and Fellows of Harvard College; all rights reserved.

The challenge for today's management is to create an organizational climate in which the need to blow the whistle is reduced. Constructive steps include the following:

- Encourage the free expression of controversial and dissenting viewpoints.
- Streamline the organization's grievance procedure so that problems receive a prompt and fair hearing.
- Find out what employees think about the organization's social responsibility policies and make appropriate changes.
- Let employees know that management respects and is sensitive to their individual consciences.
- Recognize that the harsh treatment of a whistle-blower will probably lead to adverse public opinion.[60]

In the final analysis, individual behavior makes organizations ethical or unethical. Organizational forces can help bring out the best in people by clearly identifying and rewarding ethical conduct.

Summary

Corporate social responsibility is the idea that management has broader responsibilities than just making a profit. A strict interpretation holds that an action must be voluntary to qualify as socially responsible. Accordingly, reluctant submission to court orders or government coercion is not an example of social responsibility. The debate over the basic purpose of the corporation is long-standing. Those who embrace the classical economic model contend that business's social responsibility is to maximize profits for stockholders. Proponents of the socioeconomic model disagree, saying that business has a responsibility, above and beyond making a profit, to improve the general quality of life. Stakeholder audits help management identify all parties possibly affected by the organization's actions. There are specific arguments for and against social responsibility.

Management scholars who advocate greater corporate social responsibility cite the iron law of responsibility. This law states that if business does not use its socioeconomic power responsibly, society will take away that power. A continuum of social responsibility includes four strategies: reaction, defense, accommodation, and proaction. Actions by Du Pont and Johnson & Johnson exemplify proactive social responsibility. In the short run, proactive social responsibility usually costs the firm money. But, according to the notion of enlightened self-interest, both society and the company will gain in the long run. Research indicates that corporate philanthropy actually is a profit-motivated form of advertising. The future looks promising for corporate social responsibility because of broad acceptance of the concept by present and future executives.

Corporate misconduct in recent years has focused attention on business ethics, the systematic consideration of right and wrong action in an organizational context. Business ethics research evidence indicates two practical lessons for managers: (1) perceived pressure from above can erode ethics and (2) employees desire clear ethical standards in ambiguous situations. The call for better business ethics is clearly a *personal* challenge.

Managers cannot afford to overlook each employee's personal value system; values serve as anchors for one's beliefs and conduct. Instrumental values relate to desired behavior, whereas terminal values involve desired end states. Three types of value conflict are intrapersonal, individual-organizational, and intercultural. According to survey data, managers consider drug and alcohol abuse to be the most severe ethical problem today. Employee theft, conflicts of interest, quality control, and misuse of proprietary information also are high on the list of ethical hot spots.

The typical manager is said to be *amoral*—neither moral nor immoral—just ethically lazy or indifferent. Management can encourage ethical behavior in the following four ways: conduct ethics training; use ethical advocates in high-level decision making; formulate, disseminate, and consistently enforce specific codes of ethics; and create an open climate for dissent in which whistle-blowing becomes unnecessary.

Terms to Understand

Corporate social responsibility
Stakeholder audit
Iron law of responsibility
Reactive social responsibility strategy
Defensive social responsibility strategy
Accommodative social responsibility strategy
Proactive social responsibility strategy
Altruism

Enlightened self-interest
Corporate philanthropy
Ethics
Values
Instrumental value
Terminal value
Amoral managers
Ethical advocate
Whistle-blowing

Questions for Discussion

1. Why is it important to know that an action is voluntary before you label it socially responsible?

2. Which model of business—classical economic or socioeconomic—appeals more to you? Why?

3. Considering the arguments for and against corporate social responsibility, which side seems to present the more convincing case? Why do you find those arguments more convincing?

4. What evidence can you cite to validate the iron law of responsibility?

5. From an organizational standpoint, what are the principal advantages and disadvantages of each of the four social responsibility strategies?

6. What role does enlightened self-interest play in your life?

7. How would you characterize the general state of business ethics today?

8. How do you think your personal value system would affect the way you would perform as a manager?

9. Do you agree with the contention that the typical manager is amoral? Explain why you agree or disagree.

10. Do you believe management can make employees behave more ethically? Explain your rationale.

Back to the Opening Case

Now that you have read Chapter 4, you should be able to answer the following questions about the Dennis Levine case:

1. What were Levine's strongest instrumental and terminal values during his insider trading days? Were those values good predictors of his criminal behavior? Explain.

2. Do you suppose Levine's values have changed since being convicted and going to prison? Explain.

3. Might Dennis Levine have acted differently if his employer, Drexel Burnham Lambert, had provided ethics training on insider trading? Explain your reasoning.

4. What should Drexel Burnham Lambert have done to create the proper climate for ethical conduct?

CLOSING CASE

The Body Shop: A British Business To Believe In

Anita Roddick and her husband Gordon own more than $120 million worth of stock in their company, The Body Shop, but by her own admission, Anita doesn't "give a toss about the money." Unlike most companies in The Body Shop's business—selling body lotions and shampoos—that rely heavily on marketing, The Body Shop never spends a cent on advertising and doesn't even have a marketing department. In an industry that thrives on "secret formulas" and sells products by displaying beautiful models with perfect skin, The Body Shop sees education as one of its major goals and covers its shop walls with posters of rain forests, not sexy models. What's the secret behind these apparent contradictions?

Although Gordon actually runs the company, he and everyone else who deals with

The Body Shop recognize that Anita is the company's magic. It's not just that she has a charismatic personality and the kind of energy that could turn a $6,000 investment into a multimillion-dollar fortune in just over a decade. The woman is passionately committed to what her company does, and she has been able to infect both employees and customers with her fervor.

Roddick does things not because they make a profit or help her company look good or earn her a reputation for being socially responsible. She does them because she believes they are right. No gap divides the policies her company pursues and her personal beliefs in such principles as feminism, environmentalism, and the rights of native peoples. Because of her belief in education, The Body Shop outlets offer cards, pamphlets, and videos about products and ingredients. The shops avoid hard-sell hype and are basically self-serve. Each shop does have staff trained at the company's London training center, where they learn about what goes into their products and what those products do, not how to sell them.

Roddick's dedication to animals and the environment takes her well beyond other companies' commitments to avoid animal ingredients and to stop testing products on animals. She dedicates herself to her beliefs, even if they have nothing to do with her company. Whatever the cause—saving the whales or working for the survival of Brazilian Indians—Roddick devotes her time and money, educating the public with messages on company trucks and sometimes leading employees in public demonstrations. She believes in helping developing communities, both in Third World countries and in impoverished communities in the industrialized world, through trading with them. Acting on this belief, The Body Shop built a soap factory in a high-unemployment section of Glasgow, Scotland. It also sent people to Nepal to teach the Nepalese an alternative way to make paper, using the water hyacinths clogging their waterways instead of cutting down scarce trees.

Roddick is quick to admit that she knew nothing about the Brazilian rain forests or ozone depletion until a few years ago. Nevertheless, her crusades are based on knowledge and experience, not on a sense of what is trendy or politically expedient. The company's policy of selling its products in refill-able bottles might seem to be a response to recent pressures to recycle but in fact it began because at startup the company couldn't afford to buy all the new bottles it needed. Ingredients for most of the company's products come from the Third World, not because she wants the products to sound exotic but because during extensive travels before starting the company she saw that local unorthodox approaches to personal care—such as washing your hair with mud—often worked.

Unlike many environmentalists, Roddick sees no fundamental conflict between business and environmental concerns. In fact, she believes businesses should lead the way in solving the world's problems. Such a belief is unusual—perhaps even unique— among the world's multimillionaires, but Roddick already has thousands of customers and employees who believe in her vision. Perhaps the success of The Body Shop will encourage other companies to follow her lead.

For Discussion

1. Which social responsibility strategy is The Body Shop pursuing?

2. What role does enlightened self-interest play in this case?

3. Judging from what you have just read, what instrumental and terminal values drive Anita Roddick?

4. What lessons can the average manager learn from Roddick?

References

Opening Quotation. Mark Pastin, *The Hard Problems of Management: Gaining the Ethics Edge* (San Francisco: Jossey-Bass, 1986), p. 228.

Opening Case. Dennis B. Levine, "The Inside Story of an Inside Trader," *Fortune* (May 21, 1990): 80, 82. Reprinted by permission of the author.

Closing Case. Bo Burlingham, "This Woman Has Changed Business Forever," *INC.* (June 1990): 34–46; Cilla Duff Kent, "An Environmental Concern," *The Christian Science Monitor* (July 31, 1990): 14; Robert Heller, "The Body Shop's Best," *Management Today* (June 1987): 56; Mark Maremont, "A Cosmetics Company with a Conscience," *Business Week* (May 23, 1988): 136.

1. Neil H. Jacoby, *Corporate Power and Social Responsibility* (New York: Macmillan, 1973), p. 6.

2. Thomas M. Jones, "Corporate Social Responsibility Revisited, Redefined," *California Management Review,* 22 (Spring 1980): 59–60. Also see Archie B. Carroll, "A Three-Dimensional Conceptual Model of Corporate Performance," *Academy of Management Review,* 4 (October 1979): 497–505; Keith B. Murray and John R. Montanari, "Strategic Management of the Socially Responsible Firm: Integrating Management and Marketing Theory," *Academy of Management Review,* 11 (October 1986): 815–827; and Edwin M. Epstein, "The Corporate Social Policy Process: Beyond Business Ethics, Corporate Social Responsibility, and Corporate Social Responsiveness," *California Management Review,* 29 (Spring 1987): 99–114.

3. Maria Recio and Vicky Cahan, "Bhopal Has Americans Demanding the 'Right to Know,'" *Business Week* (February 18, 1985): 36.

4. Based on discussion in Gregg Easterbrook, "Cleaning Up," *Newsweek* (July 24, 1989): 26–42.

5. Chris Welles, "What Led Beech-Nut Down the Road to Disgrace," *Business Week* (February 22, 1988): 128.

6. See Joe Queenan, "Juice Men," *Barron's* (June 20, 1988): 37–38.

7. See Robert A. Giacalone and Stephen L. Payne, "Are Business Leaders Staging a Morality Play?" *Business and Society Review,* 62 (Summer 1987): 22–26.

8. Jones, "Corporate Social Responsibility Revisited," p. 65.

9. This distinction between the economic and the socioeconomic models is based partly on discussion in Courtney C. Brown, *Beyond the Bottom Line* (New York: Macmillan, 1979), pp. 82–83.

10. Milton Friedman, *Capitalism and Freedom* (Chicago: University of Chicago Press, 1962), p. 133.

11. For example, see Nancy C. Roberts and Paula J. King, "The Stakeholder Audit Goes Public," *Organizational Dynamics,* 17 (Winter 1989): 63–79.

12. For an interesting critique, see Kenneth J. Arrow. "The Limitations of the Profit Motive," *Challenge,* 22 (September–October 1979): 23–27.

13. These arguments have been adapted in part from Jones, "Corporate Social Responsibility Revisited," p. 61; and Keith Davis and William C. Frederick, *Business and Society: Management, Public Policy, and Ethics,* 5th ed. (New York: McGraw-Hill, 1984), pp. 28–41.

14. Mark N. Vamos and Stuart Jackson, "The Public is Willing to Take Business On," *Business Week* (May 29, 1989): 29.

15. Davis and Frederick, *Business and Society,* p. 34.

16. Data from Vamos and Jackson, "The Public is Willing to Take Business ON."

17. Drawn from Ian Wilson, "What One Company Is Doing about Today's Demands on Business," in *Changing Business-Society Interrelationships,* ed. George A. Steiner (Los Angeles: UCLA Graduate School of Management, 1975).

18. See Richard J. Durbin, "The Tobacco Industry's Smoke Screen," *The Christian Science Monitor* (August 16, 1989): 18.

19. Russell W. Baker, "Critics Fault Exxon's 'PR Campaign,'" *The Christian Science Monitor* (June 14, 1989): 8.

20. Based on discussion in Harris Collingwood, "Pfizer's Heart Problem," *Business Week* (August 20, 1990): 42.

21. Ron Scherer, "Du Pont Does 'The Right Thing' for the Ozone," *The Christian Science Monitor* (March 1, 1990): 1.

22. See Kenneth E. Aupperle, Archie B. Carroll, and John D. Hatfield, "An Examination of the Relationship Between Corporate Social Responsibility and Profitability," *Academy of Management Journal,* 28 (June 1985): 446–463; Wallace N. Davidson III and Dan L. Worrell, "The Impact of Announcements of Corporate Illegalities On Shareholder Returns," *Academy of Management Journal,* 31 (March 1988): 195–200; and Jean B. McGuire, Alison Sundgren, and Thomas Schneeweis, "Corporate Social Responsibility and Firm Financial Performance," *Academy of Management Journal,* 31 (December 1988): 854–872.

23. Data from Milton Moskowitz, "Company Performance Roundup," *Business and Society Review,* 73 (Spring 1990): 63–69. Also see Michael Useem, "Market and Institutional Factors in Corporate Contributions," *California Management Review,* 30 (Winter 1988): 77–88.

24. Louis W. Fry, Gerald D. Keim, and Roger E. Meiners, "Corporate Contributions: Altruistic or For-Profit?" *Academy of Management Journal,* 25 (Mach 1982): 105.

25. For complete details, see Richard E. Wokutch and Barbara A. Spencer, "Corporate Saints and Sinners: The Effects of Philanthropic and Illegal Activity on Organizational Performance," *California Management Review,* 29 (Winter 1987): 62–77.

26. Quoted in Stanley J. Modic, "Movers and Shakers of Corporate Social Responsibility," *Business and Society Review,* 65 (Spring 1988): 63–64.

27. See Mark N. Vamos and Christopher Power, "A Kinder, Gentler Generation of Executives?" *Business Week* (April 23, 1990): 86–87.

28. Data from David E. Rosenbaum, "All Roads Lead to Washington and Politics in S&L Calamity," *The Arizona Republic* (June 10, 1990): F1, F3–F5.

29. See William D. Litzinger and Thomas E. Schaefer, "Business Ethics Bogeyman: The Perceptual Paradox," *Business Horizons,* 30 (March–April 1987): 16–21; Kenneth R. Andrews, "Ethics in Practice," *Harvard Business Review,* 67 (September–October 1989): 99–104; Frederick B. Bird and James A. Waters, "The Moral Muteness of Managers," *California Management Review,* 32 (Fall 1989): 73–88; and W. Edward Stead, Dan L. Worrell, and Jean Garner Stead, "An Integrative Model for Understanding and Managing Ethical Behavior in Business Organizations," *Journal of Business Ethics,* 9 (March 1990): 233–242.

30. O. C. Ferrell and John Fraedrich, *Business Ethics: Ethical Decision Making and Cases* (Boston: Houghton Mifflin, 1991), pp. 10–11.

31. Business ethics research findings are reviewed in Phillip V. Lewis, "Defining 'Business Ethics': Like Nailing Jello to a Wall," *Journal of Business Ethics,* 4 (October 1985): 377–383. Also see William A. Kahn, "Toward an Agenda for Business Ethics Research," *Academy of Management Review,* 15 (April 1990): 311–328.

32. Steven N. Brenner and Earl A. Molander, "Is the Ethics of Business Changing?" *Harvard Business Review,* 55 (January–February 1977): 60.

33. James S. Bowman, "Managerial Ethics in Business and Government," *Business Horizons,* 19 (October 1976): 53. This study is a replication of one by Archie B. Carroll, "Managerial Ethics: A Post-Watergate View," *Business Horizons,* 18 (April 1975): 75–80.

34. Data from Justin G. Longenecker, Joseph A. McKinney, and Carlos W. Moore, "The Generation Gap in Business Ethics," *Business Horizons,* 32 (September–October 1989): 9–14.

35. John Schwartz, "The 'Final Nail in the Coffin'?" *Newsweek* (August 6, 1990): 46.

36. William Rudelius and Rogene A. Buchholz, "Ethical Problems of Purchasing Managers," *Harvard Business Review,* 57 (March–April 1979): 12. Also see Alan J. Dubinsky, Eric N. Berkowitz, and William Rudelius, "Ethical Problems of Field Sales Personnel," *MSU Business Topics,* 28 (Summer 1980): 11–16; and James R. Davis, "Ambiguity, Ethics, and the Bottom Line," *Business Horizons,* 32 (May–June 1989): 65–70.

37. Thomas R. Horton, "The Ethics Crisis Continues: What to Do?" *Management Review,* 75 (November 1986): 3.

38. For details, see Richard F. Beltramini, Robert A. Peterson, and George Kozmetsky, "Concerns of College Students Regarding Business Ethics," *Journal of Business Ethics,* 3 (August 1984): 195–200. Also see Robert A. Peterson, Richard F. Beltramini, and George Kozmetsky, "Concerns of College Students Regarding Business Ethics: A Replication," *Journal of Business Ethics* (in press).

39. See Sir Adrian Cadbury, "Ethical Managers Make Their Own Rules," *Harvard Business Review,* 65 (September–October 1987): 69–73.

40. For good management-oriented discussions of values, see Barry Z. Posner and J. Michael Munson, "The Importance of Values in Understanding Organizational Behavior," *Human Resource Management,* 18 (Fall 1979): 9–14; and Barry Z. Posner and Warren H. Schmidt, "Values and the American Manager: An Update," *California Management Review,* 26 (Spring 1984): 202–216.

41. Frank Rose, "A New Age For Business?" *Fortune* (October 8, 1990): 164.

42. For excellent treatment of values, see Milton Rokeach, *Beliefs, Attitudes, and Values* (San Francisco: Jossey-Bass, 1968), p. 124; and Milton Rokeach and Sandra J. Ball-Rokeach, "Stability and Change in American Value Priorities, 1968–1981," *American Psychologist,* 44 (May 1989): 775–784.

43. Rokeach, *Beliefs, Attitudes, and Values,* p. 124.

44. See Rick Wartzman, "Nature or Nurture? Study Blames Ethical Lapses on Corporate Goals," *The Wall Street Journal* (October 9, 1987): 27.

45. "Corporate Culture," *Business Week* (October 27, 1980): 154.

46. Reprinted with permission from the October 1990 issue of *Training,* The Magazine of Human Resources Development. Copyright 1990, Lakewood Publications Inc., Minneapolis, MN (612) 333-0471. All rights reserved.

47. See Archie B. Carroll, "In Search of the Moral Manager," *Business Horizons,* 30 (March–April 1987): 7–15.

48. Data from Brad Lee Thompson, "Ethics Training Enters the Real World," *Training,* 27 (October 1990): 82–94.

49. For example, see Ronald E. Berenbeim, "An Outbreak of Ethics," *Across the Board,* 25 (May 1988): 15–19.

50. Based on discussion in Thompson, "Ethics Training Enters the Real World." For information on General Dynamics' ethics program, see William H. Wagel, "A New Focus on Business Ethics at General Dynamics," *Personnel,* 64 (August 1987): 4–8.

51. For informative reading on ethical advocates, see Theodore V. Purcell, "Electing an 'Angel's Advocate' to the Board," *Management Review,* 65 (May 1976): 4–11; and Theodore V. Purcell, "Institutionalizing Ethics into Top Management Decisions," *Public Relations Quarterly,* 22 (Summer 1977): 15–20.

52. For an instructive content analysis of 281 corporate ethical codes, see Robert Chatov, "What Corporate Ethics Statements Say," *California Management Review,* 22 (Summer 1980): 20–29. Another content analysis of 39 corporate codes of ethics may be found in Glen R. Sanderson and Iris I. Varner, "What's Wrong with Corporate Codes of Conduct?" *Management Accounting,* 66 (July 1984): 28–31, 35. Also see Donald Robin, Michael Giallourakis, Fred R. David, and Thomas E. Moritz, "A Different Look at Codes of Ethics," *Business Horizons,* 32 (January–February 1989): 66–73; and James R. Redeker, "Code of Conduct as Corporate Culture," *HRMagazine,* 35 (July 1990): 83–87.

53. "Business' Big Morality Play," *Dun's Review* (August 1980): 56.

54. The importance of top-management support, ethical codes, and compliance monitoring are discussed in John A. Byrne, "Businesses Are Signing Up for Ethics 101," *Business Week* (February 15, 1988): 56, 57.

55. See Richard P. Nielsen, "Changing Unethical Organizational Behavior," *The Academy of Management Executive,* 3 (May 1989): 123–130.

56. An interesting study of the characteristics of whistle-blowers among a random sample of 8,587 U.S. government employees can be found in Marcia Parmerlee Miceli and Janet P. Near, "The Relationships Among Beliefs, Organizational Position, and Whistle-Blowing Status: A Discriminant Analysis," *Academy of Management Journal,* 27 (December 1984): 687–705.

57. Ralph Nader, "An Anatomy of Whistle Blowing," in *Whistle Blowing,* ed. Ralph Nader, Peter Petkas, and Kate Blackwell (New York: Bantam, 1972), p. 7. For interesting case studies of whistle-blowers, see William McGowan. "The Whistle-blowers Hall of Fame," *Business and Society Review,* 52 (Winter 1985): 31–36.

58. The federal Whistleblowers Protection Act of 1989 is discussed in David Israel and Anita Lechner, "Protection for Whistleblowers," *Personnel Administrator,* 34 (July 1989): 106.

59. For details, see Zachary Schiller, "Ashland Just Can't Seem to Leave Its Checkered Past Behind," *Business Week* (October 31, 1988): 122–123, 126.

60. Adapted from Kenneth D. Walters, "Your Employees' Right to Blow the Whistle," *Harvard Business Review,* 53 (July–August 1975): 26–34, 161–162. Also see M. Cash Mathews, "Whistle-blowing: Acts of Courage Are often Discouraged," *Business and Society Review,* 63 (Fall 1987): 40–44; and Janet P. Near, "Whistle-Blowing: Encourage It!," *Business Horizons,* 32 (January–February 1989): 2–6.

VIDEO SKILL BUILDER

• •

The People Factor:
The Hawthorne Studies for
Today's Managers

Learning Objective

To help acquaint you with the famous Hawthorne Studies by way of a contemporary analysis of the so-called "Hawthorne Effect."

Link to Textual Material

Productivity, management history, the behavioral approach, the human relations movement, the Hawthorne Studies, Elton Mayo, group dynamics.

Until recently, the term "Hawthorne Effect" was an unchallenged assumption that management, by paying attention to individual employees, could influence the employee to greater productivity. This assumption has since been shown to be simplistic. The "Hawthorne Effect" operates only under certain conditions.

Discussion Questions

1. How would you answer a manager who declared: "People are easy to manage. All they want is money."?
2. In today's workplace, is it possible to boost performance by giving employees special attention?
3. How widespread is the problem of group-inspired restriction of output in today's workplace?
4. What "people" skills do you need to develop to be a successful manager?

PART II

Planning and Decision Making

Part II focuses on planning and decision making, two fundamental management functions that complement one another. Planning helps managers determine where they want to go, and decision making helps them get there. In Chapter 5, a definitional and conceptual framework for the planning function is presented. Special attention is devoted to management by objectives, a proven planning and control technique. Strategic management is discussed in Chapter 6 to underscore the importance of determining the organization's overall purpose and of planning for long-term success. Concepts and techniques for better decision making and more creative problem solving are covered in Chapter 7. Ways to enhance managerial creativity are explored.

5

Planning: The Primary Management Function

●●●●●●●●●●●●●●●●●●

*The only limits are, as
always, those of vision.*

JAMES BROUGHTON

CHAPTER OBJECTIVES

When you finish studying this chapter, you should
be able to

- Distinguish among state, effect, and response
  uncertainty.
- Identify and define the three types of planning.
- Write good objectives and discuss the role of
  objectives in planning.
- Describe the four-step management by objectives (MBO) process and explain how it can
  foster individual commitment and motivation.
- Compare and contrast flow charts and Gantt
  charts and discuss the value of PERT networks.
- Explain how break-even points can be calculated.

●●●●●●●●●●●●●●●●●●●●●●●●●●●●●●●●●

Coca-Cola Plans to Win the Global Cola Wars

The average person who drops into a convenience store for a soft drink probably doesn't find the choice of the afternoon's beverage particularly momentous. But to Coca-Cola and Pepsi, the big two in the world of soft drinks, every purchase is crucial. From Peoria to Peking, the two giants continue to battle, winning and losing on such a large scale that the whole business world enjoys watching. Meanwhile, Coca-Cola plans to keep things interesting in the global cola wars.

The stakes are high. In 1990, Coke earned about $1.4 billion on $10.5 billion of revenues. With a soft drink market that is worth about $27 billion in the United States alone, a gain or loss of a single percentage point of the market can mean millions of dollars to a company. Coke leads the way with the world's most valuable trademark and about 40 percent of the overall market. Pepsi trails by only 10 points in the overall market and is almost even in supermarket sales. The competition is fierce and the strategies sometimes get nasty.

Probably the most famous move in the recent history of the cola wars was Coke's 1985 introduction of New Coke, which boasted a sweeter, more Pepsi-like taste clearly intended to win market share back from the drink of the "new generation." Analysts still debate whether the move was a colossal blunder or a clever marketing ploy. When Coke lovers around the country protested the change, demanding that the company return to the old formula, they made headlines with their ferocious loyalty to their brand. After three months—long enough for New Coke (now called simply Coke) to win some devotees—the company reintroduced the old formula as Classic Coke, which went on to pass Pepsi as the best-selling single drink in America. Although Classic Coke outsells the new Coke by about 10 to 1, the company expects the new version to take off when sweet-toothed children of the baby boomers grow up. In any case, Coke now has two top entrants in the cola competition, making some people wonder if the "blunder" was planned all along.

The soft drink giants also battle on other grounds, and one of those is the movie set. Until the late 1980s, Coke diversified, buying such nonsoda businesses as Columbia Pictures. Many analysts believed that such diversification strayed too far from Coke's corporate mission, and they credit much of Coke's present success to its recent reorganization and refocusing, which included selling off the movie-making giant. Nevertheless, soft drink money still pours into movies. When Tom Cruise raced a Chevy Lumina to victory in *Days of Thunder,* the world saw Coke's Mello Yello logo cross the finish line first. Spending $3 million to promote the connection between the movie, cars, and Mello Yello (Coke's answer to Pepsi's Mountain Dew), Coke boosted Mello Yello's market share by half a percentage point.

In the 1990s, both companies expect their real growth to occur overseas. The average American drinks 283 servings of Coke's products a year, but non-Americans consume less than one-fifth that amount. Although the 1.1 billion Chinese have barely begun to enjoy the taste of America's cola successes, Coke and Pepsi are already competing for the Chinese market. Pepsi has seven bottling plants in China, and Coke sponsors big sporting events and sends sales reps around the country on motorcycles. Coke is already well established in Taiwan, where it has sponsored such things as the creation of Chinese dishes using Coke. Anyone for fried frog legs in a Coke-and-garlic sauce?

The main competition the big two encounter overseas is not each other but traditionally popular drinks—tea, coffee, milk, and even water. So far, neither company has expressed any ethical reservations about, for instance, weaning Brazilians away from their beloved milk and giving them instead a can of cola. In the United States, however, the giants raced to appeal to Americans' environmental consciousness. Each wanted to be the first to announce that it was making bottles out of recycled materials—Pepsi won by 22 minutes.

So what will the cola wars of the future look like? Coke, which created a new-products group in 1989, has introduced a reformulated version of Fresca (its grapefruit-flavored drink), PowerAde (an imitation of Gatorade), and a caffeine-free version of Classic Coke. Coke also tried a new advertising approach in 1989, contending that Diet Coke was winning converts from regular Pepsi. The move, which effectively changed the battlefield once again, seemed to make sense because the market for diet soft drinks is growing faster than the overall soda market. Both cola giants must constantly be on the lookout for such changes in habits and tastes. Although older diet drinks like Diet Pepsi were marketed to appeal particularly to women, Diet Coke's ads have targeted calorie-conscious men as well.

Besides coming up with new products and new advertising strategies, Coke is also thinking about new ways to bring its products into the home, such as miniature soda fountain taps that could be hooked up to sinks or refrigerators in private homes or soft drink utility lines that could be installed in planned communities. It may be a while before new homeowners sign up for Coke or Pepsi along with cable TV, but in the competitive world of soft drinks, anything seems possible.

•••••••••••••••••• The only certainty for today's organizations is change. For example, when Switzerland's Nestlé Enterprises, Inc. bought Carnation Company in 1985 for $3 billion, the plan was to merge Carnation with Nestlé's other U.S. food businesses by 1993. But unexpectedly stiff competition and the promise of a $30 million savings in administrative overhead prompted Nestlé to push through its U.S. consolidation two years ahead of schedule.[1] Like Nestlé, Coca-Cola will undoubtedly make many changes in its quest for greater world market share as circumstances dictate in the years ahead. Managers everywhere face an increasingly fluid social, political, economic, and technological environment. Ignoring or resisting change practically guarantees organizational failure. Effective managers keep informed about what is going on inside and outside their organizations, actively anticipate change, and plan future courses of action accordingly.

planning coping with uncertainty by formulating courses of action to achieve specified results

Planning is the process of coping with uncertainty by formulating future courses of action to achieve specified results. Because planning paves the way for all downstream management functions (see Figure 5.1) by serving as a bridge between the present and the future, it has been called the primary management function.[2]

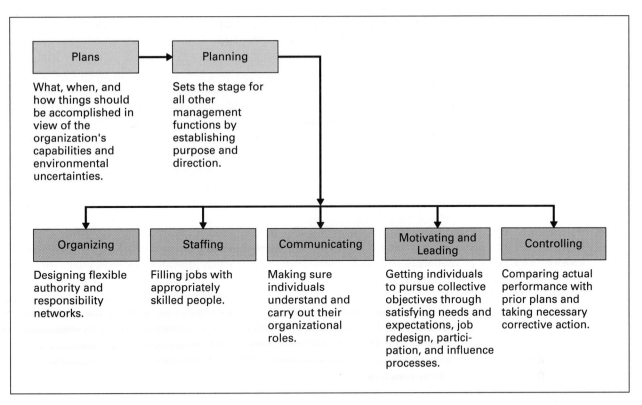

FIGURE 5.1 • Planning: The Primary Management Function

As a backdrop for what lies ahead, let us briefly examine what 250 executives from America's largest companies had to say in a survey about the evolution of planning. Because of limited growth opportunities and increased competition, the executives identified the following new directions for the planning function:

- Academically trained planning specialists are being replaced by planners with hands-on managerial experience.
- Teamwork and cooperation throughout the planning/control cycle are breaking down the traditional distinction between those who plan and those who carry out plans.
- Canned planning techniques and theories are giving way to customized planning programs based on competitive marketing strategies specific to the organization.
- Plans are becoming more flexible to accommodate greater emphasis on entrepreneurship (risk taking).
- Planners are being asked to translate broad marketing strategies into how-to-do-it plans that can be easily communicated and understood.[3]

With these trends in mind, we shall discuss uncertainty, highlight five essential aspects of the planning function, and take a close look at management by objectives. We shall also introduce four practical planning tools (flow charts, Gantt charts, PERT networks, and break-even analysis).

Coping with Uncertainty

It is often remarked that the only sure things in life are death and taxes. Although this is a gloomy prospect, it does capture a key theme of modern life: We are faced with a great deal of uncertainty. Organizations, like individuals, are continually challenged to accomplish something in spite of general uncertainty. Organizations meet this challenge largely through planning. As a context for our discussion of planning in this and the following chapter, let us explore environmental uncertainty from two different perspectives: (1) types of uncertainty and (2) organizational responses to environmental uncertainty.

Three Types of Uncertainty

●●●●●●●●●●●●●●●●●●●●
Distinguish among state, effect, and response uncertainty.

state uncertainty unpredictable environment

effect uncertainty impacts of environmental changes are unpredictable

response uncertainty consequences of decisions are unpredictable

Through the years, *environmental uncertainty* has been a catch-all term among managers and researchers. However, research indicates that people actually perceive three different types of environmental uncertainty: state uncertainty, effect uncertainty, and response uncertainty. **State uncertainty** occurs when the environment or a portion of the environment is considered unpredictable. A manager's attempt to predict the *effects* of specific environmental changes or events on his or her organization involves **effect uncertainty**. **Response uncertainty** relates to being unable to predict the *consequences* of a particular decision or organizational response.[4]

A simple analogy can help us conceptually sort out these three types of uncertainty. Suppose you are a golfer and on your way to the course you wonder if it is going to rain; this is *state uncertainty*. Next, you experience *effect uncertainty* because you are not sure it will rain hard enough, if it does rain, to make you quit before finishing nine holes. You begin weighing your chances of making par if you have to adjust your choice of golf clubs to poor playing conditions; now you are experiencing *response uncertainty*. Each of the three types of perceived uncertainty could affect your golfing attitude and performance. Similarly, managers are affected by their different perceptions of environmental factors. Their degree of uncertainty may vary from one type of uncertainty to another. A manager may, for example, be unsure about the timing of a labor strike (state uncertainty) but certain that a strike would ruin quarterly profits (effect uncertainty).

Organizational Responses to Uncertainty

Some organizations do a better job than others of planning amid various combinations of uncertainty. This is due in part to differing patterns of response to environmental factors beyond the organization's immediate control. As outlined in Table 5.1, organizations cope with environmental uncertainty by adopting one of four positions vis-à-vis the environment in which they operate. These positions are defenders, prospectors, analyzers, and reactors,[5] each with its own characteristic impact on planning.

Defenders. Organizations that are defenders can be successful as long as their narrowly defined market remains strong. Caterpillar is a good example of a

As the last survivor among some 50 airlines born during the deregulation era, Phoenix-based America West Airlines always had to deal with immense uncertainties. America West executives, such as vice president and controller Raymond Nakano, took pride in being prospectors. Its cross-trained, nonunion employees who all owned stock in the company, gave America West a competitive edge for a time. But a heavy load of debt, combined with soaring jet fuel prices and fewer passengers during the Persian Gulf War, forced this prospector into bankruptcy in mid-1991.

defender because it has stuck to its three basic product lines—earth-moving equipment, diesel engines, and materials-handling devices—and has resisted the trend among its less successful competitors to diversify to other areas.[6] But defenders can become stranded on a dead-end road if their primary market seriously weakens or dissolves.

Prospectors. Prospector organizations are easy to spot because they have a reputation for aggressively making things happen rather than waiting for them to happen. Prospectors enjoy the advantage of getting the edge on the competition by being innovative. At the same time, prospectors suffer the disadvantage of sometimes throwing money away on ideas that fail. RJR Nabisco found itself in such a position when it failed to capitalize on an estimated $325 million R&D investment after killing its new Premier brand of cigarette in 1989. Supposedly a cleaner-burning cigarette, Premier was intended to be a partial answer to growing concerns about the health effects of smoking.[7]

A study of 1,452 business units shed some light on the comparative effectiveness of these first two strategies. "Specifically, in every type of environment examined, defenders outperformed prospectors in terms of current profitability and cash flow. The costs and risks of product innovation appear significant."[8] Prospectors in the business sector need to pick their opportunities very carefully, selecting those with the best combination of feasibility and profit potential.

Analyzers. An essentially conservative strategy of following the leader marks an organization as an analyzer. General Motors, for example, followed Ford's lead in aerodynamic styling and Chrysler's in the minivan market.[9] This "me too" response to environmental uncertainty is fine as long as (1) the leader is headed in the right direction, and (2) changes in the leader's direction are detected and acted upon in time. The hundreds of companies around the world that assemble and distribute IBM-compatible personal computers (so-called clones) qualify as analyzers. Their success is attested to by the fact that the clone-makers have collectively sold more PCs than IBM has.[10] It is no accident that IBM designed its new Personal System/2 personal computer line to be more difficult to copy.[11] Analyzers conserve capital by letting prospectors assume the risks of expensive R&D projects and then copying and developing the most promising ideas. On the negative side, analyzers typically face stiff competition and narrow profit margins because, if one can follow the leader, *many* can follow the leader.

Reactors. The reactor is the exact opposite of the prospector. Reactors wait for adversity, such as declining sales, before taking corrective steps. They are slow to develop new products to supplement their tried-and-true ones. Their strategic responses to changes in the environment are often late. An interesting example in this area is Joseph E. Seagram & Sons, Inc. Seagram grew into the world's largest distiller by specializing in brown liquors such as Seagram's 7 Crown. But drinking habits have changed in recent years. Consequently, white liquors such as Bacardi rum and Smirnoff vodka pushed Seagram's 7 Crown from first place to third. Moreover, with more Americans drinking wine, the public outcry against drunk driving, and higher excise taxes on liquor, Seagram's sales dropped. By the time Seagram reacted by bolstering its wine business in the 1980s, the wine market was glutted because of European imports and overplanted vineyards in California.[12]

According to a recent field study, reactors tended to be less profitable than defenders, prospectors, and analyzers.[13]

The Need for Focus and Flexibility in the 1990s

Overall, the planner's job is to gauge the nature and degree of major environmental uncertainties, assess the organization's response capabilities, and develop appropriate plans. According to William Lawrence, TRW's top planning executive, "The key words for the nineties are 'focus' and 'flexibility.' "[14] By *focus*, Lawrence means identifying what the company does best and developing the resource base and competencies to do it even better. What about *flexibility?* Firm plans can be made for areas of low uncertainty, though areas marked by high uncertainty require flexible plans that can be adjusted as changing conditions dictate. As a general rule, the higher the degree of environmental uncertainty, the greater the need for flexibility in planning.

The Essentials of Planning

Planning is an ever-present feature of modern life, although there is no universal approach. Virtually everyone is a planner, at least in the informal sense. We plan

TABLE 5.1 • Different Organizational Responses to an Uncertain Environment

Type of organizational response	Characteristics of response
1. Defenders	Highly expert at producing and marketing a few products in a narrowly defined market
	Opportunities beyond present market not sought
	Few adjustments in technology, organization structure, and methods of operation because of narrow focus
	Primary attention devoted to efficiency of current operations
2. Prospectors	Primary attention devoted to searching for new market opportunities
	Frequent development and testing of new products and services
	Source of change and uncertainty for competitors
	Loss of efficiency because of continual product and market innovation
3. Analyzers	Simultaneous operations in stable and changing product market domains
	In relatively stable product/market domain, emphasis on formalized structures and processes to achieve routine and efficient operation
	In changing product/market domain, emphasis on detecting and copying competitors' most promising ideas
4. Reactors	Frequently unable to respond quickly to perceived changes in environment
	Make adjustments only when finally forced to do so by environmental pressures

Source: Adapted from *Organizational Strategy, Structure, and Process,* by Raymond E. Miles and Charles C. Snow. Copyright © 1978, McGraw-Hill Book Company, p. 29. Used with permission of McGraw-Hill Book Company.

A great deal of planning is required to keep this huge Georgia-Pacific paper mill running properly. The firm's Port Hudson, Louisiana, facility, measures over a football field in length. Georgia-Pacific's mission is to become the world's number one papermaker. That mission cannot be achieved if the managers do not formulate and implement sound intermediate and operational plans. Clear priorities and specific objectives also are necessary.

leisure activities after school or work; we make career plans. Personal or informal plans give purpose to our lives. In a similar fashion, more formalized plans enable managers to mobilize their intentions to accomplish organizational purposes. According to the head of Alcan Aluminum Corporation, a company with an exemplary planning program, "plans are truly the working documents by which we manage our business."[15] A **plan** is a specific, documented intention consisting of an objective and an action statement. The objective portion is the end, and the action statement represents the means to that end. Stated another way, objectives give management targets to shoot at, whereas action statements provide the arrows for hitting the targets. Properly conceived plans tell *what, when,* and *how* something is to be done.

In spite of the wide variety of formal planning systems managers encounter on the job, we can identify some essentials of sound planning. Among these

plan an objective plus an action statement

A New Mission for the U.S. Army Corps of Engineers

Ask most environmentalists about the U.S. Army Corps of Engineers and you're likely to get an unprintable reply. Traditionally, the Corps has viewed nature as "the enemy": it dammed rivers, drained swamps, and made marshes into farmland, destroying the nesting and feeding grounds of thousands of animal species. But for both philosophical and practical reasons, the Corps is changing with the times, sometimes reworking what it built just a few years ago.

Under pressure from its many stakeholders, who include Audubon society members as well as agribusinesses, the new Corps knows its own future is tied to attempts to improve the environment. The Corps's basic values and purpose have been adapting to the country's rediscovery of the value of nature, and the Corps has begun using its planning and engineering skills for very different ends. Recognizing that programs aimed at improving the environment almost always need engineers, the Corps's new leaders want to supply those engineers. As part of its new focus, the Corps has been working with the Environmental Protection Agency and local communities to develop wastewater treatment plants and to handle solid wastes. Instead of draining wetlands, it now tries to save them in areas like the Mississippi Delta.

The Corps's most important about-face to date occurred in southern Florida. Historically, summer rains would fill Lake Okeechobee and drain slowly south, creating a rich natural environment that supported the wide variety of plant and animal species for which the Everglades became famous. But Florida's big cities wanted to use the water, and farmers and land developers didn't like the unpredictable floods. At the state's request, the Corps built 1,500 miles of canals and levees and turned the winding Kissimmee River into a straight channel half its original length. Florida's cities and farms prospered, but nature suffered dramatically. The population of the area's wading birds alone has declined by 95 percent since the 1930s.

So now Florida has asked the Corps to undo its work, tear down the levees, let the Kissimmee take its natural course, and bring water back into the Everglades. Environmentalists are still suspicious, but the Corps may in time earn the title it now desires: "friend of the environment."

Sources: Vicki Monks, "Engineering the Everglades," *National Parks* (September/October 1990): 32–44; Tom Ichniowski, "Agencies Mount a Joint Effort to Push Environmental Work," *ENR* (May 31, 1990): 17–18; Frank Rose, "The Corps of Engineers Goes Green," *Fortune* (October 8, 1990): 160.

common denominators are organizational mission, types of planning, objectives, priorities, and the planning/control cycle.

Organizational Mission

To some, defining an organization's mission might seem to be an unnecessary exercise. But exactly the opposite is true. Some organizations drift along without a clear mission. Others lose sight of their original mission. Sometimes an organization, such as the U.S. Army Corps of Engineers, finds its original mission no longer acceptable to key stakeholders (see Management Ethics). Periodically redefining an organization's mission is both common and necessary in an era of rapid change.

A clear, formally written, and publicized statement of an organization's mission is the cornerstone of any planning system that will effectively guide the organization through uncertain times.[16] A good mission statement helps define the organization's special niche in the economy or culture. Moreover, it provides a focal point for the entire planning process. When Vincent A. Sarni took the top job at PPG, the large glass and paint company, for example, he created a document he called "Blueprint for the Decade." In it, he specified the company's mission and corporate objectives for such things as service, quality, and financial performance.

> *Sarni . . . trudged from plant to plant preaching the virtues in his Little Blue Book. "My first two or three years I always started with a discussion of the Blueprint," he says. "I don't have to do that anymore. The Blueprint's on the shop floor, and it has meaning."*[17]

Types of Planning

Ideally, planning begins at the top of the organizational pyramid and filters down. The rationale for beginning at the top is the need for coordination. It is top management's job to state the organization's mission, establish strategic priorities, and draw up major policies. After these statements are in place, successive rounds of strategic, intermediate, and operational planning can occur. Figure 5.2 presents an idealized picture of the three types of planning, as carried out by different levels of management.

Strategic, Intermediate, and Operational Planning. **Strategic planning** is the process of determining how to pursue the organization's long-term goals with the resources expected to be available. A well-conceived strategic plan communicates

· · · · · · · · · · · · · · · · ·
Identify and define the three types of planning.

strategic planning determining how to pursue long-term goals with available resources

FIGURE 5.2 • Types of Planning

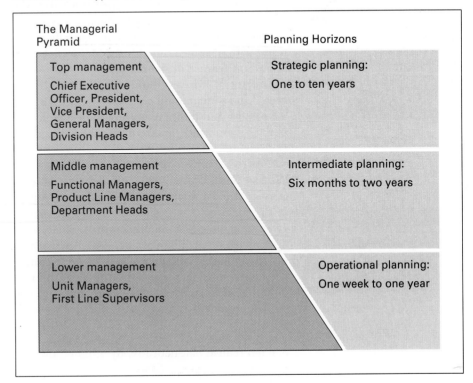

The Managerial Pyramid

Planning Horizons

Top management
Chief Executive Officer, President, Vice President, General Managers, Division Heads

Strategic planning:
One to ten years

Middle management
Functional Managers, Product Line Managers, Department Heads

Intermediate planning:
Six months to two years

Lower management
Unit Managers, First Line Supervisors

Operational planning:
One week to one year

much more than general intentions about profit and growth (see The World of Management). It specifies *how* the organization will achieve a competitive advantage, with profit and growth as necessary by-products. **Intermediate planning** is the process of determining the contributions subunits can make with allocated resources. Finally, **operational planning** is the process of determining how specific tasks can best be accomplished on time with available resources. Each level of planning is vital to an organization's success and cannot effectively stand alone without the support of the other two levels.

intermediate planning determining subunit's contributions with allocated resources

operational planning determining how to accomplish specific tasks with available resources

Planning Horizons. As Figure 5.2 illustrates, planning horizons vary for the three types of planning. The term **planning horizon** refers to the time that elapses between the formulation and the execution of a planned activity. As the planning process evolves from strategic to operational, planning horizons shorten, and plans become increasingly specific. Naturally, management can be more confident, and hence more specific, about the near future than it can about the distant future.

planning horizon elapsed time between planning and execution

Notice, however, that the three planning horizons overlap, their boundaries being elastic rather than rigid. The trend today is toward involving employees from all levels in the strategic planning process. Also, it is not uncommon for top and lower managers to have a hand in formulating intermediate plans. Middle managers often help lower managers draw up operational plans as well. So, Figure 5.2 is an ideal model with countless variations in the workplace.

Objectives

Just as a distant port is the target or goal for a ship's crew, objectives are targets that organizational members steer toward. Although some theorists distinguish between goals and objectives, managers typically use the terms interchangeably. A goal or an **objective** is defined as a specific commitment to achieve a measurable result within a given time frame. Many experts view objectives as the single most important feature of the planning process. According to a team of management consultants, "It is very difficult to see how an organization or an individual can even begin to plan until concrete objectives are clearly defined."[18] It is important for present and future managers to be able to write good objectives, to be aware of their importance, and to understand how objectives combine to form a means-ends chain.

objective commitment to achieve a measurable result within a specified period

Writing Good Objectives. An authority on objectives recommends that "as far as possible, objectives are expressed in quantitative, measurable, concrete terms, in the form of a written statement of desired results to be achieved within a given time period."[19] In other words, objectives represent a firm commitment to accomplish something specific. A well-written objective should state what is to be accomplished and when it is to be accomplished. In the following sample objectives, note that the desired results are expressed *quantitatively,* in units of output, dollars, or percentage of change.

● ● ● ● ● ● ● ● ● ● ● ● ● ● ● ● ●
Write good objectives and discuss the role of objectives in planning.

- To increase subcompact car production by 240,000 units during the next production year.
- To reduce bad-debt loss by $50,000 during the next six months.

Study Finds Scottish Companies Put the Strategic Cart in Front of the Horse

A recent study of 94 companies throughout Scotland uncovered a problem that plagues strategic planners around the world. Their strategic objectives were *too vague*. When asked to rank their strategic objectives, the majority of responding managers put profitability and growth at the top of their lists. These objectives were specified, despite the fact that many of the companies were continuing to suffer declining profits. A businessperson citing profit and growth as strategic objectives is like a college student citing wealth and fame as postgraduate objectives.

What the Scottish managers should have been focusing their strategic sights on was *how* to improve profits and stimulate growth. For example, a machine tool company might seek to introduce three new products and improve the quality of its field service efforts. If these strategic objectives were achieved, more abundant profits and growth would be natural by-products of doing things better. Profit and growth, like getting rich and famous after graduation, are aspirations that flow from doing things better and smarter. Good strategic objectives clearly specify *what* management intends to do better and smarter.

Source: Adapted in part from David M. Reid, "Where Planning Fails in Practice," *Long Range Planning*, 23 (April 1990): 85–93.

- To achieve an 18 percent increase in Brand X sales by December 31 of the current year.

The following is a handy three-way test to judge how well objectives are written:

- *Test 1:* Does this objective tell me exactly *what* the intended result is?
- *Test 2:* Does this objective specify *when* the intended result is to be accomplished?
- *Test 3:* Can the intended result be *measured?*

Statements of intention that fail one or more of these three tests do not qualify as objectives and will tend to hinder rather than help the planning process.

The Importance of Objectives.   From the standpoint of planning, carefully prepared objectives benefit managers by serving as targets and measuring sticks, fostering commitment, and enhancing motivation.[20]

- *Targets.*   As mentioned earlier, objectives provide managers with specific targets. Without objectives, managers at all levels would find it difficult to make coordinated decisions. People quite naturally tend to pursue their own ends in the absence of formal organizational objectives.

- *Measuring Sticks.*   An easily overlooked, after-the-fact feature of objectives is that they are useful tools for measuring how well an organizational subunit or individual has performed. When appraising performance, managers need an established standard against which they can measure performance. Concrete objectives enable managers to weigh performance objectively on the basis of accomplishment rather than subjectively on the basis of personality or prejudice.

- *Commitment.* The very process of getting an employee to agree to pursue a given objective gives that individual a personal stake in the success of the enterprise. Thus objectives can be helpful in encouraging personal commitment to collective ends. Without individual commitment, even well-intentioned and carefully conceived strategies are doomed to failure.

- *Motivation.* Good objectives represent a challenge—something to reach for. As such, they have a motivational aspect. People usually feel good about themselves and what they do when they successfully achieve a challenging objective. Moreover, objectives give managers a rational basis for rewarding performance. Employees who believe they will be equitably rewarded for achieving a given objective will be motivated to perform well.

The Means-Ends Chain of Objectives. Like the overall planning process, objective setting is a top-to-bottom proposition. Top managers set broader objectives with longer time horizons than do successively lower levels of managers. In effect, this downward flow of objectives creates a means-ends chain. As illustrated in Figure 5.3, supervisory-level objectives provide the means for achieving middle-level objectives (ends) which, in turn, provide the means for achieving top-level objectives (ends).

The organizational hierarchy in Figure 5.3 has, of course, been telescoped and narrowed at the middle and lower levels for illustrative purposes. Usually, two or three layers of management would separate the president and the product-line managers. Another layer or two would separate product-line managers from area sales managers. But the telescoping helps show that lower-level objectives provide the means of accomplishing higher-level ends or objectives.

FIGURE 5.3 • A Typical Means-Ends Chain of Objectives

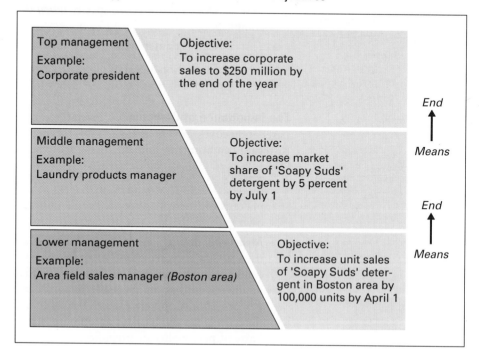

Managing Priorities

Most of us are kept so busy managing our own lives that we can't imagine how top executives manage the work of thousands of people and millions of dollars and still have time to eat, sleep, and live. There is no one secret that successful executives share. But in talking about how they run their lives and their companies, they do tend to focus on common themes.

Unfortunately, popular time management courses are not the answer. Even the founder of the time management movement, Alec Mackenzie, agrees that few people who take his courses stick with the techniques and really benefit from them.

You will find different things at the top of CEOs' priority lists. Like many other company executives, Alcoa's CEO, Paul O'Neill, lists "quality" among his highest priorities. But at the very top of his list is a surprise, "safety." Alcoa leads its industry in safety and has been cutting its injury record by 50 percent every five years. O'Neill feels that to make an operation truly safe, you must understand it perfectly and make sure that the operation isn't inefficient in any way that would encourage dangerous shortcuts. In other words, quality and safety go hand in hand.

One principle that works for many busy managers is the 80/20 rule, which states that 80 percent of a company's business generally comes from a small group—20 percent of its customers. A business that can identify the 20 percent and what they order can focus attention on those products. Illinois Tool Works, for example, used the 80/20 rule to identify which of its thousands of products it should concentrate on as it realigned its manufacturing processes. In another instance, Office Club, a discount office-supplies supermarket, decided to carry 2,200 items instead of its competitors' 5,000 because it found that 85 percent of its sales came from only 650 core items.

Every CEO has techniques for making time in a hectic schedule, doing important thinking while jogging or showering or flying to meetings. Some count on expert secretaries to arrange their time; others learn to walk out of a meeting if participants are late. According to management expert Peter Drucker, the most important skill for setting priorities and managing time is simply learning to say No.

Sources: Eric Calonius, "How Top Managers Manage Their Time," *Fortune* (June 4, 1990): 250–262; Susan Caminiti, "Seeking Big Money in Paper and Pens," *Fortune* (July 31, 1989): 173–174; Ronald Henkoff, "The Ultimate Nuts & Bolts Co.," *Fortune* (July 16, 1990): 70–73; Thomas A. Stewart, "A New Way to Wake Up A Giant," *Fortune* (October 22, 1990): 90–103.

Priorities

priorities ranking goals, objectives, or activities in order of importance

Defined as a ranking of goals, objectives, or activities in order of importance, **priorities** play a special role in planning. By listing long-range organizational objectives in order of their priority, top management prepares to make later decisions regarding the allocation of resources. Limited time, talent, and financial and material resources need to be channeled proportionately into more important endeavors and away from other areas. Establishment of priorities is a key factor in managerial and organizational effectiveness (see Managers in Action). Strategic priorities give both insiders and outsiders answers to the questions "Why does the organization exist?" and "Where is it headed?"

Establishing priorities normally is a subjective process affected by organizational politics and value conflicts. Although there is no universally acceptable formula for carrying out this important function, the following A-B-C priority system is helpful.

A: "Must do" objectives critical *to successful performance.* They may be the result of special demands from higher levels of management or other external sources.

B: "Should do" objectives necessary *for improved performance.* They are generally vital, but their achievement can be postponed if necessary.

C: "Nice to do" objectives desirable *for improved performance, but not critical to survival or improved performance.* They can be eliminated or postponed to achieve objectives of higher priority.[21]

The Planning/Control Cycle

To put the planning process in perspective, it is important to show how it is connected with the control function. Figure 5.4 illustrates the cyclical relationship between planning and control. Planning gets things headed in the right direction, and control keeps them headed in the right direction. (Because of the importance of the control function, it is covered in detail in Part Five.) Basically, each of the three levels of planning is a two-step sequence followed by a two-step control sequence.

The initial planning/control cycle begins when top management establishes strategic plans. When those strategic plans are carried out, intermediate and operational plans are formulated, thus setting in motion two more planning/control cycles. As strategic, intermediate, and operational plans are carried out, the control function begins. Corrective action is necessary when either the preliminary or the final results deviate from plans. For planned activities still in progress, the corrective action can get things back on track before it is too late. Deviations between final results and plans, on the other hand, are instructive feedback for the improvement of future plans. The dotted lines in Figure 5.4 represent the important sort of feedback that makes the planning/control cycle a dynamic and evolving process. Our attention now turns to some practical planning tools.

Management by Objectives

management by objectives (MBO) comprehensive management system based on measurable and participatively set objectives

Management by objectives (MBO) is a comprehensive management system based on measurable and participatively set objectives. MBO has come a long way since it was first suggested by Peter Drucker in 1954 as a way of promoting managerial self-control.[22] MBO theory[23] and practice subsequently mushroomed and spread around the world. In one form or another, and under various labels, MBO has been adopted by most public and private organizations of any significant size. For example, at Cypress Semiconductor Corporation, the San Jose, California, electronics firm, computerization paved the way for high-tech MBO. T. J. Rodgers, the company's founder and chief executive officer, explains:

All of Cypress's 1,400 employees have goals, which, in theory, makes them no different from employees at most other companies. What makes our people different is that every week they set their own goals, commit to achieving them by a specific date, enter them into a database, and report whether or not they completed prior goals. Cypress's computerized goal

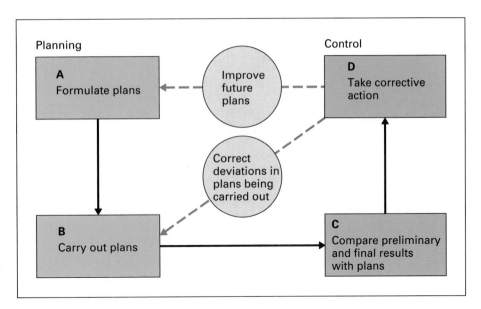

FIGURE 5.4 • The Basic Planning/Control Cycle

system is an important part of our managerial infrastructure. It is a detailed guide to the future and an objective record of the past. In any given week, some 6,000 goals in the database come due. Our ability to meet those goals ultimately determines our success or failure. . . .

I developed the goal system long before personal computers existed. It has its roots in management-by-objectives techniques I learned in the mid-1970s at American Microsystems.[24]

The common denominator that has made MBO programs so popular in both management theory and practice is the emphasis on objectives that are both *measurable* and *participatively set*. Unfortunately, as pointed out by a management consultant, a gap exists between MBO theory and practice: "Today, MBO is being used as an exploitive, manipulative management control mechanism as often as a liberating, humanistic philosophy of management. It seems to be venerated more by its abuse than for its proper use."[25] Whether properly or improperly applied, MBO is by far the most widely used of the planning tools discussed in this chapter.

The MBO Cycle

Because MBO combines planning and control, the four-stage MBO cycle corresponds to the planning/control cycle outlined in Figure 5.4. Steps 1 and 2 make up the planning phase of MBO, and steps 3 and 4 are the control phase.

Step 1: Setting Objectives. A hierarchy of challenging, fair, and internally consistent objectives is the necessary starting point for the MBO cycle and serves as the foundation for all that follows. All objectives, according to MBO theory, should be reduced to writing and put away for later reference during steps 3 and

● ● ● ● ● ● ● ● ● ● ● ● ● ● ● ●
Describe the four-step management by objectives (MBO) process and explain how it can foster individual commitment and motivation.

Strengths	Limitations
• MBO blends planning and control into a rational system of management.	• MBO is too often sold as a cure-all.
• MBO forces an organization to develop a top-to-bottom hierarchy of objectives.	• MBO is easily stalled by authoritarian (Theory X) managers and inflexible bureaucratic policies and rules.
• MBO emphasizes end results rather than good intentions or personalities.	• MBO takes too much time and effort and generates too much paperwork.
• MBO encourages self-management and personal commitment through subordinate participation in setting objectives.	• MBO's emphasis on measurable objectives can be used as a threat by overzealous managers.

FIGURE 5.5 • MBO's Strengths and Limitations

4. Consistent with what was said earlier about objectives, objective setting in MBO begins at the top of the managerial pyramid and filters down, one layer at a time.

MBO's main contribution to the objective-setting process is its emphasis on the participation and involvement of subordinates. There is no place in MBO for the domineering manager ("Here are the objectives I've written for you") or for the passive manager ("I'll go along with whatever objectives you set"). MBO calls for a give-and-take negotiation of objectives between superior and subordinate.

Step 2: Developing Action Plans. With the addition of action statements to the participatively set objectives, the planning phase of MBO is complete. Managers at each level develop plans that incorporate objectives established in step 1. Higher managers are responsible for ensuring that their direct subordinates' plans complement one another and do not work at cross-purposes.

Step 3: Periodic Review. As plans turn into action, attention turns to step 3, monitoring performance. Advocates of MBO usually recommend face-to-face meetings between superior and subordinate at three-, six-, and nine-month intervals. (Some organizations, such as Cypress, rely on shorter cycles.) These periodic checkups permit those who are responsible for a particular set of objectives to reconsider them, checking their validity in view of unexpected events—added duties or the loss of a key assistant—that could make them obsolete. If an objective is no longer valid, it is amended accordingly. Otherwise, progress toward valid objectives is assessed. Periodic checkups also give managers an excellent opportunity to give subordinates needed and appreciated feedback.

Step 4: Performance Appraisal. At the end of one complete cycle of MBO, typically one year after the original goals were set, final performance is matched with the previously agreed-upon objectives. The pairs of superior and subordinate managers who mutually set the objectives one year earlier meet face-to-face once again to discuss how things have turned out. MBO emphasizes results, not personalities or excuses.[26] The control phase of the MBO cycle is completed when success is rewarded with promotion, merit pay, or other suitable benefits and when failure is noted for future corrective action.

When appraising performance during steps 3 and 4, managers are urged to keep the following behavioral principles in mind:

- *Principle of Participation.* Motivation tends to increase as participation in decision making and objective setting increases.
- *Principle of Feedback.* Motivation tends to increase when employees know where they stand.
- *Principle of Reciprocated Interest.* Motivation tends to increase when the pursuit of organizational objectives is accompanied by the achievement of personal objectives.
- *Principle of Recognition.* Motivation to achieve organizational objectives tends to increase when employees are recognized for their contributions.[27]

After one round of MBO, the cycle repeats itself, with each cycle contributing to the learning process. A common practice in introducing MBO is to start at the top and to pull in a new layer of management to the MBO process each year. Experience has shown that plunging several layers of management into MBO all at once often causes confusion, dissatisfaction, and failure. In fact, even a moderate-size organization usually takes five or more years to evolve a full-blown MBO system that ties together such areas as planning, control, performance appraisal, and the reward system. MBO proponents believe that effective leadership and greater motivation—through the use of realistic objectives, more effective control, and self-control—are the natural by-products of a proper MBO system.[28]

Strengths and Limitations of MBO

Any widely used management technique is bound to generate debate about its relative strengths and weaknesses, and MBO is no exception.[29] Present and future managers will have more realistic expectations for MBO if they are familiar with both sides of this debate. The four primary strengths of MBO and four common complaints about it are compared in Figure 5.5.

This debate will probably not be resolved in the near future. Critics of MBO point to both theoretical and methodological flaws.[30] Meanwhile, MBO advocates are quick to point out that the misapplication of MBO, not the MBO concept itself, leads to problems. In the final analysis, MBO will probably work when organizational conditions are favorable and will probably fail when those conditions are unfavorable. A favorable climate for MBO includes top management commitment, openness to change, Theory Y management, and employees who are willing and able to shoulder greater responsibility.[31]

Ford Motor Corporation's North American operations is rethinking the way it develops and builds cars. Stressing product development, Ford is breaking down barriers between functional units: design, product engineering, factory engineering, and sales and marketing. Seen here, a cross-functional team of product planners, engineers, and product designers create the 1995 Ford Mustang. It started at the top, when fifty line executives from all functions held meetings in rooms papered with wall-size flow charts to conceive a more efficient and speedier way of bringing new cars to market.

Graphic Planning/Scheduling/Control Tools

Management science specialists have introduced needed precision to the planning/control cycle through graphic analysis. Three graphic tools for planning, scheduling, and controlling operations are flow charts, Gantt charts, and PERT networks.

Sequencing with Flow Charts

flow chart graphic device for sequencing events and decisions

Although flow charts achieved their greatest popularity among computer programmers,[32] they are readily adaptable to general management. A **flow chart** is a graphic device for sequencing significant events and yes-or-no decisions. Sequencing is simply arranging events in the order of their desired occurrence. For instance, this book had to be purchased before it could be read. Thus the event "purchase book" would come before the event "read book" in flow-chart sequence.

A sample flow chart is given in Figure 5.6. Notice that the chart consists of boxes and diamonds in addition to the start and stop ovals. Each box contains a major event, and each diamond contains a yes-or-no decision.

Managers at all levels and in all specialized areas can identify and properly sequence important events and decisions with flow charts of this kind. In doing so, they are forced to consider all relevant links in a particular endeavor as well as their proper sequence. This is an advantage because it encourages analytical thinking. But flow charts have two disadvantages. First, they do not indicate the time dimension, that is, the varying amounts of time required to complete each step and make each decision. Second, flow charts are not practical for complex situations in which several activities take place at once.

FIGURE 5.6 • A Sample Flow Chart

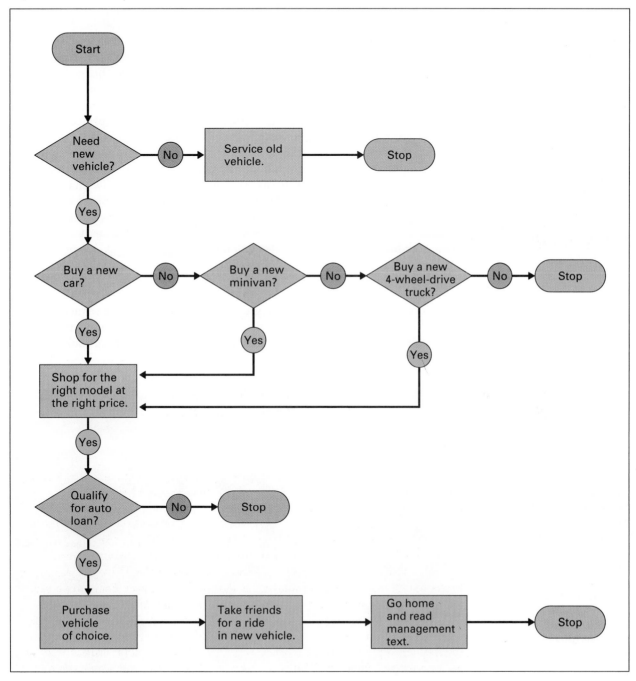

Scheduling with Gantt Charts

Scheduling is an important part of effective planning. When later steps depend on the successful completion of earlier steps, schedules help managers determine when and where resources are needed. Without schedules, inefficiency creeps in as equipment and people stand idle. Also, like any type of plan or budget, schedules provide management with a measuring stick for corrective action. Gantt charts, named for Henry L. Gantt who developed the technique, are a convenient scheduling tool for managers.[33] Gantt worked with Frederick W. Taylor at Midvale Steel beginning in 1887 and, as discussed in Chapter 2, helped refine the practice of scientific management. A **Gantt chart** is a graphic scheduling technique historically used in production operations. Things have changed since the early 1900s, and so have Gantt chart applications. Updated versions like the one in Figure 5.7 are widely used today for planning and scheduling all sorts of organizational activities. They are especially useful for large projects such as moving into a new building or installing a new computer network.

Gantt chart graphic scheduling technique

Figure 5.7 also shows how a Gantt chart can be used for more than just scheduling the important steps of a job. By filling in the time lines of completed activities, *actual* progress can be assessed at a glance. Like flow charts, Gantt charts force managers to be analytical as they reduce jobs or projects to separate steps. Moreover, Gantt charts improve on flow charts by allowing the planner to specify the time to be spent on each activity. A disadvantage Gantt charts share with flow charts is that overly complex situations are cumbersome to chart.

● ● ● ● ● ● ● ● ● ● ● ● ● ● ● ● ●

Compare and contrast flow charts and Gantt charts and discuss the value of PERT networks.

PERT Networks

The more complex the project, the greater the need for reliable sequencing and scheduling of key activities. Simultaneous sequencing and scheduling amounts to programming. One of the most widely recognized programming tools used by

This 700-horsepower Formula 1 race car zooming around a Grand Prix curve is the culmination of an incredible amount of planning and scheduling. Racing at this level takes money. Sponsors, such as Benetton, sink $10 million per car into Grand Prix racing. And it takes extensive logistics because Grand Prix races occur on five continents. Finally it takes endless hours of mechanical refinements, pit-crew practice, and skillful driving to shave off valuable seconds. Still, there is no guarantee of winning.

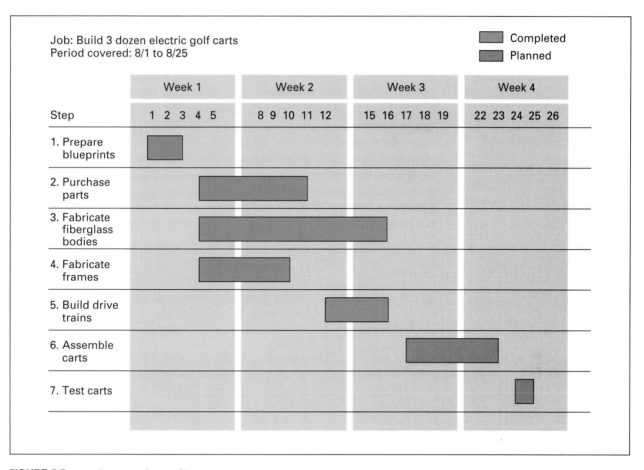

FIGURE 5.7 • A Sample Gantt Chart

PERT (Program Evaluation and Review Technique) graphic sequencing and scheduling tool for complex projects

managers is a technique referred to simply as PERT. An acronym for **Program Evaluation and Review Technique**, **PERT** is a graphic sequencing and scheduling tool for large, complex, and nonroutine projects.

History of PERT. PERT was developed in 1958 by a team of management consultants for the U.S. Navy Special Projects Office. At the time, the navy was faced with the seemingly insurmountable task of building a weapon system that could fire a missile from the deck of a submerged submarine. PERT not only contributed to the development of the Polaris submarine project but was also credited with helping bring the system to combat readiness nearly two years ahead of schedule. News of this dramatic administrative feat caught the attention of managers around the world. But, as one user of PERT reflected: "No management technique has ever caused so much enthusiasm, controversy, and disappointment as PERT."[34] Realizing that PERT is not a panacea, but rather a specialized planning and control tool that can be appropriately or inappropriately applied, helps managers accept it at face value.

PERT Terminology. Because PERT has its own special language, four key terms must be understood.

PERT event performance milestone; start or finish of an activity

PERT activity work in process

PERT times weighted time estimates for completion of PERT activities

critical path most time-consuming route through a PERT network

- *Event.* A **PERT event** is a performance milestone representing the start or finish of some activity. Handing in a difficult management exam is an event.

- *Activity.* A **PERT activity** represents work in process. Activities are time-consuming jobs that begin and end with an event. Studying for a management exam and taking the exam are activities.

- *Time.* **PERT times** are estimated times for the completion of PERT activities. PERT times are weighted averages of three separate time estimates: (1) *optimistic time* (T_o)—the time an activity should take under the best of conditions; (2) *most likely time* (T_m)—the time an activity should take under normal conditions; and (3) *pessimistic time* (T_p)—the time an activity should take under the worst possible conditions. The formula for calculating *estimated* PERT time (T_e) is

$$T_e = \frac{T_o + 4T_m + T_p}{6}$$

- *Critical Path.* The **critical path** is the most time-consuming chain of activities and events in a PERT network. In other words, the longest path through a PERT network is critical because if any of the activities along it are delayed, the entire project will be delayed accordingly.[35]

PERT in Action. A PERT network is shown in Figure 5.8. The task in this example, the design and construction of three dozen customized golf carts for use by physically challenged adults, is relatively simple for instructional purposes. PERT networks are usually reserved for more complex projects with dozens or even hundreds of activities. PERT events are coded by circled letters, and PERT activities, shown by the arrows connecting the PERT events, are coded by number. A PERT time (T_e) has been calculated and recorded for each PERT activity.

See if you can pick out the critical path in the PERT network in Figure 5.8. By calculating which path will take the most time from beginning to end, the critical path turns out to be *A-B-C-F-G-H-I*. This particular chain of activities and events will require an estimated 21.75 workdays to complete. The overall duration of the project is dictated by the critical path, and a delay in any of the activities along this critical path will delay the entire project.

Positive and Negative Aspects of PERT. During the more than thirty years that PERT has been used in a wide variety of settings, its positive and negative aspects both have become apparent.

On the plus side, PERT is an excellent scheduling tool for large, nonroutine projects, ranging from constructing an electric generation station to launching a space vehicle. PERT is a helpful planning aid because it forces managers to envision projects in their entirety. It also gives them a tool for predicting resource needs, potential problem areas, and the impact of delays on project completion. If an activity runs over or under its estimated time, the ripple effect of lost or gained time on downstream activities can be calculated. PERT also gives managers an opportunity, through the calculation of optimistic and pessimistic times, to factor in realistic uncertainties about planning horizons.

On the minus side, PERT is an inappropriate tool for repetitive assembly-line operations in which scheduling is dictated by the pace of machines. PERT also

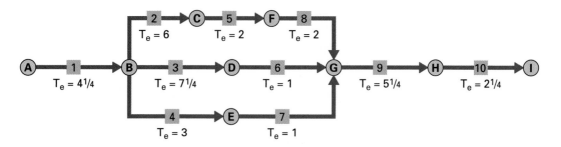

Task: Build three dozen customized golf carts
for use by physically challenged adults

PERT events		PERT activities and Times					
		Activities	T_o	T_m	T_p	T_e*	
A. Receive contract		1. Prepare final blueprints	3	4	6	4 1/4	
B. Begin construction		2. Purchase parts	4	5	12	6	
C. Receive parts		3. Fabricate bodies	5	7 1/2	9	7 1/4	
D. Bodies ready for testing		4. Fabricate frames	2 1/2	3	4	3	
E. Frames ready for testing		5. Build drive trains	1 1/2	2	3	2	
F. Drive trains ready for testing		6. Test bodies	1/2	1	1 1/2	1	
G. Components ready for assembly		7. Test frames	1/2	1	1 1/2	1	
H. Carts assembled		8. Test drive trains	1	1 1/2	5	2	
I. Carts ready for shipment		9. Assemble carts	3	5	9	5 1/4	
		10. Test carts	1	2	5	2 1/4	

* Rounded to nearest 1/4 workday

FIGURE 5.8 • A Sample PERT Network

shares with other planning and decision-making aids the disadvantage of being only as good as its underlying assumptions. False assumptions about activities and events and miscalculations of PERT times can render PERT ineffective. Despite the objective impression of numerical calculations, PERT times are derived rather subjectively. Moreover, PERT's critics say it is too time-consuming: A complex PERT network prepared by hand may be obsolete by the time it is completed, and frequent updates can tie PERT in knots. Commercially available computerized PERT packages are essential for complex projects because they can greatly speed the graphic plotting process and updating of time estimates.[36]

Break-even Analysis

In well-managed businesses, profit is a forethought rather than an afterthought. A widely used tool for projecting profits relative to costs and sales volume is break-even analysis.[37] In fact, break-even analysis is often referred to as cost-volume-profit analysis. By using either the algebraic method or the graphic method, planners can calculate the **break-even point,** the level of sales at which the firm neither suffers a loss nor realizes a profit. In effect, the break-even point is the profit-making threshold. If sales are below that point, the organization loses money. If sales go beyond the break-even point, it makes a profit. Break-even points, as discussed later, are often expressed in units. For example, Chrysler Corporation began to win its battle against bankruptcy in 1982 when severe cost-cutting measures were adopted that "lowered Chrysler's North American break-even point by 50 percent to 1.1 million vehicles."[38]

From a procedural standpoint, a critical part of break-even analysis is separating fixed costs from variable costs.[39]

Fixed versus Variable Costs

Some expenses, called fixed costs, must be paid even if a firm fails to sell a single unit. Other expenses, termed variable costs, are incurred only as units are produced and sold. **Fixed costs** are contractual costs that must be paid regardless of the level of output or sales. Typical examples include rent, utilities, insurance premiums, managerial and professional staff salaries, property taxes, and licenses. **Variable costs** are costs that vary directly with the firm's production and sales. Common variable costs include costs of production (such as labor, materials, and supplies), sales commissions, and product delivery expenses. As output/sales increase, fixed costs remain the same but variable costs accumulate. Looking at it another way, fixed costs are a function of *time,* and variable costs are a function of *volume.* You can now calculate the break-even point.

The Algebraic Method

Relying on the following labels,

$$FC = \text{total fixed costs}$$
$$P = \text{price (per unit)}$$
$$VC = \text{variable costs (per unit)}$$
$$BEP = \text{break-even point}$$

the formula for calculating break-even point (in units) is

$$BEP \text{ (in units)} = \frac{FC}{P - VC}$$

The difference between the selling price P and per unit variable costs VC is referred to as the **contribution margin.** In other words, the contribution margin is the portion of the unit selling price that falls above and beyond the variable costs and that can be applied to fixed costs. Above the break-even point, the contribution margin contributes to profits.

Variable costs are normally expressed as a percentage of the unit selling price. As a working example of how the break-even point (in units) can be calculated, assume that a firm has total fixed costs of $30,000, a unit selling price of $7, and variable costs of 57 percent (or $4 in round numbers):

$$BEP \text{ (in units)} = \frac{30,000}{7 - 4} = 10,000$$

This calculation shows that 10,000 units must be produced and sold at $7 each if the firm is to break even on this particular product.

Price Planning. Break-even analysis is an excellent "what if" tool for planners who want to know what impact price changes will have on profit. For instance, what would the break-even point be if the unit selling price was lowered to match a competitor's price of $6?

$$BEP \text{ (in units)} = \frac{30,000}{6 - 4} = 15,000$$

In this case, the $1 drop in price to $6 means that 15,000 units must be sold before a profit can be realized.

Profit Planning. Planners often set profit objectives and then work backward to determine the required level of output. Break-even analysis greatly assists such planners. The modified break-even formula for profit planning is

$$BEP \text{ (in units)} = \frac{FC + \text{desired profit}}{P - VC}$$

Assuming that top management has set a profit objective for the year at $30,000 and that the original figures above apply, the following calculation would result:

$$BEP \text{ (in units)} = \frac{30,000 + 30,000}{7 - 4} = 20,000$$

make sell

To meet the profit objective of $30,000, the company would need to sell 20,000 units at $7 each.

The Graphic Method

If you place the dollar value of costs and revenues on a vertical axis and unit sales on a horizontal axis, you can calculate the break-even point by plotting fixed costs, total costs (fixed + variable costs), and total revenue. As illustrated in Figure 5.9, the break-even point is where the total costs line and the total sales revenue line intersect. Although the algebraic method does the same job as the graphic method, some planners prefer the graphic method because it presents in a convenient visual aid the various cost-volume-profit relationships at a glance.

Break-even Analysis: Strengths and Limitations

Like the other planning tools discussed in this chapter, break-even analysis is not a cure-all. It has both strengths and limitations.

On the positive side, break-even analysis forces planners to interrelate cost, volume, and profit in a realistic way. All three variables are connected so that a change in one sends ripples of change through the other two. As mentioned earlier, break-even analysis allows planners to ask "what if" questions concerning the impact of price changes and varying profit objectives.

The primary problem with break-even analysis is that a neat separation of fixed and variable costs can be very difficult. General managers should get the help of accountants to isolate relevant fixed and variable costs. Moreover, be-

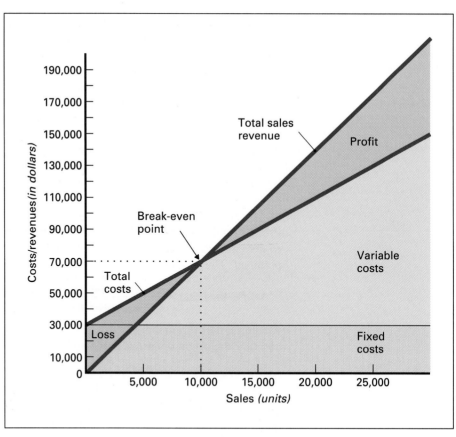

FIGURE 5.9 • Graphic Break-even Analysis

cause of complex factors in supply and demand, break-even analysis is not a good tool for setting prices. It serves better as a general planning and decision-making aid.

Summary

Planning has been labeled the primary management function because it sets the stage for all other aspects of management. Recent research has uncovered the following trends in corporate planning: more planners with actual management experience; greater teamwork, customizing, and flexibility; and more translation of broad strategies into how-to-do-it plans. Along with many other practical reasons for planning, managers need to plan in order to cope with an uncertain environment. Three types of uncertainty are state uncertainty ("What will happen?"), effect uncertainty ("What will happen to our organization?"), and response uncertainty ("What will be the outcome of our decisions?"). To cope with environmental uncertainty, organizations can respond as defenders, prospectors, analyzers, or reactors.

A properly written plan tells what, when, and how something is to be accomplished. A clearly written organizational mission statement tends to serve as a useful focus for the planning process. Strategic, intermediate, and operational plans are formulated by top, middle, and lower-level management, respectively. Objectives have been called the single most important feature of the planning process. Well-written objectives spell out in measurable terms what should be accomplished and when it is to be accomplished. Good objectives help managers by serving as targets, acting as measuring sticks, encouraging commitment, and strengthening motivation. Objective setting begins at the top of the organization and filters down, thus forming a means-ends chain. Priorities affect resource allocation by assigning relative importance to objectives. Plans are formulated and executed as part of a more encompassing planning/control cycle.

Management by objectives (MBO), an approach to planning and controlling, is based on measurable and participatively set objectives. MBO basically consists of four steps: (1) setting objectives participatively, (2) developing action plans, (3) periodically reevaluating objectives and plans and monitoring performance, and (4) conducting annual performance appraisals. Objective setting in MBO flows from top to bottom. MBO has both strengths and limitations and requires a supportive climate favorable to change, participation, and the sharing of authority.

Flow charts, Gantt charts, and PERT networks are three graphic tools for more effectively planning, scheduling, and controlling operations. Flow charts visually sequence important events and yes-or-no decisions. Gantt charts, named for F. W. Taylor's disciple Henry L. Gantt, are a graphic scheduling technique used in a wide variety of situations. Both flow charts and Gantt charts have the advantage of forcing managers to be analytical. But Gantt charts realistically portray the time dimension, whereas flow charts do not. PERT, which stands for Program Evaluation and Review Technique, is a sequencing and scheduling tool appropriate for large, complex, and nonroutine projects. Weighted PERT times enable management to factor in their uncertainties about time estimates.

Break-even analysis, or cost-volume-profit analysis, can be carried out algebraically or graphically. Either way, it helps planners gauge the potential impact of price changes and profit objectives on sales volume. A major limitation of break-even analysis is that specialized accounting knowledge is required to identify relevant fixed and variable costs.

Terms to Understand

Planning	Flow chart
State uncertainty	Gantt chart
Effect uncertainty	PERT
Response uncertainty	PERT event
Plan	PERT activity
Strategic planning	PERT times
Intermediate planning	Critical path
Operational planning	Break-even point
Planning horizon	Fixed costs
Objective	Variable costs
✓Priorities	Contribution margin
Management by objectives (MBO)	

Questions for Discussion

1. Why is planning the primary management function and why is it particularly important today?

2. What kinds of state, effect, and response uncertainty can you detect in your present life?

3. What are the advantages and disadvantages of responding to the environment as a defender, a prospector, an analyzer, or a reactor?

4. Can you write five good objectives for things you intend to accomplish in the next six months? Does each pass the three tests of a good objective?

5. Why is it important to establish priorities when planning?

6. What is the relationship between planning and control?

7. What behavioral principles should managers keep in mind when appraising performance under MBO?

8. What advantage do Gantt charts have over flow charts?

9. How do PERT networks help managers cope with uncertain timing?

10. In pursuing a college degree, what are the student's major fixed and variable costs? (*Note:* Consider the number of credit-hours taken as units of output/sales.)

Back to the Opening Case

Now that you have read Chapter 5, you should be able to answer the following questions about the Coca-Cola case:

1. What is Coca-Cola's mission?

2. What sources of state, effect, and response uncertainty can you identify in this case?

3. Is Coca-Cola a defender, prospector, analyzer, or reactor? Explain.

4. Do you have any ethical problems with Coke and Pepsi attempting to lure people away from traditional beverages such as milk and water? Explain your moral reasoning.

CLOSING CASE

Blurred Vision at American Express

Almost everyone has heard of American Express (AmEx) and has seen its ads featuring famous cardholders, accompanied by its most recent slogan, "Membership has its privileges." Those who follow Wall Street know AmEx for its consistent earnings gains and a return on equity that, thanks to its well-known card and other "travel-related services," often reaches an impressive 20 percent. This is a company that does one thing and does it well, right? Well, not quite.

No one questions the solid foundation of AmEx's success—its credit cards and traveler's checks are universally known, widely accepted, and appeal especially to the wealthy. But, like many successful American companies, AmEx saw the 1980s as a time to expand and diversify, and it spent the decade using income from its primary business to shore up its ailing subsidiaries.

James D. Robinson III, who has headed the company since 1977, had a grand, broad vision for AmEx. He wanted to turn it into a huge financial empire, offering a vast array of financial services to a great variety of customers. But such a broad vision turned out to be blurred.

AmEx could perhaps learn a lesson from two of its acquisitions during the eighties. In 1983, it bought a private Swiss bank, Trade Development Bank (TDB), for $550 million. TDB, like other Swiss banks, catered to the very wealthy who valued their privacy and individual attention from their bank. AmEx's next purchase, Investors Diversified Services Inc. (IDS), was a Minneapolis-based company with a solid reputation for selling insurance and other investments to midwesterners, often at its customers' kitchen tables.

These two purchases conformed to Robinson's vision of creating a financial services company with something for everyone, but their problems highlighted the vision's weakness. One reason for buying companies with strong established customer bases was to allow AmEx to increase its own customer base, offering its cards and other services to TDB and IDS customers. But some of TDB's old customers were insulted by the impersonal mass-mailing techniques AmEx had perfected for selling its services. IDS decided not to offer American Express cards to its customers for fear that many of them wouldn't meet the income requirements. Trying to have it both ways, AmEx ended up satisfying neither group.

AmEx also hoped to benefit from the managerial talent of the companies it bought; here again, the grand strategy proved flawed. Edmond J. Safra of TDB was given a high-level position at AmEx but soon left, frustrated with the AmEx bureaucracy and the stifling of his entrepreneurial abilities. AmEx was more successful with IDS. Leaving most of the company's management in place, AmEx essentially let IDS pursue the same course at which it had been successful for almost 100 years. Left to its "knitting," IDS grew and its assets doubled in the first six years after the AmEx takeover.

A key element, and the most troublesome, in Robinson's envisioned empire was his first major purchase, Wall Street's Shearson Loeb Rhoades, Inc. Again, Shearson brought its parent company major talent, and again many of the best executives quickly left to create their own companies. Timing and luck have also played major roles in Shearson's troubles. Shearson was counting on funding the acquisition of Prime Computer by selling junk bonds—then the stock market crashed and the era of junk bonds ended. AmEx, trying repeatedly to sell Shearson, found that investors weren't buying, and AmEx has actually increased its stake. Some analysts think Robinson wants to take full control of the troubled company, try to solve some of its problems, and then sell it.

If AmEx does eventually rid itself of Shearson, it may be able to spend the rest of the 1990s focusing on what it does well and on making itself more flexible to deal with the changes this decade is sure to bring. The 1980s taught American Express some hard lessons, but the company is still very good at one thing, and on that strength it can continue to build.

For Discussion

1. Which response to uncertainty—defender, prospector, analyzer, reactor—did Robinson's grand vision for AmEx involve? Why did it run into trouble? Which response would have been better? Why?

2. Putting yourself in Robinson's place, what sort of mission statement would you write for AmEx?

3. What role should management by objectives (MBO) play in AmEx's far-flung financial empire?

References

Opening Quotation.   James Broughton in M. R. Rosenberg, ed., *Quotations for the New Age* (Secaucus, N.J.: Citadel Press, 1978), p. 100.

Opening Case.   Harris Collingwood, "Coke and Pepsi Rush to Go Green," *Business Week* (December 17, 1990): 38; Pete Engardio, "In Asia, the Sweet Taste of Success," *Business Week* (November 26, 1990): 96; Walecia Konrad, "The Real Thing is Getting Real Aggressive," *Business Week* (November 26, 1990): 94–104; Thomas Moore, "He Put the Kick Back into Coke," *Fortune* (October 26, 1987): 46–56; Scott Ticer, "The Cola Superpowers' Outrageous New Arsenals," *Business Week* (March 20, 1989): 162–166. Bruce Crumley, "French Cola Wars," *Advertising Age* (December 17, 1990): 22.

Closing Case.   Jon Friedman, "James Robinson," *Business Week* (April 13, 1990): 86; Jon Friedman, "Now AmEx Has Even More of What It Didn't Want," *Business Week* (March 12, 1990): 108; John Meehan and Jon Friedman, "The Failed Vision," *Business Week* (March 19, 1990): 108–113; Russell Mitchell, "IDS: Sparkling Jewel in a Tarnished Crown," *Business Week* (March 19, 1990): 113; Ron Zemke, *The Service Edge* (New York: The New American Library, 1989), pp. 182–185; "Saving: AmEx Makes It Just as Easy as Spending," *Money*, 19 (July 1990): 21.

1. Adapted from Zachary Schiller, "Nestlé's Crunch in the U.S.," *Business Week* (December 24, 1990): 24–25.

2. For some interesting and thought-provoking ideas about managerial planning, see Karl E. Weick, "Misconceptions About Managerial Productivity," *Business Horizons,* 26 (July–August 1983): 47–52.

3. Adapted from a more extensive list of results found in C. Don Burnett, Dennis P. Yeskey, and David Richardson, "New Roles for Corporate Planners in the 1980s," *The Journal of Business Strategy,* 4 (Spring 1984): 64–68. A similar list of planning imperatives for the 1990s may be found in F. Paul Carlson, "The Long and Short of Strategic Planning," *The Journal of Business Strategy,* 11 (May/June 1990): 15–19.

4. Based on discussion in Frances J. Milliken, "Three Types of Perceived Uncertainty About the Environment: State, Effect, and Response Uncertainty," *Academy of Management Review,* 12 (January 1987): 133–143.

5. See Raymond E. Miles and Charles C. Snow, *Organizational Strategy, Structure, and Process* (New York: McGraw-Hill, 1978); p. 29. A recent validation of the Miles and Snow model can be found in Stephen M. Shortell and Edward J. Zajac, "Perceptual and Archival Measures of Miles and Snow's Strategic Types: A Comprehensive Assessment of Reliability and Validity," *Academy of Management Journal,* 33 (December 1990): 817–832.

6. See Brian Bremner, "Can Caterpillar Inch Its Way Back to Heftier Profits?" *Business Week* (September 25, 1989): 75, 78.

7. Based on Harris Collingwood, "RJR Got Burned on High-Tech Cigarettes," *Business Week* (March 13, 1989): 46.

8. Donald C. Hambrick, "Some Tests of the Effectiveness and Functional Attributes of Miles and Snow's Strategic Types," *Academy of Management Journal,* 26 (March 1983): 24. Also see Eli Segev, "Strategy, Strategy Making, and Performance—An Empirical Investigation," *Management Science,* 33 (February 1987): 258–269.

9. See David Woodruff, "A Car That's Just the Way Its Designers Wanted It," *Business Week* (June 5, 1989): 103–104.

10. See Geoff Lewis, "The PC Wars: IBM vs. the Clones," *Business Week* (July 28, 1986): 62–68.

11. See John W. Verity and Geoff Lewis, "Computers: The New Look," *Business Week* (November 30, 1987): 112–123.

12. See "How Seagram Is Scrambling to Survive 'The Sobering of America,' " *Business Week* (September 3, 1984): 94–95; and Andrea Rothman, "The Maverick Boss at Seagram, *Business Week* (December 18, 1989): 90–98.

13. For details, see Jeffrey S. Conant, Michael P. Mokwa, and P. Rajan Varadarajan, "Strategic Types, Distinctive Marketing Competencies and Organizational Performance: A Multiple Measures Based Study," *Strategic Management Journal,* 11 (September 1990): 365–383. Also see Shaker A. Zahra and John A. Pearce II, "Research Evidence On the Miles–Snow Typology," *Journal of Management,* 16 (December 1990): 751–768.

14. Ronald Henkoff, "How to Plan for 1995," *Fortune* (December 31, 1990): 70.

15. Roy A. Gentles, "Alcan's Integration of Management Techniques Raises Their Effectiveness," *Management Review,* 73 (April 1984): 33.

16. Helpful practical tips can be found in Mark Frohman and Perry Pascarella, "How to Write a Purpose Statement," *Industry Week* (March 23, 1987): 31–34. An excellent overview of corporate mission statements is John A. Pearce II and Fred David, "Corporate Mission Statements: The Bottom Line," *Academy of Management Executive,* 1 (May 1987): 109–115.

17. Bill Saporito, "PPG: Shiny, Not Dull," *Fortune* (July 17, 1989): 107.

18. Charles D. Flory, ed., *Managers for Tomorrow* (New York: NAL, 1965), p. 98.

19. Anthony P. Raia, *Managing by Objectives* (Glenview, Ill.: Scott, Foresman, 1974), p. 24.

20. For an excellent and comprehensive treatment of goal setting, see Edwin A. Locke and Gary P. Latham, *Goal Setting: A Motivational Technique That Works!* (Englewood Cliffs, N.J.: Prentice-Hall, 1984). Also see Robert D. Pritchard, Philip L. Roth, Steven D. Jones, Patricia J. Galgay, and Margaret D. Watson, "Designing a Goal-Setting System to Enhance Performance: A Practical Guide," *Organizational Dynamics,* 17 (Summer 1988): 69–78.

21. Raia, *Managing by Objectives*, p. 54.

22. See Peter F. Drucker, *The Practice of Management* (New York: Harper & Row, 1954).

23. As an indication of the widespread interest in MBO, more than 700 books, articles, and technical papers had been written on the subject by the late 1970s. For a brief history of MBO, see George S. Odiorne, "MBO: A Backward Glance," *Business Horizons,* 21 (October 1978): 14–24. An excellent collection of readings on MBO may be found in George Odiorne, Heinz Weihrich, and Jack Mendleson, *Executive Skills: A Management by Objectives Approach* (Dubuque, Iowa: Wm. C. Brown, 1980).

24. T. J. Rodgers, "No Excuses Management," *Harvard Business Review,* 68 (July–August 1990): 87, 89.

25. Jack Bologna, "Why MBO Programs Don't Meet Their Goals," *Management Review,* 69 (December 1980): 32.

26. Problems and solutions in the MBO/performance appraisal linkage are discussed in Jeffrey S. Kane and Kimberly A. Freeman, "MBO and Performance Appraisal: A Mixture That's Not a Solution, Part 1," *Personnel,* 63 (December 1986): 26–36; and Jeffrey S. Kane and Kimberly A. Freeman, "MBO and Performance Appraisal: A Mixture That's Not a Solution, Part 2," *Personnel,* 64 (February 1987): 26–32.

27. Adapted from William E. Reif and John W. Newstrom, "Integrating MBO and OBM—A New Perspective," *Management by Objectives,* 5, No. 2 (1975): 34–42.

28. For example, see Jan P. Muczyk and Bernard C. Reimann, "MBO as a Complement to Effective Leadership," *The Academy of Management Executive,* 3 (May 1989): 131–139.

29. An interesting study of the positive and negative aspects of MBO may be found in Robert C. Ford and Frank S. McLaughlin, "Avoiding Disappointment in MBO Programs," *Human Resource Management,* 21 (Summer 1982): 44–49; Positive research evidence is summarized in Robert Rodgers and John E. Hunter, "Impact on Management By Objectives on Organizational Productivity," Human Resource Management, 76 (April 1991): 322–336.

30. For a critical appraisal of MBO core assumptions, see David Halpern and Stephen Osofsky, "A Dissenting View of MBO," *Public Personnel Management,* 19 (Fall 1990): 321–330.

31. See Richard Babcock and Peter F. Sorensen, Jr., "An MBO Check-list: Are Conditions Right for Implementation?" *Management Review,* 68 (June 1979): 59–62.

32. Marilyn Bohl, *Flowcharting Techniques* (Chicago: Science Research Associates, 1971).

33. For examples of early Gantt charts, see H. L. Gantt, *Organizing for Work* (New York: Harcourt, Brace and Howe, 1919), chap. 8.

34. Ivars Avots, "The Management Side of PERT," *California Management Review,* 4 (Winter 1962): 16–27.

35. Adapted in part from John Fertakis and John Moss, "An Introduction to PERT and PERT/Cost Systems," *Managerial Planning,* 19 (January–February 1971): 24–31.

36. For a brief description of a computerized PERT package, see "Making Project Management Easy," *Datamation,* 24 (April 1978): 47, 50. Also see Paul A. Strassman, "The Best-Laid Plans," *Inc.,* 10 (October 1988): 135–138.

37. For interesting and informative reading on the practical application of break-even analysis, see Robert T. Patterson, "Break-Even Analysis: Decision-Making Tool," *Food Service Marketing,* 42 (April 1980): 39–42.

38. "The Banks Like Chrysler's Line," *Business Week* (August 2, 1982): 18. Also see William J. Hampton, "Why Chrysler Can't Afford to Go Off Its Diet," *Business Week* (October 5, 1987): 84.

39. An informative and interesting critique of cost-accounting practices can be found in Ford S. Worthy, "Accounting Bores You? Wake Up," *Fortune* (October 12, 1987): 43–53.

6

Strategic Management: Planning for Long-term Success

CHAPTER OBJECTIVES

When you finish studying this chapter, you should be able to

- Define the term *strategic management* and explain its relationship to strategic planning, implementation, and control.
- Explain the concept of synergy and identify four kinds of synergy.
- Discuss how the product life cycle concept can help managers think strategically.
- Describe Porter's model of generic competitive strategies.
- Identify and describe the four steps in the strategic management process.
- Explain the nature and purpose of a SWOT analysis.
- Describe the three types of forecasts.

Modifying McStrategy for the Nineties

McDonald's became McDonald's, the world's largest fast-food chain, by developing a winning strategy and sticking to it. Although Ray Kroc, who built the nationwide chain from its humble beginnings, died in 1984, his presence is still pervasive. His motto—"quality, service, cleanliness, and value"—is still central to the company's employee training and image. Kroc's office is still as he left it, preserved behind glass in Oak Brook, Illinois, and managers and trainees who attend the company's Hamburger University still "Talk with Ray" by way of an interactive video. McDonald's grew to serve 6 percent of the American public daily by following Kroc's mottos, buying up suburban street corners around the nation, ensuring that a Big Mac in Portland, Maine, tastes the same as one in Portland, Oregon, and sticking to its meat-and-potatoes menu.

Over the past few years, however, McDonald's winning strategy has been sorely tested by changes in eating habits and competition and by the gradual saturation of attractive fast-food sites. McDonald's competitors eagerly awaited the day when they could declare McDonald's dead and outdated—a dinosaur too big and too old to change with the times. But so far they've been disappointed. The giant does not change hastily, but it does change. Its strategy has evolved fast enough to keep pace with its customers' tastes and maintain the company's lead over its fast-food rivals.

Now that *saturated fat* and *cholesterol* are part of every American's vocabulary, red meat burgers and potatoes fried in beef tallow are not accepted as thoughtlessly as they were a decade ago. Some health food advocates have even singled McDonald's out for attacks, criticizing the fat content and calories in the standard meal of burger, fries, and a shake. But while defending itself against such attacks, McDonald's has also begun to appeal to the health-conscious appetite. It has replaced ice cream with lowfat yogurt, put lowfat shakes and bran muffins on the menu, switched to 100 percent vegetable oil to fry its potatoes, and introduced 91 percent fat-free burgers.

To attract busy people who don't want burgers and fries even if they are cooked right, McDonald's has expanded its menu by 25 percent since 1980, offering thirty-three items in the average store. It was relatively slow to add salads to its menu and dropped traditional salad bars after a trial period. Now, however, it sells plastic-packaged salads that keep better than most fast food and account for 7 percent of its restaurant sales. The 1980s saw three different attempts at McPizza, as McDonald's tried to cope with the fact that pizza has overtaken hamburgers in dinnertime popularity. Rivals like Pizza Hut scoffed at the pizza's quality but took the competition seriously. When McDonald's finds a new product it likes, that product may change the whole industry, as Egg McMuffins did in 1971, virtually creating the fast-food breakfast market.

McDonald's is used to competing with fast-food rivals like Burger King and Wendy's. With a $1 billion annual budget for advertising and promotion, it generally manages to stay a step ahead of those rivals. Lately, however, the competition has changed. Most American homes—and many gas stations and convenience stores—now have microwave ovens, and people can "zap" their own lunches more quickly than they can get a burger from the speediest McDonald's. McDonald's has responded by opening more drive-through lanes and promising customers higher quality and more variety than they can get from a plastic-wrapped lunch. Speed and cleanliness alone aren't enough any more.

An equally troubling trend is the slowing growth of the American fast-food market and the fast-food saturation of the suburban strips and malls that have traditionally provided homes for the Golden Arches. In the United States, therefore, the battle is on for nontraditional growth. McDonald's can now be found in urban areas, in zoos, on aircraft carriers, on Guantanamo Bay Naval Base in Cuba, in hospitals, on college campuses, along toll roads, even in a Las Vegas gambling casino. But opening such stores can be expensive: it costs $1.4 million to open the average McDonald's now, compared with less than $1 million in the mid-1980s. The average number of customers per store hasn't grown in half a decade, and the inflation-adjusted sales for many McDonald's restaurants has actually been falling.

Having taken a hard look at all this, McDonald's recognizes that its real growth potential lies overseas. Sales at company-owned restaurants overseas rose by 19 percent in 1989, as opposed to 4 percent in the United States. The Golden Arches now appear in 51 countries, including Hungary and Yugoslavia. The Moscow McDonald's is the world's largest, seating 900 people and serving one million hungry Soviets per month. The Japanese can purchase Big Macs in 653 places. All told, the 11,000+ overseas McDonald's now account for nearly one-third of total sales.

Therefore, although domestic growth may be slowing, it's much too early to be worrying that the Golden Arches are about to fall. After more than one hundred consecutive quarters of record operating results, the fast-food king has proved its ability to adjust, and it shows no signs of letting up. What's next? Who knows. If some in the McDonald's think tank have their way, the next time you visit the Golden Arches you may be greeted by a smiling hostess, have your dinner served in a basket, or offered several varieties of McFish. No doubt the next decade will present new challenges, such as the diminishing number of young people willing to work for minimum wages.

Strategic management serves as the cutting edge for the entire management process. Organizations like McDonald's that are guided by a coherent strategic framework tend to execute even the smallest details of their mission in a coordinated fashion. For example, by strictly adhering to the rule that burgers left in the warming bin for more than ten minutes should be thrown away, every restaurant manager turns McDonald's strategic emphasis on "quality" into reality. Without the guidance of a strategic management orientation, organization members tend to work at cross-purposes and important things do not get accomplished.

Many people automatically assume that strategy is the exclusive domain of top-level management, but that is simply not true. Its relevance for those lower in the organization may not be as apparent, but it is equally important. A management student who is ten to twenty years away from a top-level executive position might ask, "If top managers formulate strategies and I'm headed for a supervisory or staff position, why should I care about strategic management?"

TABLE 6.1 • Key Dimensions of Strategic Farsightedness

	Shortsighted	*Farsighted*
1. **Organizational strategy**	No formally documented strategies.	A formally written and communicated statement of long-term organizational mission.
2. **Competitive advantage**	"Follow the leader." No attention devoted to long-term competitive edge.	"Be the leader." Emphasis on gaining and holding a strategic competitive edge.
3. **Organizational structure**	Rigid structure emphasizing status quo, downward communication, and predictability.	Flexible structure encouraging change, upward and lateral communication, adaptability, and speed.
4. **Research and development**	Emphasis on applying competitors' good ideas.	Heavy emphasis on developing new products and services and on innovations in production, marketing, and personnel management.
5. **Return**	Emphasis on short-term profits.	Emphasis on increased market share, growth, and future profit potential.
6. **Personnel administration**	Emphasis on stopgap hiring and training. Labor viewed as a commodity. Layoffs common.	Emphasis on long-term development of employees. Labor viewed as a valuable human resource. Layoffs seen as a last resort.
7. **Problem solving**	Emphasis on chasing symptoms and blaming scapegoats.	Emphasis on finding solutions to problems.
8. **Management style**	Emphasis on day-to-day fire fighting, owing to short-term orientation.	Multilevel strategic thinking that encourages managers to consider long-term implications of their actions and decisions.

There are three good reasons why staff specialists and managers at all levels need a general understanding of strategic management.

First, in view of widespread criticism that American managers tend to be shortsighted, a strategic orientation encourages farsightedness (see Table 6.1). Second, employees who think in strategic terms tend to understand better how top managers think and why they make the decisions they do. In other words, the rationale behind executive policies and decisions is more apparent when things are put into a strategic perspective. McDonald's ten-minute rule makes more sense when explained within the context of the firm's best-in-the-industry quality strategy.

A third reason for promoting a broader understanding of strategic management relates to a recent planning trend discussed in the last chapter. Specifically, greater teamwork and cooperation throughout the planning/control cycle is eroding the traditional distinction between those who plan and those who implement plans. Today, more middle and lower-level managers and technical specialists are playing a direct role in both formulating and carrying out long-term strategies. Andrew Grove, chief executive officer of Intel Corporation, the computer chip giant, is one who has changed his thinking about strategy. Instead of seeing himself as the driver of strategy, he now believes the real action is in the trenches. According to Grove:

> People formulate strategy with their fingertips. Day in and day out they respond to things, by virtue of the products they promote, the price concessions they make, the distribution channels they choose.[1]

Thus, you, today's management student, are not as far away from the strategic domain as you may think. The time to start thinking strategically is *now*.

This chapter defines strategic management, looks at ways to think strategically, explores the strategic management process, and discusses forecasting.

Strategic Management = Strategic Planning + Implementation + Control

strategic management seeking a competitively superior organization-environment fit

strategy the pattern of decisions a firm makes

Strategic management is the ongoing process of ensuring a competitively superior fit between an organization and its changing environment.[2] In a manner of speaking, strategic management is management on a grand scale, management of the "big picture." Accordingly, **strategy** has been defined by MIT strategy scholar Arnoldo C. Hax as "the pattern of decisions a firm makes."[3] Hax's definition is instructive because it reminds us that strategy is the product of *actions* and *results*, not just of good intentions. The strategic management perspective is the product of a historical evolution and is now understood to include budget control, long-range planning, and strategic planning.[4]

Significantly, strategic management does not do away with earlier, more restricted approaches. Instead, it synthesizes and coordinates them all in a more systematic fashion. For example, consider the relationship between strategic planning, as defined in Chapter 5, and strategic management. Recall that *strategic planning* is the process of determining how to pursue the organization's long-term goals with the resources expected to be available. Notice that nothing is said in this definition about adjustment or control. But just as astronauts and space scientists need to make mid-flight corrections to ensure that space shuttles reach their destinations, strategic adjustment and control are necessary. The more encompassing strategic management concept is useful today because it effectively blends strategic planning, implementation, and control.

Today's competitive pressures necessitate a dynamic strategic management process. According to *Fortune*:

> The old methods won't do. At too many companies strategic planning has become overly bureaucratic, absurdly quantitative, and largely irrelevant.

1990s-Style Strategic Management

The editor of *The Journal of Business Strategy* recently interviewed Ingeborg A. Marquardt, vice president of quality and planning, Bell & Howell Company, Skokie, Illinois. Her comments include the following observations:

The difficulty for the strategic planner of today is that the 1990s will require a very broad, multi-functional perspective with emphasis on operating excellence; it can't be the single-minded financial perspective that we had in the late 1970s and 1980s, with a focus on productivity through cost reduction. We now have to focus on other roads toward increased productivity, and that new focus means paying greater attention to quality, people management, technology, and competitive analysis; and, above all, knowing and serving the customer better than the competition. . . .

If strategic plans come either from the top down or from the bottom up, they are going to fail. I think that the CEO and top management need to set the vision—to set a framework for what the company is and in which direction it should go. That framework should be set only after there is a thorough understanding of the company's strengths as well as its internal memory, internal knowledge, and internal skill base.

But once a vision is formulated, then that vision needs to be communicated to the full organization. You need to allow the business units and perhaps even the other departments to interpret that information and ask: What does this mean for us? What can we contribute toward that goal?

We then need to develop specific targets once there is a feeling for what the organization can accomplish. We have to commit to some specific targets, which must be done at a fairly high level in each division. Finally, those targets need to be translated into action plans in a cascading way down through the organization so that everybody knows what [they need] to accomplish to meet those targets.

In other words, planning should be an iterative process—a continuous dialogue with participation from all levels of the organization. . . .

In the past, only a few people were involved in the development of the strategic plans, and then we didn't communicate them well enough. They would often gather dust on a bookshelf or would be placed in a drawer. Those documents were top secret because we did not want our competitors to know what we were going to do—how we were going to attack them and how we were going to try to increase our competitive strength over theirs. But the problem was that our own employees didn't even know what was to be accomplished, so how could they work toward that goal?

In executive suites across America, countless five-year plans, updated annually and solemnly clad in three-ring binders, are gathering dust—their impossibly specific prognostications about costs, prices, and market share long forgotten.[5]

Managers who adopt a strategic management perspective appreciate that strategic plans are living documents. They require systematic updating and fine tuning as conditions change. They also need to draw upon all available talent in the organization (see Insights & Issues).

The strategic management process is discussed in greater detail later in this chapter. But first we need to consider several practical ways to encourage strategic thinking.

Thinking Strategically

Effective strategic management involves more than just following a few easy steps. It requires that managers think strategically. According to a former IBM executive consultant: "Strategic thinking in the nineties will enable success not through new answers, but through better questions."[6] Strategic thinking also involves seeing things in motion and making sense out of a cloudy and uncertain future by seeing the *interdependency* of key factors. This kind of vision requires more than a passing awareness of significant social, political/legal, economic, and technological trends. (These trends were discussed in Chapter 3.) Managers who think strategically are able to envision their organizations in the context of world trends and events and to spot important interdependencies. They focus on how their organization should act and react to emerging opportunities and obstacles. As two strategic planning experts have cautioned, "With diminishing resources, world competition, and rising costs, even the most efficient operations may no longer survive the handicap of operating without a clear, strategic direction."[7]

There is also a selfish reason for becoming a better strategic thinker—it can be good for one's managerial career, as the chairman of Avon Products, Inc., pointed out: "Those who succeed in thinking strategically and executing strategically are the people who are going to move ahead at this company."[8] Although some people seem to have a special gift for being able to perceive meaningful patterns in complex circumstances, strategic thinking (the ability to identify shifting organization/environment interdependencies) can be learned through practice. Three helpful tools for strategic thinking are the concepts of synergy and product life cycle and Porter's generic strategies.

Synergy

●●●●●●●●●●●●●●●●●●
Explain the concept of synergy and identify four kinds of synergy.

synergy the whole is greater than the sum of its parts

Although not necessarily a familiar term, *synergy* is a valuable and well-established concept. **Synergy** occurs when two or more variables (for example, chemicals, drugs, people, organizations) interact to produce an effect greater than the sum of the effects of the variables acting independently. Some call this the $2 + 2 = 5$ effect; others prefer to say that with synergy, the whole is greater than the sum of its parts. Either definition is acceptable as long as one appreciates the bonus effect in synergistic relationships. In strategic management, managers are urged to achieve as much *market, cost, technology,* and *management* synergy[9] as possible when making strategic decisions. Those decisions may involve mergers, acquisitions, new products, new technology or production processes, or executive replacement. Jeffrey Silverman, president of Ply Gem, a family of small building supply companies in New York City, believes in synergy. "He even has executives in charge of synergy: Two high-ranking national coordinators assist in such things as joint purchasing and the cross-selling of Ply Gem products."[10]

Each kind of synergy—market, cost, technology, and management—makes its own contribution both to strategic thinking and, ultimately, to organizational health. For example, at Cadbury Schweppes, a well-managed British company, chief executive Dominic Cadbury speaks of maximizing his company's synergy in its confectionery (candies, jellies, and so on) and soft drink businesses: "We must make sure we are transferring skills and product knowledge and sharing assets."[11]

Turning good ideas into marketable products is a lot like shaving: without proper preparation, both can be daunting. The Gillette Company managed to score a winner on both fronts in January 1990 with the introduction of its Sensor shaving system. The Gillette Sensor represented the company's most expensive product development project ever, taking some ten years and costing some $200 million. Buoyed by an introductory advertising budget of approximately $100 million, shipments of the Gillette Sensor outpaced the company's forecasts by more than 30 percent.

Market Synergy. When one product or service fortifies the sales of one or more other product or service, market synergy has been achieved. For example, *Sports Illustrated* parlayed its hugely successful annual swimsuit issue into a best-selling video.[12] Also, some observers wondered why Sony Corporation wanted a piece of Hollywood when the Japanese firm bought Columbia Pictures in the late 1980s. But, as *Business Week* explained, market synergy was involved:

The first payoff from the Columbia deal may be a shot in the arm for Sony's 8-mm video goods, including portable videotape decks and movie cameras. The 8-mm format was introduced four years ago. It offered advantages in size and quality over mainstream VHS products, but consumers have been slow to make the switch. Sony thinks a shelfful of movie titles in the 8-mm cassettes might persuade them.[13]

Cost Synergy. This second type of synergy can occur in almost every dimension of organized activity. When two or more products can be designed by the same engineers, produced in the same facilities, distributed through the same channels, or sold by the same salespeople, overall costs will be lower than if each product received separate treatment. In an interesting example of cost synergy, a number of U.S. railroads are making extra dollars by permitting telecommunications companies to lay fiberoptic cables along their rights-of-way. "Amtrak, under a 25-year agreement with MCI on the Washington–New York corridor is getting $4.4 million plus use of the cable for its internal communications."[14]

Cost synergy also can be achieved by recycling by-products that would normally be thrown away. Crab and shrimp shells, once a foul-smelling waste product of Alaskan seafood companies, are now being recycled to yield a natural substance called chitin (pronounced KITE-in). Selling at $8 a pound, chitin can be used as a dissolvable surgical suture, a skin-healing agent for burns or wounds, a cleanser for treatment of polluted waters, and a crop protector that fights fungus diseases.[15] Human imagination is the only limit to cost synergy!

Technological Synergy. The third variety of synergy involves transferring technology from one application to another, thus opening up new markets. For example, Alfa-Laval, a Swedish manufacturing company specializing in centrifugal separators, broadened its market base through technological synergy.

Alfa designed a separator to remove yeast particles from beer. Brewers were uninterested, but genetic researchers were fascinated; with some modifications, the same equipment is well-suited for preparing cells and harvesting bacteria in genetic research.[16]

Thanks to this sort of technological synergy, profitable new markets can be tapped without the expense of developing totally new products.

Management Synergy. As in technological synergy, management synergy requires knowledge transfer. Management synergy would be achieved, for example, if a hospital with a weak accounting department hired a new president with a strong accounting background. Ideally, the new president would transfer his or her technical skills to good advantage.

You may find it difficult, if not impossible, to take advantage of all four types of synergy when developing new strategies. Nonetheless, your strategies are more likely to be realistic and effective if you give due consideration to all four types of synergy as early as possible.

Product Life Cycles

• • • • • • • • • • • • • • •

Discuss how the product life cycle concept can help managers think strategically.

Those who advocate a contingency approach to management believe that strategies should be derived from the situation at hand instead of from fixed rules or principles. As time passes, circumstances inside and outside the organization change, and the pace of change has accelerated in recent years. Product life cycles (PLCs) are a very useful contingency management tool for strategists.[17] In addition to increasing awareness of interdependencies among operating areas such as research and development, production, finance, and marketing, PLCs help managers set a rational sequencing pattern for updating and reformulating strategies.

product life cycle a graph of a product's sales and profit

The Product Life Cycle. A **product life cycle** is a graphic representation of the sequential rise and fall of a product's sales and profit. The PLC in Figure 6.1 is typical. Yet one should not infer from Figure 6.1 that the four main stages of the PLC—introduction, growth, maturity, and decline—all last the same length of time. For instance, IBM's highly successful 360-series computers had a growth period of several years following a comparatively short introduction period. Further, the overall length of PLCs varies from product to product. Fad items, such as Cabbage Patch dolls and Swatch watches, may complete a full product cycle in six months, whereas the cycle for Rolls Royce automobiles may last for decades. PLCs reflect the unique nature and market potential of given products and services. One safe generalization about PLCs is that they probably will speed up in the coming years. Experts attribute this trend to the microelectronics revolution considered in Chapter 3. It has been observed that "except for commodity-type items, mature industries will be forced to march to a faster drummer."[18] Strategy based upon speed is discussed later in this chapter.

We need to make an important introductory point about the PLC in Figure 6.1, concerning the five categories of strategic concerns. Though they do in fact occur in the sequence listed, each set of concerns requires advance attention. Lead times for short-cycle goods or services are necessarily short, although a year or more of lead time may be appropriate for a long-cycle item. In other words, a management team that waits for profits to begin heading downward (thus signaling the end of the growth stage) before plotting a defensive strategy for the maturity stage is being shortsighted.

The Precommercialization Dilemma. Although the precommercialization stage is technically not part of the PLC, it deserves special attention. Importantly, long-term investments during this early stage pave the way for new products. Research and development (R&D) generates the innovation needed for potentially marketable goods and services. Investments in facilities and equipment help turn innovative ideas into products. American managers have been criticized for being shortsighted about such investments. Japanese managers, in contrast, are admired for their patience and farsightedness. Japan was expected to outspend the United States by $80 billion in plant and equipment in 1990—a stunning statistic, considering that America has twice the population and an economy more than half again as large as Japan's.[19] Many attribute this troubling investment gap to hard-to-explain cultural differences. But economists cite a more mundane reason, *lower cost of capital:*

> *Japan's high savings rate, coupled with individuals' willingness to accept interest rates of only 2 percent or 3 percent, makes an abundance of low-cost capital available to corporate borrowers. Hence Japanese managers' much vaunted patience. With the cost of capital at roughly half what their American counterparts pay, they can afford to wait longer to recoup their investments.*[20]

FIGURE 6.1 • Tying Strategy to the Product Life Cycle

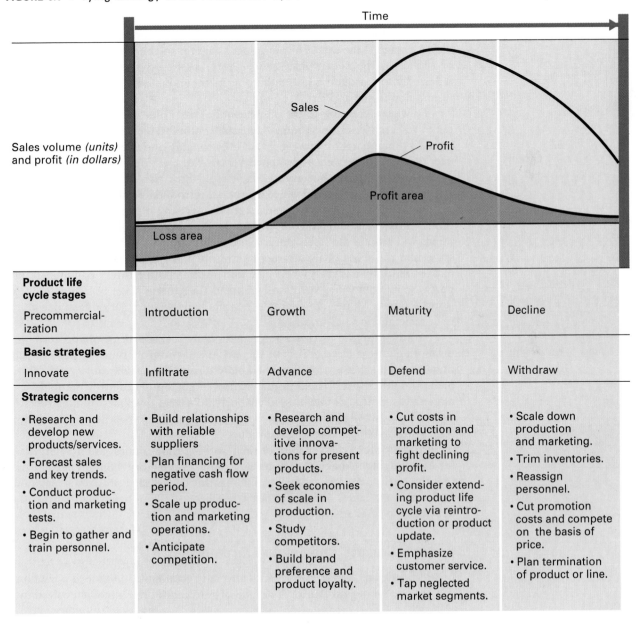

Product life cycle stages				
Precommercial-ization	Introduction	Growth	Maturity	Decline
Basic strategies				
Innovate	Infiltrate	Advance	Defend	Withdraw
Strategic concerns				
• Research and develop new products/services. • Forecast sales and key trends. • Conduct production and marketing tests. • Begin to gather and train personnel.	• Build relationships with reliable suppliers • Plan financing for negative cash flow period. • Scale up production and marketing operations. • Anticipate competition.	• Research and develop competitive innovations for present products. • Seek economies of scale in production. • Study competitors. • Build brand preference and product loyalty.	• Cut costs in production and marketing to fight declining profit. • Consider extending product life cycle via reintroduction or product update. • Emphasize customer service. • Tap neglected market segments.	• Scale down production and marketing. • Trim inventories. • Reassign personnel. • Cut promotion costs and compete on the basis of price. • Plan termination of product or line.

American corporate strategists face a dilemma: long-term investments with no immediate payoff are unattractive, given scarce resources and high interest rates. But failure to adequately fund basic research and production facilities today may mean the loss of future domestic and foreign competitiveness. Strategists are thus faced with a difficult trade-off between short-term costs and long-term benefits. Monsanto's chief executive officer, Dick Mahoney, has clear priorities on this issue. According to Mahoney, for his giant chemical company, "R&D isn't part of the strategy, R&D *is* the strategy."[21]

Strategy during the Product Life Cycle. Many hitherto unknown factors may arise as strategists shift their attention to the PLC's successive stages. The introduction or *infiltration stage,* with its sluggish early sales, is a particularly risky time because large cash outlays for supplies, facilities, and wages are not offset by cash receipts. Compounding the negative cash-flow problem during the introductory stage is the threat of a product's failure: the rejection of a new product or service in the marketplace can be very costly. The Ford Motor Company reportedly lost around $350 million on its infamous Edsel car, which proved a dismal flop in the 1950s.

However, contrary to the popular notion that nine out of ten new products fail,[22] research discloses a more favorable ratio. A study of 148 medium- and large-size manufacturers revealed that only roughly one of every three new products failed.[23] (Improved or modified versions of existing products were not included in the study.) But even a one-out-of-three risk of new product failure underscores the need for intelligent product introduction strategies.

In the PLC's *growth stage,* management faces an interesting problem. Large profit margins and limited competition can easily lull management into believing things will remain the same. But it is precisely during a product's most profitable stage that the seeds of its destruction are often sown. Detroit's Big Three auto makers fell into this trap when they underestimated the threat of Japanese imports. Some companies successfully extend the growth stage by refining an existing product. Mattel, for example, kept its long-running Barbie Doll line going with male and ethnic variations.[24]

Strategy for the *maturity stage* necessarily focuses on trimming costs and promoting efficiencies because of the erosion of profit margins by the competition. As both sales and profits fall rapidly during the *decline stage,* withdrawal plans should ensure that the organization is not burdened with unusable raw materials, supplies, or facilities; idle labor; and a large inventory of unmarketable finished goods. All operations are appropriately scaled down during the decline stage, thus making way for new products.

Product life cycles, in spite of their varying time frames, are a helpful tool for encouraging managers at all levels to think strategically. Simply recognizing that the birth, maturation, decline, and death cycle of each product is inevitable encourages managers to update their strategies instead of believing that they are dealing with final answers.[25]

Porter's Generic Competitive Strategies

In 1980, Michael Porter, a Harvard University economist, developed a model of competitive strategies. During a decade of research, Porter's model evolved into

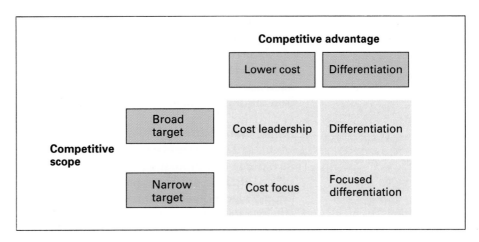

FIGURE 6.2 ● Porter's Generic Competitive Strategies

Source: Reprinted with permission of The Free Press, a Division of MacMillan, Inc. from *The Competitive Advantage of Nations* by Michael E. Porter. Copyright © 1990 by Michael E. Porter.

one with four generic strategies: (1) cost leadership, (2) differentiation, (3) cost focus, and (4) focused differentiation.[26] As shown in Figure 6.2, Porter's model combines two variables, *competitive advantage* and *competitive scope.*

On the horizontal axis is competitive advantage, which can be achieved via low costs or differentiation. A competitive advantage based on low costs, which means lower prices, is self-explanatory. **Differentiation,** according to Porter, "is the ability to provide unique and superior value to the buyer in terms of product quality, special features, or after-sale service."[27] Differentiation helps explain why consumers willingly pay more for branded products such as Sunkist oranges or Crest toothpaste. On the vertical axis is competitive scope. Is the firm's target market broad or narrow? IBM, which sells many types of computers all around the world, serves a very broad market. A neighborhood pizza parlor that offers one type of food in a small geographical area has a narrow target market.

Like the concepts of synergy and product life cycle, Porter's model helps managers think strategically: it enables them to see the big picture as it affects the organization and its changing environment. Each of Porter's four generic strategies deserves a closer look.

Cost Leadership Strategy. Managers pursuing this strategy have an overriding concern for keeping costs, and therefore prices, lower than those of competitors. Normally, this means extensive production or service facilities with efficient economies of scale (low unit costs of making products or delivering services). Productivity improvement is a high priority for managers following the cost leadership strategy. Wal-Mart Stores, Inc. is a prime example of the cost leadership strategy.

> *The Wal-Mart formula is deceptively simple: Sell good-quality, name-brand, modestly-priced merchandise in a clean, no-frills setting that offers one-stop family shopping. Rather than entice shoppers with an ever-changing array of discounts and sales, Wal-Mart operates from an "everyday low price" philosophy.*[28]

Wal-Mart's computerized warehousing network gives it an additional cost advantage over its less efficient competitors.

In manufacturing firms, the preoccupation with minimizing costs flows beyond production into virtually all areas: purchasing, wages, overhead, R&D, advertising, and selling. A relatively large market share is required to accommodate this high-volume, low-profit-margin strategy.

Differentiation Strategy. For this strategy to succeed, a company's product or service must be considered unique by most of the customers in its industry. Advertising and promotion help the product to stand out from the crowd. Specialized design (BMW automobiles), a widely recognized brand (Diet Coke), leading-edge technology (Intel), or reliable service (Caterpillar) also may serve to differentiate a product in the industry. Because customers with brand loyalty will usually spend more for what they perceive to be a superior product, the differentiation strategy can yield larger profit margins than the low-cost strategy. It is important to note, however, that cost reduction is not ignored by an organization pursuing the differentiation strategy; it simply is not the highest priority.

Cost Focus Strategy. Organizations with a cost focus strategy attempt to gain a competitive edge in a narrow or regional market by exerting strict cost control. Atlantic Richfield Company (ARCO), the Los Angeles–based oil company, adopted this strategy in 1984, when it sold all of its 1,100 gas stations east of the Rocky mountains. The idea was to better serve the fast-growing Western states. By getting most of its oil from Alaska, rather than from the volatile Middle East, pruning its payroll by 12,000 people, and refusing to accept credit cards, ARCO manages to undersell its competitors by about 6 cents a gallon.[29]

Focused Differentiation Strategy. This fourth generic strategy involves achieving a competitive edge by delivering a superior product and/or service to a limited audience. The Mayo Clinic's world-class health care facilities in Rochester, Minnesota, Jacksonville, Florida, and Scottsdale, Arizona, are an expression of this strategy.

A contingency management approach is necessary for determining which of Porter's generic strategies is appropriate. Recent research on Porter's model indicates a positive relationship between long-term earnings growth and a good strategy/environment fit.[30]

Managers in all types and sizes of organizations need to be proficient strategic thinkers. Specific strategic thinking tools such as synergy, the product life cycle, and Porter's generic strategies pave the way for understanding and implementing the strategic management process discussed next.

The Strategic Management Process

Strategic plans are formulated during an evolutionary process with identifiable steps. In line with the three-level planning pyramid covered in Chapter 5, the strategic management process is broader and more general at the top and filters

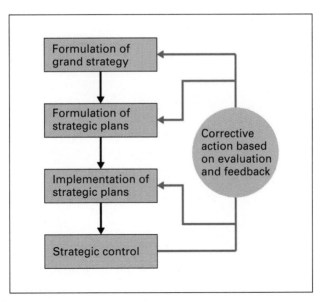

FIGURE 6.3 • The Strategic Management Process

down to narrower and more specific terms. Figure 6.3 outlines the four major steps of the strategic management process: (1) formulation of a grand strategy, (2) formulation of strategic plans, (3) implementation of strategic plans, and (4) strategic control. Corrective action based on evaluation and feedback takes place throughout the entire strategic management process to keep things headed in the right direction.

Of important note, this model represents an ideal approach. Because of organizational politics, as discussed in Chapter 13, and different planning orientations among managers, a somewhat less systematic process typically results. Nevertheless, it is helpful to study the strategic management process as a systematic and rational sequence to better understand what it involves. Although noting that rational strategic planning models should not be taken literally, Henry Mintzberg recently acknowledged their profound instructional value. They teach necessary vocabulary and implant the notion "that strategy represents a fundamental congruence between external opportunity and internal capability."[31]

Formulation of a Grand Strategy

As pointed out in Chapter 5, a clear statement of organizational mission serves as a focal point for the entire planning process. Key stakeholders inside and outside the organization are given a general idea of why the organization exists and where it is headed. Working from the mission statement, top management formulates the organization's **grand strategy,** a general explanation of *how* the organization's mission is to be accomplished. Grand strategies are not drawn out of thin air. They are derived from a careful *situational analysis* of the organization and its environment. A clear vision of where the organization *is* headed and where it *should be* headed is the gateway to competitive advantage.

• • • • • • • • • • • • • • • •
Identify and describe the four steps in the strategic management process.

grand strategy how the organization's mission will be accomplished

Peters and Waterman urged managers to "stick to their knitting." That's what Home Depot's chief executive officer Bernard Marcus (left) and president Arthur Blank have done while building America's largest chain of do-it-yourself warehouses. With weekly traffic of 25,000 to 30,000 customers per store, Home Depot could have diversified. But Home Depot's strategies are faithful to the chain's original focus, home improvement products. This strategic focus blended with economic trends. Higher home prices have forced many to settle for fix ups and room additions instead of new homes.

situational analysis finding the organization's niche by performing a SWOT analysis

---

Explain the nature and purpose of a SWOT analysis.

Situational Analysis. A **situational analysis** is a technique for matching organizational strengths and weaknesses with environmental opportunities and threats to determine the organization's right niche (see Figure 6.4). Many strategists refer to this process as a SWOT analysis (SWOT stands for *Strengths, Weaknesses, Opportunities, and Threats.*).[32] Every organization should be able to identify the purpose for which it is best suited. But this matching process is more difficult than it may at first appear. Strategists are faced not with snapshots of the environment and the organization but with a movie of rapidly changing events. As one researcher said: "The task is to find a match between opportunities that are still unfolding and resources that are still being acquired."[33] As a case in point, consider chief executive Bob Crandall's strategic goal for American Airlines:

> *By the year 2000, Crandall aims to generate about 30 percent of American's revenues from foreign routes, up from virtually nothing ten years ago. To reach that ambitious target, he has committed $11 billion—more than half American's capital spending budget—to expanding and upgrading his international operations over the next five years.[34]*

Forecasting techniques, such as those reviewed later in this chapter, help managers cope with uncertainty about the future while conducting situational analyses.

Strategic planners, whether top managers, key operating managers, or staff planning specialists, have many ways to scan the environment for opportunities and threats. They can study telltale shifts in the economy, recent innovations, growth and movement among competitors, market trends, labor availability, and demographic shifts.

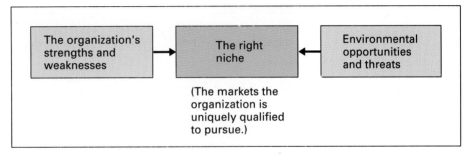

FIGURE 6.4 ● Determining Strategic Direction through Situational (SWOT) Analysis

Environmental opportunities and threats need to be sorted out carefully.[35] A perceived threat may turn out to be an opportunity, or vice versa. Steps can be taken to turn negatives into positives. Archer Daniels Midland Company (ADM), for example, literally faces an environmental threat. The huge Decatur, Illinois, grain company ships much of its inventory down the Mississippi River on barges. It is afraid that global warming, associated with the greenhouse effect, could permanently lower the river's water level. As a hedge against this threat to barge traffic, ADM recently bought part of the Illinois Central Transportation Company. That company runs a railroad paralleling the Mississippi.[36]

Capability Profile. After scanning the external environment for opportunities and threats, management's attention turns inward to identifying the organization's strengths and weaknesses. This subprocess has been called a **capability profile**.[37] When tackling this job, the usual question is "Where do we begin?" The list of organizational attributes presented in Table 6.2 is an excellent starting point. By categorizing these organizational dimensions as strengths or weaknesses, strategists produce a capability profile to compare with external environmental opportunities and threats. They also sharpen management's focus on the organization's core competencies and driving forces.

capability profile identifying the organization's strengths and weaknesses

Core Competencies. Successful organizations tend to be very good at doing certain things. These **core competencies**, defined as firsthand experience with integrating and exploiting technologies, give the organization a competitive advantage. In sports, we see competitive advantage based on competency all the time. Basketball has its Michael Jordan, ice hockey its Wayne Gretzky, and track and field its Florence Joyner. In each case, an athlete has fully exploited a core competency to become a world-class competitor. Companies also need to identify their core competencies and refine and exploit them to the fullest. Examples abound. For Sony, it's miniaturization. For 3M, it's adhesives and coatings. For Honda, it's engines.

core competencies areas of expertise that create a competitive advantage

Experts on the subject recommend the following three-way test for identifying a core competency. A core competency should (1) provide access to new markets, (2) significantly improve customer satisfaction, and (3) be very hard to imitate.[38] In the case of Honda, this helps explain how the Accord became the top-selling car in America.

Driving Forces. In addition to identifying core competencies, an organization must set an agenda for strategic improvement. Items at the top of this agenda have been termed *driving forces*. Ten major driving forces are:

TABLE 6.2 • A Framework for Identifying Organizational Strengths and Weaknesses

General category	Attributes
Organization	Structure/Climate/Culture Degree of decentralization Policies and procedures The planning system The control system The communication network
Management	Experience Expertise Track record Commitment to long-term strategic planning, implementation, and control Management succession/development programs
Personnel	Number of employees Employee attitude profile Employee age and skill profiles Union/nonunion status Absenteeism and turnover rates Grievance rate
Marketing	Size of sales force Sales force turnover Knowledge of customers' needs Market share Breadth of product line Channels of distribution Product quality Credit and refund policies Customer service Reputation
Technical	Production facilities Condition of machinery Production techniques Quality control program New product innovation Research program Purchasing system Inventory system
Finance	Financial size Liquidity Return on investment Price-earnings ratio Credit rating Lines of credit Growth record

Source: Based in part on Howard H. Stevenson, "Defining Corporate Strengths and Weaknesses," *Sloan Management Review,* 17 (Spring 1976): 51–68. Used with permission.

1. Seeking new markets,
2. Developing new products and services, *~ identify need* (handwritten)
3. Improving customer service,
4. Developing technology,
5. Improving production capability,
6. Improving methods of sale,
7. Improving methods of distribution,
8. Acquiring natural resources,
9. Enhancing size and growth, and
10. Enhancing return on investment and profit.[39]

To this list should be added the recent emphasis on time-based strategy or "organizational speed and responsiveness"[40] (see Managers in Action).

Formulation of Strategic Plans

In the second major step in the strategic management process, general intentions are translated into more concrete and measurable strategic plans, policies, and budget allocations.[41] This translation is the responsibility of top management, though input from staff planning specialists and middle managers is common. From our discussion in the last chapter we recall that a well-written plan consists of both an objective and an action statement. Plans at all levels should specify who, what, when, and how things are to be accomplished and for how much. Many managers prefer to call these specific plans "action plans" to emphasize the need to turn good intentions into action. Even though strategic plans may have a time horizon of one or more years, they must meet the same criteria that shorter-run intermediate and operational plans meet. They should:

1. Develop clear, results-oriented objectives in measurable terms.
2. Identify the particular activities required to accomplish the objectives.
3. Assign specific responsibility and authority to the appropriate personnel.
4. Estimate times to accomplish activities and their appropriate sequencing.
5. Determine resources required to accomplish the activities.
6. Communicate and coordinate the above elements and complete the action plan.[42]

All of this does not happen in a single quick-and-easy session. Specific strategic plans usually evolve over a period of months as top management consults with key managers in all areas of the organization to gather their ideas and recommendations and, one hopes, to win their commitment.

Strategic Implementation and Control

As illustrated earlier in Figure 6.3, the third and fourth stages of the strategic management cycle involve implementation and control. The entire process is only as strong as these two traditionally underemphasized areas.

The Strategic Need for Speed

Speed has become an important competitive advantage. To succeed, companies must give their customers what they want *when they want it*. Days, hours, even minutes can make or break a sale. Every successful fast-food restaurant demonstrates this principle, but now it is as important for cars as for hamburgers.

Speed has allowed American clothing manufacturers who pay garment workers $6.00 an hour to compete with factories in Bangladesh that pay 16 cents an hour. Overseas factories prefer to deal in large orders, which they may take a year to fill. But many customers now want variety—something new and different. To avoid getting stuck with thousands of outfits in last month's outmoded style, retailers buy small quantities of many different styles. Such buying requires manufacturers to be fast and flexible, not necessarily least expensive.

Liz Claiborne Inc. is one company that has responded to such pressures. It ships small quantities weekly from its 150 factories, almost ensuring that the items will sell out and demand will stay high. It knows that, because few companies last long in the clothing world, it has to be flexible and stay one step ahead of fashion trends.

Every industry can provide similar examples. Honda succeeds in America in part because it replaces old models in four years, half the time it takes most U.S. manufacturers. By setting dead-lines and holding to them religiously, Motorola now fills orders for electronic pagers in two hours instead of three weeks. Companies like computer maker Hewlett-Packard, which set out to cut in half the time between a product's conception and its profitability, have found that making speed a priority actually improves quality. Designers and engineers usually must develop a whole new—and better—production process to manufacture the product faster. They no longer have time to make mistakes. Such a new process has allowed Hewlett-Packard to manufacture computer terminals more cheaply than its foreign rivals.

Importantly, the new strategic emphasis on speed involves more than doing the same old things, only faster. Cutting through layers of bureaucracy, using autonomous development teams, giving more responsibility to people who actually make the product, building on core competencies, and meshing those competencies with environmental opportunities are among the many new approaches to speed. In the decade ahead, more companies will find that "on budget" is no longer as important as "on time."

Sources: Mark Clayton, "U.S. Apparel Industry Finds Edge," *The Christian Science Monitor* (October 17, 1989): 9; Brian Dumaine, "How Managers Can Succeed Through Speed," *Fortune* (February 13, 1989): 54–59; David Woodruff, "A New Era For Auto Quality," *Business Week* (October 22, 1990): 84–96; Laura Zinn, "Liz Claiborne Without Liz: Steady As She Goes," *Business Week* (September 17, 1990): 70–74.

Implementation of Strategic Plans

According to the editor of *Long Range Planning,* a respected international journal, implementation is the most important new frontier for corporate planning during the 1990s.[43] Because strategic plans are too often shelved without adequate attention to implementation, top managers need to do a better job of facilitating the implementation process and building middle-manager commitment.

A Systematic Filtering-Down Process. Because planning is a filtering-down process, strategic plans require further translation into successively lower-level

Imagine you are a comparatively small advertising agency competing with the industry heavyweights. And you are two women in the male-dominated business and you are working out of Miami rather than Madison Avenue. If you are Joyce Beber (right) and Elaine Silverstein, and your firm is Beber Silverstein & Partners, you go out and snare the best talent possible. Beber and Silverstein challenged Ed McCabe, called the world's best ad copywriter, to leave retirement and help make their company great. Surprisingly, he accepted, and thus is helping to implement Beber's and Silverstein's strategic goal of becoming a national force.

plans. Top management strategists can do some groundwork to ensure that the filtering-down process occurs smoothly and efficiently. Planners need answers to four questions, each tied to a different critical organizational factor:

1. *Organizational Structure.* Is the organizational structure compatible with the planning process, with new managerial approaches, and with the strategy itself?

2. *People.* Are people with the right skills and abilities available for key assignments, or must attention be given to recruiting, training, management development, and similar programs?

3. *Culture.* Is the collective viewpoint on "the right way to do things" compatible with strategy, must it be modified to reflect a new perspective, or must top management learn to manage around it?

4. *Control Systems.* Is the necessary apparatus in place to support the implementation of strategy and to permit top management to assess performance in meeting strategic objectives?[44]

Strategic plans that successfully address these four questions have a much greater chance of helping the organization achieve its intended purpose than those that do not. In addition, field research indicates the need to *sell* strategies to all affected parties. New strategies represent change, and people tend to resist change for a variety of reasons. "The strategist thus faces a major selling job; that is, trying to build and maintain support among key constituencies for a plan that is freshly emerging."[45] This brings us to the challenge of obtaining commitment among middle managers.

Building Middle-Manager Commitment. Resistance among middle managers can kill an otherwise excellent strategic management program. A study of ninety middle managers who wrote 330 reports about instances in which they had resisted strategic decisions documented the scope of this problem. It turned out that, to protect their own self-interests, the managers in the study frequently derailed strategies. This finding prompted the researchers to conclude:

> If general management decides to go ahead and impose its decisions in spite of lack of commitment, resistance by middle management can drastically lower the efficiency with which the decisions are implemented, if it does not completely stop them from being implemented. Particularly in dynamic, competitive environments, securing commitment to the strategy is crucial because rapid implementation is so important.[46]

Participative management (see Chapter 12) and influence tactics (see Chapter 14) can foster middle-manager commitment.

Strategic Control

Strategic plans, like our more informal daily plans, can go astray. But a formal control system helps keep strategic plans on track. Strategic control systems need to be carefully designed ahead of time, not merely tacked on as an afterthought.[47] Before strategies are translated downward, planners should set up and test channels for information on progress, problems, and strategic assumptions about the environment or organization that have proved to be invalid. If a new strategy varies significantly from past ones, new production, financial, or marketing reports will probably have to be drafted and introduced.

The ultimate goal of a strategic control system is to detect and correct downstream problems in order to keep strategies updated and on target, without stifling creativity and innovation in the process. A survey of 207 planning executives found that in high-performing companies there was no trade-off between strategic control and creativity. Both were delicately balanced.[48]

Corrective Action Based on Evaluation and Feedback

As illustrated in Figure 6.3, corrective action makes the strategic management process a dynamic cycle. A rule of thumb is that negative feedback should prompt corrective action at the step immediately before. Should the problem turn out to be more deeply rooted, then the next earlier step also may require corrective action. The key is to detect problems and initiate corrective action, such as reformulating plans, rewriting policies, making personnel changes, or modifying budget allocations, as soon as possible. In the absence of prompt corrective action, problems can rapidly worsen.[49]

We now turn to forecasting. Without the ability to obtain or develop reliable environmental forecasts, managerial strategists have a minimal chance of successfully negotiating their way through the strategic management process.

Forecasting

forecasts predictions, projections, or estimates of future situations

An important aspect of strategic management is anticipating what will happen. **Forecasts** may be defined as predictions, projections, or estimates of future events or conditions in the environment in which the organization operates.[50] Forecasts may be little more than educated guesses or may be the result of highly sophisticated statistical analyses. They vary in reliability. (Consider the track record of TV weather forecasters!)[51] They may be relatively short run—a few hours to a year—or long run—five or more years. A combination of factors determines a forecast's relative sophistication, time horizon, and reliability. These factors include the type of forecast required, management's knowledge of forecasting techniques, and the money that management is willing to invest.[52]

Types of Forecasts

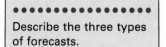

Describe the three types of forecasts.

event outcome forecasts predictions of the outcome of highly probable future events

event timing forecasts predictions of when a given event will occur

There are three types of forecasts: (1) event outcome forecasts, (2) event timing forecasts, and (3) time series forecasts.[53] Each type answers a different general question (see Table 6.3). **Event outcome forecasts** are used when strategists want to predict the outcome of highly probable future events. Examples are "What will be the first year's sales for a new product?" or "How will an impending strike affect output?" Information bases for reliably answering these two questions could be built by, respectively, conducting market tests and interviewing other strike victims in the industry.

Event timing forecasts predict when, if ever, given events will occur. Strategic questions in this area might include "When will the prime interest rate begin to fall?" or "When will our primary competitor introduce a certain product?" Timing questions like these typically can be answered by identifying leading indicators that historically have preceded the events in question. For instance, a declining inflation rate often prompts major banks to lower their prime interest rate, or a competitor may flag the introduction of a new product by conducting market tests or ordering large quantities of a new raw material.

time series forecasts estimates of future values in a statistical sequence

Time series forecasts seek to estimate future values in a sequence of periodically recorded statistics. For example, to gauge the availability of labor, strategists may want to forecast future values in a time series of quarterly unemployment data for a region. Trend analysis, discussed below, helps chart the future course of a time series.

TABLE 6.3 • Types of Forecasts

Type of forecast	General question	Example
1. Event outcome forecast	"What will happen when a given event occurs?"	"Who will win the next World Series?"
2. Event timing forecast	"When will a given event occur?"	"When will the United States have a permanently manned space station?"
3. Time series forecast	"What value will a series of periodic data have at a given point in time?"	"What will the closing Dow Jones Industrial Average be on January 5, 1995?"

Years of planning and preparation went into the 115 hours of coverage from Albertville, France, site of the 1992 Winter Olympics. Faced with a dwindling television audience, CBS won the bidding war to broadcast the audience-attracting Olympics.

Forecasting Techniques

Modern managers may use one or a combination of four techniques to forecast future outcomes, timing, and values. These techniques are informed judgment, scenario analysis, surveys, and trend analysis.

Informed Judgment.   Limited time and money often force strategists to rely on their own intuitive judgment when forecasting. Judgmental forecasts are both fast and inexpensive, but their accuracy depends greatly on how well informed the strategist is. Frequent visits with employees—in sales, purchasing, and public relations, for example—who regularly tap outside sources of information are a good way of staying informed. A broad reading program to stay in touch with current events and industry trends and refresher training through management development programs are also helpful.

Stephen Hassenfeld, who heads Hasbro, Inc., the world's largest toy company, relies heavily on informed judgment when selecting new toys. When Hassenfeld had market research done to determine whether to introduce Hasbro's new My Little Pony, the girls sampled in the study said they were much happier with the already popular Strawberry Shortcake dolls than with the new ponies. Hassenfeld brought out the pony toys anyway, and My Little Pony quickly outdistanced Strawberry Shortcake.

The intuitive approach can pay off, although it has its critics. A former corporate board member is less confident of Hasbro's forecasting style: "They do little or no research. It's how everything feels in the gut. They're eventually going to run into a brick wall."[54] Informed judgment is no panacea. It needs to be used in conjunction with other forecasting techniques.

Scenario Analysis.   This technique also relies on informed judgment but is more systematic and disciplined than the approach just discussed. **Scenario analysis** is the preparation and study of written descriptions of *alternative* but *equally likely* future conditions. Scenarios are visions of what "could be." The late futurist Herman Kahn is said to have first used the term *scenario* in conjunction with forecasting during the 1950s. The two types of scenarios are longitudinal and cross-sectional. **Longitudinal scenarios** describe how the present is expected to evolve into the future. **Cross-sectional scenarios,** the more common type, simply describe possible future situations at a given time (see The World of Management).

While noting that *multiple forecasts* are the cornerstone of scenario analysis, one researcher has offered the following perspective:

> *Scenario writing is a highly qualitative procedure. It proceeds more from the gut than from the computer, although it may incorporate the results of quantitative models. Scenario writing is based on the assumption that the future is not merely some mathematical manipulation of the past, but the confluence of many forces, past, present and future that can best be understood by simply thinking about the problem.*[55]

This same researcher recommends developing two to four scenarios (three being optimal) for narrowly defined topics. Likely candidates for scenario analysis are specific products, industries, or markets. For example, a grain exporting company's strategists might look five years into the future by writing scenarios for

scenario analysis preparing written descriptions of equally likely future situations

longitudinal scenarios describing how the future will evolve from the present

cross-sectional scenarios describing future situations at a given point in time

Scenario Planning: Domestic and Foreign

The managers of Southern California Edison, an electric utility serving 3.9 million customers in central and southern California, came to the mind-numbing realization four years ago that their strategic planning system was a bad joke. Every long-range plan they had painstakingly constructed over the past two decades had been rendered virtually useless by unexpected events—from OPEC price-fixing to new restrictions on sulfur emissions to accidents at Three Mile Island and Chernobyl. Says Vikram Budhraja, manager of electrical systems planning: "These were events that no one could have foreseen, but they had a dramatic impact on our business."

So Edison adopted a technique known as scenario planning. Looking ahead ten years, the utility came up with 12 possible versions of the future—incorporating an economic boom, a Middle East oil crisis, expanded environmentalism, and other developments. Each scenario carries implications for how much power Edison would need to generate, from 5,000 megawatts more to 5,000 megawatts less than the 15,000 megawatts it was producing in 1987.

To cope with such radical variations in demand, Edison has built flexibility into its system. It can repower or depower oil-and-gas generating plants, buy juice from other utilities, and intensify or diminish its campaign to help customers use less electricity. Edison is stepping up conservation in response to new state regulations that reward utilities for encouraging reduced consumption. Says

Vikram Budhraja: "We couldn't have done this as well if we hadn't planned for this possibility."

Royal Dutch/Shell, which has been doing scenario planning for 19 years currently has two 20-year scenarios in place. The first, called "Sustainable World," predicts increased concern about global warming trends and an expanded emphasis on conservation, recycling, and emissions controls. The second scenario, ominously entitled "Mercantilist World," postulates an increase in protectionism, a slump in world growth, and a de-emphasis of environmentalism.

Group planning coordinator Peter Hadfield believes that scenario planning has helped Shell be better prepared than its competitors for external shocks. In the early Eighties, for example, while most forecasters were predicting a steadily increasing price for crude oil, Shell, in one of its scenarios, had entertained the possibility that the price would slide to $15 a barrel. As a hedge against such an eventuality, the company began looking into cost-saving exploration technologies. When the slump hit, Shell was able to sustain a higher level of drilling activity than many of its competitors. Shell realizes that its two scenarios don't encompass everything that might happen in the future, and that neither will be a perfect predictor. Says Hadfield: "They're there to condition the organization to think."

three different likely situations: (1) above-average grain harvests, (2) average harvests, and (3) below-average harvests. These scenarios could serve as focal points for strategic plans concerning construction of facilities, staffing and training, and so on. As the future unfolds, the strategies accompanying the most realistic scenario would be followed. This approach has been called "no surprise" strategic planning.[56]

The key to good scenario writing is to focus on the few readily identifiable but unpredictable factors that will have the greatest impact on the topic in question. Because scenarios look far into the future, typically five or more years, they need to be written in general and rather imprecise terms.

Surveys.   Surveys are a forecasting technique that involves face-to-face and telephone interviews and mailed questionnaires. They can be used to pool expert opinion or fathom consumer tastes, attitudes, and opinions. When carefully constructed and properly administered to representative samples, surveys can give management comprehensive and fresh information. They suffer the disadvantages, however, of being somewhat difficult to construct, time-consuming to administer and interpret, and expensive. Although costs can be trimmed by purchasing an off-the-shelf or "canned" survey, standardized instruments too often either fail to ask precisely the right questions or ask unnecessary questions.

trend analysis hypothetical extension of a past series of events into the future

Trend Analysis.   Essentially, a **trend analysis** is the hypothetical extension of a past pattern of events or time series into the future. An underlying assumption of trend analysis is that past and present tendencies will continue into the future. Of course, surprise events such as the October 1987 stock market crash can destroy that assumption. Trend analysis can be fickle and cruel to reactive companies. As a case in point, Chrysler's commitment to fuel-efficient, four-cylinder cars in the early 1980s was based on the assumption that the 1970s trend toward higher gas prices would continue. However, when the price of gasoline stabilized during the 1980s, Chrysler came up short as American car buyers demanded more horsepower.[57] By the time Chrysler had geared up its production of more powerful V-6 engines, Iraq's 1990 invasion of Kuwait sent the price of gasoline skyward and car buyers scrambling for four-cylinder cars. Again Chrysler tripped over a faulty trend analysis. If sufficient valid historical data are readily available trend analysis can, barring disruptive surprise events, be a reasonably accurate, fast, and inexpensive strategic forecasting tool. An unreliable or atypical data base, however, can produce misleading trend projections.

Each of these forecasting techniques has inherent limitations. Consequently, strategists are advised to validate one source of forecast information with one or more additional sources.

Summary

Strategic management sets the stage for virtually all managerial activity. Managers at all levels need to think strategically and to be familiar with the strategic management process for three reasons: farsightedness is encouraged, the rationale behind top-level decisions becomes more apparent, and strategy formulation and implementation are more decentralized today. Strategic management is defined as the ongoing process of ensuring a competitively superior fit between the organization and its ever-changing environment. Strategic management effectively merges strategic planning, implementation, and control.

Strategic thinking, the ability to look ahead and spot key organization/environment interdependencies, is necessary for successful strategic management and planning. Three tools that can help managers think strategically are synergy (the 2 + 2 = 5 effect); product life cycles that trace the life of a product through its introduction, growth, maturity, and decline stages; and Porter's generic competitive strategies. Porter's four strategies are cost leadership, differentiation, cost focus, and focused differentiation.

The strategic management process consists of four major steps: (1) formulation of grand strategy, (2) formulation of strategic plans, (3) implementation of strategic plans, and (4) strategic control. Corrective action based on evaluation of progress and feedback helps keep the strategic management process on track.

Strategists formulate the organization's grand strategy by conducting a situational (SWOT) analysis and identifying the organization's core competencies and driving forces. Results-oriented strategic plans that specify what, when, and how are then formulated and translated downward into more specific and shorter-term intermediate and operational plans. Participative management can build needed middle-manager commitment during implementation. Problems encountered along the way should be detected by the strategic control mechanism or by ongoing evaluation and subjected to corrective action.

Event outcome, event timing, and time series forecasts help strategic planners anticipate and prepare for future environmental circumstances. Popular forecasting techniques among today's managers are informed judgment, scenario analysis, surveys, and trend analysis. Each technique has its own limitations, so forecasts need to be crosschecked against one another.

Terms to Understand

Strategic management
Strategy
Synergy
Product life cycle
Differentiation (strategic)
Grand strategy
Situational analysis
Capability profile
Core competencies

Forecasts
Event outcome forecasts
Event timing forecasts
Time series forecasts
Scenario analysis
Longitudinal scenarios
Cross-sectional scenarios
Trend analysis

Questions for Discussion

1. Why is strategic management particularly important today?
2. Consider a business you are familiar with. How could it achieve market, cost, technology, or management synergy?
3. Why is the concept of product life cycles useful to strategic planners?
4. Which of Porter's four generic competitive strategies would be most difficult to implement? Why? Which would be the easiest? Why?
5. What would a situational (SWOT) analysis of you and your career options look like?
6. Taking a strategic perspective of your own career, what are your core competencies and driving forces?
7. Why is ongoing evaluation important during the strategic management process?
8. Can you make outcome forecasts for three significant upcoming events? On what did you base these forecasts?
9. Why do you think managers tend to rely heavily on judgmental forecasts?
10. What is the main appeal of scenario forecasting?

Back to the Opening Case

Now that you have read Chapter 6, you should be able to answer the following questions about the McDonald's case:

1. Does the product life cycle concept apply to any of the McDonald's offerings? Explain in terms of specific products.

2. Which of Porter's four generic strategies is McDonald's pursuing? How can you tell?

3. Based on this case and reasonable assumptions from your own experience with McDonald's, what would a situational (SWOT) analysis of McDonald's tell us about the future direction the firm should take? *Tip:* First arrange your evidence under these four headings: organizational strengths, organizational weaknesses, environmental opportunities, and environmental threats.

4. What scenario can you envision for McDonald's in the year 2005?

CLOSING CASE
Citicorp's Global Strategy Falls to Pieces

Citicorp is America's largest bank. During the financial boom of the mid-1980s, when whiz-kid John S. Reed, then 44, took over, its future looked bright. Reed had an exciting vision—to make his bank the one truly global bank in the world. But by the end of the decade, Citicorp was in trouble, and people began wondering if the government would have to apply its "too big to fail" policy to a company that had $228 billion in assets.

Citicorp's problems had a lot to do with what Reed calls "externalities"—changes in the environment that made a lot of Citicorp's loans go sour. But in a way the problems with America's leading bank reflect the changes in the country's overall economic stature. During the decade, the United States became a debtor nation, and wealthy foreign companies gobbled up prime pieces of the country from New York to Los Angeles. Though Citibank is the largest bank in the United States, it no longer ranks among the top ten worldwide. So Reed's grandiose vision for Citicorp may have been a relic of an earlier age. The first truly global bank will probably have to be Japanese.

Some of Citicorp's problems had been visible on the horizon for a long time; others appeared only as a result of the economic slowdown at the end of the Reagan era. Like a number of other large American banks, Citicorp lent billions of dollars to less developed countries, many of which have either been slow to repay or have stopped paying the loans altogether. Citicorp had known about these problem foreign loans for a long time, but it was not prepared to have trouble getting loan repayments from wealthy Americans. By 1990, three of Citicorp's biggest individual borrowers—including Donald Trump—together owed the bank $1 billion. Their problems, and the bank's, stemmed from the drop in the value of real estate and the financial difficulties faced by companies that were heavily in debt, often via junk bonds.

Citicorp couldn't control these environmental factors, but analysts wonder whether Reed's grand vision blinded him and other

Citicorp executives to warning signals. Reed also had little control over the Citicorp philosophy he inherited from his predecessor, Walter Wriston. Wriston believed that earnings should increase 15 percent per year, a pace that could be maintained only by making some high-risk investments. Moreover, Citicorp has a history of inefficient management. Indeed, operating expenses rose as much as 25 percent per year during the 1980s. Citicorp's humbling, therefore, has included painful layoffs and a major reduction in dividends.

Reed has now narrowed his vision a bit, focusing on commercial banking. Although he still tends to be a big-picture thinker, he has named Richard Braddock, a hands-on, detail-oriented manager, as Citicorp's president and chief operating officer.

Even though Citicorp was in serious trouble in 1990, financial analysts agreed the government wouldn't let it fail. The government has a history of rescuing any bank whose failure would be catastrophic to the economy at large. Whether this kind of no-fault insurance is good for Citicorp's management is an open question. Certainly, no bank wants to look to the federal government for help. At the same time, however, not having to worry about bankruptcy might make bankers less efficient and more reckless than they would otherwise be.

Ironically, Citicorp never had to look far to learn how to run a profitable bank. Its strongest asset is its own consumer bank, which Reed started. The bank dedicated itself to service, took lessons from acknowledged service leaders like Federal Express, and became innovative in its approach to serving its customers, even though the average deposit was only about $10,000. Its managers realized that what Citicorp measured as good performance often clashed with what consumers defined as good service. And by catering to average Americans—rather than the super-rich—Citicorp's consumer bank has made out just fine. It provides about 60 percent of the money that Citicorp needs to stay afloat from day to day. Perhaps after its experience with Citicorp's grand vision, the government will develop a new policy toward banks—"too big to succeed."

For Discussion

1. What kinds of synergy could have helped Reed achieve his global vision for Citicorp?

2. What are Citicorp's core competencies? What sort of strategy could be shaped around them?

3. Which of Porter's four generic competitive strategies was Reed attempting to pursue during his push to make Citicorp a truly global bank? What was its major downfall?

4. How important a role did strategic implementation play in Reed's problems? Explain with details from the case.

References

Opening Quotation. Michael E. Porter, *The Competitive Advantage of Nations* (New York: The Free Press, 1990), pp. 52–53.

Opening Case. Ronald Henkoff, "Big Mac Attacks with Pizza," *Fortune* (February 26, 1990): 87–89; "McDonald's Eastern Front," *Newsweek* (March 5, 1990): 8; Martha T. Moore, "Environment, Health on Front Burner," *USA Today* (April 18, 1990): 1b, 2b; Lois Therrien, "McDonald's Isn't Looking Quite So Juicy Anymore," *Business Week* (August 6, 1990): 30; John Schwartz, "A Burger Lover's Lament," *Newsweek* (March 25, 1991): 48.

Closing Case. Carol J. Loomis, "Citicorp's World of Troubles," *Fortune* (January 14, 1991): 90–99; John Meehan, "Can John Reed Rock Citicorp Out of Its Rut?" *Business Week* (November 12, 1990): 116–118; Ron Zemke, *The Service Edge* (New York: New American Library, 1989), pp. 190–193.

1. Ronald Henkoff, "How To Plan For 1995," *Fortune* (December 31, 1990): 76.

2. Based on a definitional framework found in David J. Teece, "Economic Analysis and Strategic Management," *California Management Review,* 26 (Spring 1984): 87. Also see Henry Mintzberg, "The Strategy Concept I: Five Ps For Strategy," *California Management Review,* 30 (Fall 1987): 11–24.

3. Arnoldo C. Hax, "Redefining the Concept of Strategy and the Strategy Formation Process," *Planning Review,* 18 (May/June 1990): 35.

4. See Bernard Taylor, "Corporate Planning for the 1990s: The New Frontiers," *Long Range Planning,* 19 (December 1986): 13–18.

5. Henkoff, "How To Plan For 1995," p. 70.

6. Donald R. Schmincke, "Strategic Thinking: A Perspective For Success," *Management Review,* 79 (August 1990): 18.

7. Benjamin B. Tregoe and John W. Zimmerman, "Strategic Thinking: Key to Corporate Survival," *Management Review,* 68 (February 1979): 10.

8. Quoted in "The New Breed of Strategic Planner," *Business Week* (September 17, 1984): 62.

9. See William R. King and David I. Cleland, *Strategic Planning and Policy* (New York: Van Nostrand Reinhold, 1978), pp. 180–183.

10. Anthony Ramirez, "Ply Gem Industries," *Fortune* (August 14, 1989): 76.

11. Michael Goold and Andrew Campbell, "Many Best Ways to Make Strategy," *Harvard Business Review,* 65 (November–December 1987): 71.

12. See David Lieberman, "SI's Swimsuit Issue: More Than Meets the Eye," *Business Week* (January 16, 1989): 52.

13. Neil Gross and William J. Holstein, "Why Sony is Plugging Into Columbia," *Business Week* (October 16, 1989): 58.

14. "A Ready-Made Track for High-Tech Communications," *Business Week* (September 12, 1983): 43.

15. See Mimi Bluestone, "Stop—Don't Throw Those Crab Shells Away," *Business Week* (March 23, 1987): 112, 116. Also see Evan I. Schwartz, "A Data Base That Truly Is 'Garbage In, Garbage Out,' " *Business Week* (September 17, 1990): 92.

16. "Alfa-Laval: Updating Its Knowhow for the Biotechnology Era," *Business Week* (September 19, 1983): 80.

17. See Ward C. Smith, "Product Life-Cycle Strategy: How to Stay on the Growth Curve," *Management Review,* 69 (January 1980): 8–13; Lester A. Neidell, "Don't Forget the Product Life Cycle for Strategic Planning," *Business,* 33 (April–June 1983): 30–35; and George W. Potts, "Exploit Your Product's Service Life Cycle," *Harvard Business Review,* 66 (September–October 1988): 32–36.

18. "Technology Gives the U.S. a Big Edge," *Business Week* (June 30, 1980): 104; Susan Fraker, "High-Speed Management for the High-Tech Age," *Fortune* (March 5, 1984): 62–68.

19. Data from Mel Levine, "How the US Could Catch Up With Japanese Investment," *The Christian Science Monitor* (November 29, 1989): 8.

20. Anne B. Fisher, "Is Long-Range Planning Worth It?" *Fortune* (April 23, 1990): 282.

21. James E. Ellis, "Why Monsanto is Plunking Down Its Chips on R&D," *Business Week* (August 21, 1989): 66.

22. For a typical reference to this statistic, see Lois Therrien, "Want Shelf Space at the Supermarket? Ante Up," *Business Week* (August 7, 1989): 60–61.

23. "New Product Success Rate—One Out of Three," *Research Management,* 23 (March 1980): 3. For a more detailed study with similar results, see C. Merle Crawford, "New Product Failure Rates—Facts and Fallacies," *Research Management,* 22 (September 1979): 9–13.

24. See Patrick E. Cole, "Mattell is Putting Its Dollhouse in Order," *Business Week* (August 28, 1989): 66–67.

25. For a critical appraisal of PLCs, see Alexander Hiam, "Exposing Four Myths of Strategic Planning," *The Journal of Business Strategy,* 11 (September/October 1990): 23–28.

26. See Michael E. Porter, *Competitive Strategy* (New York: Free Press, 1980), p. 35; and Michael E. Porter, *The Competitive Advantage of Nations* (New York: The Free Press, 1990), p. 39.

Also see Alan I. Murray, "A Contingency View of Porter's 'Generic Strategies,' " *Academy of Management Review*, 13 (July 1988): 390–400.

27. Porter, *The Competitive Advantage of Nations*, p. 37.

28. Ron Zemke and Dick Schaaf, *The Service Edge* (New York: New American Library, 1989), p. 360.

29. See Ronald Grover, "Lod Cook: Mixing Oil and PR," *Business Week* (October 8, 1990): 110–116.

30. For details, see Luis Ma. R. Calingo, "Environmental Determinants of Generic Competitive Strategies: Preliminary Evidence from Structured Content Analysis of Fortune and Business Week Articles (1983–1984)," *Human Relations,* 42 (April 1989): 353–369.

31. Henry Mintzberg, "The Design School: Reconsidering the Basic Premises of Strategic Management," *Strategic Management Journal*, 11 (March–April 1990): 192.

32. See Thomas L. Wheelen and J. David Hunger, "Using the Strategic Audit," *SAM Advanced Management Journal,* 52 (Winter 1987): 4–12.

33. Richard F. Vancil, "Strategy Formulation in Complex Organizations," *Sloan Management Review,* 17 (Winter 1976): 18.

34. Kenneth Labich, "American Takes on the World," *Fortune* (September 24, 1990): 41.

35. See Frances J. Milliken, "Perceiving and Interpreting Environmental Change: An Examination of College Administrators' Interpretation of Changing Demographics," *Academy of Management Journal,* 33 (March 1990): 42–63.

36. See Vicky Cahan, "When the Rivers Go Dry and the Ice Caps Melt. . . . ," *Business Week* (February 13, 1989): 95, 98.

37. For example, see Howard H. Stevenson, "Defining Corporate Strengths and Weaknesses," *Sloan Management Review,* 17 (Spring 1976): 51–68.

38. See C. K. Prahalad and Gary Hamel, "The Core Competence of the Corporation," *Harvard Business Review,* 68 (May–June 1990): 79–91.

39. Adapted from Tregoe and Zimmerman, "Strategic Thinking," p. 13.

40. See George Stalk, Jr., "Time—The Next Source of Competitive Advantage," *Harvard Business Review,* 66 (July–August 1988): 41–51; and George Stalk, Jr. and Thomas M. Hout, *Competing Against Time* (New York: The Free Press, 1990).

41. According to Henry Mintzberg, there are four reasons why organizations need strategies: (1) to set direction; (2) to focus effort of contributors; (3) to define the organization; and (4) to provide consistency. For more, see Henry Mintzberg, "The Strategy Concept II: Another Look at Why Organizations Need Strategies," *California Management Review,* 30 (Fall 1987): 25–32.

42. Waldron Berry, "Beyond Strategic Planning," *Managerial Planning,* 29 (March–April 1981): 14.

43. See Taylor, "Corporate Planning for the 1990s," p. 17.

44. Charles H. Roush, Jr., and Ben C. Ball, Jr., "Controlling the Implementation of Strategy," *Managerial Planning,* 29 (November–December 1980): 4.

45. Donald C. Hambrick and Albert A. Cannella, Jr., "Strategy Implementation as Substance and Selling," *The Academy of Management Executive,* 3 (November 1989): 282–283. Another good discussion of strategic implementation may be found in Dale D. McConkey, "Planning in a Changing Environment," *Business Horizons,* 31 (September–October 1988): 64–72.

46. William D. Guth and Ian C. Macmillan, "Strategy Implementation Versus Middle Management Self-Interest," *Strategic Management Journal,* 7 (July–August 1986): 321.

47. See Michael Goold and John J. Quinn, "The Paradox of Strategic Controls," *Strategic Management Journal,* 11 (January 1990): 43–57; and Georg Kellinghusen and Klaus Wubbenhorst, "Strategic Control for Improved Performance," *Long Range Planning,* 23 (June 1990): 30–40.

48. See Vasudevan Ramanujan and N. Venkatraman, "Planning and Performance: A New Look at an Old Question," *Business Horizons,* 30 (May–June 1987): 19–25.

49. A critique of the conventional strategic-management model may be found in David K. Hurst, "Why Strategic Management Is Bankrupt," *Organizational Dynamics,* 15 (Autumn 1986): 4–27.

50. Based on George A. Steiner, *Top Management Planning* (New York: Macmillan, 1969), p. 17.

51. For a brief discussion of success factors in forecasting, see Steven P. Schnaars, "Off-the-Mark Forecasting," *The Journal of Business Strategy,* 11 (May–June 1990): 64.

52. An excellent overview of forecasting techniques may be found in David M. Georgoff and Robert G. Murdick, "Manager's Guide to Forecasting," *Harvard Business Review,* 64 (January–February 1986): 110–120.

53. Based on C. W. J. Granger, *Forecasting in Business and Economics* (New York: Academic Press, 1980): 6–10.

54. Lois Therrien, "How Hasbro Became King of the Toymakers," *Business Week* (September 22, 1986): 91.

55. Steven P. Schnaars, "How to Develop and Use Scenarios," *Long Range Planning,* 20 (February 1987): 106.

56. See Manuel Werner, "Planning for Uncertain Futures: Building Commitment Through Scenario Planning," *Business Horizons,* 33 (May–June 1990): 55–58; and P. R. Stokke, W. K. Ralston, T. A. Boyce, and I. H. Wilson, "Scenario Planning for Norwegian Oil and Gas," *Long Range Planning,* 23 (April 1990): 17–26.

57. See Wendy Zellner, "Chrysler's Next Generation," *Business Week* (December 19, 1988): 52–57.

7

Decision Making and Creative Problem Solving

● ● ● ● ● ● ● ● ● ● ● ● ● ● ● ●

If I had to sum up in one word the qualities that make a good manager, I'd say that it all comes down to decisiveness.

LEE IACOCCA

CHAPTER OBJECTIVES

When you finish studying this chapter, you should be able to

- Specify at least five sources of decision complexity for modern managers.
- Explain what a condition of risk is and what managers can do to cope with it.
- Define and discuss the three decision traps: framing, escalation of commitment, and overconfidence.
- Discuss why programmed and nonprogrammed decisions require different decision-making procedures.
- Explain the need for a contingency approach to group-aided decision making.
- Identify and briefly describe five of the ten "mental locks" that can inhibit creativity.
- List and explain the four basic steps in the creative problem-solving process.

● ●

Apple Computer Polishes Its Act

Its humble beginnings and phenomenal growth have made Apple Computer, Inc., a Silicon Valley legend. The Cupertino, California, company in only seven years zoomed from a shoestring operation in a computer whiz kid's garage to a position on *Fortune*'s list of the 500 largest companies in America.

In 1975, twenty-one-year-old Steve Jobs and twenty-six-year-old Steve Wozniak took the $1,300 from the sale of Wozniak's Volkswagen bus and started building personal computers in Jobs's garage. The combination of Jobs's visionary thinking—"computerize the masses"—and Wozniak's technical genius enabled the pair to gather financial support to launch their business in 1977. Little did the young entrepreneurs know at the time where their adventure would lead. By 1990, Apple was number 96 on the Fortune 500, its annual sales were $5.3 billion, and an organizational revolution had severed Wozniak and Jobs's connections with Apple.

A Corporate Shoot-out

In the early years, when it was undisputed master of the personal computer market, a youthful shoot-from-the-hip atmosphere pervaded Apple. New employees received an "Apple Values" list extolling the virtues of innovation, vision, team spirit, and excellence. Blue jeans were the preferred attire. Conflict and coordination were common— so much so that, from 1979 to 1982, two new products were designed by divisions that acted more like separate companies. One, the Lisa, was to be a higher-priced business computer. The other, the Macintosh (or Mac) targeted the lower-priced personal computer market.

Cofounder Steve Jobs, then a vice president, was assigned to head the Mac project; other top executives thought he was too inexperienced and erratic for the larger Lisa project. In his typical enthusiastic and emotional style, Jobs promptly made a $5,000 race-to-completion bet with the Lisa division head and rushed off to recruit top talent. "The competition that developed between divisions sometimes verged on fratricide. At one point a pirate flag flapped above the Mac building as an expression of battle. The Mac team was often condescending about the quality of Lisa."[1]

Working around the clock, Jobs skillfully used parties, stock options, promises of fame and fortune, impulsive deadlines, and bursts of ranting and raving to drive his team to success. His strong sense of aesthetics and feel for the average person kept the Mac designers dedicated to building a machine with unprecedented "user-friendliness."

In the end, Lisa did beat Mac to the marketplace by a full year, but its sales were so disappointing that it was discontinued in 1985. In the meantime, though, larger battles were raging.

Enter: John Sculley

In 1981, Apple was the number-one personal computer company with 41 percent of the U.S. market. By 1983, IBM, with its highly successful Personal Computer, had taken the lead, cutting Apple's share to 24 percent in two years. Realizing that Apple was being outmarketed, Jobs, who had become chairman of the board in 1981, recruited John Sculley from PepsiCo. in mid-1983. Sculley, who had "paid his dues" by driving a Pepsi truck and working in a bottling plant in Pittsburgh, had worked his way up to the presidency of Pepsi-Cola, PepsiCo's U.S. soft-drink division. Most important, from Jobs's viewpoint, Sculley knew mass marketing inside out.

As the new president of Apple, Sculley took quick steps to introduce some discipline. He reorganized Apple from four to two divisions, breaking up the product cliques and giving the company a sense of direction. He also focused on small details: phones were to be answered promptly and memos confined to one page.

Relying on his marketing background, Sculley insisted that product introductions made prior to his arrival be analyzed carefully to discover where mistakes had been made. According to *Fortune*:

Sculley also engendered loyalty through his low-key, unegotistical style and his willingness to roll up his sleeves and work. After the volatile leadership of Jobs, who was known to rave and break into tears while haranguing his troops, Sculley's even temperament was a welcome change.[2]

Exit: Steve Jobs

For nearly two years, Jobs and Sculley were hailed as a model entrepreneur/manager team. But by early 1985 it became apparent that Jobs's erratic style had to be reined in if Apple was to become more disciplined. In May 1985, following Jobs's unsuccessful bid to dump Sculley, a major reorganization engineered by Sculley stripped Jobs of authority for daily operations. Jobs and Sculley began to quarrel openly. Four months later, Jobs resigned from the company he had co-

founded eight years earlier (Wozniak had departed in early 1985). Combined with Apple's first losing quarter ever, this event dealt Apple's self-confidence a severe blow.

More New Blood

Sculley's comeback strategy involved introducing cutting-edge products, such as the Macintosh II, to capture a share of the lucrative business market. The new Mac was sophisticated, expensive, and profitable. Indeed, profits tripled between 1986 and 1989. Reality set in during 1990, however, as sales growth slumped and Apple's share of the U.S. personal computer market dropped to 9 percent. Again, Sculley swung into action with yet another reorganization and a new two-pronged strategy calling for a broader line of computers and lower prices. German-born Michael H. Spindler, architect of Apple's successful European effort, was promoted to chief operating officer (one rung below Sculley) and put in charge of marketing and daily operations. Sculley, Apple's marketing guru, surprised everyone by taking charge of technology development. Spindler's immediate layoff of 400 employees sent a clear signal that belt-tightening time had come to Apple. As *Business Week* observed at the time: "Starting with the 1991 corporate business plan, more stringent controls are in place. And planning has become more of a discipline and less of a fantasy."[3]

Morale sagged among the firm's 12,000 employees. At risk was Apple's free-wheeling culture that many believed had spawned the firm's most creative ideas. Observers were left to wonder if Sculley's latest moves would turn out to be the solution or the problem.

Years ago, the story goes, a jack-of-all-trades who had a difficult time staying employed finally landed the perfect job. He excitedly told his best friend that he had found a job sorting potatoes and that he was sure he would never quit. A couple of weeks passed before the two saw each other again. "How's the new job going?" asked the friend. "It was terrible," answered the jack-of-all-trades. "I quit last week." "Why?" asked the friend. "I thought it was easy. In fact, you said you'd never quit." "It was okay for a while," replied the jack-of-all-trades. "All I had to do was put the big potatoes in one bag, the medium in another, and the small in a third, but eventually all that decision making burned me out!"

As this story indicates, decision making is not for the fainthearted. Nevertheless, decision making is one of the primary responsibilities of managers at all levels. The quality of a manager's decisions not only contributes to the success or failure of the organization but greatly affects his or her personal success as well. Both Apple Computer's and John Sculley's future ride on his decision-making ability.

decision making identifying and choosing alternative courses of action

Decision making is the process of identifying and choosing alternative courses of action in a manner appropriate to the demands of the situation. The act of choosing implies that alternative courses of action must be weighed and weeded out. Thus judgment and discretion are fundamental to decision making. This chapter highlights major challenges for decision makers, introduces a general decision-making model, discusses group-aided decision making, and examines creativity and problem solving.

Challenges for Decision Makers

Though decision making has never been easy, it is especially challenging for today's managers. In an era of accelerating change, the pace of decision making has also accelerated. According to Alvin Toffler, "The very speed of change introduces a new element into management, forcing executives, already nervous in an unfamiliar environment, to make more and more decisions at a faster and faster pace. Response times are honed to a minimum."[4] In addition to having to cope with this acceleration, today's decision makers face a host of tough challenges. Ones we will discuss here include: (1) complex streams of decisions, (2) uncertainty, (3) information processing styles, and (4) perceptual and behavioral decision traps.

Dealing with Complex Streams of Decisions

Above all else, today's decision situations are not neat and tidy. A pair of experts recently lent realism to the subject by using the analogy of a stream:

Specify at least five sources of decision complexity for modern managers.

> *If decisions can be viewed as streams—streams containing countless bits of information, events, and choices—then how should decision makers be viewed? . . . The streams flowing through the organization do not wait for them; they flow around them. The streams do not serve up problems neatly wrapped and ready for choice. Rather, they deliver the bits and pieces, the problems and choices, in no particular order. . . .*

Corporate decision makers are under pressure to make not only sound business decision, but the *right* decisions as well. In the cosmetics and pharmaceuticals industries, the controversial practice of animal testing is under fire. Socially conscious consumers do not want their toiletries certified irritation-free at the expense of laboratory animals that experience pain, disfigurement, even death. This industry-wide conference, sponsored by Bristol-Myers Squibb Company, advanced the search for non-animal testing procedures.

In short, decision makers in an organization are floating in the stream, jostled capriciously by problems popping up, and finding anchors through action at a given time in a given place.[5]

Importantly, the foregoing is a recognition of complexity, *not* an admission of hopelessness. A working knowledge of seven intertwined factors[*] contributing to decision complexity can help decision makers successfully navigate the stream (see Figure 7.1). They include:

1. *Multiple Criteria.* Typically, a decision today must satisfy a number of often conflicting criteria representing the interests of different groups. For example, a decision to install expensive smokestack pollution-control equipment may please environmentalists but anger some stockholders because of lower dividends. Identifying stakeholders and balancing their conflicting interests is a major challenge for today's decision makers.

2. *Intangibles.* Factors such as customer good will, employee morale, increased bureaucracy, and aesthetic appeal (for example, a billboard on a scenic highway), although difficult to measure, often determine decision alternatives.

3. *Risk and Uncertainty.* Along with every decision alternative goes the chance that it will fail in some way. Poor choices can prove costly, as PepsiCo found out in 1989 when it released a TV commercial featuring Madonna enjoying a Pepsi to the beat of her hit "Like a Prayer":

   Faced with a raging controversy over the religious imagery in Madonna's new music video and the threat of a consumer boycott, Pepsi pulled the plug on the spot after running it only twice. Pepsi claimed viewers confused the commercial with Madonna's more racy and sexually suggestive "Prayer" video. The total cost of the slip-up: a reported $10 million.[6]

   Because of the importance of this particular aspect of decision complexity, we shall devote special attention to it in the next section.

4. *Long-term Implications.* Managers are becoming increasingly aware that their decisions have not only intended short-term impact but also unintended long-term impact. For example, Chrysler's management responded to lower sales during the 1974–1975 recession by cutting capital spending and laying off engineers and designers. Although these cost-cutting decisions helped Chrysler reduce its short-run losses, the firm's long-term competitiveness was nearly destroyed because of obsolete facilities and a shortage of creative talent.[7]

5. *Interdisciplinary Input.* Decision complexity is greatly increased when technical specialists such as lawyers, consumer advocates, tax advisers, accountants, engineers, and production and marketing experts are consulted before making a decision. This also is a time-consuming process.

[*]"How to Cope with Increasing Complexity" by Robert L. Kenney. Reprinted, by permission of publisher, from *Personnel*, September 1979 © 1979. American Management Association, New York. All rights reserved.

FIGURE 7.1 • Sources of Complexity for Today's Managerial Decision Makers

6. *Pooled Decision Making.* Rarely is a single manager totally responsible for an entire package of decisions. A single decision is usually a link in a chain that is passed from hand to hand. For example, one team of researchers charted the path of a major decision to purchase costly medical equipment in a hospital[8] (see Figure 7.2). Notice how a complex series of recommendations preceded final budget approval by the governing board.

7. *Value Judgments.* As long as decisions are made by people with differing backgrounds, perceptions, aspirations, and values, the decision-making process will be marked by disagreement over what is right or wrong, good or bad, and ethical or unethical[9] (see Management Ethics).

Considering all of the foregoing sources of decision complexity together, it is clear that they are not merely passing problems. Each promises to loom even larger on the decision-making horizon in the years to come.

Coping with Uncertainty

Among the valuable contributions of decision theorists are classification schemes for types and degrees of uncertainty. (Recall our distinction, in Chapter 5, about three types of uncertainty: state, effect, and response uncertainty). We are all aware of varying degrees of uncertainty in our daily personal lives. We attach

▶**FIGURE 7.2** • Many People Typically Have a Hand in Important Organizational Decisions: A Real-Life Example

Source: Alan D. Meyer, "Mingling Decision Making Metaphors," *Academy of Management Review,* 9 (January 1984): 9. Reprinted by permission.

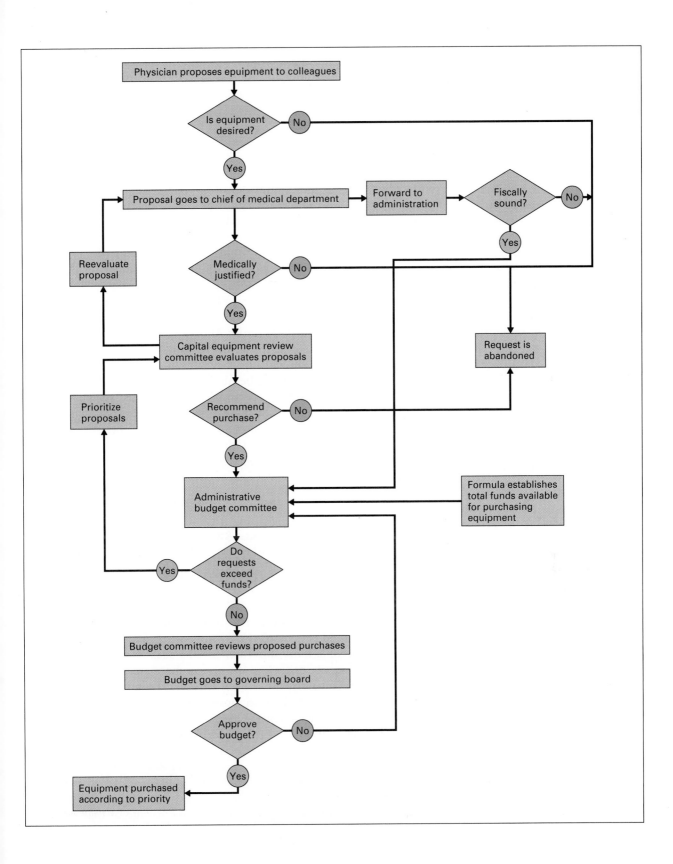

The Economics of Ethical Decisions

For some companies, social responsibility is as important as profit. In Chapter 4 we saw how The Body Shop and Ben & Jerry's not only donate money to worthy causes, but try to use every aspect of their business to make the world a better place. But for other companies, paying lip service to corporate social responsibility is simply a marketing ploy, a way to get people to buy their products. Consumers who want to invest their money in a socially responsible company or spend it on socially responsible products now must often analyze *why* a company made a decision to pursue a particular kind of responsible behavior.

According to a recent poll, two-thirds of American shoppers consider a company's social performance and 52 percent are willing to pay an extra 10 percent for a socially responsible product. A "do-good" image can bring a company profit. Procter & Gamble received a large boost of positive publicity when Alaskan rescuers used its Dawn detergent to wash oil-covered animals. And companies like Coca-Cola, Anheuser-Busch, and Evian may have been looking for publicity when they gave cases of their beverages to thirsty American soldiers during the Persian Gulf War.

A number of groups currently make it their business to ensure that the public hears about a company's behavior toward society, good and bad. The Council on Economic Priorities hands out yearly awards, both positive (to, for example, Eastman Kodak, for its equal-opportunity programs) and negative—one of the 1989 awards went to John Morrell & Co. for "willfully ignoring" unsafe conditions in its plants.

Corporate donations—one aspect of social responsibility—peaked in 1986, when the average corporation gave almost 2 percent of its pretax profits to philanthropic organizations. But the threat of takeover has scared many companies into cutting back on any spending that does not lead directly to profit. And, of course, some companies make no effort to be socially responsible, either because they believe the business of business is *business,* or because they fear that it is impossible to satisfy everyone's definition of "socially correct." Such fears are justified. Despite donating $135 million in 1989, IBM was criticized for doing business with South Africa, and even Ben & Jerry's has felt the heat because—what else?—its ice cream is fattening.

Sources: Dan Cordtz, "Corporate Citizenship," *Financial World* (May 29, 1990): 30–36; Guy Halverson, "Companies Recognized for 'Corporate Conscience,'" *The Christian Science Monitor* (March 3, 1989): 9; Mark Landler, "Publicity? Why, It Never Even Occurred to Us," *Business Week* (September 24, 1990): 46; Karen Springen and Annetta Miller, "Doing the Right Thing," *Newsweek* (January 7, 1991): 42–43.

high degrees of certainty and confidence to the prospect that the sun will rise tomorrow and that a brand new battery will start our car. But confidence drops when circumstances become more uncertain. Events such as obtaining a loan, getting an *A* on a final exam, or finding the perfect mate are plagued by doubt and apprehension. Unfortunately, life is filled with uncertainties, and managers are continually asked to make the best decisions they can in spite of uncertainties about both present and future circumstances.

Managers who are able to assess the degree of certainty in a situation, whether conditions are certain, risky, or uncertain, are able to make more effective decisions. As illustrated in Figure 7.3, there is a negative correlation between uncertainty and the decision maker's confidence in a decision. In other words, the more uncertain a manager is about the principal factors in a decision, the less confident he or she will be about the successful outcome of that decision.

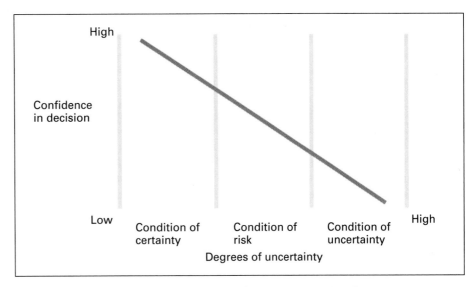

FIGURE 7.3 • The Relationship Between Uncertainty and Confidence

The key, of course, lies not in eliminating uncertainty, because it cannot be eliminated, but rather in learning to work within an acceptable range of uncertainty.

condition of certainty solid factual basis allows accurate prediction of decision's outcome

Certainty. **A condition of certainty** exists when there is no doubt about the factual basis of a particular decision and its outcome can be predicted accurately. Much like the economic concept of pure competition, the concept of certainty is useful mainly as a theoretical anchor point for a continuum. In a world filled with uncertainties, certainty is relative rather than absolute. For example, the decision to order more rivets for a manufacturing firm's fabrication department is based on the relative certainty that the current rate of use will exhaust the rivet inventory on a specific date. But even in this case, uncertainties about the possible misuse or theft of rivets creep in to reduce confidence. Since nothing is truly certain, conditions of risk and uncertainty are the general rule for managers, not the exception.

● ● ● ● ● ● ● ● ● ● ● ● ● ● ● ● ●

Explain what a condition of risk is and what managers can do to cope with it.

condition of risk decision made on basis of incomplete but reliable information

Risk. **A condition of risk** is said to exist when a decision must be made on the basis of incomplete but reliable factual information. Reliable information, though incomplete, is still useful to managers in coping with risk since they can use it to calculate the probability that a given event will occur and then to select a decision alternative with favorable odds.[10]

objective probabilities odds derived mathematically from reliable data

subjective probabilities odds based on judgment

The two basic types of probabilities are objective and subjective. **Objective probabilities** are derived mathematically from reliable historical data, whereas **subjective probabilities** are estimated from past experience or judgment. Decision making based on probabilities is common in all areas of management today. For instance, laundry product manufacturers would not think of launching a new detergent without determining its probability of acceptance by means of consumer panels and test marketing. A number of inferential statistical techniques can help managers objectively cope with risk.

The National Geographic Society Runs to Keep Up with World Events

. . . [In the summer of 1990], cartographers at the National Geographic Society . . . were putting the final touches on the latest edition of the Society's atlas, the first in nearly a decade and one of its biggest publishing events in years.

But at the last minute history refused to cooperate.

As the presses started rolling there was still no word on the final detail of the biggest map-making story of the post-war era decade: whether the capital of a united Germany would be Bonn or Berlin. With time running out, the editors decided to put stars on both cities.

"We wanted to be timely and up to date with the atlas but no one was willing to make the call," recalls John Garver, National Geographic's chief cartographer.

Finally, on September 21, a late call came from the German Embassy: the East and West German parliaments had just voted for Berlin. After a hasty conference, senior Geographic officials decided to stop the presses, close down the bindery, and print new maps.

The switch cost $100,000 and left the Society with 2,000 unusable atlases, probably soon to become collectors' items. But when the new atlas goes on sale . . . , it will be the first to record the historic events that have reshaped Europe.

"It was all quite nerve racking," says Barbara Hand of the Geographic's public affairs office. "This is probably our most challenging world atlas."

The small drama played out . . . in Washington illustrates the problem of keeping up in a world of political change that threatens to make every existing map, atlas, and globe obsolete.

Source: Excerpted from George D. Moffett III, "U.S. Mapmakers Scurry To Keep Up With Events," *The Christian Science Monitor* (October 4, 1990): 5. Reprinted by permission from *The Christian Science Monitor.* © 1990 The Christian Science Publishing Society. All rights reserved.

condition of uncertainty no reliable factual information available

Uncertainty. A condition of uncertainty exists when little or no reliable factual information is available. Although there is no data base from which to calculate objective probabilities, judgmental or subjective probabilities can still be estimated. Decision making under conditions of uncertainty can be nerve-racking for managers. Decision confidence is lowest when a condition of uncertainty prevails because decisions are then based on educated guesses rather than on hard factual data. For example, see The World of Management.

Information Processing Styles

Thinking is one of those activities we engage in constantly, yet seldom pause to examine systematically. But within the context of managerial decision making and problem solving, it is important that one's thinking does not get into an unproductive rut. The quality of our decisions is a direct reflection of how we process information.

Researchers have identified two general information processing styles: the thinking style and the intuitive style.[11] One is not superior to the other (see Figure 7.4). Both are needed during organizational problem solving. Managers who rely predominantly on the *thinking* style tend to be logical, precise, and objective. They prefer routine assignments that require attention to detail and systematic

Brain skill emphasized	Type of organization where predominant	Task preference	Problem solving/ decision making style	Example applications	Sample occcupational specialty
Thinking	• Traditional • Pyramid	• Routine • Precision • Detail • Implementation • Repetitve	• Deductive • Objective • Prefers solving problems by breakdown into parts, then approaching the problem sequentially using logic.	• Model building • Projection	• Planning • Management science • Financial management • Engineering • Law enforcement • Military
Intuitive	• Open • Temporary • Rapidly changing	• Non-routine • Broad issues • General policy options • Constant new assignments	• Inductive • Subjective • Prefers solving problems by looking at the whole, then approching the problem through hunches.	• Brain-storming • Challenging traditional assumptions	• Personnel • Marketing • Organization development • Intelligence

FIGURE 7.4 • Two General Information Processing Styles

Source: Weston H. Agor, "Managing Brain Skills: The Last Frontier," *Personnel Administrator,* 32 (October 1987): 58, Figure 1. Used with permission.

implementation. Conversely, managers who are predominantly *intuitive* find comfort in rapidly changing situations in which they can be creative and follow their hunches. Intuitive managers see things in complex patterns rather than as logically ordered bits and pieces.[12] Of course, not everyone falls neatly into one of these two categories; many people process information through a combination of the two styles.

The important thing to recognize here is that managers approach decision making and problem solving in very different ways, depending on their information processing styles. Their approaches, perceptions, and recommendations vary because their minds work differently. In traditional pyramid work organizations, where the thinking style tends to prevail, intuitive employees may be criticized for being imprecise and rocking the boat. A concerted effort needs to be made to tap the creative skills of "intuitives" and the implementation abilities of "thinkers." An appreciation for alternative information processing styles needs to be cultivated because they complement one another.[13]

• • • • • • • • • • • • • • •

Define and discuss the three decision traps: framing, escalation of commitment, and over-confidence.

Avoiding Perceptual and Behavioral Decision Traps

Behavioral scientists have identified some common human tendencies capable of eroding the quality of decision making. Three well-documented ones are framing, escalation, and overconfidence. Awareness and conscious avoidance of these traps can give decision makers a competitive edge.

framing error how information is presented influences
one's interpretation of it

Framing Error.   One's judgment can be altered and shaped by how information
is presented or labeled. In other words, labels create frames of reference with the
power to bias our interpretations. **Framing error** is the tendency to evaluate
positively presented information favorably and negatively presented information
unfavorably.[14] Those evaluations, in turn, influence one's behavior. A recent
study with 80 male and 80 female University of Iowa students documented the
framing-interpretation-behavior linkage. Half of each gender group was told
about a cancer treatment with a 50 percent success rate. The other two groups
heard about the same cancer treatment but were told it had a 50 percent failure
rate. The researchers summed up results of the study as follows:

> *Describing a medical treatment as having a 50 percent success rate led
> to higher ratings of perceived effectiveness and higher likelihood of
> recommending the treatment to others, including family members, than
> describing the treatment as having a 50 percent failure rate.*[15]

Framing thus influenced both interpretations and intended behavior. Given the
importance of the information in this study (cancer treatment), ethical questions
arise about the potential abuse of framing error.

In organizations, framing error can be used constructively or destructively.
Advertisers, for instance, take full advantage of this perceptual tendency when
attempting to sway consumers' purchasing decisions. A leading brand of cat litter
boasts of being 99 percent dust free. Meanwhile, a shampoo claims to be fortified
with 1 percent natural protein. Thanks to framing error, we tend to perceive
very little dust in the cat litter and a lot of protein in the shampoo! Managers
who couch their proposals in favorable terms hope to benefit from framing error.
And who can blame them? On the negative side, prejudice and bigotry thrive on
framing error. A male manager who believes women can't manage might frame
interview results so that John looks good and Mary looks bad.

Escalation of Commitment.   Why are people slow to write off bad investments?
Why do companies stick to unprofitable strategies? And why has the government
typically continued to fund over-budget and behind-schedule weapons systems?
Escalation of commitment is a possible explanation for these diverse situations.[16]
Escalation of commitment is the tendency of individuals and organizations to get
locked into losing courses of action because *quitting is personally and socially
difficult.* This decision-making trap has been called the "throwing good money
after bad" dilemma. Those victimized by escalation of commitment often are
heard talking about "sunk costs" and "too much time and money invested to
quit now." Within the context of management, psychological, social, and organizational factors conspire to encourage escalation of commitment (see Figure 7.5).

escalation of commitment
people get locked into losing
courses of action to avoid embarrassment of quitting or admitting error

The model in Figure 7.5 can be brought to life by using it to analyze a
highly unusual decision by the Pentagon in 1991. Two giant defense contractors,
McDonnell Douglas and General Dynamics, were under contract to design and
build the A-12 attack plane. All told, 620 of the aircraft carrier-based bombers
were to be built for the U.S. Navy at a cost of $60 billion. With the A-12 program
18 months behind schedule and $2.7 billion over budget, Secretary of Defense
Richard Cheney terminated the contract. It was the Pentagon's biggest cancellation ever. An appreciation of the contributing factors in Figure 7.5 underscores

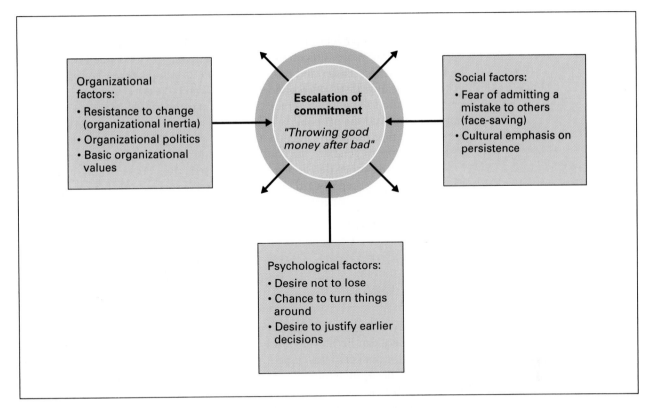

FIGURE 7.5 ● Why Escalation of Commitment is So Common

Source: Adapted from discussion in Barry M. Staw and Jerry Ross, "Understanding Behavior in Escalation Situations," *Science,* 246 (October 13, 1989): 216–220.

how truly unusual Cheney's decision was. Psychologically, his termination decision flew in the face of three possible motives for throwing good money after bad. Cheney went against the social grain as well by publicly admitting the Defense Department's mistake and doing something culturally distasteful to Americans, giving up. (American folk heroes tend to be persistent to the bitter end.) Finally, Cheney had to overcome bureaucratic resistance in the defense establishment. He also had to withstand political opposition from the contractors about their having to lay off 8,000 A-12 project employees. Nevertheless, despite many pressures to continue the program, Cheney killed it. Normally, as in the case of the Vietnam War, the forces of escalation carry the day.

Reality checks, in the form of comparing actual progress with effectiveness and efficiency standards, are the best way to keep escalation in check. In Cheney's case, he concluded: "No one can tell me exactly how much more it will cost to keep this [A-12] program going. And I do not believe that a bailout is in the national interest. If we cannot spend the taxpayers' money wisely, we will not spend it."[17] This is an instructive lesson for all potential victims of escalation.

Overconfidence. The term *overconfidence* is commonplace and requires no technical definition. We need to comprehend the psychology of overconfidence because it can expose managers to unreasonable risks. Ironically, researchers have found a positive relationship between overconfidence and task difficulty. In other words, the more difficult the task, the greater the tendency for people to be overconfident.[18] Easier and more predictable situations foster confidence, but generally not unrealistic overconfidence. People may be overconfident about one or more of the following: accuracy of input data; individual, team, or organizational ability; and the probability of success. There are various theoretical explanations for this research evidence. One likely reason is that overconfidence is often necessary to generate the courage needed to tackle difficult situations.

As with the other decision traps, managerial awareness of this problem is the important first step toward avoiding it. Careful analysis of situational factors, critical thinking about decision alternatives, and honest input from stakeholders can help managers avoid overconfidence.

Making Decisions

••••••••••••••••••
Discuss why pro-
grammed and nonpro-
grammed decisions
require different
decision-making pro-
cedures.

It stands to reason that if the degree of uncertainty varies from situation to situation, there can be no single way to make decisions. A second variable with which decision makers must cope is the number of times a particular decision is made. Some decisions are made frequently, perhaps several times a day. Others are made infrequently or just once. Consequently, decision theorists have distinguished between programmed and nonprogrammed decisions.[19] Each of these types of decisions requires a different procedure.

Making Programmed Decisions

programmed decisions repetitive and routine decisions

Programmed decisions are those that are repetitive and routine. Examples include hiring decisions in a personnel office, billing decisions in a hospital, supply re-order decisions in a purchasing department, consumer loan decisions in a bank, and pricing decisions in a university bookstore. Managers tend to devise fixed procedures for handling these everyday decisions. Most decisions made by the typical manager on a daily basis are of the programmed variety.

decision rule tells when and
how programmed decisions
should be made

At the heart of the programmed decision procedure are decision rules. A **decision rule** is a statement that identifies the situation in which a decision is required and specifies how the decision will be made. Behind decision rules is the idea that standard, recurring problems need to be solved only once. Decision rules permit busy managers to make routine decisions quickly without having to go through comprehensive problem solving over and over again. Generally, decision rules should be stated in "if-then" terms. A decision rule for a consumer loan officer in a bank, for example, might be: "*If* the applicant is employed, has no record of loan default, and can put up 20 percent collateral, *then* a loan not to exceed $10,000 can be authorized." Carefully conceived decision rules can streamline the decision-making process by allowing lower-level managers to shoulder the responsibility for programmed decisions and freeing higher-level managers for relatively more important, nonprogrammed decisions.

Making Nonprogrammed Decisions

Nonprogrammed decisions are those made in complex, important, and nonroutine situations, often under new and largely unfamiliar circumstances. This kind of decision is made much less frequently than are programmed decisions. Examples of nonprogrammed decisions include deciding whether to merge with another company, how to replace an executive who died unexpectedly, whether a foreign branch should be opened, and how to market an entirely new kind of product or service. The following six questions need to be asked prior to making a nonprogrammed decision:

1. What decision needs to be made?
2. When does it have to be made?
3. Who will decide?
4. Who will need to be consulted prior to making the decision?
5. Who will ratify or veto the decision?
6. Who will need to be informed of the decision?[20]

The decision-making process becomes more sharply focused when managers take the time to answer these questions.

One respected decision theorist has described nonprogrammed decisions as follows: "There is no cut-and-dried method for handling the problem because it hasn't arisen before, or because its precise nature and structure are elusive or complex, or because it is so important that it deserves a custom-tailored treatment."[21]

Nonprogrammed decision making calls for creative problem solving. The four-step problem-solving process introduced later in this chapter helps managers make effective and efficient nonprogrammed decisions.

A General Decision-Making Model

Although different decision procedures are required for different situations, it is possible to construct a general decision-making model. Figure 7.6 shows an idealized, logical, and rational model of organizational decision making. Importantly, it describes how decisions can be made, but it does not portray how managers actually make decisions. In fact, on-the-job research found managers did not follow a rational and logical series of steps when making decisions.[22] Why, then, should we even consider a rational, logical model? Once again, as in the case of the strategic management process in Chapter 6, a rational descriptive model has instructional value because it identifies key components of a complex process. It also suggests a better way of doing things.

The first step, a scan of the situation, is important, although it often is underemphasized or ignored altogether in discussions of managerial decision making. Scanning answers the question "How do I know a decision should be made?" Over fifty years ago, Chester I. Barnard gave one of the best answers to this question, stating that "the occasions for decision originate in three distinct fields: (a) from authoritative communications from superiors; (b) from cases referred for decision by subordinates; (c) from cases originating in the initiative of

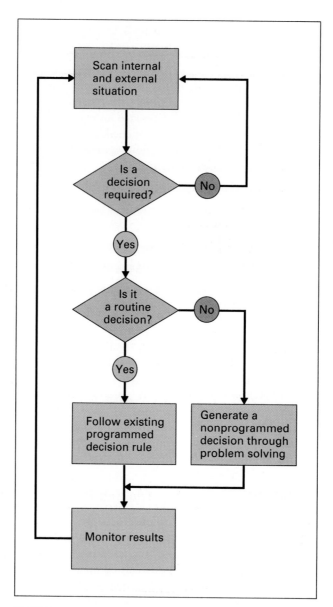

FIGURE 7.6 • A General Decision-making Model

the [manager] concerned."[23] In addition to signaling when a decision is required, scanning reveals the degree of uncertainty and provides necessary information for pending decisions.

When the need for a decision has been established, the manager must determine whether the situation is routine. If it is routine and there is an appropriate decision rule, the rule is applied. But if it turns out to be a new situation demanding a nonprogrammed decision, comprehensive problem solving begins. In either case, the results of the final decision need to be monitored to see if any follow-up action is necessary.

Group-aided decision making in today's global economy typically is an international affair. This particular meeting involves joint venture partners from China and the United States discussing a $530 million expansion of a paper pulp mill in Castlegar, British Columbia, Canada. By combining money, technical expertise, and decision-making ability, the Chinese firm (Celgar Pulp Company) and the American company (Stone Container Corp.) hope to reduce their exposure to unreasonable risk and maximize their return.

●●●●●●●●●●●●●●●●●

Explain the need for a contingency approach to group-aided decision making.

Group-Aided Decision Making: A Contingency Perspective

Decision making, like any other organizational activity, does not take place in a vacuum. Typically, decision making is a highly social activity with committees, study groups, review panels, or task teams contributing in a variety of ways. At least five aspects of the decision-making process can be assigned to groups:

1. Analyzing the problem.
2. Identifying components of the decision situation.
3. Estimating components of the decision situation [for example, determining probabilities, feasibilities, time estimates, and payoffs].
4. Designing alternatives.
5. Choosing an alternative.[24]

Assuming that two (or more) heads may be better than one and that managers can make better use of their time by delegating various decision-making chores, there is a strong case for turning to groups when making decisions. But before bringing others into the decision process, managers need to be aware of the problems of dispersed accountability and consider the trade-off between the advantages and disadvantages of group-aided decision making. In view of these problems and of research evidence comparing individual and group performance, a contingency approach is recommended. (See Managers in Action.)

The Problem of Dispersed Accountability

There is a critical difference between group-aided decision making and group decision making. In the first instance, the group does everything except make the final decision. In the second instance, the group actually makes the final decision. Managers who choose the second route face a dilemma. Although a decision made by a group probably will reflect the collective experience and wisdom of all those involved, personal accountability is lost. Blame for a joint decision that fails is too easily passed on to others.

The traditional formula for resolving this problem is to make sure that a given manager is personally accountable for a decision when the responsibility for it has to be traced. According to this line of reasoning, even when a group is asked to recommend a decision, the responsibility for the final outcome remains with the manager in charge. For managers who want to maintain the integrity of personal accountability, there is no such thing as group decision making; there is only group-*aided* decision making. Three situations in which individual accountability for a decision is necessary are when:

- The decision will have significant impact on the success or failure of the unit or organization.
- The decision has legal ramifications (such as possible prosecution for price-fixing, antitrust, or product safety violations).

Decision Making in the Bush White House

The policies and beliefs of George Bush may not differ radically from those of his predecessor in the White House, Ronald Reagan, but as a manager and decision maker, Bush has emerged as his own man. Bush's natural inclinations lead him to dive into a problem and solve it himself. He has a masterful grasp of the workings of Washington, but he often circumvents bureaucracy, getting answers for himself. Especially when dealing with foreign policy questions, Bush loves to get on the phone and talk directly to an expert or government leader he knows personally as a result of his years of government service as vice president, United Nations ambassador, and CIA director.

Although many in Washington welcome this interest in details and penchant for personal involvement, at times Bush can get too entangled. Before the American invasion of Panama, he personally took control of reacting to a coup against Panamanian dictator Manuel Noriega. Overwhelmed with raw information, much of it contradictory, Bush was unable to make a quick decision. Without adequate U.S. support, the coup failed.

Having learned from such incidents, Bush now delegates more responsibility, and his general decision-making process is consultative and consensual. When dealing with difficult policy questions, he calls together cabinet members or other trusted aides who hold opposing views and has them argue in front of him, while he takes notes and asks questions. After listening to such debates, Bush makes his own decision, sometimes taking the middle ground between the debaters, as he did on the new clean air act, sometimes going his own way, as he did by taking a more hawkish stance on Iraq than did his Joint Chiefs of Staff.

Loyalty is a key virtue in George Bush's world, and most of his advisers are his old friends. After the debates, when the President has made a decision, his advisers stand behind it, projecting a greater sense of unity and team solidarity than was common in the Reagan White House. Although such solidarity is comforting to the nation, especially in times of crisis, it may contribute to the most problematic aspect of Bush's decision-making style. Surrounded by loyal old friends from a single homogeneous social group—affluent, well-educated, white males—Bush must guard against too-easy agreement and the emergence of groupthink.

Sources: Ann Reilly Dowd, "How Bush Manages the Presidency," *Fortune* (August 27, 1990): 68–75; Michael Duffy, "Mr. Consensus," *Time* (August 21, 1989): 16–22; Evan Thomas, "The One True Hawk in the Administration," *Newsweek* (January 7, 1991): 19.

- A competitive reward is tied to a successful decision. (For example, only one person can get a promotion.)

In less critical areas, the group itself may be responsible for making decisions.

Advantages and Disadvantages of Group-aided Decision Making

Various combinations of positive and negative factors are encountered when a manager brings others into the decision-making process. The advantages and disadvantages are listed in Table 7.1. If there is a conscious effort to avoid or at least minimize the disadvantages, managers can gain a great deal by sharing the decision-making process with peers, outside consultants, and subordinates. However, some important contingency factors need to be taken into consideration.

TABLE 7.1 • Advantages and Disadvantages of Group-aided Decision Making and Problem Solving

Advantages	Disadvantages
1. **Greater pool of knowledge.** A group can bring much more information and experience to bear on a decision or problem than can an individual acting alone.	1. **Social pressure.** Unwillingness to "rock the boat" and pressure to conform may combine to stifle the creativity of individual contributors.
2. **Different perspectives.** Individuals with varied experience and interests help the group see decision situations and problems from different angles.	2. **Domination by a vocal few.** Sometimes the quality of group action is reduced when the group gives in to those who talk the loudest and longest.
3. **Greater comprehension.** Those who personally experience the give-and-take of group discussion about alternative courses of action tend to understand the rationale behind the final decision.	3. **Logrolling.** Political wheeling and dealing can displace sound thinking when an individual's pet project or vested interest is at stake.
4. **Increased acceptance.** Those who play an active role in group decision making and problem solving tend to view the outcome as "ours" rather than "theirs."	4. **Goal displacement.** Sometimes secondary considerations such as winning an argument, making a point, or getting back at a rival displace the primary task of making a sound decision or solving a problem.
5. **Training ground.** Less experienced participants in group action learn how to cope with group dynamics by actually being involved.	5. **"Groupthink."** Sometimes cohesive "in-groups" let the desire for unanimity override sound judgment when generating and evaluating alternative courses of action. (Groupthink is discussed in Chapter 13.)

A Contingency Approach Is Necessary

Are two or more heads actually better than one? The answer depends on the nature of the task, the ability of the contributors, and the form of interaction (see Figure 7.7). An analysis of dozens of individual-versus-group performance studies conducted over a sixty-one-year period led one researcher to the following conclusions: (1) groups tend to do quantitatively and qualitatively better than the *average* individual; and (2) *exceptional* individuals tend to outperform the group, particularly when the task is complex and the group is made up of relatively low-ability people.[25]

Consequently, busy managers need to delegate aspects of the decision-making process (specified earlier) according to the contingencies in Figure 7.7. More is said about delegation in Chapter 9.

Nature of task	Insights from research
Problem-solving task	Individuals are faster, but groups tend to produce better results
Complex task	Best results achieved by polling the contributions of individuals working alone
Brainstorming task	Same as for complex task
Learning task	Groups consistently outperform individuals
Concept mastery/ creative task	Contributions from average-ability group members tend to improve when they are teamed with high-ability group members

FIGURE 7.7 ● Individual versus Group Performance: Contingency Management Insights from Sixty-one Years of Research

Source: Based in part on research conclusions found in Gayle W. Hill, "Group versus Individual Performance: Are N + 1 Heads Better than One?" *Psychological Bulletin,* 91 (May 1982): 517–539.

Managerial Creativity

Demands for creativity and innovation make the practice of management endlessly exciting (and sometimes extremely difficult).[26] Nearly all managerial problem solving requires a healthy measure of creativity as managers mentally take things apart, rearrange the pieces in new and potentially productive configurations, and look beyond normal frameworks for new solutions. This process is like turning the kaleidoscope of one's mind. Thomas Edison used to retire to an old couch in his laboratory to do his creative thinking. Henry Ford reportedly sought creative insights by staring at a blank wall in his shop. Although the average manager's attempts at creativity may not be as dramatically fruitful as Edison's or Ford's, workplace creativity needs to be understood and nurtured. As a steppingstone for the next section on creative problem solving, this section defines creativity, discusses the management of creative people, and identifies barriers to creativity.

What Is Creativity?

Creativity is a rather mysterious process known chiefly by its results, and is therefore difficult to define. About as close as we can come is to say that **creativity** is the reorganization of experience into new configurations.[27] According to a management consultant specializing in creativity:

creativity the reorganization of experience into new configurations

Creativity is a function of knowledge, imagination, and evaluation. The greater our knowledge, the more ideas, patterns, or combinations we can achieve. But merely having the knowledge does not guarantee the formation of new patterns; the bits and pieces must be shaken up and interrelated in new ways. Then, the embryonic ideas must be evaluated and developed into usable ideas.[28]

Creativity is often subtle and may not be readily apparent to the untrained eye. But the combination and extension of seemingly insignificant day-to-day breakthroughs lead to organizational progress.

Identifying general types of creativity is easier than explaining the basic process. One pioneering writer on the subject isolated three overlapping domains of creativity: art, discovery, and humor.[29] These have been called the "ah!" reaction, the "aha!" reaction, and the "haha!" reaction, respectively.[30]

The discovery ("aha!") variation is the most relevant to management. Entirely new businesses can spring from creative discovery. A prime example is Donald L. Beaver Jr.'s low-tech discovery that grew into a thriving multimillion dollar business.[31] He found that nylon stockings stuffed with ground-up corncobs could soak up oil and grease spills faster than any known technique and at much less cost. Machine shops and gas stations, where slippery oil spills are a costly occupational hazard, clamored for Beaver's new product. Beaver's creativity did not stop there. It extended to the company's name: New PIG Corp. According to Beaver, PIG stands for "Partners in Grime." Creative ideas often have humble beginnings.

Managing the Creative Individual

Creative people present managers with a dilemma. Those who are very creative tend to be nonconformists in behavior, dress, and grooming. They are commonly called *wild ducks,* a term traced to Thomas J. Watson Jr., the former head of IBM.[32] Attempts to get creative employees to conform to rules and regulations may instead stifle their creativity. Creative individuals often like to get lost in intriguing aspects of the job and resent managerial attempts to get them to do bureaucratic chores. Seymour Cray, the man behind the supercomputers that bear his name, is a classic case in point. Cray reportedly keeps nothing on his desk but a sheet of graph paper on which he pursues his all-consuming passion of designing yet another version of the world's fastest computer. His children recall being told to be totally silent during family drives so their father could concentrate. Cray's concentration at work is sometimes so intense that he walks into people in the hallway. William C. Norris, founder of Control Data Corp. (CDC), got a short lesson in his prize employee's impatience with administrative detail: "Norris recalls, he asked Cray to write a five-year plan for CDC. The result: 'Five year goal: Build the biggest computer in the world. One year goal: Achieve one-fifth of the above.' "[33] Norris was patient because Cray's pioneering work got CDC off to a fast start in the computer industry.

If organizations are to grow and prosper because of creative ideas, then managers need to be flexible in their handling of creative subordinates. Creative people are an asset to be nurtured. Because many creative people dislike close supervision, the manager may need to serve primarily as a resource person who

Bill Gates, the young billionaire founder and chairman of Microsoft Corporation, the world's largest PC software company, sees himself as just another computer nerd. While it is true he routinely checks for math errors on reports and overhead slides during managers' presentations, he has kept the creative spark alive at the now-large company. He does so by being able to see the big picture, keeping organizational units small, freely delegating to professional managers, and staying in close touch with the technical core of the business.

provides help when it is requested. If creative employees like to work at night or on Sunday, perhaps they can be given a key or special pass to get into the building. If they spend a lot of time staring out the window, it might make sense to measure their productivity by the week or even longer, instead of by the hour. They may be working out their best ideas while apparently daydreaming. Consider, for example, how the Pac-Man concept came into being:

> *The idea was born when Toru Iwatami, 27, was daydreaming at his desk just before lunch. As his appetite grew, he visualized little round shapes devouring smaller ones. He took the idea to Namco, his employer [in Tokyo], and the rest is marketing history.*[34]

If Iwatami's creativity had been stifled in some way, Namco would not have collected the more than $15 million in royalties it earned from licensing the Pac-Man concept. Of course, creative people, like all other employees, must be held accountable for results. Unfortunately, some managers become so preoccupied with superficial aspects of personality, appearance, scheduling, or performance that they end up with conforming but uncreative employees.

Learning to Be More Creative

● ● ● ● ● ● ● ● ● ● ● ● ● ● ● ● ●
Identify and briefly describe five of the ten "mental locks" that can inhibit creativity.

Some people naturally seem to be more creative than others. But that does not mean that those who feel the need cannot develop their creative capacity. It does seem clear that creative ability can be learned, in the sense that our creative energies can be released from the bonds of convention, lack of self-confidence, and narrow thinking. We all have the potential to be more creative.[35]

The best place to begin is by trying to consciously overcome what creativity specialist Roger von Oech calls *mental locks*. The following mental locks are attitudes that get us through our daily activities but tend to stifle our creativity:

1. *Looking for the "Right" Answer.* Depending on one's perspective, a given problem may have several right answers.

2. *Always Trying to Be Logical.* Logic does not always prevail, given human emotions and organizational inconsistencies, ambiguity, and contradictions.

3. *Strictly Following the Rules.* If things are to be improved, arbitrary limits on thinking and behavior need to be questioned.

4. *Insisting on Being Practical.* Impractical answers to "what-if" questions can become steppingstones to creative insights.

5. *Avoiding Ambiguity.* Creativity can be stunted by too much objectivity and specificity.

6. *Fearing and Avoiding Failure.* Fear of failure can paralyze us into not acting on our good ideas. This is unfortunate because we learn many valuable and lasting lessons from our mistakes.

7. *Forgetting How to Play.* The playful experimentation of childhood too often disappears by adulthood.

8. *Becoming Too Specialized.* Cross-fertilization of specialized areas helps in defining problems and generating solutions.

9. *Not Wanting to Look Foolish.* Humor can release tensions and unlock creative energies. Seemingly foolish questions can enhance understanding.

10. *Saying "I'm Not Creative."* By nurturing small and apparently insignificant ideas we can convince ourselves that we are indeed creative.[36] (Try the creativity exercise in Figure 7.8.)

If these mental locks are conquered, the creative problem-solving process discussed in the next section can be used to its full potential.

Creative Problem Solving

problem solving conscious process of closing the gap between actual and desired situations

We are all problem solvers. But this does not mean that all of us are good problem solvers or even, for that matter, that we know how to solve problems systematically. Most daily problem solving is done on a haphazard, intuitive basis. A difficulty arises, we look around for an answer, jump at the first workable solution to come along, and move on to other things. In a primitive sense, this sequence of events qualifies as a problem-solving process, and it works quite well for informal daily activities. But in the world of management, a more systematic problem-solving process is required for tackling difficult and unfamiliar nonprogrammed decision situations. In the context of management, **problem solving** is the conscious process of bringing the actual situation closer to the desired situation.[37] Managerial problem solving consists of a four-step sequence: (1) identifying the problem, (2) generating alternative solutions, (3) selecting a solution, and (4) implementing and evaluating the solution (see Figure 7.9).

Exercise: Assume that a steel pipe is embedded in the concrete floor of a bare room as shown below. The inside diameter is .06" larger than the diameter of a ping-pong ball (1.50") which is resting gently at the bottom of the pipe. You are one of a group of six people in the room, along with the following objects:

- 100' of clothesline
- Carpenter's hammer
- Chisel
- Box of Wheaties
- File
- Wire coat hanger
- Monkey wrench
- Light bulb

List as many ways you can think of (in five minutes) to get the ball out of the pipe without damaging the ball, tube, or floor.

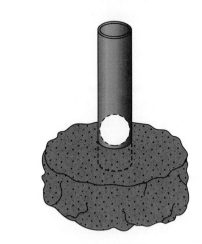
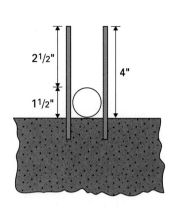

FIGURE 7.8 • How Creative Are You?

Source: From *Conceptual Blockbusting,* 2nd ed., by James L. Adams, by permission of W. W. Norton & Company, Inc. Copyright © 1974, 1976, 1979 by James L. Adams. Originally published as part of *The Portable Stanford* by the Stanford Alumni Association.

Identifying the Problem

As strange as it may seem, the most common problem-solving difficulty lies in the identification of problems. Busy managers have a tendency to rush into generating and selecting alternative solutions before they have actually isolated and understood the real problem. According to Peter Drucker, a respected management scholar, "the most common source of mistakes in management decisions is emphasis on finding the right answers rather than the right questions."[38] As problem finders, managers should probe for the right questions. Only then can the right answers be found.

What Is a Problem? Ask a half-dozen people how they identify problems and you are likely to get as many answers.[39] Consistent with the definition given above for problem solving, a **problem** is defined as the difference between an actual state of affairs and a desired state of affairs. In other words, a problem is the gap between where one is and where one wants to be. Problem solving is meant to close this gap. For example, a person in New York who has to be in San Francisco in twenty-four hours has a problem. The problem is not being in

problem the difference between actual and desired states of affairs

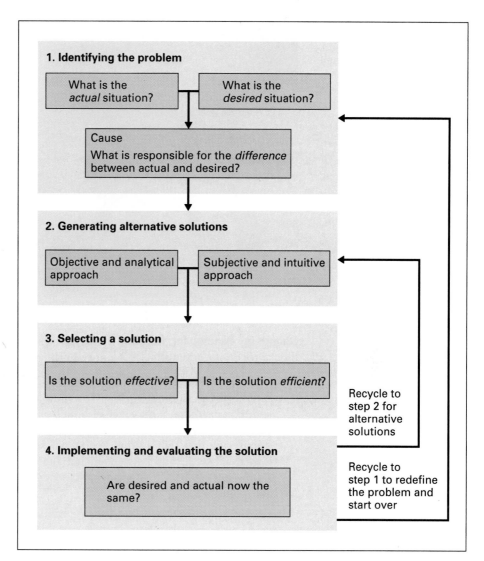

1. Identifying the problem

| What is the *actual* situation? | What is the *desired* situation? |

Cause

What is responsible for the *difference* between actual and desired?

2. Generating alternative solutions

| Objective and analytical approach | Subjective and intuitive approach |

3. Selecting a solution

| Is the solution *effective*? | Is the solution *efficient*? |

Recycle to step 2 for alternative solutions

4. Implementing and evaluating the solution

Are desired and actual now the same?

Recycle to step 1 to redefine the problem and start over

FIGURE 7.9 • The Problem-solving Process

New York (the actual state of affairs), nor is it being in San Francisco in twenty-four hours (the desired state of affairs). Instead, the problem is the 2,934 miles between New York and San Francisco. Considering the twenty-four-hour time constraint, flying is the only practical way of solving the problem (closing the gap). If more time were available, other modes of transportation could be considered.

Managers need to define problems according to the gaps between the actual and the desired situations. A production manager, for example, would be wise to concentrate on the gap between the present level of weekly production and the desired level. This focus is much more fruitful than complaining about the current low production or wishfully thinking about high production. The challenge is discovering a workable alternative for closing the gap between actual and desired production.[40]

Dade County Public School System (in south Florida) faced a shortage of money and classrooms while area companies faced a growing army of working parents worried about shuttling kids to and from school. A creative solution was needed. Community leaders developed the concept of classrooms for kindergarten through second grade on the premises of local companies. The school district provides the teachers, desks, and books; the employer provides classrooms and students.

Stumbling Blocks for Problem Finders. There are three common stumbling blocks for those attempting to identify problems:

1. *Defining the Problem according to a Possible Solution.* One should be careful not to rule out alternative solutions in the way one states a problem. For example, a manager in a unit plagued by high absenteeism who says, "We have a problem with low pay," may prevent management from discovering that tedious and boring work is the real cause. By focusing on how to close the gap between actual and desired attendance, instead of simply on low pay, management stands a better chance of finding a workable solution.

2. *Focusing on Narrow, Low-Priority Areas.* Successful managers are those who can weed out relatively minor problems and reserve their attention for problems that really make a difference. Formal organizational goals and objectives provide a useful framework for determining the priority of various problems. Don't be concerned with waxing the floor when the roof is caving in.

3. *Diagnosing Problems in Terms of Their Symptoms.* As a short-run expedient, treating symptoms rather than underlying causes may be appropriate. A bottle of aspirin is cheaper than trying to find a less stressful job, for example. In the longer run, however, symptoms tend to reappear and problems tend to get worse. There is a two-way test for discovering whether one has found the cause of a problem: "If I *introduce* this variable, will the problem (the gap) disappear?" or "If I *remove* this variable, will the problem (the gap) disappear?" **Causes** then are variables that, because of their presence or absence from the situation, are primarily responsible for the difference between the actual and the desired conditions. For example, the absence of a key can cause a problem with a locked door, and the presence of a nail can cause a problem with an inflated tire.[41]

causes variables responsible for the difference between actual and desired

Generating Alternative Solutions

After the problem and its most probable cause have been identified, attention turns to generating alternative solutions. This is the creative step in problem solving. Unfortunately, as the following statement points out, creativity is often shortchanged.

> *The natural response to a problem seems to be to try to get rid of it by finding an answer—often taking the first answer that occurs and pursuing it because of one's reluctance to spend the time and mental effort needed to conjure up a rich storehouse of alternatives from which to choose.*[42]

It takes time, patience, and practice to become a good generator of alternative solutions: a flexible combination of analysis and intuition is helpful. A good sense of humor can aid the process as well.[43] Several popular and useful techniques can stimulate individual and group creativity. Among them are the following approaches:

- *Brainstorming.* A group technique in which any and all ideas are recorded, in a *nonjudgmental* setting, for later critique and selection.
- *Free association.* Analogies and symbols are used to foster unconventional thinking. For example, think of your studies as a mountain requiring special climbing gear and skills.
- *Edisonian.* Named for Thomas Edison's tedious and persistent search for a durable light bulb filament, this technique involves trial-and-error experimentation.
- *Attribute listing.* Ideal characteristics of a given object are collected and then screened for useful insights.[44]
- *Scientific method.* Systematic hypothesis testing, manipulation of variables, situational controls, and careful measurement are the essence of this rigorous approach.
- *Creative leap.* This technique involves thinking up idealistic solutions to a problem and then working back to a feasible solution.[45]

Selecting a Solution

Simply stating that the best solution should be selected in step 3 (refer to Figure 7.9) can be misleading. Because of time and financial constraints and political considerations, *best* is a relative term. Generally, alternative solutions should be screened for the most appealing balance of effectiveness and efficiency, in view of relevant constraints and intangibles. Russell Ackoff, a specialist in managerial problem solving, contends that three things can be done about problems: they can be resolved, solved, or dissolved.[46]

Resolving the Problem. When a problem is resolved, a course of action that is good enough to meet the minimum constraints is selected. The term **satisfice** has been applied to the practice of settling for solutions that are good enough rather than the best possible. A badly worn spare tire may satisfice as a replacement for a flat tire for the balance of a trip, although getting the flat repaired is the best possible solution. According to Ackoff, most managers rely on problem

satisfice settling for a solution that is good enough

resolving. This nonquantitative, subjective approach is popular because managers claim they do not have the necessary information or time for the other approaches. Satisficing, however, has been criticized as a shortsighted and passive technique emphasizing expedient survival instead of improvement and growth.

Solving the Problem. A problem is solved when the best possible solution is selected. Managers are said to **optimize** when through scientific observation and quantitative measurement they systematically research alternative solutions and select the one with the best combination of benefits.

optimize systematically identifying the solution with the best combination of benefits

Dissolving the Problem. A problem is dissolved when the situation in which it occurs is changed so that the problem no longer exists. Problem dissolvers are said to **idealize** because they actually change the nature of the system in which a problem resides. Managers who dissolve problems rely on whatever combination of nonquantitative and quantitative tools is needed to get the job done. The replacement of automobile assembly-line welders with robots, for instance, has dissolved the problem of costly absenteeism among people in that job category.

idealize changing the nature of a problem's situation

Whatever approach a manager chooses, the following advice from Ackoff should be kept in mind: "Few if any problems . . . are ever permanently resolved, solved, or dissolved; every treatment of a problem generates new problems."[47] A Japanese manager at the General Motors–Toyota joint venture auto plant in California put it this way: "No problem is a problem."[48] However, as pointed out by the cofounder of a successful import business, an administrative life made up of endless problems is cause for optimism, not pessimism: "Spare yourself some grief. Understand that, in business, you will always have problems. They are where the opportunities lie."[49]

Implementing and Evaluating the Solution

Time is the true test of any solution. Until a particular solution has had time to prove its worth, the manager can rely only on his or her judgment concerning its effectiveness and efficiency. Ideally, the solution selected will completely eliminate the difference between the actual and the desired in an efficient and timely manner. Should the gap fail to disappear, two options are open. If management remains convinced that the problem has been correctly identified, they can recycle to step 2 to try another solution that was identified earlier. This recycling can continue until all feasible solutions have been given a fair chance or until the nature of the problem changes to the extent that the existing solutions are obsolete. If the gap between actual and desired persists in spite of repeated attempts to find a solution, then it is advisable to recycle to step 1 to redefine the problem and engage in a new round of problem solving.

Summary

Decision making is a fundamental part of management because it requires choosing among alternative courses of action. In addition to having to cope with an era of accelerating change, today's decision makers face the challenges of dealing with complexity, uncertainty, the need for flexible thinking, and decision traps.

Seven factors contributing to decision complexity are multiple criteria, intangibles, risk and uncertainty, long-term implications, interdisciplinary input, pooled decision making, and value judgments. Managers must learn to assess the degree of certainty in a situation—whether conditions are certain, risky, or uncertain. Confidence in one's decisions decreases as uncertainty increases. Today's managers need to tap the creative potential of intuitive employees and the implementation skills of those who process information as thinkers.

Researchers have identified three perceptual and behavioral decision traps that can hamper the quality of decisions. Framing error occurs when people let labels and frames of reference sway their interpretations. People are victimized by escalation of commitment when they get locked into losing propositions for fear of quitting and looking bad. Oddly, researchers find overconfidence tends to grow with the difficulty of the task.

Decisions, generally, are either programmed or nonprogrammed. Because programmed decisions are relatively clear-cut and routinely encountered, fixed decision rules can be formulated for them. In contrast, nonprogrammed decisions require creative problem solving because they are novel and unfamiliar.

Managers may choose to bring other people into virtually every aspect of the decision-making process. However, when a group rather than an individual is responsible for making the decision, personal accountability is lost. Dispersed accountability is undesirable in some key decision situations. Group-aided decision making has both advantages and disadvantages. Because group performance does not always exceed individual performance, a contingency approach to group-aided decision making is advisable.

Creativity requires the proper combination of knowledge, imagination, and evaluation to reorganize experience into new configurations. The domains of creativity may be divided into art, discovery (the most relevant to management), and humor. Because they tend to be nonconformists, creative employees often require special handling while still being held accountable for results. By consciously overcoming ten mental locks, we can become more creative.

The creative problem-solving process consists of four steps: (1) identifying the problem, (2) generating alternative solutions, (3) selecting a solution, and (4) implementing and evaluating the solution. Inadequate problem finding is common among busy managers. By seeing problems as gaps between an actual situation and a desired situation, managers are in a better position to create more effective and efficient solutions. Depending on the situation, problems can be resolved, solved, or dissolved. It is important to remember that today's solutions often become tomorrow's problems.

Terms to Understand

Decision making	Decision rule
Condition of certainty	Nonprogrammed decisions
Condition of risk	Creativity
Objective probabilities	Problem solving
Subjective probabilities	Problem
Condition of uncertainty	Causes (of problems)
Framing error	Satisfice
Escalation of commitment	Optimize
Programmed decisions	Idealize

Questions for Discussion

1. What evidence of the seven sources of decision complexity do you detect in your own life?

2. How do you cope with risk and uncertainty?

3. Is your information processing style predominantly thinking or intuitive? How do you know? How will this help or hinder you as a manager?

4. What is your personal experience with being victimized by framing error? Escalation of commitment? Overconfidence?

5. Can you write a decision rule for a programmed decision at the place where you now work or where you have worked in the past?

6. What is wrong with having a group of people make a specific decision?

7. Thinking of the most creative person you know, do you think he or she would be hard to manage? Explain.

8. Regarding your own creativity, which mental lock do you find the most troublesome? What can you do to overcome it?

9. Why is problem finding especially important?

10. Can you think of a managerial situation in which it would be better to resolve rather than solve or dissolve a problem? How about a situation in which dissolving would be most appropriate?

Back to the Opening Case

Now that you have read Chapter 7, you should be able to answer the following questions about the Apple Computer case:

1. Is Steve Jobs probably intuitive or a thinker? How can you tell? How could this tendency both help and hinder him as a manager?

2. Why do you think Steve Jobs and John Sculley were initially a good decision-making and problem-solving team but later became quarrelsome?

3. What impact do you think Sculley's recent moves will have on creativity at Apple Computer?

| CLOSING CASE |

The Man Behind Disney's New Magic

Since 1984, when Michael Eisner took over as chief executive officer, Walt Disney Co. has become a favorite of investors as well as kids of all ages. Disney exemplifies for many people the American corporate ideal of the 1990s. Yes, it is well managed, but more important, Disney is creative, especially in the ways that it makes national and international opportunities out of its strengths. Seemingly outmoded and asleep when Eisner took it over, Disney is now a leader in many different facets of the entertainment business, and a share of its stock is worth ten times its value in 1984. Because of this tremendous success—and Eisner's astronomical pay that accompanies it—Eisner's decision-making style and creativity are receiving a lot of attention.

Eisner doesn't have any trouble coming up with ideas. On the contrary, he needs level-headed associates in part to help him weed out the bad ideas from among the good. Someone had to tell him, for instance, that a 43-story hotel in the shape of Mickey Mouse was not a good idea, even for Disney World. But wherever he goes, Eisner seems to add his own touch. He asks carpenters to put backs on the benches at Disney World, he dreams up scenes for *Three Men and a Little Lady,* he invents a new chain of stores to sell both health foods and Disney souvenirs. His inspiration often springs from his own experiences and those of his family. After being stopped for speeding while president of Paramount, Eisner came up with the idea for *Beverly Hills Cop,* the top grossing comedy ever. And his son's love of Gummi Bears prompted him to make them into a Saturday morning cartoon show.

Of course, Eisner is not the only creative person on the Disney payroll, and good ideas alone don't make a multibillion-dollar company. An effective manager, Eisner also knows how to use others' talents to the best advantage. He brought together a dozen of the world's best architects to plan the layout of the new Disney theme park in Europe. He has hired *Cats* composer Andrew Lloyd Weber, as well as Michael Jackson, Bette Midler, and even Kermit the Frog. Eisner has surrounded himself with people who know how to be creative with money, and they've put together imaginative financing schemes for Disney's overseas attractions. One such scheme earned the company $800 million the first day the stock of Euro Disneyland went on sale in Paris.

Disney's decision-making processes manage to be both flexible and firm. Eisner often calls together everyone involved in a new project and has them hash out the details under the pressure of a deadline. Eisner admits the process can be "kind of cruel," but decisions tend to get made quickly. Disney cannot ignore financial considerations, of course, but it tries to keep such considerations from being a barrier to creative thinking. Ideas are often generated by the company's main think tank, Walt Disney Imagineering, which develops the project's design and engineering. Next, a six-person strategic planning group, headed by Disney's chief financial officer, takes a hard look at the idea and assesses its economic potential. The two groups then get together to propose a budget and a schedule, which go, finally, to Eisner or Disney's president, Frank Wells, for a decision.

The necessary flexibility of Disney decision making and the huge size of the company occasionally lead one branch of the empire to make a decision the other branches regret. Disney's worst recent public relations incident occurred when the state of Florida accused Disney World of capturing and killing wild and endangered birds that were making a mess in Disney World's zoos. The company has since apologized, hired a wildlife consultant, and will no doubt find a creative way to pass on to the public its new outlook on birds.

The joining of intuitive and analytical thinking apparent in the Disney creative process is just one of many important synergies that Disney exploits. The company's three main divisions, involving movie productions, consumer products, and theme parks and resorts, constantly create business for each other. As soon as he took over, Eisner spent $1 billion on expanding the company's hotels into convention complexes. Now, when schools are in session and kids can't come to Florida, conventioneers fill the theme parks. Disney's fabulously successful retail stores make plenty of money on their own, but their main function in the Disney strategy is to create enthusiasm for Disney's other businesses. A character like Roger Rabbit makes his debut on film and almost instantaneously also appears on T-shirts and in the theme parks. At a time when most big corporations are headed by lawyers or bankers who focus solely on profit, Disney's life-blood is still creativity. Nevertheless, few companies can turn ideas into dollars more quickly.

For Discussion

1. Which sources of decision complexity (see Figure 7.1) do you think are most troublesome for Eisner?

2. How would you characterize Eisner's information processing style, using Figure 7.4 as a guide?

3. How would you respond to a manager who said: "Walt Disney Company is creative because they hire creative people"?

4. Could unrestrained creativity become a problem at Disney? Explain.

References

Opening Quotation. Lee Iacocca with William Novak, *Iacocca: An Autobiography* (New York: Bantam, 1984), p. 50.

Opening Case. For additional information on Apple, see Barbara Buell, "Apple: New Team, New Strategy," *Business Week* (October 15, 1990): 86–96; Brenton R. Schlender, "Yet Another Strategy for Apple," *Fortune* (October 22, 1990): 81–87; Michael Moritz, "Apple Launches a Mac Attack," *Time* (January 30, 1984): 68–69; Joel Dreyfuss, "John Sculley Rises in the West," *Fortune* (July 9, 1984): 180–184; John Schwartz, "Apple's Third Revolution," *Newsweek* (October 22, 1990): 53; Barbara Buell, "The Second Comeback of Apple," *Business Week* (January 28, 1991): 68.

Closing Case. Stephen Kindel, "Michael Eisner," *Financial World* (April 3, 1990): 76; Christopher Knowlton, "How Disney Keeps the Magic Going," *Fortune* (December 4, 1989): 111–132; Ron Zemke, *The Service Edge* (New York: New American Library, 1989), pp. 529–533.

1. Moritz, "Apple Launches a Mac Attack," p. 69.

2. Dreyfuss, "John Sculley Rises in the West," pp. 182–183, 184.

3. Buell, "Apple: New Team, New Strategy," p. 92.

4. Alvin Toffler, *The Third Wave* (New York: Bantam, 1980), p. 229.

5. Morgan W. McCall, Jr. and Robert E. Kaplan, *Whatever It Takes: The Realities of Managerial Decision Making,* 2nd ed. (Englewood Cliffs, N.J.: Prentice-Hall, 1990), p. 5.

6. Dody Tsiantar and Annetta Miller, "Tuning Out TV Ads," *Newsweek* (April 17, 1989): 42.

7. See Irwin Ross, "Chrysler on the Brink," *Fortune* (February 9, 1981): 38–42.

8. See Alan D. Meyer, "Mingling Decision-Making Metaphors," *Academy of Management Review,* 9 (January 1984): 6–17.

9. An instructive model of ethical decision making can be found in Linda K. Trevino, "Ethical Decision Making in Organizations: A Person-Situation Interactionist Model," *Academy of Management Review,* 11 (July 1986): 601–618.

10. Empirical tests of motives for risk reduction are reported in Raphael Amit and Birger Wernerfelt, "Why Do Firms Reduce Business Risk?" *Academy of Management Journal,* 33 (September 1990): 520–533.

11. For an informative discussion see Weston H. Agor, "Managing Brain Skills: The Last Frontier," *Personnel Administrator,* 32 (October 1987): 54–60.

12. See Harvey J. Brightman, "Better Decision Making for Better Business," *Business,* 38 (April–June 1988): 28–34; and Barbara Block, "Intuition Creeps Out of the Closet and Into the Boardroom," *Management Review,* 79 (May 1990): 58–60.

13. An instructive critique of left-brain/right-brain theory can be found in Terence Hines, "Left Brain/Right Brain Mythology and Implications for Management and Training," *Academy of Management Review,* 12 (October 1987): 600–606.

14. See Beverly Geber, "A Quick Course in Decision Science," *Training,* 25 (April 1988): 54–55; and John McCormick, "How You Gonna Make Up Your Mind?" *Business Month* (July 1990): 71–72; and Alan E. Singer, Steven Lysonski, Ming Singer, and David Hayes, "Ethical Myopia: The Case of 'Framing' by Framing," *Journal of Business Ethics,* 10 (January 1991): 29–36.

15. Irwin P. Levin, Sara K. Schnittjer, and Shannon L. Thee, "Information Framing Effects in Social and Personal Decisions," *Journal of Experimental Social Psychology,* 24 (November 1988): 527.

16. For a good overview, see Barry M. Staw and Jerry Ross, "Understanding Behavior in Escalation Situations," *Science,* 246 (October 13, 1989): 216–220. Also see William S. Silver and Terence R. Mitchell, "The Status Quo Tendency in Decision Making," *Organizational Dynamics,* 18 (Spring 1990): 34–46.

17. "Navy Cancels Contract for Attack Planes," *The Christian Science Monitor* (January 9, 1991): 3. Also see Russell Mitchell, "Desperately Seeking an Attack Bomber," *Business Week* (January 21, 1991): 35.

18. See David Dunning, Dale W. Griffin, James D. Milojkovic, and Lee Ross, "The Overconfidence Effect in Social Prediction," *Journal of Personality and Social Psychology,* 58 (April 1990): 568–581. For an interesting exercise, see J. Edward Russo and Paul J. H. Schoemaker, "The Overconfidence Quiz," *Harvard Business Review,* 68 (September–October 1990): 236–237.

19. For example, see Herbert A. Simon, *The New Science of Management Decision,* rev. ed. (Englewood Cliffs, N. J.: Prentice-Hall, 1977), p. 40.

20. Andrew S. Grove, *High Output Management* (New York: Random House, 1983), p. 98.

21. Simon, *The New Science of Management Decision,* p. 46.

22. See Charles R. Schwenk, "The Use of Participant Recollection in the Modeling of Organizational Decision Processes," *Academy of Management Review,* 10 (July 1985): 496–503. Also see the discussion of "adaptive decision making" in Amitai Etzioni, "Humble Decision Making," *Harvard Business Review,* 67 (July–August 1989): 122–126.

23. Chester I. Barnard, *The Functions of the Executive* (Cambridge, Mass.: Harvard University Press, 1938), p. 190.

24. George P. Huber, *Managerial Decision Making* (Glenview, Ill.: Scott, Foresman, 1980), pp. 141–142.

25. See Gayle W. Hill, "Group Versus Individual Performance: Are N + 1 Heads Better Than One?" *Psychological Bulletin,* 91 (May 1982): 517–539. Also see John P. Wanous and Margaret A. Youtz, "Solution Diversity and the Quality of Group Decisions," *Academy of Management Journal,* 29 (March 1986): 149–158.

26. For a discussion of the connection between creativity and competitiveness, see "Create and Survive," *The Economist* (December 1, 1990): 77.

27. Based on discussion in N. R. F. Maier, Mara Julius, and James Thurber, "Studies in Creativity: Individual Differences in the Storing and Utilization of Information," *The American Journal of Psychology,* 80 (December 1967): 492–519.

28. Sidney J. Parnes, "Learning Creative Behavior," *The Futurist,* 18 (August 1984): 30–31; (emphasis added). Additional informative reading on creativity may be found in Emily T. Smith, "Are You Creative?" *Business Week* (September 30, 1985): 80–84; Jack Gordon and Ron Zemke, "Making Them More Creative," *Training,* 23 (May 1986): 30–45; Eugene Raudsepp, "Establishing a Creative Climate," *Training and Development Journal,* 41 (April 1987): 50–53.

29. See Arthur Koestler, *The Act of Creation* (London: Hutchinson, 1969), p. 27.

30. See James L. Adams, *Conceptual Blockbusting* (San Francisco: Freeman, 1974), p. 35.

31. See Charles R. Day, Jr., "What a Dumb Idea," *Industry Week* (January 2, 1989): 27–28.

32. See Beverly Geber, "How to Manage Wild Ducks," *Training,* 27 (May 1990): 29–36.

33. Russell Mitchell, "The Genius," *Business Week* (April 30, 1990): 82.

34. "E.T. and Friends Are Flying High," *Business Week* (January 10, 1983): 77.

35. See Jennifer Katz, "The Creative Touch," *Nation's Business* (March 1990): 42–43.

36. Adapted from *A Whack on the Side of the Head* by Roger von Oech, Warner Books, 1983. Reprinted by permission.

37. Huber, *Managerial Decision Making,* p. 12.

38. Peter F. Drucker, *The Practice of Management* (New York: Harper & Row, 1954), p. 531.

39. Problem finding, from a human resource management perspective, is discussed in Jane Elizabeth Allen, "How to Solve the Right Problem," *Training,* 24 (February 1987): 39–45.

40. For an empirical classification of organizational problems, see David A. Cowan, "Developing a Classification Structure of Organizational Problems: An Empirical Investigation," *Academy of Management Journal,* 33 (June 1990): 366–390.

41. Adapted from Huber, *Managerial Decision Making,* pp. 13–15.

42. Adams, *Conceptual Blockbusting,* p. 7.

43. Interesting examples are cited in Magaly Olivero, "Get Crazy! How to Have a Breakthrough Idea," *Working Woman,* 15 (September 1990): 145–147, 222.

44. The first four techniques are discussed in William G. Hyzer, "First State the Problem," *Industrial Research/Development,* 20 (September 1978): 144.

45. See James F. Bandrowski, "Taking Creative Leaps," *Planning Review,* 18 (January–February 1990): 34–38.
46. See Russell L. Ackoff, "The Art and Science of Mess Management," *Interfaces,* 11 (February 1981): 20–26.
47. Ibid., p. 22.
48. James B. Treece, "Shaking Up Detroit," *Business Week* (August 14, 1989): 78.
49. Paul Hawken, "Problems, Problems," *Inc.,* 9 (September 1987): 24.

VIDEO SKILL BUILDER

•••

Uncover your Creativity

Learning Objective

To stimulate your creativity via the "ha ha" reaction.

Link to Textual Material

Creativity, learning to be more creative, breaking mental locks on creativity, creative problem solving.

How can you increase your creativity? How can you improve your ability to discover new ideas and solve problems? This video suggests six fundamental ways to uncover creative ideas:

1. Look at the big picture.
2. Look for more than one answer.
3. Put your head together with other people and combine ideas.
4. Keep it simple.
5. Go hunting for new ideas.
6. Find a way to sell your idea.

Discussion Questions

1. Why is it a good idea to occasionally "grease the creative wheels" of our minds with humor?
2. Which of the six pointers in this video is/are the most important? Why?
3. Do you believe everyone has creative potential? What can you, as a manager, do to draw out that potential?
4. How can the six-step model in the video help you solve a troublesome problem you have had lately?

PART III

Organizing, Staffing, and Communicating

• • • • • • • • • • • • • • • • • • • Part III looks at organizational structure and effectiveness, the individual-organization matching process, and the linking role of communication. Traditional and modern views of organizations are contrasted in Chapter 8, with special attention devoted to organizational effectiveness criteria and organizational cultures. Chapter 9 introduces alternative organization design formats within a contingency management framework and explores the topic of delegation. Chapter 9 concludes with a preview of what tomorrow's organizations will look like. In Chapter 10, staffing and human resource management are examined within the context of getting the right person in the right job at the right time. Three challenging human resource problems—sexual harassment, substance abuse, and AIDS—are confronted and discussed. Attention turns to the communication process, perception, and dynamics of organizational communication in Chapter 11. Practical advice is offered for better listening, writing, and meetings.

8

Organizations: Structure, Effectiveness, and Cultures

●●●●●●●●●●●●●●●●●

Organizations are social inventions or tools developed . . . to accomplish things otherwise not possible.

JOSEPH A. LITTERER

CHAPTER OBJECTIVES

When you finish studying this chapter, you should be able to

- Identify and describe four characteristics common to all organizations.
- Identify and explain the two basic dimensions of organization charts.
- Contrast the traditional and modern views of organizations.
- Describe a business organization in terms of the open-system model.
- Explain the time dimension of organizational effectiveness.
- Define organizational decline and identify characteristics common to organizations in decline.
- Explain the nature and significance of organizational cultures.

●●

General Motors Tries to Get Back in Gear

Not so long ago, General Motors seemed to be the Rock of Gibraltar of the industrial world. Almost half of the cars on the American roads, and one out of four worldwide, bore a GM nameplate. But GM, like the Rock, was not inclined to move. Having become the world leader by building big, gas-guzzling cars, it scoffed when Japanese auto makers began selling their "econo-boxes." Even after the oil crises of the 1970s, GM was slow to realize that future American roads would not be dominated by steel monsters with massive V-8 engines. Its complacency having led to organizational decline, the giant found itself in the embarrassing position of having to play catch up.

During the 1980s, under then-chairman Roger B. Smith, GM spent roughly $50 billion to modernize its aging plants. It began the difficult process of cutting its costs and getting the company into competitive trim. But GM started these processes so late that it continued to lose market share. Buyers complained about poorly designed cars, laid-off workers griped about GM's huge bonuses for its executives, and financial analysts pointed out that GM still had the highest production and overhead costs in the industry.

With a new decade came a new strategy, a new car—the much-heralded Saturn—and a new chairman, Robert C. Stempel. As he took over, Stempel was confident GM could turn around its North American auto operations, which had lost money for three straight years.

Many General Motors employees shared Stempel's optimism, in part because of Stempel himself. Roger Smith came from a financial background and tended to be seen as a loner. In contrast, Stempel is an engineer and a team player, and he has surrounded himself with other executives with engineering backgrounds. All share a commitment to focus on the company's products, not its finances.

Just as important, GM's strategy and overall thinking have changed. It now fully realizes it operates in a global economy, with major competition from Japan, Korea, and Europe. Its new focus on quality—one of the areas in which its products have compared poorly with Japanese models—was symbolized by Stempel's taking personal responsibility for quality control. GM is figuring out ways to build its cars faster *and* better. It is redesigning its models so common parts can be used in several product lines. It consolidated its nine engine groups into five and has merged its new engine division with its transmission subsidiary to allow engineers to coordinate the two functions. GM topped all its rivals in 1991 by introducing nine redesigned cars and two new trucks, and it plans to replace all its old models by 1994.

The structural shake-up shows that GM realizes its oversized, top-heavy bureaucracy is a serious problem. Although GM has been laying off workers and closing factories, it still had 36 vice presidents in 1990, one more than in 1980. Although GM is attempting to trim this bureaucracy, its most successful decentralization so far has been the creation of its independent subsidiary, Saturn Corporation. GM gambled over $3 billion to start Saturn from scratch, and hopes it will lead the entire company into the future. Throughout the 1980s, GM touted Saturn as the car company of the future, with state-of-the-art everything. When former chairman Smith drove the first Saturn off the line in 1990, many of its initial goals had been scaled down, and the Saturn facilities resembled Japan's U.S. auto plants. But even equivalency with the Japanese would represent a big step for GM.

Initial plans called for Saturns to be built using a minimum of workers, with most assembly line tasks performed by robots. But largely as a result of a joint venture with Toyota, GM has learned it can improve production quality and efficiency more by changing its labor relations than by replacing its workers with machines. The biggest innovation in the Saturn plant may turn out to be the role workers play. Union members take part in such decisions as choosing suppliers, dealers, and ad agencies. Although their base pay is lower than at other GM plants, they can raise it substantially if they meet specified goals. Teamwork is emphasized everywhere, and the assembly line— floored with *wood* for the worker's comfort and to improve efficiency—was designed to make the workers' tasks easier. Workers like being asked to use their brains as well as their hands, and many enthusiastically participate in the company's all-out drive to cut costs.

The success of Saturn can't be judged for a few more years. As Chairman Stempel settled in, GM's other changes were beginning to show results. Buick's LeSabre was rated the highest-quality American-built car and GM's Cadillac Division won the Malcolm Baldrige National Quality Award. Although award judges stressed that quality *improvement* (rather than overall product quality) was a major criterion for the award, GM immediately ran ads to herald its triumph. Some auto analysts began talking excitedly about the company's Impact concept, an electric car that may someday outshine the Saturn.

With news of such events beginning to reach him, Chairman Stempel must have felt good as he went to work on his second day, August 2, 1990. But as luck would have it, that was the day Iraq invaded Kuwait, oil prices went through the roof, and a 10,000-Chevy shipment to Kuwait was canceled— the first of many sales losses resulting from the Gulf War. After all the planning and all the changes, GM's new boss must have had difficulty accepting this blunt reminder of just how vulnerable the once rocklike company is to environmental change.

Organizations are an ever-present feature of modern industrial society. We look to organizations for food, clothing, education, employment, entertainment, health care, transportation, and protection of our basic rights. Nearly every aspect of modern life is influenced in one way or another by organizations. As General Motors' struggle to achieve greater competitiveness demonstrates, the management of modern organizations requires bold and imaginative action.

In Chapter 1 we noted that the purpose of the management process is to achieve *organizational* objectives in an effective and efficient manner. Organizations are social entities that enable people to work together to achieve objectives they normally could not achieve working alone. This chapter explores the organizational context in which managers operate. It serves as an introduction, laying the foundation for the discussion of organization design alternatives in Chapter 9. Specifically, this chapter defines the term *organization* and discusses different types of organizations and organization charts. Traditional and modern (open-system) views in the evolution of organization theory are contrasted. Organizational effectiveness is examined as a backdrop for a discussion of organizational decline. Finally, organizational cultures are explored.

What Is an Organization?

In spite of the great number of organizations, the term *organization* is difficult to define, as evidenced by the variety of definitions that have been suggested by sociologists, psychologists, and organization and management theorists. Chester I. Barnard's definition, now more than fifty years old, still remains popular among organization and management theorists. Barnard defined an **organization** as "a system of consciously coordinated activities or forces of two or more persons."[1] In other words, when people gather together and formally agree to combine their efforts for a common purpose, an organization is the result.

There are exceptions, of course, as when two individuals agree to push a car out of a ditch. This task is a one-time effort based on temporary expediency. But if the same two people decide to pool their resources and push cars out of ditches for a living, an organization would be created. The conscious coordination Barnard referred to, which implies a degree of formal planning and division of labor, is present in the second instance but not in the first.

organization system of consciously coordinated activities of two or more people

Common Characteristics of Organizations

Although Barnard's statement is a good general definition, it does not identify all important common denominators of organizations. According to Edgar Schein, a prominent organizational psychologist, all organizations share four characteristics: (1) coordination of effort, (2) common goal or purpose, (3) division of labor, and (4) hierarchy of authority.[2]

●●●●●●●●●●●●●●●●
Identify and describe four characteristics common to all organizations.

Coordination of Effort. As discussed in the last chapter, two heads are sometimes better than one. Individuals who join together and coordinate their mental and/or physical efforts can accomplish great and exciting things. Building the great pyramids, conquering polio, sending manned flights to the moon—all these achievements far exceeded the talents and abilities of any single individual. Coordination of effort multiplies individual contributions.

Common Goal or Purpose. Coordination of effort cannot take place unless those who have joined together agree to strive for something of mutual interest. A common goal or purpose gives organization members a rallying point. For example, in 1988, billionaire entrepreneur Ross Perot recommended that General Motors should strive "to become the finest car manufacturer in the world."[3] Perot's statement leaves little doubt about GM's common goal.

Division of Labor. By systematically dividing complex tasks into specialized jobs, an organization can use its human resources efficiently. Division of labor

Who says love, peace, and understanding are ideas that won't sell in the world of rock music? Just ask the B-52's. Modest success after the band was formed in 1977 gave way to commercial disappointment. Ironically, it took the 1985 death of guitarist Ricky Wilson, their key decision maker, to cement the B-52's into a tight-knit, effective organization of artists. After dumping their manager, switching labels, and teaming up with producer Don Was, the B-52's 1990 comeback album, *Cosmic Thing,* went platinum.

permits each organization member to become more proficient by repeatedly doing the same specialized task. (But, as is discussed in Chapter 12, overspecialized jobs can cause boredom and alienation.)

The advantages of dividing labor have been known for a long time. One of its early proponents was the pioneering economist Adam Smith. While touring an eighteenth-century pin-manufacturing plant, Smith observed that a group of specialized laborers could produce 48,000 pins a day. This was an astounding figure, considering that each laborer could produce only twenty pins a day when working alone.[4]

Hierarchy of Authority.   According to traditional organization theory, if anything is to be accomplished through formal collective effort, someone should be given the authority to see that the intended goals are carried out effectively and efficiently. Organization theorists have defined **authority** as the right to direct the actions of others. Without a clear hierarchy of authority, coordination of effort is difficult, if not impossible, to achieve. Accountability also is enhanced by having people serve in what is often called the *chain of command*. For instance, a grocery store manager has authority over the assistant manager, who has authority over the produce department head, who in turn has authority over the employees in the produce department. Without such a chain of command, the store manager would have the impossible task of directly overseeing the work of every employee in the store.

The idea of hierarchy has many critics, particularly among those who advocate flatter organizations with fewer levels of management. An organization theorist recently answered those critics by noting:

> *At first glance, hierarchy may seem difficult to praise. Bureaucracy is a dirty word even among bureaucrats, and in business there is a widespread*

authority   right to direct the actions of others

view that managerial hierarchy kills initiative, crushes creativity, and has therefore seen its day. Yet 35 years of research have convinced me that managerial hierarchy is the most efficient, the hardiest, and in fact the most natural structure ever devised for large organizations. Properly structured, hierarchy can release energy and creativity, rationalize productivity, and actually improve morale.[5]

Putting All the Pieces Together.   All four of the foregoing characteristics are necessary before an organization can be said to exist. Many well-intentioned attempts to create organizations have failed because something was missing. In 1896, for example, Frederick Strauss, a boyhood friend of Henry Ford, helped Ford set up a machine shop, supposedly to produce gasoline-powered engines. But while Strauss was busy carrying out his end of the bargain by machining needed parts, Ford was secretly building a horseless carriage in a workshop behind his house.[6] Although Henry Ford eventually went on to become an automobile-industry giant, his first attempt at organization failed because not all of the pieces of an organization were in place. Ford's and his partner's efforts were not coordinated, they worked at cross-purposes, their labor was vaguely divided, and they had no hierarchy of authority. In short, they had organizational intentions, but no organization.

Classifying Organizations

Because organizations are created to pursue particular purposes, they can be classified according to their intended purposes. The classification by organizational purpose discussed here has four categories: business, nonprofit service, mutual-benefit, and commonweal organizations.[7] Some of today's large and complex organizations overlap categories. Nevertheless, classifying organizations by their purpose helps clarify the variety of roles they play in society and the similar problems shared by organizations with similar purposes (see Table 8.1).

Business Organizations.   Business organizations such as IBM, United Airlines, and the Washington Post all have one underlying purpose: to make a profit in a socially acceptable manner. Businesses cannot survive, let alone grow, without earning a profit, and profits are earned by efficiently satisfying demand for products and services. This economic production function is so important to society that many think immediately of business when the word *management* is mentioned.

Nonprofit Service Organizations.   Unlike businesses, many organizations survive, and even grow, without making any profits at all. They need to be solvent, of course, but they measure their success not in dollars and cents but by how well they provide a specific service for some segment of society. The American Heart Association, Notre Dame University, and Massachusetts General Hospital are examples of nonprofit service organizations. Because the services of such organizations are usually in great demand, one of their biggest problems lies in screening large numbers of applicants to determine who qualifies for service. Another problem for most nonprofit service organizations is securing a reliable stream of funds through fees, donations, grants, or appropriations. Given today's

TABLE 8.1 • Classifying Organizations by Their Intended Purpose

Purpose	Primary beneficiary	Common examples	Overriding management problem
Business	Owners	Computer manufacturers Newspapers Railroads Fast-food restaurant chains	Must make a profit
Nonprofit service	Clients	Universities Welfare agencies Church schools Hospitals	Must selectively screen large numbers of potential clients
Mutual benefit	Members	Unions Clubs Political parties Trade associations	Must satisfy members' needs
Commonweal	Public at large	U.S. Postal Service Police departments Fire departments Public schools	Must provide standardized services to large groups of people

limited resources, both private-sector and public-sector nonprofit service organizations are under pressure to operate more efficiently.

Mutual-Benefit Organizations.   Often, as in the case of labor unions or political parties, individuals join together strictly to pursue their own self-interests. In other cases—the National Association of Manufacturers, for example—organizations may feel compelled to join together in an umbrella organization. Mutual-benefit organizations, like all other types of organizations, must be effectively and efficiently managed if they are to survive. In this instance, survival depends on satisfying the needs of the members.

Commonweal Organizations.   Like nonprofit service organizations, commonweal organizations offer public services without attempting to earn a profit. But, unlike nonprofit service organizations, which serve some *segment* of society, a **commonweal organization** offers standardized service to *all* members of a given population. The Canadian Army, for example, protects everyone within Canada's borders, not just a select few. The same can be said for local police and fire departments. Commonweal organizations generally are very large, and their great size makes them unwieldy and difficult to manage. For instance, the U.S. Postal Service has come under fire for inefficiency in recent years—not surprising, considering that its 833,958 employees process an incredible 140 billion items a year.[8]

commonweal organization
nonprofit organization serving all members of a given population

Organization Charts

organization chart visual display of organization's positions and lines of authority

An **organization chart** is a diagram of an organization's official positions and formal lines of authority. In effect, an organization chart is a visual display of an organization's structural skeleton. With their familiar pattern of boxes and connecting lines, these charts (called tables by some) are a useful management tool because they are an organizational blueprint for deploying human resources.[9] Organization charts are common in both profit and nonprofit organizations.

Vertical and Horizontal Dimensions

●●●●●●●●●●●●●●●●●
Identify and explain the two basic dimensions of organization charts.

Every organization chart has two dimensions, one representing *vertical hierarchy* and one representing *horizontal specialization*. Vertical hierarchy establishes the chain of command, or who reports to whom. Horizontal specialization establishes the division of labor. A short case tracing the growth of a new organization helps demonstrate the relationship between vertical hierarchy and horizontal specialization.

A Case Study: The Growth of an Organization

For years, George Terrell was an avid trout fisherman. The sight of George loading up his old camper with expensive fly-casting gear and heading out to the nearest trout stream was familiar to his family and neighbors. About six years ago, George tried his hand at the difficult task of tying his own trout flies. Being a creative individual and a bit of a handyman, George soon created a fly that trout seemingly fought over to bite. Word spread rapidly among local and regional fishing enthusiasts. Eventually, George was swamped with orders for his newly patented Super Flies at $3.50 each. What had started out as a casual hobby turned into a potentially lucrative business bringing in roughly $500 per week. George no longer found any time to fish; all his time was taken up tying and selling Super Flies. An organization chart at that point would have looked like the one in Figure 8.1A. George was the entire operation, and, technically, an organization did not yet exist. There was no vertical hierarchy or horizontal specialization at that early stage.

George soon found it impossible to tie more than a couple hundred flies a week and still visit fishing-tackle retailers who might carry his Super Flies. To free some time, George hired and trained a family friend named Amy to help him run the operation in a small building he had leased. An organization chart could have been drawn up at that time because an organization came into existence when Amy was hired. (Remember that it takes at least two people to make an organization.) The chart would have resembled the one in Figure 8.1B. Vertical hierarchy had been introduced, since Amy was George's subordinate. However, there still was no horizontal specialization, because Amy did many different things.

As business picked up, George had to hire and train four full-time employees to work under Amy tying flies. He also hired Fred, a sharp salesman and an old fishing buddy, to head the marketing operation and recruit and train two regional

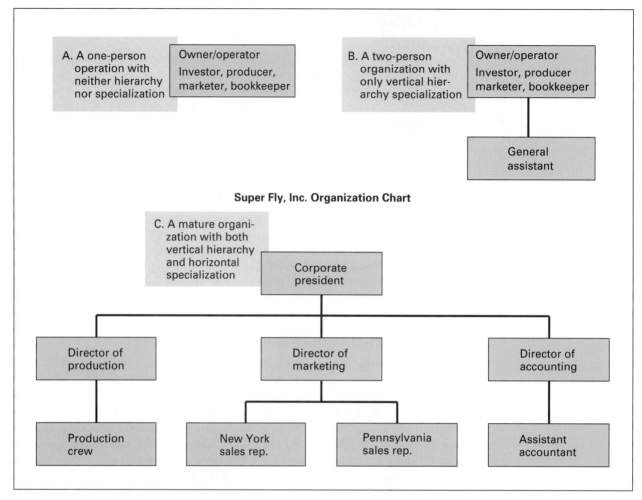

FIGURE 8.1 • The Evolution of an Organization Chart

sales representatives. Shortly afterward, an accountant was brought into the organization to set up and keep the books. Today, Super Fly, Inc., is recording annual sales in excess of $850,000. George has finally gotten around to formally organizing the company he built in patchwork fashion through the years. His current organization chart is displayed in Figure 8.1C.

Notice that the company now has three layers in the vertical hierarchy and three distinct forms of horizontal specialization. The three specialized directors now do separately what George used to do all by himself. George's job of general management will become progressively more difficult as additional vertical layers and horizontal specialists are added. Coordination is essential; the "right hand" must operate in concert with the "left hand." *Generally, specialization is achieved at the expense of coordination when designing organizations.* A workable balance between specialization and coordination can be achieved through contingency design, as discussed in the next chapter.

According to the open-system concept of equifinality, there is more than one way to get the job done. Dramatic evidence of equifinality was spotted by race fans in 1989 at the Golden Gate Fields track in Albany, California. As Nate Hubbard, a 19-year-old apprentice jockey, guided Sweetwater Oak into the final stretch, the filly stumbled on the muddy track and Hubbard lurched out of the saddle, holding on to the horse's mane. Hubbard finished second. Officials declared it a legal ride because the jockey remained aboard the horse.

Contrasting Theories of Organization

The study of organization theory is largely a twentieth-century development. As one organization theorist philosophically observed, "The study of organizations has a history but not a pedigree."[10] This history is marked by disagreement rather than uniformity of thinking. A useful way of approaching the study of organization theory is to contrast the traditional view with a modern view, two very different ways of thinking about organizations.

In the traditional view, the organization is characterized by closed-system thinking. This view assumes that the surrounding environment is fairly predictable and that uncertainty within the organization can be eliminated through proper planning and strict control. An organization's primary goal is seen to be economic efficiency. In contrast, a prevailing modern view characterizes the organization as an open system that interacts continuously with an uncertain environment. Both the organization and its surrounding environment are assumed to be filled with variables that are difficult to predict or control. As the open-system theorists see it, the organization's principal goal is survival in an environment of uncertainty and surprise. These contrasting approaches are summarized in Table 8.2.

• • • • • • • • • • • • • • •

Contrast the traditional and modern views of organizations.

The Traditional View

Let us explore the evolution of traditional organization theory by reviewing the contributions of the early management writers, Max Weber's concept of bureaucracy, and challenges to these traditional models. This will prepare the way for our examination of the modern open-system model of organizations.

TABLE 8.2 • Contrasting Theories of Organization

	Traditional view	*Modern view*
General perspective	Closed-system thinking	Open-system thinking
Primary goal of organization	Economic efficiency	Survival in an environment of uncertainty and surprise
Assumption about surrounding environment	Predictable	Generally uncertain
Assumptions about organizations	All causal, goal-directed variables are known and controllable. Uncertainty can be eliminated through planning and controlling.	The organizational system has more variables than can be comprehended at one time. Variables often are subject to influences that cannot be controlled or predicted.

Source: Adapted, by permission, from James D. Thompson, *Organizations in Action* (New York: McGraw-Hill, 1967), pp. 4–7.

The Early Management Writers.   Early contributors to management literature, such as Henri Fayol and Frederick W. Taylor, treated organizing as a subfield of management. You will recall from Chapter 1 that organizing was among Fayol's five universal functions of management. Taylor's narrow task definitions and strict work rules implied a tightly structured approach to organization design.

In general, Fayol and the other pioneering management writers who followed in his footsteps endorsed closely controlled authoritarian organizations. For instance, managers were advised to have no more than six immediate subordinates. Close supervision and obedience were the order of the day. Emphasis in these organizations was on the unrestricted downward flow of authority in the form of orders and rules. Four traditional principles of organization that emerged were (1) a well-defined hierarchy of authority, (2) unity of command, (3) authority equal to responsibility, and (4) downward delegation of authority but not of responsibility (see Table 8.3).

Max Weber's Bureaucracy.   Writing around the turn of the century, a German sociologist named Max Weber described what he considered to be the most rationally efficient form of organization, to which he affixed the label **bureaucracy.** According to Weber's model, bureaucracies are efficient because of the following characteristics: (1) division of labor, (2) hierarchy of authority, (3) a framework of rules, and (4) impersonality.[11] By *impersonality,* Weber meant hiring and promoting people on the basis of *what* they know, not *who* they know. It is important to realize that Weber's ideas about organizations were shaped by prevailing circumstances. Before the turn of the century, Germany was a semifeudal state struggling to adjust to the pressures of the Industrial Revolution. Weber was appalled at the way public administrators relied on subjective judgment, emotion, fear tactics, and nepotism (the hiring and promotion of one's relatives) rather than on sound management practices.[12] He used the widely

bureaucracy Weber's model of a rationally efficient organization respected and highly efficient Prussian army as the model for his bureaucratic form of organization.

In theory, Weber's bureaucracy was supposedly the epitome of efficiency. But experience with bureaucracies has shown that they can be slow, insensitive to individual needs, and grossly inefficient[13] (see The World of Management). Today, the term *bureaucracy* has a strongly negative connotation. This bureaucratic paradox can be reconciled somewhat by viewing bureaucracy as a matter of degree.

Every systematically managed organization, regardless of its size or purpose, is to some extent a bureaucracy. Bureaucratic characteristics are simply more pronounced or advanced in some organizations than in others. Trying to eliminate bureaucracy is impractical. The real challenge is keeping bureaucratic characteristics within functional limits. As Table 8.4 indicates, a moderate degree of bureaucratization can enhance organizational efficiency, but, taken too far, each dimension of bureaucracy can hinder efficiency. Managers who learn to read and retreat from the symptoms of dysfunction can reap the benefits of functional bureaucracy.

Challenges to the Traditional View of Organizations

Because the traditionalists' rigid recommendations for organizing and managing did not work in all situations, their recommendations were eventually challenged. Prescriptions for machinelike efficiency that worked in military units and simple shop operations often failed to work in complex organizations. Fayol's universal functions and principles turned out to be no guarantee of success. Similarly, experience proved that organizing was more than just the strict obedience to authority that Taylor had emphasized. In spite of Weber's rationally efficient organizational formula, bureaucracy in practice often became the epitome of inefficiency. In addition, challenges to traditional thinking about organizations arose from two other sources.

TABLE 8.3 • Traditional Principles of Organization

> 1. **A well-defined hierarchy of authority.** This principle was intended to ensure the coordinated pursuit of organizational goals by contributing individuals.
>
> 2. **Unity of command.** It was believed that the possibility of conflicting orders, a serious threat to the smooth flow of authority, could be avoided by making sure that each individual answered to only one superior.
>
> 3. **Authority equal to responsibility.** *Authority* was defined as the right to get subordinates to accomplish something. *Responsibility* was defined as the obligation to accomplish something. The traditionalists cautioned against holding individuals ultimately accountable for getting something done unless they were given formal authority to get it done.
>
> 4. **Downward delegation of authority but not of responsibility.** Although a superior with the requisite authority and responsibility can pass along the *right* to get something accomplished to subordinates, the *obligation* for getting it done remains with the superior. This arrangement was intended to eliminate the practice of "passing the buck."

TABLE 8.4 ● Functional versus Dysfunctional Bureaucracy: A Matter of Degree

	Indications of functional bureaucracy	Symptoms of dysfunctional bureaucracy
Degree of bureaucrati-zation	Moderate	High
Division of labor	More work, of higher quality, can be completed faster because complex tasks are separated into more readily mastered jobs.	Grievances, absenteeism, and turnover increase as a result of overly fragmented jobs that people find boring and dehumanizing. Poor quality performance leads to customer complaints.
Hierarchy of authority	A generally accepted chain of command serves to direct individuals' efforts toward organizational goal accomplishment.	Motivated by a fear of termination, a climate of blind obedience to authority, whether right or wrong, exists.
Framework of rules	Individual contributions to the collective effort are directed and coordinated by rules that answer important procedural questions.	Pursuit of the organization's mission is displaced by the practice of formulating and enforcing self-serving rules that protect, create unnecessary work, hide, or disperse accountability.
Impersonality	Hiring, promotion, and other personnel decisions are made on the basis of objective merit rather than favoritism or prejudice.	Subordinates and clients complain about being treated like numbers by bureaucrats who fail to respond to the full range of human needs.

Bottom-up Authority. Traditionalists left no doubt about the origin of authority in their organizational models. Authority was inextricably tied to property ownership and therefore naturally flowed from the top of the organization to the bottom. In businesses, those farthest removed from the ownership of stock were entitled to the least amount of authority. Naturally, this notion appealed strongly to those interested in maintaining the power base of society's more fortunate members. But when Chester I. Barnard described organizations as cooperative systems, he questioned the traditional assumption about the automatic downward flow of authority. Instead, he proposed a more democratic **acceptance theory of authority.** According to Barnard's acceptance theory, a leader's authority is determined by his or her subordinates' willingness to comply with it. Barnard believed that a subordinate recognizes a communication from above as being authoritative and decides to comply with it only when:

1. *The message is understood.*
2. *The subordinate believes it is consistent with the organization's purpose.*
3. *It serves the subordinate's interest.*
4. *The subordinate is able to comply.*[14]

acceptance theory of authority Barnard's theory that authority is determined by subordinates' willingness to comply

Glasnost Has Not Dented the Legendary Soviet Bureaucracy

In their Ladas, Trabants, and Skodas, East Europeans have become a familiar sight on the roads of Western Europe [in the summer of 1990] as they set out to see what they have been missing all these years. But Soviet tourists are still few and far between. The tribulations of an Estonian family, invited by friends to visit Denmark, help to explain why.

First, Soviet citizens must have an official invitation, stamped by a public notary, the foreign ministry, and the Soviet consulate in the country to be visited. Each stamp costs money. Back home, the would-be tourist needs an exit visa, which can be obtained only in Moscow. Inconvenient, if you happen not to live there.

The would-be tourists from Estonia failed to arrive on the appointed day. The passport police (run from Moscow) in Riga, capital of Estonia's neighboring republic, Latvia, had held them up for five hours, ensuring that they missed their flight, while the policemen argued over whether the names should be entered on travel documents in capitals or lower-case letters. New tickets had to be bought for the next flight, three days later. A friendly Aeroflot pilot advised them to keep cool: "If you protest, you may not get on the next aircraft either," they were told, "or something nasty, like narcotics, will be discovered in your luggage by the customs officials."

The intrepid travelers had already announced that they would be coming for five weeks, causing a mild case of household shock to their hosts. They explained, apologetically, that at the time they booked the trip the foreign-exchange allowance was related to the time to be spent abroad. On arrival they explained even more apologetically that, in the meantime, the rules had been changed: the foreign-exchange allowance had been abolished. That cheap holiday at home that their host had decided on this year was not so cheap after all.

Source: "Charity Begins at Home," *The Economist* (August 18, 1990): 43. © 1990 The Economist Newspaper Limited. Reprinted with permission.

Barnard's acceptance theory opened the door for a whole host of ideas, such as upward communication and the informal organization that is based on friendship rather than work rules. Prior to Barnard's contribution, such concepts had been discussed only by human relationists. In effect, **Barnard humanized organization theory by characterizing subordinates as active controllers of authority, not mere passive recipients.**

Environmental Complexity and Uncertainty. Although traditionalists liked to believe that rigid structure and rational management were important to organizational effectiveness and efficiency, environmental complexity and uncertainty often intervened to upset them. As Charles Perrow observed in writing about the history of organization theory, "The increasing complexity of markets, variability of products, increasing number of branch plants, and changes in technology all required more adaptive organizations."[15] Plans usually have to be made on the basis of incomplete or imperfect information and, consequently, things do not always work out according to plan. Similarly, many of the traditional principles of organization, such as the number of people a manager can effectively manage, have proved to be naive.

The net result of these and other challenges to traditional thinking was a desire to look at organizations in some new ways. When open-system thinking appeared on the management horizon, as discussed in Chapter 2, many eagerly embraced it because it emphasized the need for flexibility and adaptability in organization structure.

Organizations as Open Systems: A Modern View

Open-system thinking fosters a more realistic view of the interaction between an organization and its environment. Traditional closed-system perspectives—such as Fayol's universal process approach, scientific management, and bureaucracy—largely ignored environmental influences. Today's managers cannot afford that luxury. Imagine what would have happened to major airlines such as United or American if management had ignored the staggering array of environmental forces they faced in 1991. (See Managers in Action.)

Organizations are systems made up of interacting subsystems. Organizations are themselves subsystems that interact with larger social, political-legal, and economic systems.[16] Those who take an open-system perspective realize that system-to-system interactions are often as important as the systems themselves. Among these interactions are movements of people in and out of the labor force (for example, unemployment), movements of capital (for example, stock exchanges and corporate borrowing), and movements of goods and services (for example, international trade). A highly organized and vigorously interactive world needs realistically dynamic models. In this area, particularly, open-system thinking can make a contribution to organization theory.

Some Open-System Characteristics.   According to general systems theory, all open systems—whether the human body, an organization, a society, or the solar system—share certain characteristics. At the same time, the theory recognizes significant differences among the various kinds of open systems. Four characteristics that emphasize the adaptive and dynamic nature of all open systems are: (1) interaction with the environment, (2) synergy, (3) dynamic equilibrium, and (4) equifinality.

- *Interaction with the Environment.*   Open systems have permeable boundaries, whereas closed systems do not. Open systems, like the human body, are not self-sufficient. Life-sustaining oxygen, nutrients, and water must be imported from the surrounding environment, and waste must be exported. Similarly, organizations depend on the environment for survival.

- *Synergy.*   As discussed in Chapter 6, synergy is the $2 + 2 = 5$ effect. In other words, an open system adds up to more than the sum of its parts. A winning athletic team is more than its players, coaches, plays, and equipment. Only when all parts are in place and working in concert can the winning edge be achieved. Likewise, a successful business is more than the factors of production—land, labor, and capital. Synergistic thinking emphasizes that a firm's competitive edge is dictated as much by how the factors of production are mobilized as by what those factors are.

- *Dynamic Equilibrium.*   In open systems, **dynamic equilibrium** is the process of maintaining the internal balance necessary for survival by importing needed resources from the environment. Proper blood chemistry in the human body is maintained through dynamic equilibrium. When a person's

dynamic equilibrium process whereby an open system maintains its own internal balances with help from its environment

United Air Lines Battles for Global Skies

Airlines have never had the luxury of operating in a closed system. Even before government deregulation, the airline business could be affected by everything from weather conditions to economic changes to conflict in the Middle East. In fact, United Air Lines, Inc., the free world's largest airline, serves as a model of the open system, constantly reacting to and affecting its environment in significant ways.

The Persian Gulf War was a disaster for all airlines, causing the price of jet fuel to double and frightening passengers into staying at home. The effects of the war added to problems confronting the troubled airlines as a result of the recession and the continuing shakeup in the industry. Bankrupt major carriers like Eastern, Continental, and Pan Am, desperately trying to keep flying, lowered fares and contributed to a fare war that cut profits for the entire industry.

Nevertheless, United, one of the few reasonably healthy airlines, has been trying to remain proactive and avoid stagnation. With the growth of U.S. airline traffic stalled, United is looking to overseas flights as its hope for the future, and it eagerly bought Pan Am's Pacific and London routes. Even these moves could be undermined by outside influences. United must convince British regulators to agree to let its planes land at the more desirable London airport, Heathrow. British agreement may hinge on the willingness of the United States and other countries to open their airports to more foreign airlines.

Meanwhile, United has been fighting a heated internal battle, as the company's employees attempted to purchase the airline in the kind of leveraged buyout that was so popular in the 1980s. The attempts sent the company's stock price on a wild ride. When United's board rejected the employees' final offer, the news led to a drop in the overall stock market. The buyout's failure also added to the animosity between union members and United's chairman, Stephen M. Wolf, who needs to reduce labor costs if United is to outdistance its more efficient rival, American. United's future therefore depends on the company's ability to keep its sights set on growth while deftly coping with the complex array of internal and external forces that have grounded so many other airlines.

Sources: James E. Ellis, "Cleared for Takeoff," *Business Week* (November 5, 1990): 46–49; James Ellis, "Ego, Greed, and Hokum: Why the UAL Deal Crashed," *Business Week* (October 22, 1990): 33; Michael Oneal, "Dogfight!" *Business Week* (January 21, 1991): 56–62; Michael Oneal and Aaron Bernstein, "Never Before Has United Been So Divided," *Business Week* (October 22, 1990): 32; Kenneth Labich, "Can United Afford to Be Taken Over?" *Fortune* (September 11, 1989): 145–148; "Thanks, Now Get Out of Here," *Forbes* (May 28, 1990): 258.

blood sugar drops below normal, a craving for sugar prompts the ingestion of something sweet, thus increasing the blood-sugar level. Similarly, management can take out a loan when operations have drained the organization's cash reserves.

equifinality open systems can achieve similar ends through different means

- *Equifinality.* Open systems are made up of more than fixed cause-and-effect linkages. **Equifinality** means reaching the same result by different means. In their landmark book *Organization and Management,* Fremont Kast and James Rosenzweig summarize: "The concept of equifinality suggests that the manager can utilize a varying bundle of inputs into the organization, can transform them in a variety of ways, and can achieve satisfactory output."[17] For example, Nucor, a rapidly growing and highly profitable steel producer, is almost totally unlike traditional steel companies. Nucor builds its own mills, makes steel from scrap rather than ore,

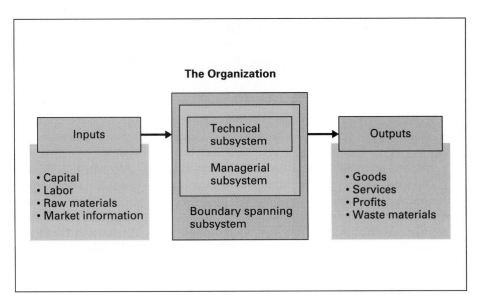

FIGURE 8.2 ● Open-System Model of a Business

uses the latest energy-saving technology, and ties its nonunion employees' weekly bonuses to productivity.[18] Whereas America's steel giants have had to retrench in the face of stiff foreign competition, Nucor has thrived because of equifinality. In short, Nucor found a different way of getting the job done.

Developing an Open-System Model.   An open-system model encourages managers to think about organization-environment interaction (see Figure 8.2). A business must acquire various *inputs:* capital, either through selling stock or borrowing; labor, through hiring people; raw materials, through purchases; and market information, through research. On the *output* side of the model, goods and services are marketed, profits (or losses) are realized, and waste materials are discarded (if not recycled). There are other inputs and outputs as well. This open-system model, although descriptive of a business organization, readily generalizes to all types of organizations.

By using the open-system premise that systems are made up of interacting subsystems, we can identify three prominent organizational subsystems: technical, boundary-spanning, and managerial. Sometimes called the production function, the technical subsystem physically transforms raw materials into finished goods and services. But the ability to turn out a product does not in itself guarantee organizational survival. Other supporting subsystems are also needed.

Whereas technical subsystems may be viewed as being at an organization's very core, boundary-spanning subsystems are directed outward toward the general environment. Most boundary-spanning jobs, or interface functions, as they are sometimes called, are easily identified by their titles. Purchasing agents are responsible for making sure that the organization has a steady and reliable flow of raw materials and subcomponents. Public relations staff are in charge of developing and maintaining a favorable public image of the organization. Strategic

••••••••••••••••••
Describe a business organization in terms of the open-system model.

planners have the responsibility of surveying the general environment for actual or potential opportunities and threats. Sales personnel probe the environment for buyers for the organization's goods or services. Purchasing agents, public relations staff, strategic planners, and sales personnel have one common characteristic: they all facilitate the organization's interaction with its environment. Each, so to speak, has one foot inside the organization and one foot outside.

Although the technical and boundary-spanning subsystems are important and necessary, one additional subsystem is needed to tie the organization together. As Figure 8.2 indicates, the managerial subsystem serves as a bridge between the other two subsystems. The managerial subsystem controls and directs the other subsystems in the organization.[19] It is within this subsystem that the subject matter of this book is practiced as a blend of science and art.

Organizational Effectiveness

The practice of management, as defined in Chapter 1, challenges managers to use organizational resources effectively and efficiently. Effectiveness is a measure of whether or not organizational objectives are accomplished. In contrast, efficiency is the relationship between outputs and inputs. Only monopolies can get away with being effective but not efficient. Moreover, in an era of diminishing resources and increasing concern about civil rights, society is reluctant to label "effective" any organization that wastes scarce resources or tramples on civil rights. Management's definition of organizational effectiveness therefore needs to be refined. The related issue of organizational decline also needs to be understood and skillfully managed.

Faced with rising overhead expenses, higher production costs, and lower prices for oil products, Patrick Early, president of Amoco Production Company, decided it was time for radical surgery. Three layers of management were eliminated. Units with about 500 people each, made up of cross-functional teams (pictured here), replaced the traditional functional hierarchy. Decision-making authority was pushed down to those closest to the action. Early feels his people are again taking the risks necessary to be competitive.

No Silver Bullet

According to one management scholar, "no single approach to the evaluation of effectiveness is appropriate in all circumstances or for all organizational types."[20] More and more, the effectiveness criteria for modern organizations are being prescribed by society in the form of explicit expectations, regulations, and laws. In the private sector, profitability is no longer the sole criterion of effectiveness. Major oil companies were highly profitable after Iraq invaded Kuwait, for example, but many members of society weren't particularly happy about it. Despite the Reagan administration's battle against unnecessary regulation, today's managers remain caught up in an enormous web of laws and regulations covering employment practices, working conditions, job safety, pensions, product safety, pollution, and competitive practices. To be truly effective, today's productive organizations need to strike a generally acceptable balance between organizational and societal goals. Direct conflicts, such as higher wages for employees and lower prices for customers, are inevitable. Therefore, the process of determining the proper weighting of organizational effectiveness criteria is an endless one requiring frequent review and updating.[21]

A Time Dimension

● ● ● ● ● ● ● ● ● ● ● ● ● ● ● ●
Explain the time dimension of organizational effectiveness.

organizational effectiveness being effective, efficient, satisfying, adaptive and developing, and ultimately surviving

To build a workable definition of organizational effectiveness, we shall introduce a time dimension. As indicated in Figure 8.3, the organization needs to be effective in the near, intermediate, and distant future. Consequently, **organizational effectiveness** can be defined as meeting organizational objectives and prevailing societal expectations in the near future, adapting and developing in the intermediate future, and surviving in the distant future.

Most people think only of the near future. It is in the near future that the organization has to produce goods or render services, use resources efficiently, and satisfy both insiders and outsiders with its activity. But this is just the beginning, not the end. To grow and be effective, an organization must adapt to new environmental demands and mature and learn in the intermediate future (two to four years).

Organizational Decline

Prior to the mid-1970s, management had a universal answer to competitive and organizational problems: growth, growth, and more growth. Fueled by strong demand, corporations mushroomed in size and diversity of operations as they strove for ever-greater market shares. In recent years, however, unsteady economic growth, resource shortages, and vigorous international competition have taken their toll among industrial giants. Especially hard hit have been U.S. auto makers and steel companies. Thirty-two U.S. auto plants were closed between 1987 and 1990.[22] Layoffs, retrenchments, cutbacks, and plant closings have become commonplace in other industries as well, including computers and electronics. Turnaround specialists, hired to restore companies to health, have come to use terms like *downsizing* and *demassing* when shrinking and breaking up organizations. All this activity points to a fundamental shortcoming of modern management theory and practice: we know a lot about managing growth but precious little about managing organizational decline.

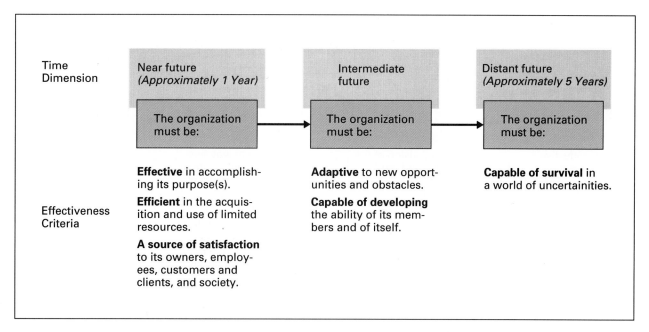

Time Dimension

Near future (Approximately 1 Year)	Intermediate future	Distant future (Approximately 5 Years)
The organization must be:	The organization must be:	The organization must be:

Effectiveness Criteria

Effective in accomplishing its purpose(s).

Efficient in the acquisition and use of limited resources.

A source of satisfaction to its owners, employees, customers and clients, and society.

Adaptive to new opportunities and obstacles.

Capable of developing the ability of its members and of itself.

Capable of survival in a world of uncertainities.

FIGURE 8.3 • The Time Dimension of Organizational Effectiveness

Source: Adapted from James L. Gibson, John M. Ivancevich, and James H. Donnelly, Jr., *Organizations: Behavior, Structure, Processes,* 5th ed. (Homewood, IL: Richard D. Irwin, Inc.), p. 37. © 1991.

●●●●●●●●●●●●●●●●●
Define organizational decline and identify characteristics common to organizations in decline.

organizational decline organization is weakened by resource or demand restrictions and/or mismanagement

Logic says what goes up must come down. According to a pair of experts on the subject: "Corporate performance almost always declines following a period of success."[23] These experts believe that *management complacency* is largely responsible for turning success into decline (see Figure 8.4). If allowed to persist, organizational decline can mean failure and bankruptcy. Today's managers must be adept at expanding, remaking, and sometimes shrinking their organizations, as conditions warrant.

Organizational decline is a weakened condition resulting from resource and/or demand restrictions and mismanagement. It typically involves a reduction in the size or scope of the organization.[24] For example, Lee Iacocca's turnaround team had to reduce Chrysler's size by 50 percent during its 1979–1981 brush with bankruptcy. Because that management era was preoccupied with growth, Iacocca had no textbook models, research base, or collection of proven techniques from which to learn. Thanks to recent interest in the management of organizational decline, an instructive body of theory, research, and practice is taking shape. Let us review that body of knowledge to better understand how managers can steer their organizations through the bad times that typically follow the good times.

Characteristics of Organizational Decline

What are the characteristics or indicators of an organization in decline? A partial answer to this question came from a survey of 3,406 administrators at 334

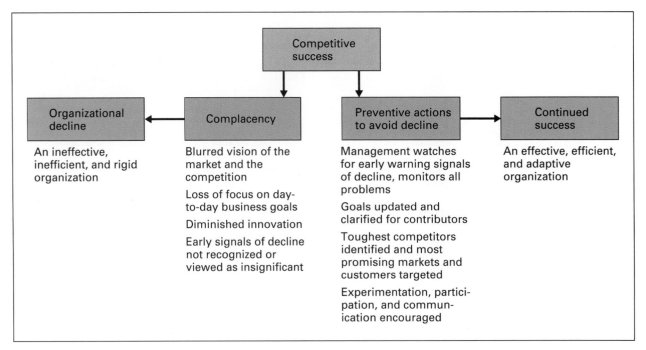

FIGURE 8.4 ● Complacency Can Lead to Organizational Decline

four-year colleges in the United States.[25] Kim Cameron and his colleagues used six years of revenue data to divide the schools into three categories: growing, stable, and declining. They found that nine attributes (listed in Table 8.5) were statistically significant characteristics of organizational decline. The researchers were surprised to find that the same characteristics were associated with stable organizations, suggesting that all organizations are actually in one of two phases—either growth or decline. In short, an organization that has entered a period of stability has taken the first step toward decline.

Decline Dilemmas. Of the nine characteristics of organizational decline presented in Table 8.5, five particularly troublesome dilemmas emerge. First, the leaders most needed by the organization tend to be the first to leave. Second, control is achieved at the expense of employee participation and morale. Third, when management needs to take long-term risks, short-term thinking and risk avoidance prevail. Fourth, conflict intensifies when teamwork is most needed. Finally, at precisely the time when changes are required, resistance to change is the greatest. Organizational decline is a cycle that feeds on itself and only gets worse if left unmanaged.

Decline Is a Never-ending Challenge. More research is required in this important area. Meanwhile, to avoid being caught by surprise, managers need to anticipate and counteract the characteristics of decline. Because the seeds of decline are sown during periods of success, when management may become overconfident and complacent, decline is an ever-present threat. Boeing, for example, holds a strong first place in the commercial aircraft industry, with a 54 percent world

TABLE 8.5 ● Nine Characteristics of Organizational Decline

	Description
Centralization	Decision making is passed upward, participation decreases, control is emphasized
No long-term planning	Crises and short-term needs drive out strategic planning
Innovation curtailed	No experimentation, risk aversion, and skepticism about non-core activities
Scapegoating	Leaders are blamed for the pain and uncertainty
Resistance to change	Conservatism and turf protection lead to rejection of new alternatives
Turnover	The most competent leaders tend to leave first, causing leadership anemia
Low morale	Few needs are met, and infighting is predominant
Nonprioritized cuts	Attempts to ameliorate conflict lead to attempts to equalize cutbacks
Conflict	Competition and in-fighting for control predominate when resources are scarce

Source: Characteristics and descriptions excerpted from Kim S. Cameron, David A. Whetten, and Myung U. Kim, "Organizational Dysfunction of Decline," *Academy of Management Journal,* 30 (March 1987): 128. Reprinted by permission.

market share. Nevertheless, Chairman Frank A. Shrontz works hard to alert Boeing's 160,000 employees to the hard reality that success can be a fleeting thing: "I must confess it's perhaps a little more difficult to do than in some industries because we have to convince our people there's a need to change and improve."[26] Shrontz's attitude should help Boeing combat complacency bred by success.

Managing Organizational Decline

Amid today's competitive pressures, it is naive to expect organizations to grow and prosper indefinitely. Instead, one should expect successive periods of growth and decline that need to be recognized and managed skillfully. Steps can be taken to try to prevent decline as long as possible. Organizations that do experience decline must be prepared to deal effectively with displaced employees.

Preventive Safeguards. Though declines are natural and cyclical, management scholars Peter Lorange and Robert T. Nelson recommend a number of organizational safeguards for recognizing declines and, if not avoiding them, at least lessening their frequency:

1. Organize the company into definable ventures that have explicit goals. The clarity and immediacy of the goals provide decision benchmarks that executives understand.

2. For each business, single out and concentrate on the toughest competitors and the most difficult customers.

3. Define each job so that it is closely tied to a venture and has a "daily effect" on the success or failure of the venture.

4. Promote individual diversity in order to challenge the hardening of outdated organizational concepts. Make room for experimentation and look for managers who are winners.

5. Strengthen the participative, interactive, and iterative sides of strategic management processes. Emphasize more effective information flow.[27]

These policies fall under the heading of good everyday management. But they also safeguard against organizational decline because they counteract complacency. The second policy in the list is especially effective.

Handling Displaced Employees in an Ethical Manner. In Chapter 3 we discussed the need to recycle technologically displaced employees through retraining. This need applies not only to those who lose their jobs because of new technology, but also to the growing number of employees whose jobs have been eliminated because of organizational decline, mergers, and acquisitions. According to one estimate, nearly 25 percent of all middle management positions in corporate America were eliminated during the 1980s.[28] Managers who see their employees as a commodity to be hired when times are good and fired when times are bad are widely criticized for being shortsighted and unethical. The preferred model today views employees as valuable human resources requiring careful nurture and career assistance in the event of a layoff. Progressive organizations have adopted one or more of the following practices to soften the blow of organizational decline:

- *Redeployment.* Displaced employees are retrained and/or transferred. IBM, for example, responded to declining sales by retraining and repositioning 45,000 employees between 1985 and 1988.[29]

- *Downgrading.* To avoid a layoff, the organization moves displaced employees to lower-level jobs, sometimes maintaining their former pay rates.

- *Work Sharing.* Instead of laying off a portion of its workforce, management divides the available work among all employees, who take cuts in hours and pay.

- *Voluntary Early Retirement and Voluntary Layoffs.* Employees are induced to leave the organization with offers of accelerated retirement benefits, severance pay, and/or prepaid health insurance. This tactic can backfire if valuable employees leave and poor performers stay. However, during IBM's reorganization, nearly 80 percent of those leaving were in jobs IBM wanted to eliminate. In addition, these people had been employees for some time and were earning high salaries, saving IBM a lot of money.[30]

- *Early Warning of Facility Closings.* Imagine the pain of an unsuspecting employee who goes to work only to find that the facility has permanently closed. Several state legislatures in the United States have passed laws requiring companies to provide employees with some sort of advance warning of factory or office closings.[31] A federal law, the Worker Adjustment and Retraining Notification Act that went into effect in 1989, requires companies with one hundred or more employees to give sixty days' notice of a closing or layoff.[32] Early warnings give displaced employees time to prepare for financial and employment disruption.

- *Outplacement.* The practice of **outplacement** involves helping displaced employees polish their job-seeking skills to increase their chances of finding suitable employment promptly.[33] This ethical practice can be costly. For example, when Detroit's Stroh Brewery was bought out by Joseph Schlitz Brewing Company, Stroh spent more than $1.5 million helping 99 percent of its 1,100 out-of-work employees find new jobs.[34]

outplacement the ethical practice of helping displaced employees find new jobs

Our discussions of organizational effectiveness and decline teach valuable lessons about the functioning of modern organizations. But the picture is not complete. A more subtle yet influential dimension of organizations remains to be explored. Managers who ignore this key dimension of organizations have little chance of success. So let's turn our attention to the interesting topic of organizational cultures to see what makes otherwise static structures come alive.

Organizational Cultures

Explain the nature and significance of organizational cultures.

Open-system thinking helps us to appreciate more fully the dynamic interaction between organizations and their environments. Recently, however, the open system model has been criticized for failing to address the *time dimension* of organizations adequately. A more encompassing *cultural* perspective has been recommended—one that realistically intertwines past, present, and future aspects of the organization.[35] Your present behavior, for instance, is affected by both your past (family and cultural history) and your future (goals and aspirations). So, too, organizational actions result from a dynamic interaction between past experience, present capabilities, and goals for future progress. Although the traditional planning/control cycle embraces the present and future dimensions, the organization's past is too often ignored by those who study organizations. When organizations are studied as distinct cultures, the powerful influence of past actions, people, and events on organizational processes becomes apparent.

In this final section, we define organizational culture and present a conceptual framework that attempts to extend the open-system model.

What Does Organizational Culture Involve?

organizational culture shared values, beliefs, and language that create a common identity and sense of community

The notion of organizational culture is rooted in cultural anthropology.[36] **Organizational culture** is the collection of shared (stated or implied) beliefs, values, rituals, stories, myths, and specialized language that fosters a feeling of community among organization members.[37] Some call organizational culture the "social glue" binding organizational members together. Others even go so far as to infer a spiritual linkage (see Management Ethics).

Table 8.6 defines some important terms used to describe various elements of organizational culture. One key cultural element missing in Table 8.6 is organizational values. Unlike instrumental and terminal values, discussed in Chapter

By any measure, Herman Miller is not your typical company. For openers, the Michigan-based office furniture maker's headquarters has the look of "farm architecture." The idea is that creative work needs a creative setting. And, CEO Max DePree writes and talks about management in spiritual and religious terms. He refers to the bond between the company and employee as a covenant. The firm's admired culture is steeped in traditions and practices involving trust, roving leadership, innovation, and morality.

organizational values shared beliefs about what the organization stands for

4 as *personal* beliefs, **organizational values** are *shared* beliefs about what the organization stands for.[38] Many of the companies discussed so far in this book provide examples of these concepts. McDonald's shrine to founder Ray Kroc is a powerful organizational *symbol* signifying the importance of *organizational values* including quality, service, cleanliness, and value. Stories or legends passed along about particular historical events are also very common in organizations. One example is the familiar *story* of Apple Computer's amazing rise from a garage-based enterprise to a *Fortune* 500 company worth billions. To those who hear it, the Apple story reinforces the values of entrepreneurship and persistence in the face of impossible odds.

When discussing organizational culture, some prefer the term *corporate* to *organizational* when referring to profit-making businesses. Whichever label one uses, it is a good idea to keep in mind some cautionary words from an anthropologist-turned-manager:

> *Corporate culture is not an ideological gimmick to be imposed from above by management or management consulting firms but a stubborn fact of human social organization that can scuttle the best of corporate plans if not taken into account.*[39]

Although the cultural components listed in our definition are largely taken for granted by members of the organization and thus "invisible," they exert a powerful influence on behavior. As one might suspect, organizational cultures vary in strength; they can be strong or weak. But, according to the authors of the best-selling book *Corporate Cultures*, ". . . a strong culture has almost always been the driving force behind continuing success in American business."[40] A strong organizational culture performs four important functions:

Should Your Company Save Your Soul?

Few people are willing to put it quite that baldly, but look at the words they use: *vision, mission, values, transformation.* Almost unnoticed, some managers' thinking has changed drastically from only a couple of years ago, when the rallying cry wasn't "values" but "shareholder value."

The language of the pulpit has become the currency of the executive suite. Michael Ray, a professor at Stanford's business school, is offering a course this winter whose syllabus argues that business can find a "new paradigm," which takes as its purpose "the enlightenment of those in it." The course includes segments on "inner wisdom" and "business as a spiritual discipline."

In his best-selling book, *Leadership Is an Art,* Herman Miller CEO Max DePree writes of a "covenant"—not a contract—between company and employee as the basis for superior management. Says James Autry, president of Meredith Corp.'s magazine group: "Work can provide an opportunity for spiritual and personal, as well as financial, growth. Good management is largely a matter of love . . . a calling . . . a sacred trust."

Even when the impulse isn't religious, the effect is. Says Minneapolis consultant Thomas Eckstein, a 3M alumnus who specializes in new-product development: "As business people look at the soft issues, they start with emotional ones—like employees' need to feel part of a community—but they don't seem to be stopping there. I think they'll end up at spiritual issues, but they don't really know it yet." Says Harrison Owen, an Episcopal priest who has become a management consultant for such companies as Shell, Du Pont, and Owens-

Corning Fiberglas: "I tell my clients, 'However much shareholder equity you've got, you're not going to cut it if the spirit isn't there'—and I get no argument."

What's driving business to think in evangelical terms? One reason, says DePree, is to ground workers in a community. Churches, families, and neighborhoods provide less and less of the psychological sustenance people need, so "for many the corporation becomes the main social involvement and even family." Only business, says Stanford's Ray, is "global enough, flexible enough, pragmatic enough, and has people's interests at heart enough" to take up the slack. . . .

A spiritual view of work and management is all very well, but when is it time for a corporation to mind its own business? According to Ray, some employees of major corporations develop marital problems as their work becomes more fulfilling. Du Pont now conducts workshops to help its people pass the benefits along to the entire family. Many companies may not want to take on such responsibility. Conversely, a church may excommunicate an occasional heretic, but it doesn't impose layoffs on the congregation. A company's care for the souls of its employees has to stop at its bottom line and their private lives. Does wrestling with these issues make a manager's life more difficult? Says DePree: "It never becomes heaven, you know."

Source: Excerpted from Thomas A. Stewart, "Should Your Company Save Your Soul?" *Fortune* (January 14, 1991): 33. © 1991 The Time Inc. Magazine Company. All rights reserved.

1. It gives organizational members a sense of identity.

2. It encourages commitment to the organization's mission.

3. It promotes organizational stability.

4. It influences behavior by helping individuals make sense of their surroundings.[41]

Organizations with weak cultures do not enjoy the advantages these four functions provide.

TABLE 8.6 • Definitions for Selected Components of Organizational Culture

	Definition
Symbol	Any object, act, event, quality, or relation that serves as a vehicle for conveying meaning, usually by representing another thing.
Rite	A relatively elaborate, dramatic, planned set of activities that combines various forms of cultural expressions and that often has both practical and expressive consequences.
Ritual	A standardized, detailed set of techniques and behaviors that manages anxieties but seldom produces intended, practical consequences of any importance.
Story	A narrative based on true events—often a combination of truth and fiction.
Legend	A handed-down narrative of some wonderful event that has a historical basis but has been embellished with fictional details.
Myth	A dramatic narrative of imagined events, usually used to explain origins or transformations of something. Also, an unquestioned belief about the practical benefits of certain techniques and behaviors that is not supported by demonstrated facts.

Source: "How an Organization's Rites Reveal Its Culture" by Janice M. Beyer and Harrison M. Trice. Reprinted by permission of publisher, from *Organizational Dynamics*, Spring, 1987 © 1987. American Management Association, New York. All rights reserved.

The Organizational Socialization Process

organizational socialization
process of transforming outsiders into accepted insiders

Organizational socialization is the process through which outsiders are transformed into accepted insiders.[42] In effect, the socialization process shapes newcomers to fit the organizational culture.

> *The culture asserts itself when the taken-for-granted cultural assumptions are in some way violated by the uninitiated and provoke a response. As the uninitiated bump into one after another taken-for-granted assumption, more acculturated employees respond in a variety of ways (tell stories, offer advice, ridicule, lecture, shun, and so forth) that serve to mold the way in which the newcomer thinks about his or her role and about "how things are done around here."*[43]

Stories deserve special attention here because they are a central feature of organizational socialization and culture. Company stories about heroic or inspiring deeds let newcomers know what "really counts."[44] For example, 3M's eleventh commandment—"Thou shalt not kill a new product idea"—has been ingrained in new employees through one inspiring story about the employee who invented transparent cellophane tape.

> *According to the story, an employee accidentally discovered the tape but was unable to get his superiors to buy the idea. Marketing studies predicted a relatively small demand for the new material. Undaunted, the employee found a way to sneak into the board room and tape down the minutes of board members with his transparent tape. The board was impressed enough with the novelty to give it a try and experienced incredible success.*[45]

Upon hearing this story, a 3M newcomer has believable, concrete evidence that innovation and persistence pay off at 3M. It has been said that stories are "social road maps" for employees, telling them where to go and where not to go and what will happen when they get there. Moreover, stories are remembered longer than abstract facts or rules and regulations. How many times have you recalled a professor's colorful story but forgotten the rest of the lecture?

Diagnosing Organizational Cultures

If one is to gain a realistic picture of an organization, both open-system thinking and a cultural diagnosis are needed. Cultural diagnoses are useful for (1) those about to join an organization and (2) those desiring to change an organization in some significant way. Whatever the reason for diagnosing an organization's culture, it is important to remember that:

> *Reading a culture is an interpretive, subjective activity. There are no exact answers, and two observers may come up with somewhat different descriptions of the same culture. The validity of the diagnosis must be judged by the utility of the insights it provides, not by its "correctness" as determined by some objective criteria.*[46]

FIGURE 8.5 ● A Framework for Diagnosing an Organization's Culture

Source: "Some Action Implications of Corporate Culture: A Manager's Guide to Action," by Vijay Sathe. Reprinted, by permission of publisher, from *Organizational Dynamics,* 12 (Autumn 1983): 8. © 1983 American Management Association, New York. All rights reserved.

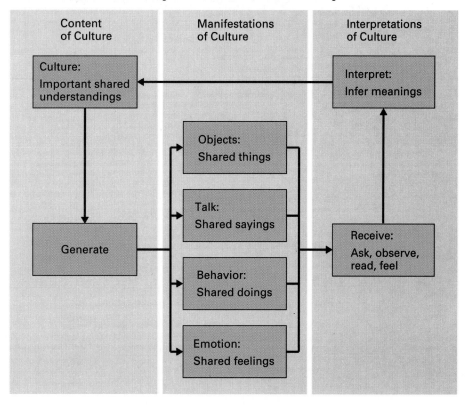

A framework for diagnosing organizational cultures is illustrated in Figure 8.5. Notice that the observer needs to "ask," "observe," "read," and "feel" when gathering information on the four manifestations of culture: objects, talk, behavior, and emotion. It is instructive and important to compare intentions with actual behavior. Taken-for-granted beliefs and values generally need to be inferred from behavior. Symptoms of a weak organizational culture include:

- *Inward Focus.* Has internal politics become more important than real-world problems and the marketplace?
- *Short-term Focus.* Is too much time and energy spent on achieving short-term results?
- *Morale Problems.* Is there chronic unhappiness and high turnover?
- *Fragmentation/Inconsistency.* Is there a lack of "fit" in the way people behave, communicate, and perceive problems and opportunities?
- *Emotional Outbursts.* Does emotionalism override sound judgment and rational thinking?
- *Ingrown Subcultures.* Is there a lack of communication among subunits?
- *Warfare among Subcultures.* Has constructive competition given way to destructive conflict?
- *Subculture Elitism.* Have organizational units become exclusive "clubs" with restricted entry? Have subcultural values become more important than the organization's values?[47]

Evidence of these symptoms may encourage a potential recruit to look elsewhere. Each of these symptoms of a weak organizational culture can be a formidable barrier to organizational effectiveness. Organizations with strong cultures, such as IBM and United Parcel Service, have done a good job of avoiding these symptoms.

Summary

Organizations need to be understood and intelligently managed because they are an ever-present feature of modern life. Whatever their purpose, all organizations have four characteristics: (1) coordination of effort, (2) common goal or purpose, (3) division of labor, and (4) hierarchy of authority. If even one of these characteristics is absent, an organization does not exist. One useful way of classifying organizations is by their intended purpose. Organizations can be classified as business, nonprofit service, mutual benefit, or commonweal. Organization charts are helpful visual aids for managers. Representing the organization's structural skeleton, organization charts delineate vertical hierarchy and horizontal specialization.

There are both traditional and modern views of organizations. Traditionalists such as Fayol, Taylor, and Weber subscribed to closed-system thinking and ignored the impact of environmental forces. Modern organization theorists tend to prefer open-system thinking because it realistically incorporates organizations' environmental dependency. Early management writers proposed tightly controlled authoritarian organizations. Max Weber, a German sociologist, applied the label *bureaucracy* to his formula for the most rationally efficient type of organization. Bureaucracies are characterized by their division of labor, hierarchy of authority, framework of rules, and impersonality. Unfortunately, in actual practice, *bureaucracy* has become a synonym for red tape and inefficiency. The answer to this bureaucratic paradox is to understand that bureaucracy is a matter of degree. When bureaucratic characteristics, which are present in all organizations, are carried to an extreme, efficiency gives way to inefficiency.

Chester I. Barnard's acceptance theory of authority and growing environmental complexity and uncertainty questioned traditional organization theory. Open-system thinking became a promising alternative because it was useful in explaining the necessity of creating flexible and adaptable rather than rigid organizations. Although the analogy between natural systems and human social systems (organizations) is imperfect, there are important parallels. Organizations, like all open systems, are unique because of their (1) interaction with the environment, (2) synergy, (3) dynamic equilibrium, and (4) equifinality. In open-system terms, business organizations are made up of interdependent technical, boundary-spanning, and managerial subsystems.

Because there is no one criterion for organizational effectiveness, profit as well as nonprofit organizations need to satisfy different effectiveness criteria in the near, intermediate, and distant future. Effective organizations are effective, efficient, and satisfying in the near term. They are adaptive and developing in the intermediate term. Ultimately, in the long term, effective organizations survive.

Because of past preoccupation with growth, the management of organizational decline has only recently received the attention it deserves. Decline is often attributable to managerial complacency. The characteristics of decline are interlocking dilemmas that foster organizational self-destruction. To avoid decline as much as possible, or at least lessen its frequency, organizations should adopt preventive safeguards that counteract complacency. Modern organizations experiencing decline are urged to treat displaced employees ethically.

Viewing organizations as cultures serves to realistically connect their past, present, and future dimensions. Successful organizations tend to have strong organizational cultures in which there are widely shared values and a sense of community. Diverse outsiders are transformed into accepted insiders through the process of organizational socialization. Stories about company heroes are a powerful and lasting socialization technique. Systematic diagnosis can reveal symptoms of a weak organizational culture. The cultural perspective extends the open-system model of organizations.

Terms to Understand

Organization	Equifinality
Authority	Organizational effectiveness
Commonweal organization	Organizational decline
Organization chart	Outplacement
Bureaucracy	Organizational culture
Acceptance theory of authority	Organizational values
Dynamic equilibrium	Organizational socialization

Questions for Discussion

1. Is the audience in a movie theater an organization? Explain your reasoning. What about an individual writing a novel? How about two people playing a friendly round of golf?

2. Why do you suppose nonprofit service organizations are considered an especially difficult challenge for managers today?

3. Why is the modern, open-system view of organizations more realistic than the traditional view?

4. In your opinion, how applicable today are the four traditional principles of organization? (Refer to Table 8.3.) Explain your reasoning.

5. What recent experiences have you had with dysfunctional bureaucracy? What should the organization do to correct the situation?

6. How can equifinality help you get a college degree?

7. How is it possible that a profitable business could be considered ineffective?

8. What is your personal experience with organizational decline? Which characteristics of decline were evident? *Tip:* Use Table 8.5 as a guide.

9. Why is the term *social glue* particularly useful when discussing organizational cultures?

10. What is your personal experience with weak (or strong) organizational cultures? What impact did the situation you describe have on the organization's effectiveness?

Back to the Opening Case

Now that you have read Chapter 8, you should be able to answer the following questions about the General Motors case:

1. Why was GM a likely victim of dysfunctional bureaucracy?

2. From an open-system viewpoint, what sources of environmental uncertainty does GM face?

3. How would you assess GM's organizational effectiveness in recent years?

4. Can GM reverse its organizational decline? Explain your reasoning. (*Tip:* Use Figure 8.4 as a guide.)

|CLOSING CASE|

The Sweet Success of Hershey's Values

If you make your way to the right part of Pennsylvania, you won't have much trouble finding Hershey Foods Corporation. As you near the town of Hershey—affectionately called Chocolate Town, U.S.A.—your nose will guide you toward the sweet aroma of Hershey's factories. You'll know you're on the right street—Chocolate Avenue—because it's the one with streetlamps shaped like Hershey's Kisses. If you have time to relax, you can enjoy the Hershey Zoo or the amusement park. But if you're looking for corporate headquarters, strictly on business, you'll find it behind the white columns of Milton Hershey's mansion. That's where President and Chief Operating Officer Kenneth Wolf works in the founder's bedroom.

If this all sounds like a nineteenth-century industrialist's dream of a company town, it should. Milton Snavely Hershey *did* start the company just after the turn of the century, and he and his wife wanted to leave a lasting legacy. The childless couple donated part of their fortune to help deprived boys, and the Milton Hershey School, now co-educational, remains the largest stockholder in Hershey Foods Corporation. So the Hershey "family" atmosphere survives.

Hershey's founder also bequeathed the company a set of values that, as current CEO Richard Zimmerman puts it, "*guide* change." The values are as predictable and American as the chocolate bar: a focus on the family and community and an emphasis on religious and moral principles, education, thrift, quality, altruism, and the golden rule. More surprising is the company's attempt to live up to the founder's principles. And the real shock is that it seems to succeed.

Carrying on such a tradition is no easy task, and company executives realize they cannot complacently assume that employees will uphold the values simply because of tradition. The 1960s and 1970s brought many changes to Hershey, as the company grew and diversified, replaced retiring personnel with outsiders, and created such new divisions as Corporate Planning and Public Relations.

In 1985, Zimmerman set up a task force to identify the values Hershey could stand behind and advocate. The task force was also asked to find the best ways to communicate those values and earn employee commitment, pinpointing and eliminating any barriers that might hamper the process. No slick outside consultants were brought in to devise a set of principles and persuade employees to follow them. The task force was kept in-house and comprised of representatives from all of Hershey's divisions. Mem-

bers spent six months interviewing Hershey employees, not urging them to change their beliefs but instead trying to discover the beliefs they already held.

The list of values that this method produced would have made Hershey's founder proud. High ethical standards were at the center of the shared principles, complemented by an orientation toward people and family, a desire to solve problems without open conflict, and a belief in a work ethic backed by strong job security. Not content to congratulate their employees and hand out the list of values on plastic cards, Hershey made the values the centerpiece of new management training seminars and vowed to demonstrate them from the top level of the company on down.

Hershey's values even affect its subsidiaries, not easy for a company with revenues of more than $2 billion yearly. Since renewing its focus on values, Hershey has worked to sell off unrelated businesses, like Friendly Restaurants, and to buy others with products and cultures that complement Hershey's own. This policy led to the 1988 purchase of Cadbury's U.S. brands, including Peter Paul Almond Joy and Mounds. That move pushed Hershey into the number one spot among American confectionery makers, ahead of rival Mars. Hershey does not attempt to eradicate the existing cultures of its acquisitions and make them swear allegiance to the Hershey principles. Instead, the company tries to develop in subsidiaries' employees a dual loyalty, a sense of identifying with their own company while also being a part of Hershey.

For Discussion

1. Why is Hershey unlikely to be a victim of organizational decline in the foreseeable future?

2. How important are stories and symbols in Hershey's organizational culture?

3. What advantages does Hershey enjoy because it has a strong organizational culture?

References

Opening Quotation. Joseph A. Litterer, *The Analysis of Organizations*, 2nd ed. (New York: Wiley, 1973), p. 5.

Opening Case. Al Fleming, "Birth of Impact of Family Affair," *Automotive News* (July 9, 1990): 141; Annetta Miller, "GM Aims for the Fast Lane," *Newsweek* (October 22, 1990): 50–51; Patricia Sellers, "To Saturn and Beyond," *Fortune* (November 5, 1990): 12–13; James B. Treece, "War, Recession, Gas Hikes . . . GM's Turnaround Will Have to Wait," *Business Week* (February 4, 1991): 94–96.

Closing Case. Sally J. Blank, "Hershey: A Company Driven by Values," *Management Review* (November 1986): 31–35; Andrew Kupfer, "The Sweet Smell of Success," *Fortune* (April 24, 1989): 30–31; Joseph Weber, "Why Hershey Is Smacking Its Lips," *Business Week* (October 30, 1989): 140.

1. Chester I. Barnard, *The Functions of the Executive* (Cambridge, Mass.: Harvard University Press, 1938), p. 73.
2. Adapted from Edgar H. Schein, *Organizational Psychology*, 3rd ed. (Englewood Cliffs, N.J.: Prentice-Hall, 1980), pp. 12–15.
3. Ross Perot, " 'How I Would Turn Around GM,' " *Fortune* (February 15, 1988): 44.
4. See Adam Smith, *The Wealth of Nations* (New York: Modern Library, 1937), p. 7.
5. Elliot Jaques, "In Praise of Hierarchy," *Harvard Business Review*, 68 (January-February 1990): 127.
6. For an interesting biography of Henry Ford, see Ann Jardim, *The First Henry Ford: A Study in Personality and Business Leadership* (Cambridge, Mass.: MIT Press, 1970), p. 40.
7. This classification scheme is adapted from Peter M. Blau and William R. Scott, *Formal Organizations* (San Francisco: Chandler, 1962).
8. See John Wilke, "What the New Boss Will Deliver at the Postal Service," *Business Week* (January 20, 1986): 28–29. An interesting follow-up report can be found in Frances Seghers, "Tisch Leaves a Faint Stamp," *Business Week* (January 18, 1988): 26–27. Also see "Can This Man Really Deliver?" *Fortune* (August 14, 1989): 87–88.
9. Of course, slavish adherence to organization charts can cause problems. For example, see Robert I. Stevens, "The Up-to-date Organization Charts," *Journal of Systems Management,* 38 (August 1987): 42.
10. James G. March, *Handbook of Organizations* (Chicago: Rand McNally, 1965), p. ix.
11. Drawn from Max Weber, *The Theory of Social and Economic Organization*, trans. A. M. Henderson and Talcott Parsons (New York: Oxford University Press, 1947). A critique based on the claim that Weber's work was mistranslated can be found in Richard M. Weiss, "Weber on Bureaucracy: Management Consultant or Political Theorist?" *Academy of Management Review,* 8 (April 1983): 242–248.
12. For a more detailed discussion, consult Warren G. Bennis, *Changing Organizations* (New York: McGraw-Hill, 1966), pp. 4–5.
13. For an excellent critique of modern bureaucracies, see Ralph P. Hummel, *The Bureaucratic Experience,* 3rd ed. (New York: St. Martin's, 1987).
14. Barnard, *The Functions of the Executive*, p. 165.
15. Charles Perrow, "The Short and Glorious History of Organizational Theory," *Organizational Dynamics,* 2 (Summer 1973): 4.
16. For example, see Christine Oliver, "Determinants of Interorganizational Relationships: Integration and Future Directions," *Academy of Management Review,* 15 (April 1990): 241–265.
17. Fremont E. Kast and James E. Rosenzweig, *Organization and Management: A Systems and Contingency Approach,* 3rd ed. (New York: McGraw-Hill, 1979), p. 103. An excellent glossary of open-system terms can be found on page 102 of this source.
18. See Richard I. Kirkland, Jr., "Pilgrims' Profits at Nucor," *Fortune* (April 6, 1981): 43–46; John Merwin, "People, Attitudes, and Equipment," *Forbes* (February 8, 1988): 68, 72; and Michael Schroeder and Walecia Konrad, "Nucor: Rolling Right into Steel's Big Time," *Business Week* (November 19, 1990): 76, 79, 81.
19. Daniel Katz and Robert L. Kahn, *The Social Psychology of Organizations,* 2nd ed. (New York: Wiley, 1978), p. 55.
20. Kim Cameron, "Critical Questions in Assessing Organizational Effectiveness," *Organizational Dynamics,* 9 (Autumn 1980): 70.
21. Detailed discussions of alternative models of organizational effectiveness may be found in Frank Shipper and Charles S. White, "Linking Organizational Effectiveness and Environmental

Change," *Long Range Planning*, 16 (June 1983): 99–106; Michael Keeley, "Impartiality and Participant-Interest Theories of Organizational Effectiveness," *Administrative Science Quarterly*, 29 (March 1984): 1–25; Kim S. Cameron, "Effectiveness as Paradox: Consensus and Conflict in Conceptions of Organizational Effectiveness," *Management Science*, 32 (May 1986): 539–553.

22. Data from Alex Taylor III, "Can American Cars Come Back?" *Fortune* (February 26, 1990): 62–65.

23. Peter Lorange and Robert T. Nelson, "How to Recognize—and Avoid—Organizational Decline," *Sloan Management Review*, 28 (Spring 1987): 41.

24. See Robert I. Sutton and Thomas D'Aunno, "Decreasing Organizational Size: Untangling the Effects of Money and People," *Academy of Management Review*, 14 (April 1989): 194–212.

25. See Kim S. Cameron, David A. Whetten, and Myung U. Kim, "Organizational Dysfunctions of Decline," *Academy of Management Journal*, 30 (March 1987): 126–138.

26. Dori Jones Yang, "To Frank Shrontz, the Blue Yonder is Anything But Wild," *Business Week* (July 9, 1990): 49.

27. Lorange and Nelson, "How to Recognize—and Avoid—Organizational Decline," p. 47.

28. Data from Joseph Weber, "Farewell, Fast Track," *Business Week* (December 10, 1990): 192–200. Also see Carol Hymowitz, "When Firms Slash Middle Management, Those Spared Often Bear a Heavy Load," *The Wall Street Journal* (April 5, 1990): B1.

29. See Aaron Bernstein, "How IBM Cut 16,200 Employees—without an Ax," *Business Week* (February 15, 1988): 98.

30. See Joel Dreyfuss, "Reinventing IBM," *Fortune* (August 14, 1989): 30–39.

31. Plant-closing legislation and programs are discussed in Angelo Kinicki, Jeffrey Bracker, Robert Kreitner, Chris Lockwood, and David Lemak. "Socially Responsible Plant Closings," *Personnel Administrator*, 32 (June 1987): 116–128.

32. For a good overview, see "Closing Law's Key Provisions," *Nation's Business* (January 1989): 58, 60.

33. See Betsy D. Gelb, "When and How to Use Outplacement," *Business Horizons*, 29 (September-October 1986): 55–59; Lisa L. Lancaster and Thomas Li-Ping Tang, "Outplacement Offers Safety Net for Displaced Workers," *Personnel Administrator*, 34 (April 1989): 60–63; and Steven D. Carr, "Managing the Business Risks of Plant Closings," *Business Horizons*, 33 (May-June 1990): 72–74.

34. Based on Joseph Jannotta, "Stroh's Outplacement Success," *Management Review*, 76 (January 1987): 52–53.

35. For a complete discussion, see Andrew M. Pettigrew, "On Studying Organizational Cultures," *Administrative Science Quarterly*, 24 (December 1979): 570–581.

36. See David M. Slipy, "Anthropologist Uncovers Real Workplace Attitudes," *HRMagazine*, 35 (October 1990): 76–79.

37. This definition is based in part on Linda Smircich, "Concepts of Culture and Organizational Analysis," *Administrative Science Quarterly*, 28 (September 1983): 339–358. For an excellent discussion of organizational cultures, see Edgar H. Schein, *Organizational Culture and Leadership* (San Francisco: Jossey-Bass, 1985); and Geert Hofstede, "Editorial: The Usefulness of the 'Organizational Culture' Concept," *Journal of Management Studies*, 23 (May 1986): 253–257.

38. See, for example, John Thorbeck, "The Turnaround Value of Values," *Harvard Business Review*, 69 (January-February 1991): 52–62; and Robert Howard, "Values Make the Company: An Interview with Robert Haas," *Harvard Business Review*, 68 (September-October 1990): 133–144.

39. Peter C. Reynolds, "Imposing a Corporate Culture," *Psychology Today*, 21 (March 1987): 38.

40. Terrence E. Deal and Allan A. Kennedy, *Corporate Cultures*, © 1982 by Addison-Wesley Publishing Co. Reprinted by permission of Addison-Wesley Publishing Co., Inc. Reading, MA. For a contingency model of organizational culture, see Bernard Arogyaswamy and Charles M. Byles, "Organizational Culture: Internal and External Fits," *Journal of Management*, 13 (Winter 1987): 647–659. Also see Frank Petrock, "Corporate Culture Enhances Profits," *HRMagazine*, 35 (November 1990): 64–66.

41. Adapted from Smircich, "Concepts of Culture and Organizational Analysis."

42. An instructive model of organizational socialization may be found in Daniel Charles Feldman, "The Multiple Socialization of Organization Members," *Academy of Management Review*, 6 (April 1981): 309–318. Also see Natalie J. Allen and John P. Meyer, "Organizational Socialization Tactics: A Longitudinal Analysis of Links to Newcomers' Commitment and Role Orientation," *Academy of Management Journal*, 33 (December 1990): 847–858.

43. Alan L. Wilkins, "The Culture Audit: A Tool for Understanding Organizations," *Organizational Dynamics,* 12 (Autumn 1983): 34–35.

44. Tactics newcomers use to make sense of their organization are discussed in Vernon D. Miller and Fredric M. Jablin, "Information Seeking During Organizational Entry: Influences, Tactics, and a Model of the Process," *Academy of Management Review,* 16 (January 1991): 92–120.

45. Alan L. Wilkins, "The Creation of Company Cultures: The Role of Stories and Human Resource Systems," *Human Resource Management,* 23 (Spring 1984): 43.

46. Vijay Sathe, "Implications of Corporate Culture: A Manager's Guide to Action," *Organizational Dynamics,* 12 (Autumn 1983): 6–7.

47. Adapted from Deal and Kennedy, *Corporate Cultures,* pp. 136–139.

9

Organizing

• • • • • • • • • • • • • • • •

There is no one way of doing things.

ANANT R. NEGANDHI

When you finish studying this chapter, you should be able to

- Explain the concept of contingency organization design.
- Distinguish between mechanistic and organic organizations.
- Discuss the roles that differentiation and integration play in organization structure.
- Identify and briefly describe the four basic departmentalization formats.
- Describe how a highly centralized organization differs from a highly decentralized one.
- Define the term *delegation* and list at least five common barriers to delegation.
- Explain how the traditional pyramid organization is being reshaped.

• •

Refining British Petroleum's Bureaucracy

British Petroleum (BP), the world's fourth-largest private oil company, sells $50 billion worth of oil and gas each year and owns about five billion barrels of oil reserves, mostly in the huge oil fields in Prudhoe Bay, Alaska, and in the North Sea. The Iraqi invasion of Kuwait, a tragedy for most of the world, immediately increased the value of BP's reserves by $100 billion. It seems that even a child could manage BP—all you have to do is pump out the oil and pump in the profits, right?

Such a strategy could keep the company afloat for a time. But if that strategy were followed, when the wells dry up in Alaska and the North Sea—and their productivity is already dropping by about 10 percent per year—BP would dry up as well. The two fields account for only about one-sixth of BP's revenues but more than 40 percent of its operating profits. In other words, the rest of the company is not in good shape.

To make sure BP has a future, new Chairman Robert B. Horton has radically altered the way his company spends its oil exploration money. In general, large oil companies drill most of their new wells in areas with proven reserves. But new wells in an old field are not as profitable as successful wells in a new field. So BP is spending half of its $1 billion yearly exploration budget on "frontier" exploration. Although the vast majority of the world's potential has already been tapped, BP is going to places like Vietnam, Ethiopia, and Papua, New Guinea, to look for fields that will turn a profit in the next century.

Just as important to Horton's strategy is a major restructuring of BP's bureaucracy. One reason BP's profits failed to keep pace with its revenues was that the company was burdened with a huge hierarchical bureaucracy, a relic from the days when oil production was a very different business. To succeed in its risky, innovative strategy, BP must be lean, flexible, and able to make decisions quickly. New structure must accompany the new strategy.

In Horton, BP has found a leader equal to the challenge. He spent the 1980s as the company's top trouble-shooter, earning the nickname "Horton the Hatchet." First he turned the company's Refining and Chemical Division around, then he moved to Cleveland to trim the fat from Standard Oil of Ohio (Sohio), which BP had just acquired. Horton has the invaluable skill of carrying out his hatchet duties without creating too much resentment. He excels at dealing with people one-on-one, and he had a teleconferencing studio installed near his office so he could talk directly to BP employees around the world. When he takes with one hand, he tries to give with the other: while cutting Sohio's charitable contributions by $4 million, he also joined the boards of Cleveland's orchestra and of its fledgling Rock 'n' Roll Hall of Fame.

No doubt restructuring the heart of BP's bureaucracy is more difficult than saying no to the United Way. But Horton saw how necessary restructuring was when he returned to Britain from Cleveland and viewed BP with fresh eyes. He was appalled at the levels of distrust and second-guessing in the old, slow-moving bureaucracy. In his first year, Horton cut corporate staff from about 2,500 to fewer than 380. Similar cuts were made in divisional staff—BP exploration axed 1,700 staff positions, at a projected savings of $150 million annually, and information systems lost 540 people. Perhaps most radical, 160 of the 540 middle managers at corporate headquarters lost their jobs or were transferred.

But Horton doesn't just want a leaner BP, he wants one that works differently, with more decentralized responsibility, trust, openness, and teamwork. Taking care to involve employees in directing the changes, BP in 1989 surveyed its top 150 managers and found widespread discontent. To address the problems this initial survey uncovered, Horton set up Project 1990, staffed by a team of seven young executives charged with redesigning how the company works.

Horton is a realist and expects the entire project to take up to five years. But some changes did take place immediately. First, the group surveyed 4,000 lower-level staff and found low morale resulting from a sense that the oppressive bureaucracy destroyed career advancement opportunities. A quick look at the organizational chart made it clear that the company's eleven layers of management and eighty standing committees presented problems. Six layers were abolished, and the committees' work was assigned to individuals and small, flexible teams who report directly to Horton or to the heads of the company's four major divisions. Information services, a unit unto itself in some organizations, was parceled out to the divisions, and BP plans to contract out much of its routine computer work. Similar changes are taking place at regional headquarters in Cleveland and Brussels as operational responsibility is passed on to people in the field. The headquarters now focus on strategy and public relations.

Horton recognizes that he must assist the employees who are undertaking new decision-making responsibilities during this massive decentralization. Training and education programs are helping employees change their attitudes and adjust their work behaviors to the new structure. And, along with their new responsibilities, managers have new authority, such as spending two and one-half times as much as they used to without authorization. Spending requests that do require authorization now need only two or three signatures instead of a dozen.

With so much corporate power transferred to the divisions, they should be ready to meet the challenge created by BP's new exploration strategy. No one can be sure BP will find new oil, but even if it doesn't, the leaner, restructured company will be able to survive better on its old strengths. No doubt the changes will take some getting used to, but as Horton said when he took his new position, "the nineties will be a decade of surprise."*

---

* Quoted in Peter Nulty, "Batman Shakes BP to Bedrock," *Fortune*, November 19, 1990, 158.

We've probably all been to picnics where everyone brings a bottle of ketchup but no one brings the mustard. Although too much of one thing and too little of another may be laughable at a picnic, such disorganized situations can spell disaster for an organization that needs to manage human and material resources effectively and efficiently in order to survive. At such times, the organizing function becomes crucial.

Organizing is the structuring of a coordinated system of authority relationships and task responsibilities. By spelling out who does what and who reports to whom, organizational structure can translate strategy into an ongoing productive operation. Structure always follows strategy in well-managed organizations, as we saw in the case of British Petroleum. Tasks and interrelationships cannot be realistically and systematically defined without regard for the enterprise's overall direction. Furthermore, strategy determines the technologies that are required and the resources that will probably be available.

As mentioned in the previous chapter, traditional closed-system prescriptions for designing organizations have proved inadequate in recent years. In the face of rapid change and increasing complexity, traditional authoritarian bureaucracies are now seen as unwieldy structural dinosaurs. *Business Week* recently issued the following blunt warning: "Americans, in short, must revolutionize the way they organize, manage, and carry out work, or their jobs will disappear in the fast-paced global economy."[1]

Fortunately, the modern open-system view with its emphasis on organization-environment interaction has helped underscore the need for more flexible organization structures. These more flexible organizations are adaptable to sudden changes and are also more interesting and challenging for employees. The traditional principles of organization are severely bent or broken during the design of flexible and adaptive organizations, and managers need new formulas for drawing up these designs. This is where the contingency approach enters the picture. The contingency approach permits the custom tailoring of organizations to meet unique external and internal situational demands.

In this chapter we introduce and discuss organizational design alternatives that enhance situation appropriateness and, hence, organizational effectiveness. We also explore the dramatic reshaping of today's organizations.

Contingency Design

Recall from our discussion in Chapter 2, that contingency thinking amounts to situational thinking. Specifically, the contingency approach to organizing involves taking special steps to make sure the organization fits the demands of the situation. In direct contrast to traditional bureaucratic thinking, contingency design is based on the assumption that there is no single best way to structure an organization. **Contingency design** is the process of determining the degree of environmental uncertainty and adapting the organization and its subunits to the situation. This does not necessarily mean that all contingency organizations will differ from each other. Instead, it means that managers who take a contingency approach select from a number of standard design alternatives to create the most situationally effective organization possible. Contingency managers typically start with the same basic collection of design alternatives but end up with unique combinations of them as dictated by the demands of their situations.

The contingency approach to designing organizations boils down to two questions: (1) How much environmental or state uncertainty is there? (See Table 9.1 for a handy way to answer this question.) (2) What combination of structural characteristics is most appropriate? We will examine two somewhat different contingency models to establish the validity of the contingency approach. Each model presents a scheme for systematically matching structural characteristics with environmental demands.

The Burns and Stalker Model

mechanistic organizations rigid bureaucracies

organic organizations flexible, adaptive organization structures

Tom Burns and G. M. Stalker, both British behavioral scientists, proposed a useful typology for categorizing organizations by structural design.[2] They distinguished between mechanistic and organic organizations. **Mechanistic organizations** tend to be rigid in design and have strong bureaucratic qualities. In contrast, **organic organizations** tend to be quite flexible in structure and adaptive to change. Actually, these two organizational types are the extreme ends of a single continuum. Pure types are difficult to find, but it is fairly easy to check off the characteristics listed in Table 9.2 to determine whether a particular organization (or subunit) is relatively mechanistic or relatively organic. It is notable that a recent field study found distinctly different communication patterns in mechanistic and organic organizations. Communication tended to be the formal command-and-control type in the mechanistic factory and participative in the organic factory.[3]

Telling the Difference. Here is a quick test of how well you understand the distinction between mechanistic and organic organizations. Read the following description of a McDonald's restaurant and decide if it describes a mechanistic or organic situation:

Here every job is broken down into the smallest of steps, and the whole process is automated. The videotape that introduces new employees to

TABLE 9.1 ● Determining Degree of Environmental Uncertainty

	Low	Moderate	High
1. How strong are social, political, and economic pressures on the organization?	Minimal	Moderate	Intense
2. How frequent are technological breakthroughs in the industry?	Infrequent	Occasional	Frequent
3. How reliable are resources and supplies?	Reliable	Occasional, predictable shortages	Unreliable
4. How stable is the demand for the organization's product or service?	Highly stable	Moderately stable	Unstable

TABLE 9.2 • Mechanistic versus Organic Organizations

Characteristic	Mechanistic organizations	Organic organizations
1. Task definition for individual contributors	Narrow and precise	Broad and general
2. Relationship between individual contribution and organization purpose	Vague	Clear
3. Task flexibility	Low	High
4. Definition of rights, obligations, and techniques	Clear	Vague
5. Reliance on hierarchical control	High	Low (reliance on self-control)
6. Primary direction of communication	Vertical (top to bottom)	Lateral (between peers)
7. Reliance on instructions and decisions from superior	High	Low (superior offers information and advice)
8. Emphasis on loyalty and obedience	High	Low
9. Type of knowledge required	Narrow, technical, and task-specific	Broad and professional

Source: Adapted from Tom Burns and G. M. Stalker, *The Management of Innovation* (London: Tavistock, 1961), pp. 119–125. Reprinted by permission.

french fries, for example, starts with boxes of frozen fries rolling off a delivery truck. Stack them in the freezer six boxes high. Leave one inch between the stacks, two inches between the stacks and the wall. Cooking and bagging the fries is explained in even greater detail: 19 steps.[4]

If you labeled the McDonald's system mechanistic, you're right. Using Table 9.2 as a guide, we see evidence in the McDonald's restaurant of narrow task definition, low task flexibility, clear definition of techniques, high reliance on instructions, and narrow knowledge requirements. An organic organization would have precisely the opposite characteristics. (See Management Ethics for an inspiring organic organization.)

Situational Appropriateness.   Burns and Stalker's research uncovered distinct organization-environment patterns indicating the relative appropriateness of both mechanistic and organic organizations. They discovered that *successful organizations in relatively stable and certain environments tended to be mechanistic.* Conversely, they also discovered that *relatively organic organizations tended to be the successful ones when the environment was unstable and uncertain.*

For practical application, this means that mechanistic design is appropriate for environmental stability, and organic design is appropriate for high environmental uncertainty. Today, the trend necessarily is toward more organic organizations because uncertainty is the rule. This is not to say that organic is good and mechanistic is bad. Some fledgling organizations, for example, are too or-

Patagonia's Golden Rule

In 1957, Yvon Chouinard began using an old forging die to make climbing equipment in his backyard. His business grew slowly for more than a decade, but it took off after he came back from a climb and decided that there was a need—a market—for functional climbing clothes. His first efforts were a rugby shirt and super-tough shorts. That was the beginning of Patagonia Inc., one of the fastest-growing and best-known makers of outdoor clothing in the country. . . .

Acknowledging that they are, in fact, in the garment business, Patagonia leaders have organized along the traditional industry model, with executives heading up nine separate clothing "lines," such as men's sportswear, women's sportswear, and fishing clothes.

Like Ben & Jerry's—with whose leaders Patagonia's managers occasionally exchange ideas—Patagonia is also not in business just to make money. It devotes 10 percent of pre-tax profits to various environmental groups.

Susan Green, Patagonia's director of human resources, says the company's goals dictate a management style which is reflected in its HR program for its 500 employees. She describes five ways in which the company's management style allows it to "walk what we talk":

- "We have a tendency to look at the whole person." One example of this approach is Patagonia's on-site day-care program, which allows workers to be near their children during the day. The center has a sliding fee scale so employees at different economic levels can afford it. Patagonia also has showers for workers who exercise at lunch and a "holistic" cafeteria with health food.

- Because the company emphasizes responsiveness to the needs of its customers, it also emphasizes responsiveness to the needs of employees. For example, employees have an opportunity to evaluate their supervisors, and those evaluations affect supervisors' merit increases.

- There are no walls between offices, and employees throughout the company are comfortable talking to top officers, fostering open communication.

- "We never wanted to create a company that we wouldn't want to work for," Green says. "We're very egalitarian as far as our benefits are concerned—all the things that are available to our top executives are available throughout the ranks of the organization."

- Not only does the company emphasize ecology but "We really believe in ecology for the individual." That means training people who already work at Patagonia—30 to 60 percent of promotions come from within.

Green says, "It sounds real sappy, but it's kind of like the Golden Rule—treat people as you would want to be treated. If you put yourself in the place of the other individuals in the organization, you're going to be making decisions that take their welfare into consideration, and not just look at the bottom line. I think that's the difference in the nineties. . . ."

Source: Excerpted from Jim Castelli, "Finding the Right Fit," *HRMagazine,* 35 (September 1990): 39–40. Reprinted with the permission of *HRMagazine* published by the Society for Human Resource Management, Alexandria, VA.

ganic and require the discipline of mechanistic qualities. Indeed, Paul Brainerd, the founder of Aldus Corporation, a software start-up in Seattle, discovered he could no longer run the company as a one-man show. He then created and staffed the new position of chief operating officer to achieve some administrative order.[5]

Woodward's Study. Since Burns and Stalker's pioneering study, several different contingency models have been proposed. Some, such as Joan Woodward's study of the relationship among technology, structure, and organizational effectiveness, focused on a single environmental variable rather than on general environmental certainty-uncertainty. Applying her own scale of technological complexity to one hundred British firms, Woodward found distinctly different patterns of structure in effective and ineffective organizations. When technological complexity was either low or high, Woodward found that effective organizations tended to have organic structure. Mechanistic structure was associated with effectiveness when technological complexity was moderate.[6] In spite of criticism of weak methodology, Woodward's study added to the case against the traditional notion of a universally applicable organization design.

The Lawrence and Lorsch Model

● ● ● ● ● ● ● ● ● ● ● ● ● ● ● ●
Discuss the roles that differentiation and integration play in organization structure.

differentiation tendency of specialists to think and act in restricted ways

integration collaboration needed to achieve a common purpose

Paul R. Lawrence and Jay W. Lorsch, researchers from Harvard University, made a valuable contribution to contingency design theory by documenting the relationship between two opposing structural forces and environmental complexity. The opposing forces they isolated were labeled differentiation and integration. **Differentiation** is the tendency among specialists to think and act in restricted ways. This structural force results from division of labor and technical specialization. Differentiation tends to fragment and disperse the organization (see Figure 9.1). **Integration,** in opposition to differentiation, is the collaboration among specialists that is needed to achieve a common purpose.[7] Integration can be partially achieved through a number of mechanisms, including hierarchical control, standard policies and procedures, departmentalization, cross-functional teams and committees, better human relations, and liaison individuals and groups. As illustrated in Figure 9.1, integration is a unifying and *coordinating* force.

According to Lawrence and Lorsch, every organization requires an appropriate *dynamic equilibrium* (an open-system term) between differentiation and integration. Moreover, their comparison of successful and unsuccessful firms in three different industries demonstrated that in the successful firms *both differentiation and integration increased as environmental complexity increased*. These findings applied not only to the overall organization but also to organizational subunits such as departments or divisions. Lawrence and Lorsch also found that "the more differentiated an organization, the more difficult it is to achieve integration."[8]

These findings suggest that organizational failure in the face of environmental complexity probably results from a combination of high differentiation and inadequate integration. Under these conditions, specialists in different areas within the organization work at cross-purposes and get embroiled in counterproductive jurisdictional conflicts. Constructive steps can be taken to achieve needed coordination, however, as General Electric's approach demonstrates.

GE's chairman, Jack Welch, has achieved a productive balance between differentiation and integration with his Corporate Executive Council. The Council, which Welch created in 1986 to bring about more cohesion and unity at GE, consists of the leaders of GE's fourteen business units, corporate staff department heads, Chairman Welch, and the company's two vice-chairmen. Formerly communicating rarely, the group of managers now meets every quarter for important,

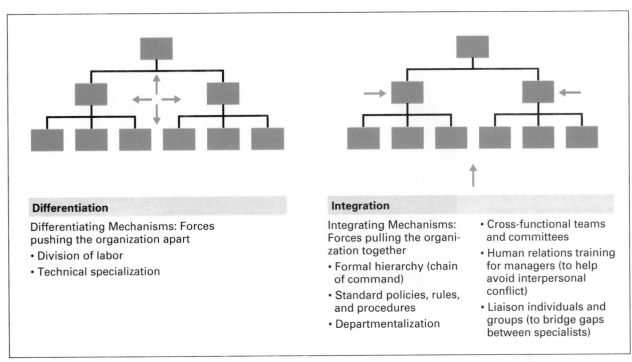

FIGURE 9.1 • Differentiation and Integration: Opposing Organizational Forces

productive discussions.[9] Welch's ultimate objective is to "create what he calls a boundaryless organization in which technology, information, managers, and management practices flow freely from one division to another." Success is evidenced by the fact that "when inspectors at the aircraft engine division check the integrity of metal parts, for example, they use x-ray technology developed by the medical systems unit."[10]

Although contingency design models may differ in perspective and language, two conclusions stand out. First, research has proved time and again that *there is no single best organization design.* Second, research generally supports the idea that the more uncertain the environment, the more flexible and adaptable the organization structure must be.[11] With this contingency perspective in mind, we now consider four structural formats.

Basic Structural Formats

As we noted earlier, differentiation occurs in part through division of labor. When labor is divided, complex processes are reduced to distinct and less complex jobs. But because differentiation tends to fragment the organization, some sort of integration must be introduced to achieve the necessary coordination. Aside from the hierarchical chain of command, one of the most common forms of integration is departmentalization. It is through **departmentalization** that related jobs, activities, or processes are grouped into major organizational subunits.

departmentalization grouping related jobs or processes into major organizational subunits

It is a long way from St. Paul, Minnesota, to Bruges, Belgium. Like other multinational companies, 3M Company goes wherever the business is. People in Belgium want Post-it Notes, so this 3M truck is on its way. 3M's 87,500 employees are sprinkled around the globe in 52 countries. Global markets require a geographically oriented organization structure that enables flexible and fast service.

● ● ● ● ● ● ● ● ● ● ● ● ● ● ● ● ●
Identify and briefly describe the four basic departmentalization formats.

For example, all jobs involving staffing activities such as recruitment, hiring, and training are often grouped into a human resources department. Grouping jobs through the formation of departments, according to management author James D. Thompson, "permits coordination to be handled in the least costly manner."[12] A degree of coordination is achieved through departmentalization because members of the department work on interrelated tasks, obey the same departmental rules, and report to the same department head. It is important to note that although the term *departmentalization* is used here, it does not always literally apply; managers commonly use labels such as *division, group,* or *unit* in large organizations.

Four basic types of departmentalization are functional departments, product-service departments, geographic location departments, and customer classification departments.

Functional Departments

Functional departments categorize jobs according to the activity performed. Among profit-making businesses, variations of the functional production-finance-marketing arrangement in Figure 9.2A are the most common forms of departmentalization. Functional departmentalization is popular because it permits those with similar technical expertise to work in a coordinated subunit. A negative aspect of functional departmentalization is that it creates "technical ghettos," in which departmental concerns tend to override more important organizational concerns. For example, production specialists may overlook financial concerns about cost containment or marketing concerns about competitive prices. Of course, functional departmentalization is not restricted to profit-making businesses. Functional departments in a nonprofit hospital might be administration, nursing, housekeeping, food service, laboratory and x-ray, admission and records, and accounting and billing.

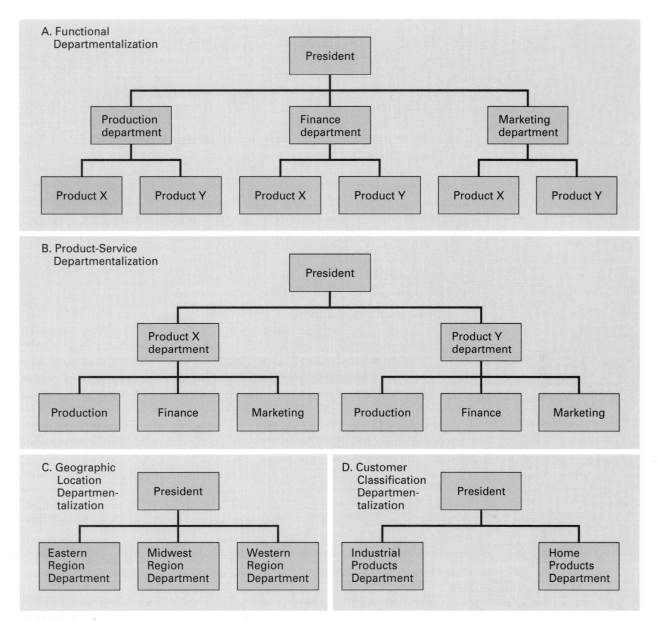

FIGURE 9.2 • Alternative Departmentalization Formats

Product-Service Departments

Because functional departmentalization has been criticized for encouraging differentiation at the expense of integration, a somewhat more organic alternative has evolved. It is called product-service departmentalization because a product (or service), rather than a functional category of work, is the unifying theme. As diagrammed in Figure 9.2B, the product-service approach permits each of, say, two products to be managed as semiautonomous businesses. Organizations that render a service instead of turning out a tangible product might find it advantageous to organize around service categories. For example, a janitorial company could have a rug-cleaning department and an office-cleaning department. In effect, the product (or service) managers are responsible for managing their own minibusinesses. Ideally, those working in a product-service department have a broad "business" orientation rather than a narrow functional orientation. It is the president's job to ensure that these minibusinesses work in a complementary fashion.

This design format was the centerpiece of IBM's 1988 reorganization of its IBM USA operations into seven product-service units: mainframe computers, minicomputers, personal computers, communications, programming, software, and computer chip manufacturing.[13] One danger of the product-service approach is that inefficient and costly duplication of effort may take place. IBM attempted to eliminate this threat by giving an eighth unit marketing responsibility for all U.S. operations.

Geographic Location Departments

Sometimes, as in the case of organizations with nationwide or worldwide markets, geography dictates structural format (see Figure 9.2C). Geographic dispersion of resources (for example, mining companies), facilities (for example, railroads), or customers (for example, chain supermarkets) may encourage the use of a geographic format to put administrators "closer to the action." One can imagine that drilling engineers in a Houston-based petroleum firm would be better able to get a job done in Alaska if they actually went up there. Similarly, a department-store marketing manager would be in a better position to judge consumer tastes in Florida if working out of a regional office in Orlando rather than a home office in San Francisco.

Long lines of communication among organizational units have traditionally been a limiting factor with geographically dispersed operations. But space-age telecommunications technology, as covered in Chapter 17, has created some interesting regional advantages. One interesting case in point is Omaha, Nebraska. Its central location, along with the absence of a distinct regional accent among Nebraskans, has made Omaha the 1-800 capital of the country. Every major hotel chain and most of the big telemarketers have telephone service centers in Omaha.[14]

Global competition is pressuring managers to organize along geographical lines. This structure allows multinational companies to better serve local markets, as Ellen Hancock decided recently when she moved her IBM group to London. (See Managers in Action.)

Customer Classification Departments

A fourth structural format centers on various customer categories (see Figure 9.2D). AT&T, for example, "has broken its long-distance business into two communications services units—one for business and the other for residential customers."[15] The rationale is to better serve the distinctly different needs of those two sets of customers. Customer classification departmentalization shares a weakness with the product-service and geographic location approaches: all

Ellen Hancock Moves Her Piece of IBM to Europe

She runs an international company with 12,000 employees and sales of $6 billion—big enough to rank around No. 77 on the *Fortune* 500 and to place her name on the short list of America's high-profile CEO's. The rub: Her "company" is part of IBM.

As head of its telecommunications business, Ellen Hancock, 47, is Big Blue's top-ranking female executive. A mathematician who likes sailing off Long Island, she started out as a programmer in 1966 and rose to her current post three years ago. Computer sales may have grown sluggish lately, but telecommunications—which for IBM means mainly computer networking products—is booming, especially in Europe.

That's one reason why Hancock recently decided to transfer her command center from the suburbs north of New York City to a site near London's Heathrow Airport. "This is a first for IBM," she says, "but having a line of business headquartered in Europe will give us a different perspective on all our markets."

Hancock also hopes that being closer to her group's three European R&D centers will help keep it a step ahead of the competition. She says, "In terms of technology, we're dealing with the most dramatic change of any business in the company." Hancock's recent career path—running telecommunications, then going abroad—traces the steps of Michael Armstrong, a member of the company's four-man management committee. Make that four-*person*, perhaps?

Source: Alan Deutschman, "IBM Goes to Europe," *Fortune* (January 14, 1991), © 1991 The Time Inc. Magazine Company. All rights reserved.

three can create costly duplication of personnel and facilities. Functional design is the answer when duplication is a problem.

Each of the preceding design formats is presented in its pure form, but in actual practice hybrid versions occur frequently (as in the case of IBM). Large organizations that serve broad markets may find it useful to combine central production and finance departments with several geographic marketing departments instead of having a single marketing department. Other organizations also combine formats to fit their needs. From a contingency perspective, the four design formats are useful starting points rather than final blueprints for organizers. A number of structural variations show how the basic formats can be adapted to meet situational demands.

Contingency Design Alternatives

Contingency design requires managers to select from a number of situationally appropriate alternatives instead of blindly following fixed principles of organization. Managers who face a relatively certain environment can enhance their effectiveness by drawing on comparatively mechanistic alternatives. Those who must cope with high uncertainty will do better to select organic alternatives. Design alternatives include span of control, decentralization, line and staff, and matrix design.

Nobel Prize-winning astrophysicist Arno Penzias is the manager of research at AT&T Bell Laboratories. *Bell Labs* is a center of cutting-edge research. But even a record of technological breakthroughs—such as talking movies, the transistor, lasers, and solar cells—cannot guarantee success in today's high-speed world. Thus, Penzias has organized his operation to give each staff scientist two jobs. Each is a researcher *and* a product team member. The idea is to make sure new technology is promptly translated into profitable new products.

Span of Control

The number of people who report directly to a manager represents that manager's **span of control.** (Some scholars prefer the term *span of management*.) Managers with a narrow span of control oversee the work of few people, whereas those with a wide span of control have many people reporting to them (see Figure 9.3). Generally, narrow spans of control foster tall organizations (many levels in the hierarchy). In contrast, flat organizations (few hierarchical levels) have wide spans of control. Everything else being equal, it stands to reason that an organization with narrow spans of control needs more managers than one with wide spans. Management theorists and practitioners have devoted a good deal of time and energy through the years attempting to answer the question "What is the ideal span of control?"[16] Ideally, the right span of control strikes an efficient balance between too little and too much supervision.

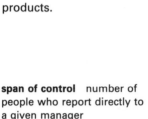

span of control number of people who report directly to a given manager

Is There an Ideal Span of Control? Early management theorists confidently specified exactly how many individuals should be in a manager's span of control. In the words of one early management scholar, "No superior can supervise directly the work of more than five or, at the most, six subordinates whose work interlocks."[17]

As time went by, research results began to supersede strictly intuitive judgments and evidence supported wider spans of control. James C. Worthy, a vice president of Sears, Roebuck and Co., reported that his company had gotten good results with spans of control far in excess of six. Specifically, Worthy found morale and effectiveness were higher in one department store in which thirty-six department managers reported to a single manager than in a second store in which the span of control averaged only five.[18]

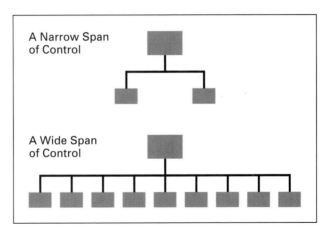

FIGURE 9.3 • Narrow and Wide Spans of Control

Today's emphasis on contingency organization design, combined with evidence that wide spans of control can be effective, have made the question of an ideal span obsolete. The relevant question is no longer how wide spans of control *should* be, but instead "How wide *can* one's span of control be?" Wider spans of control mean less administrative expense and more self-management, both popular notions today.

The Contingency Approach to Spans of Control. Both overly narrow and overly wide spans of control are counterproductive. Overly narrow spans create unnecessarily tall organizations plagued by such problems as oversupervision; long lines of communication; slow, multilevel decision making; limited initiative due to minimal delegation of authority; restricted development among managers who devote most of their time to direct supervision; and increased administrative cost.[19] Overly wide spans can erode efficiency and inflate costs through lack of training, behavioral problems among inadequately supervised subordinates, and lack of coordination. Clearly, a rationale is needed for striking a workable balance.

Situational factors such as those listed in Figure 9.4 are a useful starting point. The narrow, moderate, and wide span of control ranges in Figure 9.4 are intended to be illustrative bench marks rather than rigid limits. Each organization must do its own on-the-job experimentation. At Federal Express, for example, the span of control varies with different areas of the company. Departments that employ many people doing the same or very similar jobs—such as customer service agents, handlers/sorters, and couriers—usually have a span of control of fifteen to twenty employees per manager. Groups performing multiple tasks or tasks that require only a few people, are more likely to have spans of control of five or six.[20] No ideal span of control exists for all kinds of work.

●●●●●●●●●●●●●●●●●●
Describe how a highly centralized organization differs from a highly decentralized one.

Centralization and Decentralization

Where are the important decisions made in an organization? Are they made strictly by top management or by middle- and lower-level managers? These questions are at the heart of the decentralization design alternative. Centralization is

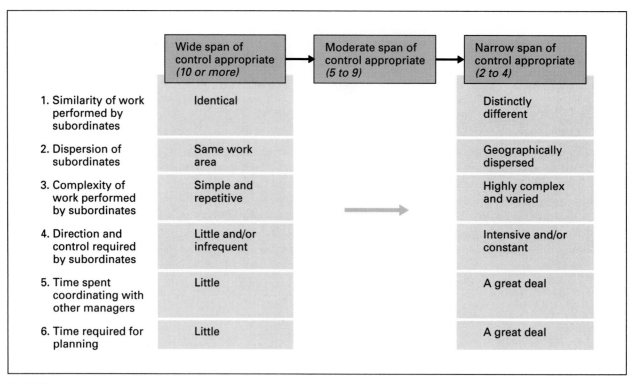

	Wide span of control appropriate (10 or more)	Moderate span of control appropriate (5 to 9)	Narrow span of control appropriate (2 to 4)
1. Similarity of work performed by subordinates	Identical		Distinctly different
2. Dispersion of subordinates	Same work area		Geographically dispersed
3. Complexity of work performed by subordinates	Simple and repetitive		Highly complex and varied
4. Direction and control required by subordinates	Little and/or infrequent		Intensive and/or constant
5. Time spent coordinating with other managers	Little		A great deal
6. Time required for planning	Little		A great deal

FIGURE 9.4 • Situational Determinants of Span of Control

centralization the retention of decision-making authority by top management

decentralization top management shares decision-making authority with subordinates

at one end of a continuum and at the other end is decentralization. **Centralization** is defined as the relative retention of decision-making authority by top management. Almost all decision-making authority is retained by top management in highly centralized organizations. In contrast, **decentralization** is the granting of decision-making authority by top management to subordinates. Decentralization increases as the degree, importance, and range of lower-level decision making *increases* and the amount of checking up by top management *decreases* (see Figure 9.5).

The Need for Balance. When we speak of centralization or decentralization, we are describing a comparative degree, not an absolute. The challenge for managers, as a management consultant recently observed, is to strike a workable balance between two extremes:

> *The modern organization in transition will recognize the pull of two polarities: a need for greater centralization to create low-cost shared resources; and, a need to improve market responsiveness with greater decentralization. Today's winning organizations are the ones that can handle the paradox and tensions of both pulls. These are the firms that analyze the optimum organizational solution in each particular circumstance, without prejudice for one type of organization over another. The result is, almost invariably, a messy mixture of decentralized units sharing cost-effective centralized resources.*[21]

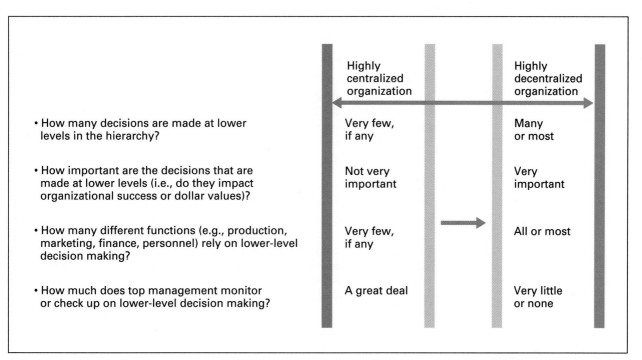

FIGURE 9.5 ● Factors in Relative Centralization/Decentralization

During IBM's 1988 reorganization, company head John Akers struck a balance between centralization and decentralization in two areas. First, the seven product-service units have decentralized control over product design and production, whereas the marketing unit has centralized control over all marketing in the United States. Second, an eighteen-member board of senior managers has retained centralized control by continuing to issue all important decisions from headquarters. "Now general managers negotiate their business plans with Akers and the board each year and then go off to run their divisions."[22] Akers reinforces this decentralization by urging his managers to be more creative and bold.

Support for greater decentralization in the corporate world has come and gone over the years in faddish waves. Today, the call is for the type of balance Akers is attempting to achieve at IBM. The case against extreme decentralization can be summed up in three words, *lack of control*. Balance helps neutralize this concern. Again, the contingency approach dictates which end of the continuum needs to be emphasized. Centralization, because of its mechanistic nature, generally works best for organizations in relatively stable situations. A more organic, decentralized approach is appropriate for firms in complex and changing conditions.

Decentralization through Strategic Business Units. Because of their growing popularity, particularly among very large businesses attempting to become more entrepreneurial, strategic business units deserve special mention. A **strategic business unit** (SBU) is an organizational subunit that acts like an independent business in all major respects, including the formulation of its own strategic plans. To qualify as a full-fledged SBU, an organizational unit must meet four criteria:

strategic business unit organizational subunit that acts like an independent business

1. It must serve a specific market outside the parent organization, rather than being simply an internal supplier.

2. It must face outside competitors.

3. It should be in a position of controlling its own destiny, especially through strategic planning and new product development. However, SBUs may choose to share the parent organization's resources, such as manufacturing facilities or sales personnel. The important point here is that the SBU, not the parent organization, makes the key choices.

4. It should be a profit center, with its effectiveness measured in terms of profit and loss.[23]

Like the underlying concept of decentralization, SBUs vary in degree. Units that fail to meet the above criteria are still called SBUs by some managers. A true SBU is highly decentralized from the parent organization.

In addition to encouraging organizational units to take greater entrepreneurial risk, SBUs can speed up the new-product development process. In response to a sharp drop in market share for plain-paper copiers, Xerox Corporation reorganized its copier business into four SBUs. One direct result was that a sophisticated new copier (a $130,000 unit designed to compete with printing machines) was developed in only three years instead of the usual five.[24] Within Xerox's SBU framework, "small engineering teams compete for the opportunity to take an idea from the concept stage to a feasibility model."[25] Unworkable product ideas can be weeded out quickly. Prior to turning to the SBU format, Xerox too often wasted valuable resources on products that eventually turned out to be unworkable.

Interference by the parent organization is the surest way to render SBUs ineffective.[26] Recent research shows that the more decentralized SBUs are from the parent organization, the more effective they are.[27] Ironically, to succeed, SBUs need the freedom to fail.

Line and Staff Organizations

Through the years, managers of large mechanistic organizations have struggled to strike a balance between technical specialization and unity of command. Remember that unity of command was emphasized by traditional management theorists. According to the unity-of-command principle, people should have only one immediate superior to avoid receiving conflicting orders. Unfortunately, in highly differentiated organizations there is often a mismatch between technical expertise and authority. For example, a production manager with the appropriate authority to take constructive action may not perceive sloppy inventory control as the source of runaway production costs. But an assistant accounting manager who has the technical expertise to identify and solve the inventory problem does not have the authority to take direct action in the production area. Line and staff organization design helps management apply technical expertise where it is most needed while maintaining relative unity of command.

line and staff organization organization in which line managers make decisions and staff personnel provide advice and support

Line versus Staff. In a **line and staff organization,** a distinction is made between line positions, those in the formal chain of command, and staff positions, those serving in an advisory capacity outside the formal chain of command. Line managers have the authority to make decisions and give orders to subordinates in the chain of command. In contrast, those who occupy staff positions merely advise and support line managers. Staff authority is normally restricted to immediate assistants. The line-staff distinction is relatively clear in mechanistic organizations but tends to blur in organic organizations.

As one might suspect, line and staff distinctions are a natural setting for conflict. Disagreement and conflict, as discussed in Chapter 15, are inevitable when two groups have different backgrounds, goals, and perspectives of the organization. For instance, line managers tend to emphasize decisiveness, whereas staff members prefer to systematically analyze problems. Thus, line managers often criticize staff for taking too much time, and staff in turn complain of line managers' impatience and hasty decisions. A recent study of 207 Israeli police officers found yet another potential source of line-versus-staff conflict. Line employees were found to have greater job commitment than their staff coworkers.[28] The differing levels of commitment could cause line managers to question staff members' loyalty to the organization's mission. Teamwork and trust could become casualties in the conflict over loyalties.

Personal versus Specialized Staff.   There are two general types of staff, personal and specialized.[29] Personal staff are individuals assigned to a specific manager to provide research support, specialized technical expertise, and counsel. For example, in Figure 9.6, the strategic planning specialist and legal counsel are on the president's personal staff. But, unlike the president's line authority, which extends to all functions, the authority of personal staff is normally limited to those working in their technical areas.

In contrast, specialized staff are "a reservoir of special knowledge, skills, and experience which the entire organization can use."[30] Consider the organization in Figure 9.6. Because it is primarily a manufacturing firm, manufacturing is a line function, whereas research and development, marketing, finance-accounting, and personnel are specialized staff functions. Notice that each of the four specialized staff functions supports but does not directly control the manufacturing function.

Functional Authority.   Strict distinctions between line and staff tend to disappear in relatively organic organizations. A device called functional authority helps prevent the collapse of unity of command. **Functional authority** is an organic design alternative that gives staff personnel temporary, limited line authority for specified tasks. In Figure 9.6, for example, the president's personal legal counsel may be given functional authority for negotiating a new union contract with factory personnel. When acting in that capacity, the legal counsel's authority would override that of cooperating line managers such as the manufacturing and personnel directors. By giving knowledgeable staff the direct authority to get something done, functional authority can reduce bureaucratic delays and enhance organizational flexibility.[31]

Matrix Organization

This last design alternative is sometimes called project management.[32] In a **matrix organization,** vertical and horizontal lines of authority are combined in checkerboard fashion. Authority flows both down and across the organization structure.

functional authority gives staff temporary and limited authority for specified tasks

matrix organization a structure with both vertical and horizontal lines of authority

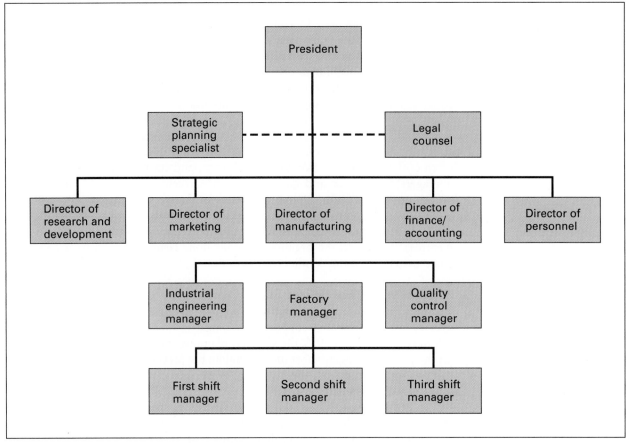

FIGURE 9.6 • A Line and Staff Organization

Matrix design originally became popular in the construction and aerospace industries. Imagine how difficult it would be for a construction firm to complete, simultaneously and in a cost-effective manner, several huge projects such as hydroelectric dams. Because each major project has its own situational and technical demands, mechanistic bureaucracies have not worked out well as principal contractors of airports and other large projects. A more organic alternative had to be found. Likewise, aerospace giants such as Lockheed, Grumman, and General Dynamics had to turn to a more organic structure to build complex weapons systems and space vehicles for the federal government. Consequently, the matrix format evolved.[33]

Take a moment to study the matrix organization chart in Figure 9.7. Notice the checkerboard configuration. In effect, the project managers borrow specialists from the line managers in charge of engineering, manufacturing, and contract administration. Technical needs dictate the number of specialists who will be borrowed from a given functional area at a given time. It is important to note that project managers have only limited (project-related) authority over the specialists, who otherwise report to their line managers. Matrix design has both advantages and disadvantages (see Table 9.3).

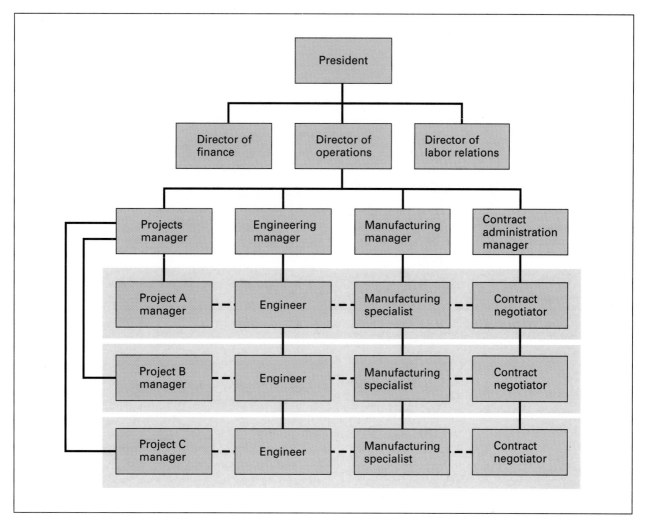

FIGURE 9.7 • A Simplified Matrix Organization Chart

Advantages. Increased *coordination* is the overriding advantage of matrix design. The matrix format places a project manager in a good position to coordinate the many interrelated aspects of a particular project, both inside and outside the organization.[34] In mechanistic organizations, the various aspects of a project normally would be handled in a fragmented fashion by functional units, such as production and marketing, with no single person being in charge of the project.

Improved information flow, the third advantage listed in Table 9.3, needs to be interpreted carefully. Research has found that matrix design increases the *quantity* of communication but decreases its *quality*.[35]

Disadvantages. First and foremost, matrix design flagrantly violates the traditional unity-of-command principle. A glance at Figure 9.7 reveals that an engineer, for instance, actually has two supervisors at the same time. This special arrangement can and sometimes does cause power struggles and conflicts of

TABLE 9.3 • Advantages and Disadvantages of Matrix Organizations

Advantages	*Disadvantages*
Efficient use of resources: Individual specialists as well as equipment can be shared across projects.	**Power struggles:** Conflict occurs since boundaries of authority and responsibility deliberately overlap.
Project integration: There is a clear and workable mechanism for coordinating work across functional lines.	**Heightened conflict:** Competition over scarce resources occurs especially when personnel is being shared across projects.
Improved information flow: Communication is enhanced both laterally and vertically.	**Slow reaction time:** Heavy emphasis on consultation and shared decision making retards timely decision making.
Flexibility: Frequent contact between members from different departments expedites decision making and adaptive responses.	**Difficulty in monitoring and controlling:** Multidiscipline involvement heightens information demands and makes it difficult to evaluate responsibility.
Discipline retention: Functional experts and specialists are kept together even though projects come and go.	**Excessive overhead:** Double management by creating project managers.
Improved motivation and commitment: Involvement of members in decision making enhances commitment and motivation.	**Experienced stress:** Dual reporting relations contribute to ambiguity and role conflict.

Source: Copyright 1987 by The Regents of the University of California. Reprinted from the *California Management Review,* Vol. 29, No. 4. By permission of The Regents.

interest. Only frequent and comprehensive communication between functional and project managers (integration) can minimize unity-of-command problems. A corollary of the unity-of-command problem is the "authority gap" facing project managers who must complete projects in spite of a lack of formal line authority. Research has shown that project managers tend to use negotiation, persuasive ability, technical competence, and the exchange of favors to compensate for their lack of authority.[36]

Finally, matrix organizations have turned out to be too complex and cumbersome for some organizations. After years of serving as a model for matrix design, Texas Instruments scrapped its complex matrix structure in favor of a more decentralized arrangement approximating strategic business units.[37] However, to conclude that matrix design is a passing fad of the 1970s and early 1980s, as some have done, would be a mistake. According to a study reported in 1987, 89 percent of 387 U.S. and Canadian companies with matrix management experience said they would continue using it.[38]

Effective Delegation

delegation assigning various degrees of decision authority to subordinates

Delegation is an important common denominator that runs through virtually all relatively organic design alternatives. It is vital to successful decentralization. Formally defined, **delegation** is the process of assigning various degrees of decision-making authority to subordinates.[39] As this definition implies, delegation is not an all-or-nothing proposition. There are at least five different degrees of delegation[40] (see Figure 9.8).

Humana is a $5-billion-a-year health care giant based in Louisville, Kentucky. To optimize the balance between care and costs at its hospitals around the U.S., Humana developed a unique Humana Nursing Practice Model. On one level, the model helps registered nurses manage their time effectively. On a deeper level, it calls for extensive delegation. The idea is to empower registered nurses and other caregivers with the opportunity to exercise their potential, within legal and professional bounds.

●●●●●●●●●●●●●●●●●

Define the term *delegation* and list at least five common barriers to delegation.

A word of caution about delegation is necessary because there is one thing it does not include. Former President Harry Truman is said to have had a little sign on his White House desk that read, "The Buck Stops Here!"[41] Managers who delegate should keep this idea in mind because, although authority may be passed along to subordinates, ultimate responsibility cannot be passed along. Thus delegation is the sharing of authority, not the abdication of responsibility. Chrysler's Lee Iacocca admittedly fell victim to this particular lapse:

> *When the company started to make money, it spent its cash on stock buybacks and acquisitions. For his part, Iacocca was distracted by nonautomotive concerns.*
> *[Iacocca] concedes that while he kept his finger on finance and marketing, he should have paid closer attention to new model planning. "If I made one mistake," he says now, "it was delegating all the product development and not going to one single meeting."*[42]

The Advantages of Delegation

Managers stand to gain a great deal by adopting the habit of delegating. By passing along well-defined tasks to subordinates, managers can free more of their time for important chores like planning and motivating. Regarding the question of exactly *what* should be delegated, Intel's chief executive officer, Andrew S. Grove, made the following recommendation: "Because it is easier to monitor something with which you are familiar, if you have a choice you should delegate those activities you know best."[43] Grove cautions that delegators who follow his advice will experience some psychological discomfort because they will quite naturally want to continue doing what they know best.

In addition to freeing valuable managerial time, delegation is also a helpful management training and development tool. Moreover, subordinates who desire

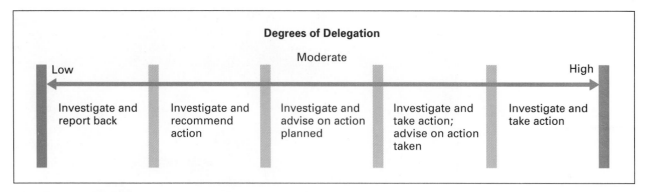

FIGURE 9.8 • The Delegation Continuum

more challenge generally become more committed and satisfied when they are given the opportunity to tackle significant problems. Conversely, a lack of delegation can stifle initiative. Consider the situation of a California home builder:

> *[The founder and chairman] personally negotiates every land deal. Visiting every construction site repeatedly, he is critical even of details of cabinet construction. "The building business is an entrepreneurial business," he says. "Yes, you can send out people. But you better follow them. You have to manage your managers."*
>
> *Says one former . . . executive: "The turnover there's tremendous. He hires bright and talented people, but then he makes them eunuchs. He never lets them make any decisions."*[44]

Perfectionist managers who avoid delegation have problems in the long run when they become overwhelmed by minute details.[45]

Barriers to Delegation

There are several reasons why managers generally do not delegate as much as they should:

- Belief in the fallacy "If you want it done right, do it yourself."
- Lack of confidence and trust in subordinates.
- Low self-confidence.
- Fear of being called lazy.
- Vague job definition.
- Fear of competition from subordinates.
- Reluctance to take the risks involved in depending on others.
- Lack of controls that provide early warning of problems with delegated duties.
- Poor example set by superiors who do not delegate.[46]

Managers can go a long way toward effective delegation by recognizing and correcting these tendencies both in themselves and in their fellow managers.[47]

Since successful delegation is habit forming, the first step usually is the hardest. Properly trained and motivated people who respond favorably to challenging work generally reward a manager's trust with a job well done.

The Changing Shape of Organizations

Management scholars have predicted the death of traditional pyramid-shaped bureaucracies for more than twenty-five years.[48] Initial changes were slow in coming and barely noticeable. Observers tended to dismiss the predictions as naive and exaggerated. However, the pace and degree of change has picked up dramatically since the early 1980s. All of the social, political/legal, economic, and technological changes discussed in Chapter 3 threaten to make traditional organizations obsolete. Why? Because they are too slow, unresponsive, uncreative, costly, and hard to manage. It is clear today that no less than a reorganization revolution is under way. Traditional pyramid organizations, though still very much in evidence, are being questioned as never before. Consequently, we need to take a look at how organizations are being reshaped because to be unaware of these changes is to be inadequately prepared for tomorrow's workplace.

Characteristics of the New Organizations

●●●●●●●●●●●●●●●●●
Explain how the traditional pyramid organization is being reshaped.

Three structural trends, already well established, are paving the way for new and different organizations. Layers are being eliminated, teamwork is becoming the norm, and size is being compartmentalized. Let us explore each of these exciting and sometimes troublesome trends.

An IBM personal computer is delivered to a customer in Paris. This scene is not new in France or elsewhere in Europe. In fact, IBM generates 50 percent of its corporate profits in Europe. An all-out assault on the European computer market by Japanese and U.S. rivals prompted a major reorganization of IBM's European operation. To better serve a unified European market, IBM scrapped its country-by-country structure in favor of a Europe-wide structure.

Toyota Reorganizes for *Kaizen*

Toyota is the best automobile maker in the world. Its cars rank just below Mercedes-Benz's on the J. D. Power Dependability Index. It dominates Japan's automobile market, is the leading import in the United States, and by the end of the century should displace Ford as the world's number-two car maker. Many factors get some credit for Toyota's phenomenal success, including its invention and perfection of just-in-time manufacturing techniques. But if the company has a single most important secret, it is *kaizen*—the Japanese term for continuous improvement.

Most companies would be satisfied with the title "world's most efficient car maker" and relax for a few years. Toyota—and especially its president, Shoichiro Toyoda—is not about to sit back and abandon the philosophy that brought the company this far. As Toyota's chief of personnel says, "Our current success is the best reason to change things."*

Recently *kaizen* led to a major reorganization of Toyota's product development unit. Toyoda, worried that the company was infected with "large-corporation disease," eliminated two layers of middle management, cut the staffs of 1,000 managers, and took personal charge of product development. Under Toyoda, 240 members of the Product Planning Division work on long-range product strategy, divided into three groups:

trucks; large rear-wheel-drive cars (like Lexus); and small front-wheel-drive cars (like Tercel).

The goal of the reorganization is to meet what Toyota considers to be the next big challenge for auto makers: creating virtually custom-made, personalized vehicles that precisely fill a customer's needs. The teamwork and manufacturing speed for which Toyota is already famous will play a role in this effort, and the reorganization created the flexible structure needed to manage the process. Each new car model is assigned to a chief engineer who has been given unusually broad authority. The engineer coordinates every aspect of the car's development, from determining physical size to choosing suppliers to designing marketing strategies. Toyota can already fill dealer orders for particular cars in four days. Under the new management structure, and with a new assembly line control system, cars will be on their way to customers in three days. Another triumph for *kaizen*.

Sources: Mary Ann Maskery, "Lexus Automation Has Pros and Cons," *Automotive News* (April 9, 1990): 24; Richard Johnson, "Toyota to Hike Production as It Chases Ford and GM," *Automotive News* (June 11, 1990): 3; Arlena Sawyers, "Mercedes, Buick, Toyota Rated Most Dependable of '85 Cars," *Automotive News* (April 9, 1990): 3; Alex Taylor III, "Why Toyota Keeps Getting Better and Better and Better," *Fortune* (November 19, 1990): 66–79.

*Quoted in Alex Taylor III, "Why Toyota Keeps Getting Better and Better and Better," *Fortune* (November 19, 1990): 66.

Fewer Layers. As mentioned in Chapter 8, an estimated one-fourth of all middle-management positions were eliminated during the 1980s. The trend continues into the 1990s. This is the most obvious feature of the reorganization revolution because it put many well-paid middle managers on the street. The simple fact is that American companies can no longer afford layer upon layer of costly managerial talent. Global competition will not permit this luxury. As an instructive case in point, General Motors has up to 22 administrative layers between its chief executive officer and the lowest line workers in some of its plants. Ford averages about 17. Japan's Toyota thrives with only *seven!*[49] Toyota's structure gives it a sizable cost advantage on each car it produces. (See The World of Management.)

The so-called delayering of corporate America has been remarkable. General Electric stripped away six layers of management, from ten to four.[50] In its Schaumburg, Illinois, mobile phone plant, Motorola cut seven layers down to four.[51] Does delayering mean that hierarchies are unnecessary? According to motivation expert Edward Lawler, hierarchies are necessary, but less hierarchy is better:

> *Hierarchies perform some very important organizational functions that must be done in some way if coordinated, organized behavior is to take place. On the other hand, if an organization design is adopted that includes work teams, new reward systems, extensive training, and . . . various other practices . . . , organizations can operate effectively with substantially less hierarchy.*[52]

Some organizations already have proved Lawler's point. Federal Express, for example, created a whole new overnight delivery industry with only five layers of management.[53]

More Teams. Envisioning tomorrow's organizations, Peter Drucker mentions three characteristics: fewer layers, information-based, and structured around teams.[54] Common team formats include quality circles, cross-functional teams, and self-managed teams. We pay close attention to each of these in later chapters. Greater emphasis on teamwork demands more effective communication, greater interpersonal trust, and efficient conflict management. These topics also are discussed in later chapters.

Smallness within Bigness. When it comes to organizations, how big is too big? Is small beautiful? Is bigger better? These questions continue to stir lively debate in management circles. Research has not produced clear-cut answers.[55] Today, however, many have come to realize the issue is not the size of the organization. Rather, *complexity* seems to be the key issue.[56] As organizations grow, they tend to become more complex. The trick for managers is to strike a balance to jointly reap the benefits of large size and small scale. A prime example is Johnson & Johnson, the $10 billion-a-year health care products giant. J&J consists of no fewer than 166 companies, each a distinct entity in its own right.[57] J&J is a feared competitor because it has created smallness within bigness. But this begs the question "How big is too big?"

Parker Hannifin Corporation, the successful maker of hydraulics and other heavy equipment, has an answer.

> *"When a division gets to a point where its general manager can't know and understand the business and be close to the customer, we split it off," says Chief Executive Paul G. Schloemer. Typically, that means plants of 300 to 400 workers, but there is no hard-and-fast rule on size. It has more to do with how well managers can deal with the organization's complexity. Parker Hannifin now has more than 200 plants in some 80 divisions.*[58]

We can expect to see many attempts to create entrepreneurial units within the financial security blanket of big companies in the years ahead.

New Organizational Configurations

Figure 9.9 illustrates three different ways in which the traditional pyramid organization is being reshaped. They are the hourglass organization, the cluster organization, and the network organization. In various combinations, these three configurations embody the characteristics just discussed. They also may overlap, as when an hourglass organization relies extensively on teams. The new structures have important implications for both the practice of management and the quality of work life. Let us examine them and take an imaginary peek into the not-too-distant future of work organizations.

hourglass organization a three-layer structure with a constricted middle layer

Hourglass Organizations. The **hourglass organization** consists of three layers, with the middle layer distinctly pinched. A strategic elite is responsible for formulating a vision for the organization and making sure it becomes reality. A significantly shrunken middle-management layer carries out a coordinating function for diverse lower-level activities. Thanks to computer networks that flash information directly from the factory floor or retail outlet to the executive suite and back again, middle managers are no longer simply conduits for warmed-over information. Also unlike traditional middle managers, hourglass middle managers are generalists rather than narrow specialists. They are comfortable dealing with complex interfunctional problems. A given middle manager might deal with an accounting problem one day, a product design issue the next, and a marketing dilemma the next—all within cross-functional team settings.

At the bottom of the hourglass is a broad layer of technical specialists who act as their own supervisors much of the time. Consequently, the distinction between supervisors and rank-and-file personnel is blurred. Employees at this operating level complain about a very real lack of promotion opportunities. Management tries to keep them motivated with challenging work assignments, lateral transfers, skill training opportunities, and pay-for-performance schemes.

FIGURE 9.9 • Reshaping the Traditional Pyramid Organization

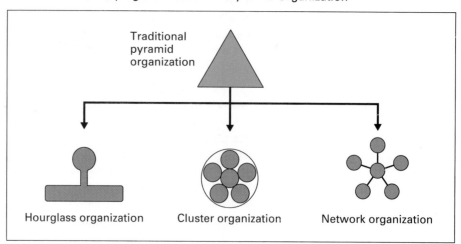

Cluster Organizations. Another new configuration shown in Figure 9.9 is the cluster organization. This label is appropriate because teams are the primary structural unit. This is how Harvard's Rosabeth Moss Kanter envisions what she calls the new collaborative organization:

cluster organization collaborative structure in which teams are the primary unit

> *The new, collaborative organization is predicated on a logic of flexible work assignments, not of fixed job responsibilities. To promote innovation and responsiveness, two of today's competitive imperatives, managers need to see this new organization as a cluster of activity sets, not as a rigid structure.*[59]

Imagining ourselves working in a cluster organization, we see multiskilled people moving from team to team as projects dictate. Pay for knowledge is a common practice. Motivation seems to be high, but some complain about a lack of job security because things are constantly changing. Stress levels rise when the pace of change quickens. Special training efforts, involving team-building exercises, are aimed at enhancing everyone's communication and group involvement skills.

network organization only function is coordination of subcontracted production/ marketing operations

Network Organizations. Network organizations get their name from the fact that their only function is administrative oversight. They do not actually produce what they sell. All production-related and marketing functions are carried out by independent companies under contract to the network organization. In short, network organizations buy a product with their own label on it and then hire other companies to handle and sell it. Consider, for example, the case of Lewis Galoob Toys Inc.:

> *A mere 115 employees run the entire [$58 million] operation. Independent inventors and entertainment companies dream up most of Galoob's products, while outside specialists do most of the design and engineering. Galoob farms out manufacturing and packaging to a dozen or so contractors in Hong Kong. . . . When the toys land in the U.S., they're distributed by commissioned manufacturers' representatives. Galoob doesn't even collect its accounts. It sells its receivables to Commercial Credit Corp., a factoring company that also sets Galoob's credit policy.*[60]

Robert and David Galoob, who call their business one of relationships, spend all of their time keeping their toy empire together via telephones and fax machines.

Business Week and others have decried these "hollow corporations" as a serious threat to America's competitiveness.[61] National security issues have been raised relative to key industries such as computers. Leaders in other countries have similar concerns. Meanwhile, inside the network organization, there is a vertical polarization. Employees tend to be either executives or clerical workers. Frictions naturally develop because of large status and pay differentials. Employees are annoyed when outsiders chide them for "not really making anything." Clerical employees are paid an unimpressive hourly wage and morale isn't very good. The fast pace of things contributes to high turnover among nonmanagerial personnel. Everyone needs negotiation skills and conflict management training, but there never seems to be any time for it. The phone bill is staggering.

Summary

Organizing is an important managerial function that translates strategy into a systematic structure of authority relationships and task responsibilities. Contingency organization design has grown in popularity as environmental complexity has increased.

The idea behind contingency design is structuring the organization to fit situational demands. Consequently, contingency advocates contend that there is no one best organizational setup for all situations. Diagnosing the degree of environmental uncertainty is an important first step in contingency design. Field studies have validated the assumption that organization structure should vary according to the situation. Burns and Stalker discovered that mechanistic (rigid) organizations are effective when the environment is relatively stable and that organic (flexible) organizations are best when unstable conditions prevail. Lawrence and Lorsch found that differentiation (division of labor) and integration (cooperation among specialists) increased in successful organizations as environmental complexity increased.

There are four basic departmentalization formats, each with its own combination of advantages and disadvantages. Functional departmentalization is the most common approach. The others are product-service, geographic location, and customer classification departmentalization. In actual practice, these pure types of departmentalization usually are combined in various ways.

Design variables available to organizers are span of control, decentralization, line and staff, and matrix. As organizers have come to realize that situational factors dictate how many people a manager can directly supervise, the notion of an ideal span of control has become obsolete. Decentralization, the delegation of decision authority to lower-level managers, has been praised as being democratic and criticized for reducing top management's control. Strategic business units foster a high degree of decentralization. Line and staff organization helps balance specialization and unity of command. Functional authority serves to make line and staff organization more organic by giving staff specialists temporary and limited line authority. Matrix organizations are highly organic because they combine vertical and horizontal lines of authority to achieve coordinated control over complex projects.

Delegation of authority, although generally resisted for a variety of reasons, is crucial to decentralization. Effective delegation permits managers to tackle higher-priority duties while helping train and develop lower-level managers. Although delegation varies in degree, it never means abdicating primary responsibility.

Many factors, with global competition leading the way, are forcing management to reshape the traditional pyramid bureaucracy. These new organizations are characterized by fewer layers, extensive use of teams, and manageably small subunits. Three emerging organizational configurations are the hourglass organization, the cluster organization, and the network organization. Each has its own potentials and pitfalls.

Terms to Understand

Organizing
Contingency design
Mechanistic organizations

Organic organizations
Differentiation
Integration

Departmentalization
Span of control
Centralization
Decentralization
Strategic business unit (SBU)
Line and staff organization

Functional authority
Matrix organization
Delegation
Hourglass organization
Cluster organization
Network organizations

Questions for Discussion

1. Why is organizing an important management function?
2. Why should structure follow strategy?
3. Would you rather work in a mechanistic organization or an organic organization? Why?
4. In your own terms, how would increased differentiation and integration help an organization face environmental complexity and uncertainty?
5. Why would a product-service department manager be better qualified than a functional department manager to assume the top position in an organization?
6. What has happened to the search for the ideal span of control? How should a manager proceed in this area?
7. What type of decentralization could take place on a college campus? For the administrators and instructors, what would be the relative advantages and disadvantages of campus decentralization?
8. If you were a project manager in a matrix organization, what would you do about closing your authority gap?
9. Would you be a good delegator or a poor delegator? How would this affect your performance as a manager?
10. Which organizational configuration—hourglass, cluster, or network—do you think will be the most common in twenty years?

Back to the Opening Case

Now that you have read Chapter 9, you should be able to answer the following questions about the British Petroleum case:

1. Is Robert Horton a good manager or just a ruthless "hatchet man" who has put a lot of people out of work?
2. Has Horton made BP a more mechanistic or more organic firm? Explain, using Table 9.2 as a guide.
3. How can you tell that Horton has made BP a more decentralized company?
4. What has Horton done to create an "organization of the future"? From a competitiveness standpoint, are these positive or negative changes? Explain your reasoning.
5. Does Horton's reorganization plan have a good chance of being successful in five years? Explain your reasoning.

No Bosses at W. L. Gore & Associates

If you've ever scrambled eggs on a nonstick frying pan, you know the benefits of polytetrafluoroethylene (PTFE), commonly known by its Du Pont trade name, Teflon. It's wonderful stuff. In the late 1950s, a Du Pont research chemist, Bill Gore, became fascinated with PTFE and began experimenting with its uses. He became convinced that the substance had great promise, especially for making insulated wires. When he couldn't interest Du Pont in his ideas, he quit to form W. L. Gore & Associates with his wife Vieve in 1958. The insulated wire idea worked, but the Gores fully realized what an amazing product they had a few years later when their son Bob heated and stretched PTFE just right. The result was Gore-tex, a fabric that "breathed" yet kept water out. Gore-tex soon became the fabric of choice for expensive raingear, space suits, artificial arteries, industrial filters. . . . You name it.

Bill Gore was right about PTFE. But as revolutionary as his company's products were, his way of doing business turned out to be just as influential. Gore's experience at Du Pont led him to vow that he would not allow his company's management structure or style to stifle anyone's ideas the way Du Pont's red tape had stifled his. So he created what he called a lattice organization—an organization without titles, hierarchies, or any conventional organizational structures. Everyone in the organization is called an associate, and anyone can talk to anyone else at any time. The only structure in W. L. Gore & Associates grows organically from the work the associates do and the way they interact. And—to the surprise and perhaps chagrin of advocates of traditional management—the lattice has been working successfully for more than thirty years.

Today, despite the death of the founder, the company and its numbers continue to be impressive. W. L. Gore has 5,300 employees and forty-one plants in six countries. Sales have tripled since 1984 and will probably top $1 billion by 1995. Although the company is still based in Newark, Delaware, you won't find a huge headquarters surrounded by acres of parking lots. Early in the company's history, Gore learned a lesson other companies, from Hewlett-Packard to Volvo, took decades to discover: the dynamics in an organization change when that organization grows too large. When the number of associates swelled to over 200 in the original plant, Gore realized he no longer knew everyone's name and that the all-important sense of community was fading. So he came up with one of the company's few rules: no Gore facility has more than 200 people. The company would rather spend its money to build another plant than lose its culture.

If new associates haven't been forewarned, their greatest surprise on their first day of work for W. L. Gore is that they don't have anything to do. There are no bosses and no one gives orders. Associates are free to devote their time and energy to any project they choose or develop their own project. Their first step is to find someone willing to act as a "sponsor" for them. The sponsor becomes an advocate for the new employee when, for instance, a committee of associates meets every six months to set pay levels. There are no stable salaries; associates are paid according to how much their peers feel they have contributed.

Sponsors also help new associates understand the organization's culture and what passes for its rules. Fairness to everyone is a key element of Gore doctrine. Associates are expected to help each other to grow in every possible way and to make and keep their own commitments. The company does have leaders, but they're not appointed or even elected. An associate becomes a leader because others follow him or her. Someone who creates a project that excites and attracts other associates becomes a leader and acquires some power over the project team. But leaders always share their power to hire, fire, or discipline with peer committees, sponsors, and members of personnel groups.

The company has progressive profit distribution and retirement plans, but people don't come to work at Gore for the money. They want to be enthusiastic about their work and they want to feel pride in their company. They like being able to set their own goals and reach them if enough other associates will commit themselves to the same goals. The lattice organization wouldn't work for all organizations, but there are no doubt thousands of potential "associates" who wish that their organization would try it.

For Discussion

1. Is W. L. Gore & Associates a mechanistic or organic organization? How can you tell?
2. How are differentiation and integration balanced at Gore?
3. Is Gore centralized or decentralized? Explain.
4. With such a loose structure, how do you suppose anything ever gets done at Gore?

References

Opening Quotation. Anant R. Negandhi, "Comparative Management and Organization Theory: A Marriage Needed," *Academy of Management Journal*, 18 (June 1975): 334.

Opening Case. "BP Signals a New Direction," *Petroleum Economist* (April 1990): 106; "Bold New Strategy for BP," *Petroleum Economist* (October 1989): 319; Peter Nulty, "Batman Shakes BP to Bedrock," *Fortune* (November 19, 1990): 155–162.

Closing Case. Robert Levering, Milton Moskowitz, and Michael Katz, *The 100 Best Companies to Work For in America* (New York: New American Library, 1985), pp. 161–164; Tom Peters and Nancy Austin, *A Passion for Excellence* (New York: Random House, 1985), pp. 233–234; Joseph Weber, "No Bosses. And Even 'Leaders' Can't Give Orders," *Business Week* (December 10, 1990): 196–197.

1. John Hoerr, "Sharpening Minds for a Competitive Edge," *Business Week* (December 17, 1990): 72. Also see Henry Mintzberg, "The Effective Organization: Forces and Forms," *Sloan Management Review*, 32 (Winter 1991): 54–67.
2. See Tom Burns and G. M. Stalker, *The Management of Innovation* (London: Tavistock, 1961), chap. 5.
3. See John A. Courtright, Gail T. Fairhurst, and L. Edna Rogers, "Interaction Patterns in Organic and Mechanistic Systems," *Academy of Management Journal*, 32 (December 1989): 773–802.
4. Kathleen Deveny, "Bag Those Fries, Squirt That Ketchup, Fry That Fish," *Business Week* (October 13, 1986): 86.
5. Additional discussion may be found in Barbara Buell, "For Aldus, Being No. 1 Isn't Enough Anymore," *Business Week* (June 11, 1990): 76–77.
6. For a complete summary of Woodward's findings, see Joan Woodward, *Industrial Organization: Theory and Practice* (London: Oxford University Press, 1965), chap 4.
7. Adapted from Paul R. Lawrence and Jay W. Lorsch, *Organization and Environment* (Homewood, Ill.: Irwin, 1967), p. 11.
8. Ibid., p. 157.
9. See Russell Mitchell, "Jack Welch: How Good a Manager?" *Business Week* (December 14, 1987): 92–103.
10. Ronald Henkoff, "How to Plan for 1995," *Fortune* (December 31, 1990): 74.
11. For detailed description of contingency design in action at a U.S. Air Force facility, see Thomas J. Von der Embse and William H. Toliver, "Contingency Organization Design: What It Is and How It Works," *Research Management*, 22 (September 1979): 31–36.
12. James D. Thompson, *Organizations in Action* (New York: McGraw-Hill, 1967), p. 59.
13. See Joel Dreyfuss, "Reinventing IBM," *Fortune* (August 14, 1989): 30–39.

14. Adapted from "Dial 800, Talk to Omaha," *Fortune* (January 29, 1990): 16.

15. John J. Keller, "Bob Allen is Turning AT&T Into a Live Wire," *Business Week* (November 6, 1989): 144.

16. For an extensive bibliography on this subject, see David D. Van Fleet and Arthur G. Bedeian, "A History of the Span of Management," *Academy of Management Review*, 2 (July 1977): 356–372.

17. L. Urwick, *The Elements of Administration* (New York: Harper & Row, 1944), pp. 52–53.

18. For details of this study, see James C. Worthy, "Organizational Structure and Employee Morale," *American Sociological Review*, 15 (April 1950): 169–179.

19. Drawn from C. W. Barkdull, "Span of Control—A Method of Evaluation," *Michigan Business Review*, 15 (May 1963): 25–32.

20. William H. Wagel, "Keeping the Organization Lean at Federal Express," *Personnel*, 64 (March 1987): 4–12.

21. Paul Kaestle, "A New Rationale for Organizational Structure," *Planning Review*, 18 (July-August 1990): 22. Also see Robert W. Keidel, "Triangular Design: A New Organizational Geometry," *Academy of Management Executive*, 4 (November 1990): 21–37.

22. Dreyfuss, "Reinventing IBM," p. 34.

23. Based on William E. Rothschild, "How to Ensure the Continued Growth of Strategic Planning," *The Journal of Business Strategy*, 1 (Summer 1980): 11–18.

24. See "How Xerox Speeds Up the Birth of New Products," *Business Week* (March 19, 1984): 58–59.

25. "Big Business Tries to Imitate the Entrepreneurial Spirit," *Business Week* (April 18, 1983): 84.

26. For discussion of SBUs at Honeywell, see F. Paul Carlson, "The Long and Short of Strategic Planning," *The Journal of Business Strategy*, 11 (May-June 1990): 15–19.

27. For complete details, see Anil K. Gupta, "SBU Strategies, Corporate-SBU Relations, and SBU Effectiveness in Strategy Implementation," *Academy of Management Journal*, 30 (September 1987): 477–500. Also see V. Govindarajan and Joseph Fisher, "Strategy, Control Systems, and Resource Sharing: Effects on Business-Unit Performance," *Academy of Management Journal*, 33 (June 1990): 259–285.

28. For details, see Meni Koslowsky, "Staff/Line Distinctions in Job and Organizational Commitment," *Journal of Occupational Psychology*, 63 (June 1990): 167–173. Also see Hillel Schmid, "Staff and Line Relationships Revisited: The Case of Community Service Agencies," *Public Personnel Management*, 19 (Spring 1990): 71–83.

29. See Louis A. Allen, "The Line-Staff Relationship," *Management Record*, 17 (September 1955): 346–349, 374–376.

30. Ibid., p. 348.

31. For additional suggestions for making the best use of staff, see Edward C. Schleh, "Using Central Staff to Boost Line Initiative," *Management Review*, 65 (May 1976): 17–23.

32. See David I. Cleland, "Why Project Management?" *Business Horizons*, 7 (Winter 1964): 81–88. For a discussion of how project management has evolved into matrix management, see David I. Cleland, "The Cultural Ambience of the Matrix Organization," *Management Review*, 70 (November 1981): 24–28, 37–39; and David I. Cleland, "Matrix Management (Part II): A Kaleidoscope of Organizational Systems," *Management Review*, 70 (December 1981): 48–56.

33. For a good update, see Christopher A. Bartlett and Sumantra Ghoshal, "Matrix Management: Not a Structure, A Frame of Mind," *Harvard Business Review*, 68 (July-August 1990): 138–145.

34. An informative description of a successful matrix organization may be found in Ellen Kolton, "Team Players," *Inc.* (September 1984): 140–144.

35. See William F. Joyce, "Matrix Organization: A Social Experiment," *Academy of Management Journal*, 29 (September 1986): 536–561.

36. Drawn from Richard M. Hodgetts, "Leadership Techniques in the Project Organization," *Academy of Management Journal*, 11 (June 1968): 211–219. Also David K. Wilemon and John P. Cicero, "The Project Manager—Anomalies and Ambiguities," *Academy of Management Journal*, 13 (September 1970): 269–282.

37. See "An About-face in TI's Culture," *Business Week* (July 5, 1982): 77.

38. Data from Erik W. Larson and David H. Gobeli, "Matrix Management: Contradictions and Insights," *California Management Review*, 29 (Summer 1987): 126–138.

39. For an interesting distinction between delegation and participation, see Carrie R. Leana, "Power Relinquishment versus Power Sharing: Theoretical Clarification and Empirical Comparison of Delegation and Participation," *Journal of Applied Psychology*, 72 (May 1987): 228–233.

40. Adapted from Marion E. Haynes, "Delegation: There's More To It Than Letting Someone Else Do It!" *Supervisory Management, 25* (January 1980): 9–15. Three types of delegation—incremental, sequential, and functional—are discussed in William R. Tracey, "Deft Delegation: Multiplying Your Effectiveness," *Personnel, 65* (February 1988): 36–42.

41. Delegation styles of selected U.S. presidents are examined in Edward J. Mayo and Lance P. Jarvis, "Delegation 101: Lessons from the White House," *Business Horizons, 31* (September-October 1988): 2–12.

42. Alex Taylor III, "Iacocca's Time of Trouble," *Fortune* (March 14, 1988): 79, 81.

43. Andrew S. Grove, *High Output Management* (New York: Random House, 1983), p. 60.

44. "How Conservatism Wins in the Hottest Market," *Business Week* (January 17, 1977): 43.

45. For a revealing case study of a top-level manager who lost his job because he could not delegate effectively, see "A 'Nuts-and-Bolts Guy' Is Out at Borg-Warner," *Business Week* (December 19, 1983): 108, 110.

46. Adapted from William H. Newman, "Overcoming Obstacles to Effective Delegation," *Management Review, 45* (January 1956): 36–41; and from Eugene Raudsepp, "Why Supervisors Don't Delegate," *Supervision, 41* (May 1979): 12–15.

47. Practical tips on delegation can be found in Everett T. Suters, "Overdoing It," *Inc.,* 8 (November 1986): 115–116; Laurie Baum, "Delegating Your Way to Job Survival," *Business Week* (November 2, 1987): 206; and Joseph T. Straub, "Delegation Dilemma: What Should You Do If It Doesn't Work?" *Supervisory Management, 34* (August 1989): 7–10.

48. See, for example, Warren G. Bennis, *Changing Organizations* (New York: McGraw-Hill, 1966).

49. Data from James B. Treece, "Will GM Learn From Its Own Role Models?" *Business Week* (April 9, 1990): 62.

50. Data from Joseph Weber, "Farewell, Fast Track," *Business Week* (December 10, 1990): 192–200.

51. Data from Otis Port, "A Smarter Way to Manufacture," *Business Week* (April 30, 1990): 110–117.

52. Edward E. Lawler III, "Substitutes for Hierarchy," *Organizational Dynamics, 17* (Summer 1988): 15.

53. Data from David Woodruff, "Ford Has a Better Idea: Let Someone Else Have the Idea," *Business Week* (April 30, 1990): 116–117.

54. See Peter F. Drucker, "The Coming of the New Organization," *Harvard Business Review, 66* (January-February 1988): 45–53.

55. See Richard Z. Gooding and John A. Wagner III, "A Meta-Analytic Review of the Relationship Between Size and Performance: The Productivity and Efficiency of Organizations and Their Subunits," *Administrative Science Quarterly, 30* (December 1985): 462–481; and Philip G. Benson, Terry L. Dickinson, and Charles O. Neidt, "The Relationship between Organizational Size and Turnover: A Longitudinal Investigation," *Human Relations, 40* (January 1987): 15–30.

56. For an informative discussion, see John A. Byrne, "Is Your Company Too Big?" *Business Week* (March 27, 1989): 84–94.

57. See Christopher Power, "At Johnson & Johnson, A Mistake Can Be a Badge of Honor," *Business Week* (September 26, 1988): 126–128.

58. Byrne, "Is Your Company Too Big?" p. 92.

59. Rosabeth Moss Kanter, "The New Managerial Work," *Harvard Business Review, 67* (November-December 1989): 92.

60. John W. Wilson, "And Now, The Post-Industrial Corporation," *Business Week* (March 3, 1986): 64.

61. See the Special Report in *Business Week*, March 3, 1986.

10

Staffing and Human Resource Management

• • • • • • • • • • • • • • • •

People are the common denominator of progress.

JOHN KENNETH GALBRAITH

CHAPTER OBJECTIVES

When you finish studying this chapter, you should be able to

- Explain what staffing involves and outline the human resource management process.
- Describe the human resource planning process.
- Distinguish among equal employment opportunity, affirmative action, and managing diversity.
- Explain how managers can be more effective interviewers.
- Discuss how performance appraisals can be made legally defensible.
- Compare and contrast the ingredients of good training programs for skill and factual learning.
- Specify the key components in organizational policies for sexual harassment, alcohol and drug abuse, and AIDS.

• •

Managing Diversity Fits at Levi Strauss

Few American companies have made as strong a commitment to putting human resource theory into practice as has Levi Strauss and Company, maker of world-famous blue jeans. Such a commitment has required a whole new style of thinking and a willingness to change in radical ways.

The new style of thinking at Levi concerns the relationship between what Chief Executive Officer (CEO) Robert Haas calls "hard stuff" (the business of selling pants) and "soft stuff" (the company's relationship to the work force). In the past, Levi, like most companies, was primarily devoted to the "hard stuff." It nevertheless thought of itself as a progressive company because it paid an unusual amount of attention to "soft stuff." Now, the company realizes that hard and soft are intertwined and that it is not going to make money unless it keeps its people happy and motivated and makes full use of them. As Haas points out, if a child's day-care arrangements fall through and a parent has to call in sick or worry about the child all day, that parent is not going to be a productive worker. So it is in the company's interest to help solve its employees' personal problems, whether they involve child care, discrimination, drug abuse, or AIDS. "Soft stuff," rather than being treated as a secondary concern, has now become vitally important stuff.

Many of the human resources innovations at Levi Strauss have been pioneered by Donna Goya, who took a job in personnel in the early 1970s while waiting for a merchandising position to open up. She soon discovered the extent to which personal factors can influence career decisions. She stayed in personnel after learning that merchandisers spend at least one-quarter of their time on the road, away from their families, something she was unwilling to do. As she worked her way up to senior vice president, she never lost sight of that key lesson about the interdependency of the personal and professional. She models her belief that the company really cares about its people, developing new ways to create, as she puts it, "an environment for success."*

One element of that environment is treating employees as responsible adults, which has meant gradually relaxing the company dress code and allowing employees to decide what clothing is appropriate. Another is coming up with clever ways to congratulate employees and urge them on, like celebrating a successful year by handing out replicas of the company's 501 blue jeans, each with a check for $501 in the back pocket. And Goya continues to follow the mysterious instruction that hangs on her computer terminal: "DWYSYWD" ("*Do What You Said You Would Do*").

Because a commitment to social values and an interest in the family are nothing new at Levi, management is aware that it cannot dictate employees' values or force employees to follow policies from on high. The Levi task force that studies ways to balance work and family life includes secretaries and sewing machine operators as well as CEO Haas. And management listens when employees talk. When a group of women and minority managers complained that advancement seemed stalled, the company responded, even though its record of hiring women and members of minorities was already good. In an off-site retreat that was to be repeated throughout the decade, white male senior managers were paired with a female or minority manager from their work group for two and a half days of discussions. Such meetings have led Levi to create new career development courses, provide support networks for particular ethnic groups, and initiate a "Valuing Diversity" course that all employees will eventually attend.

Diversity is also a key element in the company's "Aspirations Statement," a collection of company ideals against which all decisions are compared (reprinted in Chapter 14). The Aspirations commit Levi not just to hiring a diverse group of people but to taking "full advantage" of their "rich backgrounds and abilities." The statement also emphasizes "empowerment . . . that increases the authority and responsibility of those closest" to Levi products and customers.

Such empowerment provides another important link between treatment of employees and company profits. Like most successful companies, Levi knows it must be even more flexible and change with its market. Because such flexibility is difficult in a traditional, hierarchical organization, Haas flattened the company's structure and gave more responsibility to employees further down the chain of command. Company representatives now give suppliers and retailers the immediate, informed service necessary to create the close relationships that allow Levi to respond to market trends much faster than it could just a few years ago.

Levi's progressive relationships with workers extend to all major staffing functions. The hiring process emphasizes diversity, and training programs help employees explore their own values and their fit with the company's Aspirations. Levi has also come up with some unusual ways of handling performance appraisals. Rather than relying on bosses to evaluate the employees under them, Levi prefers to hold numerous interviews with the people who work for and with an individual. The process provides general feedback to the person under scrutiny and encourages an ongoing exchange of evaluations and suggestions from all involved. The company has also extended its empowerment philosophy to its blue-collar workers. A very successful gainsharing program in its Blue Ridge, Georgia, plant effectively gives sewing machine operators control over the plant and one-half of the savings they produce.

But perhaps most emblematic of Levi's attitude toward its workers is its AIDS policy. Developed in 1982, long before the federal government was taking AIDS seriously, the policy stresses education and confidentiality rather than testing. AIDS victims are allowed to work as long as possible, and they are provided with insurance coverage. Most important, when the company first set up an AIDS fund-raising table in the lobby of its San Francisco headquarters, it was manned not by gay activists but by senior executives—including then-president Bob Haas.

*Quoted in Holly Rawlinson, "Homegrown for HRM," *Personnel Administrator* (August 1989): 50.

• • • • • • • • • • • • • • • • Long-term commitment and loyalty such as that found between Levi Strauss and its workers is common in many, but not all, organizations. In our highly organized society, most of us began joining organizations and committing our loyalty at an early age. As youngsters we were encouraged by parents, friends, and teachers to join clubs, athletic teams, scout troops, and so on. As adolescents, we soon realized that taking part in organized activity is more rewarding than relying strictly on one's own resources. Sometimes, as when a child is sent to grade school, we are forced to join an organization. But membership in most organizations, including those that offer us jobs, is voluntary. With the exception of painters, sculptors, writers, and other artisans who tend to work in isolation, getting a job usually means joining an organization.

When an individual and a work organization interact, dramatically different things can happen. Both can prosper because of a mutually beneficial relationship; alternatively, counterproductive disharmony may result.[1] This chapter examines processes, problems, and solutions in the systematic individual-organization matching process.

The Staffing and Human Resource Management Function

• • • • • • • • • • • • • • • • •
Explain what staffing involves and outline the human resource management process.

staffing human resource planning, acquisition, and development

Staffing has long been an integral part of the management process. Like other traditional management functions, such as planning and organizing, the domain of staffing has grown throughout the years. This growth reflects increasing environmental complexity and greater organizational sophistication. Early definitions of staffing focused narrowly on hiring people for vacant positions. Today, **staffing** is defined more broadly as human resource planning, acquisition, and development aimed at providing the talent necessary for organizational success.[2] This broader definition underscores the point that people are valuable *resources* requiring careful nurturing. In fact, most personnel departments are now called human resource departments.[3] The day has long since passed when management could view labor simply as a commodity to be bought, exploited to exhaustion, and discarded when convenient.[4] Global competitive pressures have made the skillful management of human resources more important than ever.[5]

Progressive and successful organizations treat all employees as valuable human resources. According to the authors of the best seller *In Search of Excellence:* "If you want productivity and the financial reward that goes with it, you must treat your workers as your most important asset."[6] Frederick W. Smith, founder and chairman of Federal Express Corporation, has helped his company prosper by putting his employees first. Smith reportedly spends one-third of his week handling personnel matters, including worker-grievance appeals.[7] Field research indicates that employees tend to return the favor when they are treated with dignity and respect. Specifically, eighty-eight professional employees in one study reported higher organizational commitment when their employer's human resource practices were perceived to be fair and just.[8]

A particularly promising development in the staffing area is the linkage of the human resource perspective with strategic management.[9] Such linkage is evident in the following statement by Kathryn Connors, vice president of human resources at clothing retailer Liz Claiborne:

> *Human resources is part of the strategic planning process. . . . It's part of policy development, line extension planning and the merger and acquisition processes. Little is done in the company that doesn't involve us in the planning, policy or finalization stages of any deal.*[10]

When Tyson Foods, Inc. offered Debbie Chambers a chance to move up by transferring to Arkansas, it also promised to place her husband, who worked with her at a Tyson sow complex in North Carolina. Now each of them manages a complex, caring for sows and their litters. "If Tyson wants you to transfer, it does everything it can to make the move easy," Debbie says. Demographic changes have made human resource planning more complex than ever.

Figure 10.1 presents a model for the balance of this chapter; it reflects this strategic orientation. Notice how a logical sequence of staffing activities—human resource planning, selection, performance appraisal, and training—all derive from organizational strategy and structure. Without a strategic orientation, the staffing function becomes hapazardly inefficient and ineffective. Also, as indicated in Figure 10.1, an ongoing process following selection involves identifying and solving human resource problems. Three contemporary human resource problems, explored in the last section of this chapter, are sexual harassment, alcohol and drug abuse, and AIDS.

Human Resource Planning

Planning enables managers to cope better with an uncertain environment and to allocate scarce resources more efficiently. In recent years, management scholars have emphasized the need to plan the human side of organized endeavor: "There continues to be in organizations a failure, particularly on the part of line manag-

FIGURE 10.1 • A General Model for Human Resource Management

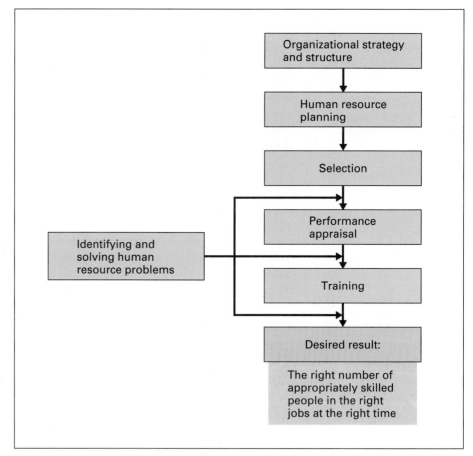

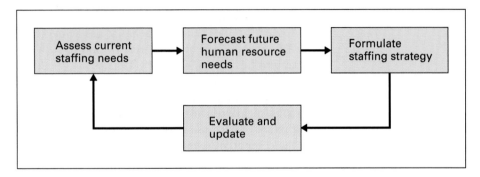

FIGURE 10.2 ● A Basic Model for Human Resource Planning Systems

ers and functional managers in areas other than personnel, to recognize the true importance of planning for and managing human resources."[11]

Human resource planning helps management find the right people for the right jobs at the right time. Formally defined, **human resource planning** is the development of a comprehensive staffing strategy for meeting the organization's future human resource needs.[12]

A Systems Perspective

Human resource planning requires a systematic approach to staffing.[13] Staffing has suffered from a lack of continuity as people are hired and trained on an "as needed" basis. With today's rapidly changing conditions, organizations need a foresighted, systematic approach that provides specific answers to this overriding question: "How can the organization assure that it will have people of the right types and numbers, organized appropriately, managed effectively, and focused on customer satisfaction?"[14] Answers to this question can be obtained through a systematic approach such as the one in Figure 10.2. First, current staffing needs are assessed. Next, future needs of human resources are forecast. Third, a comprehensive staffing strategy is formulated. Finally, evaluation and updating of the system are achieved by continually recycling through the process.

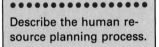

Describe the human resource planning process.

Assessing Current Needs

No meaningful forecasting and formulation of staffing strategies can take place until management has a clear picture of the organization's current staffing situation. A time-consuming procedure called job analysis comes into play here. **Job analysis** is the process of determining the fundamental elements of jobs through systematic observation and analysis.[15] Usually, a team of trained specialists isolates specific jobs by analyzing work flows, tracking procedures for accomplishing subunit objectives, and interviewing individuals about what their jobs entail. If job descriptions exist, they are updated. If not, they are written. A **job description** is a clear and concise summary of the duties of a specific job and the qualifications for holding it.[16] Job descriptions are a useful staffing tool for achieving productive individual-organization matches.

By comparing updated job descriptions with the qualifications and duties of the individuals currently holding those jobs, management can determine whether the organization is appropriately staffed. Overstaffing can be wastefully expensive, but understaffing can block the achievement of organizational objectives. An appropriately staffed organization has the right number of people working in jobs best suited to their talents.

A growing number of organizations are finding computerized personnel inventories useful. *Human resource information systems* can be compiled most conveniently during the initial assessment of human resources. By keying each present employee's name, identification number, and biographical summary into the computer along with such pertinent data as seniority, pay status, promotion record, and training experience, a time-saving staffing decision tool is created. In a matter of seconds, a manager can, for example, obtain a print-out of the age distribution among upper-level managers to use as an objective basis for predicting where replacements will be needed as older managers retire.[17]

Forecasting Future Needs

This second phase of the human resource planning cycle compares projected demand and projected supply. Many environmental and organizational factors need to be considered (see Table 10.1).[18] It is often helpful for managers to envision human resources as flowing into, through, and out of the organization. Like any other resource, human resources are subject to subtle erosion: employees leave the organization for a wide variety of reasons, and they must be replaced. Management should explore both internal and external sources of supply for these replacements. If, for instance, enough people are studying computer programming in schools and colleges, data processing firms may not need to train so many of their own computer programmers in the future.

The net result of human resource demand and supply forecasting is a detailed list of future staffing requirements. This list will tell management how many people with what sorts of abilities will be needed at specific future points in time.

TABLE 10.1 • Factors in Forecasting the Demand for and Supply of Human Resources

Forecast demand	Expected growth of the organization
	Budget constraints
	Turnover resulting from resignations, terminations, transfers, retirement, and death
	Introduction of new technology
	Minority-hiring goals
Forecast supply	Number of employees willing and able to be trained
	Promotable employees
	Availability of required talent in local, regional, and national labor markets
	Competition for talent within the industry and in general
	Demographic trends (such as movement of families in the United States from the Northeast to the Southwest)
	Enrollment trends in government training programs, trade schools, and colleges and universities

Formulating a Staffing Strategy

To satisfy future staffing requirements, management has two sets of options. First, it can rely on current employees or hire new ones. Second, employees can be trained or not trained. Combined, these two sets of options yield four staffing strategies: (1) do not train current employees, (2) train current employees, (3) hire but do not train outsiders, and (4) hire and train outsiders. In today's larger organizations all four strategies are usually used simultaneously, according to situational requirements.

Evaluation and Update

Like many other systems, human resource planning requires a feedback loop, or a means of monitoring the system. Comparisons of the actual performance of the system with previously formulated plans allow necessary corrections to be made. Unexpected shortages or excesses of qualified people signal a defect in the planning system. Sometimes management discovers it has overlooked critical demand or supply considerations. Whatever the problem, prompt corrective action will help the human resource planning cycle work more smoothly and effectively each time it is repeated.

Selection

Management finds qualified people to fill available jobs through the employee selection process. In a manner of speaking, employee selection serves as the organization's human resource gatekeeper. Today's managers are challenged to find the best available talent without unfairly discriminating against any segment of society.

A person who has applied for a particular job is not necessarily qualified to hold it. Thus, a screening mechanism is required to separate those who are qualified from those who are not. Personnel management experts commonly compare the screening process to a hurdle race. Typical hurdles job applicants have to clear are psychological tests, work sampling tests, reference checks, interviews, and physical examinations. Many companies have added pre-employment drug tests to this list. Importantly, Equal Employment Opportunity (EEO) legislation in the United States and elsewhere delineates what managers can and cannot do when screening job applicants. As indicated in Figure 10.3, there is no perfect screening device; each has the potential for adversely affecting one or more protected minorities.

Equal Employment Opportunity

● ● ● ● ● ● ● ● ● ● ● ● ● ● ● ● ●
Distinguish among equal employment opportunity, affirmative action, and managing diversity.

Although earlier legislation selectively applies, the landmark EEO law in the United States is Title VII of the Civil Rights Act of 1964. Subsequent amendments, presidential executive orders, and related laws have expanded EEO's coverage. EEO law now provides a broad umbrella of employment protection for certain categories of disadvantaged individuals:

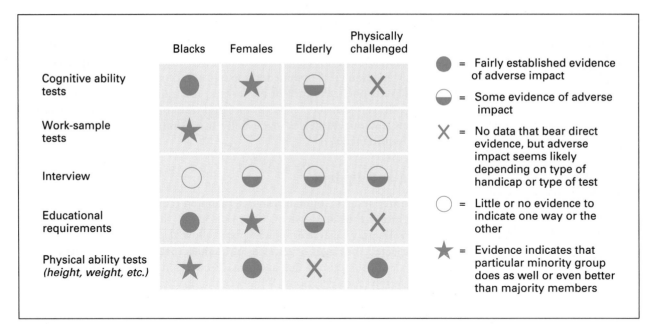

FIGURE 10.3 ● Adverse Impact of Screening Techniques on Minorities

Source: Richard D. Arvey and Robert H. Faley, *Fairness in Selecting Employees,* Second Edition, © 1988, Addison-Wesley Publishing Co., Inc., Reading, Massachusetts. Reprinted with permission of the publisher.

The result of this legislation has been that in virtually all aspects of employment, it is unlawful to discriminate on the basis of race, color, sex, religion, age, national origin, handicapped status, being a disabled veteran, or being a veteran of the Vietnam Era.[19]

What all this means is that managers cannot refuse to hire, promote, train, or transfer employees simply on the basis of the characteristics listed above. Nor can they lay off or discharge employees on these grounds. Sexual preference has been added to the list in some local jurisdictions. Selection and all other personnel decisions must be made solely on the basis of objective criteria such as ability to perform or seniority.

Affirmative Action. A more rigorous refinement of EEO legislation is affirmative action. An **affirmative action program** (AAP) is a plan for actively seeking out, employing, and developing the talents of those groups traditionally discriminated against in employment. Affirmative action amounts to a concerted effort to make up for *past* discrimination. EEO, in contrast, is aimed at preventing *future* discrimination. Typical AAPs attack employment discrimination with the following four methods: (1) *active* recruitment of women and minorities; (2) elimination of prejudicial questions on employment application forms; (3) establishment of specific goals and timetables for minority hiring; and (4) statistical validation of employment testing procedures.

Like any public policy with legal ramifications, the EEO/AAP area is fraught with complexity.[20] Varying political and legal interpretations and inconsistent

affirmative action program
making up for past discrimination by actively seeking and employing minorities

Typically, the necessary push for equal employment opportunity and managing diversity programs comes from enlightened top managers. At Avon Products Inc., there is a *grass-roots* push as well. During the 1980s, some minority employees formed informal support groups that have evolved into influential networks. The Avon Hispanic Network (AHN), Black Professionals Association (BPA), and Avon Asian Network (AAN) today are established self-help groups championing minority recruiting and career advancement. Pictured here (l to r) are the network presidents: Jose Agosto (AHN), Shirley Dong (AAN), and Sharon Hall (BPA).

employment selection test
any procedure used in the employment decision process

court decisions have left managers somewhat frustrated and confused. In late 1990, for example, President George Bush vetoed a civil rights bill because it was perceived by conservatives to be "a hiring quota bill."[21]

From Affirmative Action to Managing Diversity. Some organizations have used the debate about hiring quotas as an excuse to do nothing until confronted with a court order. Others, meanwhile, have taken progressive steps to follow the "spirit" of EEO law and AAP guidelines.[22] A progressive attitude is important for those who have been shortchanged by affirmative action, particularly for women over forty and the physically challenged.[23] But, as discussed in Chapter 3, the "managing diversity" movement promises to raise the discussion of equal opportunity and affirmative action to a higher plane. One authority on the subject put it this way:

> *Managers usually see affirmative action and equal employment opportunity as centering on minorities and women, with very little to offer white males. The diversity I'm talking about includes not only race, gender, creed, and ethnicity but also age, background, education, function, and personality differences. The objective is not to assimilate minorities and women into a dominant white male culture but to create a dominant heterogeneous culture.*[24]

In short, diversity advocates want to replace all forms of bigotry, prejudice, and intolerance with *tolerance of individual differences.*

Employment Selection Tests

EEO guidelines in the United States have broadened the definition of an **employment selection test** to include any procedure used as a basis for an employment decision. This means that, in addition to traditional pencil-and-paper tests, unscored application forms; informal and formal interviews; performance tests; and physical, educational, or experience requirements all qualify as tests.[25] This definition of an employment test takes on added significance when you realize that the federal government requires all employment tests to be statistically valid and reliable predictors of job success. Historically, women and minorities have been victimized by invalid, unreliable, and prejudicial employment selection procedures. Similar complaints have been voiced about the use of polygraphs, drug tests, and AIDS screening during the hiring process (see Table 10.2).

Ethical Hot Spots. Busy managers often seek quick, inexpensive, and supposedly sure-fire ways to make hiring decisions. Consequently, the area of employee selection and testing is plagued by unethical claims and practices. *Handwriting analysis* (also called graphoanalysis and graphology) is a good case in point. Proponents of this technique make generous claims about its ability to identify personality characteristics and predict job performance.[26] However, a statistical analysis of seventeen graphology studies raised serious doubts about the practice. In fact, psychologists, who were untrained in graphology, actually did a better job of predicting future performance from handwritten scripts than did graphologists.[27] Hiring people on the basis of their handwriting is an open invitation to a costly lawsuit. (See Management Ethics.)

TABLE 10.2 • Employment Testing Techniques: An Overview

Type of test	Purpose	Comments
Pencil-and-paper psychological and personality tests	Measure attitudes and personality characteristics such as emotional stability, intelligence, and ability to deal with stress.	Renewed interest based on claims of improved validity. Can be expensive when scoring and interpretations are done by professionals. Validity varies widely from test to test.
Pencil-and-paper honesty tests	Assess candidate's degree of risk for engaging in dishonest behavior.	Inexpensive to administer. Questionable validity. Growing in popularity since recent curtailment of polygraph testing.
Job skills tests (clerical and manual dexterity tests, math and language tests, assessment centers, and simulations)	Competence is assessed in actual "hands-on" situations.	Generally good validity if carefully designed and administered. Assessment centers and simulations can be very expensive.
Polygraph (lie detector) tests	Measure physical signs of stress, such as rapid pulse and perspiration.	Growing use in recent years severely restricted by federal (Employee Polygraph Protection Act of 1988), state, and local laws. Questionable validity.
Drug tests	Urine, blood, or hair samples submitted to chemical analysis for controlled substances.	Rapidly growing in use despite strong employee resistance and potentially inaccurate procedures.
Handwriting analysis (graphoanalysis)	Personality characteristics and styles inferred from samples of handwriting.	Popular in Europe and growing in popularity in United States. Sweeping claims by proponents leave validity in doubt.
AIDS/HIV antibody tests	Blood samples tested for evidence of AIDS virus.	An emerging area with undetermined legal and ethical boundaries. Major confidentiality issue.

Source: Adapted from discussion in Paul L. Blocklyn, "Preemployment Testing," *Personnel* (February 1988): 66–68; Eric Rolfe Greenberg, "Workplace Testing: Results of a New AMA Survey," *Personnel* (April 1988): 36–44; Karen M. Evans and Randall Brown, "Reducing Recruitment Risk Through Preemployment Testing," *Personnel* (September 1988): 55–64; and James G. Frierson, "New Polygraph Test Limits," *Personnel Journal* (December 1988): 84–92.

No Quick Fixes. In the final analysis, there are no really good shortcuts when screening job applicants. At the very least, vendors of screening techniques should be asked for objective third-party validation evidence. Library searches can turn up academic studies such as the one on graphology cited earlier. Companies that conduct their own validation studies have an obvious conflict of interest. A *multimethod approach* to employee selection is most desirable. For example, a manager might weigh a particular job candidate's employability on the basis of education and experience, one or more interviews, a performance test, and a reference check.

Effective Interviewing

Interviewing warrants special attention here because, according to one human resources author, "the interview is probably the most widely used personnel

Employee Selection Techniques That *Are* Too Good to Be True

Selecting future employees is one of the most important and difficult processes for which human resource managers are responsible. The time-honored approach of interviewing, investigating an applicant's experience and education, and talking with references, although time-consuming, may still be the best method. Besides, interviewing today is a minefield of legal do's and don'ts. You may ask an applicant about prior convictions but not about arrests. You may ask about medical background but not about race and religion. And, ironically, if you hire a person who then hurts a customer, you can be sued for not having known about his or her prior arrest record.

Faced with such difficulties, many companies buy quick-and-easy solutions to the selection dilemma. Many of these solutions *are*, in fact, too good to be true. Take the 1980s, for example. Polygraph—lie detector—tests seemed at that time to be the wave of the future. Companies began relying on machines and polygraph experts to screen applicants. Disturbed by this trend and by the inaccuracy of many of the test results, Congress severely restricted polygraph use.

In the 1990s, equally questionable selection techniques are being offered as the human resource manager's best friend. Some companies borrow a technique from county fairs and try to judge applicants on the basis of their handwriting. Others turn to "honesty tests" which claim to be able to uncover applicants who would be problem employees. Some pencil-and-paper tests do provide personnel managers with useful information, but many tests now being marketed simply do not live up to their claims.

Because of the wealth of information available from government records, credit bureaus, and other sources, an entire industry has sprung up in the business of collecting and selling information about applicants. Some of the more reputable employee information companies produce carefully researched, expensive summaries of an applicant's background. But many businesses turn to data gatherers that check their data less thoroughly and that may even sell information like lists of arrests, which a prospective employer is not allowed to use. Such screening does weed out people with checkered backgrounds, but it can be both unfair and illegal. Apparently you get what you pay for.

Sources: Caleb S. Atwood and James M. Neel, "New Lawsuits Expand Employer Liability," *HRMagazine* (October 1990): 74–75; Robin Inwald, "Those 'Little White Lies' Of Honesty Test Vendors," *Personnel* (June 1990): 52–58; Jeffrey Rothfeder, "Looking for a Job? You May Be Out before You Go In," *Business Week* (September 24, 1990): 128–130.

technique, particularly in the selection procedure."[28] Line managers at all levels are often asked to interview candidates for job openings and promotions and should be aware of the weaknesses of the traditional unstructured interview. The traditional unstructured or informal interview, which has no fixed question format or systematic scoring procedure, has been criticized because:

> Explain how managers can be more effective interviewers.

- It is highly susceptible to distortion and bias.
- It is highly susceptible to legal attack.
- It is usually indefensible if legally contested.
- It may have apparent validity, but no real validity.
- It is rarely totally job-related and may incorporate personal items that infringe on privacy.
- It is the most flexible selection technique, thereby being highly inconsistent.

- There is a tendency for the interviewer to look for qualities he or she prefers, and then to justify the hiring decision based on these qualities.
- Often the interviewer does not hear about the selection mistakes.
- There is an unsubstantiated confidence in the traditional interview.[29]

The Problem of Cultural Bias. Traditional unstructured interviews are notorious for being culturally insensitive. Evidence of this problem surfaced in a recent study of the interviewing practices of thirty-eight general managers employed by nine different fast-food chains. According to the researcher:

> *Considering the well-known demographics of today's work force, it's amazing that 9 percent of those receiving a negative hiring decision are turned down for inappropriate eye contact. To give a firm handshake and look someone straight in the eyes is a very important lesson taught by Dad to every middle-class male at a tender age. Not only do nonmainstream groups miss the lesson from Dad, some are taught that direct eye contact is rude or worse. Girls are frequently taught that direct eye contact is unbecoming in a female. In reality, having averted or shifty eyes may indicate mostly that the job applicant is not a middle-class male.*[30]

Managers can be taught, however, to be aware of and to overcome cultural biases when interviewing.

Structured Interviews. Structured interviews are the recommended alternative to traditional unstructured or informal interviews.[31] A **structured interview** is defined as a series of job-related questions with standardized answers that are consistently applied across all interviews for a particular job.[32] Structured interviews are constructed, conducted, and scored by a committee of three to six members to try to eliminate individual bias. The structured format and scoring of structured interviews eliminate the weaknesses inherent in unstructured interviews. Four types of questions are typically found in structured interviews: (1) situational, (2) job knowledge, (3) job sample simulation, and (4) worker requirements (see Table 10.3).

structured interview a series of job-related questions with standardized answers

Performance Appraisal

Although formal performance appraisal systems are considered essential in today's organizations, they are often a source of dissatisfaction, as the following survey demonstrated. In a survey of 589 personnel administrators, 87 percent reportedly used formal performance appraisal systems, yet only 56 percent of those with such systems were satisfied with them.[33] Performance appraisal can be effective and satisfying if systematically developed and implemented techniques replace haphazard methods. For our purposes, **performance appraisal** is the process of evaluating individual job performance as a basis for making objective personnel decisions.[34] This definition intentionally excludes occasional coaching, in which a supervisor simply checks an employee's work and gives immediate

performance appraisal evaluating job performance as a basis for personnel decisions

TABLE 10.3 • Types of Structured Interview Questions

Type of question	Method	Information sought	Sample question
Situational	Oral	Can the applicant handle difficult situations likely to be encountered on the job?	"What would you do if you saw two of your immediate subordinates arguing loudly in the work area?"
Job knowledge	Oral or written	Does the applicant possess the knowledge required for successful job performance?	"Do you know the computer languages COBOL and BASIC?"
Job sample simulation	Observation of actual or simulated performance	Can the applicant actually do essential aspects of the job?	"Can you show us how to prepare a letter on this word processor?"
Worker requirements	Oral	Is the applicant willing to cope with job demands such as travel, relocation, or hard physical labor?	"Are you willing to spend 25 percent of your time on the road?"

Source: "Structured Interviewing: Avoiding Selection Problems," by Elliott D. Pursell, Michael A. Campion, and Sarah R. Gaylord, copyright November 1980. Reprinted with permission of *Personnel Journal,* Costa Mesa, California; all rights reserved.

feedback. Although personal coaching is fundamental to good management, formally documented appraisals are needed both to ensure equitable distribution of opportunities and rewards and to avoid prejudicial treatment of protected minorities.[35]

A survey of nearly 600 organizations belonging to the American Management Association (AMA) found that managers use performance appraisal results as follows:

The appraisals are used for compensation (85.6 percent), counseling (65.1 percent), training and development (64.3 percent), promotion (45.3 percent), [staff] planning (43.1 percent), retention/discharge (30.3 percent), and validation of a selection technique (17.2 percent).[36]

In this section, we will examine five important aspects of performance appraisal: (1) legal defensibility; (2) general approaches; (3) alternative techniques; (4) frequency; and (5) the evaluation versus development dilemma.

Making Performance Appraisals Legally Defensible

••••••••••••••••••
Discuss how performance appraisals can be made legally defensible.

Lawsuits challenging the legality of specific performance appraisal systems and resulting personnel actions have left scores of human resource managers asking themselves: "Will my organization's performance appraisal system stand up in court?" From the standpoint of limiting legal exposure, it is better to ask this question when developing a formal appraisal system rather than after it has been implemented. Managers need specific criteria for legally defensible performance appraisal systems. Fortunately, researchers have discerned some instructive patterns in recent court decisions.

After studying the verdicts in sixty-six employment discrimination cases in the United States, one pair of researchers found that employers could successfully defend their appraisal systems if they satisfied four criteria:

1. A *job analysis* was used to develop the performance appraisal system.
2. The appraisal system was *behavior-oriented,* not trait-oriented.
3. Performance evaluators followed *specific written instructions* when conducting appraisals.
4. Evaluators *reviewed the results* of the appraisals with the ratees.[37]

Each of these conditions has a clear legal rationale. Job analysis, discussed earlier relative to human resource planning, anchors the appraisal process to specific job duties, not to personalities. Behavior-oriented appraisals properly focus management's attention on *how* the individual actually performed his or her job. Performance appraisers who follow specific written instructions are less likely to be plagued by vague performance standards and/or personal bias. Finally, by reviewing performance appraisal results with those who have been evaluated, managers provide the feedback necessary for learning and improvement. Managers who keep these criteria for legal defensibility in mind are better equipped to select a sound appraisal system from alternative approaches and techniques.

General Approaches to Appraising Job Performance

There are three general approaches to determining who has done a good job and who has not. They are the trait-oriented approach, the behavior-oriented approach, and the outcome-oriented approach. Respectively, these approaches focus on *who* did the job, *how* the job was done, and *what* was accomplished. Each deserves a closer look.

Trait-oriented Appraisals. This approach enjoys the dubious distinction of being both one of the most widely used as well as one of the weakest approaches. The case against trait-oriented appraisals has been summarized by two experts as follows:

> If the purpose of the appraisal is to evaluate past *performance, then an evaluation of simple personality traits such as [initiative, dependability, ambition, loyalty] hardly fits the bill. Personality traits are not in and of themselves measures of either behavior or performance. In fact, a great deal of research indicates that traits are unstable within individuals and across situations. In other words, the extent to which a person possesses "initiative" differs as a function of the situation. Most trait-rating approaches pay little or no attention to the context of behavior.*[38]

Consequently, trait-oriented appraisals tend to be unfair and do not stand up well in court.

Behavior-oriented Appraisals. Performance appraisals that focus on specific job-related behavior are strongly recommended by experts. The rationale is that *behavior,* not personality traits or abilities, is ultimately responsible for job success or failure. Legal defensibility is greatly enhanced when a performance appraisal system is tied to specific job behavior.

Outcome-oriented Appraisals. Whereas the trait approach focuses on *who* and the behavioral approach on *how,* the outcome approach directs the appraiser's attention to *what* was actually accomplished. The most popular outcome-oriented approach to performance appraisal is management by objectives (MBO).[39] As you may recall from our discussion in Chapter 5, managers who rely on MBO assess performance in terms of how well employees meet measurable and participatively set goals. It is important to note, however, that MBO and other outcome-oriented approaches have a major shortcoming. Because goals are individualized, comparisons between two or more people are difficult if not impossible. As a result, MBO is said to be a poor vehicle for making decisions about promotions or merit pay that require employees to be ranked.[40]

Alternative Performance Appraisal Techniques

The list of alternative performance appraisal techniques is long and growing. Unfortunately, many are simplistic, invalid, and unreliable. In general terms, an *invalid* appraisal instrument does not accurately measure what it is supposed to measure. *Unreliable* instruments do not measure criteria in a consistent manner. Many other performance appraisal techniques are so complex that they are impractical and burdensome to use. But armed with a working knowledge of the most popular appraisal techniques, a good manager can distinguish the strong from the weak. Once again, the strength of an appraisal technique is gauged by its conformity to the criteria for legal defensibility discussed previously. Different techniques are discussed here in diminishing order of popularity, as determined in the AMA study cited earlier.

- *Goal Setting.* Within an MBO framework, performance is typically evaluated in terms of formal objectives set at an earlier date. This is a comparatively strong technique if desired outcomes are clearly linked to specific behavior. For example, a product design engineer's "output" could be measured in terms of the number of product specifications submitted per month.

- *Written Essays.* Managers describe the performance of subordinates in narrative form, sometimes in response to predetermined questions. Evaluators often criticize this technique for consuming too much time. This method is also limited by the fact that some managers have difficulty expressing themselves in writing.

- *Critical Incidents.* Specific instances of inferior and superior performance are documented by the supervisor when they occur. Accumulated incidents then provide an objective basis for evaluations at appraisal time. The strength of critical incidents is enhanced when evaluators document specific behavior in specific situations and ignore personality traits.

behaviorally anchored rating scales performance appraisal scales with notations about observable behavior attached

- *Graphic Rating Scales.* Various traits or behavior are rated on incremental scales. For example, "initiative" could be rated on a 1(=low)--2--3--4--5(=high) scale. This technique is among the weakest when personality traits are employed. However, **behaviorally anchored rating scales** (BARS), defined as performance rating scales divided into increments of observable job behavior determined through job analysis, are considered to be one of the strongest performance-appraisal techniques.[41] (See Figure 10.4.)

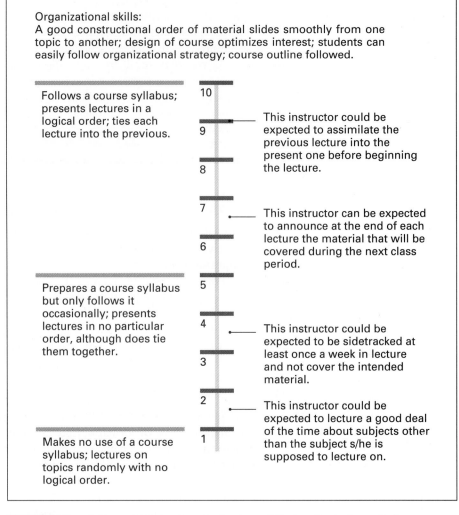

Organizational skills:
A good constructional order of material slides smoothly from one topic to another; design of course optimizes interest; students can easily follow organizational strategy; course outline followed.

Follows a course syllabus; presents lectures in a logical order; ties each lecture into the previous.

10

9 — This instructor could be expected to assimilate the previous lecture into the present one before beginning the lecture.

8

7 — This instructor can be expected to announce at the end of each lecture the material that will be covered during the next class period.

6

Prepares a course syllabus but only follows it occasionally; presents lectures in no particular order, although does tie them together.

5

4 — This instructor could be expected to be sidetracked at least once a week in lecture and not cover the intended material.

3

2 — This instructor could be expected to lecture a good deal of the time about subjects other than the subject s/he is supposed to lecture on.

Makes no use of a course syllabus; lectures on topics randomly with no logical order.

1

FIGURE 10.4 • A Sample Behaviorally Anchored Rating Scale for a College Professor

Source: Adapted from H. John Bernardin and Richard W. Beatty, *Performance Appraisal: Assessing Human Behavior at Work* (Boston: Kent Publishing Company, 1984), p. 84 © 1984 by Wadsworth, Inc. Reprinted by permission of PWS—KENT Publishing Company, a division of Wadsworth, Inc.

- *Weighted Check Lists.* Evaluators check appropriate adjectives or behavioral descriptions that have predetermined weights. The weights, which gauge the relative importance of the randomly mixed items on the check list, are usually unknown to the evaluator. Following the evaluation, the weights of the checked items are added or averaged to permit interpersonal comparisons. As with the other techniques, the degree of behavioral specificity largely determines the strength of weighted check lists.
- *Rankings/Comparisons.* Coworkers in a subunit are ranked or compared in head-to-head fashion according to specified accomplishments or job

behavior. A major shortcoming of this technique is that the absolute distance between ratees is unknown. For example, the employee ranked number one may be five times as effective as number two, who in turn is only slightly more effective than number three. Rankings/comparisons are also criticized for causing resentment among lower-ranked, but adequately performing, coworkers. This technique can be strengthened by combining it with a more behavioral technique, such as critical incidents or BARS.

Frequency of Performance Reviews

Regarding the frequency of performance appraisals, the long-standing tradition has been the annual review. But MBO scholar George Odiorne recently made a disturbing finding:

> *In one survey, 70 percent of the bosses reported that they faithfully reviewed their subordinates annually. Yet in the same organizations, less than 30 percent of the subordinates reported that they had their performance reviewed annually by their boss.*[42]

Why did such a glaring disagreement exist between raters and ratees? Odiorne speculates that either the annual review meetings were too informal or the managers viewed the annual salary adjustment announcement as a performance review. Either way, employees perceived that they did not have a formal performance evaluation meeting and desired more specific feedback. Odiorne recommends that managers conduct quarterly review meetings. His rationale is based on the rapid pace of change today.

The frequency of performance review meetings is ultimately a judgment call for managers. Given adequate managerial time and motivation, the more frequent the review sessions, the better. Whether they decide to conduct quarterly reviews or stick with the traditional annual format, however, managers need to resolve the following dilemma to render effective appraisals.

Evaluation versus Development: A Dilemma

Ideally, performance appraisal occurs in three phases:

1. Objective evaluation of job performance for a specified period of time.
2. Evaluation feedback interview.
3. Developmental interview.

All too often, unfortunately, subjective bias contaminates the evaluation, feedback is vague or absent, and development is shortchanged. Worse yet, busy managers sometimes confuse and frustrate their subordinates by trying to accomplish all three phases in one brief sitting. These problems result from a failure to resolve the conflict between being both an evaluator and a developer of subordinates (see Figure 10.5). Objective evaluation calls for hard-nosed analysis of an individual's performance, free of political and emotional considerations.[43] Conversely, employee development can occur only in a climate of mutual trust, understanding, teamwork, and honest communication.

Experts suggest that the best way to resolve this dilemma is to play the evaluator role in one face-to-face interview and the developer role in a later

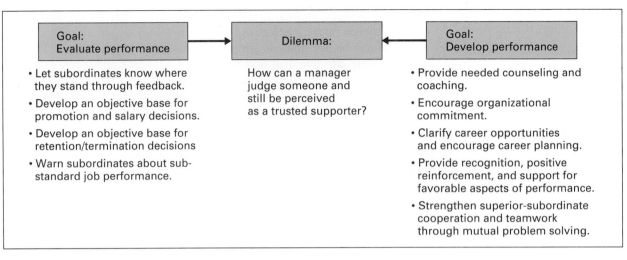

FIGURE 10.5 • The Performance Appraisal Dilemma

Source: Based on Michael Beer, "Performance Appraisal: Dilemmas and Possibilities." Reprinted, by permission of the publisher, from *Organizational Dynamics,* Winter/1981. American Management Association, New York. All rights reserved.

interview.[44] Each meeting should have its own appropriate tone. When time and other factors preclude separate evaluation and developmental meetings, as is often the case, a single interview with the following format can be used:

> *Begin interview . . .*
> 1. *Open-ended discussion and exploration of problems, in which the subordinate leads and the supervisor listens.*
> 2. *Problem-solving discussion, in which the subordinate leads, but supervisor takes somewhat stronger role.*
> 3. *Agreement between supervisor and subordinate on performance problems and a plan for improvements.*
> 4. *Closing evaluation, in which the supervisor gives his or her views and final evaluation if the subordinate has not dealt with important issues.*[45]
>
> *. . . interview ends.*

Assuming that the subordinate is told ahead of time what to expect, evaluation and development can occur simultaneously. *Self-evaluation* is the key to success here because it encourages candor and honesty without betraying trust or driving the subordinate into a passive or defensive posture.

Training

There is often a gap between what employees *do* know and what they *should* know. Filling this knowledge gap by means of training has become big business. According to U.S. government statistics, American companies spend an incredible $30 to $40 billion a year on training.[46] An estimated one-third of the U.S. work

Details can make or break a fast-food company like Domino's Pizza. Air bubbles in the crust, bald spots in the sauce, or skimpy toppings can mean a lost customer in the fiercely competitive pizza market. The challenge is to adequately train thousands of employees to exacting standards. Domino's relies on its own satellite television network to teach its franchisees everything from how to slice vegetables to minding the store. Corporate television industry experts forecast rapid growth for business TV, with a projected 141 networks by 1992.

training using guided experience to change employee behavior/attitudes/opinions

force (about 39.5 million people) participated in employer-sponsored training programs in 1990.[47] As the term is used here, **training** is the process of changing employee behavior, attitudes, or opinions through some type of guided experience.

In this section, we discuss training content and delivery, identify the ingredients of a good training program, and draw an important distinction between skill and factual learning.

Modern Training: Content and Delivery

A 1990 survey by *Training* magazine of 2,645 U.S. businesses with one hundred or more employees shed instructive light on today's training practices. Respondents represented all major industries and worked in small, medium-size, and large organizations.[48] Figure 10.6 presents the top fifteen training content areas and the most frequently used methods of instruction. Management development is the most common type of training today.[49] Basic computer-skills training, now ranked fifth, has become increasingly important. Renewed competitive emphasis on customer service has elevated customer relations/services training to the number-seven spot. Videotape, a comparative newcomer to organizational training, has quickly become the most extensively used instructional method.[50]

Which instructional method is best? There probably are as many answers to this question as there are trainers. Given variables such as interpersonal differences, budget limitations, and instructor capabilities, it is safe to say that there is no one best training technique.[51] For example, the lecture method, though widely criticized for being dull and encouraging learner passivity, ranked a strong

FIGURE 10.6 • The Content and Delivery of Today's Organizational Training

Source: Reprinted with permission from the October 1990 issue of *Training,* The Magazine of Human Resources Development. Copyright 1990, Lakewood Publications Inc., Minneapolis, MN (612) 333-0471. All rights reserved.

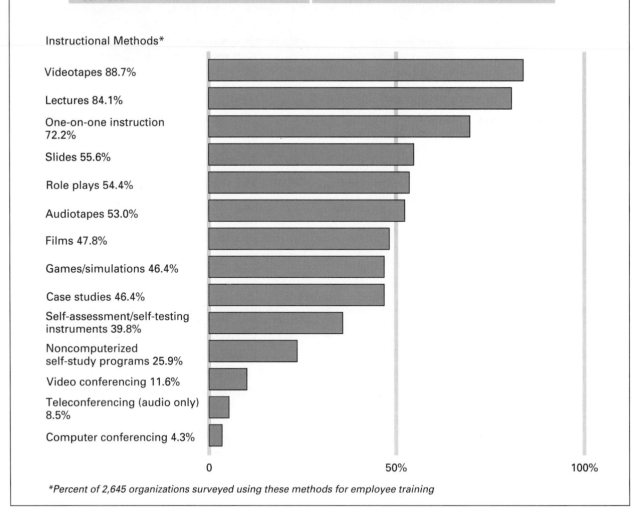

General Types of Training

Types of training	Percent providing	Types of training	Percent providing
Management skills/development	86.2	Executive development	69.1
Technical skills/knowledge	83.0	Clerical/secretarial skills	68.2
Supervisory skills	82.4	Personal growth	65.6
Communication skills	78.2	Employee/labor relations	56.4
Basic computer skills	74.5	Wellness	52.8
New methods/procedures	72.6	Sales skills	47.5
Customer relations/services	70.8	Customer education	45.2
		Remedial basic education	35.1

Instructional Methods*

- Videotapes 88.7%
- Lectures 84.1%
- One-on-one instruction 72.2%
- Slides 55.6%
- Role plays 54.4%
- Audiotapes 53.0%
- Films 47.8%
- Games/simulations 46.4%
- Case studies 46.4%
- Self-assessment/self-testing instruments 39.8%
- Noncomputerized self-study programs 25.9%
- Video conferencing 11.6%
- Teleconferencing (audio only) 8.5%
- Computer conferencing 4.3%

0   50%   100%

Percent of 2,645 organizations surveyed using these methods for employee training

Training Pays Off for Marriott in Poland

Says Richard Whiteley, president of Forum Corp., a Boston consulting firm: "Training is much more powerful if it starts at the top and sifts down." That was the approach that Marriott adopted to meet a remarkable challenge in opening the Warsaw Marriott, Poland's first Western-owned hotel. In late 1987, two years before it opened, the company recruited twenty Polish managers, none with lodging-industry background. Says Haile Aguilar, a seventeen-year Marriott veteran who is now the Warsaw Marriott's general manager: "A sense of hospitality is not characteristic of hotels in Poland. We wanted people with no experience and a willingness to learn from us."

The Poles flew to Boston, where Marriott managers led classroom discussions in matters such as running a smooth room-service operation and taking accurate messages for guests. Says Dorota Kowalska, the Warsaw hotel's director of human resources: "Role-playing helped more than three hours of lectures because it made the trainees think like customers."

When the trainees returned home, they hired and instructed a staff of one thousand. Quickly they proved that bosses don't have to be behind-closed-door dictators. Says Kowalska, 32, the daughter of a Polish diplomat and previously a teacher of English, French, and Arabic in Warsaw: "Seeing the executive director of food and beverage actually clear tables in the breakfast room was something our people had never experienced before." Now her compatriots are passing up lunch breaks and working extra-long hours, for the sake of caring for the guests. And the Warsaw Marriott, which attracts mostly Westerners, has been earning even higher customer satisfaction ratings than Marriott's U.S. hotels.

Source: Excerpted from Patricia Sellers, "What Customers Really Want," *Fortune* (June 4, 1990) © The Time Inc. Magazine Company. All rights reserved.

second in the study just discussed. Role playing, ranked fifth in the study above, remains popular among both trainers and trainees (see The World of Management).

The Ingredients of a Good Training Program

Although training needs and approaches vary, managers can get the most out of their training budgets by following a few guidelines. According to two training specialists, every training program should be designed along the following lines to maximize retention and transfer learning to the job:

1. Maximize the similarity between the training situation and the job situation.

2. Provide as much experience as possible with the task being taught.

3. Provide for a variety of examples when teaching concepts or skills.

4. Label or identify important features of a task.

5. Make sure that general principles are understood before expecting much transfer.

6. Make sure that the trained behaviors and ideas are rewarded in the job situation.

7. Design the training content so that the trainees can see its applicability.

8. Use adjunct questions to guide the trainee's attention.[52]

Skill versus Factual Learning

•••••••••••••••••
Compare and contrast the ingredients of good training programs for skill and factual learning.

The ingredients of a good training program vary according to whether skill learning or factual learning is involved. It has been pointed out that:

Effective skill learning should incorporate four essential ingredients: (1) goal setting, (2) modeling, (3) practice, and (4) feedback. Let's take as an example the task of training someone to ride horseback. How would you do it? It basically must entail telling someone specifically what you want them to do (goal setting), showing them how you want them to do it (modeling), giving them the opportunity to try out what you have told them and shown them (practice), and then telling them what they are doing correctly (feedback).[53]

When factual learning is involved, the same sequence is used, except that in step 2, "meaningful presentation of the materials" is substituted for modeling. Keep in mind that the object of training is *learning*.[54] Learning requires thoughtful preparation, carefully guided exposure to new ideas or behavior, and motivational support. Let us turn our attention to some modern human resource management problems that have serious implications for the well-being of today's organizations and employees.

Contemporary Human Resource Problems

•••••••••••••••••
Specify the key components in organizational policies for sexual harassment, alcohol and drug abuse, and AIDS.

Modern organizations are a direct reflection of society in general. People take societal influences to work in the form of values, attitudes, and ethics. Along with these predispositions, they take their social, emotional, behavioral, and health-related problems to work. Like it or not and prepared or not, managers face human resource problems such as sexual harassment, alcohol and drug abuse, and AIDS. These three problems deserve a closer look from a human resource management perspective. Each is a serious threat to individual well-being and organizational performance.

Discouraging Sexual Harassment

sexual harassment unwanted sexual attention that creates an offensive or intimidating work environment

A great deal of misunderstanding surrounds the topic of sexual harassment because of sexist attitudes, vague definitions, and inconsistent court findings. **Sexual harassment,** defined generally as unwanted sexual attention or conduct, has both behavioral and legal dimensions (see Table 10.4). Important among these are the following:

- Although female employees are typically the victims of sexual harassment, both women and men (in the United States) are protected under Title VII of the Civil Rights Act of 1964.

The partnership for a Drug-Free America urges managers to be part of the solution to drug problems, not part of the problem. The results of drug addiction are poor performance, absenteeism, theft, industrial accidents, or death. Addicts seldom get well or even into treatment by themselves. The National Institute on Drug Abuse hotline for managers stands ready to help businesses set up drug programs. Along with sexual harassment and AIDS, drug and alcohol abuse are the major human resource problems confronting managers today.

Sometimes, the worst thing you can do to a drug user is the only way to help.

Drug use is a question of extremes. People who use drugs are either addicted or in danger of addiction.

The results of drug addiction are poor performance, absenteeism, theft, robbery, industrial accidents, and death.

And addicts often take others down with them. Loved ones, co-workers, even employers.

Addicts seldom get well or even get into treatment by themselves. Someone has to help. You could be that person. If you're willing to get involved.

When you say, in no uncertain terms, "Get well or get out," you may be awakening the addict to the one reality that can save her.

Threatening to fire an addict is the worst thing you can do to her. Or the best. If it gets her into treatment.

To find out how to set up a treatment program in your company, please call 1-800-843-4971. That's the National Institute on Drug Abuse hot line for managers and CEOs. It's manned by trained Employee Assistance Program planners and designers, from Monday through Friday, 9:00 a.m. to 8:00 p.m. Eastern Time. They won't tell you what to do, but they can outline the options.

Partnership for a Drug-Free America

- Sexual harassment includes, but is not limited to, unwanted physical contact. Gestures, displays, joking, and language also may create a sexually offensive or intimidating work environment.

- It is the manager's job to be aware of and correct cases of sexual harassment. Ignorance of such activity is not a valid legal defense.[55]

Research evidence indicates that sexual harassment is commonplace. In a recent survey of 1,232 employees, 33 percent of the women and 25 percent of the men said they had been sexually harassed in their current job.[56] A survey of college students found far greater problems on campus (89 percent for women; 85 percent for men).[57] Researchers find people generally agree that unwanted sexual propositions, promises or threats tied to sexual favors, lewd comments/gestures/jokes, and touching/grabbing/brushing qualify as sexual harassment. Beyond that, opinions differ.[58] Personal tastes and sensibilities vary widely from individual to individual. In view of the foregoing evidence, corrective action needs to be taken by both the victims of sexual harassment and management.

What Can the Victim Do? Employees who believe they are victims of sexual harassment can try to live with it, fight back, complain to higher-ups, find another job, or sue their employer. One study revealed a low success rate for the last option. Of 81 sexual harassment cases (76 female; 5 male) processed by the state of Illinois between 1981 and 1983, only 20 rulings were favorable to the

TABLE 10.4 • Behavioral and Legal Dimensions of Sexual Harassment

What exactly is sexual harassment? The Equal Employment Opportunity Commission (EEOC) says that unwelcome sexual advances, requests for sexual favors, and other verbal or physical conduct of a sexual nature constitute sexual harassment when submission to such conduct is made a condition of employment; when submission to or rejection of sexual advances is used as a basis for employment decisions; or when such conduct creates an intimidating, hostile, or offensive work environment. These EEOC guidelines interpreting Title VII of the Civil Rights Act of 1964 further state that employers are responsible for the actions of their supervisors and agents and that employers are responsible for the actions of other employees if the employer knows or should have known about the sexual harassment.

Source: "Sexual Harassment, 1: Discouraging It in the Work Place," by B. Terry Thornton. Reprinted by permission of the publisher, from *Personnel,* April 1986. American Management Association, New York. All rights reserved.

complainants.[59] This study identified three factors associated with favorable judgments of sexually harassed employees. The courts tended to look favorably on cases in which:

1. There was *serious misconduct* ("such as sexual assault, unwanted physical contact, and propositions linked to threats or promises of a change in an individual's conditions of employment"[60]).

2. There were *witnesses.*

3. *Notice had been given to management* before charges were filed.

Courtrooms are the last line of defense for victims of sexual harassment. Preventive and remedial actions also are needed. Harassers need to be told by their victims, coworkers, and supervisors that their actions are illegal, unethical, and against company policy. As more organizations develop and enforce sexual harassment policies, the problem can be greatly reduced without costly court battles and the loss of valued employees.

What Can the Organization Do?   Starting with top management, an organizationwide commitment to eliminating sexual harassment should be established. A clear policy statement, with behavioral definitions of sexual harassment and associated penalties, is essential. As with all policies, sexual-harassment policies need to be disseminated and uniformly enforced if they are to have the desired impact. Appropriate training, particularly for new employees, can alert people to the problem and consequences of sexual harassment. Finally, in accordance with EEOC guidelines, management can remain adequately informed of any sexual harassment in the organization by establishing a grievance procedure. Harassed employees should be able to get a fair hearing of their case without fear of retaliation.[61]

Controlling Alcohol and Drug Abuse

The statistics tell a grim story about the number-one drug problem—alcohol. Serious drinking problems afflict approximately 10 percent of the U.S. population. About 10.5 million Americans qualify as alcoholics. Twenty-five percent of Americans polled say alcohol has been a problem in their family.[62] Once believed to be a character disorder, **alcoholism** is now considered a disease in which an individual's normal social and economic roles are disrupted by the consumption of alcohol. Very few alcoholics are actually the skid-row-bum type; the vast majority are average citizens with jobs and families. Alcoholism cuts across all age brackets, both sexes, and all racial and ethnic categories. Experts say a glance in the mirror shows what the average alcoholic looks like.[63]

alcoholism a disease in which alcohol abuse disrupts one's normal life

Close on the heels of employee alcoholism is workplace drug abuse.

> *Although alcohol is the nation's most abused drug, an increasingly greater number of Americans are also abusing mood-altering drug substances apart from, and in addition to, the usage of alcohol. These other drug substances can be described as "illegal"—heroin, cocaine, marijuana, morphine, and so on—or "legal"—prescription drugs such as amphetamines, tranquilizers, and barbiturates.[64]*

The National Institute on Drug Abuse "estimates that if every worker from age eighteen to forty were tested for drugs on any given day, 14 to 25 percent would test positive."[65] Compared with nonabusers, alcoholic employees and drug abusers are significantly less productive, ten times more likely to be absent, and three times more likely either to have or to cause an accident.[66] In terms of lost productivity due to absenteeism, accidents, shoddy work, sick leave, and theft of organizational resources, employee alcohol and drug abuse costs the U.S. economy an estimated $60 billion to $100 billion a year.[67] Employers can play a key role in curbing this tragic and costly erosion of our human resources.

The Legal Side of Workplace Substance Abuse. Businesses doing contract work for the U.S. government are squeezed on two sides by the law. On one side, alcoholics and drug addicts are protected from employment discrimination by the Vocational Rehabilitation Act of 1973. They are presumed to have the same employment rights that any disabled person has.[68] On the other side, employers with federal contracts exceeding $25,000 are subject to the Federal Drug-Free Workplace Act of 1988. These employers "must certify that they will maintain a drug-free workplace."[69] The idea is to rid federal contractors' workplaces of the production, distribution, and possession of controlled substances. Alcohol is not considered a controlled substance by the 1988 Act. Companies found to be in violation of the Act may lose their right to do business with the U.S. government.

Do these two legal thrusts work in opposite directions? Actually, the two laws work in combination because they make *rehabilitation* the best option.

Referral and Rehabilitation. Alcoholism or drug abuse typically reveals itself to the manager in the form of increased absenteeism, tardiness, sloppy work, and complaints from coworkers. As soon as a steady decline in performance is observed, the manager should confront the individual with his or her poor performance record. Experts advise supervisors not to make accusations about alcohol or drug abuse. It is the employee's challenge to admit having such a problem. Management's job is to refer troubled employees to appropriate sources of help. Managers are cautioned against "playing doctor" when trying to help the alcohol- or drug-abusing employee. If the organization has an *employee assistance program* (EAP),[70] counselors, or a company doctor, an in-house referral can be made. Counselors in General Motors' highly successful EAP estimate that the company gets back $3 for every $1 spent on alcohol/drug-abuse treatment.[71] Kimberly-Clark and DuPont claim EAP recovery rates of 65 to 70 percent for alcohol abusers.[72]

Managers in small organizations without sophisticated employee services can refer the alcoholic employee to community resources such as Alcoholics Anonymous. Similar referral agencies for drug abusers exist in most communities. The overriding objective for the manager is to put troubled employees in touch with trained rehabilitation specialists as soon as possible.

If employee searches and workplace drug testing are part of a company's substance-abuse program, complex and difficult considerations arise (see Insights & Issues). A 1989 survey found nearly 52 percent of the companies polled were testing for drugs.[73] Meanwhile, the appropriate balance between management's need for greater control and the individual's rights to privacy and fair treatment is being worked out by lawmakers.

Developing a Responsible AIDS Policy

The current acquired immune deficiency syndrome (AIDS) epidemic raises two critical questions for managers: (1) How should the organization treat an individual who has tested positive for the AIDS virus? and (2) What can be done to prevent an AIDS victim's coworkers from panicking? In view of the following statistics, these questions have become vital for all managers.

The virus responsible for AIDS is truly an epidemic, having spread from being a virtually unknown disease in 1981 to infecting 6 million to 8 million victims worldwide by 1990. By the year 2000, about 20 million people worldwide will carry the AIDS virus, which has a 20 to 40 percent chance of becoming active and deadly. More than 1.5 million Americans were infected with the AIDS-causing virus by 1990, with 3,000 new cases every month. Companies are sagging under the additional $40,000 to $50,000 cost of employing someone with advanced AIDS. One estimate puts the annual cost of the AIDS epidemic for American business at about $55 billion.[74] Managers have no choice but to develop a responsible AIDS policy.

Three Key Components. *Equal treatment, education,* and *confidentiality* are the three key components of a well-conceived AIDS policy (see the principles in Table 10.5). As stated in a report titled "AIDS: Corporate America Responds":

> *Treatment of employees with AIDS should be the same as that for others with a chronic or life-threatening illness . . . including eligibility for the same work privileges and medical benefits.*[75]

The approach taken by the International Business Machines Corporation, for example, was to draft an AIDS policy in 1985 and, in the fall of 1987, to distribute to the company's 240,000 domestic employees an AIDS pamphlet written by the U.S. Centers for Disease Control. IBM's medical director Glenn E. Haughie included a "Dear IBMer" introduction in the brochure, in which he

Putting Workplace Drug Testing to the Test

Workplace drug testing has developed into a major controversy, with many companies now using one or more of five testing approaches.

- *Random testing:* Employees are selected at random to be tested.
- *Periodic testing:* Every employee is tested regularly, usually at the time of an annual physical exam.
- *Pre-employment testing:* Job applicants are tested during the screening process.
- *Post-accident testing:* Workers involved in accidents are required to undergo tests.
- *Reasonable-cause testing:* Used only when an employer has good reason to suspect that an employee is using drugs.

Although everyone agrees that drug abuse and accidents should be reduced, it isn't clear that drug testing is all that effective. Employees and employers alike have raised serious questions about such testing. Many feel that asking an employee to urinate into a bottle while being watched violates the employee's constitutional rights. Moreover, because it seems to demonstrate a lack of trust in the employee, it may destroy the employee's relationship with the company. The least expensive—and therefore most popular—drug tests yield inaccurate results as much as one-quarter of the time, thus putting many innocent people at risk. An employee who is seriously impaired after snorting cocaine at lunch may test negative in an early

afternoon drug test, whereas an employee who breathed second-hand marijuana smoke at last Saturday's party may test positive. And, most ironically, few companies test for the drug that causes most workplace accidents—*alcohol*—and almost none tests for the substance that kills more people than all others—*tobacco*. Even if test results were reliable, most managers are not trained in drug detection and must take time from other issues to enforce drug-testing policies.

Many human resource experts would prefer to approach drug abuse the same way they treat other workplace problems—with education, confidentiality, and employee involvement. "Performance testing" has emerged as an important alternative approach to ensuring that employees come to work unimpaired in any way—by drugs, lack of sleep, or even emotional problems. By spending less than a minute on a performance test similar to a video game, employees can prove they are alert and reacting well. These tests, which are less expensive than drug tests and don't foster the kinds of problems listed above, may become the approach of choice in future attempts to improve job safety and create drug-free workplaces.

Sources: Michael R. Carrell and Christina Heavrin, "Before You Drug Test . . . ," *HRMagazine* (June 1990): 64–68; Lewis L. Maltby, "Put Performance to the Test," *Personnel* (July 1990): 30–31; Miriam Rothman, "Random Drug Testing in the Workplace: Implications for Human Resource Management," *Business Horizons* (March-April 1988): 23–27; Cheryl Sullivan, "Federal Workers Fight Drug Testing," *The Christian Science Monitor* (January 25, 1989): 8.

---

wrote, "IBMers affected by AIDS will be encouraged to work as long as they are able, and their privacy will be respected."[76]

Fear Is the Worst Enemy. Coworkers of an individual who tests positive for the AIDS virus are less likely to panic if they are given the latest facts.[77] According to the best available medical evidence, the virus is spread only through sexual contact, infected blood products, and from infected mothers to their unborn children. Other modes of transmission, such as those encountered in medical and

TABLE 10.5 • AIDS: Ten Principles for the Workplace

The Citizens Commission on AIDS for New York City and Northern New Jersey has formulated guidelines to help employers deal with AIDS. The recommendations, "Responding to AIDS: Ten Principles for the Workplace," have been endorsed by more than 370 companies and organizations. The commission's executive director, Carol Levine, calls the principles a bill of rights regarding the illness. Here are their essential points:

1. People with AIDS or HIV infection are entitled to the same rights and opportunities as people with other serious or life-threatening illnesses.

2. Employment policies must, at a minimum, comply with federal, state, and local laws and regulations.

3. Employment policies should be based on the scientific and epidemiological evidence that people with AIDS or HIV infection do not pose a risk of transmission of the virus to coworkers through ordinary workplace contact.

4. The highest levels of management and union leadership should unequivocally endorse nondiscriminatory employment policies and educational programs about AIDS.

5. Employers and unions should communicate their support of these policies to workers in simple, clear, and unambiguous terms.

6. Employers should provide employees with sensitive, accurate, and up-to-date education about risk reduction in their personal lives.

7. Employers have a duty to protect the confidentiality of employees' medical information.

8. To prevent work disruption and rejection by coworkers of an employee with AIDS or HIV infection, employers and unions should undertake education for all employees before such an incident occurs and as needed thereafter.

9. Employers should not require HIV screening as part of pre-employment or general workplace physical examinations.

10. In occupational settings where there may be a potential risk of exposure to HIV, such as in health-care facilities, employers should implement universal precautions, offer specific and ongoing education, and provide the necessary protective equipment to reinforce appropriate infection-control procedures.

Source: Ira D. Singer, "AIDS Concerns for Business," Reprinted by permission. *Nation's Business,* June 1989. Copyright 1989, U.S. Chamber of Commerce.

dental settings, are being investigated. Employees' fears about normal casual contact in the workplace, including the sharing of drinking fountains, dining facilities, tools, and rest rooms, are unrealistic. Organizations without a responsible AIDS policy will have to cope with an even greater problem, unwarranted fear.

Summary

Within the context of strategic human resource management, staffing encompasses human resource planning, acquisition, and development. Four key staffing activities necessarily linked to organizational strategy and structure are (1) human resource planning, (2) selection, (3) performance appraisal, and (4) training. After an employee has joined the organization, part of the human resource management process involves dealing with human resource problems such as sexual harassment, alcohol and drug abuse, and AIDS.

A systems approach to human resource planning will help management devise staffing strategies for future human resource needs. As the organization's gatekeeper for vital human resources, employee selection should be more than a haphazard process of looking around for people to fill vacancies. Federal Equal

Employment Opportunity laws require managers to make hiring and other personnel decisions on the basis of ability to perform rather than personal prejudice. Affirmative action, making up for past discrimination, is evolving into managing diversity. All employment tests must be valid predictors of job performance. Because interviews are the most popular employee screening device, experts recommend structured rather than traditional, informal interviews.

Legally defensible performance appraisals enable managers to make objective personnel decisions. Of the three general approaches to performance appraisal—trait, behavior, and outcome—the behavior-oriented approach is most strongly recommended. Listed in declining order of popularity, six common performance appraisal techniques are goal setting, written essays, critical incidents, graphic rating scales, weighted check lists, and rankings/comparisons. Managers are challenged both to evaluate performance and to develop human potential during the performance appraisal process. This dilemma can be partially resolved by encouraging subordinates to engage in self-evaluation before offering constructive feedback on performance.

Today, training is a huge business in itself. Managers can ensure that their training investment pays off by using techniques appropriate to the situation. Training programs should be designed with an eye toward maximizing the retention and transfer of learning to the job. Successful skill learning and factual learning both depend on goal setting, practice, and feedback. But skills should be modeled, whereas factual information should be presented in a logical and meaningful manner.

Sexual harassment, alcohol and drug abuse, and AIDS are contemporary human resource problems that require top management attention and strong policies. Special care needs to be taken in each area to avoid discrimination. These three problems represent an erosion of human potential that today's organizations cannot afford if they are to achieve a competitive edge.

Terms to Understand

Staffing
Human resource planning
Job analysis
Job description
Affirmative action program (AAP)
Employment selection test
Structured interview

Performance appraisal
Behaviorally anchored rating scales
  (BARS)
Training
Sexual harassment
Alcoholism

Questions for Discussion

1. In your view, why is the staffing function a key determinant of organizational success?
2. Why is each portion of the human resource planning system important to effective staffing?
3. What is the essential difference between equal employment opportunity and affirmative action? What is your personal experience with these programs?

4. What are your feelings about the use of handwriting analysis (graphology) in the hiring process?

5. In reference to a specific job that you can think of, what structured interview questions should be asked of an applicant for that job?

6. What has been your experience with performance appraisals (including student evaluations of teacher effectiveness)? Would the instruments you have used meet the four legal defensibility criteria?

7. What could be done to promote the transfer of learning from the course(s) you are currently taking to your future employment as a manager?

8. Have you ever been the victim of sexual harassment on campus or on the job? Explain the circumstances and what, if anything, management did about it.

9. What are your feelings about workplace drug testing?

10. Should someone who has tested positive for the AIDS virus be fired? Explain your reasoning.

Back to the Opening Case

Now that you have read Chapter 10, you should be able to answer the following questions about the Levi Strauss case:

1. Why is Levi Strauss likely to have a loyal and hard-working group of employees?

2. Does the human resource management process at Levi Strauss have strategic importance? Explain, using evidence from the case.

3. Has Levi Strauss done a good job of giving the concept of "managing diversity" more than lip service? Explain. If you were a proponent of this concept and a Levi Strauss employee, what else would you like the company to do?

4. How would you respond to a manager who said: "Levi Strauss shouldn't associate itself with the AIDS epidemic. It could tarnish the firm's reputation and be bad for business."

CLOSING CASE

GE's Training Camp: 'Outward Bound' for Managers

Jack Welch is a tough, pragmatic, intuitive manager. And what does the chairman of General Electric think of management theory and academics? "Not much," reports Noel M. Tichy, a University of Michigan business professor who has worked at GE.

So it may seem surprising that Welch is putting more money into GE's Management Development Institute in Croton-on-Hudson, N.Y. But Crotonville, as it's called, is no ordinary corporate training center. Yes, there are lecture halls and blackboards—but there are also river-rafting races and mandates to tackle real GE problems. And, yes, there are some courses in finance—but far more that encourage team-building and networking. Instead of using Crotonville to teach traditional business subjects, Welch wants it to be a "change agent."

Crotonville's mission: to make GE managers more action-oriented, more risk-oriented, more people-oriented. It's supposed to develop leaders, not just managers. Says Welch: "Yesterday's idea of the boss, who became the boss because he or she knew one more fact than the person working for them, is yesterday's manager. Tomorrow's person leads through a vision, a shared set of values, a shared objective."

Lessons in Change

Instilling those skills is no easy task, and GE had to invent much of its course work. New managers, for example, come to Crotonville about six months after their promotions—time enough for them to have made mistakes. They come with critiques of their performance from subordinates and supervisors. They learn what they've been doing wrong and promise to change. They discuss issues in teams, partly so they know they're not alone in their experiences.

Since last year, Crotonville has offered what Tichy—who headed Crotonville for two years until September—calls "a business Outward Bound experience." It's a four-week course that lets employees crack a real GE business problem. First, participants do preparatory case studies, bone up on the business problem, and learn to work in teams. That's where the rafting comes in: The teams build rafts, then race each other up the Hudson River. Or they spend a few days performing other physical tasks to build trust among team members. Later, they visit the business and meet with customers—or anyone else they wish. Then they make recommendations and present them, in competition with another team, to the appropriate vice president. Besides team-

work and analytical skills, the course teaches people that they can handle bigger problems than they thought.

Participants seem to relish the course. Bonnie L. Ayres, a radar programs manager in GE's aerospace business, was part of a team devising ways to expand a service business in GE's power systems group. "It's an 'up' experience," she says. "You feel tremendously stimulated and excited about what's happening at the company." Ayres took some lessons home, too: Feedback from teammates prompted Ayres, who manages 400 people, to delegate more.

Global Issues

In words that would warm Welch's heart, Ayres adds that "there was a large reinforcement of the company's desire to look outward—at markets—instead of inward, and to think competitively." That's deliberate. Many of the business problems focus on global issues. And Welch harps on competitiveness when he visits Crotonville, a dozen times a year, to meet with students. "Yesterday, he was up there [at the board] sketching global organizational forms—strategic alliances, and what they might look like," Tichy says.

As competition increases, many experts believe, old-fashioned bureaucratic management is simply not going to cut it anymore. "The evidence that leadership is so much more important today is overwhelming," says Harvard business school professor John Kotter. "Yet the average corporation is not doing anything." Once again, he adds, GE is ahead of the pack.

For Discussion

1. What do you think about Welch's distinction between leaders and managers?
2. What ingredients of a good training program do you see in this case? Which ranks as the most important?
3. Why is GE's approach to management development probably effective?

References

Opening Quotation. John Kenneth Galbraith, *Economic Development*, in M. R. Rosenberg, ed., *Quotations for the New Age* (Secaucus, N.J.: Citadel Press, 1978), p. 120.

Opening Case. Charles Davis, "Deficiency Syndrome: Business Isn't Facing Up to the AIDS Crisis," *Canadian Business* (August 1989): 9; Robert Howard, "Values Make the Company: An Interview with Robert Haas," *Harvard Business Review* (September-October 1990): 132–144; Holly Rawlinson, "Homegrown for HRM," *Personnel Administrator* (August 1989): 48–53.

Closing Case. Judith H. Dobrzynski, "GE's Training Camp: 'Outward Bound' for Managers." Reprinted from December 14, 1987 issue of *Business Week* by special permission, copyright © 1987 by McGraw-Hill, Inc.

1. An excellent critical appraisal of organizational life may be found in William G. Scott and David K. Hart, *Organizational America* (Boston: Houghton Mifflin, 1979).

2. See R. Wayne Mondy, Robert M. Noe, and Robert E. Edwards, "What the Staffing Function Entails," *Personnel,* 63 (April 1986): 55–58.

3. Six alternative models of personnel departments are discussed in Janet R. Andrews, "Is There a Crisis in the Personnel Department's Identity?" *Personnel Journal,* 65 (June 1986): 86–93.

4. See, for example, David R. Francis, "Efficiency Gains Rare After Business Layoffs," *The Christian Science Monitor* (May 25, 1990): 8.

5. See Peter J. Dowling and Randall S. Schuler, *International Dimensions of Human Resource Management* (Boston: PWS-Kent, 1990).

6. Thomas J. Peters and Robert H. Waterman, Jr., *In Search of Excellence* (New York: Harper & Row, 1982), p. 238.

7. Dean Foust, "Why Federal Express Has Overnight Anxiety," *Business Week* (November 9, 1987): 62–66.

8. Data from Daniel J. Koys, "Human Resource Management and a Culture of Respect: Effects on Employees' Organizational Commitment," *Employee Responsibilities and Rights Journal,* 1 (March 1988): 57–68. Also see Dennis J. Kravetz, "Increase Finances through Progressive Management," *HRMagazine,* 36 (February 1991): 57–62.

9. See Paul F. Buller, "Successful Partnerships: HR and Strategic Planning at Eight Top Firms," *Organizational Dynamics,* 17 (Autumn 1988): 27–43, Michael C. Busch, "Linking Strategic Planning to the Management of People," in *The 1990 Annual: Developing Human Resources,* ed. J. William Pfeiffer (San Diego: University Associates, 1990), pp. 265–270; and Randall S. Schuler and James W. Walker, "Human Resources Strategy: Focusing on Issues and Actions," *Organizational Dynamics,* 19 (Summer 1990): 4–19.

10. Stephanie Lawrence, "Voices of HR Experience," *Personnel Journal,* 68 (April 1989): 69.

11. Edgar H. Schein, "Increasing Organizational Effectiveness through Better Human Resource Planning and Development," *Sloan Management Review,* 19 (Fall 1977): 1.

12. Three informative articles on human resource planning are James W. Walker, "Moving Closer to the Top," *Personnel Administrator,* 31 (December 1986): 52–57, 117; John A. Hooper, Ralph F. Catalanello, and Patrick L. Murray, "Shoring Up the Weakest Link," *Personnel Administrator,* 32 (April 1987): 49–55, 134; and Susan E. Jackson and Randall S. Schuler, "Human Resource Planning," *American Psychologist,* 45 (February 1990): 223–239.

13. An instructive discussion of an actual human resource planning system may be found in David R. Leigh, "Business Planning Is People Planning," *Personnel Journal,* 63 (May 1984): 44–54.

14. James W. Walker, "Developing Human Resource Strategies," in *Human Resource Forecasting and Strategy Development,* eds. Manuel London, Emily S. Bassman, and John P. Fernandez (New York: Quorum Books, 1990), p. 82.

15. See Richard J. Mirabile, "The Power of Job Analysis," *Training,* 27 (April 1990): 70–74.

16. For practical tips on writing good job descriptions, see Stephen F. Mona, "The Job Description," *Association Management,* 43 (February 1991): 33–37.

17. Human resource information systems are discussed in Stephen G. Perry, "The PC-based HRIS," *Personnel Administrator,* 33 (February 1988): 60–63; Edward Blair, "Bootstrapping Your HRIS Capabilities," *Personnel Administrator,* 33 (February 1988): 68–72; Timothy R. Adams, "Buying Software without the Glitches," *HRMagazine,* 35 (January 1990): 40–42; and Gary Meyer, "Hard-working Micros Aid Managers," *HRMagazine,* 35 (August 1990): 54–60.

18. For excellent material on human resource forecasting, see Manuel London, Emily S. Bassman, and John P. Fernandez, eds. *Human Resource Forecasting and Strategy Development* (New York: Quorum Books, 1990).

19. David A. Brookmire and Amy A. Burton, "A Format for Packaging Your Affirmative Action Program," *Personnel Journal,* 57 (June 1978): 294.

20. Useful background information on EEO law can be found in Ann Weaver Hart, "Intent vs. Effect: Title VII Case Law That Could Affect You (Part I)," *Personnel Journal*, 63 (March 1984): 31–47; Ann Weaver Hart, "Intent vs. Effect: Title VII Case Law That Could Affect You (Part II)," *Personnel Journal*, 63 (April 1984): 50–58; and Jere W. Morehead and Peter J. Shedd, "Civil Rights and Affirmative Action: Revolution or Fine-Tuning?" *Business Horizons*, 33 (September-October 1990): 53–60.

21. General updates on U.S. affirmative action law can be found in Stephen Wermiel, "Supreme Court, in 6–3 Vote, Backs Hiring Goals to Correct Sex Bias," *The Wall Street Journal* (March 26, 1987): 3, 24; Paula Dwyer, "Affirmative Action: after the Debate, Opportunity," *Business Week* (April 13, 1987): 37; and Paula Dwyer, "Republicans May Have Found the Perfect Democrat-Slayer," *Business Week* (December 3, 1990): 36.

22. See Frances C. Shipper and Frank M. Shipper, "Beyond EEO: Toward Pluralism," *Business Horizons*, 30 (May-June 1987): 53–61; George E. Stevens, "Exploding the Myths About Hiring the Handicapped," *Personnel*, 63 (December 1986): 57–60.

23. See Gary N. Powell, "Upgrading Management Opportunities for Women," *HRMagazine*, 35 (November 1990): 67–70; and Michelle Neely Martinez, "Creative Ways to Employ People with Disabilities," *HRMagazine*, 35 (November 1990): 40–44, 101.

24. R. Roosevelt Thomas, Jr., "From Affirmative Action to Affirming Diversity," *Harvard Business Review*, 68 (March-April 1990): 114.

25. See David P. Twomey, *Equal Employment Opportunity Law*, 2nd ed. (Cincinnati: South-Western, 1990).

26. For example, see M. Susan Taylor and Kathryn K. Sackheim, "Graphology," *Personnel Administrator*, 33 (May 1988): 71–76.

27. Data from Efrat Neter and Gershon Ben-Shakhar, "The Predictive Validity of Graphological Inferences: A Meta-Analytic Approach," *Personality and Individual Differences*, 10 (1989): 737–745.

28. Leon C. Megginson, *Personnel and Human Resources Administration*, 3rd ed. (Homewood, Ill.: Irwin, 1977), p. 232. Also see Michael M. Harris, "Reconsidering the Employment Interview: A Review of Recent Literature and Suggestions for Future Research," *Personnel Psychology*, 42 (Winter 1989): 691–726.

29. "Structured Interviewing: Avoiding Selection Problems," by Elliott D. Pursell, Michael A. Campion, and Sarah R. Gaylord, copyright November 1980. Reprinted with permission of *Personnel Journal*, Costa Mesa, California; all rights reserved.

30. Barbara Whitaker Shimko, "New Breed Workers Need New Yardsticks," *Business Horizons*, 33 (November-December 1990): 35–36.

31. Practical tips on interviewing can be found in James M. Jenks and Brian L. P. Zevnik, "ABCs of Interviewing," *Harvard Business Review*, 67 (July-August 1989): 38–42; and Thomas F. Casey, "Making the Most of a Selection Interview," *Personnel*, 67 (September 1990): 41–43.

32. Pursell et al., "Structured Interviewing." (Emphasis added.)

33. See Barry C. Campbell and Cynthia L. Barron, "How Extensively Are HRM Practices Being Utilized by the Practitioners?" *Personnel Administrator*, 27 (May 1982): 67–71.

34. See Charles Lee, "Smoothing Out Appraisal Systems," *HRMagazine*, 35 (March 1990): 72–76; and Peter M. Tafti, "Face to Face," *Training & Development Journal*, 44 (November 1990): 66–71.

35. For instructive reading on performance appraisal, see H. John Bernardin and Richard W. Beatty, *Performance Appraisal: Assessing Human Behavior at Work* (Boston: Kent, 1984); Roberta V. Romberg, "Performance Appraisal, 1: Risks and Rewards," *Personnel*, 63 (August 1986): 20–26; David C. Martin, "Performance Appraisal, 2: Improving the Rater's Effectiveness," *Personnel*, 63 (August 1986): 28–33; and Bill Shaw, "Employee Appraisals, Discrimination Cases, and Objective Evidence," *Business Horizons*, 33 (September-October 1990): 61–65.

36. "Performance Appraisal: Current Practices and Techniques," *Personnel*, 61 (May-June 1984): 57.

37. Adapted from Hubert S. Field and William H. Holley, "The Relationship of Performance Appraisal System Characteristics to Verdicts in Selected Employment Discrimination Cases," *Academy of Management Journal*, 25 (June 1982): 392–406. A more recent analysis of fifty-one cases that derived similar criteria can be found in Gerald V. Barrett and Mary C. Kernan, "Performance Appraisal and Terminations: A Review of Court Decisions Since Brito v. Zia with Implications for Personnel Practices," *Personnel Psychology*, 40 (Autumn 1987): 489–503.

38. Bernardin and Beatty, *Performance Appraisal*, p. 64.

39. See Jeffrey S. Kane and Kimberley A. Freeman, "MBO and Performance Appraisal: A Mixture That's Not a Solution, Part 1," *Personnel*, 63 (December 1986): 26–36; Jeffrey S. Kane and

Kimberly A. Freeman, "MBO and Performance Appraisal: A Mixture That's Not a Solution, Part 2," *Personnel*, 64 (February 1987): 26–32.

40. See Bernardin and Beatty, *Performance Appraisal*, pp. 116–124.

41. See Kevin R. Murphy and Virginia A. Pardaffy, "Bias in Behaviorally Anchored Rating Scales: Global or Scale-specific?" *Journal of Applied Psychology*, 74 (April 1989): 343–346.

42. George S. Odiorne, "The Trend toward the Quarterly Performance Review," *Business Horizons*, 33 (July-August 1990): 38.

43. See Clinton O. Longenecker, "Truth or Consequences: Politics and Performance Appraisals," *Business Horizons*, 32 (November-December 1989): 76–82.

44. An excellent discussion of the two-interview performance appraisal format may be found in H. Kent Baker and Philip I. Morgan, "Two Goals in Every Performance Appraisal," *Personnel Journal*, 63 (September 1984): 74–78.

45. Michael Beer, "Performance Appraisal: Dilemmas and Possibilities," *Organizational Dynamics*, 9 (Winter 1981): 33.

46. Data from John Hoerr, "Sharpening Minds for a Competitive Edge," *Business Week* (December 17, 1990): 72, 74, 78.

47. Data from Jack Gordon, "Where the Training Goes," *Training*, 27 (October 1990): 51–69.

48. See Chris Lee, "Industry Report," *Training*, 27 (October 1990): 29–32.

49. For additional discussion, see George C. Thornton III and Jeanette N. Cleveland, "Developing Managerial Talent through Simulation," *American Psychologist*, 45 (February 1990): 190–199.

50. See Robert Neff, "Videos Are Starring in More and More Training Programs," *Business Week* (September 7, 1987): 108–110.

51. Training issues are discussed in John Hoerr, "With Job Training, A Little Dab Won't Do Ya," *Business Week* (September 24, 1990): 95; and Irwin L. Goldstein and Patrice Gilliam, "Training System Issues in the Year 2000," *American Psychologist*, 45 (February 1990): 134–143.

52. Kenneth N. Wexley and Gary P. Latham, *Developing and Training Human Resources in Organizations* (Glenview, Ill.: Scott, Foresman, 1981): 75–77.

53. Ibid., p. 77. Also see Joel Rakow, "Not Just the Facts, Ma'am," *Training*, 27 (June 1990): 59–61.

54. See Jack Gordon, "How to Learn," *Training*, 27 (May 1990): 51–62.

55. Specific cases are discussed in Cliff Tuttle, "Sexual Harassment Is No Joke," *Management Review*, 79 (August 1990): 44–48.

56. Data from Barbara A. Gutek, Aaron Groff Cohen, and Alison M. Konrad, "Predicting Social-Sexual Behavior at Work: A Contact Hypothesis," *Academy of Management Journal*, 33 (September 1990): 560–577.

57. Data from Donald B. Mazer and Elizabeth F. Percival, "Students' Experiences of Sexual Harassment at a Small University," *Sex Roles*, 20 (January 1989): 1–22.

58. See, for example, Gary N. Powell, "Sexual Harassment: Confronting the Issue of Definition," *Business Horizons*, 26 (July-August 1983): 24–28; Robert C. Ford and Frank S. McLaughlin, "Sexual Harassment at Work," *Business Horizons*, 31 (November-December 1988): 14–19; and Douglas D. Baker, David E. Terpstra, and Bob D. Cutler, "Perceptions of Sexual Harassment: A Re-Examination of Gender Differences," *The Journal of Psychology*, 124 (July 1990): 409–416; and Ruth Marcus, "When Is Flirting at Work Sexual Harassment?" *The Washington Post National Weekly Edition* (February 25–March 3, 1991): 32.

59. See David E. Terpstra and Douglas D. Baker, "Outcomes of Sexual Harassment Charges," *Academy of Management Journal*, 31 (March 1988): 185–194.

60. Ibid., p. 191.

61. These recommendations are based on B. Terry Thornton, "Sexual Harassment, 1: Discouraging It in the Work Place," *Personnel*, 63 (April 1986): 18–25. Also see Jacqueline F. Strayer and Sandra E. Rapoport, "Sexual Harassment, 2: Limiting Corporate Liability," *Personnel*, 63 (April 1986): 26–33; and Donna M. Stringer, Helen Remick, Jan Salisbury, and Angela B. Ginorio, "The Power and Reasons Behind Sexual Harassment: An Employer's Guide to Solutions," *Public Personnel Management*, 19 (Spring 1990): 43–52.

62. Data from Jim Castelli, "Employer-Provided Programs Pay Off," *HRMagazine*, 35 (April 1990): 55–58; and "Alcohol and the Moderate Drinker," *The Futurist*, 24 (November-December 1990): 47.

63. See David Gelman, "Roots of Addiction," *Newsweek* (February 20, 1989): 52–57; and William C. Symonds, "Is Business Bungling Its Battle With Booze?" *Business Week* (March 25, 1991): 76–78.

64. James A. Belohlav and Paul O. Popp, "Employee Substance Abuse: Epidemic of the Eighties," *Business Horizons,* 26 (July-August 1983): 29.

65. Stephenie Overman, "Federal Drug-Test Bill First to Cover All Employees," *HRNews* (February 1990): A9.

66. See Janice Castro, "Battling the Enemy Within," *Time* (March 17, 1986): 52–61.

67. Data from Theodore H. Rosen, "Identification of Substance Abusers in the Workplace," *Public Personnel Management,* 16 (Fall 1987): 197–207.

68. See Richard J. Tersine and James Hazeldine, "Alcoholism: A Productivity Hangover," *Business Horizons,* 25 (November-December 1982): 68–72.

69. Janet Deming, "Drug-Free Workplace Is Good Business," *HRMagazine,* 35 (April 1990): 61.

70. See, for example, Diane Kirrane, "EAPs: Dawning of a New Age," *HRMagazine,* 35 (January 1990): 30–34; and Steve Bergsman, "Help Employees Who Help Themselves," *HRMagazine,* 35 (April 1990): 46–49.

71. Data from John Brecher, "Taking Drugs on the Job," *Newsweek* (August 22, 1983): 52–50.

72. Data from Castelli, "Employer-Provided Programs Pay Off."

73. Data from Eric Rolfe Greenberg, "Workplace Testing: The 1990 AMA Survey, Part 2," *Personnel,* 67 (July 1990): 26–29. Also see Abby Brown, "To Test or Not to Test," *Personnel Administrator,* 32 (March 1987): 67–70; John Hoerr, "Privacy," *Business Week* (March 28, 1988): 61–65, 68; and Timothy L. Baker, "Preventing Drug Abuse at Work," *Personnel Administrator,* 34 (July 1989): 56–59.

74. Data from Geoffrey Cowley, "AIDS: The Next Ten Years," *Newsweek* (June 25, 1990): 20–27; Jeffrey A. Mello, "AIDS Education For the Workplace," *Training & Development Journal,* 44 (December 1990): 65–70; and Anne E. Jordheim, "Removing the Mystery From AIDS Education," *Management Review,* 79 (February 1990): 20–25.

75. Marilyn Chase, "Corporations Urge Peers to Adopt Humane Policies for AIDS Victims," *The Wall Street Journal* (January 20, 1988): 29.

76. Ibid.

77. See, for example, George E. Stevens, "Understanding AIDS," *Personnel Administrator,* 33 (August 1988): 84–88; Ira D. Singer, "AIDS Concerns For Business," *Nation's Business,* 77 (June 1989): 75–77; Lisa I. Fried, "When AIDS Strikes the Office," *Management Review,* 79 (February 1990): 12–18; and Jonathan A. Segal, "AIDS Education Is a Necessary High-Risk Activity," *HRMagazine,* 36 (February 1991): 82–85.

11

Communicating

CHAPTER OBJECTIVES

When you finish studying this chapter, you should be able to

- Identify each major link in the communication process.

- Explain the concept of media richness and the Lengel-Daft contingency model of media selection.

- Describe the roles of selectivity, organization, and interpretation in perception.

- Discuss why it is important for managers to know about grapevine and nonverbal communication.

- Explain how management can encourage upward communication.

- Identify and briefly describe four barriers to communication.

- List at least three practical tips for improving each of the following communication skills: listening, writing, and running a meeting.

Fun and Profits at Uncle Herb's Southwest Airlines

In the era of "downsizing" and "lean and mean" companies, do you have to be a cold-hearted tyrant to run a successful company? Not if you're Herb Kelleher, chairman of Southwest Airlines. Southwest has grown to become the nation's eighth largest airline and was one of only three U.S. airlines to make a profit in 1990. Its growth and profitability have been among the best in the industry for years, as have its on-time records and its low number of customer complaints. Yet to many of Southwest's employees, the chairman is not a distant "Mr. Kelleher" but "Uncle Herb" or "Herbie." In fact, Kelleher doesn't fit the top brass stereotype in a number of ways. If it's Friday, Southwest's "fun uniform" day, Kelleher may wear khaki pants and bright red sweatshirt even if he's going to a bank board meeting. To celebrate the opening of Sea World in San Antonio, Kelleher painted one of the company's 737s to look like a killer whale. And he's been known to spend time on baggage duty or behind a ticket counter and to show up for a flight in jungle-print jams.

Yet Herb Kelleher is no fool. Southwest makes money by keeping its operating costs the lowest in the business, a result of a no-frills approach that pleases customers, employees, and stockholders. First-time Southwest flyers may be surprised at the lack of in-flight meals. But low ticket prices attract customers. The company's profit-sharing and no-layoff policies keep employees happy and, as a result, they work more productively for Southwest. The company has an unusually low 10 percent turnover rate and, although 85 percent of its employees are unionized, both management and employees sign new contracts without any fuss. Up to 80 percent of promotions come from within the company, and the company feels like a family to most of Southwest's 8,200 employees in thirty-three cities.

Many companies would like their employees to feel that way but few succeed. What's different about Southwest? Besides having an eccentric, fun-loving chairman, the key is communication. Although many of Kelleher's antics may be spontaneous improvisations, all communicate to customers and employees alike a sense of what the company is all about. The stunts demonstrate that good service and good fun are not incompatible. Efficient does not have to mean uptight. The company readies its planes for the next flight in one-third of the time taken by the average airline, yet that doesn't mean employees are cracking the whip to herd passengers on board.

Southwest even uses its television commercials to show off Kelleher and his message of value and fun. In response to a competitor's ad that said people should be embarrassed to fly on a no-frills airline like Southwest, Kelleher filmed a commercial with a bag over his head, offering the bag to anyone who was ashamed to be seen on Southwest. He coyly added that perhaps they could use the bag to carry money they'd save flying Southwest.

Besides Kelleher's *show*, Southwest also *tells* its employees a lot about its approach, using any number of different communication media. It believes in treating its employees with the same care and attention companies usually reserve for their best customers. Most new recruits see Kelleher first on a training film, strutting like a chicken, flapping his chicken-wing arms, singing, "The Southwest Shuffle. Shuffle down, down." Kelleher is known for making unexpected flights on Southwest planes, and he's willing to turn the table—employees may drop in on him any time. The chairman's "open door" is located in the company's headquarters in Dallas, a building dedicated to its employees.

Like a family, the company has its traditions, including cookouts and an annual awards dinner at which Kelleher personally hands out awards. Southwest's newsletter is also a family affair, passing on information about employees' awards, acts of community service, or recent illnesses. The company fills most openings from within by posting all job vacancies in all its locations. And Southwest's top human resources person says that what it looks for in employees is, logically enough, a sense of humor. Even its quarterly report is different. Instead of a slick brochure, Southwest sends out a video.

Kelleher is not the only one allowed to express his sense of humor. Flight attendants wear sneakers in the summer, even if it's not Friday. And instead of a dry "sit down and buckle up" announcement, a Southwest pilot may greet passengers by saying "As soon as y'all get both cheeks into the seat, we'll get this old bird in the air."* If you're flying Southwest at Christmas time, don't be too surprised if you're greeted by flight attendants dressed as reindeer and elves or serenaded by the captain's Christmas carols on the loudspeaker.

Kelleher's zany approach to running an airline hasn't yet caught on at his larger rivals, but he's trying to change that, too. After hearing about Southwest's killer whale 737, Robert L. Crandall, head of American Airlines, called Kelleher to congratulate him on his clever marketing but asked what he would do with the killer whale waste. On the following Monday, during a staff meeting at American, a messenger appeared with Kelleher's response: a huge bowl of chocolate mousse and a spoon.

*Quoted in Amy Engeler, "A Busy Boss Can Never Fly Solo," *Business Month* (August 1990): 22.

One of the most difficult challenges for management is getting individuals to understand and voluntarily pursue organizational objectives. Effective communication, of the sort seen at Southwest Airlines, is vital to meeting this challenge. Organizational communication takes in a great deal of territory—virtually every management function and activity can be considered communication in one way or another. Planning and controlling require a good deal of communicating, as do organization design and development, decision making and problem solving, leadership, and staffing. Organizational cultures would not exist without communication. Studies have shown that both organizational and individual performance improve when managerial communication is effective.[1]

Field research of managers in action gives a clear picture of the nature and extent of managerial communication (see Figure 11.1). Mintzberg was right! Managers do indeed spend their days engaged in rapid-fire episodes of primarily oral communication. According to a classic work-sampling study of 136 managers, 81 percent of the typical manager's workday was devoted to communication.[2] A more recent study of 120 managers found face-to-face communication to be far and away the leading mode of managerial communication. Face-to-face communication took place primarily in scheduled and unscheduled meetings. Telephone conversations accounted for a comparatively small 10 percent of the managers' total communication activities.[3] Most recently, researchers found middle managers emphasizing different audiences in small and large organizations. Managers in small, entrepreneurial companies (fewer than fifty employees) relied most heavily on *horizontal* communication (46 percent). This type of communication took the form of interaction between technical and functional specialists

FIGURE 11.1 • Managerial Communication Insights from 25 Years of Research

Source: Data from John R. Hinrichs, "Communications Activity of Industrial Research Personnel," *Personnel Psychology,* 17 (Summer 1964): 199; Fred Luthans and Janet K. Larsen, "How Managers Really Communicate," *Human Relations,* 39 (February 1986): 168; and Larry R. Smeltzer and Gail L. Fann, "Comparison of Managerial Communication Patterns in Small, Entrepreneurial Organizations and Large, Mature Organizations," *Group & Organization Studies,* 14 (June 1989): 207.

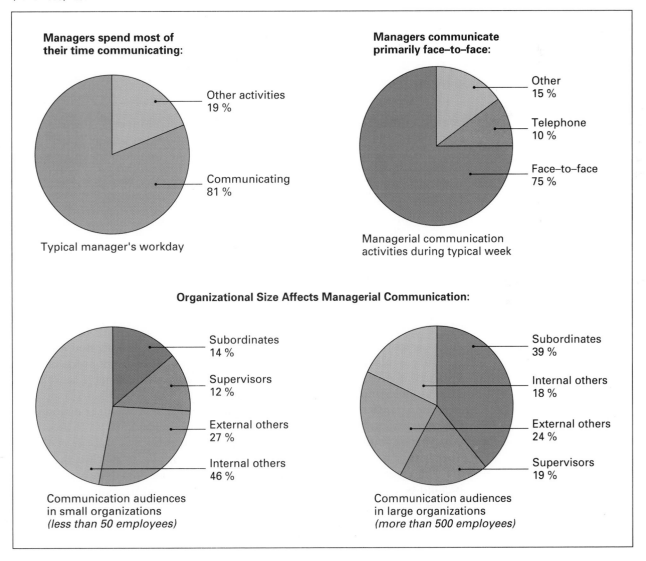

Managers spend most of their time communicating:

Other activities
19 %

Communicating
81 %

Typical manager's workday

Managers communicate primarily face-to-face:

Other
15 %

Telephone
10 %

Face-to-face
75 %

Managerial communication activities during typical week

Organizational Size Affects Managerial Communication:

Subordinates
14 %

Supervisors
12 %

External others
27 %

Internal others
46 %

Communication audiences in small organizations
(less than 50 employees)

Subordinates
39 %

Internal others
18 %

External others
24 %

Supervisors
19 %

Communication audiences in large organizations
(more than 500 employees)

rather than between bosses and subordinates. In contrast, middle managers in large multidivision companies (more than 500 employees) directed 58 percent of their communication *vertically,* either to supervisors or subordinates. Thus, the formal chain of command tends to have a stronger influence over communication as the organization grows and becomes more bureaucratic.[4]

Just because managers spend most of their time communicating does not necessarily mean they are effective communicators. One indication that managers believe this area should be improved is the continuing popularity of communication seminars in management development programs. One management writer summed up the state of managerial communication with this critical appraisal: "Talk is cheap, so we spend it recklessly, overloading our message systems and thereby depreciating their contents. With so much garbage in the system, much of it will inevitably be sent out."[5] Before managers, or anyone else for that matter, can become more effective communicators they need to appreciate that communication is a complex process subject to a great deal of perceptual distortion and many problems. This is especially true for the apparently simple activity of communicating face to face.

The Communication Process

• • • • • • • • • • • • • • •

Identify each major link in the communication process.

Management scholar Keith Davis has defined **communication** as "the transfer of information and understanding from one person to another person."[6] Communication is inherently a social process.[7] Whether one communicates face to face with a single person or with a group of people via television, it is still a social activity involving two or more people. By analyzing the communication process, one discovers that it is a chain made up of identifiable links (see Figure 11.2). Links in this process include sender, encoding, medium, decoding, receiver, and feedback. The essential purpose of this chainlike process is to send an idea from one person to another in a way that will be understood by the receiver. Like any other chain, the communication chain is only as strong as its weakest link.[8]

Encoding

Thinking is a personal process. It takes place within the privacy of your brain and is greatly affected by how you perceive your environment. But when you want to pass along a thought to someone else, an entirely different process begins. This second process, communication, requires that you, the sender, package the idea for understandable transmission. Encoding starts at this point. The purpose of encoding is to translate internal thought patterns into a language or code that the intended receiver of the message will probably understand.

Managers usually rely on words, gestures, or other symbols for encoding. Their choice of symbols depends on several factors, one of which is the nature of the message itself. Is it technical or nontechnical, emotional or factual? Perhaps it could be expressed better with numbers than with words, as in the case of a budget report. To express skepticism, merely a shrug might be enough.

The purpose of the message is also important. Is it intended to convey spe-

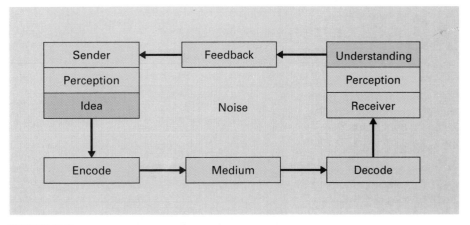

FIGURE 11.2 • The Basic Communication Process

cific information needed for the completion of a job? Or is it intended to persuade, to change attitudes, or to indicate general direction? The purpose often dictates the approach. If a manager wants to propose a bold new program to his or her superiors, for example, a dry technical report would probably not have the needed persuasive impact. Broad generalizations with a certain emotional appeal for motivational purposes would be more productive; technical details could be communicated later.

Selecting a Medium

Managers can choose among a number of media: face-to-face conversations, telephone calls, memos, letters, computer reports and networks, photographs, bulletin boards, meetings, organizational publications, and others. Communicating with those outside the organization opens up further possibilities, such as news releases, press conferences, and advertising on television and radio or in magazines and newspapers.

Media Selection in Action. Each particular medium has its own advantages and disadvantages. Walt Disney Company exemplifies a skillful mix of media. All Disney employees, called cast members, are kept informed via four communication strategies: environmental, audiovisual, print, and personal contact.

> *Environmental communications include bulletin and communications boards; audiovisual presentations involve executive and stockholder's updates and use of the Cast Communications Network (Disney's cast television network). Some of the more important examples of print communications are policy manuals and brochures, weekly division newsletters, and* Eyes & Ears *(a company-wide weekly newsletter). Major types of communication by personal contact include management forums, focus groups, and the basic "hands-on" approach of "management by walking around."*[9]

EDS, General Motors' information technology subsidiary, is pioneering a new concept in meeting rooms. Capture Centers are futuristic rooms that allow members to electronically focus their energies on the problem at hand. Group members capture and manipulate their ideas on computer network terminals. A main screen displays the collective progress. As electronic meeting rooms become commonplace, they will revolutionize group-aided decision making.

media richness a media's capacity to convey information and promote learning

●●●●●●●●●●●●●●●●●●
Explain the concept of media richness and the Lengel-Daft contingency model of media selection.

A Contingency Approach. A contingency model for media selection has been proposed by Robert Lengel and Richard Daft.[10] It pivots on the concept of media richness. **Media richness** describes the capacity of a given medium to convey information and promote learning. As illustrated in the top portion of Figure 11.3, media vary in richness from high (or rich) to low (or lean). Face-to-face conversation is a rich medium because it (1) simultaneously provides *multiple information cues,* such as message content, tone of voice, facial expressions, and so on; (2) facilitates immediate *feedback*; and (3) is *personal* in focus. In contrast, bulletins and general computer reports are lean media, meaning they convey limited information and foster limited learning. Lean media, such as bulletins, provide a single cue, do not facilitate immediate feedback, and are impersonal.

Management's challenge, indicated in the bottom portion of Figure 11.3, is to match media richness with the situation. Nonroutine problems are best handled with such rich media as face-to-face, telephone, or video interactions. Lean media—including memos, letters, and computer reports—are appropriate for routine problems. Examples of mismatched media include reading a corporate annual report at a stockholders' meeting (data glut) or announcing a massive layoff with an impersonal memo (data starvation).

Decoding

Even the most expertly fashioned message will not accomplish its purpose unless it is understood. After physically receiving the message, the receiver must comprehend it. If the message has been properly encoded, decoding will take place rather

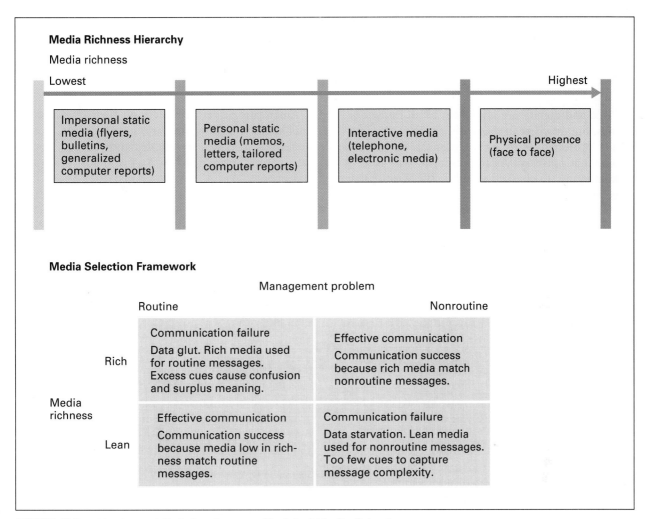

Media Richness Hierarchy

Media richness

Lowest ————————————————————————————→ Highest

| Impersonal static media (flyers, bulletins, generalized computer reports) | Personal static media (memos, letters, tailored computer reports) | Interactive media (telephone, electronic media) | Physical presence (face to face) |

Media Selection Framework

Management problem

Media richness	Routine	Nonroutine
Rich	Communication failure Data glut. Rich media used for routine messages. Excess cues cause confusion and surplus meaning.	Effective communication Communication success because rich media match nonroutine messages.
Lean	Effective communication Communication success because media low in richness match routine messages.	Communication failure Data starvation. Lean media used for nonroutine messages. Too few cues to capture message complexity.

FIGURE 11.3 • The Lengel-Daft Contingency Model of Media Selection

Source: Robert H. Lengel and Richard L. Daft, "The Selection of Communication Media as an Executive Skill," *Academy of Management Executive,* 2 (August 1988): 226, 227, exhibits 1 and 2. Reprinted by permission.

routinely. But perfect encoding is nearly impossible to achieve in our world of many languages and cultures (see The World of Management). The receiver's willingness to receive the message is a principal prerequisite for successful decoding. The chances of successful decoding are greatly enhanced if the receiver knows the language and terminology used in the message. It helps too if the receiver understands the sender's purpose and background situation. Effective listening is given special attention later in this chapter.

Feedback

Some sort of verbal or nonverbal feedback from the receiver to the sender is required to complete the communications process. Appropriate forms of feedback are determined by the same factors that govern the sender's encoding decision.

"Saving Face" in Asia: A Matter Requiring Careful Encoding and Decoding

Pride and dignity are important to all human beings, but nowhere in the world are they so culturally protected as in Asia. To speak or act in a way that causes an Asian person to "lose face" is tantamount to physical assault in the West. Asians go to great extremes to save their own face *and* everyone else's. This causes problems for the Westerner, who may not get a straight answer to a straightforward question.

"Can you tell me the way to the nearest post office?" If Asians know, it would not be unusual for them to escort you there, even though it may be far out of their way. If they do not know, they probably will point and say "that way." To be seen not to know is to lose face.

"Can you make this piece of furniture that I have designed?" Yes, they can. And they will, even though they know it will collapse almost immediately because the design is poor. To suggest a flaw in your design is to cause *you* to lose face.

The solution to these problems lies in the way the question is asked. "Do you know someone who might help me find a post office?" "I've designed a piece of furniture, but I would appreciate any suggestions. . . ."

Americans pride themselves on their frankness and honesty. Asians also are honest people, but honesty is mediated by the demands of face. For this reason, "frankness" in Asia is almost always rudeness.

It's possible for self-assured Americans in Asia to leave wide paths of resentment and never know that they have offended anyone. No one will tell [the Americans what they have done]. Or, if anyone does, the message will be delivered so obliquely that it probably will not be received. Such Americans will find that life becomes "difficult," that no one seems very cooperative. More than likely they will not blame themselves nor examine their actions and words. They may well conclude that the people are lazy and stupid and dismiss them with the thought, "I can't wait to get back to the good old U.S.A. where people can understand plain English."

These Americans will continue to see nothing in Asia but smiles and a pretense of assistance, in spite of the reversal of goodwill.

Source: John A. Reeder, "When West Meets East: Cultural Aspects of Doing Business in Asia," *Business Horizons,* 30 (January-February 1987): 69–70. Reprinted with permission.

Without feedback, senders have no way of knowing whether their ideas have been accurately understood. Knowing whether others understand us significantly affects both the form and content of our follow-up communication.

A survey of 105 executives from various major companies documented the importance of feedback from superiors to managers. Specifically, 64 percent of the respondents, when asked what they expected from their superiors, ranked "good communication and feedback" number one. The runners-up were leadership (60 percent), encouragement and support (50 percent), delegation and autonomy (37 percent), professional competence (21 percent), and information (17 percent).[11]

Noise

noise any interference with normal flow of communication

Noise is not an integral part of the chainlike communication process, but it may influence the process at any or all points. As the term is used here, **noise** is any interference with the normal flow of understanding from one person to another. This is a relatively broad definition. Thus, a speech impairment, garbled technical transmission, negative attitudes, misperception, illegible print or pictures, telephone static, partial loss of hearing, and poor eyesight all qualify as noise. Understanding tends to diminish as noise increases. In general, the effectiveness of organizational communication can be improved in two ways. Steps can be taken to make verbal and written messages more understandable. At the same time, noise can be minimized by foreseeing and neutralizing sources of interference.

Perception: A Vital Link in Communication

perception process of giving meaning to one's environment

Walter Nord defines **perception** as "the process by which an individual gives meaning to [his or her] environment."[12] Although perception often is equated with "seeing," we perceive with all our senses. Perception is essential to communication because it helps senders interpret the circumstances on which ideas and messages are based. Receivers, in turn, rely on perception to interpret the messages they receive. With highly personalized perceptual filters operating at both ends of the communication chain, it is no wonder that messages often fail to have their intended impact. In 1977, one such failure resulted in the worst disaster in aviation history. In the Canary Islands, a jet airliner that was taking off collided with one that was taxiing on the runway. According to the investigation, the pilot of the plane that was taking off had understood the tower's command to "*stand by* for takeoff" as the go-ahead to "take off." Twenty seconds later 583 people lost their lives.[13] Although perception may not be a life-and-death matter for the average manager, an understanding of perception is essential to effective communication.

● ● ● ● ● ● ● ● ● ● ● ● ● ● ● ● ●
Describe the roles of selectivity, organization, and interpretation in perception.

A general model of the perceptual process is displayed in Figure 11.4. Three subprocesses of perception are selectivity, organization, and interpretation. Each is potentially an obstacle to eventual understanding. Misperception is said to have occurred when appropriate understanding is not forthcoming.

Selectivity

selectivity sensory screening and sorting out process

Selectivity is a sensory screening process that allows us to sort out and process only some details in our surroundings and to disregard the rest. We are constantly bombarded by environmental stimuli—verbal or written messages, noises, lights, symbols, signs, or the nonverbal behavior of others—that compete for our attention. We would literally go mad if we did not have some mental faculty for sorting out and screening these competing stimuli.[14] This selectivity occurs in two ways, through perceptual defense and perceptual set, both of which can help or hinder the communication process.

FIGURE 11.4 ● The Perceptual Process

Perception

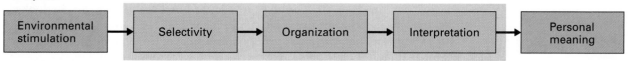

Perceptual Defense.   How many times have you seen someone study with the radio or television going full blast? Those who can retain what they read in spite of competing stimuli have highly developed perceptual defenses. **Perceptual defense** is the screening out of environmental stimuli. A training director's perceptual defense to criticisms of his or her department's work may effectively block critical communication from other managers.

perceptual defense screening out stimuli

One can readily see that perceptual defense has both a good side and a bad side. On the good side, busy managers cannot hope to be effective if they give their full attention to every fact, problem, bit of information, criticism, and question they encounter during a typical day. Managers must be selective to avoid being swamped by endless details. This need for selective perception makes the establishment of priorities very important.

The bad side of perceptual defense is that, although blinders may help horses stay on the road, they do little to promote managerial effectiveness. A manager may lose *too* much in screening out important situational variables. For example, managers in nonunion organizations who ignore rumors about growing pay dissatisfaction among hourly personnel may end up bargaining with a union.

Perceptual Set.   Unlike perceptual defense, which is a screening-out process, **perceptual set** is more of a "screening-in" process; one forms a full perception with only limited or minimal information. Perceptual set often occurs when someone bases a conclusion on a hastily gathered first impression.[15] Research has demonstrated this effect by showing that when people have been told to expect a new acquaintance to be "warm," they in fact perceive the person to be warm, intelligent, and generally likable.[16] The reverse is true for a negative perceptual set. As the term implies, we often become set in our perception of people and the messages they send. Jokes told by good friends somehow tend to be funnier than the same ones told by adversaries.

perceptual set forming a lasting impression from limited information

Perceptual set, like perceptual defense, has advantages and disadvantages. A certain degree of perceptual set allows a manager to have an eye for relevant detail without getting tangled up in irrelevant minutiae. Too much perceptual set leads to prejudice and inflexibility.

Organization

Selectivity is only the first hurdle in the overall perception process. After something has been selected from among competing stimuli, the subprocess of organization takes over. Through **perceptual organization**, we arrange otherwise meaningless or disorganized stimuli into meaningful patterns. This organization takes place in three ways: grouping, figure-ground, and closure. Optical illusions like the entertaining ones in Figure 11.5 play havoc with perceptual organization.

perceptual organization mentally creating meaningful patterns from disorganized stimuli

Grouping.   Look at Image 1 in Figure 11.5 and follow the instructions. (Look now before reading on.) If you look closely, the sentence contains the word *the* twice. Because *the* is such a common word and because we normally group words line by line, the duplicate wording between the two lines tends to be overlooked. So, too, managers may overlook subtle individual differences by grouping or stereotyping people. However, grouping helps us quickly and efficiently sort out unusual stimuli, such as defective products when testing for quality.

Image 1 Read this sentence out loud.

A BIRD IN THE
THE HAND IS WORTHLESS

Image 2

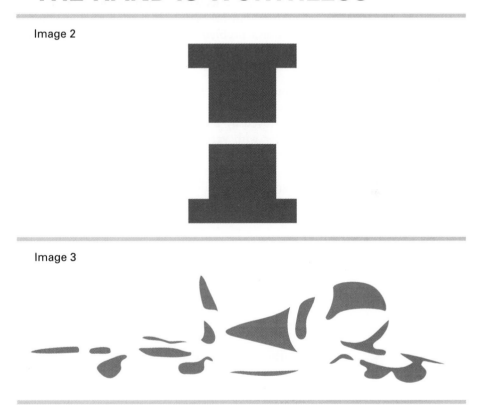

Image 3

FIGURE 11.5 • "What You See Isn't Always What You Get!"

Source: Image 1 reproduced by permission of the publisher *Optricks,* by Melinda Wentzell and D. K. Holland. © 1973. Troubador Press, 385 Fremont Street, San Francisco, CA 94105.

Figure-ground.   Glance quickly at Image 2 in Figure 11.5. (Look now before reading on.) What did you see? Did you first see dark T-shaped blocks (one right side up, the other upside down)? Or did you see a light capital letter H against a dark background? What you saw depended on what you perceived as the figure and what you perceived as the background. In the same fashion people often reverse figure-ground relationships in their surroundings. Entering a new organizational setting, one may initially perceive the recruiter as the principal figure and others in the organization as the undifferentiated background. Eventually, though, the recruiter fades into the background as supervisors, new friends, and others emerge as personally important figures. Similarly, important problems and communications often get lost in a background of trivial matters.

Closure.   Now take a fast glance at Image 3 in Figure 11.5. (Look now before reading on.) What did you see? If you saw a commercial jet airliner flying toward you from left to right you relied on the perceptual process of closure. In effect, closure means mentally filling in the blanks of an incomplete whole. Since you are accustomed to seeing complete pictures of airplanes, you perceptually complete an incomplete picture. We are all familiar with the tendency of people to fill in the blanks when they hear only part of a story. Rumors start this way. But closure can be extremely helpful to a manager trying to identify and solve a complex problem with only limited information.

Interpretation

Managers often interpret situations differently because they have highly specialized and thus restricted perspectives. For instance, an engineer and a salesperson employed by a computer manufacturer may come out of a meeting with a customer with very different interpretations of what lies ahead. Suppose the customer wants additional software for an already complex computer installation. To the salesperson, this means more sales revenue; to the engineer, it means significant technical difficulties. The salesperson interprets the situation as an opportunity, but the engineer interprets it as a problem. They therefore can be expected to react quite differently to the situation.

Dynamics of Organizational Communication

As a writer on the subject has pointed out, "civilization is based on human cooperation and without communication, no effective cooperation can develop."[17] Accordingly, effective communication is essential for cooperation within productive organizations. At least four dynamics of organizational communication—structural considerations, the grapevine, nonverbal communication, and upward communication—largely determine the difference between effectiveness and ineffectiveness in this important area.

Organizing for Coordinated Communication

As we mentioned earlier, the term *organizational communication* takes in a lot of territory. Research on major companies has identified seven categories of organizational communication: advertising and promotion, employee communications, media relations, shareholder relations, consumer affairs, community relations, and government relations.

In terms of organization structure, the same study revealed a trend toward greater centralization of the communication function. Firms are showing an increasing preference for a separate corporate communications department headed by an executive-level manager, who may be called the director of communications, director of public affairs, or director of public relations. Behind this drive toward greater centralization of the communications function is a desire to support and coordinate companywide communications through a central source. After specific communications programs were developed at the corporate level, however, the firms studied tended to administer those programs at the divisional or local levels.[18]

Members of the Teamsters union, representing truck drivers and other employees around the United States, have a well-deserved reputation as a tough, independent-minded group. But at Preston Trucking, a Maryland company, listening to employees is practically a religion. Even members of the Teamsters union have been won over. In a single year, Preston's managers receive about 5,800 suggestions, averaging one per employee. The estimated value of each suggestion to the company is $300.

The Grapevine

grapevine unofficial and informal communication system

In every organization, large or small, there are actually two communication systems, one formal, and the other informal. Sometimes these systems complement and reinforce one another; at other times they come into direct conflict. Although theorists have found it convenient to separate the two, distinguishing one from the other in real life can be difficult. Information required to accomplish official objectives is channeled throughout the organization via the formal system. Official or formal communication, by definition, flows in accordance with established lines of authority and structural boundaries. Media for official communication include all of those discussed earlier. But superimposed on this formal network is the **grapevine**, the unofficial and informal communication system. The term *grapevine* can be traced back to Civil War days, when vinelike telegraph wires were strung from tree to tree across battlefields.

Grapevine Patterns. An authority on grapevine communication has offered the following vivid description:

> *The grapevine operates fast and furiously in almost any work organization. It moves with impunity across departmental lines and easily bypasses superiors in chains of command. It flows around water coolers, down hallways, through lunch rooms, and wherever people get together in groups. It performs best in informal social contacts, but it can operate almost as effectively as a sideline to official meetings. Wherever people congregate, there is no getting rid of the grapevine. No matter how management feels about it, it is here to stay.*[19]

Grapevine communication is not a formless, haphazard process: close study has uncovered definite orderly patterns (see Figure 11.6), the most common of which

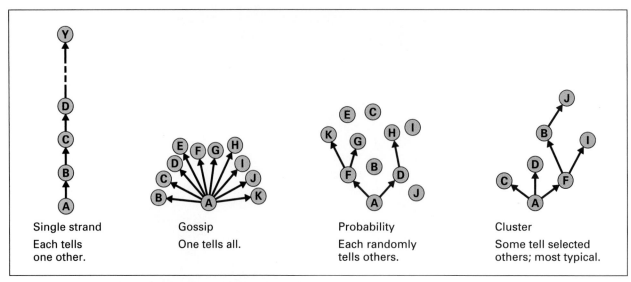

FIGURE 11.6 • Grapevine Patterns

Source: Keith Davis and John W. Newstrom, *Human Behavior at Work: Organizational Behavior,* 8th ed. (New York: McGraw-Hill, 1989), p. 373. Reprinted by permission of McGraw-Hill, Inc.

is the cluster configuration. When the cluster pattern is operating, only select individuals repeat what they hear; others do not.[20] Those who consistently pass along what they hear to others serve as grapevine liaisons or gatekeepers.

> *About 10 percent of the employees on an average grapevine will be highly active participants. They serve as liaisons with the rest of the staff members who receive information but spread it to only a few other people. Usually these liaisons are friendly, outgoing people who are in positions that allow them to cross departmental lines. For example, secretaries tend to be liaisons because they can communicate with the top executive, the janitor, and everyone in between without raising eyebrows.*[21]

Alert managers can keep abreast of grapevine communication by regularly conversing with known gatekeepers.

Managerial Attitudes toward the Grapevine. One survey of 341 participants in a management development seminar uncovered predominantly negative feelings among managers toward the grapevine. Moreover, first-line supervisors perceived the grapevine to be more influential than did middle managers. This second finding led the researchers to conclude that "apparently the grapevine is more prevalent, or at least more visible, at lower levels of the managerial hierarchy where supervisors can readily feel its impact."[22] Finally, the survey found that employees of relatively small organizations (fewer than fifty people) viewed the grapevine as less influential than did those from larger organizations (more than one hundred people). A logical explanation for this last finding is that smaller organizations are usually more informal.

In spite of the negative attitude that many managers have toward it, the grapevine does have a positive side. In fact, experts estimate that grapevine communication is about 75 percent accurate.[23] Though the grapevine has a reputation among managers as a bothersome source of inaccurate information and gossip, it helps satisfy a natural desire to know what is really going on and gives employees a sense of belonging. The grapevine also serves as an emotional outlet for employee fears and apprehensions. Consider, for example, what happened when investor Laurence A. Tisch became chairman of CBS:

> *Tisch's reputation as a ferocious cost cutter, which he despises, forces him to watch every word and gesture. Simple questions—such as why a department needs so many people—are sometimes interpreted as orders to slash. One day Tisch and [the CBS News department head] were talking outside CBS's broadcast center on Manhattan's West 57th Street when Tisch pointed to a tower atop the building, asking what it was. Apparently staffers at a window saw him pointing in their general direction, and the next day newspaper reporters called CBS checking out a rumor that Tisch planned to sell the building.[24]*

Nevertheless, grapevine communication can carry useful information through the organization with amazing speed. Moreover, grapevine communication can help management learn how employees truly feel about policies and programs.[25]

Coping with the Grapevine. Considering that the grapevine can be an influential and sometimes negative force, what can management do about it? First and foremost, the grapevine *cannot be extinguished.* In fact, attempts to stifle grapevine communication may serve instead to stimulate it. Subtly monitoring the grapevine and officially correcting or countering any potentially damaging misinformation is about all any management team can do. "Management by walking around," as discussed in the Disney example, is an excellent way to monitor the grapevine in a nonthreatening manner. Some managers selectively feed information into the grapevine. For example, a health care administrator has admitted: "Sure, I use the grapevine. Why not? The employees sure use it. It's fast, reaches everyone, and employees believe it—no matter how preposterous. I limit its use, though."[26] Rumor-control hot lines have proved useful for neutralizing disruptive and inaccurate grapevine communication.

Nonverbal Communication

body language nonverbal communication based on facial expressions, posture, and appearance

In today's hurried world, our words often have unintended meanings. Facial expressions and body movements that accompany our words can worsen matters. This nonverbal communication, sometimes referred to as **body language,** is an important part of the communication process. In fact, one expert contends that only 7 percent of the impact of our face-to-face communication comes from the words we utter; the other 93 percent comes from our vocal intonations, facial expressions, posture, and appearance.[27] The whole idea of "dressing for success" is an attempt to send a desired nonverbal message about oneself. Image consultants have developed a thriving business of helping aspiring executives look the part:

> *Vanda Sachs had a problem. The 35-year-old senior marketing executive for a well-known fashion magazine had her sights set on the publisher's office. Her trouble? Projecting enough authority to be considered for*

the job. *"I'm petite and blonde and I'm baby-faced,"* she says, *"none of which goes over very well in a world of 45-year-old men who are 6-foot-2."* Being short, in particular, is a *"major liability,"* she adds, *"more so than being a woman."*

Beyond wearing high heels. Sachs (a pseudonym) couldn't do much about her height, but she decided she could improve on her appearance. The first step was to hire a personal-image consultant. Her choice: Emily Cho, founder of New Image, a respected New York City personal-image shopping service that for nineteen years has been helping women choose clothes compatible with their private and professional aspirations. Four days and $3,000 later, Sachs had a knockout wardrobe and a newly acquired savvy that would help her look the part of a publisher. "Like it or not," she explains, *"we're a society that's built on first impressions."*[28]

Types of Body Language. There are three kinds of body language: facial, gestural, and postural.[29] Without the speaker or listener consciously thinking about it, seemingly insignificant changes in facial expression, gestures, and posture send various messages. A speaker can tell whether a listener is interested by monitoring a combination of nonverbal cues, including an attentive gaze, an upright posture, and confirming or agreeing gestures. One manager used such information to delay a vote on an important decision:

A project director in a huge aerospace company called a meeting of higher management people who supported his research project. Consonant with the oft-expressed company policy of commercially exploiting advanced research work, he wanted them to fund development of a new product internally. Early in the meeting, as he began to outline the sizable costs involved, he sensed their disapproval from facial expressions and body postures. His intuition told him that if they were asked to make an explicit decision on the project, it would be negative. So he changed his line of argument and began stressing the possibilities for external rather than internal funding of the project. And he assiduously avoided asking for a funding decision at that time.[30]

Unfortunately, many people in positions of authority—parents, teachers, and managers—ignore or misread nonverbal feedback. When this happens, they become ineffective communicators.

Receiving Nonverbal Communication. Like any other interpersonal skill, sensitivity to nonverbal cues can be learned. (See Table 11.1.) Listeners need to be especially aware of subtleties, such as the fine distinctions between an attentive gaze and a glaring stare and between an upright posture and a stiff one. Knowing how to interpret a nod, a grimace, or a grin can be invaluable to managers. If at any time the response seems inappropriate to what one is saying, it is time to back off and reassess one's approach. It may be necessary to explain things more clearly, adopt a more patient manner, or make other adjustments.

Giving Nonverbal Feedback. What about the nonverbal feedback that managers give rather than receive? A research study carried out in Great Britain suggests that nonverbal feedback from authority figures significantly affects subordinate

TABLE 11.1 • Reading Body Language

Unspoken message	Behavior
"I want to be helpful."	Uncrossing legs Unbuttoning coat or jacket Unclasping hands Moving closer to other person Smiling face Removing hands from pockets Unfolding arms from across chest
"I'm confident."	Avoiding hand-to-face gestures and head scratching Maintaining an erect stance Keeping steady eye contact Steepling fingertips below chin
"I'm nervous."	Clearing throat Expelling air (such as "Whew!") Placing hand over mouth while speaking Hurried cigarette smoking
"I'm superior to you."	Peering over tops of eyeglasses Pointing a finger Standing behind a desk and leaning palms down on it Holding jacket lapels while speaking

Source: Adapted from William Friend, "Reading Between the Lines," *Association Management,* 36 (June 1984): 94–100. Reprinted by permission of the publisher.

behavior. Among the people who were interviewed, those who received nonverbal approval from the interviewers in the form of smiles, positive head nods, and eye contact behaved quite differently from those who received nonverbal disapproval through frowns, head shaking, and avoidance of eye contact. Those receiving positive nonverbal feedback were judged by neutral observers to be significantly more relaxed, more friendly, more talkative, and more successful in creating a good impression.[31]

Positive nonverbal feedback to and from managers is a basic building block of good interpersonal relations.[32] A smile or nod of the head in the appropriate situation tells the individual that he or she is on the right track and to keep up the good work. Such feedback is especially important for managers, who must avoid participating in the subtle but powerful nonverbal discrimination experienced by women leaders. When samples of men and women leaders in a recent study offered the same arguments and suggestions in a controlled setting, the women leaders received more negative and less positive nonverbal feedback than did the men.[33] Managing diversity workshops target this sort of "invisible barrier" to women and minorities.

Upward Communication

upward communication encouraging subordinates to share their feelings and ideas

As used here, the term **upward communication** refers to a process of systematically encouraging subordinates to share with management their feelings and ideas.[34] Upward communication has become increasingly important in recent years as employees have demanded—and, in some cases, received—a greater say in their work lives. Yet recent research suggests that improvement is needed in this area.

Explain how management can encourage upward communication.

When Opinion Research Corp. of Chicago surveyed 100,000 middle managers, supervisors, professionals, salespeople, and technical, clerical, and hourly workers of Fortune 500 companies in 1988, it found the lines of communications fraying. With the exception of the sales group, employees believed top management now was less willing to listen to their problems than five years earlier.[35]

At least seven different options are open to managers who want to improve upward communication.

Formal Grievance Procedures. When unions represent rank-and-file employees, provisions for upward communication are usually spelled out in the collective bargaining agreement. Typically, unionized employees have a formal grievance procedure for contesting managerial actions and oversights. Grievance procedures usually consist of a series of progressively more rigorous steps. For example, union members who have been fired may talk with their supervisor in the presence of the union steward. If the issue is not resolved at that level, the next step may be a meeting with the department head. Sometimes the formal grievance process includes as many as five or six steps, with a third-party arbitrator as the last resort. Formal grievance procedures are also found in nonunion situations.[36]

Employee Attitude and Opinion Surveys. Both in-house and commercially prepared surveys can bring employee attitudes and feelings to the surface. According to an employee-benefits specialist, employee surveys are regularly used by about 45 percent of large U.S. companies.[37] Employees usually will complete surveys if they are convinced meaningful changes will result. Du Pont, for example, recently took the right approach:

Du Pont surveyed 6,600 of its people, including some at Towanda, [Pennsylvania,] and found that flexible work hours were a top priority. Working mothers and single parents said it was hard to cope with the kids while keeping to a rigid plant schedule. A team at Towanda got together and devised a novel solution: Take vacation time by the hour. During slack times when three of the four [task] team members could easily handle the job, one could take off a few hours in the afternoon to go to a school play or bring a sick kid to the doctor. Today other Du Pont workers and managers visit Towanda to learn about flextime. A few have already borrowed it for their own plants.[38]

Surveys with no feedback or follow-up action tend to alienate employees, who feel they are just wasting their time.[39]

Suggestion Systems. Provided that those who submit suggestions receive prompt feedback and appropriate monetary incentives for good ideas, suggestion systems can be a valuable tool. A study of U.S. government employees found a positive correlation between suggestions and productivity.[40]

Open-Door Policy. The open-door approach to upward communication has been both praised and criticized.[41] Proponents say problems can be nipped in the bud when managers keep their doors open and subordinates feel free to walk in at any time and talk with them. Delta Air Lines reportedly has had success with its open-door program.[42] But critics contend that an open-door policy encourages subordinates to leapfrog the formal chain of command. They argue further that it is an open invitation to annoying interruptions when managers can least afford them. A limited open-door policy—afternoons only, for example—can effectively remedy this last objection.

Informal Gripe Sessions. Employees may feel free to air their feelings if they are confident that management will not criticize or penalize them for being frank. But the term *gripe session* seems to encourage only negative communication, and so a more positive label is recommended. One Honeywell division holds regular, informal "coffee talks" to stimulate upward communication. Delta Air Lines relies on a somewhat more formal approach. Department heads allow time for a question-and-answer session at the end of business-update meetings, held approximately every six weeks.[43]

task force multilevel and/or cross-functional team assigned to a specific problem

Task Forces. In spite of its limited use, a task-force approach to upward communication has excellent potential. A **task force** is a team of management and nonmanagement personnel assigned to a specific problem or issue.[44] Task forces generally are fact-finding and advisory panels with no final decision-making authority. Multilevel and cross-functional participation in a task force can foster integration and teamwork, enhance creativity, and develop interpersonal skills.

exit interview brief structured interview with a departing employee

Exit Interviews. An employee leaving the organization, for whatever reason, no longer fears possible recrimination from superiors and so can offer unusually frank and honest feedback, obtained in a brief, structured **exit interview**.[45] On the other hand, exit interviews have been criticized for eliciting artificially negative feedback, because the employee may have a sour-grapes attitude toward the organization.

In general, attempts to promote upward communication will be successful only if subordinates truly believe their contributions will have a favorable impact on their employment. Halfhearted or insincere attempts to get subordinates to open up and become involved will do more harm than good.

Communication Problems

Because communication is a complex, give-and-take process, there will naturally be problems. Managers who are aware of common barriers to communication and who are sensitive to the problem of sexist communication are more likely to be effective communicators.

Barriers to Communication

Earlier in this chapter, the concept of noise was introduced. Noise is common, but it varies in degree. On the low end of the scale, noise such as radio static is a minor irritant that hampers but does not completely block the transfer of understanding. But at the high end of the scale, noise can become an impenetrable barrier to communication. There are four types of communication barriers that represent extreme forms of noise: (1) process barriers, (2) physical barriers, (3) semantic barriers, and (4) psychosocial barriers.

• • • • • • • • • • • • • • • • •
Identify and briefly describe four barriers to communication.

In-house video teleconferencing facilities like those pictured here at Hewlett Packard and a closed-circuit television network help employees from different locations work together easily and efficiently. Communication barriers caused by distance are easier to overcome in today's business environment with the use of technology.

Process Barriers. Every step in the communication process is necessary for effective communication. Blocked steps become barriers. Consider the following situations:

- *Sender Barrier.* A management trainee with an unusual new idea fails to speak up at a meeting for fear of criticism.
- *Encoding Barrier.* A Spanish-speaking factory worker cannot get an English-speaking supervisor to understand a grievance about working conditions.
- *Medium Barrier.* After getting no answer three times and a busy signal twice, a customer concludes that a store's consumer hot line is a waste of time.
- *Decoding Barrier.* An older manager is not sure what a young supervisor means when she refers to an employee as an "air head."
- *Receiver Barrier.* A manager who is preoccupied with the preparation of a budget asks a clerk to repeat an earlier statement. (See Managers in Action.)
- *Feedback Barrier.* During on-the-job training, the failure of the trainee to ask any questions causes a manager to wonder if any real understanding has taken place.

The complexity of the communication process itself is a potentially formidable barrier to communication. Malfunctions anywhere along the line can singly or collectively block the transfer of understanding.

Listening to an Inner Voice

John Yeh has a disability, but he doesn't consider himself disabled. Born deaf in 1947, Yeh has always had to work a little harder. When his hearing disability closed doors to him in the business world, he did not give up. Instead he created his own opportunities.

The result was Integrated Microcomputer Systems, a computer-software engineering and integration company that Yeh founded in 1979. Then, the IMS staff consisted of Yeh, a business manager, and a secretary who knew sign language. Today, the firm is a multimillion-dollar enterprise with 450 employees.

For John Yeh the road to achievement was difficult and sometimes frustrating. Yeh, one of six children, was born to Chinese parents. His family fled mainland China for Taiwan in 1949 [and] then moved to Brazil on a cargo ship in 1960. He arrived in the United States in 1962.

In his new country, Yeh had to learn not just one language but two. Although he could lip-read Chinese and knew Chinese sign language, he now had to translate Chinese to English and then English to sign language.

He was 15 at the time, and he was eager to start school and make friends. "But I was put in a class with the 8- and 9-year-olds," he says, speaking through a sign-language interpreter. He was so embarrassed, Yeh continues, that he worked exceptionally hard and set high goals for himself.

He earned a bachelor's degree in mathematics and a master's in computer science from the University of Maryland, and he became a U.S. citizen. But when he decided to make his own place in the business world, new struggles began. With hands moving in fluid motion, he communicates the frustration he experienced when attempting to come up with the funds to start his company. Every bank rejected Yeh's request for money, even though his parents offered their home as collateral.

Yeh looked to those in his family for moral support. Without them, he says, "I probably would have quit."

Finally, in 1979, friends told him of loans available to the handicapped and members of minority groups through the U.S. Small Business Administration. When Yeh was told he needed three bank-loan rejection letters to be eligible, he simply turned over that day's mail. He got a loan for $100,000.

Yeh has gone on to develop the Personal Tele-Communicator, a machine that allows deaf people to communicate through telephones and computer networks, and he is working on other technology that will further merge the hearing and nonhearing worlds. . . .

More than 10 percent of Yeh's employees are deaf, and 39 percent are minorities. "We do not look at color of skin," Yeh says. "We do not give special treatment to the deaf. I want the world to understand that capable people should be given an opportunity, whether they are handicapped, black, or whatever.

"We must finally learn to look at people's abilities and not their disabilities."

Source: Alison A. Knocke, "Listening to an Inner Voice," Excerpted by permission from *Nation's Business* (February 1989). Copyright 1989, U.S. Chamber of Commerce.

Physical Barriers. Sometimes a physical object blocks effective communication. For example, a riveter who wears ear protectors probably could not hear someone yelling "Fire!" Distance is another physical barrier. The 3,000 miles between New York and Los Angeles and the time-zone difference can complicate coast-to-coast communication in a nationwide organization. Although people often take physical barriers for granted, they can sometimes be removed. For example, an inconveniently positioned wall in an office can be torn out. Choosing an appropriate medium is especially important for managers who must overcome physical barriers. A manager with a soft voice can reach hundreds of people by using a sound system.

Semantic Barriers. Formally defined, **semantics** is the study of meaning of words. Words are indispensable, though they can sometimes cause a great deal of trouble. In a well-worn army story, a growling drill sergeant once ordered a frightened recruit to go out and paint his entire jeep. Later, the sergeant was shocked to find that the private had painted his *entire* jeep, including the head-lights, windshield, seats, and dashboard gauges. Obviously, the word *entire* meant something different to the recruit than it did to the sergeant.

In today's highly specialized world, managers in such fields as accounting, computer science, or advertising may become so accustomed to their own techni-cal language that they forget that people outside their field may not understand them. Unexpected reactions or behavior by others may signal a semantic barrier. It may become necessary to re-encode the message using more generally used terms. Sometimes, if the relationship among specialists in different technical fields is an ongoing one, remedial steps can be taken. For example, hospital administra-tors often take a special course in medical terminology so that they can better understand the medical staff.

Psychosocial Barriers. Psychological and social barriers are probably respon-sible for more blocked communication than any other type of barrier.[46] People's backgrounds, perceptions, values, biases, needs, and expectations differ. Child-hood experiences may result in negative feelings toward authority figures (such as supervisors), racial prejudice, distrust of the opposite sex, or lack of self-confidence. Family and personal problems, including poor health, alcoholism, and emotional strain, may be so upsetting that an employee is unable to concen-trate on work. Experience on present or past jobs may have created anger, dis-trust, and resentment that speak more loudly in the employee's mind than any work-related communication. Sincere sensitivity to the receiver's needs and per-sonal circumstances goes a long way toward overcoming psychosocial barriers to communication.[47]

Sexist Communication

In recent years the English language has been increasingly criticized for being sexist.[48] Words like *he, chairman, brotherhood, mankind,* and the like have tradi-tionally been used in reference to both men and women. The usual justification is that everyone understands that these words refer to both sexes, and it is simpler to use the masculine form. Critics maintain that wholly masculine wording subtly denies women a place and image worthy of their equal status and importance in society.[49] This criticism is largely based on psychological and sociological considerations. Calling the human race *mankind,* for instance, is seldom a real barrier to understanding. But a Stanford University researcher found that "males appear to use 'he' in response to male-related imagery, rather than in response to abstract or generic notions of humanity."[50] In other words, *he* is commonly interpreted to mean literally *he* (a man), not *they* (men and women). Ethical male

"Come On In, Angel"

Ed Derwinski, secretary of the U.S. Department of Veterans' Affairs, may think he's just being cute—but women in his office are livid over what they consider his demeaning treatment of them. In office ceremonies, the cabinet secretary anoints female staffers with nicknames—and then insists on calling them by those names, even in meetings that include nondepartment personnel. Assistant Mary Jo Munnelly is "Little Miss Coffee Maker"; operations and policy staffers Kathrene Hansen and Camille Barry are "Little Miss Muffet" and "Zsa Zsa," respectively; assistant Sandy Peyton is "Miss America," assistant Jane Saunders is "Shirley" because Derwinski thinks she looks like Shirley Temple Black. The only black woman in the office, assistant Judy Williamson, is called "Lena"—as in Lena Horne.

Derwinski, 64, an affable, old-style Illinois politician who served twelve terms in Congress, has awarded women on his staff nicknames throughout his career. He boasts his unreconstructed treatment of women creates an informal office atmosphere. "It really adds to office morale," he says. "One girl [27 years old] I call 'Little Miss Muffet,' because she looks like that, petite and dainty . . . If I don't know a girl's name I just wave and say, 'Hi angel.' Nobody has ever complained. Just the opposite, we laugh about it." Well, maybe *he* laughs about it. One top female staffer expresses the frustration she and her colleagues feel: "It's hard enough to get credibility in the professional world. Then you walk into a meeting and hear, 'Oh come on in, angel, have a chair.' It's horrible."

Source: "Come On In, Angel," *Newsweek* (September 17, 1990): 6, © 1990, Newsweek, Inc. All rights reserved. Reprinted by permission.

and female managers are weeding sexist language out of their vocabularies and correspondence so as not to subordinate or demean women inadvertently (see Management Ethics).

Becoming a Better Communicator

Three communication skills especially important in today's highly organized world are listening, writing, and running meetings. Managers who master these skills usually have fewer interpersonal relations problems. Moreover, effective communicators tend to move up the hierarchy faster than poor ones do.

Effective Listening

●●●●●●●●●●●●●●●●
List at least three practical tips for improving each of the following communication skills: listening, writing, and running a meeting.

Almost all training in oral communication in high school, college, and management development programs is in effective speaking. But what about listening, the other half of the communication equation? Listening is the forgotten stepchild in communication skills training. This is unfortunate, because the most glowing oration is a waste of time if it is not heard. Interestingly, a Cornell University researcher recently asked 827 employees in the hospitality industry to rate their managers' listening ability. Managers considered to be good listeners by subordi-

How can managers be effective communicators when their employees could be anywhere on the roads of America? At Yellow Freight Systems, the nation-wide trucking firm based in Overland Park, Kansas, company audio cassettes are one answer. Dubbed Yellow Line Radio, the cassettes feature news and information about company and employee happenings. Updated versions are regularly sent to long-haul Yellow Freight drivers. So to help drivers pass long hours on the road, Yellow Freight offers its own version of talk radio.

nates tended to be female, under 45 years of age, and relatively new to their position.[51]

Listening takes place at two steps in the communication process. First, the receiver must listen in order to decode and understand the original message. Then the sender becomes a listener when attempting to decode and understand subsequent feedback. Identical listening skills come into play at both ends.

We can hear and process information much more quickly than the normal speaker can talk. According to researchers our average rate of speaking is about 125 words per minute, whereas we are able to listen to about 400 to 600 words a minute.[52] Thus, listeners have up to 75 percent slack time during which they alternatively can daydream or analyze the information and plan a response.[53] Effective listeners know how to put that slack time to good use. Here are some practical tips for more effective listening:

- Tolerate silence. Listeners who rush to fill momentary silences cease being listeners.

- Ask stimulating open-ended questions, ones that require more than merely a yes or no answer.

- Encourage the speaker with attentive eye contact, alert posture, and verbal encouragers such as "um-hum," "yes," and "I see." Occasionally repeating the speaker's last few words also helps.

- Paraphrase. Periodically restate in your own words what you have just heard.

- Show emotion to demonstrate that you are a sympathetic listener.

- Know your biases and prejudices and attempt to correct for them.

- Avoid premature judgments about what is being said.

- Summarize. Briefly highlight what the speaker has just finished saying to bring out possible misunderstandings.[54]

Effective Writing

Managers often complain about college graduates' poor writing skills.[55] Writing difficulties stem from an educational system that requires students to do less and less writing. Essay tests have given way in many classes to the multiple-choice variety, and term papers are being pushed aside by team activities and projects. Moreover, computerized "spelling checkers" used by those who compose at the computer keyboard do little to improve grammar. (There is no substitute for careful proofreading.) As a learned skill, effective writing is the product of regular practice.[56] Students who do not get the necessary writing practice in school are handicapped when they step onto the managerial firing line.

Good writing is clearly part of the encoding step in the basic communication process. If it is done skillfully, potentially troublesome semantic and psychosocial barriers can be surmounted. Caterpillar Company's publications editor has offered four helpful reminders.

1. *Keep words simple.* Simplifying the words you use will help reduce your thoughts to essentials; keep your readers from being "turned off" by the complexity of your letter, memo, or report; and make it more understandable.

2. *Don't sacrifice communication for rules of composition.* Most of us who were sensitized to the rules of grammar and composition in schools never quite recovered from the process. As proof, we keep trying to make our writing conform to rigid rules and customs without regard to style or the ultimate purpose of the communication. (Of course, managers need to be sensitive to the stylistic preferences of their bosses.)

3. *Write concisely.* This means express your thoughts, opinions, and ideas in the fewest number of words consistent with composition and smoothness. But don't confuse conciseness with brevity; you may write briefly without being clear or complete.

4. *Be specific.* Vagueness is one of the most serious flaws in written communication because it destroys accuracy and clarity, leaving the reader to wonder about your meaning or intent.[57]

Also, avoid irritating your readers with useless phrases (see Table 11.2).

Running a Meeting

Meetings are an ever-present feature of modern organizational life.[58] Whether they are convened to find facts, devise alternatives, or pass along information, meetings typically occupy a good deal of a manager's time. For example, during

TABLE 11.2 ● Six Expressions Managers Dislike the Most

Robert Flax, president of Motivational Systems, a management development and communication training firm in West Orange, NJ, is one soldier in the army of business-writing consultants trying to eliminate outdated, imprecise, and unnecessary expressions from America's memos, letters and reports. "Hackneyed, awkward, antiquated writing is bad business," he says. "It confuses, bores and irritates readers, while reducing the writer's credibility."

As part of his campaign, Flax asked thousands of managers and executives who have participated in his writing programs to nominate the expressions they find most annoying. The leading offenders are:

- *To be perfectly honest.* . . . It implies that everything else you've written has been a tissue of lies.

- *Needless to say.* . . . Really? Then don't say it.

- *Enclosed herewith, please find.* . . . Swell, if your memo is traveling via time warp to a recipient in the 18th century. Otherwise, just use "Enclosed is . . ."

- *As you know.* . . . *As you are well aware.* . . . *As per our conversation.* . . . Stop telling people what they already know, unless you are keen on insulting their intelligence.

- *At your earliest convenience.* . . . *As soon as possible.* . . . Give a specific date or don't even bother. The reader's earliest convenience might be [two years from now].

- *Please be advised that.* . . . My, we are officious, aren't we? Is the reader under arrest?

Flax's final word of advice: "If you'd be embarrassed to say it, don't write it."

one of his typical 60-hour weeks, Sara Lee Corporation's chief executive officer, John H. Bryan, Jr., spent 33.5 hours in meetings.[59] Meetings are the principal format for committee action. Whatever the reason for a meeting, managers who chair meetings owe it to themselves and their organization to use everyone's time and talent efficiently. Some useful pointers for conducting successful meetings are the following:

1. *Make certain a meeting is necessary.* Don't call a meeting if the same result can be achieved by personal visit, memo, phone call, etc.

2. *Develop an agenda and send it out in advance.* The agenda should clearly indicate the item(s) to be covered, appropriate supporting materials, time and place of the meeting, approximate time the meeting will require, and some indication of what is expected in the way of participation from the members, e.g., to give advice or make a decision.

3. *Give careful consideration to those being invited to the meeting.* Invite only those people who need to attend. Inviting individuals who have no reason for attending can actually be disruptive or counterproductive, especially if they are vocal.

4. *Give the meeting your undivided attention.* Hold the meeting where distractions and interruptions can be held to a minimum.

5. *Be prepared.* There is no substitute for adequate preparation. Know what it is you want to accomplish and do your homework in such a way that all necessary information is available. Anticipate questions and issues that may arise.

6. *If participation by members is important, be prepared to ask the right questions to stimulate discussion.* Encourage everyone to get involved. Avoid questions which stifle discussion. Reserve personal opinions and judgments until later in the discussion; otherwise, the members might be unduly biased by your comments and fail to provide the type of input really desired. Don't allow one or a few members to monopolize the conversation.

7. *Keep to the agenda.* Encourage members to express themselves, but don't permit them to wander off the subject or waste time with long-winded dissertations.

8. *Conclude the meeting by summarizing the highlights,* including action to be taken as a result of the discussion. Follow up the meeting with a set of accurate and detailed minutes, distributing them to all who were present.[60]*

With practice, these guidelines will become second nature. Running a meeting brings into focus all the components of the communication process, including coping with noise and barriers. Effective meetings are important to organizational communication and, ultimately, to organizational success.

Summary

On-the-job research reveals managers spend most of their time communicating face to face. Middle-manager communication in small businesses tends to be primarily horizontal. In contrast, it tends to be vertical in large organizations. Communication is a social process involving the transfer of information and understanding. Links in the communication process include sender, encoding, medium, decoding, receiver, and feedback. According to the contingency model of media selection, rich media such as face-to-face communication are best for nonroutine problems. Lean media such as impersonal bulletins are suitable for routine problems. Noise is any source of interference.

Perception is important to communication because it helps senders and receivers give meaning to environmental stimuli, including messages. Three perceptual subprocesses are selectivity, organization, and interpretation. Perceptual defense enables one to screen out irrelevant stimuli, and perceptual set causes one to form lasting impressions from limited information. Grouping, figure-ground, and closure help people perceptually organize otherwise meaningless stimuli. Specialists often differ in their interpretations because of their restricted perspectives.

Four dynamics of organizational communication are structural considerations, the grapevine, nonverbal communication, and upward communication. Research suggests a trend toward greater centralization of the overall communication function. The unofficial and informal communication system that sometimes complements and sometimes disrupts the formal communication system has been labeled the grapevine. A sample of managers surveyed had predominantly negative feelings toward it. Recognizing that the grapevine cannot be suppressed, managers are advised to monitor it constructively. Nonverbal communication, including facial, gestural, and postural body language, accounts for most of the impact of face-to-face communication. Managers can become more effective communicators by doing a better job of receiving and giving nonverbal communication. Upward communication can be stimulated by using formal grievance procedures, employee attitude and opinion surveys, suggestion systems, an open-door policy, informal gripe sessions, task forces, and exit interviews.

Process, physical, semantic, and psychosocial barriers and sexist communication are common organizational communication problems. Awareness of the various barriers and a sincere effort to eliminate sexist language can improve communication effectiveness. Constructive steps also can be taken to become a better listener, writer, and meeting chairperson. Managers who master these steps usually have fewer interpersonal relations problems. Also, effective communicators tend to move up the hierarchy faster.

Terms to Understand

Communication
Media richness
Noise
Perception
Selectivity
Perceptual defense
Perceptual set

Perceptual organization
Grapevine
Body language
Upward communication
Task force
Exit interview
Semantics

Questions for Discussion

1. In your daily face-to-face communication, which link in the communication process tends to be the weakest? Why? What corrective action could you take?

2. Why is media selection a particularly important consideration for managers? How does the Lengel-Daft contingency model help in this regard?

3. In what situations would perceptual set be a serious communication problem for a manager?

4. Can you explain the role of perception in a disagreement between you and a friend, coworker, or relative?

5. Have you ever been victimized by the grapevine? Explain. What could have been done to prevent this?

6. Why is it important for managers to understand body language?

7. What kind of process barriers can block the transfer of understanding in the classroom?

8. What forms of verbal or nonverbal sexist communication have you observed lately? Do you believe that the elimination of sexist communication is a legitimate concern for managers? Explain.

9. How can you become a better listener?

10. In your experience, what do people often do wrong when running a meeting? Give examples.

Back to the Opening Case

Now that you have read Chapter 11, you should be able to answer the following questions about the Southwest Airlines case:

1. Does Herb Kelleher do an effective or ineffective job with media selection?

2. Why is Kelleher likely to get straightforward and honest feedback from Southwest's employees?

3. How would you respond to a manager who made the following statement: "Kelleher's humorous style encourages employees to slack off and be disrespectful to management."?

4. Is the company tradition of "fun uniform Fridays" an effective form of nonverbal communication? Explain. Does it communicate similar or different messages to employees and customers?

5. Would you like to work for Southwest Airlines? Why or why not?

|CLOSING CASE|

The Case of the Errant Messenger*

The following case study has been reported by Robert I. Stevens, a systems consultant and writer.

Whenever anyone on the executive floor wanted to tease Henry Reeves, they would ask him, "Are you sure you don't have any messages for me from the president?" Hank would become somewhat flustered and ignore the question. This by-play, which lasted for a year or so, was the result of the following incident—known by many, but not including the president.

The president of the company was a grizzled, dour army veteran who ran the operation as if he was still commanding a unit in the service. He made all major decisions and was almost always right in his judgment. I had seen him join a meeting of top staff just after a policy decision had been reached and ask a few big questions that resulted in a complete reversal of the original decision. The only executive who contested the president, usually at meetings where the president was not present, was vice president James Dubler, who was almost always wrong.

The president believed in "seeing what the troops were doing" and spent a good portion of his time visiting the many dispersed locations of the company. . . . Whenever the president wanted to inform an officer of the company who was not present of a decision, request for information, or at times a reprimand, he would turn to a member of his traveling party and give him an oral message to deliver to the appropriate person. Usually, the selected messenger was Henry Reeves, a shy, introverted MBA, recently hired.

On one trip that I attended just before Reeves was hired, a situation developed that displeased the president. He turned to me and said, "You tell Jim Dubler, he better get this problem corrected before it blows up in his face." Although I was only a senior analyst, it would never have occurred to me to question the president's order to deliver such a message to a vice president.

When I delivered the president's message to Mr. Dubler, he became very agitated and gave me the type of verbal thrashing that a vice president can give an analyst. I finally blurted out "Mr. Dubler, I'm only the messenger." He immediately calmed down and told me to leave.

From what we pieced together later, the first time Hank Reeves delivered a message to Mr. Dubler, he received the same type of tongue-lashing from Dubler without being able to withdraw from the confrontation. Evidently, the occasion so traumatized Reeves that when the president gave him other messages to be relayed to Dubler, he never delivered them. The situation of Reeves not delivering the president's messages to Dubler went on for several months without Reeves telling anyone about his problem. During that time, the president was heard to grumble about Dubler not reacting too fast to various situations.

Then one Friday afternoon the president asked Reeves to get Dubler to prepare a report over the weekend that he wanted on his desk Monday morning. Reeves again did not deliver the message. Monday morning, when the president arrived at his office and no report was present, he checked with his secretary if Dubler had left a message as to why he had not finished the report. He muttered to me (I had just entered his office as requested), "Well, this is the last straw." He then called the personnel officer on the phone and said "Fire Dubler. Give him whatever severance benefits you think he should have, but get him off the property—and I don't want him coming up to see me."

As in most corporations, such situations become common knowledge in short order—and that's why Reeves was asked occasionally if he had any messages to deliver from the president.

*"The Case of the Errant Messenger" is reprinted by permission of the author, Robert I. Stevens.

For Discussion

1. Who is primarily to blame for Dubler's unfortunate firing: the president, Reeves, or Dubler himself? Why?

2. Did the grapevine have a positive or negative impact in this case? Explain.

3. Considering what you now know about organizational communication, what advice would you give the president? Reeves? Dubler?

References

Opening Quotation. Laurence J. Peter, *Peter's Quotations* (New York: Bantam, 1977), p. 100.

Opening Case. Jim Castelli, "Finding the Right Fit," *HRMagazine* (September 1990): 38–41; Amy Engeler, "A Busy Boss Can Never Fly Solo," *Business Month* (August 1990): 22–23; Frank Gibney, Jr., "Southwest's Friendly Skies," *Newsweek* (May 30, 1988): 49; Kevin Kelly, "Southwest Airlines: Flying High with 'Uncle Herb'," *Business Week* (July 3, 1989): 53–55; Joseph Weber, "Where 'Frill' Is a Four-Letter Word," *Business Week* (September 21, 1987): 58–62.

Closing Case. Robert I. Stevens, "The Case of the Errant Messenger," *Journal of Systems Management,* 35 (July 1984): 42.

1. For example, see Robert A. Snyder and James H. Morris, "Organizational Communication and Performance," *Journal of Applied Psychology,* 69 (August 1984): 461–465; and Elmore R. Alexander, Marilyn M. Helms, and Ronnie D. Wilkins, "The Relationship between Supervisory Communication and Subordinate Performance and Satisfaction among Professionals," *Public Personnel Management,* 18 (Winter 1989): 415–429.

2. For more details on this study, see John R. Hinrichs, "Communications Activity of Industrial Research Personnel," *Personnel Psychology,* 17 (Summer 1964): 193–204.

3. See Fred Luthans and Janet K. Larsen, "How Managers Really Communicate," *Human Relations,* 39 (February 1986): 161–178.

4. See Larry R. Smeltzer and Gail L. Fann, "Comparison of Managerial Communication Patterns in Small, Entrepreneurial Organizations and Large, Mature Organizations," *Group & Organization Studies,* 14 (June 1989): 198–215.

5. David S. Brown, "Barriers to Successful Communication: Part I. Macrobarriers," *Management Review,* 64 (December 1975): 28.

6. Keith Davis, *Human Behavior at Work: Organizational Behavior,* 6th ed. (New York: McGraw-Hill, 1981), p. 399.

7. A manager's view of the communication process may be found in Michael L. Peters, "How Important Is Interpersonal Communication?" *Personnel Journal,* 62 (July 1983): 554–560.

8. For discussion of an alternative model of communication, see Johan van Hoorde, "The Targowski & Bowman Model of Communication: Problems and Proposals for Adaptation," *The Journal of Business Communication,* 27 (Winter 1990): 51–70.

9. Paul L. Blocklyn, "Making Magic: The Disney Approach to People Management," *Personnel,* 65 (December 1988): 32.

10. See Robert H. Lengel and Richard L. Daft, "The Selection of Communication Media as an Executive Skill," *Academy of Management Executive,* 2 (August 1988): 225–232.

11. See Fernando Bartolomé and André Laurent, "The Manager: Master and Servant of Power," *Harvard Business Review,* 64 (November-December 1986): 77–81.

12. Walter R. Nord, *Concepts and Controversy in Organizational Behavior,* 2nd ed. (Santa Monica: Goodyear, 1976), p. 22.

13. For more on this accident and its behavioral aspects, see "Spaniards Analyze Tenerife Accident," *Aviation Week & Space Technology* (November 20, 1978): 113–121; and Karl E. Weick, "The Vulnerable System: An Analysis of the Tenerife Air Disaster," *Journal of Management,* 16 (September 1990): 571–593.

14. Research evidence on managerial selective perception is presented in James P. Walsh, "Selectivity and Selective Perception: An Investigation of Managers' Belief Structures and Information Processing," *Academy of Management Journal,* 31 (December 1988): 873–896.

15. Impression management research results are presented in William L. Gardner and Mark J. Martinko, "Impression Management: An Observational Study Linking Audience Characteristics with Verbal Self-Presentations," *Academy of Management Journal,* 31 (March 1988): 42–65.

16. For a typical example of this research, see H. H. Kelley, "The Warm-Cold Variable in First Impressions of Persons," *Journal of Personality,* 18 (1950): 431–439.

17. Frank Snowden Hopkins, "Communication: The Civilizing Force," *The Futurist,* 15 (April 1981): 39.

18. See "Communications Patterns," *Management Review,* 66 (August 1977): A useful discussion of General Motors' internal communications program may be found in Bruce H. Goodsite, "General Motors Attacks Its Frozen Middle," *Communication World,* 4 (October 1987): 20–23.

19. Keith Davis, "Grapevine Communication among Lower and Middle Managers," *Personnel Journal,* 48 (April 1969): 269.

20. For more extensive discussion, see Keith Davis, "Management Communication and the Grapevine," *Harvard Business Review,* 31 (September-October 1953): 43–49.

21. Hugh B. Vickery, III, "Tapping into the Employee Grapevine," *Association Management,* 36 (January 1984): 59–60.

22. John W. Newstrom, Robert E. Monczka, and William E. Reif, "Perceptions of the Grapevine: Its Value and Influence," *Journal of Business Communication,* 11 (Spring 1974): 12–20.

23. See Roy Rowan, "Where Did *That* Rumor Come From?" *Fortune* (August 13, 1979): 130–137.

24. Patricia Sellers, "Lessons from TV's New Bosses," *Fortune* (March 14, 1988): 115, 118.

25. See Alan Zaremba, "Working With the Organizational Grapevine," *Personnel Journal,* 67 (July 1988): 38–41.

26. "Executives Favor Plucking the Fruits from Employee Grapevine," *Association Management,* 36 (April 1984): 105.

27. See Albert Mehrabian, "Communication without Words," *Psychology Today,* 2 (September 1968): 53–55.

28. Brian Hickey, "People Packaging," *America West Airlines Magazine,* 5 (September 1990): 61. Reprinted by permission of the author.

29. This three-way breakdown comes from Dale G. Leathers, *Nonverbal Communication Systems* (Boston: Allyn & Bacon, 1976), chap. 2.

30. Michael B. McCaskey, "The Hidden Messages Managers Send," *Harvard Business Review,* 57 (November-December 1979): 145.

31. See A. Keenan, "Effects of the Non-Verbal Behaviour of Interviewers on Candidates' Performance," *Journal of Occupational Psychology,* 49, No. 3 (1976): 171–175.

32. For a pointed and humorous contrast between male and female body language, see Gwen Rubinstein, "Body Politics," *Association Management,* 39 (April 1987): 55–58.

33. For details, see Dore Butler and Florence L. Geis, "Nonverbal Affect Responses to Male and Female Leaders: Implications for Leadership Evaluations," *Journal of Personality and Social Psychology,* 58 (January 1990): 48–59.

34. For an instructive discussion of upward communication, see John B. McMaster, "Getting the Word to the Top," *Management Review,* 68 (February 1979): 62–65.

35. Alan Farnham, "The Trust Gap," *Fortune* (December 4, 1989): 57.

36. See Mary P. Rowe and Michael Baker, "Are You Hearing Enough Employee Concerns?" *Harvard Business Review,* 62 (May-June 1984): 127–135.

37. Data from Farnham, "The Trust Gap," pp. 56–78.

38. Brian Dumaine, "Creating a New Company Culture," *Fortune* (January 15, 1990): 130.

39. See Stephen L. Guinn, "Surveys Capture Untold Story," *HRMagazine,* 35 (September 1990): 64–66.

40. Suggestion systems are discussed in Woodruff Imberman, "The Golden Nuggets on the Factory Floor," *Business Horizons,* 29 (July-August 1986): 63–69. Also see James S. Larson, "Employee Participation in Federal Management," *Public Personnel Management,* 18 (Winter 1989): 404–414.

41. An informative overview may be found in Everett T. Suters, "Hazards of an Open-Door Policy," *Inc.,* 9 (January 1987): 99–101.

42. See Bill Leonard, "Making the Message Clear," *Personnel Administrator,* 34 (November 1989): 46–49.

43. See Ibid.

44. For practical advice on task forces, see William J. Altier, "Task Forces: An Effective Management Tool," *Management Review,* 76 (February 1987): 52–57; and Walter Kiechel, III, "The Art of the Corporate Task Force," *Fortune* (January 28, 1991): 104–105.

45. See Walter Kiechel, III, "The Art of the Exit Interview," *Fortune* (August 13, 1990): 114–115.

46. See John S. Fielden, "Why Can't Managers Communicate?" *Business,* 39 (January-March 1989): 41–44.

47. Practical tips on overcoming barriers to communication may be found in Paul R. Timm, "Driving Out the Devils of Communication," *Management World,* 13 (July 1984): 27–29; and Cheryl L. McKenzie and Carol J. Qazi, "Communication Barriers in the Workplace," *Business Horizons,* 26 (March-April 1983): 70–72.

48. For example, see Bobbye Persing, "Sticks and Stones and Words: Women in the Language," *Journal of Business Communication,* 14 (Winter 1977): 11–19.

49. For a brief discussion of male-versus-female communication styles, see Cynthia Berryman-Fink, "Changing Sex-Role Stereotypes," *Personnel Journal,* 62 (June 1983): 502, 504.

50. Wendy Martyna, "What does 'He' Mean? Use of the Generic Masculine," *Journal of Communication,* 28 (Winter 1978): 138. A later study with similar results is Janet A. Sniezek and Christine

H. Jazwinski, "Gender Bias in English: In Search of Fair Language," *Journal of Applied Social Psychology,* 16, No. 7 (1986): 642–662.

51. Data from Judi Brownell, "Perceptions of Effective Listeners: A Management Study," *Journal of Business Communication,* 27 (Fall 1990): 401–415. For examples of managers who listen, see Kenneth Labich, "Making over Middle Managers," *Fortune* (May 8, 1989): 58–64.

52. Cynthia Hamilton and Brian H. Kleiner, "Steps to Better Listening," *Personnel Journal,* 66 (February 1987): 20–21.

53. College students' barriers to listening are reported in Steven Golen, "A Factor Analysis of Barriers to Effective Listening," *Journal of Business Communication,* 27 (Winter 1990): 25–36.

54. This list has been adapted from John F. Kikoski, "Communication: Understanding It, Improving It," *Personnel Journal,* 59 (February 1980): 126–131; and John L. DiGaetani, "The Business of Listening," *Business Horizons,* 23 (October 1980): 40–46.

55. See "Wanted: Great Communicators," *The Christian Science Monitor* (June 22, 1990): 8.

56. Several instructive pointers for more readable writing may be found in Arn Tibbetts, "Ten Rules for Writing Readably," *Journal of Business Communication,* 18 (Fall 1981): 53–62. Also see Ronald E. Dulek and John S. Fielden, "How Well Do You Manage Writing?" *Business Horizons,* 29 (September-October 1986): 38–42; Rosalind Gold, " 'Reader-Friendly' Writing," *Supervisory Management,* 34 (January 1989): 39–43; and Larry R. Smeltzer and Jeanette W. Gilsdorf, "How to Use Your Time Efficiently When Writing," *Business Horizons,* 33 (November-December 1990): 61–64.

57. Robert F. DeGise, "Writing: Don't Let the Mechanics Obscure the Message," *Supervisory Management,* 21 (April 1976): 26–28.

58. See Gary English, "How About a Good Word for Meetings?" *Management Review,* 79 (June 1990): 58–60.

59. Data from Judith H. Dobrzynski, "A Week in the Life of a CEO," *Business Week* (October 23, 1987): 46–52.

60. Other practical tips on running a meeting may be found in Andrew S. Grove, "How (and Why) to Run a Meeting," *Fortune* (July 11, 1983): 132–140; Glenn W. Soden, "Avoid Meetings or Make Them Work," *Business Horizons,* 27 (March-April 1984): 47–49; Robert C. Ford and M. Gene Newport, "Strategic Steps for Resolving the Committee Dilemma," *SAM Advanced Management Journal,* 51 (Spring 1986): 9–14; Norman B. Sigband, "The Uses of Meetings," *Nation's Business* (February 1987): 28R; and Richard D. Massimilian, "The New Language Barrier: Closer to Home Than You Think," *Business Horizons,* 33 (July-August 1990): 52–57.

VIDEO SKILL BUILDER

• •

Manager of the Year: A Film About Effective Listening

Learning Objective

To help you recognize the importance of effective listening and develop your listening skills.

Link to Textual Material

Managerial roles, communicating, listening, teamwork, managing conflict.

Effective listening can:

1. Give us information about ourselves.
2. Give us information about others.
3. Ensure that the information we receive from others is complete.
4. Ensure that the information we receive from others is correct, and not distorted by bias.
5. Avoid misunderstandings and miscommunication that can result in interpersonal conflict and stress.
6. Enable more effective problem solving and decision making.
7. Enhance personal popularity and interpersonal effectiveness.

Discussion Questions

1. After viewing this video, do you consider yourself an effective listener? Explain.
2. Which particular listening skills do you need to work on? Explain.
3. How would you respond to someone who made the following statement? ''Listening is easy, all you need to do is keep your mouth shut.''

PART IV

Motivating and Leading

• • • • • • • • • • • • • • • • Part IV focuses on the process of getting individuals to contribute effectively and efficiently to organizational objectives. Like any other valuable resource, people can be employed appropriately and to full capacity, or they can be wastefully depleted. In Chapter 12 an introduction to motivation theory is used as a springboard for a discussion of rewards and participative management. Because management is essentially a social process, Chapter 13 deals with important group dynamics, including group development, organizational politics, and conformity. Effective teamwork is discussed, with an emphasis on trust. Chapter 14 examines how managers can more effectively influence employees through power, leadership, and behavior modification. And in Chapter 15, the problem of overcoming resistance to change is discussed within the context of planned change. Useful information on managing conflict is also provided.

12

Motivating Job Performance

*There are no simple,
cookbook formulas for
working with people.*

KEITH DAVIS

CHAPTER OBJECTIVES

When you finish studying this chapter, you should
be able to

- Explain the motivational lessons taught by
  Maslow's theory, Herzberg's theory, and expectancy theory.

- Describe how goal setting motivates performance.

- Discuss how managers can improve the motivation of routine-task personnel.

- Explain how job enrichment can be used to enhance the motivating potential of jobs.

- Distinguish extrinsic rewards from intrinsic rewards and list four rules for administering extrinsic rewards effectively.

- Discuss the contributions quality control circles and self-managed teams can make to participative management.

- Explain how companies are striving to motivate an increasingly diverse workforce.

Lincoln Electric's Motivational Secrets

Since 1934, Lincoln Electric, a maker of industrial welding equipment in Cleveland, has never had a losing quarter. It has not laid anyone off in 40 years, and it has maintained a stable 40 percent market share. Its factory workers are as much as three times more productive than their counterparts in other manufacturing plants, and some earn as much as $80,000 a year.

Visitors flock to Cleveland to discover Lincoln's secret. What they find is not a hothouse for high-tech inventions or a company that follows every new employee motivation plan imported from Japan. Lincoln's secrets are far from mysterious. And, though different aspects of Lincoln's approach appeal to different workers, one key to the company's success sounds almost absurdly simple: it pays its workers to be responsible for high-quality work.

Instead of earning a flat hourly or weekly rate, Lincoln's factory workers get paid for each piece they produce. Industrial engineers set the piece-rate standard when a product or technology is introduced and change it only by adding a cost-of-living factor each year. Therefore, employees don't have to worry about getting paid less per piece if they increase their output. If they develop a more efficient approach or come to work at 5 a.m. every day, they reap the benefits. There is no upper limit on what they can earn.

But they cannot benefit from fast, sloppy work. If a customer returns a product or a factory inspection discovers a defect, the worker responsible for the poor work pays for it, either through losing bonus pay or by staying after hours to repair the product. The return of a defective product can cost a worker up to $1,600 in lost bonus pay. It's not surprising then that Lincoln has earned a reputation for high quality and reliability and that its products tend to sell even during recessions.

Like the piece-work system, the bonus system directly rewards workers for the quality and quantity of their work. Twice a year, supervisors rate each employee on five criteria: work quality, dependability, output, and cooperation, and idea generation. The score for each category is independent of the others, and the system is set up so that supervisors cannot simply give everyone high ratings. For example, employees lose points for absences, regardless of reason—an approach that keeps the absentee rate down to 1.5 percent. Workers and supervisors discuss the ratings, which become the basis for the company's incentive bonuses. The average worker makes almost as much in bonuses as in regular earnings, so the bonuses are well worth working for.

Good pay tied directly to good work is one key to Lincoln's success but not the only one. Job security is another. The company takes hiring very seriously, trying to find only those workers who will fit into the system. Four vice presidents interview and must unanimously agree on every candidate offered a job. The company looks not for experience but for dependability, skills or abilities, and evidence of desire for success. Lincoln does most of its own training.

Despite such careful screening, about one-quarter of new employees quit within the first three months, after learning that the company's famous wages require hard, steady work. When Lincoln is busy, employees are expected to work extra hours. In slack times, employees may be asked to learn a new task or even paint fences. The company doesn't pay workers for holidays, sick days, health benefits, or educational tuition. The workforce is nonunion, and the span of control is wide—about one hundred employees per supervisor. Newly hired MBAs spend weeks sweating on the factory floor (Lincoln's main plant has no windows or air conditioning). But people who can adapt to these conditions and make it through the first three months are likely to stick with Lincoln for a long time. The average worker is forty years old and has been with the company for seventeen years. Although Lincoln has no seniority system, everyone with two years' experience is virtually guaranteed a lifetime job.

Lincoln's no-layoff policy is especially remarkable given the cyclical nature of its customers' businesses. Its major buyers are in industries like oil, steel, construction, and automobile manufacturing, all of which tend to experience major slowdowns during recessions. In the middle of the early-1980s recession, Lincoln's revenues dropped by 40 percent, workweeks were cut to 30 hours, and employees' earnings dropped by half. But no one was laid off and, as it has done every year, the company paid a bonus, which amounted to 55 percent of employees' earnings in 1982.

Lincoln Electric also attracts employees by treating its workers with trust and respect. Executives are treated pretty much the same as other employees—they don't have special bathrooms, cafeterias, or parking spaces, and their offices are as drab as the plant itself. More important, the company's respect for its employees' abilities extends to its treatment of employee ideas. Employees don't get paid for suggestions—although good ideas can figure in at bonus time—but Lincoln employs three engineers whose sole task is to review the feasibility of suggestions. The company implements as many as one-quarter of the two hundred to three hundred employee suggestions it receives each month.

Lincoln also listens when employees complain. The company's president personally reviews all merit evaluations, and employees who disagree with their ratings can take their grievance right to the top, an option exercised by about 140 employees every year.

Lincoln's success is demonstrated not just by steady profits but by the waiting list of job applicants it has had since 1933. The company's founder, an engineer and son of a minister, wanted to manage by the Golden Rule, and his brother, author of *Incentive Management,* believed in giving employees incentives to search constantly for more productive methods. At Lincoln, this simple combination of philosophies lets everyone win—employees, shareholders, and customers.

• • • • • • • • • • • • • • • • • • Japan's stunning economic success in recent decades has prompted American managers to search high and low for Japan's "secret." Management consultants are grilled and best-selling management books scoured for answers. Are superior technology and robots the secret? Is it Japan's group-centered culture? Is it the legendary Japanese work ethic? Could it be Japan's questionable trade practices? Although all these factors work in Japan's favor, the real secret is as plain as day—*people. Business Week* explains:

American companies are now discovering what the Japanese learned long ago: that people—not technology alone or marketing ploys—are the keys to success in global competition. Indeed, American workers can be just as productive as Japanese workers. This has been demonstrated conclusively by the success of Honda, Toyota, and Nissan using American labor in U.S. plants.[1]

In short, Japanese managers know how to motivate their people. They do it with such things as continuous training, a team approach, participation down to the lowest levels, no-layoff policies, group profit-sharing plans, and respect and trust.[2] Nothing magical in this list. Well-managed and successful American companies such as Lincoln Electric have relied on these motivational techniques for decades. Let us explore the concept of motivation and its exciting potential.

The term *motivation* derives from the Latin *movere,* "to move." It is virtually impossible to determine a person's motivation until that person behaves or literally moves. By observing what someone says or does in a given situation, one can draw reasonable inferences about the person's underlying motivation. As used here, the term **motivation** refers to the psychological process that gives behavior purpose and direction.[3] By appealing to this process, managers attempt to get individuals to willingly pursue organizational objectives. Motivation theories are generalizations about the "why" and "how" of purposeful behavior.[4]

Figure 12.1 is an overview model for this chapter. The final element in this model, job performance, is the product of a combination of an individual's motivation and ability. Both are necessary. All the motivation in the world, for example, will not enable a computer-illiterate person to sit down and compose a computer spreadsheet. Ability and skills, acquired through training and/or on-the-job experience, also are required. The individual's motivational factors—

motivation psychological process giving behavior purpose and direction

FIGURE 12.1 • Individual Motivation and Job Performance

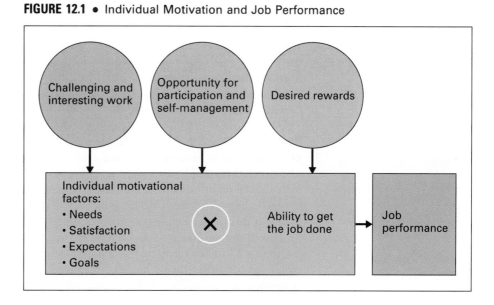

They call it recreation but sport climbing is hard work! Why would Nanette Raybaud risk life and limb during this sport climbing competition at Snowbird, Utah? The same motivational needs that drove her to this death-defying position are present in the workplace. Sport climbers and employees alike are propelled by needs for social recognition, self-esteem, and self-actualization. Progressive managers realize that individuals express common needs in uncommon ways.

• • • • • • • • • • • • • • • • •

Explain the motivational lessons taught by Maslow's theory, Herzberg's theory, and expectancy theory.

needs, satisfaction, expectations, and goals—are affected by challenging work, rewards, and participation. We need to take a closer look at each key element in this model. A review of four basic motivation theories is a good starting point.

Motivation Theories

Although there are dozens of different theories of motivation, four have emerged as the most influential: Maslow's needs hierarchy theory, Herzberg's two-factor theory, expectancy theory, and goal-setting theory. Each approaches the motivation process from a different angle, each has supporters and detractors, and each teaches important lessons about motivation to work.

Maslow's Needs Hierarchy Theory

In 1943 psychologist Abraham Maslow proposed that people are motivated by a predictable five-step hierarchy of needs.[5] Little did he realize at the time that his tentative proposal, based on an extremely limited clinical study of neurotic patients, would become one of the most influential concepts in the field of management.[6] Perhaps because it is so straightforward and intuitively appealing, Maslow's theory has strongly influenced those interested in work behavior. Maslow's message was simply this: people always have needs, and when one need is relatively fulfilled, others emerge in a predictable sequence to take its place. From bottom to top, Maslow's needs hierarchy includes physiological, safety, love, esteem, and self-actualization needs (see Figure 12.2). According to Maslow, most individuals are not consciously aware of these needs; yet we all supposedly proceed up the hierarchy of needs, one level at a time.

Physiological Needs.　At the bottom of the hierarchy are needs based on physical drives, including the need for food, water, sleep, and sex. Fulfillment of these lowest-level needs enables the individual to survive, and nothing else is important when these bodily needs have not been satisfied. As Maslow observed, "It is quite true that man lives by bread alone—when there is no bread."[7] But today the average employee experiences little difficulty in satisfying physiological needs. Figuratively speaking, the prospect of eating more bread is not motivating when one has plenty of bread to eat.

Safety Needs.　After our basic physiological needs have been relatively well satisfied, we next become concerned about our safety from the elements, enemies, and other threats. Most modern employees, by earning a living, also achieve a high degree of fulfillment in this area. Unemployment assistance is a safety net for those between jobs. One nagging safety need in the United States, however, is health insurance. Employers are straining to pay the per-employee average of $3,100 in annual health-care premiums.[8] As mentioned in Chapter 3, some 31 million to 33 million Americans, many of whom are employed or dependents of employed persons, have no health insurance.[9] To the extent this lack of insurance represents an unfulfilled safety need, job satisfaction and productivity could suffer.

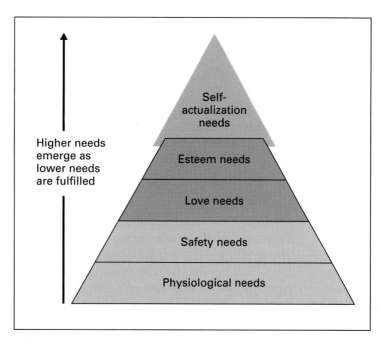

Higher needs
emerge as
lower needs
are fulfilled

Self-actualization needs

Esteem needs

Love needs

Safety needs

Physiological needs

FIGURE 12.2 ● Maslow's Hierarchy of Needs Theory

Source: Data for diagram drawn from A. H. Maslow, "A Theory of Human Motivation," *Psychological Review,* 50 (July 1943): 370–396.

Love Needs. A physiologically satisfied and secure person focuses next on satisfying needs for love and affection. This category is a powerful motivator of human behavior. People typically strive hard to achieve a sense of belonging with others. As with the first two levels of needs, relative satisfaction of love needs paves the way for the emergence of the next higher level.

Esteem Needs. People who perceive themselves as worthwhile are said to possess high self-esteem.[10] Self-respect is the key to esteem needs. Much of our self-respect, and therefore our esteem, comes from being accepted and respected by others. It is important for those who are expected to help achieve organizational objectives to have their esteem needs relatively well fulfilled. But esteem needs cannot emerge if lower-level needs go unattended.

Self-actualization Needs. At the top of Maslow's hierarchy is the open-ended category *self-actualization needs.* It is open-ended because it relates to the need "to become more and more what one is, to become everything that one is capable of becoming."[11] One may satisfy this need by striving to become a better homemaker, plumber, rock singer, or manager. According to one management writer, the self-actualizing manager has the following characteristics:

1. Has warmth, closeness, and sympathy.
2. Recognizes and shares negative information and feelings.
3. Exhibits trust, openness, and candor.
4. Does not achieve goals by power, deception, or manipulation.

5. Does not project own feelings, motivations, or blame onto others.

6. Does not limit horizons; uses and develops body, mind, and senses.

7. Is not rationalistic; can think in unconventional ways.

8. Is not conforming; regulates behavior from within.[12]

Granted, this is a rather tall order to fill. It has been pointed out that "a truly self-actualized individual is more of an exception than the rule in the organizational context."[13] Whether productive organizations need more self-actualized individuals is subject to debate. On the positive side, self-actualized employees might help break down barriers to creativity and steer the organization in new directions. On the negative side, too many unconventional nonconformists could wreak havoc with the typical administrative setup dedicated to predictability.

Relevance of Maslow's Theory for Managers. Behavioral scientists who have attempted to test Maslow's theory in real life claim it has some deficiencies.[14] Even Maslow's hierarchical arrangement has been questioned. Practical evidence points toward a two-level rather than a five-level hierarchy. In this competing view, physiological and safety needs are arranged in hierarchical fashion, as Maslow contends. But beyond that point, any one of a number of needs may emerge as the single most important need, depending on the individual. Edward Lawler, a leading motivation researcher, has observed, "Which higher-order needs come into play after the lower ones are satisfied and in which order they come into play cannot be predicted. If anything, it seems that most people are simultaneously motivated by several of the same-level needs."[15]

Although Maslow's theory has not stood up well under actual testing, it teaches managers one important lesson: a *fulfilled* need does not motivate an individual. For example, the promise of unemployment benefits may partially fulfill an employee's need for economic security (the safety need). But the added security of additional unemployment benefits will probably not motivate fully employed individuals to work any harder. Effective managers try to anticipate each employee's personal need profile and to provide opportunities to fulfill emerging needs. Because challenging and worthwhile jobs and meaningful recognition tend to enhance self-esteem, the esteem level presents managers with the greatest opportunity to motivate better performance.

Herzberg's Two-Factor Theory

During the 1950s, Frederick Herzberg proposed a theory of employee motivation based on satisfaction.[16] His theory implied that a satisfied employee is motivated from within to work harder and that a dissatisfied employee is not self-motivated. Herzberg's research uncovered two classes of factors associated with employee satisfaction and dissatisfaction (see Table 12.1). As a result, his concept has come to be called Herzberg's two-factor theory.

Dissatisfiers and Satisfiers. Herzberg compiled his list of dissatisfiers by asking a sample of about 200 accountants and engineers to describe job situations in which they felt exceptionally bad about their jobs. An analysis of their responses revealed a consistent pattern. Dissatisfaction tended to be associated with complaints about the job context or factors in the immediate work environment.

TABLE 12.1 • Herzberg's Two-Factor Theory of Motivation

Dissatisfiers: factors mentioned most often by dissatisfied employees	*Satisfiers:* factors mentioned most often by satisfied employees
1. Company policy and adminis-tration	1. Achievement
2. Supervision	2. Recognition
3. Relationship with supervisor	3. Work itself
4. Work conditions	4. Responsibility
5. Salary	5. Advancement
6. Relationship with peers	6. Growth
7. Personal life	
8. Relationship with subordinates	
9. Status	
10. Security	

Source: Reprinted by permission of the *Harvard Business Review.* An exhibit from "One More Time: How Do You Motivate Employees?" by Frederick Herzberg (September-October 1987); copyright © 1987 by the President and Fellows of Harvard College; all rights reserved.

Herzberg then drew up his list of satisfiers, factors responsible for self-motivation, by asking the same accountants and engineers to describe job situations in which they had felt exceptionally good about their jobs. Again, a patterned response emerged, but this time different factors were described: the opportunity to experience achievement, receive recognition, work on an interesting job, take responsibility, and experience advancement and growth. Herzberg observed that these satisfiers centered on the nature of the task itself. Employees appeared to be motivated by *job content*—that is, by what they actually did all day long. Consequently, Herzberg concluded that enriched jobs were the key to self-motivation. The work itself—not pay, supervision, or some other environmental factor—was the key to satisfaction and motivation.

Implications of Herzberg's Theory. By insisting that satisfaction is not the opposite of dissatisfaction, Herzberg encouraged managers to think carefully about what actually motivates employees. According to Herzberg, "the opposite of job satisfaction is not job dissatisfaction, but rather *no* job satisfaction; and similarly, the opposite of job dissatisfaction is not job satisfaction, but *no* dissatisfaction."[17] Rather, the dissatisfaction-satisfaction continuum contains a zero midpoint at which both dissatisfaction and satisfaction are absent. An employee stuck on this midpoint, though not dissatisfied with pay and working conditions, is not particularly motivated to work hard because the job itself lacks challenge. Herzberg believes that the most that managers can hope for when attempting to motivate employees with pay, status, working conditions, and other contextual factors is to reach the zero midpoint. But the elimination of dissatisfaction is not the same as truly motivating an employee. To satisfy and motivate employees, an additional element is required: meaningful, interesting, and challenging work. Herzberg is convinced that money is a weak motivational tool because, at best, it can only eliminate dissatisfaction.

Like Maslow, Herzberg has triggered lively debate among motivation theorists. His assumption that job performance improves as satisfaction increases has been criticized for its weak empirical basis. For example, one researcher, after reviewing twenty studies that tested this notion, concluded that the relationship, though positive, was too weak to have any theoretical or practical significance.[18] Others have found that one person's dissatisfier may be another's satisfier (for example, money).[19] Nonetheless, Herzberg has made a useful contribution to motivation theory by emphasizing the motivating potential of enriched work. (Job enrichment is discussed in detail in the next section.)

Expectancy Theory

Both Maslow's and Herzberg's theories have been criticized for making unsubstantiated generalizations about what motivates people. Practical experience tells us that the same people are motivated by different things at different times and that different people are motivated by different things at the same time. Fortunately, expectancy theory, which is based largely on Victor H. Vroom's 1964 classic *Work and Motivation,* effectively deals with the highly personalized rational choices that individuals make when faced with the prospect of having to work to achieve rewards. Individual perception, though secondary in the Maslow and Herzberg models, is central to expectancy theory. Accordingly, **expectancy theory** is a motivation model based on the assumption that motivational strength is determined by perceived probabilities of success. The term **expectancy** refers to the subjective probability (or expectation) that one thing will lead to another. Work-related expectancies, like all other expectancies, are shaped by ongoing personal experience. For instance, an employee's expectation of a raise, diminished after being turned down, later rebounds when the supervisor indicates a willingness to reconsider the matter.

expectancy theory model that assumes motivational strength is determined by perceived probabilities of success

expectancy one's belief or expectation that one thing will lead to another

A Basic Expectancy Model. Although Vroom and other expectancy theorists have developed their models in somewhat complex mathematical terms, the descriptive model in Figure 12.3 is helpful for basic understanding. In this model, one's motivational strength increases as one's perceived effort-performance and performance-reward probabilities increase. All this is not as complicated as it sounds. For example, estimate your motivation to study if you expect to do poorly on a quiz no matter how hard you study (low effort-performance probability) and you know the quiz will not be graded (low performance-reward probability). Now contrast that estimate with your motivation to study if you believe that you can do well on the quiz with minimal study (high effort-performance probability) and that by doing well on the quiz your course grade will significantly improve (high performance-reward probability). Like students, employees are motivated to expend effort when they believe it will ultimately lead to rewards they themselves value. This expectancy approach not only appeals strongly to common sense, it has received encouraging empirical support from researchers.[20]

Relevance of Expectancy Theory for Managers. According to expectancy theory, effort → performance → reward expectations determine whether motivation will be high or low. Although these expectations are in the mind of the employee,

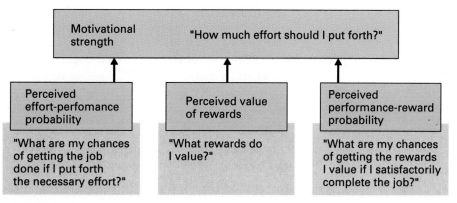

FIGURE 12.3 • A Basic Expectancy Model

they can be influenced by managerial action and organizational experience. Training, combined with challenging but realistic objectives, helps give people the idea that they can get the job done if they put forth the necessary effort. But perceived effort-performance probabilities are only half the battle. Listening skills enable managers to discover each individual's perceived performance-reward probabilities. Employees tend to work harder when they believe they have *a good chance* of getting *personally meaningful* rewards. Both sets of expectations require managerial attention. Each is a potential barrier to work motivation.

Goal-Setting Theory

Think of the three or four most successful people you know personally. Their success may have come via business or professional achievement, politics, athletics, or community service. Chances are they got where they are today by being goal-oriented. In other words, they committed themselves to (and achieved) progressively more challenging goals in their professional and personal affairs. Biographies and autobiographies of successful people in all walks of life generally attest to the virtues of goal setting. Accordingly, goal setting is acknowledged today as a respected and useful motivation theory.

goal setting process of improving performance with objectives, deadlines, or quality standards

Within an organizational context, **goal setting** is the process of improving individual or group job performance with formally stated objectives, deadlines, or quality standards.[21] Management by objectives (MBO), discussed in Chapter 5, is a specific application of goal setting that advocates participative and measurable objectives. Also, recall from Chapter 5 that managers tend to use the terms *goal* and *objective* interchangeably.

A General Goal-Setting Model. Thanks to motivation researchers such as Edwin A. Locke, there is a comprehensive body of knowledge about goal setting.[22] Goal setting has been researched more rigorously than the three motivation theories just discussed.[23] Important lessons from goal-setting theory and research are incorporated in the general model in Figure 12.4. This model shows how properly conceived goals trigger a motivational process that improves performance. Let us explore the key components of this goal-setting model.

•••••••••••••••••••
Describe how goal setting motivates performance.

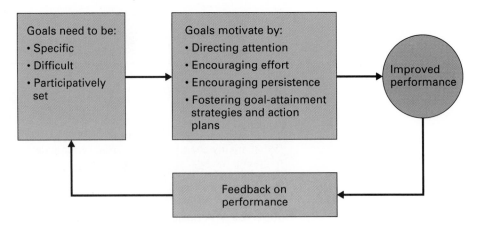

FIGURE 12.4 • A Model of How Goals Can Improve Performance

Personal Ownership of Challenging Goals. In Chapter 5, the discussion of MBO and writing good objectives stressed that goal effectiveness is enhanced by *specificity, difficulty,* and *participation.* Measurable and challenging goals encourage an individual or a group to stretch while trying to attain progressively more difficult levels of achievement. For instance, parents who are paying a college student's tuition and expenses are advised to specify a challenging grade point goal rather than to simply tell their son or daughter to "just do your best." Otherwise, the student could show up at the end of the semester with two Cs and three Ds, saying, "Well, I did my best!" It is important to note that goals need to be difficult enough to be challenging but not impossible. Impossible goals hamper performance; they are a handy excuse for not even trying.

Participation in the goal-setting process gives the individual *personal owner-ship.* From the employee's viewpoint, it is "something I helped develop, not just my boss's wild idea." Feedback on performance operates in concert with well-conceived goals. Feedback lets the person or group know if things are on track or if corrective action is required to reach the goal. An otherwise excellent goal-setting program can be crippled by lack of timely and relevant feedback from managers. Recent research documented the motivational value of matching *specific goals* with *equally specific feedback.*[24] A huge scoreboard in the Palatine, Illinois, headquarters of Square D, a manufacturer of electrical switching equipment, is an imaginative response to the need for specific feedback.

> Up on the board are the quarterly results broken down by profit per employee, sales per employee, and return on equity for Square D and its competitors, among them Emerson Electric, General Electric, and Westinghouse. Square D workers know exactly what they're up against.[25]

Moreover, its stadium-like scoreboard injects a bit of competitive zeal into Square D's goal-setting program.

How Do Goals Actually Motivate? Goal-setting researchers say goals perform a motivational function by doing the four things listed in the center of Figure 12.4. First, a goal is an exercise in selective perception because it direct one's *attention* to a specific target. Second, a goal encourages one to exert *effort* toward achieving something specific. Third, because a challenging goal requires sustained or repeated effort, it encourages *persistence*. Fourth, because a goal creates the problem of bridging the gap between actual and desired, it fosters the creation of *strategies and action plans*. Consider, for example, how all these motivational components were activated by the following program at Marriott's hotel chain.

> *For years, Marriott's room-service business didn't live up to its potential. But after initiating a 15-minute-delivery guarantee for breakfast in 1985, Marriott's breakfast business—the biggest portion of its room-service revenue—jumped 25 percent. [Hotel guests got their breakfast free if it was delivered late.] Marriott got employees to devise ways to deliver the meals on time, including having deliverers carry walkie-talkies so they can receive instructions more quickly.*[26]

Marriott's goal, increased room-service revenue, was the focal point for this program. In effect, the service-guarantee program told Marriott employees that prompt room service was important, and they rose to the challenge with persistent and creative effort. Clear, reasonable, and challenging goals, reinforced by specific feedback and meaningful rewards, are indeed a powerful motivational tool.

Practical Implications of Goal-Setting Theory. Because the model in Figure 12.4 is a generic one, the performance environment may range from athletics, to academics, to the workplace. The motivational mechanics of goal-setting are the same, regardless of the targeted performance. If you learn to be an effective goal setter in school, that ability will serve you faithfully throughout life.

Motivation through Job Design

job design creating task responsibilities based upon strategy, technology, and structure

A job serves two separate but related functions. It is a productive unit for the organization and a career unit for the individual. Thus **job design,** the delineation of task responsibilities as dictated by organizational strategy, technology, and structure, is a key determinant of individual motivation and ultimately of organizational success. Considering that the average adult spends about half of his or her waking life at work, jobs are a central feature of modern existence. A challenging and interesting job can add zest and meaning to one's life. Boring and tedious jobs, on the other hand, can become a serious threat to one's motivation to work hard, not to mention the effect on one's physical and mental health. Concern about uneven productivity growth, eroded product quality, and declining employee satisfaction have persuaded managers to consider two job design strategies.[27]

Strategy One: Fitting People to Jobs

• • • • • • • • • • • • • • • • •
Discuss how managers can improve the motivation of routine-task personnel.

For technological or economic reasons, work must sometimes be divided into routine and repetitive tasks. Nevertheless, steps can be taken to avoid chronic dissatisfaction and to bolster motivation. Three proven alternatives include realistic job previews, job rotation, and limited exposure. Each involves adjusting the

Saturn is General Motors' start-from-scratch attempt to beat the Japanese automakers at their own game: a marketable combination of sporty design, high quality, and low price. The real key to Saturn's long-term success is a good working relationship between General Motors and the United Auto Worker's union. The Square and Circle logos on Saturn employee Ron Bizzell's company badge symbolize the need for teamwork between opposites. Saturn works to make life more interesting for its employees by redesigning jobs for greater challenge and autonomy.

person rather than the job in the person-job match. Hence each entails creating a more compatible fit between an individual and a routine or fragmented job. (In line with this approach is the use of mentally disadvantaged workers, often in sheltered workshops.)

Realistic Job Previews.   Unrealized expectations are a major cause of job dissatisfaction, low motivation, and turnover. Managers commonly create unrealistically high expectations in recruits to entice them to accept a position. This has proved particularly troublesome with regard to routine tasks. Dissatisfaction too often sets in when lofty expectations are brought down to earth by dull or tedious work. **Realistic job previews,** honest explanations of what a job actually entails, have been successful in helping to avoid employee dissatisfaction resulting from unrealized expectations. On-the-job research has demonstrated the practical value of giving a realistic preview of both positive and negative aspects to applicants for highly specialized jobs. In one early experiment, telephone operators who saw a realistic job preview film before being hired had fewer thoughts of resigning and in fact accounted for fewer resignations than did a similar group of operators who viewed a traditional "good news only" recruiting film.[28]

Subsequent research has provided a fairly clear picture of the strengths and limitations of this technique. According to an analysis of twenty-one separate studies involving 9,166 employees, those who had realistic job previews tended to have lower initial expectations, greater organizational commitment and job satisfaction, and a lower turnover rate. However, the impact of realistic job previews on job performance was mixed. Audiovisual previews tended to enhance job performance, whereas written descriptions (in booklet form) had a slightly negative impact.[29]

realistic job previews   honest explanations of what a job actually entails

job rotation moving people from one specialized job to another

Job Rotation. As the term is used here, **job rotation** involves periodically moving people from one specialized job to another. Such movement prevents stagnation. Other reasons for rotating personnel include compensating for a labor shortage, safety, and preventing fatigue.[30] (The FBI rotates its agents off the drug squad periodically to prevent corruption.[31]) If highly repetitive and routine jobs are unavoidable, job rotation, by introducing a modest degree of novelty, can help prevent boredom and resulting alienation. Of course, a balance needs to be achieved between rotating people often enough to fight boredom but not so often that they feel unfairly manipulated or disoriented.

contingent time off rewarding people with early time off when they get the job done

Limited Exposure. Another way of coping with the need to staff a highly fragmented and tedious job is to limit the individual's exposure to it. A number of organizations have achieved high productivity among routine-task personnel by allowing them to earn an early quitting time.[32] This technique, called **contingent time off** (CTO) or earned time off, involves establishing a challenging yet fair daily performance standard, or quota, and letting employees go home when it is reached. The following CTO plan was implemented at a large manufacturing plant where the employees were producing about 160 units a day with 10 percent rejects:

> *If the group produced at 200 units with three additional good units for each defective unit, then they could leave the work site for the rest of the day. Within a week of implementing this CTO intervention, the group was producing 200 + units with an average of 1.5 percent rejects. These employees, who had formerly* put in *an 8-hour day, were now* working *an average of 6.5 hours per day and, importantly, they increased their performance by 25 percent.*[33]

Some employees find the opportunity to earn eight hours of pay for six hours of steady effort extremely motivating.

Companies that use contingent time off report successful results. Impressive evidence comes from a recent large-scale survey of 1,598 U.S. companies employing about 10 percent of the civilian workforce. Among nine nontraditional reward systems, "earned time off" ranked only eighth in terms of use (5 percent of the companies). But among those using it, earned time off ranked *second* in terms of positive impact on job performance—an 85 percent approval rating.[34] Thus, the use of contingent time off has not kept pace with its excellent potential as a motivational tool.

Strategy Two: Fitting Jobs to People

The second job-design strategy calls for managers to consider changing the job instead of the person. Two job-design experts have proposed that managers address the question, "How can we achieve a fit between persons and their jobs that fosters *both* high work productivity and a high-quality organizational experience for the people who do the work?"[35] Two techniques for moving in this direction are job enlargement and job enrichment.

job enlargement combining two or more specialized tasks to increase motivation

Job Enlargement. As used here, **job enlargement** is the process of combining two or more specialized tasks in a work flow sequence into a single job. Aetna used this technique to give some of its office employees a measure of relief from staring into a video display terminal (VDT) all day:

> *Aetna Life & Casualty in Hartford last year reorganized its payroll department to combine ten full-time data-entry jobs with ten jobs that involve paperwork and telephoning. Now nobody in the department spends more than 70 percent of [the] day on a VDT. Morale and productivity have gone up dramatically since the change, says Richard Assunto, Aetna's payroll services manager.*[36]

A moderate degree of complexity and novelty can be introduced in this manner. But critics claim that two or more potentially boring tasks do not necessarily make one challenging job. Furthermore, organized labor has criticized job enlargement as a devious ploy for getting more work for the same amount of money. But if pay and performance are kept in balance, boredom and alienation can be pushed aside a bit by job enlargement.

job enrichment redesigning jobs to increase their motivational potential

• • • • • • • • • • • • • • • •
Explain how job enrichment can be used to enhance the motivating potential of jobs.

Job Enrichment. In general terms, **job enrichment** is redesigning a job to increase its motivating potential.[37] Job enrichment increases the challenge of one's work by reversing the trend toward greater specialization. Unlike job enlargement, which merely combines equally simple tasks, job enrichment builds more complexity and depth into jobs by introducing planning and decision-making responsibility normally carried out at higher levels. For example, "Montgomery Ward Chairman Bernard F. Brennan has authorized 7,700 sales clerks to approve checks and handle merchandise-return problems—functions that once were reserved for store managers."[38] Ward's customers like the resulting speedier service. Thus, enriched jobs are said to be *vertically loaded,* whereas enlarged jobs are *horizontally loaded.*

Jobs can be enriched by upgrading five core dimensions of work: (1) skill variety, (2) task identity, (3) task significance, (4) autonomy, and (5) job feedback. Each of these core dimensions deserves a closer look.

- *Skill Variety.* The degree to which a job requires a variety of different activities in carrying out the work, involving the use of a number of different skills and talents of the person.
- *Task Identity.* The degree to which a job requires completion of a "whole" and identifiable piece of work; that is, doing a job from beginning to end with a visible outcome.
- *Task Significance.* The degree to which the job has a substantial impact on the lives of other people, whether those people are in the immediate organization or in the world at large.
- *Autonomy.* The degree to which the job provides substantial freedom, independence, and discretion to the individual in scheduling the work and in determining the procedures to be used in carrying it out.
- *Job Feedback.* The degree to which carrying out the work activities required by the job provides the individual with direct and clear information about the effectiveness of his or her performance.[39]

Figure 12.5 shows the theoretical connection between enriched core job characteristics and high motivation and satisfaction. At the heart of this job-

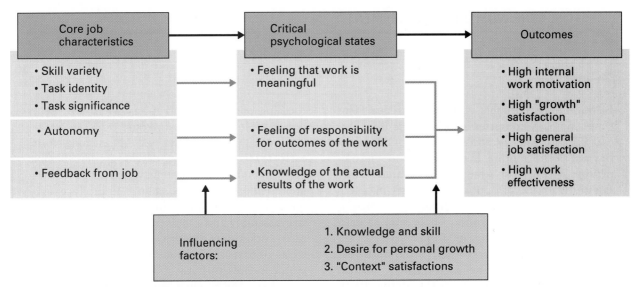

FIGURE 12.5 • How Job Enrichment Works

Source: J. R. Hackman/G. R. Oldham, *Work Redesign,* © 1980 Addison-Wesley Publishing Company, reprinted with permission of the publisher.

enrichment model are three psychological states that highly specialized jobs usually do not satisfy: meaningfulness, responsibility, and knowledge of results.

It is important to note that not all employees will respond favorably to enriched jobs. Personal traits and motives influence the connection between core job characteristics and desired outcomes. Only those with the necessary knowledge and skills plus a desire for personal growth will be motivated by enriched work.[40] Furthermore, in keeping with Herzberg's two-factor theory, dissatisfaction with factors such as pay, physical working conditions, or supervision can neutralize enrichment efforts. Researchers have reported that fear of failure, lack of confidence, and lack of trust in management's intentions can stand in the way of effective job enrichment.[41] But job enrichment can and does work when it is carefully thought out, when management is committed to its success, and when employees desire additional challenge (see The World of Management).

Motivation through Rewards

rewards material and psychological payoffs for working

All workers, including volunteers who donate their time to worthy causes, expect to be rewarded in some way for their contributions. **Rewards** may be defined broadly as the material and psychological payoffs for performing tasks in the workplace. Managers have found that job performance and satisfaction can be improved by properly administered rewards. For example, Au Bon Pain, a chain of upscale sandwich shops in the Northeastern United States, has found the key to breaking the vicious cycle of failure in fast-food ventures. Contributing to that cycle are low pay, low-ability employees, bad morale, high turnover, poor service, and customer dissatisfaction. Au Bon Pain's answer? Incredibly high pay!

Baldor Enriches Its Jobs and Stays Home

Baldor Electric delights in bucking trends. This small company competes against giants like General Electric and Westinghouse in building industrial electric motors. In the 1980s, foreign competition drove most American companies either out of the business or out of the country in search of cheap labor. But Baldor stayed right where it was, in Fort Smith, Arkansas, increasing its market share and, eventually, its profits.

Part of Baldor's success results from a 70-year commitment to building high-quality, efficient motors. During the energy crises of the 1970s other companies rushed to develop motors that didn't waste a watt, but Baldor already had a long-standing reputation for efficiency and superior workmanship. When the flood of Asian motors hit the United States, Baldor didn't try to compete by lowering its prices on standard models but concentrated instead on finding small market niches it could exploit. It can deliver a new type of motor six weeks after it begins the design process.

Behind all this inventiveness, flexibility, and high quality are, of course, Baldor's people, and Baldor knows how to treat them well. The company shares its profits with employees and doesn't lay anyone off. In 1987 Baldor sent all its middle-level managers to Florida for a training program focusing on quality, and it has given most of its other employees similar in-house training.

While other companies were retrenching in the early 1980s, Baldor was developing its "flexible flow" manufacturing system, which keeps workers interested and motivated enough to produce high-quality products. The system eliminated progressive assembly lines and enriched assembly jobs: each worker puts together a complete motor from a tray of parts. A computer printout tells what the motor is, how to put it together, and how to test it. Taking one product from start to finish gives workers a sense of task identity and, because they may assemble as many as twenty different models of motors in one shift, workers are stimulated by the need for a considerable degree of skill variety. Moreover, these workers take personal pride in their company's products. Although Baldor's motors are more expensive than the ones made overseas on assembly lines, Baldor has recently established offices from Singapore to Canada. The company's strongest growth area is now export sales.

Sources: Alan Farnham, "Baldor's Success: Made in the USA," *Fortune* (July 17, 1989): 101–105; Joseph A. Glorioso, "Baldor, Sneaking Up on the Giants," *Industry Week* (February 6, 1984): 43–44; Robert E. Lee, "Baldor Thinks Small, Competes Big," *Purchasing* (May 8, 1986): 59–61.

Store managers earn from $50,000, about twice the industry average, to as much as $165,000 a year based on their contribution to sales and profits. Crew workers, the people who slap the Boursin on the baguette, are paid up to $25,000 a year, but they must work at least 50 hours a week.

The payoff for Au Bon Pain is high productivity, low absenteeism, and reduced training costs because workers stick around longer. Annual turnover of entry-level workers is about 75 percent, vs. over 200 percent industrywide. Since the luncheon crowd seems to care whether restaurant workers remember their names, a stable work force helps Au Bon Pain keep buyers loyal.[42]

In this section, we distinguish between extrinsic and intrinsic rewards, review alternative employee compensation plans, and discuss the effective management of extrinsic rewards.

Members of the United Steelworkers (USW) union take pride in turning iron ore into steel at USX Corporation, even though extrinsic rewards tend to outweigh intrinsic rewards. Therefore, on January 31, 1991, when the USX-USW contract was set to expire, employees were happy to learn that USX's new chairman, Charles A. Corry, was willing to stand up for his employees. Corry agreed to a pay raise and generous cost-of-living and pension increases.

●●●●●●●●●●●●●●●●●

Distinguish extrinsic rewards from intrinsic rewards and list four rules for administering extrinsic rewards effectively.

extrinsic rewards payoffs, such as money, that are granted by others

intrinsic rewards self-granted and internally experienced payoffs, such as a feeling of accomplishment

Extrinsic versus Intrinsic Rewards

There are two different categories of rewards. **Extrinsic rewards** are payoffs granted to the individual by other people. Examples include money, employee benefits, promotions, recognition, status symbols, and praise. The second category is called **intrinsic rewards,** which are self-granted and internally experienced payoffs. Among intrinsic rewards are a sense of accomplishment, self-esteem, and self-actualization.[43] Usually, on-the-job extrinsic and intrinsic rewards are intermingled. For instance, employees often experience a psychological lift when they complete a big project, in addition to reaping material benefits.

Employee Compensation

Compensation plans deserve special attention at this point because money is the universal extrinsic reward. Employee compensation is a complex area fraught with legal and tax implications. Although an exhaustive treatment of employee compensation plans is beyond our present purpose, we can identify major types. Table 12.2 lists and briefly describes ten different pay plans. Two are nonincentive plans, seven qualify as incentive plans, and one additional plan is in a category of its own. Each type of pay plan has advantages and disadvantages. Therefore, there is no single best plan suitable for all employees. Indeed, two experts at the U.S. Bureau of Labor Statistics say the key words in compensation for the next twenty-five years will be "flexible" and "varied."[44] A diverse work force will demand an equally diverse array of compensation plans.

Improving Performance with Extrinsic Rewards

Extrinsic rewards, if they are to motivate job performance effectively, need to be administered in ways that (1) satisfy operative needs, (2) foster positive expectations, (3) ensure equitable distribution, and (4) reward results. Let us see how these four criteria can be met relative to the ten different pay plans in Table 12.2.

Rewards Must Satisfy Individual Needs. Whether it is a pay raise or a pat on the back, a reward has no motivational impact unless it satisfies an operative need. Not all people need the same things, and one person may need different things at different times. Money is a powerful motivator for those who seek security through material wealth. But the promise of more money may mean little to a financially secure person who seeks ego gratification from challenging work. People's needs concerning when and how they want to be paid also vary.

TABLE 12.2 • Guide to Employee Compensation Plans

Pay plan	Description/ calculation	Main advantage	Main disadvantage
Nonincentive			
Hourly wage	Fixed amount per hour worked	Time is easier to measure than performance	Little or no incentive to work hard
Annual salary	Contractual amount per year	Easy to administer	Little or no incentive to work hard
Incentive			
Piece rate	Fixed amount per unit of output	Pay tied directly to personal output	Negative association with sweatshops and rate-cutting abuses
Sales commission	Fixed percentage of sales revenue	Pay tied directly to personal volume of business	Morale problem when sales personnel earn more than other employees
Merit pay	Bonus granted for outstanding performance	Gives salaried employees incentive to work harder	Fairness issue raised when tied to subjective appraisals
Profit sharing	Distribution of specified percentage of bottom-line profits	Individual has a personal stake in firm's profitability	Profits affected by more than just performance (for example, by prices and competition)
Gainsharing	Distribution of specified percentage of productivity gains and/or cost savings	Encourages employees to work harder *and* smarter	Calculations can get cumbersome
Pay-for-knowledge	Salary or wage rates tied to degrees earned or skills mastered	Encourages lifelong learning	Tends to inflate training and labor costs
Stock options	Selected employees earn right to acquire firm's stock free or at a discount	Gives individual personal stake in firm's financial performance	Can be resented by ineligible personnel
Other			
Cafeteria compensation	Employee selects personal mix of benefits from an array of options	Tailored benefits package fits individual needs	Can be costly to administer

cafeteria compensation plan that allows employees to select their own mix of benefits

Because cafeteria compensation is rather special and particularly promising, we shall examine it more closely. **Cafeteria compensation** is a plan that allows each employee to determine the make-up of his or her benefit package. Because today's nonwage benefits sometimes range as high as 50 percent of total compensation, the motivating potential of such a privilege can be sizable.

> *Under these plans, employers provide minimal "core" coverage in life and health insurance, vacations, and pensions. The employee buys additional benefits to suit [his or her] own needs, using credits based on salary, service, and age.*
>
> *The elderly bachelor, for instance, may pass up the maternity coverage he would receive, willy-nilly, under conventional plans and "buy" additional pension contributions instead. The mother whose children are covered by her husband's employee health insurance policy may choose legal and dental care insurance instead.*[45]

Although some organizations have balked at installing cafeteria compensation because of added bookkeeping expense, the number of programs in effect in the United States has grown steadily.[46] Cafeteria compensation represents a revolutionary step toward fitting rewards to people, rather than vice versa.

Employees Must Believe Effort Will Lead to Reward. According to expectancy theory, an employee will not strive for an attractive reward unless it is perceived as being attainable. For example, the promise of an expense-paid trip to Hawaii for the leading salesperson will prompt additional efforts at sales only among those who feel they have a decent chance of winning. Those who believe they have little chance of winning will not be motivated to try any harder than usual. Incentive pay plans, especially merit pay, profit sharing, gainsharing, and stock options, need to be designed and communicated in a way that will foster believable effort-reward linkages.[47]

Rewards Must Be Equitable. Something is equitable if people perceive it to be fair and just. Each of us carries in our head a pair of scales upon which we weigh equity.[48] Figure 12.6 shows one scale for *personal equity* and another for *social equity*. The personal equity scale tests the relationship between effort expended and rewards received. The social equity scale, in contrast, compares our own effort-reward ratio with that of someone else in the same situation. We are motivated to seek personal and social equity and to avoid inequity.[49] An interesting aspect of research on this topic has demonstrated that inequity is perceived by those who are *overpaid* as well as by those who are underpaid.[50] Since perceived inequity is associated with feelings of dissatisfaction and anger, jealousy, or guilt, inequitable reward schemes tend to be counterproductive and are ethically questionable (see Management Ethics).

Rewards Must Be Linked to Performance. Ideally, there should be an if-then relationship between task performance and extrinsic rewards. Traditional hourly wage and annual salary pay plans are weak in this regard. They do little more than reward the person for showing up at work. Managers can strengthen motivation to work by making sure that those who give a little extra get a little extra. In addition to piece-rate and sales-commission plans, merit pay, profit sharing,

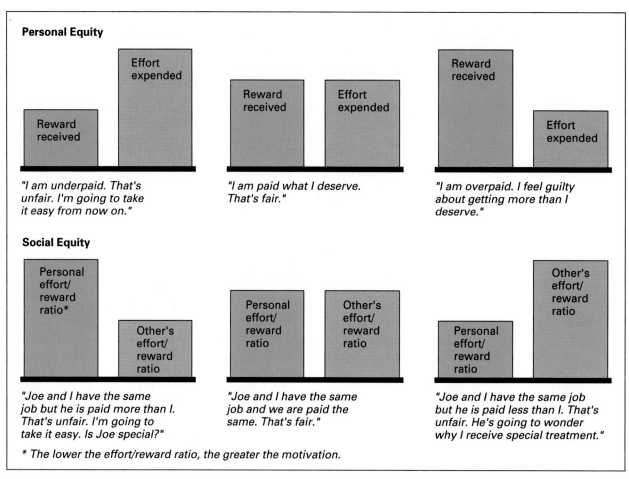

Personal Equity

"I am underpaid. That's unfair. I'm going to take it easy from now on."

"I am paid what I deserve. That's fair."

"I am overpaid. I feel guilty about getting more than I deserve."

Social Equity

"Joe and I have the same job but he is paid more than I. That's unfair. I'm going to take it easy. Is Joe special?"

"Joe and I have the same job and we are paid the same. That's fair."

"Joe and I have the same job but he is paid less than I. That's unfair. He's going to wonder why I receive special treatment."

* The lower the effort/reward ratio, the greater the motivation.

FIGURE 12.6 • Personal and Social Equity

gainsharing, and stock option plans are popular ways of linking pay and performance. There is a trend toward group-based profit sharing and gainsharing to encourage cooperation and teamwork. We now turn our attention to two of these options, merit pay and gainsharing plans.

According to its advocates, merit pay can be used to give salaried personnel an incentive to go that extra mile. But despite claims of the effectiveness of merit pay,[51] research support is lacking. A longitudinal study of a managerial merit-pay plan in the U.S. Social Security Administration found no positive impact on job performance.[52]

Gainsharing plans, described in Table 12.2, include the Scanlon Plan, Improshare®, and the Rucker® Plan.[53] Each involves a calculation for bonuses based on productivity improvements and/or cost savings. Thus, gainsharing plans forge a strong link between performance and rewards. Advocates of gainsharing believe it is superior to traditional profit-sharing programs for at least two basic reasons: (1) gainsharing emphasizes employee participation, whereas profit sharing generally does not; and (2) in large organizations, the link between individual performance and bottom-line profits typically is too weak to have motivational

A *Fair* Day's Pay?

How much is a good CEO worth? The high pay of top executives can create employee distrust and sometimes outright hostility, especially during times of financial hardship. More and more companies are facing the question of how to set ethical pay standards for their top brass.

How can anyone judge whether Walt Disney's Michael Eisner is worth the $40 million in total compensation he received in 1988? One way to make sense of such figures is to compare them with wages earned by the company's lowest paid workers. Does Eisner do work equivalent to that of more than 2,000 people who run rides and pick up trash at Disney World? The question isn't confined to Walt Disney. A 1988 *Business Week* study showed that the average CEO was making 93 times the salary of an average factory worker, 72 times that of a teacher, and 44 times that of an engineer. In 1960, those figures were 41, 38, and 19, respectively. Moreover, executives can now take advantage of many more tax breaks than they could thirty years ago. Whereas in 1960 a CEO could expect to bring home 11 times as much as a teacher, the same CEO's net pay is now equivalent to that of 66 teachers!

Some corporations—including a number of well respected and very successful ones—understand how much resentment such figures can create in employees. They have put a ceiling on the amount their top executives can make. The pretax income of office furniture maker Herman Miller's CEO is limited to 20 times that of the company's manufacturing employees. Ben & Jerry's limits its executives' pay to five times that of its lowest-paid employees. Executives at other companies—including America West Airlines, Southwest Airlines, and Nucor Corporation, a steel company—voluntarily cut their own salaries during economic hard times, demonstrating that sacrifice should start at the top.

Most American corporations still scoff at such ideas and continue to widen the gap between their best- and worst-paid employees. But before too long, such well-paid executives may start getting some of the blame for the problems American companies have competing in the global economy. With American CEOs making twice as much as their European and Japanese counterparts, perhaps they deserve such blame.

Sources: "American CEOs Rake in the Cash—and Worries to Match," *Business Week* (November 12, 1990); John A. Byrne, "Is the Boss Getting Paid Too Much?" *Business Week* (May 1, 1989): 46–52; Alan Farnham, "The Trust Gap," *Fortune* (December 4, 1989): 56–78; Dawn Gilbertson, "Airline Cuts Pay for Key Executives," *The Phoenix Gazette* (January 30, 1991): A1–A2; John A. Byrne, "The Flap Over Executive Pay," *Business Week* (May 6, 1991): 90–96.

impact.[54] It is surprising that more organizations have not installed gainsharing plans; they have a very high approval rating among managers. For example, when 108 managers from eight companies with gainsharing plans were surveyed, 91 percent agreed that their gainsharing plan should be continued. Eighty-two percent would advise other managers to install a similar plan.[55]

All incentive pay plans should be carefully conceived because undesirable behavior may inadvertently be encouraged. Consider, for example, what the head of Nucor Corporation, a successful minimill steel company, had to say about his firm's bonus system:

> *[Nucor's] bonus system . . . is very tough. If you're late even five minutes, you lose your bonus for the day. If you're late more than thirty minutes, or you're absent because of sickness or anything else, you lose your bonus for the week. Now, we do have what we call four "forgiveness" days*

Although Denny Perak (center) is a manager, he isn't a supervisor in the traditional sense. He only coaches this self-managed team at a General Mills factory in Lodi, California; the team manages itself. Perak facilitates its interaction with headquarters. Team members schedule production and operate and maintain the machinery. Productivity has risen 40 percent and the night shift runs smoothly without managers present.

participative management empowering employees to assume greater control of the workplace

• • • • • • • • • • • • • • • • •
Discuss the contributions quality control circles and self-managed teams can make to participative management.

quality control circles voluntary problem-solving groups committed to improving quality and reducing costs

during the year when you can be sick or you have to close on a house or your wife is having a baby. But only four. We have a melter, Phil Johnson, down in Darlington, and one of the workers came in one day and said that Phil had been in an automobile accident and was sitting beside his car off of Route 52, holding his head. So the foreman asked, "Why didn't you stop and help him?" And the guy said, "And lose my bonus?"[56]

Like goals, incentive plans foster selective perception.

Motivation through Employee Participation

While noting that the term *participation* has become a "stewpot" into which every conceivable kind of management fad has been tossed, one management scholar has helpfully identified four key areas of participative management. Employees may participate in (1) setting goals, (2) making decisions, (3) solving problems, and (4) designing and implementing organizational changes.[57] Thus, **participative management** is defined as the process of empowering employees to assume greater control of the workplace. By being personally and meaningfully involved, above and beyond just doing assigned tasks, employees are said to be more motivated and productive (see Figure 12.7). Notice the individual, organizational, and environmental contingency factors. Participation will not work if individual values and attitudes are not in tune with it. Organizational factors such as job design and corporate culture can also help or hinder the process. Finally, environmental factors such as technological change and competition affect the participation process.

This section focuses on two team-oriented approaches to participation. They are quality control circles and self-managed teams. The former are typically found in manufacturing operations, whereas the latter are found in both factory and office settings. These two approaches to employee participation have been singled out for three reasons. First, they mesh well with the trend toward team-based organizations. Second, when executed properly, they have a good track record. Third, they have broad applicability. This section concludes with a discussion of four keys to successful employee participation programs.

Quality Control Circles

Developed in Japan during the early 1960s, this innovation took the U.S. industrial scene by storm during the late 1970s and early 1980s. Today, thousands of quality control circles can be found in hundreds of North American and European companies. **Quality control circles,** commonly referred to as QC circles or simply quality circles, are voluntary problem-solving groups of five to ten employees from the same work area who meet regularly to discuss quality improvement and ways to reduce costs.[58] A weekly one-hour meeting, during company time, is common practice. By relying on *voluntary* participation, QC circles attempt to tap the creative potential every employee possesses. Although QC circles do not work in every situation, benefits such as direct cost savings, improved worker-management relations, and greater individual commitment have been reported.[59]

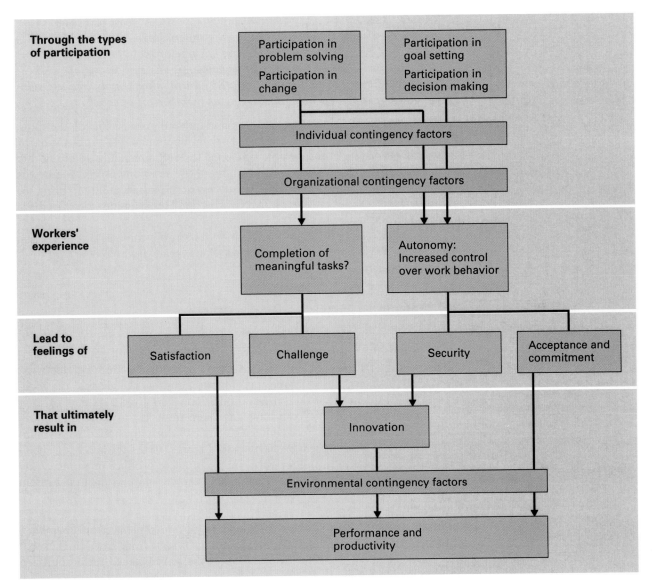

FIGURE 12.7 ● How Participative Management Works

Source: "Participative Management Is an Ethical Imperative," by Marshall Sashkin. Reprinted, by permission of publisher, from *Organizational Dynamics,* Spring 1984 © 1984. American Management Association, New York. All rights reserved.

QC circles should be introduced in evolutionary fashion rather than by management edict. As the following description of Northrop Corporation's successful QC circle program illustrates, training, supportive supervision, and team building are all part of this evolutionary development:

In a well-managed program like Northrop's, team members are given a good dose of training in the basic techniques of problem solving. They learn to gather and analyze data, weed out trivial issues to focus on major ones, generate innovative ideas in brainstorming sessions, forge consensus decisions, and communicate effectively. At least one team member—usually though not always the supervisor—gets extra training in leadership. And any well-run program has one or more people trained as "facilitators," who help the leader organize groups and get people who were accustomed to performing isolated jobs on an assembly line to begin thinking, talking, listening, and caring as members of a team.[60]

The idea is to give those who work day in and day out at a specific job the tools, group support, and opportunity to have a say in nipping quality problems in the bud. Each QC circle is responsible not only for recommending solutions but also for actually implementing and evaluating those solutions. According to one observer, "The invisible force behind the success of QC's is its ability to bring the psychological principles of Maslow, McGregor, and Herzberg into the workplace through a structured process."[61]

QC circles foster employee participation within the confines of the existing power structure. In contrast, self-managed teams create a whole new decentralized power structure.

Self-Managed Teams

According to the logic of this comprehensive approach to participation, self-management is the best management because it taps people's full potential. Advocates say self-management fosters creativity, motivation, and productivity. **Self-managed teams,** also known as autonomous work groups or high-performance work teams, take on traditional managerial tasks as part of their normal work routine.[62] They can have anywhere from five to more than thirty members, depending on the job. Unlike QC circles, which are staffed with volunteers, employees are assigned to self-managed teams. Cross-trained team members typically rotate jobs as they turn out a complete product or service. Any supervision tends to be minimal, with managers acting more as *facilitators* than as order givers.

self-managed teams high-performance teams that assume traditional managerial duties such as staffing and planning

Vertically Loaded Jobs. In the language of job enrichment, team members' jobs are vertically loaded. For example, Cummins Engine company's chief executive officer, Henry B. Schacht, helped pioneer the self-managed team approach in the following manner:

> *Beginning in 1974, after a prolonged strike in Columbus, [Indiana,] Schacht organized assembly workers in teams of ten to thirty people. Each team is responsible for scheduling shifts, ordering materials, and even hiring more workers when necessary. One group reworked its engine-housing line so drastically that it cut costs by 75 percent.*[63]

General Mills has extended the idea of self-managed teams to the point that the night shift in its cereal plant in Lodi, California, runs with no managers at all. Other progressive organizations such as General Foods, Texas Instruments, Corning, General Electric, Boeing, Procter & Gamble, and Volvo have operations built around self-managed teams. *Fortune* quoted the head of Texas Instruments as saying, "No matter what your business, these teams are the wave of the future."[64]

Managerial Resistance. Not surprisingly, managerial resistance is the number one barrier to self-managed teams. More than anything else, self-managed teams represent *change,* and lots of it.

> *Adopting the team approach is no small matter; it means wiping out tiers of managers and tearing down bureaucratic barriers between departments. Yet companies are willing to undertake such radical changes to gain workers' knowledge and commitment—along with productivity gains that exceed 30 percent in some cases.*[65]

Traditional authoritarian supervisors view autonomous teams as a threat to their authority and job security. For this reason, *new* facilities built around the concept of self-managed teams, so-called greenfield sites, tend to fare better than re-worked existing operations.

Hiring, training, and job design need to be skillfully interlocked with self-managed teams, thus driving up front-end costs. Such has been the case at Corning, where more than 3,000 teams are in place companywide. *Business Week* followed the action at Corning's new team-based factory in Blacksburg, Virginia:

> *Corning sorted through 8,000 job applicants and hired 150 with the best problem-solving ability and a willingness to work in a team setting. The majority had finished at least one year of college. They received extensive training in technical and interpersonal skills; in the first year of production, 25 percent of all hours worked were devoted to training, at a cost of about $750,000.*[66]

Managers who take the long view and switch to self-managed teams are finding it well worth the investment of time and money. Self-managed teams even show early promise of boosting productivity in the huge service sector.[67] (Teamwork is discussed in the next chapter.)

Keys to Successful Employee Participation Programs

According to researchers, four factors build the *employee* support necessary for any sort of participation program to work:

1. A profit-sharing or gainsharing plan.
2. A long-term employment relationship with good job security.
3. A concerted effort to build and maintain group cohesiveness.
4. Protection of the individual employee's rights.[68]

Working in combination, these factors help explain motivational success stories such as Lincoln Electric's, in our chapter-opening case.

It should be clear by now that participative management involves more than simply announcing a new program, such as quality control circles. To make sure a supportive climate exists, a good deal of background work often needs to be done. This is particularly important in view of the conclusion drawn by researchers who analyzed forty-one participative management studies:

> *Participation has . . . [a positive] effect on both satisfaction and productivity, and its effect on satisfaction is somewhat stronger than its*

effect on productivity.... Our analysis indicates specific organizational factors that may enhance or constrain the effect of participation. For example, there is evidence that a participative climate has a more substantial effect on workers' satisfaction than participation in specific decisions.[69]

In the end, effective participative management is as much a managerial attitude about sharing power as it is a specific set of practices. In some European countries, such as Germany, the supportive climate is reinforced by government-mandated participative management.

Other Motivation Techniques for a Diverse Work Force

Work force diversity has made "flexibility" a must for managers in the 1990s and beyond. This chapter concludes with a look at ways of accommodating emerging employee needs. By meeting these needs in creative ways, such as flexible work schedules, family support services, and sabbaticals, managers can hope to enhance motivation and job performance.

Flexible Work Schedules

flextime allows employees to choose their own arrival and departure times within specified limits

The standard 8 a.m. to 5 p.m., forty-hour workweek has come under fire as single parents and others attempt to juggle hectic schedules. Taking its place is **flextime,** a work-scheduling plan that allows employees to determine their own arrival and departure times within specified limits.[70] All employees must be present during a fixed core time (see the center portion of Figure 12.8). If an eight-hour day is required, as in Figure 12.8, an early bird can put in the required eight hours by arriving at 7:00 a.m., taking a half-hour for lunch, and departing at 3:30 p.m. Alternatively, a late starter can come in at 9:00 a.m. and leave at 5:30 p.m.

Benefits. In addition to many anecdotal reports citing the benefits of flextime, research studies have uncovered promising evidence. Among the documented benefits of flextime are:

- better employee-supervisor relations
- reduced absenteeism
- selective positive impact on job performance (a 24 percent improvement for computer programmers over a two-year period but no effect on the performance of data-entry workers).[71]

Flextime, though generally popular among employees because of the degree of freedom it brings, is not appropriate for all situations. Problems reported by adopters include greater administrative expense, supervisory resistance, and inadequate coverage of jobs.

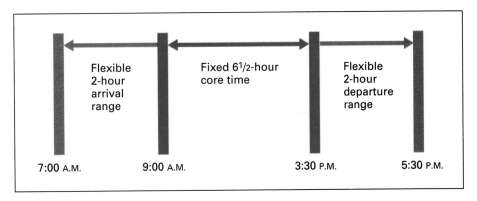

FIGURE 12.8 • Flextime in Action

Alternatives. Other work-scheduling innovations include *compressed work-weeks* (forty hours in fewer than five days) and *permanent part-time* (workweeks with fewer than forty hours). *Job sharing* (complementary scheduling that allows two or more part-timers to share a single full-time job), yet another work-scheduling innovation, is growing in popularity among employers of working mothers. Steelcase Inc., the Grand Rapids, Michigan, office furniture maker, responded favorably to a joint résumé from Anne Saliers and Peggy Hoogerhyde. Both women have preschoolers at home and wanted to work two or three days a week.

> *Saliers and Hoogerhyde each work two days a week and alternate Fridays, preparing presentations for customer groups and working with sales representatives from the field. "We do most of our coordination by phone, or leave messages for each other," says Saliers.*[72]

Considering that the standard forty-hour, five-day workweek has been a prominent feature on the American workscape for nearly a half century, these alternative work schedules represent a significant accommodation to individual needs and circumstances. Naturally, employers expect a motivational return for this sort of accommodation.

Family Support Services

With dual-income families and single parents caught between obligations to family and the job, companies are increasingly coming to the rescue. Parenting and working are no longer viewed by employers as totally independent roles. In a recent survey of 259 major U.S. companies, 56 percent provided some type of assistance with child day care. (Some 47 percent offered financial help, but only 9 percent provided company-sponsored child-care facilities.[73]) Fifty-six percent offered the opportunity for flexible work schedules. Seventy-seven percent provided employee assistance programs (recall our discussion of EAPs in Chapter 10). Forty-two percent of the polled firms provided unpaid parental leave; only 5 percent provided *paid* parental leave. Fourteen percent provided adoption benefits (typically $2,000 per adopted child). Elder care reportedly was just beginning to receive corporate attention. (See Insights & Issues.)

Stride Rite Sets the Pace in Corporate Day Care

In 1971, Arnold Hiatt, CEO of Stride Rite, made a radical move. He started the first corporate, on-site, day-care center at his Cambridge, Massachusetts, shoe company. Such an idea seems commonplace now only because other companies have followed Stride Rite's lead. But Hiatt, not content with his past innovations, recently added a new twist to his center: it now cares for dependent elderly as well as the young.

The idea is simple and ancient. Children and dependent elderly share many needs—such as supervision, sturdy furniture, and amusement. The two age groups also have much to offer each other. Children bring vitality and change into the lives of people who can no longer move about as they'd like to. Older people have their years of accumulated patience, knowledge, and skills that they can use to teach or entertain young children. Throughout history, the two age groups have lived in the same household and have mixed naturally. But in modern American culture, with its tendency to isolate the very old and the very young, bringing them together is a startling idea.

Stride Rite spent three years and $700,000 to create its new center, which has room for 55 children and 24 elderly people. The two groups have separate wings—with gym equipment for the kids and a library for the elders' discussions—but they can meet in a common area for stories, reading aloud, and eating.

Like many new ideas, elder care has caught on slowly, but Hiatt isn't nervous. Day care wasn't an instant hit either. Hiatt believes that he and his company have a responsibility to their employees and to their community, and he knows that 40 percent of the American workforce currently takes care of both children and aging parents. The older people will come.

Hiatt's innovations are tremendous motivators. His proactive responses to the increasing diversity of his employees show workers that their company cares. Grateful employees who take advantage of the company day care save time and worry and feel a loyalty and a commitment to their company that no amount of motivational training could instill. The maker of Keds and other "old-fashioned" shoes, Stride Rite no longer tries to keep up with Nike and Reebok. But in some ways, it may be miles ahead.

Sources: Barbara Hetzer, "Old Friends," *Business Month* (August 1990): 48–51; Barbara Kantrowitz, "Day Care: Bridging the Generation Gap," *Newsweek* (July 16, 1990): 52; Patti Watts, "A Giant Step for Day Care at Stride Rite," *Executive Female* (July-August 1990): 9, 30.

Sabbaticals

Several companies, including IBM, Apple, Intel, and McDonald's, give selected employees paid sabbaticals after a certain number of years of service. Two to six months of paid time off gives the employee time for family, recreation, and travel. The idea is to refresh long-term employees and hopefully bolster their motivation and loyalty in the process.[74]

Summary

Motivation is an important area of study for managers because it helps them better understand our most valuable resource, people. Much of Japan's economic success can be attributed to how Japanese managers effectively motivate employees. But motivation alone does not guarantee good performance; ability to get the job done is also necessary.

Among alternative motivation theories, Maslow's needs hierarchy theory, Herzberg's two-factor theory, expectancy theory, and goal-setting theory stand out as particularly relevant for managers. Maslow's five-level needs hierarchy, although empirically criticized, makes it clear to managers that people are motivated by emerging rather than fulfilled needs. Assuming that job satisfaction and performance are positively related, Herzberg believes that the most that wages and working conditions can do is eliminate sources of dissatisfaction. According to Herzberg, the key to true satisfaction, and hence motivation, is an enriched job that provides an opportunity for achievement, responsibility, and personal growth.

Expectancy theory is based on the idea that the strength of one's motivation to work is the product of perceived probabilities of acquiring personally valued rewards. Both effort-performance and performance-reward probabilities are important to expectancy theory. Goals can be an effective motivational tool when they are specific, difficult, participatively set, and accompanied by feedback on performance. Goals motivate performance by directing attention, encouraging effort and persistence, and prompting goal-attainment strategies and action plans.

Depending on how it is designed, a job can either hamper or promote personal growth and satisfaction. Although historically a key to higher productivity, specialization of labor has been associated with costly human problems in recent years. Managers attempting to counter the specialization dilemma have the option of fitting people to jobs or fitting jobs to people. The first option includes realistic job previews, job rotation, and limited exposure. Managers who pursue the second option, fitting jobs to people, can either enlarge or enrich jobs. Job enrichment vertically loads jobs to meet individual needs for meaningfulness, responsibility, and knowledge of results. Personal desire for growth and a supportive climate must exist for job enrichment to be successful.

Both extrinsic (externally granted) and intrinsic (self-granted) rewards, when properly administered, can have a positive impact on performance and satisfaction. There is no single best employee compensation plan. A flexible and varied approach to compensation will be necessary in the coming years because of workforce diversity. The following rules can help managers maximize the motivational impact of extrinsic rewards: (1) rewards must satisfy individual needs, (2) one must believe that effort will lead to reward, (3) rewards must be equitable, and (4) rewards must be linked to performance. Gainsharing plans have great motivational potential because they emphasize participation and link pay to actual productivity.

Participative management programs foster direct employee involvement in one or more of the following areas: goal setting, decision making, problem solving, and change implementation. Quality control circles and self-managed teams are appropriate participative techniques in today's team-based organizations. Profit sharing or gainsharing, job security, cohesiveness, and protection of employee rights are keys to building crucial employee support for participation programs.

A diverse workforce requires diverse motivational techniques. Flextime, a flexible work-scheduling scheme that allows employees to choose their own arrival and departure times, has been effective in improving employee-supervisor relations while reducing absenteeism. Employers are increasingly providing family support services such as child day care and elder care, parental leaves, and adoption benefits. Employee sabbaticals are offered by some companies.

Terms to Understand

Motivation	Job enrichment
Expectancy theory	Rewards
Expectancy	Extrinsic rewards
Goal setting	Intrinsic rewards
Job design	Cafeteria compensation
Realistic job previews	Participative management
Job rotation	Quality control circles
Contingent time off (CTO)	Self-managed teams
Job enlargement	Flextime

Questions for Discussion

1. Relative to Figure 12.1, which of the following factors is the most powerful motivator for you? (a) challenging and interesting work, (b) rewards, (c) opportunity for participation and self-management.

2. How could self-actualization get one into trouble at work?

3. What did you like most about the best job you ever had? Does your answer conform to Herzberg's theory? Explain.

4. Which motivation theory—Maslow's, Herzberg's, expectancy, or goal setting—do you feel has the most practical value for today's managers?

5. Why would job enrichment probably be more appealing to you than job enlargement?

6. Which of the compensation plans in Table 12.2 would you like to work under? Why? Would you select a different one if you were a manager choosing a compensation plan for your organization? Explain.

7. Why is equity an important consideration when developing a reward plan?

8. What are the comparative advantages and disadvantages of QC circles and self-managed teams? Which is the more promising motivational tool?

9. Why do you think some organizations would not adopt flextime?

10. How would you respond to a manager who says, "Companies have no business providing child day care facilities."

Back to the Opening Case

Now that you have read Chapter 12, you should be able to answer the following questions about the Lincoln Electric case.

1. Drawing upon the motivation theory, research, and practice discussed in this chapter, can you explain why Lincoln Electric's motivation program is so effective?

2. Which particular aspect of Lincoln Electric's approach to motivating job performance is most critical to its success?

3. Relative to the four criteria for a properly administered extrinsic reward program, how does Lincoln Electric's reward system stack up? Explain.

4. How would you respond to the following comment? "People aren't motivated by money."

5. Do intrinsic rewards play any role in this case? Explain.

Teams Replace the Assembly Line at Sweden's Volvo

Ever since Henry Ford brought mass production techniques to car manufacturing in 1914, almost all cars have been put together on a moving assembly line. Over the years, the lines have become more efficient, but the workers' tasks have tended to get more specialized, repetitive, and tedious. Workers get bored if their work cycle is short—if they repeat the same operations every minute or two. The quality of their work tends to be low, whereas their absenteeism and turnover rates are high.

In trying to reduce the 20 percent absenteeism and 30 percent turnover rates in its Swedish plants, Volvo—Sweden's leading car maker—is gradually eliminating assembly lines. It is effectively turning back the clock to a time when vehicles were made one at a time by craftspeople. In the mid-1970s at Kalmar, Sweden, Volvo built a plant that replaced assembly lines with computer-guided carriers that travel to groups of fifteen to twenty employees who add on large sections of the car. The work cycles at Kalmar average 30 minutes, and the company claims that Kalmar workers are more productive than workers at more conventional assembly plants. But absenteeism rates at Kalmar are still high.

While the rest of the world was coming to admire and learn from the Kalmar plant, Volvo was building an even more revolutionary plant in Uddevalla, Sweden. To demonstrate the new plant's capabilities, Volvo's president, Roger Holtback, assembled a car at Uddevalla all by himself in 1987 and drove it off when he was finished.

Despite Holtback's demonstration, the work teams at Uddevalla have not yet shrunk to just one person. Eight to ten people work in each group, and the group assembles four cars per shift. A worker normally performs the same task only once every three hours or so, and each worker should eventually learn how to do half the tasks necessary to build the whole car. The entire factory is divided into six assembly stations, each with eight work teams. The teams handle most of their own scheduling, hiring, and quality control decisions, eliminating the need for most supervisors. The team spokesperson—a post passed on to another team member each month—reports to one of the six plant managers, who reports directly to the president of the factory. Perhaps most important, the team constantly modifies and adjusts its own procedures, using the plant's high-tech machines as tools, rather than being controlled by the machines. Unlike most modern car-assembly plants, the Uddevalla plant has only one robot, which installs windshields.

Volvo insists that "we're not doing this because we are nice guys"* but because cars assembled at Uddevalla have fewer quality problems and require fewer hours of labor than cars assembled at Volvo's traditional factories. But clearly one of the motivations for designing such a factory was to deal with Sweden's unique labor situation. The Swedish unemployment rate is below 2 percent. Because most workers are well-trained and highly educated, they tend to get dissatisfied quickly in traditional factories, where one-third of the workers quit yearly. Taxes eat up 70 percent of workers' overtime pay, so extra pay alone doesn't motivate many workers.

Therefore to staff its factory and keep its reputation for high-quality products, Volvo had to find a way to attract good workers and keep them interested. It carefully assembles each team: at least one-quarter of the team must be 20 to 25 years old and one-quarter over 45. Forty percent of the team members must be women. The company has even designed special power tools to fit women's smaller hands.

So far, the Uddevalla experiment seems to be working. Morale is high, and absenteeism is only 8 percent, less than half the rate at Volvo's other plants. American workers may also one day find themselves working in such teams if American auto manufacturers become convinced that the Uddevalla method is efficient, not just humane.

For Discussion

1. What role does job enrichment play in this case? Have the auto assembly jobs been vertically or horizontally loaded?

2. Are intrinsic rewards an important part of Volvo's motivational program? Explain.

3. Would a gainsharing plan be likely to have a positive motivational impact at the new Uddevalla plant? Explain.

4. Do Volvo's auto assembly teams qualify as self-managed teams, or are they merely QC circles?

5. Would Volvo's new team program work in the United States (or any other particular country you might choose)? Explain your reasoning.

* Quoted in Jonathan Kapstein, "Volvo's Radical New Plant: 'The Death of the Assembly Line'?" *Business Week* (August 28, 1989): 92–93.

References

Opening Quotation. Keith Davis, Human Behavior at Work: *Organizational Behavior*, 6th ed. (New York: McGraw-Hill, 1981), p. 2.

Opening Case. Kent R. Davies, "Is Individual Responsibility a Radical Idea in American Business?" *Training* (November 1988): 63–65; Toni A. Perry, "Staying with the Basics," *HRMagazine* (November 1990): 73–76; Bruce G. Posner, "Right from the Start," *Inc.* (August 1988): 95–96.

Closing Case. Richard Johnson, "Volvo's New Assembly Plant Has No Assembly Line," *Automotive News* (July 10, 1989): 22–24; Jonathan Kapstein, "Volvo's Radical New Plant: 'The Death of the Assembly Line'?" *Business Week* (August 28, 1989): 92–93; Norman Mayersohn, "Volvo's Alternate Route," *Automotive Industries* (November 1989): 58–60; Jennifer Reese, "Saab and Volvo Hit a Pothole in the U.S.," *Fortune* (March 25, 1991): 16.

1. John Hoerr, "The Payoff From Teamwork," *Business Week* (July 10, 1989): 60.

2. See James B. Treece, "Shaking Up Detroit," *Business Week* (August 14, 1989): 74–80; and Edmund Faltermayer, "Is 'Made In U.S.A.' Fading Away?" *Fortune* (September 24, 1990): 62–73.

3. A very good overview of motivation theory may be found in Terence R. Mitchell, "Motivation: New Directions for Theory, Research, and Practice," *Academy of Management Review*, 7 (January 1982): 80–88. Also see Martin G. Evans, "Organizational Behavior: The Central Role of Motivation," *Journal of Management*, 12 (Summer 1986): 203–222; and Raymond A. Katzell and Donna E. Thompson, "Work Motivation: Theory and Practice," *American Psychologist*, 45 (February 1990): 144–153.

4. For an excellent historical and conceptual treatment of basic motivation theory, see Richard M. Steers and Lyman W. Porter, *Motivation and Work Behavior*, 5th ed. (New York: McGraw-Hill, 1991), chap. 1.

5. See A. H. Maslow, "A Theory of Human Motivation," *Psychological Review,* 50 (July 1943): 370–396.

6. For a revealing study of what managers think about management theory, see M. T. Matteson, "Some Reported Thoughts on Significant Management Literature," *Academy of Management Journal,* 17 (1974): 386–389.

7. Maslow, "A Theory of Human Motivation," p. 375.

8. Data from Christine Gorman, "Can't Afford To Get Sick," *Time* (August 21, 1989): 43.

9. Data from Edmund Faltermayer, "How To Close the Health Care Gap," *Fortune* (May 21, 1990): 123–134. Also see Frank Swoboda, "Reforming a Cure That's Become Worse Than the Disease," *The Washington Post National Weekly Edition* (February 25-March 3, 1991): 19.

10. An organizational model of self-esteem is presented in Jon L. Pierce, Donald G. Gardner, Larry L. Cummings, and Randall B. Dunham, "Organization-Based Self-Esteem: Construct Definition, Measurement, and Validation," *Academy of Management Journal,* 32 (September 1989): 622–648.

11. Maslow, "A Theory of Human Motivation," p. 382.

12. George W. Cherry, "The Serendipity of the Fully Functioning Manager," *Sloan Management Review,* 17 (Spring 1976): 73.

13. Vance F. Mitchell and Pravin Moudgill, "Measurement of Maslow's Need Hierarchy," *Organizational Behavior and Human Performance,* 16 (August 1976): 348.

14. For example, see Mahmoud A. Wahba and Lawrence G. Bridwell, "Maslow Reconsidered: A Review of Research on the Need Hierarchy Theory," *Organizational Behavior and Human Performance,* 15 (April 1976): 212–240; Ellen L. Betz, "Two Tests of Maslow's Theory of Need Fulfillment," *Journal of Vocational Behavior,* 24 (April 1984): 204–220.

15. Edward E. Lawler, *Motivation in Work Organizations* (Monterey, Calif.: Brooks/Cole, 1973), p. 34.

16. See Frederick Herzberg, Bernard Mausner, and Barbara Bloch Snyderman, *The Motivation to Work,* 2nd ed. (New York: Wiley, 1959).

17. Frederick Herzberg, "One More Time: How Do You Motivate Employees?" *Harvard Business Review,* 46 (January-February 1968): 56.

18. For details, see Victor H. Vroom, *Work and Motivation* (New York: Wiley, 1964), p. 186.

19. See Robert J. House and Lawrence A. Wigdor, "Herzberg's Dual-Factor Theory of Job Satisfaction and Motivation: A Review of the Evidence and a Criticism," *Personnel Psychology,* 20 (1967): 369–389.

20. For example, see J. Richard Hackman and Lyman W. Porter, "Expectancy Theory Predictions of Work Effectiveness," *Organizational Behavior and Human Performance,* 3 (November 1968): 417–426; Peter W. Hom, "Expectancy Prediction of Reenlistment in the National Guard," *Journal of Vocational Behavior,* 16 (April 1980): 235–248; John P. Wanous, Thomas L. Keon, and Janina C. Latack, "Expectancy Theory and Occupational/Organizational Choices: A Review and Test," *Organizational Behavior and Human Performance,* 32 (August 1983): 66–86.

21. See Robert D. Pritchard, Philip L. Roth, Steven D. Jones, Patricia J. Galgay, and Margaret D. Watson, "Designing a Goal-Setting System to Enhance Performance: A Practical Guide," *Organizational Dynamics,* 17 (Summer 1988): 69–78.

22. See, for example, Edwin A. Locke and Gary P. Latham, *Goal Setting: A Motivational Technique That Works!* (Englewood Cliffs, N.J.: Prentice-Hall, 1984).

23. See, for example, Edwin A. Locke, Keryll N. Shaw, Lise M. Saari, and Gary P. Latham, "Goal Setting and Task Performance: 1969–1980," *Psychological Bulletin,* 90 (July 1981): 125–152; and Anthony J. Mento, Robert P. Steel, and Ronald J. Karren, "A Meta-Analytic Study of the Effects of Goal Setting on Task Performance: 1966–1984," *Organizational Behavior and Human Decision Processes,* 39 (February 1987): 52–83.

24. See Christopher Earley, Gregory B. Northcraft, Cynthia Lee, and Terri R. Lituchy, "Impact of Process and Outcome Feedback on the Relation of Goal Setting to Task Performance," *Academy of Management Journal,* 33 (March 1990): 87–105.

25. Ronald Henkoff, "Cost Cutting: How To Do It Right," *Fortune* (April 9, 1990): 48.

26. Stephen Phillips and Amy Dunkin, "King Customer," *Business Week* (March 12, 1990): 91.

27. Adapted from J. Richard Hackman, "The Design Of Work in the 1980s," *Organizational Dynamics,* 7 (Summer 1978): 3–17. An instructive four-way analysis of job design may be found in Michael A. Campion and Paul W. Thayer, "Job Design: Approaches, Outcomes, and Trade-offs," *Organizational Dynamics,* 15 (Winter 1987): 66–79.

28. For more details, see John P. Wanous, "Effects of a Realistic Job Preview on Job Acceptance, Job Attitudes, and Job Survival," *Journal of Applied Psychology,* 58 (December 1973): 327–332.

29. See Stephen L. Premack and John P. Wanous, "A Meta-Analysis of Realistic Job Preview Experiments," *Journal of Applied Psychology,* 70 (November 1985): 706–719. Also see James A. Breaugh, "Realistic Job Previews: A Critical Appraisal and Future Research Direction," *Academy of Management Review,* 8 (October 1982): 612–619; and John P. Wanous, "Installing a Realistic Job Preview: Ten Tough Choices," *Personnel Psychology,* 42 (Spring 1989): 117–134.

30. For examples of job rotation, see Norm Alster, "What Flexible Workers Can Do," *Fortune* (February 13, 1989): 62–66.

31. See Lee Smith, "The FBI Is a Tough Outfit To Run," *Fortune* (October 9, 1989): 133–140.

32. See M. A. Howell, "Time Off as a Reward for Productivity," *Personnel Administration,* 34 (November-December 1971): 48–51.

33. Fred Luthans and Robert Kreitner, *Organizational Behavior Modification and Beyond: An Operant and Social Learning Approach* (Glenview, Ill.: Scott, Foresman, 1985), p. 192. Also see Diane L. Lockwood and Fred Luthans, "Contingent Time Off: A Nonfinancial Incentive for Improving Productivity," *Management Review,* 73 (July 1984): 48–52.

34. Data from Carla O'Dell and Jerry McAdams, "The Revolution in Employee Rewards," *Management Review,* 76 (March 1987): 30–33.

35. J. Richard Hackman and Greg R. Oldham, *Work Redesign* (Reading, Mass.: Addison-Wesley, 1980), p. 20.

36. David Kirkpatrick, "How Safe Are Video Terminals?" *Fortune* (August 29, 1988): 71.

37. See J. Barton Cunningham and Ted Eberle, "A Guide to Job Enrichment and Redesign," *Personnel,* 67 (February 1990): 56–61; and Joe G. Thomas and Ricky W. Griffin, "The Power of Social Information in the Workplace," *Organizational Dynamics,* 18 (Autumn 1989): 63–75.

38. Phillips and Dunkin, "King Customer," p. 91.

39. Hackman and Oldham, *Work Redesign,* pp. 78–80.

40. Two classic job enrichment success stories may be found in Robert N. Ford, "Job Enrichment Lessons from AT&T," *Harvard Business Review,* 51 (January-February 1973): 96–106; Pehr G. Gyllenhammar, "How Volvo Adapts Work to People," *Harvard Business Review,* 55 (July-August 1977): 102–113.

41. Informative critiques of job enrichment may be found in William E. Reif and Fred Luthans, "Does Job Enrichment Really Pay Off?" *California Management Review,* 15 (Fall 1972): 30–37; Mitchell Fein, "Job Enrichment: A Reevaluation," *Sloan Management Review,* 16 (Winter 1974): 69–88.

42. Patricia Sellers, "What Customers Really Want," *Fortune* (June 4, 1990): 60.

43. An interesting discussion of intrinsic motivation can be found in Kenneth W. Thomas and Betty A. Velthouse, "Cognitive Elements of Empowerment: An 'Interpretive' Model of Intrinsic Task Motivation," *Academy of Management Review,* 15 (October 1990): 666–681.

44. See George L. Stelluto and Deborah P. Klein, "Compensation Trends into the 21st Century," *Monthly Labor Review,* 113 (February 1990): 38–45. Also see Luis R. Gomez-Mejia, David B. Balkin, and George T. Milkovich, "Rethinking Rewards For Technical Employees," *Organizational Dynamics,* 18 (Spring 1990): 62–75; and Carla O'Dell, "Team Play, Team Pay—New Ways of Keeping Score," *Across the Board,* 26 (November 1989): 38–45.

45. "Companies Offer Benefits Cafeteria-Style," *Business Week* (November 13, 1978): 116.

46. See Betty A. Iseri and Robert R. Cangemi, "Flexible Benefits: A Growing Option," *Personnel,* 67 (March 1990): 30–32; Aric T. Wilt, "Cafeteria Plans Help Meet Needs & Control Costs," *Management Review,* 79 (September 1990): 43–46; and Richard Gisonny and Steven Fein, "Better Benefits Emerge From Tax-Wise Choices," *HRMagazine,* 36 (February 1991): 36–39.

47. See Steven Waldman, "Grading 'Merit Pay'," *Newsweek* (November 14, 1988): 45–46; and Nancy J. Perry, "Here Come Richer, Riskier Pay Plans," *Fortune* (December 19, 1988): 50–58.

48. See Marshall Sashkin and Richard L. Williams, "Does Fairness Make a Difference?" *Organizational Dynamics,* 19 (Autumn 1990): 56–71.

49. A good overview of equity theory can be found in Robert P. Vecchio, "Models of Psychological Inequity," *Organizational Behavior and Human Performance,* 34 (October 1984): 266–282.

50. See J. Stacy Adams and Patricia R. Jacobsen, "Effects of Wage Inequities on Work Quality," *Journal of Abnormal and Social Psychology,* 69 (1964): 19–25; Jerald Greenberg and Suzyn Ornstein, "High Status Job Title as Compensation for Underpayment: A Test of Equity Theory," *Journal of Applied Psychology,* 68 (May 1983): 285–297.

51. For example, see Frederick S. Hills, Robert M. Madigan, K. Dow Scott, and Steven E. Markham, "Tracking the Merit of Merit Pay," *Personnel Administrator,* 32 (March 1987): 50–57.

52. Details of this study may be found in Jone L. Pearce, William B. Stevenson, and James L. Perry,

"Managerial Compensation Based on Organizational Performance: A Time Series Analysis of the Effects of Merit Pay," *Academy of Management Journal,* 28 (June 1985): 261–278.

53. See Gary W. Florkowski, "Analyzing Group Incentive Plans," *HRMagazine,* 35 (January 1990): 36–38; Prescot Behn, "An Answer to the Japanese Challenge," *HRMagazine,* 35 (August 1990): 76–79.

54. For a comprehensive update on gainsharing, see Brian Graham-Moore and Timothy L. Ross, *Gainsharing: Plans For Improving Performance* (Washington, D.C.: Bureau of National Affairs, 1990); and Charles R. Gowen, III, "Gainsharing Programs: An Overview of History and Research," *Journal of Organizational Behavior Management,* 11, No. 2 (1990): 77–99.

55. Data from Larry Hatcher and Timothy L. Ross, "Gainsharing Plans—How Managers Evaluate Them," *Business,* 36 (October-December 1986): 30–37.

56. See Marshall Sashkin, "Participative Management Is an Ethical Imperative," *Organizational Dynamics,* 12 (Spring 1984): 4–22. Also see Dean Tjosvold, "Participation: A Close Look at Its Dynamics," *Journal of Management,* 13 (Winter 1987): 739–750; and Nicholas Baloff and Elizabeth M. Doherty, "Potential Pitfalls in Employee Participation," *Organizational Dynamics,* 17 (Winter 1989): 51–62.

57. George Gendron, "Steel Man: Ken Iverson," *Inc.* (April 1986): 47–48.

58. For a good introduction to QC circles, see Ed Yager, "Examining the Quality Control Circle," *Personnel Journal,* 58 (October 1979): 682–684, 708. Also see Edward E. Lawler III and Susan A. Mohrman, "Quality Circles: After the Honeymoon," *Organizational Dynamics,* 15 (Spring 1987): 42–54; and Gerald E. Ledford, Jr., Edward E. Lawler III, and Susan A. Mohrman, "The Quality Circle and Its Variations," in *Productivity in Organizations,* ed. John P. Campbell, Richard J. Campbell, and Associates (San Francisco: Jossey-Bass, 1988), pp. 255–294.

59. Evidence of a positive long-term impact on productivity may be found in Mitchell L. Marks, Philip H. Mirvis, Edward J. Hackett, and James F. Grady, Jr., "Employee Participation in a Quality Circle Program: Impact on Quality of Work Life, Productivity, and Absenteeism," *Journal of Applied Psychology,* 71 (February 1986): 61–69. Also see James S. Bowman, "Quality Circles: Promise, Problems, and Prospects in Florida," *Public Personnel Management,* 18 (Winter 1989): 375–403.

60. Charles G. Burck, "What Happens When Workers Manage Themselves," *Fortune* (July 27, 1981): 64.

61. Frank Shipper, "Tapping Creativity," *Quality Circles Journal,* 4 (August 1981): 12. Also see Richard Koenig, "Quality Circles Are Vulnerable to Union Tests," *The Wall Street Journal* (March 28, 1990): B1.

62. See, for example, Chris Lee, "Beyond Teamwork," *Training,* 27 (June 1990): 25–32; and Charles C. Manz, David E. Keating, and Anne Donnellon, "Preparing For an Organizational Change to Employee Self-Management: The Managerial Transition," *Organizational Dynamics,* 19 (Autumn 1990): 15–26.

63. Louis Therrien, "Mr. Rust Belt," *Business Week* (October 17, 1988): 78. Also see Robert H. Guest, "Team Management Under Stress," *Across the Board,* 26 (May 1989): 30–35.

64. Brian Dumaine, "Who Needs a Boss?" *Fortune* (May 7, 1990): 52.

65. Hoerr, "The Payoff from Teamwork," 57.

66. John Hoerr, "Sharpening Minds for a Competitive Edge," *Business Week* (December 17, 1990): 72.

67. See John Hoerr, "Work Teams Can Rev Up Paper-Pushers, Too," *Business Week* (November 28, 1988): 64–72.

68. Adapted from David I. Levine, "Participation, Productivity, and the Firm's Environment," *California Management Review,* 32 (Summer 1990): 86–100.

69. Katherine I. Miller and Peter R. Monge, "Participation, Satisfaction, and Productivity: A Meta-Analytic Review," *Academy of Management Journal,* 29 (December 1986): 748.

70. For an extensive treatment of flextime and other work scheduling alternatives, see Allan R. Cohen and Herman Gadon, *Alternative Work Schedules: Integrating Individual and Organizational Needs* (Reading, Mass.: Addison-Wesley, 1978). Also see David A. Ralston, "The Benefits of Flextime: Real or Imagined?" *Journal of Organizational Behavior,* 10 (October 1989): 369–373; and David A. Ralston, "How Flexitime Eases Work/Family Tensions," *Personnel,* 67 (August 1990): 45–48.

71. Data from V. K. Narayanan and Raghu Nath, "A Field Test of Some Attitudinal and Behavioral Consequences of Flextime," *Journal of Applied Psychology,* 67 (April 1982): 214–218; David A. Ralston, William P. Anthony, and David J. Gustafson, "Employees May Love Flextime, But What Does It Do to the Organization's Productivity?" *Journal of Applied Psychology,* 70 (May 1985): 272–279.

72. Jane Easter Bahls, "Two For One: A Working Idea," *Nation's Business* (June 1989): 28.

73. Data from Norma R. Fritz, "Help for Working Parents," *Personnel,* 67 (September 1990); *HR Focus Supplement,* pp. 1–2.

74. See Lucia Landon, "Pump Up Your Employees," *HRMagazine,* 36 (May 1990): 34–37; and Carolyn Hughes Crowley, " 'Jones, Take Six Months Off' " *The Christian Science Monitor* (August 20, 1990): 14.

13

Group Dynamics and Teamwork

Trust is the highest form of human motivation. It brings out the very best in people. But it takes time and patience, and it doesn't preclude the necessity to train and develop people so that their competency can rise to the level of that trust.

STEPHEN R. COVEY

CHAPTER OBJECTIVES

When you finish studying this chapter, you should be able to

- Define the term *group*.
- Explain the significance of cohesiveness, roles, norms, and ostracism in regard to the behavior of group members.
- Identify and briefly describe the six stages of group development.
- Define organizational politics and summarize relevant research insights.
- Explain how groupthink can lead to blind conformity.
- Discuss the criteria and determinants of team effectiveness.
- Explain why trust is a key ingredient of teamwork and discuss what management can do to build trust.

Slugging It Out at Pillsbury

To the public, Pillsbury Co. is a familiar friendly giant, as American as the entrants in its famous annual bake-off. Founded in 1869 in Minneapolis, Pillsbury has for most of its history been run by members of the Pillsbury clan. Its products include those "ho-ho-ho" vegetables from Green Giant, Burger King's fast-food fare, and virtually everything that can be made from flour, the company's original product. Its advertising symbol is the Pillsbury Doughboy, a squishy little man with a childish laugh. But behind this warm and friendly front, Pillsbury has spent the last two decades being managed by a succession of men who seem to have ignored the managerial lessons of the last thirty years and who have left Pillsbury with an internal sense of distrust and political intrigue that may haunt it for years.

William H. Spoor ran the company from 1973 to 1985. During this time of tremendous expansion, the company bought and sold any number of other firms and even had a vice president of mergers and acquisitions. Under Spoor, both the company's sales and its profits increased roughly five-fold. Although Pillsbury's success during these years may be a testament to Spoor's strength and decisiveness as a leader, he was also famous for his ego and his temper. The former director of investor relations remembers hiding under his desk one day to avoid an angry Spoor who was stomping toward his office, fuming about the poor price of Pillsbury's stock. Another former executive remembers Spoor's response to one of his ideas in a brainstorming session: "That's a terrible idea. I don't know why we hired you."[1] After a legendary late-night meeting, Spoor challenged some of his executives to race home, then laughed with delight when he beat a vice president to his own driveway.

Given his attitude toward subordinates, Spoor's failure to adequately prepare a successor is perhaps not surprising. Several directors objected when Spoor chose the relatively inexperienced John M. Stafford to take over as chairman and chief executive. Although Stafford did get the job, he lasted only three years; during that time Pillsbury's sales, earnings, and market share all declined. The tone for Stafford's tenure was set early, in a meeting on the fate of Pillsbury's J. J. Muggs restaurant chain. Insiders had been assured that Stafford supported the chain. But after Spoor, now a director, attacked the chain and called for its closing, Stafford switched sides and joined the attack.

Thereafter, many at Pillsbury viewed Stafford as both weak and untrustworthy, and any notion of top management working as a team vanished. Other executives nicknamed the stiff and inflexible Stafford "the wooden soldier." Unlike Spoor, he was cautious about expansion and slow to make decisions, stances that often angered both suppliers and insiders. The head of Pillsbury's restaurant business became known for his imitations of his boss's wooden, predictable gestures.

In such an atmosphere, many of Pillsbury's top people spent much of their time and energy trading political gossip and jockeying for Stafford's position, especially after the company's poor showing fostered the belief that the job might soon be open. In the month before his resignation, Stafford undermined Pillsbury management and ultimately his own position. He told securities analysts that Pillsbury's managers were "overpromising and underperforming" and indicated that he wanted to fire the head of the restaurant group, which would have left Pillsbury's already shaky restaurants in even worse shape.

Ironically, when Stafford resigned, Spoor took over again as the company searched for another CEO, eventually settling on Philip L. Smith. For a few months, it seemed that Pillsbury had found what it needed: Smith had vision and was personable. In a radical departure from his predecessors' behavior, Smith went out of his way to shake hands with secretaries and clerks, and he was generally liked at headquarters. But Pillsbury's years of floundering had made it a perfect target for a takeover—a company with assets that were currently undervalued because its management wasn't making enough use of them. Sure enough, before 1988 was over, Grand Metropolitan, a giant British conglomerate, had succeeded in buying Pillsbury in a hostile takeover. Pillsbury's new boss was Grand Met's chief, Allen Sheppard.

Sheppard has a reputation for being as combative as Spoor. He once described his management style as "a light grip on the throat," and he added "anybody incapable of punching me in the face is probably incapable of being a group executive for Grand Met."[2] Within three months, Sheppard had sold off Pillsbury's Steak & Ale restaurants and had fired 550 employees—23 percent of the total staff—at Pillsbury's Minneapolis headquarters.

To some, Sheppard and Grand Met looked like perfect saviours for Pillsbury. In Sheppard's first two years at Grand Met's helm, the company's earnings per share climbed 50 percent, although sales rose only 14 percent. He seemed in many ways to be the typical tough manager of the late 1980s, cutting overhead to create leaner companies, buying and selling companies worth billions of dollars while trying to consolidate Grand Met's holdings into its areas of strength, putting his company under tight financial controls while trying to allow its informal culture to survive. He believes in delegating authority but also in making bold moves himself when he sees an opportunity. In one such move he had Grand Met work up a deal in four days to buy Heublein for $1.3 billion.

Most analysts agreed at the time that Pillsbury needed some strong medicine. Its profit margins and productivity ratings were among the worst in the American food industry. It was not entering the 1990s as a "leaner" company, and it was clearly suffering from management instability. Sheppard's reforms address those problems. It remains to be seen whether he will be able to build trust, present a better role model, and encourage teamwork at Pillsbury—all necessary ingredients for turning the company around.

Pillsbury's problems offer a vivid picture of group dynamics gone sour. At the time of Stafford's resignation, distrust, politicking, and conflict seemed to dominate that company's high-level decision making. The lingering question is whether or not Allen Sheppard's "hand on the throat" management style will improve matters.

Remembering that people are at the same time individuals and social beings can help managers maintain their perspective. This sometimes frustrating combination—a central fact in any discussion of group dynamics—was thoughtfully explored by Henry David Thoreau, a nineteenth-century American philosopher. Thoreau's two-year experiment with solitary living in the woods near Walden Pond is chronicled in his classic book *Walden*. Only by removing himself from the distractions of life in town could Thoreau reevaluate his relationship with society. He found that even though no one else was around, he was never truly alone because he was the product of society. Everything Thoreau thought and did was social in origin. He was first and foremost a social being.

Although most of us will never have the opportunity to contemplate our relationship with society by living alone in the woods for a few years, each of us is challenged daily to resolve the inevitable conflict between the demands of individuality and society. A working understanding of the social forces that constantly shape and redirect our lives is particularly important for managers. The practice of management is, after all, fundamentally social in nature.[3]

Fundamental Group Dynamics

According to one organization theorist, "All groups may be collections of individuals, but all collections of individuals are not groups."[4] This observation is more than a play on words; mere togetherness does not automatically create a group. Consider, for example, this situation. A half-dozen people who worked for different companies in the same building often shared the same elevator in the morning. As time passed, they introduced themselves and exchanged pleasantries. Eventually, four of the elevator riders discovered that they all lived in the same suburb. Arrangements for a car pool were made, and they began to take turns picking up and delivering one another. A group technically came into existence only when the car pool was formed. To understand why this is so, we must examine the definition of the term *group*.

What Is a Group?

group two or more freely interacting individuals with a common identity and purpose

From a sociological perspective, a **group** can be defined as two or more freely interacting individuals who share a common identity and purpose.[5] Careful analysis of this definition reveals four important dimensions (see Figure 13.1). First, a group must be made up of two or more people if it is to be considered a social unit. Second, the individuals must freely interact in some manner. An organization may qualify as a sociological group if it is small and personal enough to permit all its members to interact regularly with each other. Generally, however, larger organizations with bureaucratic tendencies are made up of many overlapping groups. Third, the interacting individuals must share a common

These creatures are actually cotton harvesters sweeping an Arizona cotton field. Although each harvester is operated by an individual, the drivers must work as a coordinated team. Otherwise, portions of the field go unharvested, expensive equipment might be damaged, and serious injuries sustained. Like any other formal work group, these harvester drivers operate according to roles and norms specifying everything from the timing of breaks to safety habits.

identity. Each must recognize himself or herself as a member of the group. Fourth, interacting individuals who have a common identity must also have a common purpose. That is, there must be at least a rough consensus on why the group exists.

Types of Groups

Human beings belong to groups for many different reasons. Some people join a group as an end in itself. For example, an accountant may enjoy the socializing that is part of belonging to a group at a local health spa. That same accountant's membership in a work group is a means to a professional end. Both the exercise group and the work group satisfy the sociological definition of a group, but they fulfill very different needs. The former is an informal group, and the latter is a formal group.

informal group collection of people seeking friendship

Informal Groups. As Maslow pointed out, a feeling of belonging is a powerful motivator. People generally have a great need to fit in, to be liked, to be one of the gang. Whether the group meets at work or during leisure time, it is still an **informal group** if the principal reason for belonging is friendship. Informal groups usually evolve spontaneously. They serve to satisfy esteem needs because one develops a better self-image when accepted, recognized, and liked by others. Sometimes, as in the case of a group of friends forming a service club, an informal group may evolve into a formal one.

formal group collection of people created to do something productive

Formal Groups. A **formal group** is a group created for the purpose of doing productive work. It may be called a team, a committee, or simply a work group. Whatever its name, a formal group is usually formed for the purpose of contributing to the success of a larger organization. Formal groups tend to be more rationally structured and less fluid than informal groups. Rather than joining formal task groups, people are assigned to them according to their talents and the organi-

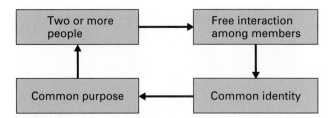

FIGURE 13.1 • What Does It Take to Make a Group?

zation's needs. One person normally is granted formal leadership responsibility to ensure that the members carry out their assigned duties. Informal friendship groups, in contrast, generally do not have officially appointed leaders, although informal leaders often emerge by popular demand.[6] For the individual, the formal group and an informal group at the place of employment may or may not overlap. In other words, one may or may not be friends with one's coworkers.

Explain the significance of cohesiveness, roles, norms, and ostracism in regard to the behavior of group members.

cohesiveness tendency of group to stick together

Attraction to Groups

What attracts a person to one group but not to another? And why do some groups members stay whereas others leave? Managers who can answer these questions can also take steps to motivate others to join and remain members of a formal work group. Individual commitment to either an informal or formal group hinges on two factors. The first is *attractiveness,* the outside-looking-in view. A nonmember will want to join a group that is attractive and will shy away from a group that is unattractive. The second factor is **cohesiveness,** the tendency of group members to follow the group and resist outside influences. This is the inside-looking-out view. In a highly cohesive group, individual members tend to see themselves as "we" rather than "I." Cohesive group members stick together.[7]

Factors that either enhance or destroy group attractiveness and cohesiveness are listed in Table 13.1. It is important to note that each factor is a matter of degree. For example, a group may offer the individual little, moderate, or great opportunity for prestige and status. Similarly, group demands on the individual may range from somewhat disagreeable to highly disagreeable. What all this means is that both the decision to join a group and the decision to continue being a member depend on a net balance of the factors in Table 13.1. Naturally, the resulting balance is colored by one's perception and frame of reference, as it was in the case of Richard Dale, a former manager of distribution at Commodore International, during his first meeting with the company's founder, Jack Tramiel:

> *Dale's first meeting with Tramiel began with a summons to appear at Tramiel's office. Dale flew from his office in Los Angeles to Santa Clara . . . , only to find that Tramiel had decided to visit him instead.*
>
> *Terrified, Dale caught a plane back to find his secretary shaking in her shoes and the burly Tramiel sitting at his desk. For an hour Tramiel grilled Dale on his philosophy of business, pronounced it all wrong, and suggested a tour of the warehouse. When they passed boxes of Commodore Vic-20s and Pets waiting for shipment, recalls Dale, Tramiel seemed to "go crazy," pounding the boxes with his fists and yelling, "Do you think this is bourbon? Do you think it gets better with age?"*[8]

TABLE 13.1 • Factors That Enhance or Detract from Group Attractiveness and Cohesiveness

Factors that enhance	*Factors that detract*
1. Prestige and status	1. Unreasonable or disagreeable demands on the individual
2. Cooperative relationship	2. Disagreement over procedures, activities, rules, and the like
3. High degree of interaction	3. Unpleasant experience with the group
4. Relatively small size	4. Competition between the group's demands and preferred outside activities
5. Similarity of members	5. Unfavorable public image of the group
6. Superior public image of the group	6. Competition for membership by other groups
7. A common threat in the environment	

Source: Figure adapted from *Group Dynamics: Research and Theory,* Second Edition, by Dorwin Cartwright and Alvin Zander. Copyright © 1962 by Dorwin Cartwright and Alvin Zander. Reprinted by permission of HarperCollins Publishers, Inc.

Dale's departure within a few months of this episode is not surprising in view of the fact that Tramiel's conduct destroyed work group attractiveness and cohesiveness.

Roles

According to Shakespeare, "All the world's a stage, and all the men and women merely players." In fact, Shakespeare's analogy between life and play-acting can be carried a step further—to organizations and their component formal work groups. Although employees do not have scripts, they do have formal positions in the organizational hierarchy, and they are expected to adhere to company policies and rules. Furthermore, job descriptions and procedure manuals spell out how jobs are to be done. In short, every employee has one or more organizational roles to play. An organization that is appropriately structured, in which everyone plays his or her role(s) effectively and efficiently, will have a greater chance for organizational success.

A social psychologist has described the concept of role as follows:

> *The term* role *is used to refer to (1) a set of expectations concerning what a person in a given position must, must not, or may do, and (2) the actual behavior of the person who occupies the position. A central idea is that any person occupying a position and filling a role behaves similarly to anyone else who could be in that position.*[9]

role socially determined way of behaving in a specific position

A **role**, then, is a socially determined prescription for behavior in a specific position. Roles evolve out of the tendency for social units to perpetuate themselves, and roles are socially enforced. Role models are a powerful influence. They are indispensable to those trying to resolve the inherent conflicts between work and family roles (see Managers in Action).

How One Woman Learned about Work and Family Roles

Christine Hegenbart, 23, is an assistant municipal bond trader at Gannett, Welsh, and Kotler in Boston. Her mother, Kathleen Hegenbart, is vice president and financial consultant for Shearson Lehman Hutton, Inc., in Newton Centre, MA.

Most of my friends' mothers didn't work. We all played a lot of tennis and their mothers pretty much carted them from club to club—that was their full-time job. Comparing them with my mother showed me two different types of lives a woman could choose. The one type is to live almost solely for your children and your family. The other type of lifestyle is to live for yourself while also spending quality time with your family—which my mother always did. I could have gone either route, but seeing both personalities and sets of values, I was inspired all the more to become like my mother.

The fact that my mother worked was also good for my relationship with my father—particularly when my mother changed careers and became a stockbroker. She had to do a lot of studying then, which absolutely drained her. My dad had to pick up the emotional side of the family and the duties that were typically considered women's work. Before, my parents had pretty much stuck to traditional male and female roles. But as we became a more modern family, they had to mesh the two roles to become a more balanced unit. If I were a parent, I would try to balance work and family exactly the way my parents did in the later years—each one picking up where the other one couldn't.

Many women who work feel guilty about not spending enough time with their children. It makes a lot of sense to feel that way, but the solution to the problem is to nurture your children's interests. If they are busy when they aren't with you, then they won't miss you and will be very pleased when you are around instead of taking you for granted.

Source: Excerpted from Patti Watts, "What Kids Really Think about Mom Working," *Executive Female,* 13 (May-June 1990): 26. Reprinted by permission.

Norms

norms general standards of conduct for various social settings

Norms define "degrees of acceptability and unacceptability."[10] More precisely, **norms** are general standards of conduct that help individuals judge what is right or wrong or good or bad in a given social setting (such as work, home, play, or religious organization). Because norms are culturally derived, they vary from one culture to another. For example, disagreement and debate, which are normal in Western societies, are often considered rude in Eastern countries such as Japan.

Norms have a broader influence than do roles, which focus on a specific position. Although usually unwritten, norms influence behavior enormously.

Every mature group, whether informal or formal, generates its own pattern of norms that constrains and directs the behavior of its members. Norms are enforced for at least four different reasons:

1. To facilitate survival of the group.
2. To simplify or clarify role expectations.
3. To help group members avoid embarrassing situations (protect self-images).
4. To express key group values and enhance the group's unique identity.[11]

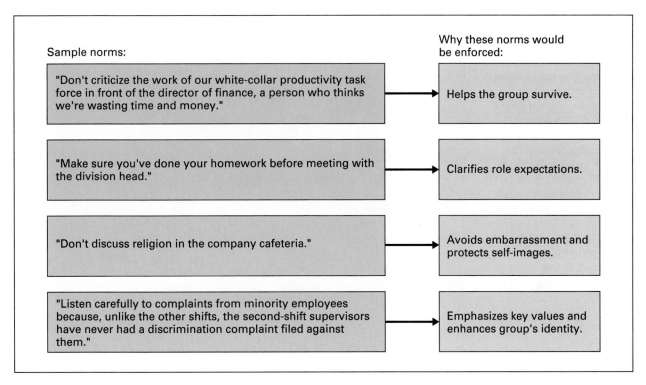

Sample norms:

"Don't criticize the work of our white-collar productivity task force in front of the director of finance, a person who thinks we're wasting time and money."

"Make sure you've done your homework before meeting with the division head."

"Don't discuss religion in the company cafeteria."

"Listen carefully to complaints from minority employees because, unlike the other shifts, the second-shift supervisors have never had a discrimination complaint filed against them."

Why these norms would be enforced:

Helps the group survive.

Clarifies role expectations.

Avoids embarrassment and protects self-images.

Emphasizes key values and enhances group's identity.

FIGURE 13.2 ● Norms Are Enforced for Different Reasons

As illustrated in Figure 13.2, norms tend to go above and beyond formal rules and written policies. Compliance is shaped with social reinforcement in the form of attention, recognition, and acceptance. Those who fail to comply with the norm may be criticized or ridiculed, as new managers at IBM soon discover. Thomas Watson, the founder of IBM, insisted that his male employees wear conservative dark suits, white shirts, and plain ties. Although times have changed and white shirts are no longer official IBM policy, white shirts are everywhere in the company's environs. Why? Because of an informally enforced norm: " 'There is no rule about white shirts,' insists an IBM manager, 'but when I wear a striped shirt, my colleagues ask if I'm going to the beach.' "[12] Worse than ridicule is the threat of being ostracized. **Ostracism,** or rejection from the group, is figuratively the capital punishment of group dynamics. Informal groups derive much of their power over individuals through the ever-present threat of ostracism.

ostracism rejection from a group

Norms have an important relationship with cohesiveness. In a highly cohesive group, there is consensus on what the relevant norms are. Disagreement over group norms tends to tear apart cohesiveness. For example, a management advisory committee made up of department heads may establish and enforce a norm that encourages each department head to carry a fair share of the workload. Deviations from this norm will diminish cohesiveness within the group and subsequently undermine its effectiveness.

Like many manufacturers today, competitive pressures are pushing NCR Corp. to speed up the process of turning good ideas into saleable products. When a cross-functional team at NCR's Atlanta, Georgia, facility used concurrent engineering to bring a new checkout terminal to market in half the usual time, drastic steps were taken to capitalize on the success. Walls between design and manufacturing departments were literally torn down in the name of group development and teamwork.

Group Development

Like inept youngsters who mature into talented adults, groups undergo a maturation process before becoming effective.[13] We have all experienced the uneasiness associated with the first meeting of a new group, be it a class, a club, or committee. Initially, there is little mutual understanding, trust, and commitment among the new group members, and their uncertainty over objectives, roles, and leadership doesn't help. The prospect of cooperative action seems unlikely in view of defensive behavior and differences of opinion about who should do what. Someone steps forward to assume a leadership role, and the group is off and running toward eventual maturity (or perhaps premature demise). A working knowledge of the characteristics of a mature group can help the manager systematically manage group development rather than leaving this vital process to chance.

Characteristics of a Mature Group

If and when a group takes on the following characteristics, it can be called a mature group:

1. Members are aware of their own and each other's assets and liabilities vis-à-vis the group's task.

2. These individual differences are accepted without being labeled as good or bad.

3. The group has developed authority and interpersonal relationships that are recognized and accepted by the members.

4. Group decisions are made through rational discussion. Minority opinions and dissension are recognized and encouraged. Attempts are not made to force decisions or a false unanimity.

5. Conflict is over substantive group issues such as group goals and the effectiveness and efficiency of various means for achieving those goals. Conflict over emotional issues regarding group structure, processes, or interpersonal relationships is at a minimum.

6. Members are aware of the group's processes and their own roles in them.[14]

A hidden but nonetheless significant benefit of group maturity is that individuality is strengthened and not extinguished. Protecting the individual's right to dissent is particularly important in regard to the problem of blind obedience, which we shall consider later in this chapter.

Six Stages of Group Development

•••••••••••••••••••
Identify and briefly describe the six stages of group development.

Experts have identified six distinct stages in the group development process[15] (see Figure 13.3). During stages 1 through 3, attempts are made to overcome the obstacle of uncertainty over power and authority. Once this first obstacle has been surmounted, uncertainty over interpersonal relations becomes the challenge. This second obstacle must be cleared during stages 4 through 6 if the group is to achieve maturity. Each stage confronts the group's leader and contributing members with a unique combination of problems and opportunities.

Stage 1: Orientation. Attempts are made to "break the ice." Uncertainty about goals, power, and interpersonal relationships is high. Members generally want and accept any leadership at this point. Emergent leaders often misinterpret this "honeymoon period" as a mandate for permanent control.

Stage 2: Conflict and Challenge. As the emergent leader's philosophy, objectives, and policies become apparent, individuals or subgroups advocating alternative courses of action struggle for control. This second stage may be prolonged while members strive to clarify and reconcile their roles as part of a complete redistribution of power and authority. Many groups never continue past stage 2 because they get bogged down in emotionalism and political infighting. Committees within the organization are often the brunt of jokes because their frequent failure to mature beyond stage 2 prevents them from accomplishing their goals. (As one joke goes, a camel is a horse designed by a committee.)

Stage 3: Cohesion. The shifts in power started in stage 2 are completed, under a new leader or the original leader, with a new consensus on authority, structure, and procedures. A "we" feeling becomes apparent as everyone becomes truly involved. Any lingering differences over power and authority are resolved quickly. Stage 3 is usually of relatively short duration. If not, the group is likely to stall.

Stage 4: Delusion. A feeling of "having been through the worst of it" prevails after the rather rapid transition through stage 3. Issues and problems that threaten to break this spell of relief are dismissed or treated lightly. Members seem committed to fostering harmony at all costs. Participation and camaraderie run high as members believe that all the difficult emotional problems have been solved.

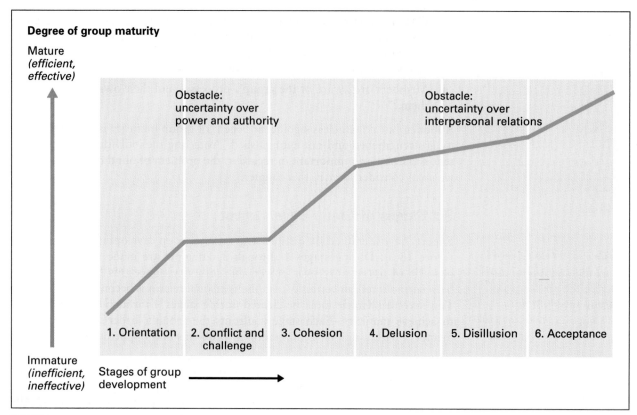

FIGURE 13.3 • Group Development from Formation to Maturity

Source: Group Effectiveness in Organizations, by Linda N. Jewell and H. Joseph Reitz, p. 20.
Used with permission of the authors.

Stage 5: Disillusion. Subgroups tend to form as the delusion of unlimited goodwill wears off, and there is a growing disenchantment with how things are turning out. Those with unrealized expectations challenge the group to perform better and are prepared to reveal their personal strengths and weaknesses if necessary. Others hold back. Tardiness and absenteeism are symptomatic of diminishing cohesiveness and commitment.

Stage 6: Acceptance. It usually takes a trusted and influential group member who is concerned about the group to step forward and help the group move from conflict to cohesion. This individual, acting as the group catalyst, is usually someone other than the leader. Members are encouraged to test their self-perceptions against the reality of how others perceive them. Greater personal and mutual understanding helps members adapt to situations without causing problems. Members' expectations are more realistic than ever before. Since the authority structure is generally accepted, subgroups can pursue different matters without threatening group cohesiveness. Consequently, stage 6 groups tend to be highly effective and efficient.

Prior to his assuming the top post at Xerox in 1990, Paul Allaire's company went through a decade of major changes. So what does Allaire plan for the next five years? He envisions Xerox as more than a copier company; he calls Xerox the "Document Company," signifying their growing ability to create and use all sorts of information. Characterized as a skillful listener, Allaire has little patience for organizational politicians who do not get results.

•••••••••••••••••
Define organizational politics and summarize relevant reseach insights.

organizational politics the pursuit of self-interest in response to real or imagined opposition

Time-wasting problems and inefficiencies can be minimized if group members are consciously aware of this developmental process. Just as it is impossible for a child to skip being a teen-ager on the way to adulthood, committees and other work groups will find that there are no short cuts to group maturity. Some emotional stresses and strains are inevitable along the way.

Organizational Politics

Only in recent years has the topic of organizational politics (also known as office politics) begun to receive serious attention from management theorists and researchers. But as we all know from practical experience, organizational life is often highly charged with political wheeling and dealing. A corporate executive has underscored this point by asking:

> *Have you ever done a very satisfactory piece of work only to have it lost in the organizational shuffle? Have you ever come up with a new idea only to have your boss take credit for it? Have you ever faced a situation where someone else made a serious mistake and somehow engineered it so you got the blame?*[16]

Whether politically motivated or not, managers need to be knowledgeable about organizational politics because their careers will be affected by it.[17] New managers, particularly, should be aware of the political situation in their organization. As "new kids on the job" they might be more easily taken advantage of than other more experienced managers.[18] Certain political maneuvers also have significant ethical implications. (See Management Ethics.)

What Does Organizational Politics Involve?

As the term implies, self-interest is central to organizational politics. In fact, **organizational politics** has been defined as "the pursuit of self-interest at work in the face of real or imagined opposition."[19] Political maneuvering is said to encompass all self-serving behavior above and beyond competence, hard work, and luck.[20] Although the term organizational politics has a negative connotation, researchers have identified both positive and negative aspects:

> *Political behaviors widely accepted as legitimate would certainly include exchanging favors, "touching bases," forming coalitions, and seeking sponsors at upper levels. Less legitimate behaviors would include whistle-blowing, revolutionary coalitions, threats, and sabotage.*[21]

Recall our discussion of whistle-blowing in Chapter 4.

Employees resort to political behavior when they are unwilling to trust their career solely to competence, hard work, or luck. One might say that organizational politicians help luck along by relying on political tactics. Whether employees will fall back on political tactics has a lot to do with an organization's climate or culture. For example, imagine yourself trying to climb the managerial ladder at PepsiCo Inc., where political maneuvering is said to be active amid a climate of "creative tension":

How Do You Feel about "Hard Ball" Organizational Politics?

Circle one number for each item, total your responses, and compare your score with the scale below:

	Unacceptable attitude/conduct				*Acceptable attitude/conduct*
1. The boss is always right.	1	2	3	4	5
2. If I were aware that an executive in my company was stealing money, I would use that information against him or her in asking for favors.	1	2	3	4	5
3. I would invite my boss to a party in my home even if I didn't like that person.	1	2	3	4	5
4. Given a choice, take on only those assignments that will make you look good.	1	2	3	4	5
5. I like the idea of keeping a "blunder (error) file" about a company rival for future use.	1	2	3	4	5
6. If you don't know the correct answer to a question asked by your boss, bluff your way out of it.	1	2	3	4	5
7. Why go out of your way to be nice to any employee in the company who can't help you now or in the future?	1	2	3	4	5
8. It is necessary to lie once in a while in business in order to look good.	1	2	3	4	5
9. Past promises should be broken if they stand in the way of one's personal gain.	1	2	3	4	5
10. If someone compliments you for a task that is another's accomplishment, smile and say thank you.	1	2	3	4	5

Scale
10–20 = Straight arrow with solid ethics
21–39 = Closet politician with elastic ethics
40–50 = Hard ball politician with no ethics

Total score = _____

Source: From the book *Winning Office Politics* by Andrew Dubrin. © 1990. Used by permission of the publisher, Prentice-Hall/A division of Simon & Schuster, Englewood Cliffs, N.J.

Managers are pitted against each other to grab more market share, to work harder, and to wring more profits out of their businesses. Because winning is the key value at Pepsi, losing has its penalties. Consistent runners-up find their jobs gone. Employees know they must win merely to stay in place—and must devastate the competition to get ahead. . . .

The immediate past chairman set a constant example. He once resorted to using a snowmobile to get to work in a blizzard, demonstrating the ingenuity and dedication to work he expects from his staff. This type of pressure has pushed many managers out. But a recent survey shows that others thrive under such conditions.[22]

One can only speculate about the value of such a highly political climate. In view of Pepsi's titanic battle with Coca-Cola, a strong competitive spirit seems appropriate. Of course, those who were forced out or had their toes stepped on might have a different view.

Research on Organizational Politics

Researchers in one widely cited study of organizational politics conducted structured interviews with eighty-seven managers employed by thirty electronics firms in southern California. Included in the sample were thirty chief executive officers, twenty-eight middle managers, and twenty-nine supervisors. Significant results included:

- The higher the level of management, the greater the perceived amount of political activity.
- The larger the organization, the greater the perceived amount of political activity.
- Personnel in staff positions were viewed as more political than those in line positions.
- People in marketing were the most political; those in production were the least political.
- "Reorganization changes" reportedly prompted more political activity than any other type of change.
- A majority (61 percent) of those interviewed believed organizational politics helps advance one's career.
- Forty-five percent believed that organizational politics distracts from organizational goals.[23]

Regarding the last two findings, it was clear that political activities were seen as helpful to the individual. On the other hand, the interviewed managers were split on the question of the value of politics to the organization. Managers who believed political behavior had a positive impact on the organization cited the following reasons: "gaining visibility for ideas, improving coordination and communication, developing teams and groups, and increasing *esprit de corps*. . . . "[24] As listed above, the most often cited negative effect of politics was its distraction of managers from organizational goals. Misuse of resources and conflict were also mentioned as typical problems.

Political Tactics

As defined earlier, organizational politics takes in a lot of behavioral territory. The following six political tactics are common expressions of politics in the workplace:

- *Posturing.* Those who use this tactic look for situations in which they can make a good impression. "One-upmanship" and taking credit for other people's work are included in this category.

- *Empire Building.* Gaining and keeping control over human and material resources is the principal motivation behind this tactic. Those with large budgets usually feel more safely entrenched in their positions and believe they have more influence over peers and superiors.

- *Making the Supervisor Look Good.* Traditionally referred to as "apple polishing," this political strategy is prompted by a desire to favorably influence those who control one's career ascent. Anyone with an oversized ego is an easy target for this tactic.

- *Collecting and Using Social IOUs.* Reciprocal exchange of political favors can be done in two ways: (1) by helping someone look good or (2) by preventing someone from looking bad by ignoring or covering up a mistake. Those who rely on this tactic feel that all favors are coins of exchange rather than expressions of altruism or unselfishness.

- *Creating Power and Loyalty Cliques.* Because there is power in numbers, the idea here is to face superiors and competitors as a cohesive group rather than alone.

- *Destructive Competition.* As a last-ditch effort, some people will resort to character assassination through suggestive remarks, vindictive gossip, or outright lies. This tactic also includes sabotaging the work of a competitor.[25]

Obvious illegalities notwithstanding, one's own values and ethics and organizational sanctions are the final arbiters of whether or not these tactics are acceptable. (See Table 13.2 for a practicing manager's advice on how to win at office politics.)

Antidotes to Political Behavior

Each of the foregoing political tactics varies in degree. The average person will probably acknowledge using at least one of these strategies.[26] But excessive political maneuvering can become a serious threat to productivity when self-interests clearly override the interests of the group or organization.[27] Organizational politics can be kept within reasonable bounds by applying the following five tips:

- Strive for a climate of openness and trust.
- Measure performance results rather than personalities.
- Encourage top management to refrain from exhibiting political behavior that will be imitated by subordinates.
- Strive to integrate individual and organizational goals through meaningful work and career planning.

TABLE 13.2 ● One Manager's Rules for Winning at Office Politics

> 1. Find out what the boss expects.
> 2. Build an information network. Knowledge is power. Identify the people who have power and the extent and direction of it. Title doesn't necessarily reflect actual influence. Find out how the grapevine works. Develop good internal public relations for yourself.
> 3. Find a mentor. This is a trusted counselor who can be honest with you and help train and guide you to improve your ability and effectiveness as a manager.
> 4. Don't make enemies without a very good reason.
> 5. Avoid cliques. Keep circulating in the office.
> 6. If you must fight, fight over something that is really worth it. Don't lose ground over minor matters or petty differences.
> 7. Gain power through allies. Build ties that bind. Create IOUs, obligations, and loyalties. Do not be afraid to enlist help from above.
> 8. Maintain control. Don't misuse your cohorts. Maintain the status and integrity of your allies.
> 9. Mobilize your forces when necessary. Don't commit your friends without their approval. Be a gracious winner when you do win.
> 10. Never hire a family member or a close friend.

Source: Adapted from David E. Hall, "Winning at Office Politics," *Credit & Financial Management,* 86 (April 1984): 23. Reprinted with permission from *Credit & Financial Management,* Copyright April 1984, published by the National Association of Credit Management, 475 Park Avenue South, New York, NY 10016.

● Practice job rotation to encourage broader perspectives and understanding of the problems of others.[28]

Conformity

Much is accomplished in this world because people conform to accepted standards of behavior. Imagine how chaotic it would be if all automobile drivers suddenly stopped conforming to traffic laws: our chances of arriving alive would greatly diminish. Similarly, relatively strict conformity to norms, rules, and regulations at work is necessary to ensure the efficient accomplishment of organizational objectives.

conformity complying with prevailing role expectations and norms

As used here, **conformity** means complying with the role expectations and norms perceived by the majority to be appropriate in a particular situation. Conformity enhances predictability, generally thought to be good for rational planning and productive enterprise. How can anything be accomplished if people cannot be counted on to perform their assigned duties? On the other hand, why do so many employees actively participate in or passively condone illegal and unethical organizational practices involving discrimination, environmental degradation, and unfair competition? The answers to these questions lie along a continuum with anarchy at one end and blind conformity at the other. Socially responsible management is anchored to a point somewhere between them.

Research on Conformity

Social psychologists have discovered much about human behavior by studying individuals and groups in controlled laboratory settings. One classic laboratory study conducted by Solomon Asch was designed to answer the question: How often will an individual take a stand against a unanimous majority that is obviously wrong?[29] Asch's results were both intriguing and unsettling.

The Hot Seat. Asch began his study by assembling groups of seven to nine college students, supposedly to work on a perceptual problem. Actually, though, Asch was studying conformity. All but one member of each group were Asch's confederates, and Asch told them exactly how to behave and what to say. The experiment was really concerned with the reactions of the remaining student—called the naive subject—who didn't know what was going on.

All the students in each group were shown cards with lines similar to those in Figure 13.4. They were instructed to match the line on the left with the one on the right that was closest to it in length. The differences in length among the lines on the right were obvious. Each group went through twelve rounds of the matching process, with a different set of lines for every round. The researcher asked one group member at a time to state aloud to the group his or her choice. Things proceeded normally for the first two rounds as each group member voiced an opinion. Agreement was unanimous. Suddenly, on the third round only one individual, the naive subject, chose the correct pair of lines. All the other group members chose a different (and obviously wrong) pair. During the rounds in which there was disagreement, all of Asch's confederates conspired to select an incorrect pair of lines. It was the individual versus the rest of the group.

Following the Immoral Majority. Each of the naive subjects was faced with a personal dilemma. Should he or she fight the group or give in to the obviously incorrect choice of the overwhelming majority? Among 31 naive subjects who made a total of 217 judgments, two-thirds of the judgments were correct. The other one-third were incorrect; that is, they were consistent with the majority opinion. Individual differences were great, with some subjects yielding to the incorrect majority opinion more readily than others. *Only 20 percent of the naive subjects remained entirely independent in their judgments.* All the rest turned

FIGURE 13.4 • The Asch Line Experiment

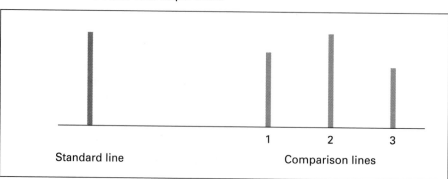

their backs on their own perceptions and went along with the group at least once. In other words, 80 percent of Asch's subjects knuckled under to the pressure of group opinion at least once, even though they knew the majority was dead wrong.

Replications of Asch's study in the Middle East (Kuwait) and in Japan have demonstrated that this tendency toward conformity is not unique to American culture.[30] (You may find it instructive to ponder how you would act in such a situation.)

Because Asch's study was a contrived laboratory experiment, it failed to probe the relationship between cohesiveness and conformity. Asch's naive subjects were outsiders. But recent research on "groupthink" has shown that a cohesive group of insiders can fall victim to blind conformity.

Groupthink

• • • • • • • • • • • • • •
Explain how groupthink can lead to blind conformity.

groupthink Janis's term for blind conformity in cohesive in-groups

After studying the records of several successful and unsuccessful American foreign policy decisions, psychologist Irving Janis uncovered an undesirable by-product of group cohesiveness. He labeled this problem **groupthink** and defined it as a "mode of thinking that people engage in when they are deeply involved in a cohesive in-group, when the members' strivings for unanimity override their motivation to realistically appraise alternative courses of action."[31] Groupthink helps explain how intelligent policy makers, in both government and business, can sometimes make incredibly unwise decisions.[32]

One dramatic result of groupthink in action was the Vietnam War. Strategic advisors in three successive administrations unwittingly rubber-stamped battle plans laced with false assumptions. Critical thinking, reality testing, and moral judgment were temporarily shelved as decisions to escalate the war were enthusiastically railroaded through. Although Janis acknowledges that cohesive groups are not inevitably victimized by groupthink, he warns group decision makers to be alert for the signs of groupthink—the risk is always there.

Symptoms of Groupthink. According to Janis, the onset of groupthink is foreshadowed by a definite pattern of symptoms. Among these are excessive optimism, an assumption of inherent morality, suppression of dissent, and an almost desperate quest for unanimity.[33] Given such a decision-making climate, the probability of a poor decision is high. Managers face a curious dilemma here. While a group is still in stage 1 or stage 2 of development, its cohesiveness is too low to get much accomplished because of emotional and time-consuming power struggles. But by the time the group achieves enough cohesiveness in stage 3 to make decisions promptly, the risk of groupthink is high. The trick is to achieve needed cohesiveness without going to the extreme of groupthink.

Preventing Groupthink. According to Janis, one of the group members should periodically ask, "Are we allowing ourselves to become victims of groupthink?"[34] More fundamental preventive measures include:

- Avoiding the use of groups to rubber-stamp decisions that have already been made by higher management.
- Urging each group member to be a critical evaluator.
- Bringing in outside experts for fresh perspectives.

- Assigning to someone the role of devil's advocate to challenge assumptions and alternatives.[35]
- Taking time to consider possible side effects and consequences of alternative courses of action.[36]

Ideally, decision quality will improve when these steps become second nature in cohesive groups. Intel's chief executive officer, Andrew Grove, employs the following confrontational technique to prevent groupthink: "I get a much better understanding of an issue with which I am not familiar by listening to two people with opposing views discuss it than I do by listening to one side only."[37] Managers who cannot imagine themselves being victimized by blind conformity are prime candidates for groupthink.

Managerial Implications

Like other aspects of group dynamics, conformity has both a good side and a bad side. When the work group identifies with the organization's overall direction, and that direction is socially responsible, great things can be accomplished. In this context, conformity is a positive force. But, as one authority points out, "The group has a potential to produce blind loyalty, abject submission, and total obedience, and such conditions have invariably been dehumanizing in the end."[38] Conformity becomes a negative force when it encourages group members to deny their personal convictions, better judgment, or ethical values for fear of group reprisal.

Clearly, one challenge facing today's managers is to make sure that they and their peers and subordinates can tell the difference between productive conformity and blind, destructive conformity.

Teams, Teamwork, and Trust

As mentioned in Chapter 9, Peter Drucker envisions tomorrow's organizations as primarily team-oriented in structure. He sees this trend already taking shape as follows:

> In pharmaceuticals, in telecommunications, in papermaking, the traditional sequence of research, development, manufacturing, and marketing is being replaced by synchrony: specialists from all these functions work together as a team, from the inception of research to a product's establishment in the market.[39]

Thus, teams and teamwork are vital group dynamics in the modern workplace. Unfortunately, team skills in today's typical organization tend to lag far behind technical skills. It is one thing to be a creative software engineer, for example. It is quite another for that software specialist to be able to team up with other specialists in accounting, finance, and marketing to beat the competition to market with a profitable new product. In this final section, we explore teams and teamwork by discussing cross-functional teams, a model of team effectiveness, and the importance of trust.

For years Motorola took a strictly adversarial approach to its computer chip rivals in Japan. Now the electronics giant is trying teamwork. Here a team of semiconductor specialists from Motorola and Toshiba is all smiles posing in Japan with the fruit of its joint effort. Toshiba is striving to learn more about American microprocessor technology while Motorola is pushing for a bigger market share in Japan. This sort of international teamwork, when carried out in a measured and systematic way, can be a win-win situation.

Cross-Functional Teams

cross-functional team task group staffed with a mix of specialists pursuing a common objective

A **cross-functional team** is a task group staffed with a mix of specialists focused on a common objective. This structural innovation deserves special attention here because cross-functional teams are becoming commonplace. They may or may not be self-managed, although self-managed teams generally are cross-functional. Because cross-functional teams are based on assigned rather than voluntary membership, quality control (QC) circles made up of volunteers, discussed in Chapter 12, technically are in a different category. Cross-functional teams stand in sharp contrast to the tradition of lumping specialists into functional departments, thereby creating the problem of integrating and coordinating those departments. Boeing, for example, is relying on cross-functional teams to integrate its various departments to achieve an important strategic goal. The giant aircraft manufacturer wants to speed up its product development process for the new Boeing 777 jetliner:

> [Boeing] has handed the 777 over to Japanese-style design-build teams. The idea: Bunch marketing, engineering, manufacturing, finance, and service representatives on teams so that each department knows what the other is doing. Boeing also plans to arm the teams with "digital preassembly" design technology so that the 777 can be conceived, engineered, and "assembled" in three-dimensional computer models. Before a single piece of metal is cut, Boeing people in all disciplines will know if each phase of the design is feasible.[40]

Speedier cross-functional teams will help Boeing meet its 1995 delivery date for the first 777.

Cross-functional teams have exciting potential. But they present management with the immense challenge of getting technical specialists to be effective boundary spanners.

What Makes Workplace Teams Effective?

●●●●●●●●●●●●●●●●●●
Discuss the criteria and determinants of team effectiveness.

Widespread use of team formats—including QC circles, self-managed teams, and cross-functional teams—necessitates greater knowledge of team effectiveness. A model of team effectiveness criteria and determinants is presented in Figure 13.5. This model is the product of two recent field studies involving 360 new-product development managers employed by 52 high-tech companies.[41] Importantly, it is a generic model, applying equally well to all workplace teams.[42]

FIGURE 13.5 ● A Model of Team Effectiveness

Source: Reprinted by permission of the publisher from "Managing Technologically Innovative Team Efforts toward New Product Success," by Hans J. Thamhain, *Journal of Product Innovation Management,* 7 (March 1990): 5–18. Copyright 1990 by Elsevier Science Publishing Co., Inc.

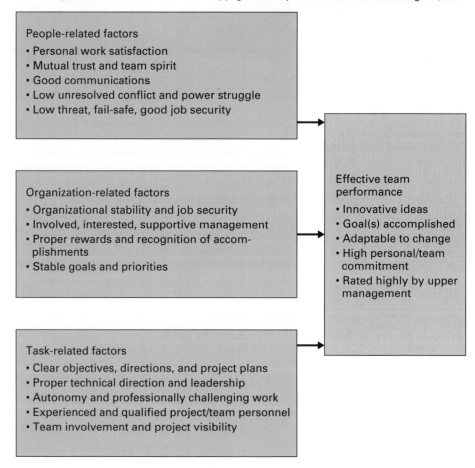

People-related factors
- Personal work satisfaction
- Mutual trust and team spirit
- Good communications
- Low unresolved conflict and power struggle
- Low threat, fail-safe, good job security

Organization-related factors
- Organizational stability and job security
- Involved, interested, supportive management
- Proper rewards and recognition of accomplishments
- Stable goals and priorities

Task-related factors
- Clear objectives, directions, and project plans
- Proper technical direction and leadership
- Autonomy and professionally challenging work
- Experienced and qualified project/team personnel
- Team involvement and project visibility

Effective team performance
- Innovative ideas
- Goal(s) accomplished
- Adaptable to change
- High personal/team commitment
- Rated highly by upper management

The five criteria for effective team performance in the center of Figure 13.5 parallel the criteria for organizational effectiveness discussed in Chapter 8. Thus, team effectiveness feeds organizational effectiveness. For example, if the Boeing 777 product development teams are not effective, the entire corporation will stumble.

Determinants of team effectiveness, in Figure 13.5, are grouped into people-, organization-, and task-related factors. Considered separately, these factors involve rather routine aspects of good management. But the collective picture reveals each factor to be part of a complex and interdependent whole. Managers cannot maximize just a few of them, ignore the rest, and hope to have an effective team. In the spirit of the Japanese concept of *Kaizen*, managers and team leaders need to strive for "continuous improvement" on all fronts. Because gains on one front will inevitably be offset by losses in another, the pursuit of team effectiveness and teamwork is an endless battle with no guarantees of success.[43] (See The World of Management.)

Let us focus on trust, one of the people-related factors in Figure 13.5 that can make or break work teams.

Trust: A Key to Team Effectiveness

trust belief in the integrity, character, or ability of others

Trust, a belief in the integrity, character, or ability of others, is essential if people are to achieve anything together in the long run. Participative management programs are very dependent on trust. Sadly, trust is not one of the hallmarks of the current American management scene. In a recent survey of 400 managers, for example, 33 percent said they distrusted their immediate bosses. Fifty-five percent reportedly did not believe their firm's top management![44] *Fortune* has sounded the alarm about this "trust gap."[45] To a greater extent than they may initially suspect, managers determine the level of trust in the organization and its component work groups and teams.

Zand's Model of Trust. Trust is not a free-floating variable. It affects, and in turn is affected by, other group processes. Dale Zand's model of work group interaction puts trust into proper perspective (see Figure 13.6). Zand believes that trust is the key to establishing productive interpersonal relationships.[46]

● ● ● ● ● ● ● ● ● ● ● ● ● ● ● ● ●

Explain why trust is a key ingredient of teamwork and discuss what management can do to build trust.

Primary responsibility for creating a climate of trust falls on the manager. Team members usually look to the manager, who enjoys hierarchical advantage and greater access to key information, to set the tone for interpersonal dealings. Threatening or intimidating actions by the manager are likely to encourage the group to bind together in cohesive resistance. Therefore, trust needs to be developed right from the beginning, when team members are still receptive to positive managerial influence.

Trust is initially encouraged by the manager's being open and honest. Trusting managers talk *with* their people rather than *at* them. A trusting manager, according to Zand's model, demonstrates a willingness to be influenced by others and to change if the facts show that a change is appropriate. Mutual trust between a manager and team members encourages *self-control,* as opposed to control through direct supervision. Hewlett-Packard (HP), a computer company with a reputation for excellent management, has carefully nurtured an organizational culture based on trust. According to the authors of *In Search of Excellence:*

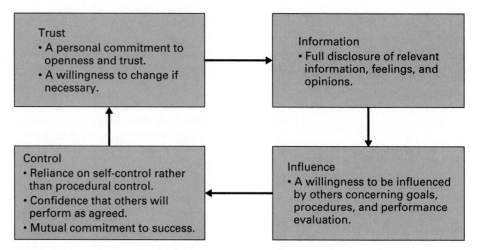

FIGURE 13.6 • Trust and Effective Group Interaction

Source: Reprinted from "Trust and Managerial Problem Solving," by Dale E. Zand and published in *Administrative Science Quarterly,* 17, no. 2 (June 1972) by permission of *The Administrative Science Quarterly* © 1972 by Cornell University.

> *The faith that HP has in its people is conspicuously in evidence in the corporate "open lab stock" policy. . . . The lab stock area is where the electrical and mechanical components are kept. The open lab stock policy means that not only do the engineers have free access to this equipment, but they are actually encouraged to take it home for their personal use![47]*

HP's rationale for this trusting policy is that the company will reap innovative returns no matter how the engineers choose to work with the valuable lab equipment.

Paradoxically, managerial control actually expands when committed group or team members enjoy greater freedom in pursuing consensual goals. Those who trust each other generally avoid taking advantage of others' weaknesses or shortcomings.[48]

Six Ways to Build Trust. Trust is a fragile thing. As most of us know from personal experience, trust grows at a painfully slow pace, yet can be destroyed in an instant with a thoughtless remark. Mistrust can erode the long-term effectiveness of work teams and organizations. According to management professor and consultant Fernando Bartolomé, managers need to concentrate on six areas: communication, support, respect, fairness, predictability, and competence. He explains:

- Communication *is a matter of keeping subordinates informed, providing accurate feedback, explaining decisions and policies, being candid about one's own problems, and resisting the temptation to hoard information for use as a tool or a reward. . . .*

- Support *means showing concern for subordinates as people. It means being available and approachable. It means helping people, coaching them, encouraging their ideas, and defending their positions. . . .*

Teamwork Has British Airways Flying High

Getting the most out of employees—without pushing them too hard—needs to be an ongoing process. It is at British Airways, which purged itself of 22,000 workers in 1983 and doesn't want to have to do it again. The airline, which lost embarrassing amounts of money in the early 1980s, believes customer service was the key to its turnaround. And the best way to a customer's heart? Good employee relations. Says Brian Robson, head of corporate development: "We use the phrase 'transparent organization'; that is, customers can actually see into BA. If they see a cold, authoritarian style of management, they know not to expect a warm, caring type of service."

Initially, BA put 35,000 employees through a training program designed to make them more sensitive not only to their own needs on the job but also to those of coworkers and customers. BA also taught group decision-making techniques to 2,000 managers. The idea was to get managers thinking like workers while involving workers in the search for greater efficiency. All employees took seminars with titles like Fit for Business, Putting People First, and Managing People First. These emphasized customer service and stress management together, and schooled employees to recognize when co-workers needed help.

BA began with its cabin crews, then in 1987 turned to service in airport terminals. The airline trained a cadre of about 100 supervisors to coach managers and workers in sharing ideas on improving baggage handling and ticket taking, rather than having the boss impose his ideas. Within six months, says Tony Clarry, head of customer service, employees at [London's] Heathrow Airport were saying that things seemed less busy—when, in fact, volume was up 10 percent. Today, BA is highly profitable and has one of the best reputations for service among the world's airlines.

Source: Excerpted from Thomas A. Stewart, "Do You Push Your People Too Hard?" *Fortune* (October 22, 1990): 128. © 1990 The Time Inc. Magazine Company. All rights reserved.

- Respect *feeds on itself. The most important form of respect is delegation, and the second most important is listening to subordinates and acting on their opinions. . . .*
- Fairness *means giving credit where it's due, being objective and impartial in performance appraisals, giving praise liberally. The opposite kind of behavior—favoritism, hypocrisy, misappropriating ideas and accomplishments, unethical behavior—is difficult to forgive and hugely destructive of trust. . . .*
- Predictability *is a matter of behaving consistently and dependably and of keeping both explicit and implicit promises. A broken promise can do considerable damage. . . .*
- Competence, *finally, means demonstrating technical and professional ability and good business sense. Employees don't want to be subordinate to people they see as incompetent. Trust grows from seeds of decent behavior, but it thrives on the admiration and respect that only a capable leader can command.*[49]

Managers find that trust begets trust. In other words, those who feel they are trusted tend to trust others in return.

Summary

Managers need a working understanding of group dynamics because groups are the basic building blocks of organizations. Both informal (friendship) and formal (work) groups are made up of two or more freely interacting individuals who have a common identity and purpose. After someone has been attracted to a group, cohesiveness—a "we" feeling—encourages continued membership. Roles are social expectations for behavior in a specific position, whereas norms are more general standards for conduct in a given social setting. Norms are enforced because they help the group survive, clarify role expectations, protect self-images, and enhance the group's identity by emphasizing key values. Compliance with role expectations and norms is rewarded with social reinforcement; noncompliance is punished by criticism, ridicule, and ostracism.

Mature groups that are characterized by mutual acceptance, encouragement of minority opinion, and minimal emotional conflict are the product of a developmental process with identifiable stages. During the first three stages—orientation, conflict and challenge, and cohesion—power and authority problems are resolved. Groups are faced with the obstacle of uncertainty over interpersonal relations during the last three stages—delusion, disillusion, and acceptance. Committees have a widespread reputation for inefficiency and ineffectiveness because they tend to get stalled in an early stage of group development.

Organizational politics centers on the pursuit of self-interest. Research shows greater political activity to be associated with higher levels of management, larger organizations, staff and marketing personnel, and reorganizations. Political tactics such as posturing, empire building, making the boss look good, collecting and using social IOUs, creating power and loyalty cliques, and destructive competition need to be kept in check if the organization is to be effective.

Although a fairly high degree of conformity is necessary if organizations and society in general are to function properly, blind conformity is ultimately dehumanizing and destructive. Research shows that individuals have a strong tendency to bend to the will of the majority, even if the majority is clearly wrong. Cohesive decision-making groups can be victimized by groupthink when unanimity becomes more important than critical evaluation of alternative courses of action.

Teams are becoming the structural format of choice. Today's employees generally have better technical skills than team skills. Cross-functional teams are particularly promising because they enable greater strategic speed. Three sets of factors—relating to people, organization, and task—combine to determine the effectiveness of a work team.

Trust, a key ingredient of effective teamwork, is disturbingly low in the American workplace today. When work group members trust one another, there will be a more active exchange of information, more interpersonal influence, and hence greater self-control. Managers can build trust through communication, support, respect (primarily in the form of delegation), fairness, predictability, and competence.

Terms to Understand

Group	Cohesiveness
Informal group	Role
Formal group	Norms

Ostracism
Organizational politics
Conformity

Groupthink
Cross-functional team
Trust

Questions for Discussion

1. Applying the sociological definition of *group,* how many groups do you belong to at this time? What positive and negative influences do they have on your behavior?

2. What unwritten norms are there for student behavior in the classroom? How are they communicated and enforced?

3. Using the example of a particular group you belong to, in what stage of development is it? How do you know?

4. According to your own experience, why do many committees fail to achieve stage 6 maturity?

5. What positive and/or negative experiences have you had with organizational politics?

6. What are the practical management implications of your score on the organizational politics quiz in the Management Ethics box?

7. Have you ever been a victim of blind conformity? Explain the circumstances.

8. As a member of a committee, what steps could you personally take to help the group avoid groupthink?

9. Using the model of team effectiveness in Figure 13.5 as a guide, what are your personal experiences with effective and ineffective teams? *Tip:* Consider all sorts of teams, including athletic teams, social groups, and work teams.

10. What does it take for you to trust someone? Is this likely to help or hinder you as a manager? Why?

Back to the Opening Case

Now that you have read Chapter 13, you should be able to answer the following questions about the Pillsbury case:

1. Why were mistrust and political maneuvering unavoidable at Pillsbury?

2. Why might blind conformity (possibly in the form of groupthink) be a problem for an organization with an executive such as William Spoor?

3. Could John Stafford have learned something from the following quotation from Tom Peters's 1987 book, *Thriving on Chaos?* "To move fast requires trust—period. Trust, though essentially interpersonal or one-on-one, is exhibited on a day-to-day basis by not signing up for what you can't deliver on."[50] Explain your answer, citing ways in which Stafford could have built trust.

4. Do you believe Grand Met's Allen Sheppard can create a climate of teamwork and trust at Pillsbury during the next few years? Explain your reasoning.

The Teamwork Transformation at AAL

Radical reorganizations tend to be associated with companies in crisis, and many people think a company that uses work teams must be taking lessons from the Japanese. Neither description fits Aid Association for Lutherans (AAL), the largest fraternal benefit society in the United States. AAL operates a huge insurance business: with assets of more than $4.6 billion and yearly revenues of over $1 billion, it ranks among the top 2 percent of American insurance companies. And in 1986, when it began to change, it was doing just fine. Like most American service companies, AAL hasn't been affected by foreign competition to the extent many manufacturing companies have. From its headquarters outside of Appleton, Wisconsin, it wasn't spending too much time wondering what the Japanese were doing. Nonetheless, in 1986 and 1987, AAL underwent a restructuring so radical it was dubbed "the transformation." It was grounded at every step in a belief in participative work teams and it improved AAL's productivity and customer relations almost overnight.

AAL was not in trouble in the mid-1980s, but it did recognize that slipping profit margins and increased competition were beginning to create a squeeze that would eventually force AAL to become more efficient for its own survival. The company workforce grew 40 percent between 1982 and 1986, and a survey revealed that employees were beginning to feel that they were working for just another big company.

The change began at the top, with a new president and CEO, Richard L. Gunderson. Convinced that AAL had to cut millions of dollars from costs, Gunderson replaced 25 of 26 top managers, mostly with people from within the company. This overhaul helped reduce resistance to radical change. From then on, most steps in the transformation involved workers from all levels, often volunteers, who formed teams to study every aspect of the reorganization. One hundred managers helped draw up the company's vision statement. A 12-person transformation team spent months asking employees about the company's strengths and weaknesses and about changes they'd like to see. Teams made decisions about strategy, structure, and tactics of the transformation.

The changes were most obvious in the company's insurance division. Like most service industries, insurance companies generally adopted functional divisions in the early part of the century, following the lead of manufacturing companies. That meant that AAL's insurance division was divided into three sections, one for life insurance, one for health insurance, and one for support services—billing and policy loans. This system took up to twenty days to process a complex application, and AAL's 1,900 field agents felt lost as they were bounced from clerk to clerk.

The transformed division has five groups, each serving a particular geographical region. Three or four cross-functional teams of twenty to thirty people make up each group. Each team can handle any of the 167 tasks formerly handled by the three divisions. Agents, who now work only with members of one team, develop personal relationships with that team. The team decides how to apportion tasks (as well as how to schedule their own flextime hours and vacations). Because applications don't have to move back and forth through divisions, the whole process can take just five days, one quarter as long as under the old system.

Although each team has a manager, three other layers of management disappeared in the transformation. As the team members took on management responsibilities, fifty-five jobs were eliminated. To help these displaced employees, AAL developed a successful Employee Placement Program, which offers career counseling and moral support as well as assistance in finding a new position inside or outside of the company. Overall, the number of personnel in the insurance division dropped 12 percent between 1987 and 1988, but the division's volume of business increased 10 percent. The company began training employees to take on even more of the tasks within their teams and pays them in part for their applied knowledge. Twice as many field agents now feel that headquarters really understands what happens in the field.

Of course, not all responses to the transformation have been positive. Job enrichment and redesign create new responsibilities and new stress, and some employees complain that they aren't paid to manage. In general, however, team morale is high, thanks in large part to the participation of employees at every stage of the team creation. The transformation was founded on the belief that people want to do a good job if they're given the right environment. AAL's success proves that if a company trains and trusts employees, anything can happen.

For Discussion

1. Using Figure 13.5 as a guide, why are AAL's insurance division teams effective?

2. What role, if any, does trust play in AAL's team approach?

3. Are organizational politics likely to thrive in AAL's team-based operations? Explain your position.

4. How would you answer the following question from an AAL team employee? "I'm not paid to manage, so why should I do my manager's job?"

References

Opening Quotation. Stephen R. Covey, *The Seven Habits of Highly Effective People* (New York: Simon & Schuster, 1989), p. 178.

Opening Case. Harris Collingwood, "Grand Met Shakes up Pillsbury," *Business Week* (March 20, 1989): 46; Richard Gibson and Robert Johnson, "Why Pillsbury's Chief from the '70s Is Again Taking Firm's Helm," *The Wall Street Journal* (March 1, 1988): 1, 21; Richard I. Kirkland, Jr., "Grand Met's Recipe for Pillsbury," *Fortune* (March 13, 1989): 61–68; Russell Mitchell, "The Gods Must Be Angry at Pillsbury's Phil Smith," *Business Week* (November 14, 1988): 61–62; Milton Moskowitz, Michael Katz, and Robert Levering, *Everybody's Business* (San Francisco: Harper & Row, 1980), pp. 68–69.

Closing Case. John Hoerr, "Work Teams Can Rev up Paper-Pushers, Too," *Business Week* (November 28, 1988): 64–72; Robert Janson and Richard L. Gunderson, "The Team Approach to Companywide Change," *National Productivity Review* (Winter 1990-91): 35–44; William H. Wagel, "Implacement at AAL," *Personnel* (November 1989): 8–12.

1. Quoted in Richard Gibson and Robert Johnson, "Why Pillsbury's Chief from the '70s Is Again Taking Firm's Helm," *The Wall Street Journal* (March 1, 1988): 21.

2. Quoted in Richard I. Kirkland, Jr., "Grand Met's Recipe for Pillsbury," *Fortune* (March 13, 1989): 61.

3. See Frank Friedlander, "The Ecology of Work Groups," in Jay W. Lorsch (ed.), *Handbook of Organizational Behavior* (Englewood Cliffs, N.J.: Prentice-Hall, 1987), pp. 301–314.

4. Joseph A. Litterer, *The Analysis of Organizations,* 2nd ed. (New York: Wiley, 1973), p. 231.

5. For an excellent elaboration of this definition, see David Horton Smith, "A Parsimonious Definition of 'Group': Toward Conceptual Clarity and Scientific Utility," *Sociological Inquiry,* 37 (Spring 1967): 141–167.

6. For a recent review of small group research, see John M. Levine and Richard L. Moreland, "Progress in Small Group Research," in *Annual Review of Psychology,* Vol. 41, eds. Mark R. Rosenzweig and Lyman W. Porter (Palo Alto, Calif.: Annual Reviews Inc., 1990), pp. 139–155.

7. See Aharon Tziner, "Differential Effects of Group Cohesiveness Types: A Clarifying Overview," *Social Behavior and Personality,* 10, no. 2 (1982): 227–239; and Peter E. Mudrack, "Group Cohesiveness and Productivity: A Closer Look," *Human Relations,* 42 (September 1989): 771–785.

8. Peter Nulty, "Cool Heads Are Trying to Keep Commodore Hot," *Fortune* (July 23, 1984): 38, 40.

9. Albert A. Harrison, *Individuals and Groups: Understanding Social Behavior* (Monterey, Calif.: Brooks/Cole, 1976), p. 16.

10. Ibid., p. 401.

11. Adapted from Daniel C. Feldman, "The Development and Enforcement of Group Norms," *Academy of Management Review,* 9 (January 1984): 47–53.

12. Joel Dreyfuss, "Reinventing IBM," *Fortune* (August 14, 1989): 34.

13. See Connie J. G. Gersick, "Marking Time: Predictable Transitions in Task Groups," *Academy of Management Journal,* 32 (June 1989): 274–309.

14. From *Group Effectiveness in Organizations* by L. N. Jewell and H. J. Reitz, Scott, Foresman, 1981. Reprinted by permission of the authors.

15. The following discussion of the six stages of group development is adapted from *Group Effectiveness in Organizations* by Linda N. Jewell and H. Joseph Reitz. Copyright 1981, Scott, Foresman and Company, pp. 15–20. Reprinted by permission. For ground-breaking research in this area, see Warren G. Bennis and Herbert A. Shepard, "A Theory of Group Development," *Human Relations,* 9 (1956): 415–437.

16. David E. Hall, "Winning at Office Politics," *Credit & Financial Management,* 86 (April 1984): 20.

17. See Abraham Zaleznik, "Real Work," *Harvard Business Review,* 67 (January-February 1989): 57–64.

18. See Don R. Beeman and Thomas W. Sharkey, "The Use and Abuse of Corporate Politics," *Business Horizons,* 30 (March-April 1987): 26–30; and Andrew J. DuBrin, *Winning Office Politics: DuBrin's Guide For the '90s* (Englewood Cliffs, N.J.: Prentice-Hall, 1990).

19. Victor Murray and Jeffrey Gandz, "Games Executives Play: Politics at Work," *Business Horizons,* 23 (December 1980): 16.

20. Andrew J. DuBrin, *Fundamentals of Organizational Behavior: An Applied Perspective,* 2nd ed. (Elmsford, N.Y.: Pergamon Press, 1978), p. 154.

21. Dan Farrell and James C. Petersen, "Patterns of Political Behavior in Organizations," *Academy of Management Review,* 7 (July 1982): 407.

22. "Corporate Culture," *Business Week* (October 27, 1980): 148, 154.

23. Adapted from Dan L. Madison, Robert W. Allen, Lyman W. Porter, Patricia A. Renwick, and Bronston T. Mayes, "Organizational Politics: An Exploration of Managers' Perceptions," *Human Relations,* 33 (February 1980): 79–100. Also see Andrew J. DuBrin, "Career Maturity, Organizational Rank, and Political Behavioral Tendencies: A Correlational Analysis of Organizational Politics and Career Experience," *Psychological Reports,* 63 (October 1988): 531–537.

24. Madison et al., "Organizational Politics," p. 97.

25. These six political tactics have been adapted from a more extensive list found in DuBrin, *Fundamentals of Organizational Behavior,* pp. 158–170.

26. Common problems of politics in employee performance appraisal are discussed in Clinton O. Longenecker, Henry P. Sims, Jr., and Dennis A. Gioia, "Behind the Mask: The Politics of Employee Appraisal," *The Academy of Management Executive,* 1 (August 1987): 183–193. Also see Paul Tosey, "Politics in Context: Our Secret Lives," *Management Education and Development,* 20 (Fall 1989): 254–269.

27. See Jerry B. Harvey, "Some Thoughts about Organizational Backstabbing: Or, How Come Every Time I Get Stabbed in the Back My Fingerprints Are on the Knife?" *Academy of Management Executive,* 3 (November 1989): 271–277.

28. Adapted from DuBrin, *Fundamentals of Organizational Behavior,* pp. 179–182.

29. See Solomon E. Asch, *Social Psychology* (Englewood Cliffs, N.J.: Prentice-Hall, 1952), Chap. 16.

30. For details, see Taha Amir, "The Asch Conformity Effect: A Study in Kuwait," *Social Behavior and Personality,* 12, no. 2 (1984): 187–190; Timothy P. Williams and Shunya Sogon, "Group Composition and Conforming Behavior in Japanese Students," *Japanese Psychological Research,* 26, no. 4 (1984): 231–234.

31. Irving L. Janis, *Groupthink,* 2nd ed. (Boston: Houghton Mifflin, 1982), p. 9. See also Gregory Moorhead, "Groupthink: Hypothesis in Need of Testing," *Group & Organization Studies,* 7 (December 1982): 429–444; Carrie R. Leana, "A Partial Test of Janis' Groupthink Model: Effects of Group Cohesiveness and Leader Behavior on Defective Decision Making," *Journal of Management,* 11 (Spring 1985): 5–17.

32. See Glen Whyte, "Groupthink Reconsidered," *Academy of Management Review,* 14 (January 1989): 40–56.

33. Adapted from a list in Janis, *Groupthink,* pp. 174–175.

34. Ibid., p. 275.

35. For excellent discussions of the devil's advocate role, see Charles R. Schwenk, "Devil's Advocacy in Managerial Decision Making," *Journal of Management Studies,* 21 (April 1984): 153–168; and Richard A. Cosier and Charles R. Schwenk, "Agreement and Thinking Alike: Ingredients for Poor Decisions," *Academy of Management Executive,* 4 (February 1990): 69–74.

36. Adapted from a list in Janis, *Groupthink,* pp. 262–271.

37. Andrew S. Grove, *High Output Management* (New York: Random House, 1983), p. 79.

38. Andrew Malcolm, *The Tyranny of the Group* (Toronto: Clarke, Irwin, 1973), p. 4.

39. Peter F. Drucker, "The Coming of the New Organization," *Harvard Business Review,* 66 (January-February 1988): 47.

40. Dori Jones Yang and Michael Oneal, "How Boeing Does It," *Business Week* (July 9, 1990): p. 49.

41. See Hans J. Thamhain, "Managing Technologically Innovative Team Efforts Toward New Product Success," *Journal of Product Innovation Management,* 7 (March 1990): 5–18.

42. For an instructive discussion of teams, see Steve Buchholz and Thomas Roth, *Creating the High-Performance Team* (New York: John Wiley & Sons, 1987).

43. See Dee Dee O'Connor, "Trouble in the American Workplace: The Team Player Concept Strikes Out," *Records Management Quarterly,* 24 (April 1990): 12–15; and Michael A. Verespej, "Yea, Teams? Not Always," *Industry Week* (June 18, 1990): 104–105.

44. Data from Norma R. Fritz, "Trust Me," *Personnel,* 67 (April 1990, HR Focus supp.): 4–5.

45. See Alan Farnham, "The Trust Gap," *Fortune* (December 4, 1989): 56–78.

46. See Dale E. Zand, "Trust and Managerial Problem Solving," *Administrative Science Quarterly,* 17 (June 1972): 229–239.

47. Thomas J. Peters and Robert H. Waterman, Jr., *In Search of Excellence* (New York: Harper & Row, 1982), p. 245.

48. See Louis B. Barnes, "Managing the Paradox of Organizational Trust," *Harvard Business Review,* 59 (March-April 1981): 108; and Marsha Sinetar, "Building Trust Into Corporate Relationships," *Organizational Dynamics,* 16 (Winter 1988): 73–79.

49. Excerpted from Fernando Bartolomé, "Nobody Trusts the Boss Completely—Now What?" *Harvard Business Review,* 67 (March-April 1989): 137–139.

50. Tom Peters, *Thriving on Chaos* (New York: Knopf, 1987), p. 514.

14

Influence Processes and Leadership

Leaders have a clear idea of what they want to do—personally and professionally—and the strength to persist in the face of setbacks, even failures. They know where they are going and why.

WARREN BENNIS

CHAPTER OBJECTIVES

When you finish studying this chapter, you should be able to

- Identify and describe eight generic influence tactics used in modern organizations.
- Define the term *power,* relate power and authority, and identify the five bases of power.
- Summarize what the Ohio State model and the Leadership Grid® have taught managers about leadership.
- Describe the path-goal theory of leadership and explain how the assumption on which it is based differs from the assumption on which Fiedler's contingency theory is based.
- Explain how the Vroom/Yetton/Jago and transformational leadership theories can help managers deal with decision making and with change, respectively.
- Identify the two key functions that mentors perform and explain how a mentor can help develop a junior manager's leadership skills.
- Explain the management of antecedents and consequences in behavior modification.

Can Bill Gates Keep Microsoft in the Fast Lane?

It is a familiar story in the computer industry of the past two decades. A high school kid gets hooked on computers; he and his hacker friends spend all their time writing programs and creating games. Eventually, he begins turning his hacking abilities to more practical and profitable pursuits and forms a company. The company creates a product that sets the world buzzing, and the whiz kids become instant millionaires.

The story of William H. Gates III follows this familiar outline. Bill has never done anything on a small scale. At the age of 14, he and three friends started a programming group. After developing a computerized payroll system for their school, they went on to design a program that helped monitor road traffic. The group kicked Bill out for a time—he was the youngest by two years. But two years later, when it formed a company to sell the traffic counter to cities, the group reinstated Bill and made him president. Even at this early age, Bill's peers recognized that he was a rare individual—one with an aptitude for both business and computers.

After a brief stint at Harvard, Gates and one of his original programming pals, Paul Allen, started writing a condensed version of the computer language BASIC that could be used by the new small computers being built around a new Intel microprocessor. In 1975, Gates and Allen founded Microsoft Corp., and in 1979 they moved to Seattle. There they were discovered by the biggest of all computer companies—IBM. Big Blue, trying to make up for its slow start in personal computers, needed someone to create an op-

erating system for its new machines. Gates was realistic—he recognized that Microsoft was not yet up to the task, but he knew someone in Seattle who had written a "quick and dirty operating system," or Q-DOS. Gates bought Q-DOS, modified it, and sold it to IBM. By 1991, 60 million copies of the operating system, now known as MS-DOS or just DOS, had been sold. Over half of all personal computers relied on DOS. Microsoft had grown to 5,200 employees and over $1 billion of business annually. The company boasted the highest profit margins in the software industry, and Bill Gates was worth about $2.8 billion.

As Microsoft grew, it maintained the feel of a small group of programmers. People worked long, irregular hours. They wore blue jeans and no ties and came to work barefoot if they liked. Terms like *superneat* and *word prossers* flew around as freely as Frisbees. They ordered out for pizza, had picnics and parties together, and worked out at a local health club, courtesy of the company. Gates put in 14-hour days and often came to work on Sundays.

If a few details were changed, the hero of this part of the story could be named Steven Jobs or Mitchell Kapor, and the company could be Jobs's Apple Computer or Kapor's Lotus Development. But neither of those technical wizards made a successful transition from entrepreneur to leader. Each left the company he had started when it got huge and muscled its way into a top slot in the computer world. Gates, however, still runs Microsoft and still stands with one foot in the business world and the other in the technical. He has proved to be a successful manager and an inspiring leader.

One of Gates's early discoveries was delegating authority without losing touch. "He learned at a young age that you've got to give up power to get power," as a former Microsoft executive puts it.[1] He hired professional managers as well as programmers. He and his seven "architects" or "gurus" decide which new technologies the company will get involved in and which of Bill's ideas will be pursued. They then turn the work over to one of the company's twelve business units, some of which include only thirty people. Each unit focuses on one type of software and is responsible for knowing everything competitors are doing in that area. Each unit tries to stay ahead of its rivals in both technology and productivity, but company guidelines ensure that programs will function effectively with those of other Microsoft groups.

To keep the small-company feel, Microsoft uses its own version of electronic mail. Anyone can send Chairman Bill a message any time, and he makes a point of trying to respond on the same day. He even sends "E-mail" to his parents. (His mother admits that his response to her messages is not always so rapid.) Unlike many successful geniuses, Gates has managed to keep his ego in check, though he is not always easy to deal with. He likes to argue and he can be caustic. The people around him have learned to be tough. Nevertheless, most of them accept the lesson and stay with the company. Microsoft has a low turnover rate—less than 10 percent yearly. Salaries aren't outlandish but, before the company went public in 1986, even programmers got stock options. Now they can purchase shares at a discount.

One of Gates's secrets is that he still takes on plenty of risks and challenges, so he can still feel much of the excitement of the entrepreneur betting his future on a start-up company. Although Microsoft has entries in every major area of personal computer software, it tends to gamble much of its development time and money on one particular area. And it still alternately competes and collaborates with the biggest names in the field, including IBM, Apple, and Lotus. Current projects include a computer that can read handwriting; software that will allow PCs to work with photos, sound, and animation; and a new concept in software that would allow users to create their own programs by combining favorite elements from other programs. Gates's dream is a computer in every home and business, each one running Microsoft software. He's not likely to become bored soon.

What do the following situations have in common?

- An employee praises her supervisor's new outfit immediately before asking for the afternoon off.
- A milling-machine operator tells a friend that he will return the favor if his friend will watch out for the supervisor while he takes an unauthorized cigarette break.
- An office manager attempts to head off opposition to a computerized word-processing system by carefully explaining how the new system will make everyone's job easier.

Aside from the fact that all of these situations take place on the job, the common denominator is "influence." In each case, someone is trying to get his or her own way by influencing someone else's behavior. Bill Gates, as documented in the

influence any attempt to change another's behavior

Opening Case, has had a tremendous influence on Microsoft and its stakeholders.

Influence is any attempt by a person to change the behavior of superiors, peers, or subordinates. Influence is not inherently good or bad. As the foregoing situations illustrate, influence can be used for purely selfish reasons, to subvert organizational objectives, or to enhance organizational effectiveness. Managerial success is firmly linked to the ability to exercise the right sort of influence at the right time.[2]

The purpose of this chapter is to examine different approaches to influencing others. We focus specifically on influence tactics, power, leadership, mentoring, and behavior modification.

Influence Tactics in the Workplace

A recent replication and refinement of an earlier ground-breaking study provides useful insights about on-the-job influence.[3] Both studies asked employees basically the same question: "How do you get your boss, coworker, or subordinate to do something you want?" The following eight generic influence tactics emerged:

• • • • • • • • • • • • • • • • •

Identify and describe eight generic influence tactics used in modern organizations.

1. *Consultation.* Seeking someone's participation in a decision or change.
2. *Rational persuasion.* Trying to convince someone by relying on a detailed plan, supporting information, reasoning, or logic.
3. *Inspirational appeals.* Appealing to someone's emotions, values, or ideals to generate enthusiasm and confidence.
4. *Ingratiating tactics.* Making someone feel important or good before making a request; acting humbly or friendly before making a request.
5. *Coalition tactics.* Seeking the aid of others to persuade someone to agree.
6. *Pressure tactics.* Relying on intimidation, demands, or threats to gain compliance or support.
7. *Upward appeals.* Obtaining formal or informal support of higher management.
8. *Exchange tactics.* Offering an exchange of favors; reminding someone of a past favor; offering to make a personal sacrifice.[4]

These influence tactics are *generic* because they are used by various organizational members to influence subordinates (downward influence), peers (lateral influence), or superiors (upward influence). Table 14.1 indicates what the researchers found out about patterns of use for the three different directions of influence. Notice how consultation, rational persuasion, and inspirational appeals were the three most popular tactics, regardless of the direction of influence. Meanwhile, pressure tactics, upward appeals, and exchange tactics consistently were the least used influence tactics. Ingratiating and coalition tactics fell in the mid-range of use. This is an encouraging pattern from the standpoint of getting things done through problem solving rather than through intimidation and conflict.

Do women and men tend to rely on different influence tactics? Available research evidence reveals no systematic gender-based differences, relative to influencing others.[5] In contrast, influence tactics used by employees to influence

TABLE 14.1 • Use of Generic Organizational Influence Tactics

Tactic	Rank order (by direction of influence)		
	Downward	*Lateral*	*Upward*
Consultation	1	1	2
Rational persuasion	2	2	1
Inspirational appeals	3	3	3
Ingratiating tactics	4	4	5
Coalition tactics	5	5	4
Pressure tactics	6	7	7
Upward appeals	7	6	6
Exchange tactics	8	8	8

Source: Adapted from discussion in Gary Yukl and Cecilia M. Falbe, "Influence Tactics and Objectives in Upward, Downward, and Lateral Influence Attempts." *Journal of Applied Psychology,* 75 (April 1990): 132–140.

their bosses were found to vary with different leadership styles. Employees influencing authoritarian managers tended to rely on ingratiating tactics and upward appeals. Rational persuasion was used most often to influence participative managers.[6]

Power

Power is inevitable in modern organizations. According to one advocate of the positive and constructive use of power:

> *Power must be used because managers must influence those they depend on. Power also is crucial in the development of managers' self-confidence and willingness to support subordinates. From this perspective, power should be accepted as a natural part of any organization. Managers should recognize and develop their own power to coordinate and support the work of subordinates; it is powerlessness, not power, that undermines organizational effectiveness.[7]*

As a manager, if you understand power, its bases, and its responsible use, you will have an advantage when it comes to getting things accomplished with and through others.

What Is Power?

Power is "the ability to marshal the human, informational, and material resources to get something done."[8] Power affects organizational members in the following three areas:

1. *Decisions.* A packaging engineer decides to take on a difficult new assignment after hearing her boss's recommendations.

●●●●●●●●●●●●●●●●●
Define the term *power,* relate power and authority, and identify the five bases of power.

power ability to marshal resources to get something done

The wonderful world of Walt Disney is no longer limited to theme parks, movies, and television shows, thanks to the creative influence of CEO Michael Eisner. Disney's fast-growing chain of retail outlets is the product of Eisner's new-idea-a-minute style of leadership. Not all of Eisner's ideas pan out so well, but his energy and enthusiastic use of expert power pumped life into a company once dismissed by many as nothing more than a Mickey Mouse operation.

2. *Behavior.* A hospital lab technician achieves a month of perfect attendance after receiving a written warning about absenteeism from his supervisor.

3. *Situations.* The productivity of a product design group increases dramatically following the purchase of computerized workstations.[9]

Another instructive way of looking at power is to distinguish between "power over" (ability to dominate), "power to" (ability to act freely), and "power from" (ability to resist the demands of others).[10]

By emphasizing the word *ability* in our definition and discussion of power, we can contrast power with authority. As defined in Chapter 8, authority is the "right" to direct the activities of others. Authority is an officially sanctioned privilege that may or may not get results. In contrast, power is the demonstrated *ability* to get results. As illustrated in Figure 14.1, one may alternatively possess authority but have no power, possess no authority yet have power, or possess both authority and power. The first situation, authority but no power, occurred in Vietnam when American soldiers refused to follow their officers into battle. Power but no authority can occur, for example, when employees respond to the wishes of the supervisor's spouse.[11] Finally, a manager who gets subordinates to work hard on an important project has both authority and power (see Managers in Action).

The Five Bases of Power

Essential to the successful use of power in organizations is an understanding of the various bases of power. One widely cited classification of power bases identifies five types of power: reward, coercive, legitimate, referent, and expert.[12]

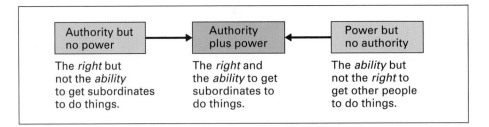

FIGURE 14.1 • The Relationship between Authority and Power

Reward Power. One's ability to grant rewards to those who comply with a command or request is the key to **reward power**. Management's reward power can be strengthened by linking pay raises, merit pay, and promotions to job performance. Sought-after expressions of friendship or trust also enhance reward power.

reward power gaining compliance through rewards

Coercive Power. Rooted in fear, **coercive power** is based on threatened or actual punishment. For example, a manager might threaten a habitually tardy employee with a demotion if he or she is late one more time.

coercive power gaining compliance through threats or punishment

Legitimate Power. **Legitimate power** is achieved when a person's superior position alone prompts another person to act in a desired manner. This type of power closely parallels formal authority, as discussed above. Parents, teachers, religious leaders, and managers who demand obedience by virtue of their superior social position are attempting to exercise legitimate power. Note, however, the following warning about legitimate power:

legitimate power compliance based on one's formal position

> *Trying to control others solely by directing them and on the basis of the power associated with one's position simply will not work—first, because managers are always dependent on some people over whom they have no formal authority, and second, because virtually no one in modern organizations will passively accept and completely obey a constant stream of orders from someone just because he or she is the "boss."*[13]

One might reasonably conclude that legitimate power has been eroded by its frequent abuse (or overuse) through the years.

Referent Power. An individual has **referent power** over those who identify with him or her if they comply on that basis alone. Personal attraction is an elusive thing to define, let alone consciously cultivate. *Charisma* is a term often used in conjunction with referent power. Although leaders with the personal magnetism of Abraham Lincoln, John Kennedy, or Martin Luther King, Jr., are always in short supply, charisma in the workplace can be problematic. For example, Mitchell D. Kapor, the founder and former head of Lotus Development Corporation, voiced these complaints about charisma:

referent power compliance based on charisma or personal identification

> *I fundamentally don't like charisma, no matter who has it. To me, having charisma means that I can get you to do things that violate your own self-interest. . . . I like to be in environments where everybody is at a peer level and people get to make up their own minds. . . .*

General "Stormin' Norman": A Study in Authority and Power

During the U.N.-sanctioned war against Iraq, the image that Americans found most reassuring was of a tall, powerfully built four-star general gesturing at charts and responding to questions rapidly and articulately. He was equally sincere as he joked with reporters one minute and then vented his anger toward Saddam Hussein the next. Even many people who were against the armed conflict found themselves listening to General Norman Schwarzkopf with respect and admiration. Here was a different kind of a military leader—one who didn't hide behind technical jargon or political euphemisms, was as intelligent as anyone questioning him, and even in refusing to answer questions, was direct in his response. He was an exceptional manager, coordinating a huge fighting force from many nations. Perhaps most important, he was clearly a man with emotions as well as intellect and cunning. Unlike so many high-profile leaders, he seemed real.

Before the war, some who worked with Schwarzkopf weren't sure he was the right man to head the largest-scale military operation in twenty years. He has a hot temper, and he's so competitive that his family refuses to play Trivial Pursuit with him anymore. One of his mottoes is "A good leader never walks by a mistake." Some view that attitude as perfectionist; others simply call him a tyrant. At the same time, he can be charming, charismatic, sensitive, and self-deprecating. He admires officers who know what mud tastes like, and he has a reputation for putting his life on the line to save others. His thirty-five years on active duty and lifelong interest in military strategy paid off when what he described as his "Hail Mary" play worked against Iraq.

Schwarzkopf had the authority to do his job effectively. By the time President Bush called for a ground assault, he had the power as well. No doubt he owes some of his popularity to the Allied victory. Nevertheless, many who watched him on television liked not just the outcome of his leadership but the dignity and intelligence with which he used his power. He has received offers to write books, run corporations, and head universities. More than one commentator has suggested that Stormin' Norman would make a good president.

Sources: Peter Grier, " 'Management' Key to Gulf Victory," *The Christian Science Monitor* (March 8, 1991): 4; Tom Mathews, "A Soldier of Conscience," *Newsweek* (March 11, 1991): 32–34; Molly Moore, "Commanding the Storm," *The Washington Post National Weekly Edition* (February 25–March 3, 1991): 6–7.

> *[The other problem with] charisma is that people will more happily follow whichever direction you are heading off in, whether it's a good direction or not. And that's very dangerous. I never liked the fact that, at Lotus, people might take temporary leave of their senses because they wanted to agree with me. Or sometimes it would happen that people would interpret a little twitch that I had as some sort of royal command—and before you know it, they were going off and reorienting an entire department because of something that I didn't actually say.*[14]

Still, as we will see in our discussion of transformational leadership later in the chapter, charisma does have its positive side.

Expert Power.   Those who possess and can dispense valued information generally exercise **expert power** over those in need of such information. Computer hardware experts and programmers, for instance, are in a position today to wield a great deal of expert power. Anyone who has ever been taken advantage of by

expert power compliance based on ability to dispense valued information

More than 5,000 strikeouts, 300 + wins, and seven no hitters, each a new record. Not bad for a homespun guy in his mid-40s from Alvin, Texas. There is more to Nolan Ryan than a legendary collection of statistics amassed during a quarter-century of professional baseball. He is a successful hands-on owner/manager of a cattle ranch and a bank. In an era of bank failures, Ryan's little bank in Danbury, Texas, posted impressive growth numbers and focused on expansion. He is described as a natural leader who excels at everything he does.

leadership social influence process involving voluntary pursuit of collective objectives

formal leadership the process of influencing others to pursue official objectives

an unscrupulous automobile mechanic knows what expert power in the wrong hands can mean.[15]

Using Power Responsibly

Experts on power are quick to point out that power is neutral. Like a hammer, it is a tool. Just as a hammer can be used either constructively to build a house or destructively to shatter a window, power also can be used in a positive or negative manner. David C. McClelland, a respected researcher on power, has defined the responsible use of power as it applies to leadership:

> *An effective leader is an educator. One leads by helping them set their goals, by communicating widely throughout the group, and by taking initiative in formulating means of achieving the goals, and finally, by inspiring the members of the group to feel strong enough to work hard for those goals. Such an image of the exercise of power and influence in a leadership role should not frighten anybody and should convince more people that power exercised in this way is not only not dangerous but of the greatest possible use to society.*[16]

Power exercised for power's sake, on the other hand, can be quite dangerous and of little use to society.

Leadership

Leadership has fascinated people since the dawn of recorded history. References to both good and bad leadership in the literature of every age give testimony to the search for good leaders that has been a common thread running through human civilization. In view of research evidence that effective leadership is associated with both better performance and more ethical performance, the search for ways to identify (or develop) good leaders needs to continue.[17]

Leadership Defined

The research on leadership has produced many definitions of the term. Much of the variation is semantic; the definition offered here is a workable compromise. **Leadership** is "a social influence process in which the leader seeks the voluntary participation of subordinates in an effort to reach organizational objectives."[18] *Voluntary* is the operative term here. To encourage voluntary participation, leaders supplement any authority and power they possess with their personal attributes and social skills. As a wit once observed, a good leader is someone who can tell you to go to hell and make you look forward to the trip!

Formal versus Informal Leaders

Experts on leadership distinguish between formal and informal leadership. **Formal leadership** is the process of influencing relevant others to pursue official

informal leadership the process of influencing others to pursue unofficial objectives

organizational objectives. **Informal leadership,** in contrast, is the process of influencing others to pursue unofficial objectives that may or may not serve the organization's interests. Formal leaders generally have a measure of legitimate power because of their formal authority, whereas informal leaders typically lack formal authority. Beyond that, both types rely on expedient combinations of reward, coercive, referent, and expert power. Informal leaders who identify with the job to be done are a valuable asset to an organization. Conversely, an organization can be brought to its knees by informal leaders who turn cohesive work groups against the organization.

Like the study of management, the study of leadership has evolved as theories were developed and refined by successive generations of researchers.[19] Something useful has been learned at each stage of development. We now turn to significant milestones in the evolution of leadership theory by examining the trait, behavioral styles, situational, and transformational approaches (see Figure 14.2).

Trait Theory

During most of recorded history the prevailing assumption was that leaders are born and not made. Leaders such as Alexander the Great, Napoleon Bonaparte, and George Washington were said to have been blessed with an inborn ability to lead. This so-called great-man approach to leadership eventually gave way to trait theory. According to one observer, "under the influence of the behavioristic school of psychological thought, the fact was accepted that leadership traits are not completely inborn but can also be acquired through learning and experience. Attention turned to the search for universal traits possessed by leaders."[20]

FIGURE 14.2 ● The Evolution of Leadership Theory

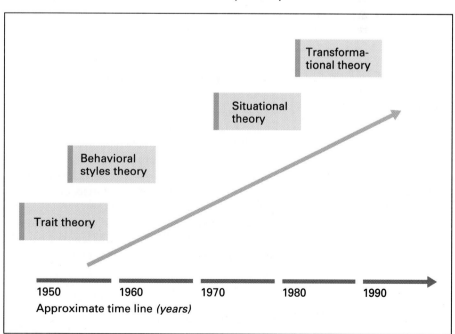

As the popularity of the trait approach mushroomed during the second quarter of the twentieth century, literally hundreds of physical, mental, and personality traits were said to be the key determinants of successful leadership. Unfortunately, few theorists agreed on the most important traits of a good leader. The predictive value of trait theory was severely limited because traits tend to be a chicken-and-egg proposition: Was George Washington a good leader because he had self-confidence, or did he have self-confidence because he was thrust into a leadership role at a young age? In spite of inherent problems, trait profiles provide a useful framework for examining what it takes to be a good leader.

An Early Trait Profile. Not until 1948 was a comprehensive review of competing trait theories conducted. After comparing more than one hundred studies of leader traits and characteristics, the reviewer uncovered moderate agreement on only five traits. In the reviewer's words, "the average person who occupies a position of leadership exceeds the average member of his group in the following respects: (1) intelligence, (2) scholarship, (3) dependability in exercising responsibilities, (4) activity and social participation, and (5) socioeconomic status."[21]

Renewed Interest in Leader Traits. Interest in the trait approach to leadership has been stirred recently on two different fronts. First, James M. Kouzes and Barry Z. Posner surveyed over 7,500 managers from across the United States during the 1980s to determine the traits they admired in superior leaders. *Honesty* was selected by 87 percent of the respondents, easily outdistancing *competent* (74 percent), *forward-looking* (67 percent), *inspiring* (61 percent), and *intelligent* (46 percent).[22] This sequence could be a positive sign, from the standpoint of business ethics.

A second source of renewed interest in leadership traits is the ongoing debate about female versus male leadership traits (see Insights & Issues).

Behavioral Styles Theory

During World War II, the study of leadership took on a significant new twist. Rather than concentrating on the personal traits of successful leaders, researchers began turning their attention to patterns of leader behavior (called leadership styles). In other words, attention turned from who the leader was to how the leader actually behaved. One early laboratory study of leader behavior demonstrated that followers overwhelmingly preferred managers who had a democratic style to those with an authoritarian style or a laissez-faire (hands-off) style.[23] An updated review of these three classic leadership styles can be found in Table 14.2.

For a number of years, theorists and managers hailed democratic leadership as the key to productive and happy employees. Eventually, however, their enthusiasm was dampened when critics pointed out that the original study relied on children as subjects and virtually ignored productivity. Although there is general agreement that these basic styles exist, debate has been vigorous over their relative value and appropriateness. Practical experience has shown, for example, that the democratic style does not always stimulate better performance. Some employees prefer to be told what to do rather than to participate in decision making.

Do Women and Men Use Different Leadership Styles?

Few topics in the field of management have sparked more heated debate than the question of whether male and female managers differ in their leadership styles. Judy Rosener is one of a number of researchers who have recently proposed that women and men do differ in their styles and that the difference results from the ways the two sexes are socialized in our still male-dominated society.

Rosener studied the results of a survey by the International Women's Forum (IWF), an organization of prominent female leaders. The women were matched with male leaders, and both groups then filled out an eight-page questionnaire. Among Rosener's conclusions: women tend to be transformational leaders who focus on getting subordinates "to transfer their own self-interest into the interest of the group through concern for a broader goal."* In contrast, men tend to be transactional leaders who "view job performance as a series of transactions with subordinates—exchanging rewards for services rendered."** As part of their interactive style, women tend to encourage participation, share information and power, enhance the self-worth of others, energize others, and prefer to use personal rather than structural power, according to the study.

Rosener's study and conclusions have been attacked on a number of grounds. Some of her critics charge that her attempt to claim special

abilities for women is just another form of stereotyping. A thorough survey of the large body of research performed on gender differences over the past fifteen years fails to support most of Rosener's conclusions. Some observers suggest that the IWF results are more a reflection of the organizations that employed the women and men than of the people themselves. Compared with the organizations that employed the men, the organizations employing the women tended to be more nontraditional, smaller, and less hierarchical. Such organizations, some argue, encourage transformational leadership in *all* of their leaders.

As Rosener points out, it is ironic that many organizations now value and encourage traits that have long been identified with women and that women have often been criticized for possessing—such as preferences for consensus rather than competition and for intuition rather than linear logic. Many experts agree that flatter, less hierarchical organizations are now looking for leaders with traits that used to be thought of as "feminine." But smart organizations hire people with successful traits and abilities regardless of gender.

Sources: Jaclyn Fierman, "Do Women Manage Differently?," *Fortune* (December 17, 1990): 115–118; Gary N. Powell, "One More Time: Do Female and Male Managers Differ?," *Academy of Management Executive* (August 1990): 68–75; Judy B. Rosener, "Ways Women Lead," *Harvard Business Review* (November-December 1990): 119–125; "Stereotyping Charge in Management Study Denied," *The Arizona Republic* (December 9, 1990): F2; "Ways Women and Men Lead," *Harvard Business Review* (January-February 1991): 150–160.

*Judy B. Rosener, "Ways Women Lead," *Harvard Business Review* (November-December 1990): 120.

**Rosener, 120

● ● ● ● ● ● ● ● ● ● ● ● ● ● ● ●
Summarize what the Ohio State model and the Leadership Grid® have taught managers about leadership.

The Ohio State Model. While the democratic style of leadership was receiving attention, a slightly different behavioral approach to leadership emerged. This second approach began in the late 1940s when a team of Ohio State University researchers defined two independent dimensions of leader behavior.[24] One dimension, called "initiating structure," was the leader's efforts to get things organized and get the job done. The second dimension, labeled "consideration," was the degree of trust, friendship, respect, and warmth that the leader extended to subordinates. By making a matrix out of these two independent dimensions of leader

TABLE 14.2 ● The Three Classic Styles of Leadership

	Authoritarian	Democratic	Laissez-faire
Nature	Leader retains all authority and responsibility	Leader delegates a great deal of authority while retaining ultimate responsibility	Leader grants responsibility and authority to group
	Leaders assign people to clearly defined tasks	Work is divided and assigned on the basis of participatory decision making	Group members are told to work things out themselves and do the best they can
	Primarily a downward flow of communication	Active two-way flow of upward and downward communication	Primarily horizontal communication among peers
Primary strength	Stresses prompt, orderly, and predictable performance	Enhances personal commitment through participation	Permits self-starters to do things as they see fit without leader interference
Primary weakness	Approach tends to stifle individual initiative	Democratic process is time-consuming	Group may drift aimlessly in the absence of direction from leader

behavior, the Ohio State researchers identified four styles of leadership (see Figure 14.3).

This particular scheme proved to be fertile ground for leadership theorists, and variations of the original Ohio State approach soon appeared.[25] Leadership theorists began a search for the "one best style" of leadership. The high-structure, high-consideration style was generally hailed as the best all-around style. This "high-high" style has intuitive appeal because it embraces the best of both categories of leader behavior. But one researcher cautioned in 1966 that, although there seemed to be a positive relationship between consideration and subordinate satisfaction, a positive link between the high-high style and work group performance had not been proved conclusively.[26]

The Leadership Grid®. Developed by Robert R. Blake and Jane S. Mouton, and originally called the Managerial Grid®, the Leadership Grid® is a trademarked and widely recognized typology of leadership styles.[27] Today, amid the growing popularity of situational and transformational leadership theories, Blake and his colleagues remain convinced that there is one best style of leadership.

As illustrated in Figure 14.4, the Leadership Grid® has "concern for production" on the horizontal axis and "concern for people" on the vertical axis. Concern for production involves a desire to achieve greater output, cost effectiveness, and profits in profit-seeking organizations. Concern for people involves promoting friendship, helping coworkers get the job done, and attending to things that matter to people, like pay and working conditions. By scaling each axis from 1 to 9, the grid is highlighted by five major styles:

9,1 style: primary concern for production; people secondary

1,9 style: primary concern for people; production secondary

1,1 style: minimal concern for either production or people

5,5 style: moderate concern for both production and people to maintain the status quo

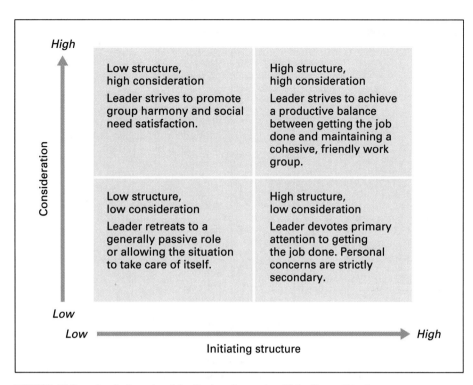

High

Low structure,
high consideration

Leader strives to promote
group harmony and social
need satisfaction.

High structure,
high consideration

Leader strives to achieve
a productive balance
between getting the job
done and maintaining a
cohesive, friendly work
group.

Low structure,
low consideration

Leader retreats to a
generally passive role
or allowing the situation
to take care of itself.

High structure,
low consideration

Leader devotes primary
attention to getting
the job done. Personal
concerns are strictly
secondary.

Consideration

Low

Low   High

Initiating structure

FIGURE 14.3 • Basic Leadership Styles from the Ohio State Study

9,9 style: high concern for both production and people as evidenced by personal commitment, mutual trust, and teamwork

Although they stress that managers and leaders need to be versatile enough to select the courses of action appropriate to the situation, Blake and his colleagues contend that a *9,9* style correlates positively with better results, better mental and physical health, and effective conflict resolution. They do not believe the conclusion that there is no one best leadership style. As they see it, the true *9,9* style has never been adequately tested by the situationalists. In a more recent study by Blake and Mouton, one hundred experienced managers overwhelmingly preferred the *9,9* style, regardless of how the situation varied.[28] Consequently, Blake's management training and organization development programs are designed to help individuals and entire organizations move into the *9,9* portion of the Leadership Grid®.

Situational Theory

Convinced that no one best style of leadership exists, a number of management scholars have advocated situational or contingency thinking. Although a number of different situational-leadership theories have been developed, they all share one fundamental assumption: successful leadership occurs when the leader's style matches the situation. Situational-leadership theorists stress the need for flexibility. They reject the notion of a universally applicable style. Research is under way to determine precisely when and where various styles of leadership are

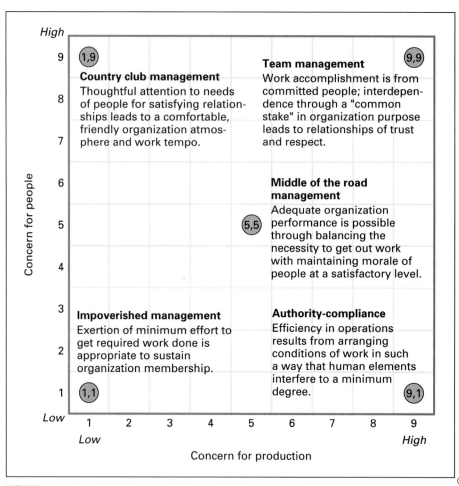

FIGURE 14.4 • Blake and McCanse's Leadership Grid®

Source: The Leadership Grid® figure from *Leadership Dilemmas—Grid Solutions,* by Robert R. Blake and Anne McCanse. Houston: Gulf Publishing Company, page 29. Copyright © 1991 by Scientific Methods, Inc. Reproduced by permission of the owners.

appropriate. Fiedler's contingency theory, the path-goal theory, and the Vroom/ Yetton/Jago decision-making model are introduced and discussed here because they represent distinctly different approaches to situational leadership.

Fiedler's Contingency Theory. Among the various leadership theories proposed so far, Fiedler's is the most thoroughly tested. It is the product of more than thirty years of research by Fred E. Fiedler and his associates. Fiedler's contingency theory gets its name from the following assumption:

> *The performance of a leader depends on two interrelated factors: (1) the degree to which the situation gives the leader control and influence—that is, the likelihood that [the leader] can successfully accomplish the job; and (2) the leader's basic motivation—that is, whether [the leader's] self-esteem depends primarily on accomplishing the task or on having close supportive relations with others.*[29]

Regarding the second factor, the leader's basic motivation, Fiedler believes that leaders are either task-motivated or relationship-motivated. These two motivational profiles are roughly equivalent to initiating structure (or concern for production) and consideration (or concern for people).

A consistent pattern has emerged from the many studies of effective leaders carried out by Fiedler and others.[30] As illustrated in Figure 14.5, task-motivated leaders seem to be effective in extreme situations when they have either very little control or a great deal of control over situational variables. In moderately favorable situations, however, relationship-motivated leaders tend to be more effective. Consequently, Fiedler and one of his colleagues summed up their findings by noting that "everything points to the conclusion that there is no such thing as an ideal leader."[31] Instead, there are leaders, and there are situations. The challenge, according to Fiedler, is to analyze a leader's basic motivation and then match that leader with a suitable situation to form a productive combination. He believes it is more efficient to move leaders to a suitable situation than to tamper with their personalities by trying to get task-motivated leaders to become relationship-motivated, or vice versa.

Path-Goal Theory. Another situational leadership theory is the path-goal theory, a derivative of expectancy motivation theory (see Chapter 12). Path-goal theory gets its name from the assumption that effective leaders can enhance subordinate motivation by (1) clarifying the subordinate's perception of work goals, (2) linking meaningful rewards with goal attainment, and (3) explaining how goals and desired rewards can be achieved. In short, leaders should motivate their followers by providing clear goals and meaningful incentives for reaching them. Path-goal theorists believe that motivation is essential to effective leadership.

According to two path-goal theorists, leaders can enhance motivation by "increasing the number and kinds of personal payoffs to subordinates for work-goal attainment and making paths to these payoffs easier to travel by clarifying the paths, reducing road blocks and pitfalls, and increasing the opportunities for personal satisfaction enroute."[32] Personal characteristics of subordinates, environmental pressures, and demands on subordinates will all vary from situation to situation. Thus, path-goal proponents believe that managers need to rely contingently on four different leadership styles:

- *Directive:* Tell people what is expected of them and provide specific guidance, schedules, rules, regulations, and standards.[33]
- *Supportive:* Treat subordinates as equals in a friendly manner while striving to improve their well-being.
- *Participative:* Consult with subordinates to seek their suggestions and then seriously consider those suggestions when making decisions.
- *Achievement-oriented:* Set challenging goals, emphasize excellence, and seek continuous improvement while maintaining a high degree of confidence that subordinates will meet difficult challenges in a responsible manner.[34]

The assumption that managers can and do shift situationally from style to style clearly sets path-goal theory apart from Fiedler's model. Recall that Fiedler claims managers cannot and do not change their basic leadership styles.

Describe the path-goal theory of leadership and explain how the assumption on which it is based differs from the assumption on which Fiedler's contingency theory is based.

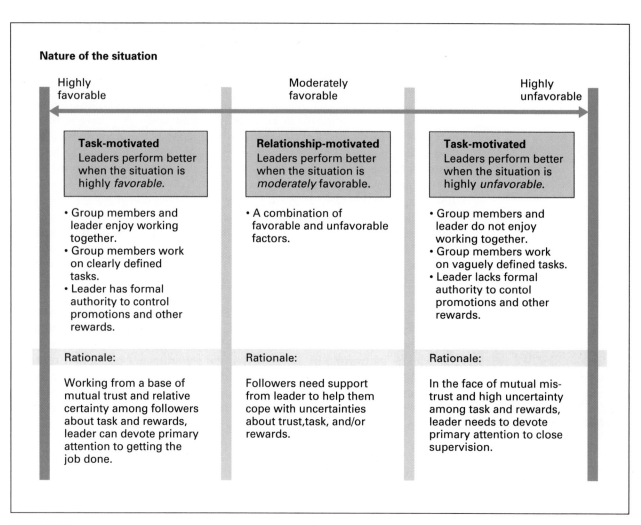

Nature of the situation

Highly favorable	Moderately favorable	Highly unfavorable

Task-motivated
Leaders perform better when the situation is highly *favorable*.

- Group members and leader enjoy working together.
- Group members work on clearly defined tasks.
- Leader has formal authority to control promotions and other rewards.

Relationship-motivated
Leaders perform better when the situation is *moderately* favorable.

- A combination of favorable and unfavorable factors.

Task-motivated
Leaders perform better when the situation is highly *unfavorable*.

- Group members and leader do not enjoy working together.
- Group members work on vaguely defined tasks.
- Leader lacks formal authority to contol promotions and other rewards.

Rationale:

Working from a base of mutual trust and relative certainty among followers about task and rewards, leader can devote primary attention to getting the job done.

Rationale:

Followers need support from leader to help them cope with uncertainties about trust, task, and/or rewards.

Rationale:

In the face of mutual mistrust and high uncertainty among task and rewards, leader needs to devote primary attention to close supervision.

FIGURE 14.5 • Fiedler's Contingency Theory of Leadership

Limited research on the path-goal model has produced mixed results.[35] So far, though, some enlightening contingency relationships have surfaced (see Table 14.3). One valuable contribution of path-goal theory is its identification of the achievement-oriented leadership style. As managers deal with an increasing number of highly educated and self-motivated employees in advanced-technology industries, they will need to become skilled facilitators rather than just order givers or hand holders.

The Vroom/Yetton/Jago Decision-making Model. A model originally proposed by Victor H. Vroom and Philip W. Yetton and later refined by Vroom and Arthur G. Jago portrays leadership as a *decision-making* process.[36] (Recall from Chapter 12 that Vroom helped develop the expectancy theory of motivation.) Their model qualifies as a situational-leadership theory because they prescribe different decision styles for varying situations managers typically encounter.

TABLE 14.3 ● Contingency Relationships in Path-Goal Leadership Model

Leadership style	Effect in various situations
Directive	Positively affects satisfaction and expectancies of subordinates working on ambiguous tasks.
	Negatively affects satisfaction and expectancies of subordinates working on clearly defined tasks.
Supportive	Positively affects satisfaction of subordinates working on dissatisfying, stressful, or frustrating tasks.
Participative	Positively affects satisfaction of subordinates who are ego involved with nonrepetitive tasks.
Achievement-oriented	Positively affects confidence that effort will lead to effective performance of subordinates working on ambiguous and nonrepetitive tasks.

Source: From *Managerial Process and Organizational Behavior,* by Alan C. Filley, Robert J. House, and Steven Kerr. Copyright © 1976 Scott, Foresman and Company. Reprinted by permission of the publisher.

●●●●●●●●●●●●●●●●●
Explain how the Vroom/Yetton/Jago and transformational leadership theories can help managers deal with decision making and with change, respectively.

The Vroom model identifies five distinct decision-making styles (see Figure 14.6), each of which requires a different degree of subordinate participation. Two styles are autocratic (AI and AII). Two others are consultative (CI and CII). The fifth style, group-directed (GII), involves decisions based on group consensus. In addition, the Vroom model gives managers tools for matching styles with various individual and group situations. One tool is a user-friendly computer software program,[37] the other is a set of four decision trees for hand calculations. Both the computerized and decision-tree versions are based on a series of diagnostic questions about the situation. (See the eight questions at the top of Figure 14.7.) Vroom and Jago are quick to point out, however, that the computer program and the decision trees are not adequate substitutes for managerial judgment:

> *The program, like the model itself, is intended to provide nothing more than a standard against which one's choices or intended choices can be compared. Sometimes such a standard is not required. An awareness of the benefits and liabilities of participation and an understanding of the contingencies involved are often enough to help the manager select which decision process to use.*[38]

We can use the sample decision tree in Figure 14.7 to better understand the mechanics of Vroom's model. This particular decision tree is suitable for group problem-solving situations in which there is limited time for a decision. (The other three decision trees involve time-driven individual problems and development-driven group or individual problems.) For our problem, let's imagine you are the director of accounting at Microsoft and the executive committee has given you a month to decide whether or not to switch to an entirely new budgeting process. The new system would require extensive updating of the firm's computerized financial control system, thus meaning lots of work for all your key people. The likely answers to the eight diagnostic questions follow: QR = high; CR = high; LI = no; ST = yes; CP = no; GC = yes; CO = no; SI =

Degree of subordinate participation	Symbol	Decision-making style

Autocratic leader

| None | AI | You solve the problem or make the decision yourself, using information available to you at that time. |
| Low | AII | You obtain the necessary information from your subordinate(s), then decide on the solution to the problem yourself. You may not tell your subordinates what the problem is in getting the information from them. The role played by your subordinates in making the decision is clearly one of providing the necessary information to you, rather than generating or evaluating alternative solutions. |

Consultative leader

| Moderate | CI | You share the problem with relevant subordinates individually, getting their ideas and suggestions without bringing them together as a group. Then you make a decision that may or may not reflect your subordinates' influence. |
| Moderate | CII | You share the problem with your subordinates as a group, collectively obtaining their ideas and suggestions. Then you make the decision that may or may not reflect your subordinates' influence. |

Group Directed

| High | GII | You share a problem with your subordinates as a group. Together you generate and evaluate alternatives and attempt to reach agreement (consensus) on a solution. Your role is much like that of a chairman. You do not try to influence the group to adopt "your" solution and you are willing to accept and implement any solution that has the support of the entire group. |

FIGURE 14.6 • Alternative Decision-making Styles in the Vroom/Yetton/Jago Model

Source: Victor H. Vroom, "A New Look at Managerial Decision Making." Reprinted, by permission of publisher, from *Organizational Dynamics,* Spring 1973, p. 67. © 1973 American Management Association, New York. All rights reserved.

no. This particular sequence in the decision tree in Figure 14.7 recommends a CII style. (Refer to Figure 14.6 for a summary of the CII decision-making style.) In sum, you should involve your people in this important decision because you need their collective expertise and research capabilities. And later, if the change is made, you will need their support. They will tend to support a change they fully understand and had a direct hand in selecting.

Vroom's model may appear overly complex at first glance, but a closer look reveals a good deal of practical significance. For example, it reminds managers to ask such important questions as: "Is time a critical factor?" "Who has the

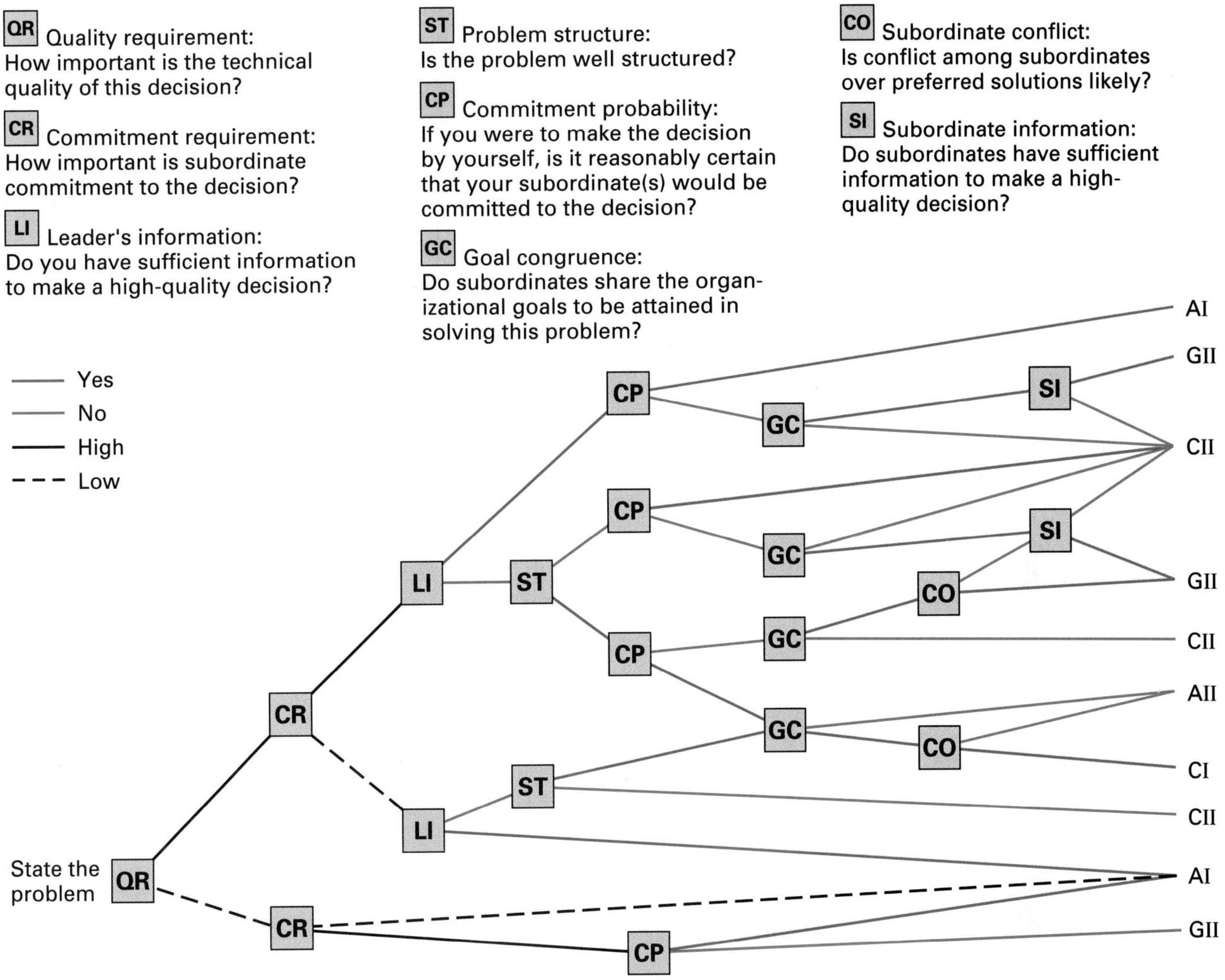

——— Yes
——— No
——— High
- - - Low

FIGURE 14.7 ● The Vroom/Jago Decision Tree for Dealing with a Group Problem When Time Is Limited

Source: Reprinted from *The New Leadership: Managing Participation in Organizations* by Victor H. Vroom and Arthur G. Jago, 1988, Englewood Cliffs, NJ: Prentice-Hall. Copyright 1987 by V. H. Vroom and A. G. Jago. Used with permission of the authors.

needed information?" "How will my people respond?" "Do I need their support during implementation?" "Will this decision cause conflict?" By cross-checking pending decisions with a trip through Vroom's diagnostic questions, leaders can sharpen their decision skills.

Transformational Leadership Theory

In his 1978 book, *Leadership,* James McGregor Burns drew a distinction between transactional and transformational leadership. Burns characterized **transformational leaders** as visionaries who challenge people to achieve exceptionally high levels of morality, motivation, and performance.[39] Only transformational leaders,

transformational leaders visionaries who challenge people to do exceptional things

Levi Strauss & Company's Aspiration Statement: Striving for Transformational Leadership

We all want a Company that our people are proud of and committed to, where all employees have an opportunity to contribute, learn, grow, and advance based on merit, not politics or background. We want our people to feel respected, treated fairly, listened to, and involved. Above all, we want satisfaction from accomplishments and friendships, balanced personal and professional lives, and to have fun in our endeavors.

When we describe the kind of LS&CO. we want in the future, what we are talking about is building on the foundation we have inherited: affirming the best of our Company's traditions, closing gaps that may exist between principles and practices, and updating some of our values to reflect contemporary circumstances.

What Type of Leadership Is Necessary to Make Our Aspirations a Reality?

New behaviors: Leadership that exemplifies directness, openness to influence, commitment to the success of others, willingness to acknowledge our own contributions to problems, personal accountability, teamwork, and trust. Not only must we model these behaviors but we must coach others to adopt them.

Diversity: Leadership that values a diverse workforce (age, sex, ethnic group, etc.) at all levels of the organization, diversity in experience, and a diversity in perspectives. We have committed to taking full advantage of the rich backgrounds and abilities of all our people and to promote a greater diversity in positions of influence. Differing points of view will be sought; diversity will be valued and honesty rewarded, not suppressed.

Recognition: Leadership that provides greater recognition—both financial and psychic—for individuals and teams that contribute to our success. Recognition must be given to all who contribute: those who create and innovate and also those who continually support the day-to-day business requirements.

Ethical management practices: Leadership that epitomizes the stated standards of ethical behavior. We must provide clarity about our expectations and must enforce these standards. . . .

Communications: Leadership that is clear about Company, unit, and individual goals and performance. People must know what is expected of them and receive timely, honest feedback on their performance and career aspirations.

Empowerment: Leadership that increases the authority and responsibility of those closest to our products and customers. By actively pushing responsibility, trust, and recognition into the organization we can harness and release the capabilities of all our people.

Source: Reprinted with permission from Levi Strauss & Co.

Burns argued, are capable of charting necessary new courses for modern organizations. Why? Because they are masters of change.[40] They can envision a better future, effectively communicate that vision, and get others to willingly make it a reality (see Management Ethics).

Transactional versus Transformational Leaders. Extending the work of Burns, Bernard Bass more recently emphasized the importance of charisma in transformational leadership. Transformational leaders rely heavily on referent power. Chrysler's Lee Iacocca and GE's Jack Welch exemplify charismatic leaders who engineered bold changes at their respective companies.[41] While acknowledging that transformational leaders exhibit widely different styles and tend to stir their fair share of controversy, Bass rounded out Burns's distinction between

TABLE 14.4 ● Transactional versus Transformational Leaders

Transactional leader		Transformational leader	
Contingent reward	Contracts exchange of rewards for effort, promises rewards for good performance, recognizes accomplishments.	**Charisma**	Provides vision and sense of mission, instills pride, gains respect and trust.
Management by exception (active)	Watches and searches for deviations from rules and standards, takes corrective action.	**Inspiration**	Communicates high expectations, uses symbols to focus efforts, expresses important purposes in simple ways.
Management by exception (passive)	Intervenes only if standards are not met.	**Intellectual stimulation**	Promotes intelligence, rationality, and careful problem solving.
Laissez-faire	Abdicates responsibilities, avoids making decisions.	**Individualized consideration**	Gives personal attention, treats each employee individually, coaches, advises.

Source: Bernard M. Bass et al., "From Transactional to Transformational Leadership: Learning to Share the Vision." Reprinted, by permission of the publisher, from *Organizational Dynamics*, 18 (Winter 1990). American Management Association, New York. All rights reserved.

transactional and transformational leaders (see Table 14.4). Transactional leaders monitor people so they do the expected, according to plan. In contrast, transformational leaders inspire people to do the unexpected, above and beyond the plan. This distinction can mean the difference between maintaining the status quo and fostering creative and productive growth.

Positive Evidence. It is important to note that the distinction in Table 14.4 is not between bad and good leaders—both are needed today. This is where transformational leadership theory effectively combines the behavioral styles and situational approaches just discussed. To the traditional behavioral patterns of initiating structure and consideration have been added charismatic and other behaviors.[42] Transformational leadership also needs to be situationally appropriate. Specifically, transformational leadership is needed in rapidly changing situations; transactional leaders can best handle stable situations.

Available laboratory and field research evidence generally supports the transformational leadership pattern. Followers of transformational leaders tend to perform better and to report greater satisfaction than those of transactional leaders.[43]

Putting to Work What You've Learned about Leadership

Finding ways to practice leadership both on and off the job can help present and future managers develop their abilities. Serving in campus, community, or religious organizations, for example, will give you an opportunity to experiment with different leadership styles in a variety of situations. Leading effectively, like riding a bike, is learned only by doing.

The scene: a John Deere tractor factory in Mannheim, Germany. The program: a tough apprenticeship lasting three-and-a-half years. The primary influence process: mentoring. Here an apprentice receives one-on-one instruction in transmission assembly. The program involves a great deal of cross-training so everyone, from electricians to mechanical engineers to sales personnel, have a firm grasp of the entire tractor business. Deere's efforts in this regard have been recognized with prestigious German industrial awards.

Mentoring

In spite of mountains of leadership research, much remains to be learned about why some people are good leaders whereas many others are not. One thing is clear, though: mentors can make an important difference. Let us explore this interesting process whereby leadership skills are acquired by exposure to role models.

Learning from a Mentor

mentor someone who develops another through tutoring, coaching, and guidance

The many obstacles and barriers blocking the way to successful leadership make it easy to understand why there is no simple formula for developing leaders. Abraham Zaleznik, a widely respected sociologist, insists that leaders must be nurtured under the wise tutelage of a mentor. A **mentor** is an individual who systematically develops a subordinate's abilities through intensive tutoring, coaching, and guidance.[44] Zaleznik explains the nature of this special relationship:

> *Psychological biographies of gifted people repeatedly demonstrate the important part a mentor plays in developing an individual. Andrew Carnegie owed much to his senior, Thomas A. Scott. As head of the Western Division of the Pennsylvania Railroad, Scott recognized talent and the desire to learn in the young telegrapher assigned to him. By giving*

Carnegie increasing responsibility and by providing him with the opportunity to learn through close personal observation, Scott added to Carnegie's self-confidence and sense of achievement. Because of his own personal strength and achievement, Scott did not fear Carnegie's aggressiveness. Rather, he gave it full play in encouraging Carnegie's initiative.

Mentors take risks with people. They bet initially on talent they perceive in [junior] people. Mentors also risk emotional involvement in working closely with their juniors. The risks do not always pay off, but the willingness to take them appears crucial in developing leaders.[45]

Research suggests that *informal* mentor relationships that arise naturally work better than formally structured pairings.[46] Also, a survey of 246 health care industry managers found higher satisfaction, greater recognition, and more promotion opportunities among managers with mentors than among those without.[47]

Dynamics of Mentoring

According to Kathy Kram, who conducted intensive biographical interviews with both members in eighteen different senior manager–junior manager mentor relationships, mentoring fulfills two important functions: (1) a career enhancement function and (2) a psychosocial support function (see Table 14.5). Mentor relationships were found to average about five years in length.[48] Thus a manager might have a series of mentors during the course of an organizational career.

Interestingly, the junior member of a mentor relationship is not the only one to benefit. Mentors often derive great intrinsic pleasure from seeing their protégés move up through the ranks and conquer difficult challenges. Moreover, by passing along their values and technical and leadership skills to promising junior managers, mentors can wield considerable power. Mentor relationships do sometimes turn sour. A mentor can become threatened by a protégé who surpasses him or her. Also, cross-gender[49] and cross-racial mentor relationships can be victimized by bias and social pressures.

● ● ● ● ● ● ● ● ● ● ● ● ● ● ● ●

Identify the two key functions that mentors perform and explain how a mentor can help develop a junior manager's leadership skills.

TABLE 14.5 ● Mentors Serve Two Important Functions

*Career functions**	*Psychosocial functions***
Sponsorship	Role modeling
Exposure-and-visibility	Acceptance and confirmation
Coaching	Counseling
Protection	Friendship
Challenging assignments	

Source: Kathy E. Kram, "Phases of the Mentor Relationship," *Academy of Management Journal* 26 (December 1983), Exhibit 1, p. 614. Reprinted by permission.

*Career functions are those aspects of the relationship that primarily enhance career advancement.

**Psychosocial functions are those aspects of the relationship that primarily enhance sense of competence, clarity of identity, and effectiveness in the managerial role.

Behavior Modification

This last approach to influencing behavior can be traced to two psychologists, John B. Watson and Edward L. Thorndike, who did their work in the early twentieth century. From Watson came the advice to concentrate on observable behavior. Accordingly, the philosophy of **behaviorism** holds that observable behavior is more important than hypothetical inner states such as needs, motives, or expectations. From Thorndike came an appreciation of the way in which consequences control behavior. According to Thorndike's classic law of effect, favorable consequences encourage behavior, whereas unfavorable consequences discourage behavior.[50] However, it remained for B. F. Skinner, the late Harvard psychologist, to integrate Watson's and Thorndike's contributions into a precise technology of behavior change.

behaviorism belief that observable behavior is more important than inner states

What Is Behavior Modification?

Skinner was the father of *operant conditioning*, the study of how behavior is controlled by the surrounding environment.[51] Although some find Skinner's substitution of environmental control for self-control repulsive and dehumanizing,[52] few deny that operant conditioning actually occurs. Indeed, much of our behavior is the product of environmental shaping. Rather, the debate centers on whether or not natural shaping processes should be systematically managed to alter the course of everyday behavior. Advocates of behavior modification in the workplace believe they should be.

Behavior modification is the practical application of Skinnerian operant-conditioning techniques to everyday behavior problems. **Behavior modification** (B. Mod.) involves systematically managing environmental factors to get people to do the right things more often and the wrong things less often. This is accomplished by managing the antecedents and/or consequences of observable behavior.

behavior modification systematic management of the antecedents and consequences of behavior

Managing Antecedents

An **antecedent** is an environmental cue that prompts an individual to behave in a given manner. Antecedents do not automatically *cause* an individual to behave in a predictable manner, as a hot stove causes you to withdraw your hand reflexively when you touch it. Rather, we learn through experience to interpret antecedents as signals that tell us it is time to behave in a certain way if we are to get what we want or to avoid what we do not want. This process is sometimes referred to as cue control. Domino's Pizza Inc. makes effective use of cue control for maintaining product quality.

antecedent an environmental cue for a specific behavior

• • • • • • • • • • • • • • • • • •

Explain the management of antecedents and consequences in behavior modification.

> *[Every Domino's] features a myriad of strategically placed, visually appealing posters displaying helpful, job-related tips and reminders. . . .*
> *Centrally located, particularly for the benefit of the oven tender who slices and boxes the just-baked pizza, are two photos, one of "The Perfect Pepperoni" pizza, the other showing a pizza with 10 common flaws, one per slice.*[53]

After wage cutbacks and a strike in the early 1980s, morale was low and tension was high among Warren Trucking Company's drivers and support staff. Seeking to create a sense of community, E.R. "Buddy" Eanes, president, broke the ice by going to the warehouse in Martinsville, VA, to help handle freight. Adjusting drivers' schedules to permit more nights at home and holding monthly support meetings for drivers' spouses enabled Warren to double its business. Participative management, a program of "catching people doing things right," and Eanes' humorous style keep Warren Trucking on the right road.

Although often overlooked, the management of antecedents is a practical and relatively simple way of encouraging good performance. As Table 14.6 indicates, there are two ways to manage antecedents. Barriers can be removed, and helpful aids can be offered. These steps simply ensure that the path to good performance is clearly marked and free of obstacles (which meshes with the path-goal theory of leadership).

TABLE 14.6 • Managing Antecedents

Barriers: remove barriers that prevent or hinder the completion of a good job, such as	Aids: provide helpful aids that enhance the opportunity to do a good job, such as
Unrealistic objectives, plans, schedules or deadlines	Challenging yet attainable objectives
Uncooperative or distracting co-workers	Clear and realistic plans
Training deficiencies	Understandable instructions
Contradictory or confusing rules	Constructive suggestions, hints, or tips
Inadequate or inappropriate tools	Clear and generally acceptable work rules
Conflicting orders from two or more managers	Realistic schedules and deadlines
	Friendly reminders
	Posters or signs with helpful tips
	Easy-to-use forms
	Nonthreatening questions about progress

Managing Consequences

Managing the consequences of job performance is more complex than dealing strictly with antecedents because there are four different classes of consequences. Each type of consequence involves a different process. Positive reinforcement and negative reinforcement both encourage behavior, but they do so in different ways. Extinction and punishment discourage behavior but, again, in different ways. These four terms have precise meanings that are often confused by casual observers.

Positive Reinforcement. Positive reinforcement encourages a specific behavior by immediately following it with a consequence that the individual finds pleasing. For example, a machine operator who maintains a clean work area because he or she is praised for doing so has responded to positive reinforcement. As the term implies, positive reinforcement reinforces or builds behavior in a positive way.

Negative Reinforcement. *Negative reinforcement* encourages a specific behavior by immediately withdrawing or terminating something that particular person finds displeasing. Children learn the power of negative reinforcement early in life when they discover that the quickest way to get something is to cry and scream until their parents give them what they want. In effect, the parents are negatively reinforced for complying with the child's demand by the termination of the crying and screaming. In other words, the termination or withdrawal of an undesirable state of affairs (for example, the threat of being fired) has an incentive effect. In a social context, negative reinforcement amounts to blackmail. "Do what I want, or I will continue to make your life miserable" is the byword of the person who relies on negative reinforcement to influence behavior.

Extinction. Through *extinction*, a specific behavior is discouraged by ignoring it. For example, managers sometimes find that the best way to keep subordinates from asking redundant questions is to simply not answer them. Just as a plant will wither and die without water, behavior will fade away without occasional reinforcement.

Punishment. *Punishment* discourages a specific behavior by the immediate presentation of an undesirable consequence or the immediate removal of something desirable. For example, a manager may punish a tardy employee by either assigning the individual to a dirty job or docking the individual's pay.

It is important to remember that positive and negative reinforcement, extinction, and punishment all entail the manipulation of the *immediate or direct* consequences of a desired or undesired behavior. If action is taken before the behavior, behavior control is unlikely. For instance, if a manager gives an employee a cash bonus *before* a difficult task is completed, the probability of the task being completed declines because the incentive effect has been removed. In regard to managing consequences, behavior modification works only when there is a contingent ("if . . . then") relationship between a specific behavior and a given consequence.

Positively Reinforce What Is Right about Job Performance

Behavior-modification proponents prefer to build up desirable behaviors rather than tear down undesirable ones. Every undesirable behavior has a desirable counterpart that can be reinforced. For example, someone who comes in late once a week actually comes in *on time four days* a week. To encourage productive behaviors, managers are advised to focus on the positive aspects of job performance when managing consequences. Thus, positive reinforcement is the preferred consequence strategy.[54] This positive approach was effectively taken to heart by Preston Trucking, a Maryland shipping company:

> *Preston, years ago, had terrible relations between management and labor. Then, one day, top management resolved to bury the hatchet. All sorts of reforms were announced, including the Four-to-One Rule: For every criticism a manager made about a driver's performance, he had to give him four compliments. You can imagine how this went over. "It was like a . . . like a* marriage encounter," *says Teamster Nick Costa, rolling his eyes. Eventually, though, drivers discovered that the rule really did reflect a change of heart.*[55]

This positive approach to modifying behavior is the central theme in the best-selling book *The One Minute Manager,* which extols the virtues of "catching people doing something *right!*"[56]

Schedule Positive Reinforcement Appropriately

continuous reinforcement every instance of a behavior is rewarded

intermittent reinforcement rewarding some, but not all, instances of a behavior

Both the type and the timing of consequences are important in successful B. Mod. When a productive behavior is first tried out by an employee, a continuous schedule of reinforcement is appropriate. Under **continuous reinforcement** every instance of the desired behavior is reinforced. For example, a bank manager who is training a new loan officer to handle a difficult type of account should praise the loan officer after every successful transaction until the behavior is firmly established. After the loan officer seems able to handle the transaction, the bank manager can switch to a schedule of intermittent reinforcement. As the term implies, **intermittent reinforcement** calls for reinforcing some, rather than all, of the desired responses.

The more unpredictable the payoff schedule is, the better the results will be. One way to appreciate the power of intermittent reinforcement is to think of the enthusiasm with which people play slot machines; these gambling devices pay off on an unpredictable intermittent schedule. In the same way, occasional reinforcement of established productive behaviors with meaningful positive consequences is an extremely effective management technique.[57]

Summary

Influence is fundamental to management because individuals must be influenced to pursue collective objectives. In addition to motivation, important influence processes include power, leadership, mentoring, and behavior modification. Recent research has identified eight generic influence tactics used on the job: consultation, rational persuasion, inspirational appeals, ingratiating tactics, coalition tactics, pressure tactics, upward appeals, and exchange tactics.

Authority is defined as the right to seek compliance, whereas power is the demonstrated ability to obtain compliance. A manager may have authority but may not have power. Organizationally, power affects decisions, behavior, and situations. The five types of power are reward, coercive, legitimate, referent, and expert. Power in itself is a neutral tool. It becomes good or bad only through responsible or irresponsible application.

Formal leadership is influencing relevant others to voluntarily pursue organizational objectives. Informal leadership can work for or against the organization. Leadership theory has evolved through four major stages: trait theory, behavioral styles theory, situational theory, and transformational theory. Trait theory is limited in that personal traits generally have poor predictive value. Reseachers who differentiated authoritarian, democratic, and laissez-faire styles concentrated on leader behavior rather than personality traits. Leadership studies at Ohio State University isolated four styles of leadership based on two categories of leader behavior: initiating structure and consideration. According to Blake and his colleagues, a 9,9 style (high concern for both production and people) is the best overall style.

Situational-leadership theorists believe there is no single best leadership style; rather, different situations require different styles. Many years of study led Fiedler to conclude that task-motivated leaders are more effective in either very favorable or very unfavorable situations, whereas relationship-motivated leaders are better suited to moderately favorable situations. The favorableness of a situation is dictated by the degree of the leader's control and influence in getting the job done. Path-goal leadership theory, an expectancy perspective, assumes that leaders are effective to the extent that they can motivate followers by clarifying goals and clearing the paths to achieving those goals and valued rewards. Unlike Fiedler, path-goal theorists believe that managers can and should adapt their leadership style to the situation. A third situational-leadership model has been put forth by Vroom, Yetton, and Jago. It helps managers select one of five decision-making styles by asking a series of diagnostic questions about the situation. The Vroom model calls for subordinate participation in situations where the manager has incomplete information and requires subordinate support for implementation.

In contrast to transactional leaders who maintain the status quo, transformational leaders are visionary, charismatic leaders dedicated to change. Becoming familiar with leadership theories is only the first step toward being an effective leader; lots of first-hand practice with various styles in different situations is needed. Mentors can help develop junior managers' leadership skills by providing career and psychosocial guidance.

Behavior modification (B. Mod.) is the practical application of Skinner's operant conditioning principles. B. Mod. involves managing antecedents and consequences to strengthen desirable behavior and weaken undesirable behavior. Proponents of B. Mod. prefer to shape behavior positively through positive reinforcement in lieu of negative reinforcement, extinction, and punishment. Continuous reinforcement is recommended for new behavior and intermittent reinforcement for established behavior.

Terms to Understand

Influence

Power

Reward power

Coercive power

Legitimate power

Referent power

Expert power

Leadership

Formal leadership

Informal leadership

Transformational leaders

Mentor

Behaviorism

Behavior modification

Antecedent

Positive reinforcement

Continuous reinforcement

Intermittent reinforcement

Questions for Discussion

1. What tactics do you usually use to influence your parents, instructors, or supervisor? Would it be better to rely on other tactics? Explain.

2. Which base(s) of power do you suppose first-line supervisors rely on the most? Explain.

3. Do you agree that power is a neutral tool, neither inherently good nor bad? Explain.

4. Think of the best leader that you have personally ever known. In terms of traits, style, and situational factors, why was that person a good leader?

5. Do you agree with the situational-leadership theorists' claim that there is no "one best" style of leadership? Why or why not?

6. Relative to a specific work group problem, with a limited time frame, which decision style would the Vroom-Jago decision tree in Figure 14.7 recommend?

7. Is it possible for a transactional leader to become a transformational leader? Explain.

8. As a new manager, would you be interested in having a mentor? Explain your answer in terms of the pros and cons.

9. What antecedents could you rearrange to improve your study (or work) behavior?

10. It has been pointed out by experts that children and pets are the world's best behavior modifiers. Why, in terms of managing antecedents and consequences, is this probably true?

Back to the Opening Case

Now that you have read Chapter 14, you should be able to answer the following questions about the Bill Gates/Microsoft case:

1. Drawing upon what you have learned in this chapter, why is Bill Gates unlike many entrepreneurs who cannot make the transition to corporate leader?

2. How would you explain the influence implications of the following statement about Gates? "He learned at a young age that you've got to give up power to get power."

3. Is Gates a transactional or transformational leader? Explain your rationale.

The Woman Who Fired Luciano Pavarotti

To some, Ardis Krainik's most visible moment as leader of Lyric Opera was potentially the riskiest: She fired Luciano Pavarotti just days before the opening of last year's gala 35th season. "I'm sure he didn't realize the cumulative effect of what he had done to Lyric Opera [canceling a total 26 out of 41 scheduled performances in five productions], but everybody in Chicago did, and if I hadn't done anything strong, the Chicago public would have been very upset. And after all, my job as the steward of Lyric Opera is to serve the public. They're the ones that are buying the tickets. There's no question from the reaction—people that didn't know me would stop me on the street and say I'd done the right thing."

As a leader of this country's premier operatic institution, Ms. Krainik has gained the respect of both the opera world and the Chicago business community as well. What are her views on leadership?

"I think anyone who thinks that they're leading something themselves is in a lot of trouble, because as far as I'm concerned, the helmsman is God. I think that it takes confidence to be a strong leader, and a lot of good humor, and a lot of determination. I think it takes intelligence, it takes knowledge of the field in which you intend to be a leader.

"It takes a willingness to compromise so that you can have all the people follow you instead of just one or two. But most of all, I think leadership is a matter of the sum-total of your experience and then always listening for the 'still, small voice': That's what . . . guides the way—the 'still, small voice.'

"The first year that I took over I was scared to death all the time. . . . Well, I am not scared to death all the time now; I am only scared to death about half of the time! And anybody in my business who doesn't have that edge of anxiety is kidding himself, because when you're putting on anything theatrical, all people in the theater run on the raw edge of nerve all the time. That's just the nature of the business.

"At 7:30 that curtain goes up, and you do 68 performances between September and February, and that is it. And you do parties around that, and you raise money around it and you have P.R. and interviews with people, you have to go out into the community and be a figure in the community, as in Chicago every business leader is.

"I think that one of the things that has driven me most is the sense that I must not fail. . . . The one way to take away a sense of looking at the possibility of failure is to recognize that this is not all in your own hands. . . . And so, through these ten years, I think I've grown as a manager, as a business person, and my understanding of God and His presence in my life has grown.

"The biggest challenge was, and always is, trying to make the greatest art with the least amount of money. And even though the budget has gone from $9 million to $20 million, that doesn't mean that we don't have that challenge to meet every year.

"I don't believe that leadership involves risk. You've got to examine everything, and even though it seems to be a risk from outside, you as an insider must know the pitfalls—whatever might be going on—and determine what to do based on facts, dollars, bottom-line figures, not taking risks."

For Discussion

1. What sort of power did Ardis Krainik use when she fired Pavarotti? What other bases of power does it appear she has?

2. How well does Krainik match the top five leader traits in the Kouzes and Posner study?

3. Would you call Krainik a transformational leader? Why or why not?

References

Opening Quotation. Warren Bennis, "Managing the Dream: Leadership in the 21st Century," *Training,* 27 (May 1990): 44.

Opening Case. Richard Brandt, "The Billion-Dollar Whiz Kid," *Business Week* (April 13, 1987): 68–76; Richard Brandt and Evan I. Schwartz, "IBM and Microsoft: They're Still Talking, But . . . ," *Business Week* (October 1, 1990): 164–166; "Meanwhile, Back among the Fir Trees at Microsoft," *Fortune* (October 9, 1989): 61; Brenton Schlender, "How Bill Gates Keeps the Magic Going," *Fortune* (June 18, 1990): 82–89; "The Corporate Elite," *Business Week* (October 19, 1990): 180; "What Comes after Seven Fat Years?" *The Economist* (March 24, 1990): 72–73; Brenton R. Schlender, "Bill Gates Sets a New Target," *Fortune* (February 25, 1991): 12–13.

Closing Case. Thor Eckert, Jr., "The Woman Who Fired Luciano Pavarotti," *The Christian Science Monitor* (November 13, 1990): 10. Reprinted with permission of the author.

1. Vern L. Raburn, quoted in Richard Brandt, "The Billion-Dollar Whiz Kid," *Business Week* (April 13, 1987): 69.

2. See Bernard Keys and Thomas Case, "How To Become an Influential Manager," *Academy of Management Executive,* 4 (November 1990): 38–51; and Linda Thornburg, "Influence, a Potent Ingredient for Success," *HRMagazine,* 35 (November 1990): 52–55.

3. See Gary Yukl and Cecilia M. Falbe, "Influence Tactics and Objectives in Upward, Downward, and Lateral Influence Attempts," *Journal of Applied Psychology,* 75 (April 1990): 132–140. Also see David Kipnis, Stuart M. Schmidt, and Ian Wilkinson, "Intraorganizational Influence Tactics: Explorations in Getting One's Way," *Journal of Applied Psychology,* 64 (August 1980): 440–452; and Chester A. Schriesheim and Timothy R. Hinkin, "Influence Tactics Used by Subordinates: A Theoretical and Empirical Analysis of the Kipnis, Schmidt, and Wilkinson Subscales," *Journal of Applied Psychology,* 75 (June 1990): 246–257.

4. Adapted from Yukl and Falbe, "Influence Tactics and Objectives in Upward, Downward, and Lateral Influence Attempts."

5. See George F. Dreher, Thomas W. Dougherty, and William Whitely, "Influence Tactics and Salary Attainment: A Gender-Specific Analysis," *Sex Roles,* 20 (May 1989): 535–550.

6. See Mahfooz A. Ansari and Alka Kapoor, "Organizational Context and Upward Influence Tactics," *Organizational Behavior and Human Decision Processes,* 40 (August 1987): 39–49.

7. Dean Tjosvold, "The Dynamics of Positive Power," *Training and Development Journal,* 38 (June 1984): 72.

8. Morgan McCall, Jr., "Power, Influence, and Authority: The Hazards of Carrying a Sword," *Technical Report,* 10 (Greensboro, N.C.: Center for Creative Leadership, 1978), p. 5.

9. For more on these three effects of power, see Anthony T. Cobb, "An Episodic Model of Power: Toward an Integration of Theory and Research," *Academy of Management Review,* 9 (July 1984): 482–493. On power coalitions, both inside and outside the organization, see Henry Mintzberg, "Power and Organization Life Cycles," *Academy of Management Review,* 9 (April 1984): 207–224.

10. Based on Edwin P. Hollander and Lynn R. Offermann, "Power and Leadership in Organizations: Relationships in Transition," *American Psychologist,* 45 (February 1990): 179–189.

11. For related discussion, see Allan R. Cohen and David L. Bradford, "Influence without Authority: The Use of Alliances, Reciprocity, and Exchange to Accomplish Work," *Organizational Dynamics,* 17 (Winter 1989): 4–17; and Allan R. Cohen and David L. Bradford, *Influence without Authority* (New York: John Wiley & Sons, 1990).

12. See John R. P. French, Jr., and Bertram Raven, "The Bases of Social Power," *Studies in Social Power,* ed. Dorwin Cartwright (Ann Arbor: University of Michigan Press, 1959), pp. 150–167. Eight different sources of power are discussed in Hugh R. Taylor, "Power at Work," *Personnel Journal,* 65 (April 1986): 42–49.

13. John P. Kotter, "Power, Dependence, and Effective Management," *Harvard Business Review,* 55 (July-August 1977): 128.

14. Robert A. Mamis and Steven Pearlstein, " '1-2-3' Creator Mitch Kapor," *Inc.,* 9 (January 1987): 38.

15. For an instructive review of research, see Philip M. Podsakoff and Chester A. Schriesheim, "Field Studies of French and Raven's Bases of Power: Critique, Reanalysis, and Suggestions for Future Research," *Psychological Bulletin,* 97 (May 1985): 387–411.

16. David C. McClelland, *Power: The Inner Experience* (New York: Irvington, 1975), p. 269. See also Charles M. Kelly, "The Interrelationship of Ethics and Power in Today's Organizations," *Organizational Dynamics,* 16 (Summer 1987): 4–18; and Carrie R. Leana, "Power Relinquishment versus Power Sharing: Theoretical Clarification and Empirical Comparison of Delegation and Participation," *Journal of Applied Psychology,* 72 (May 1987): 228–233.

17. See Jonathan E. Smith, Kenneth P. Carson, and Ralph A. Alexander, "Leadership: It Can Make a Difference," *Academy of Management Journal,* 27 (December 1984): 765–776; and Janet M. Dukerich, Mary Lippitt Nichols, Dawn R. Elm, and David A. Vollrath, "Moral Reasoning in Groups: Leaders Make a Difference," *Human Relations,* 43 (May 1990): 473–493.

18. Chester A. Schriesheim, James M. Tolliver, and Orlando C. Behling, "Leadership Theory: Some Implications for Managers," *MSU Business Topics,* 26 (Summer 1978): 35.

19. See Gary Yukl, "Managerial Leadership: A Review of Theory and Research," *Journal of Management,* 15 (June 1989): 251–289; and Gary A. Yukl, *Leadership in Organizations,* 2nd ed. (Englewood Cliffs, N.J.: Prentice-Hall, 1989).

20. Fred Luthans, *Organizational Behavior,* 3rd ed. (New York: McGraw-Hill, 1981), p. 419.

21. Ralph M. Stogdill, "Personal Factors Associated with Leadership: A Survey of the Literature," *Journal of Psychology,* 25 (1948): 63.

22. Data from James M. Kouzes and Barry Z. Posner, "The Credibility Factor: What Followers Expect from Their Leaders," *Business Credit,* 92 (July-August 1990): 24–28. Also see James M. Kouzes and Barry Z. Posner, *The Leadership Challenge: How To Get Extraordinary Things Done in Organizations* (San Francisco: Jossey-Bass, 1987).

23. Kurt Lewin, Ronald Lippitt, and Ralph K. White, "Patterns of Aggressive Behavior in Experimentally Created 'Social Climates,' " *Journal of Social Psychology,* 10 (May 1939): 271–299.

24. For an informative summary of this research, see Edwin A. Fleishman, "Twenty Years of Consideration and Structure," in *Current Developments in the Study of Leadership,* eds. Edwin A. Fleishman and James G. Hunt (Carbondale, Ill.: Southern Illinois University Press, 1973), pp. 1–40. Also see Vishwanath V. Baba and Merle E. Ace, "Serendipity in Leadership: Initiating Structure and Consideration in the Classroom," *Human Relations,* 42 (June 1989): 509–525.

25. Three popular extensions of the Ohio State leadership studies may be found in Robert R. Blake and Anne McCanse, *Leadership Dilemmas—Grid Solutions* (Houston: Gulf Publishing, 1990); William J. Reddin, *Managerial Effectiveness* (New York: McGraw-Hill, 1970); and Paul Hersey and Kenneth H. Blanchard, *Management of Organizational Behavior: Utilizing Human Resources,* 5th ed. (Englewood Cliffs, N.J.: Prentice-Hall, 1988), p. 171. Empirical lack of support for Hersey and Blanchard's situational leadership theory is reported in Jane R. Goodson, Gail W. McGee, and James F. Cashman, "Situational Leadership Theory: A Test of Leadership Prescriptions," *Group & Organization Studies,* 14 (December 1989): 446–461.

26. See Abraham K. Korman, "Consideration, 'Initiating Structure,' and Organizational Criteria— A Review," *Personnel Psychology,* 19 (Winter 1966): 349–361.

27. See Blake and McCanse, *Leadership Dilemmas–Grid Solutions.*

28. For details of this study, see Robert R. Blake and Jane Srygley Mouton, "Management by Grid® Principles or Situationalism: Which?" *Group & Organization Studies,* 6 (December 1981): 439–455. Also see Robert R. Blake and Jane Srygley Mouton, "A Comparative Analysis of Situationalism and 9,9 Management by Principle," *Organizational Dynamics,* 10 (Spring 1982): 20–43.

29. Fred E. Fiedler, "Job Engineering for Effective Leadership: A New Approach," *Management Review,* 66 (September 1977): 29.

30. For an excellent comprehensive validation study, see Michael J. Strube and Joseph E. Garcia, "A Meta-Analytic Investigation of Fiedler's Contingency Model of Leadership Effectiveness," *Psychological Bulletin,* 90 (September 1981): 307–321.

31. Fred E. Fiedler and Martin M. Chemers, *Leadership and Effective Management* (Glenview, Ill.: Scott, Foresman, 1974), p. 91.

32. Robert J. House and Terence R. Mitchell, "Path-Goal Theory of Leadership," *Journal of Contemporary Business,* 3 (Autumn 1974): 85. The entire Autumn 1974 issue is devoted to an instructive review of contrasting theories of leadership.

33. See Jan P. Muczyk and Bernard C. Reimann, "The Case for Directive Leadership," *Academy of Management Executive,* 1 (November 1987): 301–311.

34. Adapted from House and Mitchell, "Path-Goal Theory of Leadership," p. 83.

35. For path-goal research, see Abduhl-Rahim A. Al-Gattan, "Test of the Path-Goal Theory of Leadership in the Multinational Domain," *Group & Organization Studies,* 10 (December 1985): 429–445; Robert T. Keller, "A Test of the Path-Goal Theory of Leadership with Need for Clarity as a Moderator in Research and Development Organizations," *Journal of Applied Psychology,* 74 (April 1989): 208–212; and John E. Mathieu, "A Test of Subordinates' Achievement and Affiliation Needs as Moderators of Leader Path-Goal Relationships," *Basic and Applied Social Psychology,* 11 (June 1990): 179–189.

36. See Victor H. Vroom and Philip W. Yetton, *Leadership and Decision-Making* (Pittsburgh: University of Pittsburgh Press, 1973); Victor H. Vroom, "A New Look at Managerial Decision

Making," *Organizational Dynamics,* 1 (Spring 1973): 66–80; and Victor H. Vroom and Arthur G. Jago, *The New Leadership: Managing Participation in Organizations* (Englewood Cliffs, N.J.: Prentice-Hall, 1988).

37. The computer program is called MPO (Managing Participation in Organizations). It is available through Leadership Software, Inc., P.O. Box 271848, Houston, TX 77277–1848.

38. Vroom and Jago, *The New Leadership,* p. 182.

39. See J. McGregor Burns, *Leadership* (New York: HarperCollins, 1978).

40. See David A. Nadler and Michael L. Tushman, "Beyond the Charismatic Leader: Leadership and Organizational Change," *California Management Review,* 32 (Winter 1990): 77–97.

41. For the negative side of visionary and charismatic leaders, see Jay A. Conger, "The Dark Side of Leadership," *Organizational Dynamics,* 19 (Autumn 1990): 44–55; and John B. Judis, "Myth vs. Manager," *Business Month,* 136 (July 1990): 24–33.

42. See Joseph Seltzer and Bernard M. Bass, "Transformational Leadership: Beyond Initiation and Consideration," *Journal of Management,* 16 (December 1990): 693–703.

43. For example, see Jane M. Howell and Peter J. Frost, "A Laboratory Study of Charismatic Leadership," *Organizational Behavior and Human Decision Processes,* 43 (April 1989): 243–269; Bernard M. Bass, "From Transactional to Transformational Leadership: Learning to Share the Vision," *Organizational Dynamics,* 18 (Winter 1990): 19–31; and Ronald J. Deluga, "The Effects of Transformational, Transactional, and Laissez Faire Leadership Characteristics on Subordinate-Influencing Behavior," *Basic and Applied Social Psychology,* 11 (June 1990): 191–203.

44. For more on mentoring, see David Marshall Hunt and Carol Michael, "Mentorship: A Career Training and Development Tool," *Academy of Management Review,* 8 (July 1983): 475–485; Jack L. Mendleson, A. Keith Barnes, and Gregory Horn, "The Guiding Light to Corporate Culture," *Personnel Administrator,* 34 (July 1989): 70–72; Peter Kizilos, "Take My Mentor, Please!" *Training,* 27 (April 1990): 49–55; and Rick Rubow and Suzanne Jansen, "A Corporate Survival Guide for the Baby Bust," *Management Review,* 79 (July 1990): 50–52.

45. Abraham Zaleznik, "Managers and Leaders: Are They Different?" *Harvard Business Review,* 55 (May-June 1977): 76. For more on mentorship, see Charles D. Orth, Harry E. Wilkinson, and Robert C. Benfari, "The Manager's Role as Coach and Mentor," *Organizational Dynamics,* 15 (Spring 1987): 66–74.

46. See "Mentoring Process Works Best When It Is Kept Informal, Finds Study," *Management Review,* 73 (June 1984): 55.

47. For details, see Ellen A. Fagenson, "The Mentor Advantage: Perceived Career/Job Experiences of Proteges versus Non-Proteges," *Journal of Organizational Behavior,* 10 (October 1989): 309–320.

48. For more, see Kathy E. Kram, "Phases of the Mentor Relationship," *Academy of Management Journal,* 26 (December 1983): 608–625.

49. Good discussions of women and mentoring can be found in James G. Clawson and Kathy E. Kram, "Managing Cross-Gender Mentoring," *Business Horizons,* 27 (May-June 1984): 22–32; Raymond A. Noe, "Women and Mentoring: A Review and Research Agenda," *Academy of Management Review,* 13 (January 1988): 65–78; Belle Rose Ragins, "Barriers to Mentoring: The Female Manager's Dilemma," *Human Relations,* 42 (January 1989): 1–22; and R. J. Burke and C. A. KcKeen, "Mentoring in Organizations: Implications for Women," *Journal of Business Ethics,* 9 (April-May 1990): 317–332.

50. See Edward L. Thorndike, *Educational Psychology: The Psychology of Learning* (New York: Columbia University Press, 1913), II, 4.

51. For an instructive account of operant conditioning applied to human behavior, see B. F. Skinner, *Science and Human Behavior* (New York: Free Press, 1953), pp. 62–66. A good update is B. F. Skinner, "What Is Wrong with Daily Life in the Western World," *American Psychologist,* 41 (May 1986): 568–574.

52. For example, see Tom Kramlinger and Tom Huberty, "Behaviorism versus Humanism," *Training & Development Journal,* 44 (December 1990): 41–45.

53. Dale Feuer, "Training for Fast Times," *Training,* 24 (July 1987): 28.

54. For interesting case studies, see Wayne Dierks and Kathleen McNally, "Incentives You Can Bank On," *Personnel Administrator,* 32 (March 1987): 60–65; and Edward J. Feeney, "Modifying Employee Behavior: Making Rewards Pay Off," *Supervisory Management,* 30 (December 1985): 25–27.

55. Alan Farnham, "The Trust Gap," *Fortune* (December 4, 1989): 74.

56. Kenneth Blanchard and Spencer Johnson, *The One Minute Manager* (New York: Berkley, 1982), p. 45. (Emphasis added.) Also see Kenneth Blanchard and Robert Lorber, *Putting the One Minute Manager to Work* (New York: Berkley, 1984).

57. For detailed treatment of B. Mod. in the workplace, see Fred Luthans and Robert Kreitner, *Organizational Behavior Modification and Beyond: An Operant and Social Learning Approach* (Glenview, Ill.: Scott, Foresman, 1985); and Gerald A. Merwin, Jr., John A. Thomason, and Eleanor E. Sanford, "A Methodology and Content Review of Organizational Behavior Management in the Private Sector: 1978–1986," *Journal of Organizational Behavior Management,* 10, No. 1 (1989): 39–57.

15

Managing Change and Conflict

The art of progress is to
preserve order amid
change and to preserve
change amid order.

ALFRED NORTH WHITEHEAD

CHAPTER OBJECTIVES

When you finish studying this chapter, you should
be able to

- Identify and describe four types of organizational change, according to the Nadler-Tushman model.

- Explain the transition stages an individual goes through when responding to change.

- List at least six reasons why employees resist change and discuss what management can do about resistance to change.

- Define, in your own words, the term *organization development* (OD).

- Describe how the unfreezing-change-refreezing analogy applies to OD.

- Explain how OD interventions can be aimed at individuals, groups, or entire organizations.

- Explain the difference between functional and dysfunctional conflict.

- Identify and describe five conflict resolution techniques.

They Love Change at PepsiCo

In a slower world, "If it ain't broke, don't fix it," seemed a sensible motto. Managers dealt with problems and crises, and visionary leaders were those who could foresee the problems a few months down the road. Now, however, competitors and the environment can change so quickly that by the time management is aware of a problem, it may be a crisis, and a crisis may spell bankruptcy. So smart companies don't change as a reaction, they change as a matter of principle, never satisfied with last year's results. No company embodies this approach better than PepsiCo.

"Love change. Learn to dance. And leave J. Edgar Hoover behind."[1] That's the secret to Pepsi's success, according to its CEO, Wayne Calloway. The second and third ingredients may need a little explanation. Companies need to "learn to dance" with their customers, ascertaining what their customers want and then giving it to them. For instance, Pepsi's company-owned bottlers used to produce about 21 percent of its soda, but now they produce about half. It used to market products mostly to big customers; now it sells to stores, restaurant chains, schools—600,000 of them. So Pepsi-Cola North America has been sending its top seventy executives to talk to retailers about Pepsi and to observe companies like Federal Express and Walt Disney, which are famous for their customer service.

The reference to J. Edgar Hoover is a cryptic way of saying that a big corporation must be decentralized. Hoover used to sign off on every decision, whereas PepsiCo's Calloway concentrates mostly on financial goals and doesn't see Pepsi's new commercials until the viewing public does. But he is relentless about improvement of the financial position at the divisional level. As a former executive under Calloway put it, "Promise him 12 percent profit growth, and he'll say, 'Well, gee, I'd take another look at that plan, Tom. I sorta think you oughta be comin' up with a number in the high teens.' "[2]

Anyone who consumes Pepsi's products knows about the company's passion for not sitting still. Kentucky Fried Chicken, which PepsiCo acquired in 1986, is one of the parent company's least successful performers, so you would expect it to change. First Calloway gave the company a new boss, John Cranor, who had run Pepsi's eastern U.S. soft drink business. Cranor took the colonel off the packages and changed the name to KFC. Then he changed the slogan to "Nobody's cookin' like the new KFC" and brought executives over from Pizza Hut to teach KFC delivery techniques. Profits rose 28 percent in 1990.

But why mess with a company like Frito-Lay, whose volume has been rising 6 percent per year despite the backlash against junk food and the diminishing number of chip-loving teenagers? According to Calloway, complacency is the company's worst enemy. So, as successful as Frito-Lay has been at pleasing customers, its new head thinks the company can do better. Its consumer testing has led to redesigns of some of its most successful products. Doritos got thinner and crispier; Ruffles are now made from a different kind of potato. Instead of just letting computers and inspectors figure out whether the products were being made right, a manufacturing supervisor now actually samples the plant's crunchies at least once an hour. And to help Frito-Lay's salespeople learn to dance more efficiently, the company has given all 10,000 of them hand-held computers, with information downloaded to headquarters nightly. Now anyone in the company can find out exactly what is selling where and when, and the company can quickly adjust promotions or product mixes.

To bring in the kind of numbers that make chief Calloway happy, PepsiCo's managers have had to find new ways to cut costs and squeeze out profits. By keeping its trucks full, Pepsi-Cola has saved $56 million—about one-fifth of its total distribution budget—over the last four years. A truck that carried Diet Pepsi in the morning might carry Fritos or even another company's products in the afternoon. Better communication between bottlers and PepsiCo's ownership of more bottlers allow a bottling innovation in one plant to spread quickly to other plants. The soft-drink division has kept profit gains above 15 percent for the past five years, although volumes increased only 3 or 4 percent per year.

Like arch-rival Coca-Cola Co., PepsiCo is now looking to Europe for its biggest gains and changes. Pepsi wants to raise overseas volume by 150 percent by 1995, and it is willing to spend $1 billion to do so. That will mean more vending machines in Europe simply to make its products more available—the United States has eleven times more machines per capita than Europe. Both cola giants also need to change European tastes—colas currently account for only about 40 percent of the European soft drink market, compared with 70 percent in the United States.

The kind of competition that has made the cola wars so fierce may play a big role in PepsiCo's overall success. Pepsi has been competing against number-one Coke for its entire history. But now, as a major player in the fast-food arena and owner of Pizza Hut, Taco Bell, and KFC, PepsiCo has taken on another food industry giant, McDonald's. And at the moment, PepsiCo's food is moving faster, with operating profit gains increasing at more than 20 percent annually compared with McDonald's 8 percent. PepsiCo placed fifth in *Fortune* magazine's 1991 poll of America's most admired corporations, based on such attributes as quality of management, innovativeness, and quality of products or services. Coca-Cola ranked sixth. It seems that being number two really does make PepsiCo try harder.

When introducing changes, whether at PepsiCo or elsewhere, managers often are surprised and dismayed that things don't turn out as planned. Frequently, the change itself is not the problem. Rather, the change *process* is to blame. Employees resent being pushed into unfamiliar territory without adequate information or involvement. Improving this state of affairs is both possible and necessary in today's competitive world.

American Telephone & Telegraph (AT&T) is a good case in point. This is what happened to a training program at AT&T prior to the firm's 1984 divestiture and deregulation:

AT&T set up a school to teach managers to coordinate the design and manufacture of data products for customized sales. But when managers completed the course, they found that the traditional way of operating—making noncustomized mass sales—[was] what counted in the company. They were given neither the time to analyze individual customers' needs nor rewards commensurate with such efforts. The result was that 85 percent of the graduates quit, and AT&T disbanded the school.[3]

Like a fish on land, this ill-fated change died for lack of a support system. Thanks in large part to the progressive management philosophy of AT&T's current chairman, Robert E. Allen, change is handled much differently today. Allen has slimmed down AT&T's legendary bureaucracy, putting go-getters in key positions. He has pushed responsibility for results down to lower-level managers. Said one AT&T subsidiary vice president: "Bob told us: 'It's your company. I'm not going to tell you what to do with it, but I'm holding you accountable.' For some people that was a frightening statement."[4] Many others, however, have risen to the challenge and are supporting wrenching changes that would have been unthinkable in the early 1980s. AT&T managers who once saw themselves as the victims of changes imposed by top management are now the confident architects of change. The net result: AT&T is a much more responsive, flexible, and competitive company than it was a decade ago.

The purpose of this chapter is to explore the dynamics of organizational change and its natural by-product, conflict. We discuss change from organizational and individual perspectives, address resistance to change, and examine planned change via organization development (OD). We conclude with a discussion of the nature and management of conflict.

Change: Organizational and Individual Perspectives

anticipatory changes planned changes based on expected situations

reactive changes changes made in response to unexpected situations

incremental changes subsystem adjustments required to keep the organization on course

strategic changes altering the overall shape or direction of the organization

In blunt terms, organizations that fail to change are sure to fail. Unfortunately, as the restructurings and layoffs of the 1980s dramatically demonstrated, organizational change can be hard on individuals. Indeed, the *Fortune* 500 companies cut their collective employment ranks by 3.5 million people during the 1980s.[5] Is it any wonder the average employee is wary of changes in the workplace? Let us begin to tackle this managerial dilemma by looking at four types of organizational change and also at how individuals tend to respond to significant changes. These twin perspectives are important because organizational changes unavoidably have personal impacts.

Types of Organizational Change

Consultant David A. Nadler and management professor Michael L. Tushman recently developed an instructive typology of organizational change (see Figure 15.1). On the vertical axis of their model, change is characterized as either anticipatory or reactive. **Anticipatory changes** are any systematically planned changes intended to take advantage of expected situations. Oppositely, **reactive changes** are those necessitated by unexpected environmental events or pressures. The horizontal axis deals with the scope of a particular change, either incremental or strategic. **Incremental changes** involve subsystem adjustments needed to keep the organization on its chosen path. **Strategic changes** alter the overall shape or

The Japanese symbol for *kaizen*, shown here, means continuous improvement, or getting big results by tweaking the littlest details of an operation. Managers committed to this sort of organizational tuning are never totally happy with things. They not only expect organizational change, they seek it. *Kaizen* managers anticipate and correct problems before they happen. *Kaizen* is the first line of defense against organizational decline.

direction of the organization. For instance, adding a night shift to meet unexpectedly high demand for the company's product is an incremental change. Switching from building houses to building high-rise apartment complexes would be a strategic change. Four resulting types of organizational change in the Nadler-Tushman model are tuning, adaptation, reorientation, and re-creation.[6] These types of organizational changes, listed in order of increasing complexity, intensity, and risk, require a closer look.

Tuning. This is the most common, least intense, and least risky type of change. Other names for it include preventive maintenance and the Japanese concept of *kaizen* (continuous improvement). The key to effective tuning is to actively anticipate and avoid problems rather than passively waiting for things to go wrong before taking action. For example, Du Pont recently tuned its marketing efforts by developing an Adopt-a-Customer program. The program "encourages blue-collar workers to visit a customer once a month, learn his needs, and be his representative on the factory floor."[7] This is a refreshing alternative to the traditional practice of waiting for customer complaints and only then trying to figure out how to fix them.

Adaptation. Like tuning, adaptation involves incremental changes. But this time, the changes are in reaction to external problems, events, or pressures. For example, after Ford had great success with its aerodynamic styling, General Motors and Chrysler followed suit. In turn, Ford and GM broadened their product lines to compete with Chrysler's trend-setting minivans.

Reorientation. This type of change is anticipatory and strategic in scope. Nadler and Tushman call reorientation "frame bending" because the organization is significantly redirected. Importantly, there is not a complete break with the organization's past. Kodak, for example, is investing in the next generation of picture-taking technology, electronic photography. "In that brave new world, cameras sense light with microchips and record images onto floppy diskettes. Photographers will view their images on a computer screen, perhaps cropping the pictures or improving the color balance before transmitting them to a special printer."[8] Even though electronic photography would make Kodak's conventional products obsolete in about ten years, the firm's strategy still centers on photography. Hence, Kodak is reorienting or frame bending.

FIGURE 15.1 • Four Types of Organizational Change

Source: David A. Nadler and Michael L. Tushman, "Beyond the Charismatic Leader: Leadership and Organizational Change." Copyright 1990 by The Regents of the University of California. Reprinted from the *California Management Review*, Vol. 32, No. 2. By permission of The Regents.

	Incremental	Strategic
Anticipatory	Tuning	Re-orientation
Reactive	Adaptation	Re-creation

Re-creation. Competitive pressures normally trigger this most intense and risky type of organizational change. Nadler and Tushman say it amounts to "frame breaking." A prime example is USX. The company's name formerly was U.S. Steel, reflecting its primary emphasis on making steel. After years of mergers and restructuring, the once-giant steel firm ended up being primarily an oil company. Severe international competition in the steel industry forced U.S. Steel to re-create itself.

Individual Reaction to Change

Each of the above types of change, in one way or another, has personal implications and consequences for individuals. Mergers, for example, trigger ripples of change that often cost employees their jobs. So when discussing organizational change, we need to consider how individuals tend to respond to change.

A Seven-Stage Model. Despite individual differences that enable people to cope with change in various ways, researchers have detected common response patterns.[9] The model in Figure 15.2 illustrates seven transition stages in personal change. Depending on how the transition process is managed, each stage can be a closed or open door to full adaptation to changes in the workplace. (This model applies to off-the-job changes—such as moving, marriage, and divorce—as well.) Notice in Figure 15.2 how the person's mood, morale, and sense of self-worth rise, fall, and rise once again as the change is digested. The time between the onset of change and full adaptation, which may not even occur, varies widely depending on personalities and situations.

• • • • • • • • • • • • • • • •
Explain the transition stages an individual goes through when responding to change.

The Model in Action. Let us walk through the seven stages listed in Figure 15.2 with Maria, a production supervisor at a dairy products cooperative that is switching to team-based production. In stage 1, Maria feels a bit unsure and somewhat overwhelmed by the proposed switch to teams. She needs a lot more information to decide whether she really likes the idea. She feels twinges of fear. Stage 2 finds Maria joking with her fellow supervisors about how upper management's enthusiasm for teams will blow over in a few days, so there's no need to worry. Her mood, morale, and self-worth are better than usual. After an initial training session on team-based management and participation, Maria begins to worry about her job security. Even if she keeps her job, she wonders if she is up to the new way of doing things. Thus, her morale and sense of self-worth drop sharply in stage 3. In stage 4, after a stern lecture from her boss about being a team player, Maria comes to grips with her resistance to the team approach. She resolves to stop criticizing management's "crazy team scheme" and help make it work. Her mood improves and her morale and self-worth turn around in stage 5, as she tries participative management techniques and gets encouraging results. Additional training and some personal research and reading on team-based management convince Maria that it's the wave of the future (stage 6). In stage 7, six months after the switch to teams was announced, Maria has become an outspoken advocate for teams and participative management. Her job security is assured by a pending promotion to the training department, where she will coordinate all team training for supervisors. Unknown to her superiors, Maria has even toyed with the idea of starting her own consulting business,

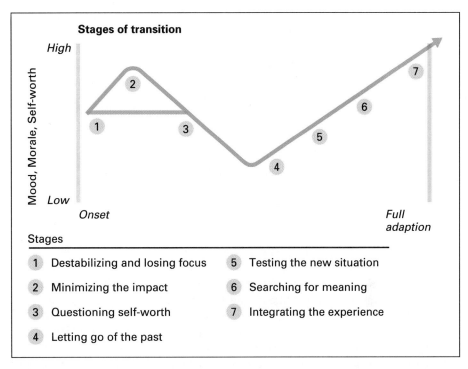

Stages of transition

Stages

1. Destabilizing and losing focus
2. Minimizing the impact
3. Questioning self-worth
4. Letting go of the past
5. Testing the new situation
6. Searching for meaning
7. Integrating the experience

FIGURE 15.2 • Transitions in Personal Change

Source: John D. Adams and Sabina A. Spencer, "People in Transition," *Training & Development Journal,* 42 (October 1988), 61–63. Copyright 1988, the American Society for Training and Development. Reprinted with permission. All rights reserved.

specializing in team management. Maria's transition from fear to full adaptation has taken months and has not been easy, but it has been a normal and positive experience.

Facilitating Personal Change Transitions. Managers need to be aware of the stages in personal change so they can facilitate smooth transitions. Maria's talk with her boss about being a team player, for example, helped her make the crucial transition from stage 3 to stage 4. Self-awareness of the normal ups and downs of change transitions can help employees avoid being overwhelmed by fear of failure and self-doubts. Training programs can empower individuals relative to the change process by getting them to envision how things could be improved (see Managers In Action). Managers also need to know how to overcome the resistance to change typically encountered during stages 1 to 3.

Overcoming Resistance to Change

Change is the order of the day for today's managers. In his book *Thriving on Chaos,* Tom Peters quotes an IBM executive as saying: "We must reexamine every relationship, every element of doing business, every process, every procedure. The only plausible criterion for success is: 'Are you changing enough,

Helping Trainees Develop a Picture of Their Future at Work

Have participants make two columns on a piece of paper.

Have them label the first column "What doesn't work." Under that heading, they should write five or six major or minor aspects of their work lives with which they are unhappy. Encourage them to state the problems negatively, and give them a lot of examples (such as, "I am burning out from all the work," and "My project doesn't have management support"). Give them plenty of time to write the list.

Ask them to label the second column "Instead, I choose." In this column, they should transform the negative statements that they wrote in the first column into positive, desirable statements. For example, across from "Things have changed so much that I'm not sure what my job consists of anymore," a trainee could write in the second column, "I am very clear about my job responsibilities." Encourage all of the participants not to concern themselves with what they think is possible.

Now instruct participants to write a description of what they need to do in order to make this future come to pass. Encourage the participants to write these statements as if they were already true. Have them put their descriptions in the form of

positive self-talk statements that can be committed to memory. Here are some examples:

- "I am creating a really clear picture of the kind of job I want to do for this company, and I am conveying it to my boss."
- "I am taking responsibility for myself as the organization changes: I am taking care of my health and remaining productive."
- "I am learning new skills that are making me attractive to future employers."
- "I am using this transition as a time to re-think my career objectives."

Then give trainees suggestions about how to use their positive self-talk statements to keep themselves centered during the turmoil of change. For example, read the statements over two or three times each day, make a poster with them on it, enter them into a diary, or tell friends about them.

Finally, have participants who are comfortable doing so share their self-talk statements with the group.

Source: Richard McKnight and Marilyn Thompson, "Navigating Organizational Change," *Training & Development Journal,* 44 (December 1990): 48. Copyright 1991, the American Society of Training and Development. Reprinted with permission. All rights reserved.

rapidly enough, to successfully confront the future?' "[10] Within the change typology just discussed, organizational change comes in all sizes and shapes. Often it's new and unfamiliar equipment, such as personal computers. It could be reorganization, a merger, a new pay plan, or perhaps a new performance-appraisal program. Whatever its form, change is like a stone tossed into a still pond. The initial impact causes ripples to radiate in all directions, often with unpredictable consequences. A common consequence of change in organizations is resistance from those whose jobs are directly affected. Both rational and irrational resistance can bring the wheels of progress to a halt. Management faces the challenge of foreseeing and neutralizing resistance to change. The question is, how? To answer that question, we must examine why employees resist change.

Why Do Employees Resist Change?

Employees resist change for many reasons.[11] Among the most common are:

Another issue of the *Chicago Tribune* hits the streets. New demands, greater need for speed, and new technology have meant nonstop change for newsrooms at the *Tribune* and elsewhere. For instance, the *Tribune* recently replaced a couple of aged minicomputer systems with a network of 400 Compaq Deskpro 386 computers. Electronic mail, databases, wire service feeds, and source material from others is now at reporters' fingertips. But all this high-tech improvement did not come about without some pain. Inevitable resistance to change had to be identified and overcome.

List at least six reasons why employees resist change and discuss what management can do about resistance to change.

Surprise. Significant changes that are introduced on the spur of the moment or with no warning can create a threatening sense of imbalance in the workplace. Regarding this problem, an executive task force at J. C. Penney Co., the well-known retailer, recommended: "Schedule changes in measurable, comfortable stages. Too much, too soon can be counterproductive."[12]

Inertia. Many members of the typical organization desire to maintain a safe, secure, and predictable status quo. The byword of this group is: "But we don't do things that way here." Technological inertia also is a common problem. Consider, for example, the history of the standard typewriter keyboard (referred to as the Qwerty keyboard because **QWERTY** are the first six letters in the upper left-hand corner).

> *The ungainly layout of the Qwerty keyboard was introduced in 1873 to slow down typists so they wouldn't jam the keys. That design imperative quickly disappeared, yet Qwerty has turned back all attempts—including one by its own inventor—to replace it with something faster. The productivity cost? Undoubtedly billions of dollars.*[13]

Thanks to resistance to change, the latest high-tech marvels in personal computing come out of the box today complete with an 1873-style keyboard! Supervisors and middle managers who fall victim to unthinking inertia can effectively kill change programs.

Misunderstanding/Ignorance/Lack of Skills. Without adequate introductory or remedial training, an otherwise positive change may be perceived in a negative light.

Emotional Side Effects. Those who are forced to accept on-the-job changes commonly experience a sense of loss over past ways of doing things. For example, consider what one AT&T employee said following the government-forced divestiture in 1984: "I felt like I had gone through a divorce that neither my wife nor my children wanted. . . . It was like waking up in familiar surroundings, but your family and all that you held dear were missing."[14]

Lack of Trust. Promises of improvement are likely to fall on deaf ears when employees do not trust management. Conversely, managers are unlikely to permit necessary participation if they do not trust their people.

Fear of Failure. Just as most college freshmen have doubts about their chances of ever graduating, challenges presented by significant on-the-job changes can also be intimidating.

Personality Conflicts. Managers who are disliked by their people are poor conduits for change.

Poor Timing. In every work setting, internal and/or external events can conspire to create resentment about a particular change. For example, Intel's across-the-board salary cut, in response to the electronics industry slump of 1981–1982, generated greater than expected resentment because "the salary cuts were timed to come just as taxes for Social Security were reimposed."[15]

Lack of Tact. As we all know, it is not necessarily what is said that shapes our attitude toward people and events. How it is said is often more important. Tactful and sensitive handling of changes is essential.

Threat to Job Status/Security. Because employment fulfills basic needs, employees can be expected to resist changes with real or imaginary impacts on job status or job security.

Breakup of Work Group. Significant changes can tear the fabric of on-the-job social relationships. Accordingly, members of cohesive work groups often exert peer pressure on one another to resist changes that threaten to break up the group.[16]

These reasons for resisting change help demonstrate that participation is not a panacea. For example, imagine the futility of trying to gain the enthusiastic support of a team of auto assembly-line welders for a robot that will eventually take over their jobs. In extreme form, each reason for resisting change can become an insurmountable barrier to genuine participation. Therefore, managers need a broad array of methods for dealing with resistance to change.

Strategies for Overcoming Resistance to Change

Only in recent years have management theorists begun to give serious attention to alternative ways of overcoming resistance to change.[17] At least six options, including participation, are available in this area:

1. *Education and Communication.* This strategy is appealing because it advocates prevention rather than cure. The idea here is to help employees understand the true need for a change as well as the logic behind it. Various media may be used, including face-to-face discussions, formal group presentations, or special reports or publications.

2. *Participation and Involvement.* Once again, personal involvement through participation tends to defuse both rational and irrational fears about a workplace change. By participating in both the design and implementation of a change, one acquires a personal stake in its success.

3. *Facilitation and Support.* When fear and anxiety are responsible for resistance to doing things in a new and different way, support from management in the form of special training, job stress counseling, and compensatory time off can be helpful.

4. *Negotiation and Agreement.* Sometimes management can neutralize potential or actual resistance by exchanging something of value for cooperation. An hourly clerical employee may, for instance, be put on a salary in return for learning how to operate a new computerized work station.

5. *Manipulation and Co-optation.* Manipulation occurs when managers selectively withhold or dispense information and consciously arrange events to increase the chance that a change will be successful. Co-optation normally involves token participation. Those who are co-opted with token participation cannot claim that they have not been consulted, yet the ultimate impact of their input is negligible.

6. *Explicit and Implicit Coercion.* Managers who cannot or will not invest the time required for the other strategies can force employees to go along with a change by threatening them with termination, loss of pay raises or promotions, transfer, and the like.

As shown in Table 15.1, each of these strategies for overcoming resistance to change has advantages and drawbacks. Situational appropriateness is the key to success.

Now we turn our attention to organization development, a systematic approach to planned change.

Planned Change through Organization Development (OD)

Organization development has become a convenient label for a host of techniques and processes aimed at making sick organizations healthy and healthy organizations healthier. According to experts in the field:

organization development (OD) planned change programs intended to help people and organizations function more effectively

> ***Organization development*** (OD) *consists of planned efforts to help persons work and live together more effectively, over time, in their organizations. These goals are achieved by applying behavioral science principles, methods, and theories adapted from the fields of psychology, sociology, education, and management.*[18]

TABLE 15.1 • Dealing with Resistance to Change

Approach	Commonly used in situations	Advantages	Drawbacks
1. Education + communication	Where there is a lack of information or inaccurate information and analysis	Once persuaded, people will often help with the implementation of the change	Can be very time-consuming if lots of people are involved
2. Participation + involvement	Where the initiators do not have all the information they need to design the change, and where others have considerable power to resist	People who participate will be committed to implementing change, and any relevant information they have will be integrated into the change plan	Can be very time-consuming if participators design an inappropriate change
3. Facilitation + support	Where people are resisting because of adjustment problems	No other approach works as well with adjustment problems	Can be time-consuming, expensive, and still fail
4. Negotiation + agreement	Where someone or some group will clearly lose out in a change, and where that group has considerable power to resist	Sometimes it is a relatively easy way to avoid major resistance	Can be too expensive in many cases if it alerts others to negotiate for compliance
5. Manipulation + co-optation	Where other tactics will not work or are too expensive	It can be a relatively quick and inexpensive solution to resistance problems	Can lead to future problems if people feel manipulated
6. Explicit + implicit coercion	Where speed is essential, and the change initiators possess considerable power	It is speedy, and can overcome any kind of resistance	Can be risky if it leaves people mad at the initiators

Source: Reprinted by permission of the *Harvard Business Review.* An exhibit from "Choosing Strategies for Change," by John P. Kotter and Leonard A. Schlesinger (March-April 1979), p. 111. Copyright © 1979 by the President and Fellows of Harvard College; all rights reserved.

• • • • • • • • • • • • • • • • • •

Define, in your own words, the term *organization development* (OD).

Others simply call OD *planned change*. Regarding the degree of change involved, OD consultant and writer Warner Burke contends that:

> *Organization development is a process of fundamental change in an organization's culture. By fundamental change, as opposed to fixing a problem or improving a procedure, I mean that some significant aspect of the organization's culture will never be the same.*[19]

OD programs generally are facilitated by hired consultants, although inside OD specialists also can be found. In this section, we examine the nature and process of OD.[20]

The Objectives of OD

OD programs vary because they are tailored to unique situations. What is appropriate for one organization may be totally out of place in another. In spite of this variation, certain objectives are common to most OD programs. In general,

Renee Tillman is a very valuable resource at Pacific Bell. She is a creative and demanding change agent. Tillman recently played a key role in implementing Pacific Bell's new customer focus program. A great deal of unfreezing, change, and refreezing had to be carried out as she reorganized 120 Los Angeles-area service representatives into self-managed teams. Now Tillman's efforts are focused on program evaluation as she heads up a taskforce to determine if Pacific Bell's customer service strategy is working as intended.

OD programs develop social processes such as trust, problem solving, communication, and cooperation to facilitate organizational change and enhance personal and organizational effectiveness. More specifically, the typical OD program tries to achieve the following seven objectives:

1. Deepen the sense of organizational purpose (or vision) and align individuals with that purpose.
2. Strengthen interpersonal trust, communication, cooperation, and support.
3. Encourage a problem-solving rather than problem-avoiding approach to organizational problems.
4. Develop a satisfying work experience capable of building enthusiasm.
5. Supplement formal authority with authority based on personal knowledge and skill.
6. Increase personal responsibility for planning and implementing.
7. Encourage personal willingness to change.[21]

Critics of OD are quick to point out that there is nothing really new in this list of objectives. Directly or indirectly, each of these objectives is addressed by one or another general management technique. OD advocates respond by noting that general management lacks a systematic approach. They feel that the usual practice of teaching managers how to plan, solve problems, make decisions, organize, motivate, lead, and control leads to a haphazard, bits-and-pieces management style. According to OD thinking, organization development gives managers a vehicle for systematically introducing change by applying a broad selection of management techniques as a unified and consistent package. This, they claim, leads to greater personal, group, and organizational effectiveness.

The OD Process

•••••••••••••••••
Describe how the unfreezing-change-refreezing analogy applies to OD.

unfreezing neutralizing resistance by preparing people for change

refreezing systematically following up a change program for lasting results

A simple analogy helps introduce the three major components of OD. Suppose someone hands you a coffee cup filled with clear, solid ice. You look down through the ice and see a penny lying tails up on the bottom of the cup. Now, suppose for some reason you want the penny to be frozen in place in a heads-up position. What can you do? There is really only one practical solution. You let the ice in the cup thaw, reach in and flip the penny over, and then refreeze the cup of water. This is precisely how social psychologist Kurt Lewin recommended that change be handled in social systems. Specifically, Lewin recommended that change agents unfreeze, change, and then refreeze social systems.

Unfreezing prepares the members of a social system for change and then helps neutralize initial resistance. Sudden, unexpected change, according to Lewin, is socially disruptive. When the change has been introduced, **refreezing** is necessary to follow up on problems, complaints, unanticipated side effects, and any lingering resistance. This seemingly simple approach to change spells the difference between systematic and haphazard change.

The OD model introduced here is based on Lewin's approach to handling change (see Figure 15.3). Diagnosis is carried out during the unfreezing phase. Change is then carefully introduced through tailor-made intervention. Finally, a systematic follow-up refreezes the situation.[22] Each phase is critical to successful organizational change and development. Still, it takes continual recycling through this three-phase sequence to make OD an ongoing system of planned change.

OD Diagnosis

Because of the expense of conducting a diagnosis, management teams (or qualified outside consultants) need to identify at the outset the specific problem areas

FIGURE 15.3 ● A General Model of OD

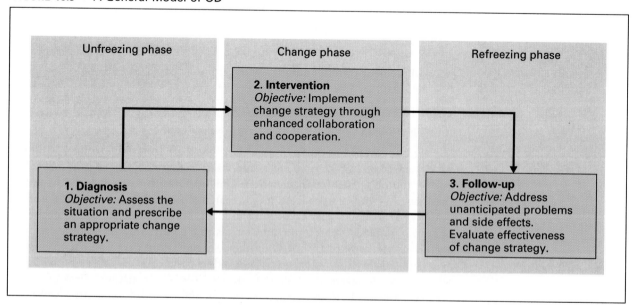

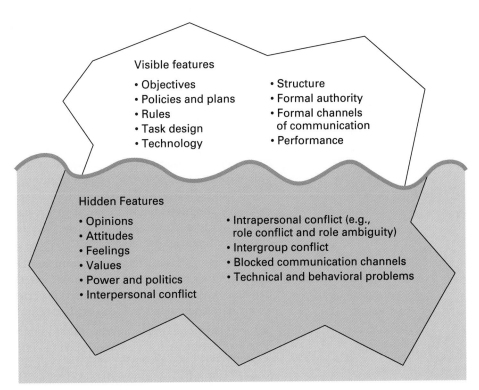

Visible features

- Objectives
- Policies and plans
- Rules
- Task design
- Technology

- Structure
- Formal authority
- Formal channels of communication
- Performance

Hidden Features

- Opinions
- Attitudes
- Feelings
- Values
- Power and politics
- Interpersonal conflict

- Intrapersonal conflict (e.g., role conflict and role ambiguity)
- Intergroup conflict
- Blocked communication channels
- Technical and behavioral problems

FIGURE 15.4 • The Organizational Iceberg: Hidden Features Are Also Important

or subunits that deserve close examination. Diagnoses that are overly comprehensive or carelessly directed are a waste of time and money.

After the relevant domain has been selected, management (or hired consultants) can turn to three important aspects of the diagnostic phase: (1) unfreezing the situation, (2) designing the diagnostic strategy, and (3) interpreting the diagnostic data.

Unfreezing the Situation. An OD program should not come as a surprise. Some unfreezing—making announcements, holding meetings, and launching a promotional campaign in the organization's newsletter and on bulletin boards—can help start things. All these activities help deliver a clear message: "We can improve the effectiveness of our organization while increasing our personal satisfaction if we all cooperate in a comprehensive program of finding out where we are, where we want to go, and how we can get there." This message prepares people for interviewers, questionnaires, unfamiliar consultants, and group activities that could be threatening if they came as surprises. One word of caution: during the unfreezing phase, care needs to be taken to avoid creating unrealistic expectations. OD is designed to introduce change, not miracles.[23]

Designing the Diagnostic Strategy. Those about to tackle an OD diagnosis will find it helpful to view the typical organization as an iceberg. Figure 15.4 shows that just as most of an iceberg lies beneath the surface of the water, a greater proportion of an organization's activities and information is also hidden from view. OD diagnosis is difficult because hidden as well as visible information must be brought to the surface. Naturally, a complete diagnosis of every feature listed in Figure 15.4 would be prohibitively expensive and time-consuming, and so it is important to select the right diagnostic strategy for the information sought. Four widely used approaches are:

1. *Review of Records.* Largely in response to the government's increased demand for reports, today's organizations possess a wealth of recorded information and data. When change agents have the time and patience to carry out a thorough records search, they are often rewarded with valuable information about the relative health or sickness of the organization. Much can be learned by reviewing human resource records for signs of excessive absenteeism and turnover or for patterns of grievances. Similarly, a study of financial records can yield telling signs of cost overruns and other financial problems.

2. *Interviews.* By using a carefully compiled list of specific questions (requiring yes or no answers) and general, open-ended questions (requiring detailed explanations), a skilled interviewer can discover a great deal about both individuals and the organization at large.

3. *Survey Questionnaires.* Survey questionnaires are the most widely used diagnostic strategy today. Questionnaires may be administered to people assembled in groups, or they may be mailed individually. They may be constructed in-house or purchased.[24] Some of the more sophisticated published survey questionnaires include in the purchase price scoring and statistical analysis.

4. *Direct Observation.* It is well known that people tend to say one thing and do another. When this kind of discrepancy is likely to be a problem, management may choose to have a neutral third party (usually an outside consultant) directly observe organizational members at work.

Each of these strategies has its appropriate place in OD diagnosis. By balancing the respective strengths and weaknesses of the various approaches (see Table 15.2), it is possible to develop a diagnostic strategy based on two or more approaches. For example, a carefully structured interview could supplement the results of a records review or fill in gaps left by a prepackaged survey questionnaire. The overall objective, of course, is to obtain as much useful information as possible at a reasonable cost.

Interpreting Diagnostic Data. Careful interpretation of the data collected during diagnosis paves the way for effective OD intervention. It is a serious mistake, however, to wait until the diagnosis has been completed before thinking about the interpretation phase. Diagnostic strategies need to be selected with ease of interpretation in mind. Furthermore, as one OD expert has pointed out, "Data should be collected for a reason, not just 'because it's there,' and analysis should be done with direction and purpose, not as a fishing expedition to 'see what we come up with.' "[25]

Comparisons are helpful. If a similar diagnosis has been conducted in the past, comparing past results with present results can show how things have changed. Comparisons among departments and other organizational subunits

TABLE 15.2 ● Evaluating Various Diagnostic Approaches

Diagnostic approach	Major strengths	Major weaknesses
Review of records	Provides historical perspective over extended period.	Time-consuming.
	Facts and figures confirm or refute employee's intentions and/or perceptions.	Faulty recordkeeping can be disruptive.
Interviews	Face-to-face contact is revealing (for example, body language).	Respondents often try to look good in the interviewer's eyes.
	Questions can be inserted on the spot to probe promising areas.	Time-consuming and costly if a large sample is required.
Survey questionnaires	Appropriate for large samples.	Prepackaged questionnaires may ask the wrong questions.
	Administration is time- and cost-efficient.	Preparation and interpretation of in-house questionnaires can be time-consuming and costly.
Direct observation	Behavior speaks for itself. (Actions speak louder than words.)	Presence of observer often causes people to behave abnormally.
	Previously unrecognized problems may be spotted by trained outside observer.	Time-consuming and costly if a large sample is required.

can also be revealing. For instance, a comparatively strong negative attitude toward supervision in one department may signal the need to train or replace a particular supervisor.

Careful interpretation of diagnostic data is the key to selecting an appropriate change or intervention strategy. Inaccurate or sloppy diagnosis will doom even the best-designed and most well-intentioned OD intervention.

Intervention

intervention an OD effort designed to correct problems uncovered through diagnosis

After the organization or target group has been unfrozen and the diagnosis is complete, the wheels of change can be set in motion. An **intervention,** in OD terms, is a systematic attempt to correct an organizational deficiency uncovered through diagnosis. Management teams, working either alone or in collaboration with an outside consultant, are responsible for selecting OD interventions.[26] However, the wheels of failure will be set in motion at this critical juncture if management is uninformed about alternative interventions, withholds its full support, or has unrealistic expectations. (See Table 15.3 for OD success factors that researchers have uncovered.) Every year new OD techniques emerge—some have great potential, but others promise more than they can deliver.

●●●●●●●●●●●●●●●●●●
Explain how OD interventions can be aimed at individuals, groups, or entire organizations.

Here we examine six popular OD interventions designed to increase effectiveness at three different organizational levels (see Figure 15.5). *Life and career*

TABLE 15.3 • OD Success Factors

A nationwide sample of 245 OD consultants responded to a questionnaire asking about their successes and failures. "Fifty-three percent of the projects reported were successful, 47 percent unsuccessful." Among the factors found to be associated with *successful* OD programs were:

1. Client system was *ready for change*.
2. OD consultant's principal contact person was a *powerful* member of the organization.
3. Top management *supported* and *accepted responsibility* for the OD program.
4. Both inside and outside OD consultants had a *high degree of access* to client organization's resources (such as information and people).
5. A high degree of consultant/client *collaboration* existed.
6. Successful consultants used *multiple interventions*.

Source: Adapted from W. Warner Burke, Lawrence P. Clark, and Cheryl Koopman, "Improve Your OD Project's Chances for Success," *Training and Development Journal,* 38 (September 1984): 62–68. Copyright 1984, the American Society for Training and Development. Reprinted with permission. All rights reserved.

planning and *skill development* focus on the individual; *role analysis* and *team building* are aimed at the group; and *survey feedback* and *Grid*® OD target the entire organization. These particular interventions have been chosen for two reasons: they are representative of what is available, and they complement one another. Conceivably, all six interventions could be included in a single, comprehensive OD program.

Life and Career Planning. Many employees today have no clear plans for their lives or their careers; things just happen. (See Appendix B for more on career management.) But individuals can be challenged to take greater responsibility for the direction of their lives. Just as challenging objectives can stimulate organizational productivity, so life and career objectives can enhance personal effectiveness and satisfaction. Life and career planning, as an OD intervention, gives the individual an opportunity to sit down and do a thorough self-analysis. Part of this self-analysis is listing personal strengths and weaknesses. Discussion with a career counselor follows, with an eye toward taking greater advantage of one's strengths and eliminating or minimizing the weaknesses. If lack of formal education is a barrier, then a plan is formulated for going back to school. Perhaps a long-lost dream to master a second language, or play a musical instrument, or learn computer programming can be rekindled.

The overall objective of life and career planning is to get individuals to define their personal goals for growth and development and to plan ways to achieve them. Underlying all this is the assumption that organizational growth and development is a function of individual growth and development.

Skill Development. When carried out alone (rather than as part of a comprehensive OD program), this intervention is generally considered part of management training and development. Unlike most OD interventions, skill development deals with content rather than process. For example, when an OD diagnosis uncovers the inability of a group of engineers in the research and development

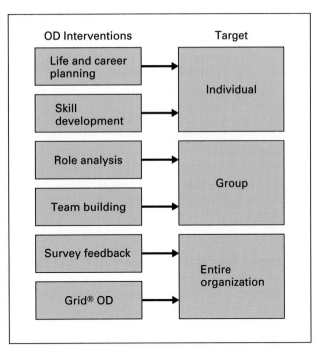

FIGURE 15.5 • OD Interventions for Different Levels

department to write objectives and formulate plans, the deficiency can be corrected through appropriate training. Similarly, managers at all levels can be trained to polish their skills in areas such as delegation, problem solving, conflict resolution, and leading. Emphasis in skill development clearly is on learning "how to do it."

Role Analysis. A role, once again, is a prescribed way of behaving. In an unhealthy organization, many people do not know what their roles are or should be, and if they do know, their roles typically are in direct conflict with those of coworkers. In a healthy organization, everyone knows his or her role, and those roles mesh in a way that encourages cooperation and reduces dysfunctional conflict. For this reason, many OD programs call for some sort of **role analysis,** which is the systematic clarification of interdependent tasks and job behavior.

role analysis systematic clarification of interdependent tasks and job behavior

team building OD technique for developing mature and effective work groups

Team Building. As an OD process for developing work group maturity and effectiveness, **team building** has become very popular in recent years.[27] In fact, in a recent survey of 179 *Fortune* 500 human resource executives, team building turned out to be the most widely used (61 percent) human resource development technique.[28] Team building takes many forms, from intensive laboratory training (such as diversity training)[29] to structured exercises (such as the formulation of strategic plans by a team of executives). Team building is viewed by many as "pure" OD because it emphasizes interactive group processes, the "how" of effective group behavior. A noted OD specialist has ranked the purposes of team building as follows:

1. To set goals and/or priorities.
2. To analyze or allocate the way work is performed.
3. To examine the way a group is working, its processes (such as norms, decision making, communications).
4. To examine relationships among the people doing the work.[30]

It is important for the group itself to achieve these purposes by relying on its own leadership to solve real-life problems. The consultant-facilitator merely gets things headed in the right direction, quietly coaches as necessary along the way, periodically summarizes what has taken place, and selectively points out the impact of group processes such as communicating, problem solving, conflict resolution, and decision making.[31] Ideally, people come away from team-building programs with a greater appreciation of how they as individuals can contribute effectively to group activity (for example, see The World of Management).

Survey Feedback. In survey feedback, data gathered through personal interviews and/or survey questionnaires are analyzed, tabulated into understandable form, and shared with those who first supplied the information. The main purpose of survey feedback is to let people know where they stand in relation to others on important organizational issues so that constructive problem solving can take place. Effective feedback should be:

- *Relevant.*   Only information that is meaningful to the recipients should be fed back.
- *Understandable.*   To ensure clear communication, language and symbols should be familiar to the recipients.
- *Descriptive.*   Data should be in the form of real-life examples with which the recipients can identify.
- *Verifiable.*   The form of presentation should allow recipients to test the validity and accuracy of the data fed back to them.
- *Limited.*   Too much feedback causes an information overload, and so only significant highlights should be presented.
- *Controllable.*   Recipients should be given information on situations that they can directly control.
- *Comparative.*   Comparative data let recipients know where they stand in relation to others.
- *Inspiring.*   Recipients must see feedback information as a beginning and a stimulus for action rather than as a final statement.[32]

Feedback that meets these criteria should be fed back to organizational subgroups, as the situation allows, until all employees have had a chance to see where and how they fit. At that point, interventions such as life and career planning, skill development, team building, and role analysis can be introduced.

Grid® OD. The Grid® approach is an OD program based on Blake and Mouton's Leadership Grid®. Since the mid-1960s it has consistently ranked among the most popular OD approaches, and tens of thousands of managers have received Grid® training. Grid® proponents believe it is a comprehensive kind of

Building Teams for Safety at Australian Airlines

The cockpit of a modern jetliner is one of the most imposingly high-tech places on earth. Hundreds of dials, lights, gauges, buttons, levers, and other gadgets are crammed into a small space. During an emergency, two or three people must make proper use of just the right combination of cockpit controls, and the lives of hundreds of people ride on their hastily made decisions. So what's the best way to ensure that their decisions will be right and all those people will return safely to earth?

According to a growing number of safety experts, the answer is management team-building training. A study by the National Aeronautics and Space Administration showed that 60 percent of all fatal airline crashes in the 1970s probably could have been prevented if the cockpit crew had made better use of available resources. Cockpit Resource Management has therefore become the newest training technique at many airlines. It has already been credited with saving lives during emergencies when the crew worked together and came up with creative solutions to seemingly unsolvable problems. In training, crews watch videos of effective and ineffective cockpit behavior, role play, solve conflicts and problems, and learn how to handle stress and make decisions as a team.

One such training program was developed by three management experts for Australian Airlines, an airline that serves all major cities in Australia. The experts overcame resistance largely by involving the pilots themselves in creating the program. Initially, most pilots said they needed many other things more than they needed team building. It soon became apparent that they recognized that communication, leadership, and interpersonal problems existed in the cockpit, but they assumed the solutions to those problems would be technical, not managerial. During the training sessions, they now handle simulated disasters such as an outbreak of fire at 30,000 feet. They also practice resolving conflicts and learn more about the way they and others approach their jobs. The effects of such training are difficult to measure, since success results in something *not* happening. Still, participants and consultants have been so pleased with the sessions that they envision using the same approach with technical crews at power plants, oil rigs, big ships, and other places where managing people has traditionally taken a back seat to managing machines.

Sources: Charles Margerison, Rod Davies, and Dick McCann, "Air-crew Team Management Development," *Journal of Management Development,* 7, No. 4 (1988): 41–54; Charles Margerison, Rod Davies, and Dick McCann, "High-Flying Management Development," *Training and Development Journal* (February 1987): 38–41; Joseph Oberle, "Teamwork in the Cockpit," *Training* (February 1990): 34–38.

OD intervention because its six major phases unfold over a period of four, five, or more years. Briefly, the six phases are:

- *Phase 1.* During a week-long seminar, participants have their management style diagnosed and discuss how they can move toward an ideal *9,9* style (see Chapter 14).
- *Phase 2.* Participants learn how to be more effective contributors by attending a team-building workshop.
- *Phase 3.* Working from the skills developed in phases 1 and 2, managers concentrate on developing intergroup problem-solving ability.
- *Phase 4.* Management teams (starting at the top and filtering down) work together to devise an organizational blueprint. This blueprint details where the organization ought to be headed.

- *Phase 5.* This action phase usually takes years to complete as the organizational blueprint conceived in phase 4 is put into practice.
- *Phase 6.* In this stabilization period, newly acquired ways of solving problems, resolving conflict, and making decisions are refined for continued use.[33]

Grid® OD is popular because it is a package encompassing several OD interventions arranged in an orderly and coherent fashion.

Follow-up

Effective OD programs do not end abruptly when the intervention phase is completed but, rather, require a carefully monitored refreezing period to ensure lasting change. This follow-up phase has two objectives. First, the effectiveness of OD interventions needs to be evaluated. Second, steps need to be taken to maintain the changes that have been introduced. We now look more closely at these two objectives.

Evaluating the OD Program. Evaluating changes in any complex social system is never easy.[34] Still, those in charge of an OD program owe it to themselves, the target group, and top management to determine whether they have really done any good. To date, evaluation has been the weakest link in OD practice.[35]

A recent statistical analysis of 126 studies involving OD interventions yielded the following insights: (1) *combined interventions* were more effective at improving employee attitudes and satisfaction than were single-technique interventions; (2) *team building* was the most effective OD intervention for improving attitudes and satisfaction; and (3) OD interventions tend to have a stronger influence on *attitudes* than on satisfaction.[36] The empirical linkages between OD interventions and productivity are not strong.[37]

Ideally, users of OD techniques attempt to evaluate their programs in hard, factual terms. Attitude questionnaire results as well as absentee, turnover, grievance, and financial data can be gathered before the OD program to serve as a base line against which data can be compared later. The use of a control group strengthens the evaluation by helping rule out changes from other causes that might otherwise be attributed to the OD intervention(s). From a research perspective, objective evaluations should be a part of every OD program, even though they are difficult, time-consuming, expensive, and hence largely unappealing from an administrative standpoint. Claims of improvement because of an OD program are virtually impossible without an objective evaluation of results.

Maintaining Positive Changes. The purpose of any OD program is to induce organizational members to behave differently (for example, more cooperatively, more collaboratively, more productively). Although the various OD interventions are designed to persuade individuals to experiment with new modes of behavior, permanent behavior change is a different matter. The key is a supportive climate for change back on the job. When the formal reward and punishment system and peer group pressure support change, it will probably take place. Top management's unqualified commitment to the OD program[38] helps bring the formal reward and punishment system into harmony with the desired behavioral change. Peer group support is the difficult part. Only skillful unfreezing and exciting, relevant, and innovative OD interventions will generate individual commitment. But after enthusiasm among organization members is achieved and the culture shifts in a positive direction, no barrier to change is too great to be overcome.

Managing Conflict

●●●●●●●●●●●●●●●●
Explain the difference between functional and dysfunctional conflict.

Conflict is intimately related to change and interpersonal dealings.[39] Harvard's Abraham Zaleznik recently offered this perspective:

> *Because people come together to satisfy a wide array of psychological needs, social relations in general are awash with conflict. In the course of their interactions, people must deal with differences as well as similarities, with aversions as well as affinities. Indeed, in social relations, Sigmund Freud's parallel of humans and porcupines is apt: like porcupines, people prick and injure one another if they get too close; they will feel cold if they get too far apart.[40]*

conflict all kinds of opposition or antagonistic interaction

As used here, **conflict** "refers to all kinds of opposition or antagonistic interaction. It is based on scarcity of power, resources or social position, and differing value structures."[41] Not all conflict is bad. Conflict has two faces, one functional (or constructive) and the other dysfunctional (or destructive). According to one authority who emphasizes the constructive side of conflict:

> *Conflicts, when appropriately managed, add substantial value to organizations. Conflict is the medium by which problems are recognized and solved. Employees who discuss conflict disclose information, challenge assumptions, dig into issues, and, as a consequence, make successful decisions. Conflict is needed because diverse opinions and information are mandatory to solve problems and get things done in organizations.[42]*

One important aspect of effectively managing functional conflict is expressing anger in constructive ways (see Management Ethics).

Dealing with the Two Faces of Conflict

An organizational perspective is required when distinguishing between functional and dysfunctional conflict. The organizational benefits of functional conflict are increased effort and improved performance, enhanced creativity, and personal development and growth. In contrast, the symptoms of dysfunctional conflict include indecision, resistance to change, destructive emotional outbursts, apathy, and increased political maneuvering. By monitoring these various signs and symptoms, management can decide when it is appropriate to encourage conflict and when it is time to resolve or neutralize it. For example, functional conflict is encouraged at Anheuser-Busch in the following manner:

> *When the policy committee of that company considers a major move—getting into or out of a business, or making a big capital expenditure—it sometimes assigns teams to make the case for each side of the question. There may be two teams or even three. Each is knowledgeable about the subject; each has access to the same information.*

How to Express Anger

Although not every angry feeling should be expressed to the person held accountable, this approach is direct and has the most potential to initiate a productive conflict. There are several rules to keep in mind when expressing anger.

- **Check assumptions.** No matter how convinced employees are that someone has deliberately interfered and tried to harm them, they may be mistaken. People can ask questions and probe. It may be that the other person had no intention and was unaware that others were frustrated. The incident may just dissolve into a misunderstanding.

- **Be specific.** People find being the target of anger stressful and anxiety provoking. They fear insults and rejection. The more specific the angry person can be, the less threatening and less of an attack on self-esteem the anger is. Knowing what angered the other can give the target of the anger concrete ways to make amends.

- **Be consistent.** Verbal and nonverbal messages should both express anger. Smiling and verbally expressing anger confuses the issue.

- **Take responsibility for anger.** Persons expressing anger should let the target know that they are angry and the reasoning and steps they took that made them feel unjustly frustrated.

- **Avoid provoking anger.** Expressing anger through unfair, insinuating remarks ("I can't believe someone can be as stupid as you!") can make the target of the anger angry too. Such situations can quickly deteriorate.

- **Watch for impulsivity.** Anger agitates and people say things they later regret.

- **Be wary of self-righteousness.** People can feel powerful, superior, and right; angry people can play, "Now I got 'ya and you will pay." But anger should be used to get to the heart of the matter and solve problems, not for flouting moral superiority.

- **Be sensitive.** People typically underestimate the impact their anger has on others. Targets of anger often feel defensive, anxious, and worried. It is not usually necessary to repeat one's anger to get people's attention.

- **Make the expression cathartic.** Anger generates energy. Telling people releases that energy rather than submerges it. Anger is a feeling to get over, not to hang on to.

- **Express positive feelings.** Angry people depend upon and usually like people they are angry with. People expect help from people who have proved trustworthy, and are angry when it is not forthcoming.

- **Move to constructive conflict management.** Feeling affronted, personally attacked, and self-righteous should not side-track you from solving the underlying problems. Use the anger to create positive conflict.

- **Celebrate joint success.** Anger tests people's skills and their relationships. Be sure to celebrate the mutual achievement of expressing and responding to anger successfully.

Source: Dean Tjosvold, *The Conflict-Positive Organization* © 1991 by Addison-Wesley Publishing Company, Inc. Reprinted with permission of the publisher.

Occasionally someone in favor of the project is chosen to lead the dissent, and an opponent to argue for it. Pat Stokes, who heads the company's beer empire, describes the result: "We end up with decisions and alternatives we hadn't thought of previously," sometimes representing a synthesis of the opposing views. "You become a lot more anticipatory, better able to see what might happen, because you have thought through the process."[43]

There are two sets of tools available for managing conflict. The first we call conflict triggers, which stimulate conflict, and the second involves conflict resolution techniques, which are used when functional conflict deteriorates into dysfunctional conflict.

Conflict Triggers

conflict trigger any factor that increases the chances of conflict

A **conflict trigger** is a circumstance that increases the chances of intergroup or interpersonal conflict. It can stimulate either functional or dysfunctional conflict. As long as a conflict trigger appears to stimulate constructive conflict, it can be allowed to continue. But as soon as the symptoms of destructive conflict become apparent, steps need to be taken to remove or correct the offending conflict trigger. Major conflict triggers include:

- *Ambiguous or Overlapping Jurisdictions.* Unclear job boundaries often create competition for resources and control. Reorganization can help to clarify job boundaries if destructive conflict becomes a problem (refer to the organization design alternatives discussed in Chapter 9).

- *Competition for Scarce Resources.* As the term is used here, resources include funds, personnel, authority, power, and valuable information. In other words, anything of value in an organizational setting can become a competitively sought-after scarce resource. Sometimes, as in the cases of money and people, destructive competition for scarce resources can be avoided by enlarging the resource base (such as increasing competing managers' budgets or hiring additional personnel).

- *Communication Breakdowns.* Because communication is a complex process beset by many barriers, these barriers often provoke conflict. It is easy to misunderstand another person or group of people if two-way communication is hampered in some way. The battle for clear communication never ends.

- *Time Pressure.* Deadlines and other forms of time pressure can stimulate prompt performance or trigger destructive emotional reactions. When imposing deadlines, managers should consider individuals' ability to cope.

- *Unreasonable Standards, Rules, Policies, or Procedures.* These triggers generally lead to dysfunctional conflict between managers and their subordinates. The best remedy is for the manager to tune into employees' perceptions of fair play and correct extremely unpopular situations before they mushroom.

- *Personality Clashes.* It is very difficult to change one's personality on the job. Therefore the practical remedy for serious personality clashes is to separate the antagonistic parties by reassigning one or both to a new job.

- *Status Differentials.* As long as productive organizations continue to be arranged hierarchically, this trigger is unavoidable. But managers can minimize dysfunctional conflict by showing a genuine concern for the ideas, feelings, and values of subordinates.

- *Unrealized Expectations.* Dissatisfaction grows when expectations are not met. Conflict is another by-product of unrealized expectations. Destructive conflict can be avoided in this area by taking time to discover, through frank discussion, what people expect from their employment. Unrealistic expectations can be countered before they become a trigger for dysfunctional conflict.[44]

Managers who understand these conflict triggers will be in a much better position to manage conflict in a systematic and rational fashion. Those who passively wait for things to explode before reacting will find conflict managing them.

Resolving Conflict

Identify and describe five conflict resolution techniques.

Even the best managers sometimes find themselves in the middle of dysfunctional conflict, whether it is due to inattention or to circumstances beyond their control. In such situations, they may choose to do nothing, called an *avoidance* strategy by some, or try one or more of the following conflict resolution techniques.

Problem Solving. When conflicting parties take the time to identify and correct the source of their conflict, they are engaging in problem solving. This approach is based on the assumption that causes must be rooted out and attacked if anything is really to change. Problem solving (refer to our discussion of creative problem solving in Chapter 7) encourages managers to focus their attention on causes, factual information, and promising alternatives rather than on personalities or scapegoats. The major shortcoming of the problem-solving approach is that it takes time, but the investment of extra time can pay off handsomely when the problem is corrected instead of ignored and allowed to worsen.

Superordinate Goals. "Superordinate goals are highly valued, unattainable by any one group [or individual] alone, and commonly sought."[45] When a manager relies on superordinate goals to resolve dysfunctional conflict, he or she brings the conflicting parties together and, in effect, says, "Look, we're all in this together. Let's forget our differences so we can get the job done." For example, a company president might remind the production and marketing department heads who have been arguing about product design that the competition is breathing down their necks. Although this technique often works in the short run, the underlying problem tends to crop up later to cause friction once again.

Compromise. This technique generally appeals to those living in a democracy. Proponents claim that everybody wins because it is based on negotiation, or give and take.[46] But everyone also loses something in a compromise. Something must be given up if anything is to be gained. Like problem solving, compromise takes time that management may not be able to afford. But, unlike problem solving, the problem is worked around rather than solved.

Forcing. Sometimes, especially when time is important, management must simply step into a conflict and order the conflicting parties to handle the situation in a certain manner. Reliance on formal authority and power of superior position is at the heart of forcing. As one might suspect, forcing does not resolve the personal conflict and, in fact, may serve to compound it by hurting feelings and/ or fostering resentment and mistrust.

Smoothing.   A manager who relies on smoothing says to the conflicting parties something like "Settle down. Don't rock the boat. Things will work out by themselves." This approach may tone down conflict in the short run, but it does not solve the underlying problem. As with each of the other conflict resolution techniques, smoothing has its place. It can be useful when management is attempting to hold things together until a critical project is completed or when there is no time for problem solving or compromise and forcing is deemed inappropriate.

Problem solving is the only approach that removes the actual sources of conflict. It is the only resolution technique that helps improve things in the long run. All the other approaches amount to short-run, stopgap measures. And managers who fall back on an avoidance strategy are simply running away from the problem. Nonetheless, as mentioned, problem solving can take up valuable time, time that management may not be willing or able to spend at that particular moment. When this is the case, management may choose to fall back on superordinate goals, compromise, forcing, or smoothing, whichever seems most suitable.[47]

Summary

Managers need to do a much better job of managing the process of change. Nadler and Tushman's model identifies four types of organizational change by cross-referencing anticipatory and reactive change with incremental and strategic change. Four resulting types of change are tuning, adaptation, reorientation, and re-creation.

People generally respond to change in a common cyclical pattern. According to the seven-step model of individual reaction to change, a person's mood, morale, and feelings of self-worth initially rise, then fall sharply, and eventually rise again as a change is encountered, resisted, and then embraced. Managers need to facilitate smooth transitions from one stage to another.

Inevitable resistance to change must be overcome if the organization is to succeed. Employees resist change for many different reasons, including but not limited to, inertia, lack of trust, and fear of failure. Modern managers facing resistance to change can select from several strategies, including education and communication, participation and involvement, facilitation and support, negotiation and agreement, manipulation and co-optation, and explicit and implicit coercion.

Organization development (OD) is a systematic approach to planned organizational change. The principal objectives of OD are increased trust, better problem solving, more effective communication, improved cooperation, and greater willingness to change. The typical OD program is a three-phase process, with unfreezing, change, and refreezing phases.

After deciding whether or not the services of an outside consultant are required and pinpointing likely trouble spots, management's attention turns to unfreezing the situation, making a diagnosis, and interpreting the diagnostic data.

A great deal of valuable diagnostic information can be obtained by balancing the strengths and weaknesses of various techniques. Among these techniques are record reviews, interviews, survey questionnaires, and direct observation. Careful interpretation of diagnostic data helps change agents select an appropriate intervention.

OD interventions can be designed to bring about systematic change at the individual, group, or organizational level. Life and career planning and skill development enhance individual potential. Role analysis and team building are popular OD techniques for improving the problem-solving ability of work groups. Survey feedback and Grid® OD have proved useful for improving overall organizational functioning. Because these interventions complement one another, they can be used in various combinations in accordance with the demands of the situation.

The third and final phase of OD, follow-up, is the evaluation of program effectiveness and maintenance of newly introduced changes. Everything considered, the purpose of OD is to get people to behave in more productive and supportive ways, with benefits accruing to both the individual and the organization.

Conflict is inevitable in organized settings. Recognizing that conflict can be either functional or dysfunctional, managers can enhance effort, performance, and creativity by permitting conflict triggers to continue until dysfunctional conflict appears. Dysfunctional conflict can be resolved through problem solving, superordinate goals, compromise, forcing, or smoothing.

Terms to Understand

Anticipatory changes
Reactive changes
Incremental changes
Strategic changes
Organization development (OD)
Unfreezing

Refreezing
Intervention
Role analysis
Team building
Conflict
Conflict trigger

Questions for Discussion

1. Relative to the Nadler-Tushman model of organizational change, why is it a good idea for managers to deal primarily with tuning and reorientation?
2. What has been your own experience with the seven stages in the personal change transition model?
3. What kinds of resistance to change have you observed recently? How could they have been overcome?
4. Drawing on your own experience, can you describe the circumstances of an organization that needs OD?
5. In your view, which of the seven objectives of OD is the most important? Why?
6. Why does an OD intervention without proper "unfreezing" have only limited chances of success?

7. Why are role analysis and team building useful OD interventions?

8. Which elements of effective feedback do you believe are the most important? Why?

9. What kinds of functional conflict have you experienced lately?

10. Why is it naive to think that on-the-job dysfunctional conflict can be completely avoided?

Back to the Opening Case

Now that you have read Chapter 15, you should be able to answer the following questions about the PepsiCo case:

1. According to the Nadler-Tushman model, what sorts of change have taken place at PepsiCo in recent years?

2. Why is resistance to change likely to be less at PepsiCo than elsewhere?

3. Can you find any evidence of functional conflict in this case? Explain.

4. Why might "unfreezing" be easier at PepsiCo than at the typical company?

CLOSING CASE
Can Larry Fit In?*

You are the manager of an auditing team for a major accounting firm. You are sitting in your office reading some complicated new reporting procedures that have just arrived from the home office. Your concentration is suddenly interrupted by a loud knock on your door. Without waiting for an invitation to enter, Larry, one of your auditors, bursts into your office. He is obviously very upset and it is not difficult for you to surmise why he is in such a nasty mood. You have just posted the audit assignments for the next month and you scheduled Larry for a job you knew he wouldn't like. Larry is one of your senior auditors and the company norm is that they get the better assignments. This particular job will require him to spend two weeks away from home, in a remote town,

working with a company whose records are notorious for being a mess.

Unfortunately, you have had to assign several of these less desirable audits to Larry recently because you are short of personnel. But that's not the only reason. You have received several complaints from the junior staff members recently about Larry's treating them in an obnoxious manner. They feel he is always looking for an opportunity to boss them around, as if he were their supervisor instead of a member of the audit team. As a result, your whole operation works smoothly when you can send Larry out of town on a solo project for several days. It keeps him from coming into your office telling you how to do your job, and the morale of the . . . staff is significantly higher.

Larry slams the door and proceeds to express his anger over this assignment. He says you are deliberately trying to undermine his status in the group by giving him all the dirty assignments. He accuses you of being insensitive to his feelings and says that if things don't change, he is going to register a formal complaint with your boss.

*From *Developing Management Skills* by David A. Whetten and Kim S. Cameron. Copyright © 1984 by Scott, Foresman and Company. Reprinted with permission.

For Discussion

1. What conflict triggers can you identify in this case? How do you know they are present?

2. How have you (Larry's manager) handled the conflict surrounding Larry so far? What are the positive and negative aspects of this approach?

3. How can you (Larry's manager) turn this present confrontation into functional conflict?

References

Opening Quotation.   Laurence J. Peter, *Peter's Quotations* (New York: Bantam, 1977), p. 75.

Opening Case.   John Marcom, Jr., "Cola Attack," *Forbes* (November 26, 1990): 48–49; Patricia Sellers, "Pepsi Keeps on Going after No. 1," *Fortune* (March 11, 1991): 62–70; Alison L. Sprout, "America's Most Admired Corporations," *Fortune* (February 11, 1991): 52–60.

Closing Case.   From *Developing Management Skills* by David A. Whetton and Kim S. Cameron. Copyright © 1984 by Scott, Foresman and Company. Reprinted by permission of HarperCollins Publishers.

1. Quoted in Patricia Sellers, "Pepsi Keeps on Going After No. 1," *Fortune* (March 11, 1991): 63.

2. Quoted in Patricia Sellers, "Pepsi Keeps on Going After No. 1," *Fortune* (March 11, 1991): 68.

3. "Corporate Culture," *Business Week* (October 27, 1980): 149–150.

4. John J. Keller, "Bob Allen Is Turning AT&T into a Live Wire," *Business Week* (November 6, 1989): 144.

5. Data from Jeremy Main, "A Golden Age for Entrepreneurs," *Fortune* (February 12, 1990): 120–125.

6. Adapted from discussion in David A. Nadler and Michael L. Tushman, "Organizational Frame Bending: Principles for Managing Reorientation," *Academy of Management Executive,* 3 (August 1989): 194–204.

7. See Brian Dumaine, "Creating a New Company Culture," *Fortune* (January 15, 1990): 127–131.

8. Keith Hammonds, "A Moment Kodak Wants to Capture," *Business Week* (August 27, 1990): 53.

9. See John D. Adams and Sabina A. Spencer, "People in Transition," *Training & Development Journal,* 42 (October 1988): 61–63; Lynn A. Isabella, "Evolving Interpretations as a Change Unfolds: How Managers Construe Key Organizational Events," *Academy of Management Journal,* 33 (March 1990): 7–41; and Connie J. G. Gersick, "Revolutionary Change Theories: A Multilevel Exploration of the Punctuated Equilibrium Paradigm," *Academy of Management Review,* 16 (January 1991): 10–36.

10. Tom Peters, *Thriving on Chaos* (New York: Knopf, 1987), p. 466.

11. For a general typology of "change resisters," see George S. Odiorne, "The Change Resisters," *Personnel Administrator,* 26 (January 1981): 57–62. Also see Jeffrey Goldstein, "A Far-from-Equilibrium Systems Approach to Resistance to Change," *Organizational Dynamics,* 17 (Autumn 1988): 16–26.

12. J. Alan Ofner, "Managing Change," *Personnel Administrator,* 29 (September 1984): 20.

13. Peter Coy, "The Perils of Picking the Wrong Standard," *Business Week* (October 8, 1990): 145.

14. Jeremy Main, "Waking Up AT&T: There's Life after Culture Shock," *Fortune* (December 24, 1984): 67.

15. "Why They're Jumping Ship at Intel," *Business Week* (February 14, 1983): 108.

16. This list is based in part on John P. Kotter and Leonard A. Schlesinger, "Choosing Strategies for Change," *Harvard Business Review,* 57 (March-April 1979): 106–114; and Joseph Stanislao and Bettie C. Stanislao, "Dealing with Resistance to Change," *Business Horizons,* 26 (July-August 1983): 74–78.

17. See H. B. Karp, "A Positive Approach to Resistance," in J. William Pfeiffer, ed. *The 1988 Annual: Developing Human Resources* (San Diego: University Associates, 1988), pp. 143–146.

18. Philip G. Hanson and Bernard Lubin, "Answers to Questions Frequently Asked about Organization Development," in *The Emerging Practice of Organization Development,* eds. Walter Sikes, Allan Drexler, and Jack Gant (Alexandria, Va.: NTL Institute, 1989), p. 16. (Emphasis added.) For good background information of current OD practices, see Richard W. Woodman, "Organizational Change and Development: New Arenas for Inquiry and Action," *Journal of Management,* 15 (June 1989): 205–228; and Michael Beer and Elise Walton, "Developing the Competitive Organization: Interventions and Strategies," *American Psychologist,* 45 (February 1990): 154–161.

19. W. Warner Burke, *Organization Development: A Normative View* (Reading, Mass.: Addison-Wesley, 1987), p. 9.

20. Instructive historical perspectives of OD can be found in Burke, *Organization Development,* chap. 3; and Thomas H. Patten, Jr., "Historical Perspectives on Organization Development," *In The Emerging Practice of Organization Development,* pp. 3–14.

21. This list is based on Wendell French, "Organization Development Objectives, Assumptions, and Strategies," *California Management Review,* 12 (Winter 1969): 23–34; and Charles Kiefer and Peter Stroh, "A New Paradigm for Organization Development," *Training and Development Journal,* 37 (April 1983): 26–35.

22. For an alternative model, see Ralph H. Kilmann, "A Completely Integrated Program for Creating and Maintaining Organizational Success," *Organizational Dynamics,* 18 (Summer 1989): 5–19.

23. See Elizabeth S. Gorovitz, "Looking beyond the OD Mystique," *Training and Development Journal,* 37 (April 1983): 12–14; and Joseph E. Garcia and Carla Haggith, "OD Interventions That Work," *Personnel Administrator,* 34 (June 1989): 90–94.

24. One useful collection of ninety-two instruments, many with diagnostic potential, is J. William Pfeiffer, Richard Heslin, and John E. Jones, *Instrumentation in Human Relations Training,* 2nd ed. (1976). This and other relevant OD materials are published by University Associates, Inc.; 8517 Production Ave., San Diego, CA 92121.

25. David Nadler, *Feedback and Organization Development: Using Data-Based Methods* (Reading, Mass.: Addison-Wesley, 1977), p. 143.

26. Good advice on handling the inevitable organizational politics surrounding OD can be found in Newton Margulies and Anthony P. Raia, "The Politics of Organization Development," *Training and Development Journal,* 38 (August 1984): 20–23.

27. For a comprehensive treatment of team building, see William G. Dyer, *Team Building: Issues and Alternatives,* 2nd ed. (Reading, Mass.: Addison-Wesley, 1987).

28. Data from Eric Stephan, Gordon E. Mills, R. Wayne Pace, and Lenny Ralphs, "HRD in the Fortune 500: A Survey," *Training and Development Journal,* 42 (January 1988): 26–32.

29. For example, see Elizabeth Ehrlich, "Anger, Shouting, and Sometimes Tears," *Business Week* (August 6, 1990): 55.

30. Richard Beckhard, "Optimizing Team-Building Efforts," *Journal of Contemporary Business,* 1 (Summer 1972): 24. The entire Summer 1972 issue is devoted to an informative overview of organization development.

31. See Gregory E. Huszczo, "Training for Team Building," *Training & Development Journal,* 44 (February 1990): 37–43.

32. This list is adapted from Nadler, *Feedback and Organization Development: Using Data-Based Methods,* pp. 147–148.

33. For more extensive discussion, see Robert R. Blake and Jane Srygley Mouton, "An Overview of the Grid®," *Training and Development Journal,* 29 (May 1975): 29–37.

34. See C. A. Carnall, "Toward a Theory for the Evaluation of Organizational Change," *Human Relations,* 39 (August 1986): 745–766; and Yoram Zeira and Joyce Avedisian, "Organizational Planned Change: Assessing the Chances for Success," *Organizational Dynamics,* 17 (Spring 1989): 31–45.

35. For an excellent review of OD evaluation problems, see David E. Terpstra, "The Organization Development Evaluation Process: Some Problems and Proposals," *Human Resource Management,* 20 (Spring 1981): 24–29. Also see James L. Eubanks, Julie B. Marshall, and Michael P.

O'Driscoll, "A Competency Model For OD Practitioners," *Training & Development Journal,* 44 (November 1990): 85–90; and Michael Beer, Russell A. Eisenstat, and Bert Spector, "Why Change Programs Don't Produce Change," *Harvard Business Review,* 68 (November-December 1990): 158–166.

36. Data from George A. Neuman, Jack E. Edwards, and Nambury S. Raju, "Organizational Development Interventions: A Meta-Analysis of Their Effects on Satisfaction and Other Attitudes," *Personnel Psychology,* 42 (Autumn 1989): 461–489.

37. For a concise, informative discussion of OD evaluation, see Bernard M. Bass, "Issues Involved in Relations between Methodological Rigor and Reported Outcomes in Evaluations of Organizational Development," *Journal of Applied Psychology,* 68 (February 1983): 197–199.

38. See Rosabeth Moss Kanter, "Championing Change: An Interview with Bell Atlantic's CEO Raymond Smith," *Harvard Business Review,* 69 (January-February 1991): 118–130.

39. See Gordon Cliff, "Managing Organizational Conflict," *Management Review,* 76 (May 1987): 51–53.

40. Abraham Zaleznik, "Real Work," *Harvard Business Review,* 67 (January-February 1989): 59–60.

41. Stephen P. Robbins, *Managing Organizational Conflict: A Nontraditional Approach* (Englewood Cliffs, N.J.: Prentice-Hall, 1974), p. 23. Also see Richard E. Walton, *Managing Conflict,* 2nd ed. (Reading, Mass.: Addison-Wesley, 1987).

42. Dean Tjosvold, *The Conflict-Positive Organization: Stimulate Diversity and Create Unity* (Reading, Mass.: Addison-Wesley, 1991), p. 2.

43. Walter Kiechel III, "How to Escape the Echo Chamber," *Fortune* (June 18, 1990): 130. For other good material on functional conflict, see Don Michael McDonald, "How To Tell Your Boss He's Wrong," *Management Solutions,* 33 (December 1988): 3–9; and Richard Tanner Pascale, "The Renewal Factor: Constructive Contention," *Planning Review,* 18 (July-August 1990): 4–13, 47–48.

44. For an alternative list of conditions that tend to precipitate conflict, see Alan C. Filley, *Interpersonal Conflict Resolution* (Glenview, Ill.: Scott, Foresman, 1975): pp. 9–12.

45. Robbins, *Managing Organizational Conflict,* p. 62.

46. See Roger Fisher and William Ury, *Getting to Yes: Negotiating Agreement without Giving in* (Boston: Houghton Mifflin, 1981).

47. See M. Afzalur Rahim, "A Measure of Styles of Handling Conflict," *Academy of Management Journal,* 26 (June 1983): 368–376; and Roger J. Volkema and Thomas J. Bergmann, "Interpersonal Conflict at Work: An Analysis of Behavioral Responses," *Human Relations,* 42 (September 1989): 757–770.

VIDEO SKILL BUILDER

•••

The Leadership Edge

Learning Objective

To help you recognize, understand, and use effective leadership techniques.

Link to Textual Material

Communicating, motivating, generating effective team-work, leading, and managing change.

The ability to lead is what separates a top-performing manager from one who achieves only average results. It is easy to see why. Effective leaders can make work a rewarding and often exciting experience. In this positive atmosphere, people deliver better results. Leaders use a number of different strategies to create this positive atmosphere. In the film, *The Leadership Edge*, these strategies are divided into three categories:

1. Communicating a clear sense of purpose.
2. Involving others.
3. Demonstrating commitment.

Discussion Questions

1. Which of the three managers profiled in this video would you like to work for? Why?
2. Does one of the three leadership skills have overriding importance? Explain.
3. Based on what you have just learned which particular skills/abilities do you need to work on to become a more effective leader? Explain.

PART V

Controlling

Part V examines the vital role that the control function plays in good management. Control involves monitoring organizational performance so that plans are carried out as intended and corrective action is taken when necessary. Chapter 16 introduces basic control concepts, examines the control of financial performance, and discusses crisis management. In Chapter 17, information is discussed as a vital resource and the lifeblood of organizations. Special attention is devoted to personal computers and computer networks. Operations management, which involves the systematic management of production and service processes, is examined in Chapter 18. Successful Japanese operations-management philosophies, including just-in-time production and total quality control are explored. Service quality is given special attention because we live in a service economy.

16

The Control Function

Judge a tree from its fruit, not from the leaves.

EURIPIDES

CHAPTER OBJECTIVES

When you finish studying this chapter, you should be able to

- Distinguish among feedforward, concurrent, and feedback control.
- Identify three components common to all organizational control systems.
- Discuss organizational control from a strategic perspective.
- Describe three ways in which a control system can become misguided.
- Explain what budget variances are and when management should take steps to correct them.
- Discuss how financial ratios and cash management can enhance financial control.
- Identify the four key elements of a crisis management program.
- Discuss the factors that lead to employee dishonesty and be familiar with a strategy for controlling it.

Marriott-style Control

In 1990, the U.S. hospitality industry was enduring an unwelcome glut of rooms. With too many hotels and not enough customers, hotel occupancy rates averaged about 64 percent, below the level most hotels need to break even. Even wealthy international buyers—Japanese, Middle Eastern, and European—who had been paying top dollar for fancy American hotels in the 1980s were starting to shy away, putting their money into European hotels instead. But while most of the industry was cutting back amid this squeeze, Marriott Corporation was planning to nearly double its number of hotels by the mid-1990s. Although continued hard times in the industry forced Marriott to scale back that goal, aggressive growth targets are still in place.

Crazy? Maybe. But many people had pronounced J. W. (Bill) Marriott Jr. crazy once before, in 1980. That was the year he announced that he planned a better than 20 percent annual return on equity for the coming decade, even though his company had averaged only 11 percent in the previous ten years. The company faltered somewhat in 1989, but Bill Marriott's prediction held up through 1988; returns averaged well over 20 percent and never fell below 18 percent. During that same period, the total value of Marriott's stock jumped from $700 million to $3.5 billion, and the company kept its occupancy rates a comfortable ten points above the industry average.

What's Marriott's secret? In part, its control. Since the company's founding, the Marriott family has been very much in control of its company, keeping an eye on the smallest of details. In 1927, J. W. Marriott and his wife Alice moved east from their home in Marriott, Utah, to open an A & W Root Beer franchise in Washington, D.C. That fall, the Marriotts made a key business decision: to offset slow root beer sales during the winter, they changed the name of their business to The Hot Shoppe and began serving chili con carne and hot tamales, using recipes from a Mexican embassy cook.

Today, under names like Courtyard, Fairfield Inn, and Residence Inn, the second J. W. Marriott runs a company with 121,000 rooms, and his 1,100 restaurants include Roy Rogers, Bob's Big Boy, and Allie's. In fact, though most people identify the Marriott name with hotels, 70 percent of the company's revenues are in food sales, including those made at hotels and catered to airlines and to big companies. Marriott and many of its 230,000 employees feed more people each day than any other organization in the world.

Yet Bill Marriott sometimes acts as though he were running just the original nine-stool soda fountain. He drops in on Marriott hotels on short notice, logging some 200,000 miles annually. It is a grueling pace for which Bill Marriott has paid the price of two mild heart attacks. Now, some of his mileage is logged during daily workouts on an exercise treadmill. Even though his hotel visits are short, he observes carefully and lets his managers know what looks good and what could be changed. He keeps notes so he can comment on the improved decor or cleanliness the next time he comes around. He also reads hundreds of comment cards from customers and takes them much more seriously than do most CEOs. And, of course, he sits in on planning meetings, listens carefully to what planners say, and makes sure future needs are met. When he heard in one such meeting that the new Marriott at Walt Disney World didn't have a large enough ballroom for large group meetings, he quickly set about buying adjacent land for expansion.

Bill Marriott's version of management by wandering around provides symbolic leadership for the company's control functions, but Marriott also keeps in touch with its customers and its costs in other ways. Marriott hotels can be almost obnoxious in their insistence that guests fill out rating sheets to compile the Guest Service Index (GSI). Guests receive the sheets at check-in, in the restaurants, and in their rooms. Some hotel managers even build contests around the sheets—put your rating sheet with a business card in this briefcase and get a chance to win the case. The company encourages such tactics because it relies on the GSI as a crucial source of information about customers' responses and desires. The more rating sheets that are filled out on a property, the more accurate its GSI will be.

The GSI information isn't just for management's impressive graphs. The latest figures are posted in every department, where employees can see them. But when the GSI indicates a change is needed, the company doesn't use the information to punish the employees who should be responsible. It makes the problem itself—for instance, a long registration wait—the enemy, and it focuses on ways to change it.

Not content with the wealth of information gathered through rating forms, Marriott also employs an outside research organization that surveys, unannounced, a certain percentage of guests who have recently visited a particular hotel. These ratings do go right to the top, and they can affect whether a particular manager is put in line for a promotion or is visited by a regional group of company experts who help straighten out problems. Timely use of such information allows Marriott to not just deal with current problems but to forecast trends and head off incipient crises.

J. W. Marriott Sr. liked to know all of his employees' names, a feat beyond even the considerable skills of his son. But Bill Jr. does try to uphold his father's belief that a company can make money while still treating both customers and employees well. Marriott pays well, invests heavily in employee training, and likes to promote managers from within the company. These practices keep employee turnover low and allow Marriott to be choosy about who it hires. A few years ago it had 40,000 applicants for 1,200 openings at a new Marriott in New York. The company also consistently ranks at the top of its industry in surveys of customers. Business people say it's simply the best place to stay or to hold a meeting. So, although there may not be room for more second-rate hotels in the United States, Marriott is betting that there's always room for the best.

According to the infamous Murphy's Law, "If anything can go wrong, it will!" Murphy's Law may be overly pessimistic, but it drives home the point that unexpected events can and do cause plans and operations to go astray. Control, with its preventive and corrective actions, is needed in today's complex world to keep plans on course. The Exxon *Valdez* disaster dramatically underscores the need for skillful organizational control. Prior to its 11-million-gallon oil spill in Alaska in 1989, Exxon was a widely respected and very profitable company. Two years later, when a final settlement was being contested in court, Exxon's

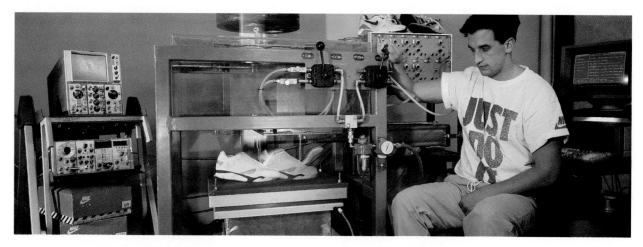

Nike has long been an innovator in the highly competitive sports shoe business. All three types of control are needed to generate customer satisfaction and profits. Countless hours of research in this Beaverton, Oregon, performance laboratory give Nike an exacting degree of feedforward control over the quality of its footwear. Concurrent control is exercised during the actual production process, making sure each pair of shoes meets product specifications. Finally, Nike carries out feedback control by making product and process changes on the basis of customer surveys.

reputation was still on the rocks. Approximately $3.2 billion in clean-up costs, legal settlements, and fines (about $291 for each gallon spilled) also wiped out months of profits.[1] All that, because one of Exxon's operations momentarily lost control. As we will see in the next section, Exxon could have saved a lot of money with some "feedforward control."

The purpose of this chapter is to expand your knowledge of the control function by identifying types of control, reviewing common control problems, discussing new ideas on managing costs, and focusing on two modern control problems, crisis management and employee theft.

Dimensions of Control

control taking preventive or corrective actions to keep things on track

The word *control* suggests the operations of checking, testing, regulation, verification, or adjustment. As a management function, **control** is the process of taking the necessary preventive or corrective actions to ensure that the organization's mission and objectives are accomplished as effectively and efficiently as possible. Objectives are yardsticks against which actual performance can be measured. If actual performance is consistent with the appropriate objective, things will proceed as planned. If not, changes must be made. Successful managers detect deviations from desirable standards and make appropriate adjustments. Those adjustments can range from ordering more raw materials to overhauling a production line; from discarding an unnecessary procedure to hiring additional personnel; from containing an unexpected crisis to firing a defrauder. Although the possible adjustments exercised as part of the control function are countless, the purpose of the control function is always the same: *get the job done despite environmental, organizational, and behavioral obstacles and uncertainties.*

Types of Control

● ● ● ● ● ● ● ● ● ● ● ● ● ●

Distinguish among feedforward, concurrent, and feedback control.

Every open system processes inputs from the surrounding environment to produce a unique set of outputs. Natural open systems, such as the human body, are kept in life-sustaining balance through automatic feedback mechanisms. In contrast, artificial open systems, such as organizations, do not have automatic controls. Instead, they require constant monitoring and adjustment to control for deviations from standards. Figure 16.1 illustrates the control function. Notice the three different types of control: feedforward, concurrent, and feedback.

feedforward control active anticipation and prevention of problems, rather than passive reaction

Feedforward Control. According to two early proponents of feedforward control, "the only way [managers] can exercise control effectively is to see the problems coming in time to do something about them."[2] **Feedforward control** is the active anticipation of problems and their timely prevention, rather than after-the-fact reaction. It is important to note that planning and feedforward control are two related but different processes. Planning answers the question "Where are we going and how will we get there?" Feedforward control addresses the issue of "What can we do ahead of time to help our plan succeed?" *Preventive maintenance* qualifies as feedforward control. New York City's bridge system illustrates the importance of prevention. According to a recent study, "the city could save $250 million a year in emergency repair and reconstruction costs by spending $36 million a year to maintain its bridges."[3] Indeed, an ounce of prevention is better than a pound of cure.

On-the-job opportunities for feedforward control are plentiful. For example, if the purchasing manager in a home appliance-manufacturing company alerts the production and marketing managers to a delay in the receipt of an important subcomponent, corrective steps can be taken to avoid costly delays. The production manager can reschedule the workload, and the marketing manager can negotiate a new delivery date for the final product. Imagine the downstream havoc if the purchasing manager remained silent.

Of the three types of control, American managers tend to do the poorest job with feedforward control. Longer-term thinking and better cross-functional communication would remedy this situation.

concurrent control monitoring and adjusting on-going activities and processes

Concurrent Control. This second type of control might well be called real-time control because it deals with the present rather than the future or past. **Concurrent control** involves monitoring and adjusting on-going activities and processes to ensure compliance with standards. When you are using a bread toaster, for instance, you can set the automatic control mechanism and run the risk of ending up with a piece of charcoal. Because toaster control mechanisms are rather primitive, they are not a very reliable form of feedforward control. To compensate, you can exercise concurrent control by keeping an eye on the toasting process and ejecting your toast by hand when it reaches the right shade. So, too, construction supervisors engage in concurrent control when they help carpenters and plumbers with difficult tasks at the building site.

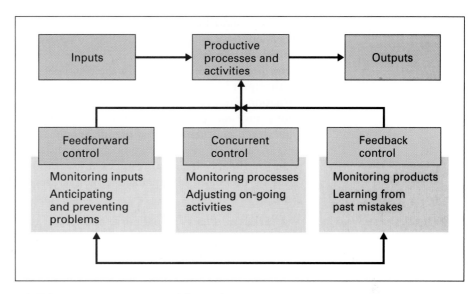

FIGURE 16.1 • Three Types of Control

feedback control checking a completed activity and learning from mistakes

Feedback Control. **Feedback control** is gathering information about a completed activity, evaluating that information, and taking steps to improve similar activities in the future. Feedback control permits managers to use information on past performance to bring future performance into line with planned objectives and acceptable standards. For example, by monitoring the complaints from discharged patients about billing errors, a hospital's comptroller learns that the performance of its billing clerks requires attention. Critics of feedback control complain that it is like closing the gate after the horse is gone. Because corrective action is taken after the fact, costs tend to pile up quickly, and problems and deviations persist.

On the positive side, feedback control tests the quality and validity of objectives and standards. Objectives that prove impossible to attain should be made more reasonable. Those that prove too easy need to be toughened. A bank's loan officer, for example, may discover that too much potentially profitable business is being turned away because the criteria for granting credit are too strict. By exercising feedback control—loosening the credit standards that loan applicants must meet—the bank's lending operation can be made more profitable. Of course, if this adjustment leads to a default rate that eats up the additional profits, the credit criteria may need yet another round of feedback control.

In summary, a successful manager must exercise all three types of control in today's complex organizations. Feedforward control helps managers avoid mistakes in the first place; concurrent control enables them to catch mistakes as they are being made; feedback control keeps them from repeating past mistakes. A workable balance among the three types of control is desirable.

Components of Organizational Control Systems

The owner-manager of a small business such as a dry cleaning establishment can keep things under control by personally overseeing operations and making necessary adjustments. An electrician can be called in to fix a broken pressing machine, poor workmanship can be improved through coaching, a customer's complaint can be handled, or a shortage of change in the cash register can be remedied. A small organization directed by a single, highly motivated individual with expert knowledge of all aspects of the operation represents the ideal control situation. Unfortunately, the size and complexity of most productive organizations have made firsthand control by a single person obsolete. Consequently, multilevel, multidimensional organizational control systems have evolved.[4]

A study of nine large companies in different industries sheds some needed light on the mechanics of complex organizational control systems.[5] After interviewing dozens of key managers, the researchers identified six distinct control subsystems:

1. *Strategic Plans.* Qualitative analyses of the company's position within the industry.
2. *Long-range Plans.* Typically, five-year financial projections.
3. *Annual Operating Budgets.* Annual estimates of profit, expenses, and financial indicators.
4. *Statistical Reports.* Quarterly, monthly, or weekly nonfinancial statistical summaries of key indicators such as orders received and personnel surpluses or shortages.
5. *Performance Appraisals.* Evaluation of employees through the use of management by objectives (MBO) or rating scales.
6. *Policies and Procedures.* Organizational and departmental standard operating procedures referred to on an as-needed basis.

According to the researchers, the first two control subsystems were the exclusive province of top management. The remaining four were used throughout the managerial ranks. A seventh organizational control subsystem is *cultural control*. As discussed in Chapter 8, stories and company legends have a profound impact on how things are done in specific organizations. Employees who deviate from cultural norms are promptly straightened out with glances, remarks, or ridicule.

Complex organizational control systems such as these help keep things on the right track because they embrace three basic components, common to all organizational control systems: objectives, standards, and an evaluation-reward system.[6]

●●●●●●●●●●●●●●●●●

Identify three components common to all organizational control systems.

Objectives. In Chapter 5, we defined an objective as a target signifying what should be accomplished and when. Objectives are an indispensable part of any control system because they provide measurable reference points for corrective action. To help Chrysler get back on the road to profitability, Chairman Lee Iacocca set the objective of committing his company in 1990 to cutting $3 billion in costs by July 1991. That particular objective served as a focal point and measuring stick for wide-ranging cost reductions, including layoffs and smaller buyer rebates.[7]

Standards. Whereas objectives serve as measurable targets, standards serve as guideposts on the way to reaching those targets. Standards provide feedforward control by warning people when they are off the track. Golfers use par as a

Benchmarking for World-Class Results

Originally, companies used benchmarking primarily as a control technique to compare themselves against competitors in their own industry. A company might figure out what a successful competitor was doing and try to copy it. Ford and Xerox made the technique popular by taking apart competitors' products and using the knowledge they'd gained to redesign their own. J. C. Penney still employs essentially the same concept. When Penney's managers question customers about how they were treated at J. C. Penney, the managers ask the same questions of people who shopped at competitors like Sears and Nordstrom. This comparative information helps Penney know what it's doing well relative to the competition and in which areas it needs to make changes.

Today, many companies aren't satisfied with just doing as well as the other retailers in the mall. They want to be the best possible, and they recognize that their entire industry may share some weaknesses in processes and products. So, to improve a particular function, they may search the country or the world to find a company that handles that function masterfully, even if that company is in a totally different industry.

For example, Xerox's parts distribution people now take lessons from L. L. Bean, which doesn't sell copiers but runs its warehouse and distribution operations better than anyone else. Motorola's finance department learned how to handle electronic data-transfer from First National Bank of Chicago's check-clearing unit. GTE compares its telephones to those of a well-respected Swedish manufacturer and its telephone service to Southern Bell's. But when GTE wanted to upgrade its billing system, it visited American Express Co., which has made billing an art. A just-in-time manufacturer can teach a financial institution a surprising amount about same-day loan approval techniques. While companies in the same industry may be wary of sharing their trade secrets with competitors, firms in unrelated businesses are often proud to show off what they do well.

Despite the advantages of this approach, experts caution companies against becoming satisfied with matching another firm's abilities. They say the true name of the game in quality control now is continuous improvement. But if you're not sure how to improve a process, taking advice from a best-in-the-world company sounds like a good start.

Sources: "Businesses Emulate the Very Best," *The Arizona Republic* (January 27, 1991): F4; Richard J. Schonberger, *Building a Chain of Customers* (New York: The Free Press, 1990), 23–25; Ron Zemke, *The Service Edge* (New York: NAL, 1989), 51–56.

standard for gauging the quality of their game. When the objective is to shoot par, a golfer who exceeds par on a hole is warned that he or she must improve on later holes to achieve the objective. Universities exercise a degree of feedforward control over student performance by establishing and following admission standards for grades and test scores. Businesses rely on many different kinds of standards, including those in purchasing, engineering, time, safety, accounting, and quality.

benchmarking imitating the standards of the best in the business or world

A proven technique for establishing challenging standards is **benchmarking,** identifying and imitating the business practices of market leaders. The central idea in benchmarking is to be competitive by striving to be as good as or better than the *best* in the business (see Managers in Action). The search for benchmarks is not restricted to a single industry. Many companies in many industries are presently emulating the world-class service standards of Scandinavian Airlines (SAS).[8]

An Evaluation-Reward System. Because employees do not get equal results, some sort of performance review is required to document individual contributions to organizational objectives. Extrinsic rewards need to be tied equitably to documented results and improvement. A carefully conceived and clearly communicated evaluation-reward scheme can shape favorable effort-reward expectancies, hence motivating better performance. (Recall our discussions of performance appraisal in Chapter 10 and rewards in Chapter 12.)

When integrated systematically, objectives, standards, and an equitable evaluation-reward system constitute an invaluable control mechanism.

Strategic Control

Managers who fail to complement their strategic planning with strategic control, as recommended in Chapter 6, will find themselves winning some battles but losing the war.[9] The performance pyramid in Figure 16.2 illustrates the necessarily tight linkage between planning and control. It is a strategic model because everything is oriented toward the strategic peak of the pyramid. Objectives based on the corporate vision (or mission) are translated downward during planning. As plans become reality, control measures of activities and results are translated up the pyramid. The flow of objectives and measures requires a good information system, as discussed in the next chapter.

● ● ● ● ● ● ● ● ● ● ● ● ● ● ● ● ● ● ●
Discuss organizational control from a strategic perspective.

FIGURE 16.2 ● The Performance Pyramid for Strategic Control

Source: C. J. McNair, Richard L. Lynch, and Kelvin F. Cross, "Do Financial and Nonfinancial Performance Measures Have to Agree?" *Management Accounting,* 72 (November 1990): 30. Reprinted by permission.

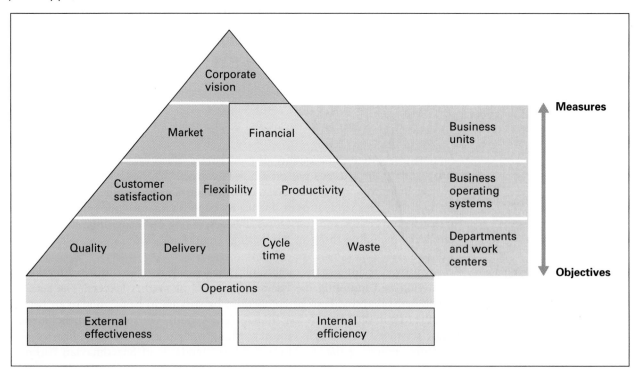

External effectiveness and internal efficiency criteria are distinguished in Figure 16.2 by color coding. Significantly, all of the external effectiveness areas are focused on the marketplace in general and on the *customer* in particular. According to the performance pyramid, control measures are needed for cycle time, waste, flexibility, productivity, and financial results. *Cycle time* is the time it takes for a product to be transformed from raw materials or parts into a finished good. Notice how *flexibility* relates to both effectiveness and efficiency. A garden tractor manufacturer, for example, needs to be externally flexible in adapting to changing customer demands and internally flexible in training employees to handle new technology.

Identifying Control Problems

Control problems have a way of quietly snowballing into overwhelming proportions. Progressive managers can take constructive steps to keep today's complex operations under control.[10] One approach is the **executive reality check,** whereby top-level managers periodically work in the trenches to increase their awareness of operations. It is a variation of Peters and Waterman's "management by wandering around," discussed in Chapter 2. Southwest Airlines goes about it this way:

> The officers of Southwest Airlines, [CEO Herb] Kelleher included, work at least once every quarter as baggage handlers, ticket agents, and flight attendants. "We're trying to create an understanding of the difficulties every person has on his job," explains Kelleher. "When you're actually dealing with customers, and you've done the job yourself, you're in a better position to appraise the effect of some new program or policy."[11]

This approach not only alerts top managers to control problems but it also fosters empathy for lower-level employees' problems and concerns. In addition to firsthand reality checks, an internal audit can identify weak spots and problems in the organizational control system.

Internal Audits

There are two general types of auditing, external and internal. External auditing, generally performed by certified public accountants (CPAs), is the verification of an organization's financial records and reports. In the United States, the protection of stockholders' interests is the primary rationale for objective external audits. Of course, the Internal Revenue Service (IRS) and the Securities and Exchange Commission (SEC) also benefit from external auditors' watchdog function. That is, external auditors help keep organizations honest by double-checking to see if reported financial results are derived through generally accepted accounting principles and are based on material fact, not fiction.

Internal auditing differs from external auditing in a number of ways. First, and most obviously, it is performed by an organization's staff rather than by outsiders. Second, internal auditing is intended to serve the interests of the organization as a whole. Also, as the following definition illustrates, internal auditing

Pacific Gas & Electric has become one of America's most profitable power companies. Its status as a regulated monopoly protects it from various competitive uncertainties. But PG&E still faces considerable control challenges as its 26,600 employees provide natural gas and electricity to 11.5 million people in a 94,000-square-mile region of northern and central California. Performance and equipment must be of uniformly high quality to achieve tough reliability and safety standards.

internal auditing independent appraisal of organizational operations and systems to assess effectiveness and efficiency

tends to be more encompassing than the external variety: "**Internal auditing** is the independent appraisal of the various operations and systems of control within an organization to determine whether acceptable policies and procedures are followed, established standards are met, resources are used efficiently and economically, planned missions are accomplished effectively, and the organization's objectives are being achieved."[12]

The product of internal auditing is called a *process audit* by some and a *management audit* by others.[13] To strengthen the objectivity of internal auditing, experts recommend that internal auditors report directly to the top person in the organization. In organization development terms, some "unfreezing" needs to be done to quiet the common complaint that internal auditing is a ploy used by top management for snooping and meddling. Timely and valid internal audits are a primary safeguard against organizational decline, as we saw in Chapter 8.

Symptoms of Inadequate Control

When a comprehensive internal audit is not available, a general check list of symptoms of inadequate control can be a useful diagnostic tool. Recognizing that every situation has some unusual problems, common symptoms include:

- An unexplained decline in revenues or profits.
- A degradation of service (customer complaints).
- Employee dissatisfaction (complaints, grievances, turnover).
- Cash shortages caused by bloated inventories or delinquent accounts receivable.
- Idle facilities or personnel.
- Disorganized operations (work flow bottlenecks, excessive paperwork).
- Excessive costs.
- Evidence of waste and inefficiency (scrap, rework).[14]

Problems in one or more of these areas may be a signal that things are getting out of control. (See Management Ethics.)

Trying to Get the Pentagon under Control

For a manager who believes in control and efficiency, no job is more challenging than overseeing the Pentagon's weapons acquisitions. That's what John A. Betti discovered when he took the post of Under Defense Secretary for acquisition in 1989. Betti had impressive credentials—as an executive vice president at Ford, he had helped make America's number two automaker competitive again—so he knew how difficult it is to put a bit in the mouth of runaway bureaucracy and rein in costs.

No one questions that the Pentagon needs reining in. Every few years, new procurement scandals and grotesque wastes of taxpayers' money come to light. In the mid-1980s, the public was outraged about stories of $400 hammers and $600 coffee pots. In 1988, the Air Force's $120 paper-cup dispensers captured the headlines, and in 1990, congressional investigators heard rumors of $3,000 pairs of pliers.

Many hoped such stories would end as a result of the U.S. Attorney General's investigations into charges of conspiracy, bribery, and trafficking in secret defense documents brought against major defense contractors. By 1990, the investigations had led to thirty-two guilty pleas and the payment of millions of dollars in fines by companies ranging from Teledyne to RCA to Raytheon.

But despite these well-publicized successes and Betti's managerial expertise, the man who left Ford a hero resigned from the Department of Defense in disgrace in 1990. He had failed to warn his superiors that the Navy's attack bomber, the A-12, was way behind schedule and way over budget. Like many other Department of Defense managers, he had hidden the bad news and stopped the upward flow of information. A month after Betti's resignation, Defense Secretary Richard B. Cheney killed the A-12 project, the biggest program cancellation in Pentagon history. McDonnell Douglas and General Dynamics, the project's two biggest contractors, lost an estimated $60 billion in business and laid off 8,000 workers. Ironically, Congress had created Betti's position in 1986 so that a civilian could oversee the Pentagon's procurement practices and not fall prey to pressures to keep projects going. But Betti was the third civilian manager in five years to quit the post. As long as the procurement system lacks built-in checks on waste and fraud, controlling its abuses may prove to be too much for anyone.

Sources: Dave Griffiths, "Business as Usual at the Pentagon," *Business Week* (April 16, 1990): 26; Russell Mitchell, "It Was Mr. Fixit vs. the Pentagon—and the Pentagon Won," *Business Week* (December 24, 1990): 33; Russell Mitchell, "Desperately Seeking an Attack Bomber," *Business Week* (January 21, 1991): 35; "Navy Cancels Contract for Attack Planes," *The Christian Science Monitor* (January 9, 1991): 3; Tim Smart, "Look What Ill Wind Is Blowing in," *Business Week* (April 16, 1990): 27.

Signs of Misguided Control Systems

● ● ● ● ● ● ● ● ● ● ● ● ● ● ● ● ●
Describe three ways in which a control system can become misguided.

measurementship manipulating data and control reports to make oneself look good

Control systems breed their own special problems among managers, three of which are goal displacement, measurementship, and budget games. *Goal displacement* occurs when the means become more important than the ends. For example, bureaucratic paperwork takes precedence over human compassion when a welfare office employee shows greater concern for gathering redundant information than for helping people get back on their feet.

Measurementship is political maneuvering motivated by a desire to "look good," even if it means manipulating reports and control data. This sort of conduct can put the entire organization at risk, as happened at Cordis Corporation, a pioneering manufacturer of cardiac pacemakers. In 1984, the U.S. Food and Drug Administration discovered that Cordis officials were guilty of altering reports describing possible technical problems with the pacemakers. When the cover-up was made public, some users had the pacemakers removed. Although those responsible for tampering with the documents were fired and Cordis sold its pacemaker business in 1987, the firm pleaded guilty in 1988 and paid a $123,000 fine.[15]

The third problem, budget games, takes many forms, one of which is the common practice whereby managers request a larger budget than necessary and still manage to spend all the funds. Devious schemes or budget games, such as those listed in Table 16.1, can subvert the control system.[16] A study of 1,339 planning executives and managers found that managers tended to rely on devious budget games when their boss had a punitive leadership style, and they reported being under stress.[17] Realistic objectives and supportive leadership, therefore, are proper tools for curbing such games. The wrong kind of control or too much control can turn out to be as bad as no control.

Our attention now turns to some conventional financial control techniques.

Financial Control

The ultimate survival of organizations in both the public and private sectors is dictated largely by how proficiently funds are acquired and managed. Dollars (or

TABLE 16.1 • Devious Budget Games That Can Erode Financial Control

	Budget game	*Ranking (most common to least common)*
Incremental	I get changes in my budget by seeking incremental changes over past budgets.	1
Circle the wagons	I try hard to keep what I had in last year's (period's) budget.	2
Sacrificial lamb	I place some items in my budgetary request which I know will not be approved so that those requests will be cut instead of items I really want approved.	3
Piggyback	I attach items that are likely to be cut from the budget if separately submitted to other projects that are certain to be approved.	4
Foot in the door	I ask for a small item in the budget knowing that I can ask for a lot more next time once it's in the budget.	5
Relying on friendship	I rely on friendship with my boss to get what I want in my budget.	6
Crisis	I get what I want in my budget by letting my boss think my operation has a crisis and must have the budgetary request.	7

Source: Excerpted and adapted from a more extensive list in Frank Collins, Paul Munter, and Don W. Finn, "The Budgeting Games People Play," *The Accounting Review,* 62 (January 1987): 35. Reprinted by permission.

Shelton J. Lee, better known as Spike, is a one-man entertainment empire. Although still in his early thirties, Spike Lee has proven himself an accomplished film director, actor, screen writer (with an Academy Award nomination for *Do The Right Thing*), and product pitchman. Not only do the critics rave about his creative and provocative work, his business associates are equally enthusiastic about his ability to maintain tight financial control in an industry known for its runaway budgets. Every one of Spike Lee's films has been profitable.

other units of currency) are handy measuring sticks for assessing organizational performance. Are the necessary resources available? Have resources been properly allocated? Are resources being wasted? How can available resources be more efficiently used? These are just a few of the many important questions answered by means of financial control. In this section, we consider four significant aspects of financial control: (1) budget variance, (2) financial ratios, (3) cash management, and (4) cost control.

Budget Variance as a Control Tool

budget formal financial projection

budget variance difference between budgeted and actual figures

A **budget** is a formal financial projection. Because all types of budgets are projections or plans of future events, they provide managers with standards for control. Control occurs when actual figures are compared with budgeted figures (see the information stage of the operating budget process illustrated in Figure 16.3). Some refer to this process as "management by exception." The difference between the actual figures and the budgeted ones is called **budget variance.** "Variances should be evaluated, however, only when the benefits of doing so outweigh the costs to investigate and correct."[18]

A look at the operating budget in Table 16.2 shows that things do not always work out favorably. Whether variances are favorable or unfavorable, a great deal can be learned by studying them. For instance, the $11,000 unfavorable variance in direct labor expense in Table 16.2 should prompt management to search for the cause. Perhaps too much was spent on costly overtime, thus suggesting a staffing deficiency. Favorable variances should trigger control action in the form of adjusting future budget figures. Following up on both favorable and unfavorable budget variances is a practical expression of feedback control.

••••••••••••••••••••
Explain what budget variances are and when management should take steps to correct them.

FIGURE 16.3 • The Operating Budget Process

Source: From an article appearing in *Cost and Management* by Ralph L. Benke, Jr. and Timothy O'Keefe, July/August 1980 issue, by permission of The Society of Management Accountants of Canada.

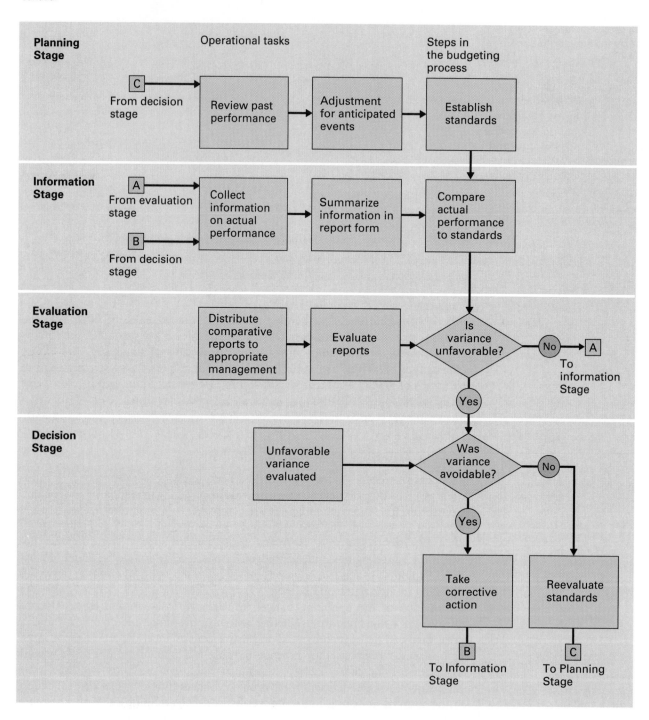

Financial management experts recommend that managers consider four factors when deciding whether or not to take action on a favorable or unfavorable budget variance. Corrective action in the form of feedback control is needed when a budget variance is *costly, consistent, controllable,* and *vital* to the success of the organization or unit.[19]

Making Budgets Flexible. One shortcoming of the standard type of budget illustrated in Table 16.2 is that it limits managers to feedback control. It permits managers to assess financial performance only after the fact. A **flexible budget** is a technique using standardized costs that allows managers to exercise concurrent control over the expenditure of funds.

In a flexible budget, standard costs are calculated from past performance or on the basis of informed judgment. These standard costs are tied to revenue. For example, assume that the standard cost for direct labor is $1 for every $2 of revenue, or a ratio of 1:2. Suppose that after three months, $95,000 has been spent for direct labor, whereas $142,500 has been received in revenue. Because the ratio of direct labor cost to revenue is now 1.33:2, management is warned that something must be done to limit spending on direct labor during the next nine months. Flexible budgets based on standard costs allow managers to keep a running tab on financial performance so that they can take corrective action immediately instead of waiting until the entire budget period has elapsed.[20]

Adjusting for Inflation. During an inflationary period, comparing actual figures with budgeted ones is like comparing oranges and apples. Parents attempting to save for their young child's college education are well aware of this problem. One expert on financial control has gone so far as to say that recurrent bouts of inflation have rendered obsolete all traditional budgetary and cost accounting methods.[21] The recommended solution is **indexed standard costing,** in which standard costs are adjusted for inflation each month rather than each year. Appropriate inflation indexes dictate the magnitude of the monthly adjustments. This approach enabled Brazilian firms to maintain meaningful budgetary control

flexible budget use of standardized costs to permit concurrent control

indexed standard costing adjusting standardized budget costs monthly for inflation

TABLE 16.2 • Budget Variances Tell an Important Story

			Variance	
XYZ Company Operating budget for the year _____				
	Budget	Actual	Favorable	Unfavorable
Revenue	$325,000	$329,350	$4,350	
Expenses				
Direct labor	195,000	206,000		$11,000
Materials	70,000	67,200	2,800	
Overhead	35,000	33,700	1,300	
	300,000	306,900		
Pretax profit	$ 25,000	$ 22,450		$ 2,550

in 1989 when inflation rates soared 40 to 50 percent a *month!*[22] (For an unconventional view of budgets, see The World of Management.)

Financial Ratios

financial ratios numerical measures of an organization's financial health

Physicians would not think of recommending tests or offering a diagnosis without first comparing the patient's pulse, temperature, and blood pressure with accepted standards. Similarly, managers are in a better position to take corrective action if they check the vital signs of their organizations. **Financial ratios** are measures of an organization's financial status that can be compared with industry standards, and they offer a convenient way of gauging an organization's financial health. In fact, after reviewing six empirical studies of the relationship between financial ratios and corporate bankruptcies, one researcher concluded "that financial ratios have predictive power as to whether a business will survive or not."[23] Financial ratios are generally categorized into five main types:

1. *Liquidity:* How well can the company meet its maturing short-term (one-year) obligations?[24]
2. *Asset Management:* How effectively is the company managing its assets?
3. *Debt Management:* To what extent is the company financed by debt?
4. *Profitability:* What are the combined effects of asset management, debt management, and liquidity on the company's profitability?
5. *Market Value:* How do investors regard the company's past performance and future prospects?[25]

By calculating various ratios in each area and then comparing them with industry standards compiled and published by firms such as Dun & Bradstreet, managers can conduct financial analyses to exercise feedforward and feedback financial control.

As with other types of control, financial ratios are not restricted to use by profit-making businesses. They can be used quite effectively to assess the financial health of not-for-profit organizations as well.[26]

Cash Management

Stubbornly high interest rates, wild fluctuations in foreign currency exchange rates, and a financial hangover from the debt binge of the 1980s have made the management of cash more important than ever.[27] A couple of percentage points in interest rates can cause a firm to gain or lose significant sums of money in just a few days when millions of dollars are involved.

> *For example, a large real estate developer recently discovered that an office in one part of the country was borrowing funds at the same time that another office was investing for the short term. The lost interest spread was close to 3 percent on $50 million for an overlap period of 30 days, representing an interest penalty of about $120,000.*[28]

The same principle applies to currency exchange rates. Philip Morris's chief financial officer, Hans G. Storr, turned heads in the financial management community with the following deft move: "In late 1984, figuring the U.S. trade deficit

It's "Management by Pride" for This French Executive

Many U.S. managers are ripping up confining, old-fashioned budgets, but few of the budget bashers have gone further faster than Europe's Jean-Marie Descarpentries. A portly Frenchman with a Rabelaisian taste for ribald jokes and country cooking, he runs the Franco-British CMB Packaging (1989 sales: $4.6 billion) as a federation of entrepreneurs who strive to multiply sales, profits, and productivity as fast as they can. For Descarpentries, 54, following a formal budget would mean curbing his epic ambitions. "If the budget is the basis of your plan, you content yourself with an extrapolation of the past," he says. "How can you budget the 26-percent-a-year compound growth we've achieved?"

By reaching for the sky, Descarpentries has turned in one of the best corporate performances of the 1980s. When he took over a debt-laden French tin-can maker called Carnaud in 1982, its market value was $19 million. Now . . . the re-christened CMB is worth $3 billion.

In lieu of binding budgets, Descarpentries sets dramatic targets designed to make managers stretch for the seemingly unreachable. Each year he asks the heads of 94 profit centers to project their best possible performance if everything, including product demand, goes just right. Those estimates become the budget. "Then we promptly forget about them," he says. "The purpose is to get managers to dream the impossible dream."

Unlike most companies, CMB doesn't measure managers against the budget. Descarpentries says that removes budgeting's biggest evil, aiming too low: "Normally, managers try to negotiate easy targets so they can surpass them and earn big bonuses. The guy who sets an ambitious goal and just misses is penalized."

Instead, CMB rates its managers mainly on how they did this year vs. last year, and how they stack up against the best managers in the industry. Besides growth in sales and operating profits, the main criteria are productivity, debt levels, and hours spent on training. Each month the division heads get a chart comparing their performance on each criterion. "It's management by pride," says Descarpentries. "They all want to be first."

Money is also at stake. Each year CMB rates the 94 profit-center heads on a scale ranging from a low of −5 to a maximum of 15. Poor performers often get no bonus at all, while the stars receive bonuses equal to 30 percent of their salary, plus lucrative stock options. How does Descarpentries fit in? "My job is offering consulting advice—not orders—and choosing people," he says. If a manager posts consistently low ratings for eighteen months, Descarpentries replaces him.

Last year, during a ten-day company outing in the Jordanian desert, he exploited the surrealistic setting to unveil his new goal: a monumental $17 billion in sales by 2000. Reaching it will require huge effort. But for Descarpentries—and the managers he taught to substitute dreams for budgets—nothing seems impossible.

Source: Shawn Tully, "The CEO Who Sees beyond Budgets," *Fortune* (June 4, 1990): 86. © 1990 The Time Inc. Magazine Company. All rights reserved.

would soon undermine the dollar, he began shifting $2 billion into foreign currencies. Riding them up for the next three years made $400 million for Philip Morris."[29] One of the outstanding features of a cash management program is that, with proper training, existing staff can reap impressive profits with relatively little front-end investment.[30]

The following six tips can help managers wring additional profits from an organization's cash resources:

- *Keep Cash Moving.* The faster cash moves from customer to bank and into appropriate short-term investments, the better. Modern computer information technologies such as electronic data interchange and electronic funds transfer permit instantaneous cash transactions.

- *Coordinate Cash Flow among Organizational Units.* As in the example cited above, one unit's cash surplus can fulfill another's needs. Cash management specialists can effect economies by maintaining an information clearinghouse on an organization's cash availability and needs.
- *Shop around for Banking Services.* Healthy competition can be created among banks by comparing services, yields, and costs.
- *Diversify Short-term Investment Portfolios.* This will help achieve a better match between investment terms and cash-flow requirements.
- *Take Advantage of Foreign Exchange Differentials.* Avoid weaker currencies and seek out stronger currencies as market conditions and organizational transactions permit.
- *Broaden the Borrowing Base.* Although effective cash management will usually reduce the need to borrow, necessary borrowing should take advantage of favorable terms and foreign currency exchange rates.[31]

Inflation, even at a modest 4 to 5 percent a year, erodes idle cash. Consequently, an important aspect of financial control is to place cash where it will earn the best return without unreasonable risk.

New Perspectives on Managing Costs

Stiff competition in recent years has made managers highly cost conscious. Seemingly insignificant cost disadvantages in large-scale operations can mean the difference between success and failure. For example, it costs United Airlines about $\frac{1}{2}$ cent more per seat-mile than it does American Airlines. That translates to a loss of nearly $500 million in annual operating profits for United.[32]

Such situations caused many managers to go on cost-cutting sprees in the 1980s. Companies laid off employees, closed facilities, sold money-losing units, discontinued products, froze wages, and reduced benefits. All in the name of creating leaner and more efficient and competitive organizations. Unfortunately, much of the cost cutting was rather imprecise, and muscle was trimmed along with the fat. Experts on the subject say managers now need fresh new perspectives on managing costs. Two promising areas are waste reduction and activity-based costing.

Cut Costs by Cutting Waste. According to C. Jackson Grayson, Jr., head of the American Productivity and Quality Center in Houston, managers need to "focus not on 'cost reduction' but on 'eliminating waste.' You might think they are the same, but they are not."[33] Sea-Land, a transportation company, recently put Grayson's advice to work:

Sea-Land laid off 93 of its 8,000 employees in March [1990], and 440 took severance packages. CEO Alex Mandl has made work elimination his priority, not job elimination. Workers and company managers rewrote the job descriptions for each of the remaining 4,500 nonunion positions.

The aim of the exercise was to get rid of wasteful, unnecessary tasks—a particularly important goal since there would be fewer employees to do them. The unexpected result: Many job descriptions shrank from five pages to a single sheet. For example, salespeople no longer have to write overly detailed reports that often went unread. A blunt but effective test that Sea-Land now uses to determine the necessity of any task: If somebody else's department needs it more than you, let that group do it. Often, they don't need the job done either.[34]

Sea-Land's decentralized approach to cutting waste reflects operations management expert Richard J. Schonberger's philosophy of getting everyone into the act. According to Schonberger: "Teach the employees, singly or in teams, to do microanalysis to smoke out waste, delay, and variability in their own operations. Strive to have hundreds of little improvements going on all the time, not a few grand projects led by analysts."[35] Waste-reduction opportunities abound in the typical organization. Managers need to relentlessly track down wasted time, space, effort, money, talent, facilities, reports, and so on.

Needed: More Accurate Product Cost Systems. Critics of conventional cost-accounting systems, such as Harvard University's Robert S. Kaplan, contend that managers need a clearer idea of what it actually costs to produce a given product.[36] He criticizes today's cost-accounting data for being *precise* (down to the penny or fourth decimal place), *but not accurate*. Traditional cost accounting deals only with labor, material, and overhead costs. Typically, those major cost categories are not broken down by product. Thus, product-to-product cost comparisons are difficult if not impossible. How are managers to know which product is profitable and which is not? Which should be retained and which should be dropped? Kaplan and his colleagues have developed an alternative approach to managing costs called activity-based costing (ABC).

Activity-based costing is defined as determining the cost of a given product in terms of the chain of activities responsible for its creation.[37] An ABC activity might be a five-minute trip through a robotic spot-welding station on an auto assembly line. A cost figure for that five minutes would encompass a proportionate share of the labor, machine, and material costs associated with the creation, maintenance, and operation of the welding unit. The final cost of a given automobile would be the total costs of the various activities required to produce it.

We can look forward to significant developments in this rapidly changing area of financial control. Meanwhile, two feedforward control problems that deserve our careful consideration are organizational crises and employee theft.

activity-based costing costing a given product in terms of the chain of activities responsible for its creation

Contemporary Control Problems

Control systems in well-managed organizations are attuned to social, political/legal, economic, and technological realities. A good planning/control system enables management to identify and respond in a timely and effective manner to situations that threaten the organization's survival. Organizational crises and employee theft are two serious threats that require systematic control.

Crisis Management

crisis management preparing for events that could seriously threaten the organization

Traditionally, crisis management has been viewed negatively, as "managerial fire fighting"—waiting for things to go wrong and scurrying to limit the damage. More recently, the term has taken on a more precise and positive meaning. In fact, a body of theory and practice is evolving around the idea that managers should think about the unthinkable and expect the unexpected. **Crisis management** is the systematic anticipation of and preparation for internal and external problems that seriously threaten an organization's reputation, profitability, or survival. It is important to note that crisis management involves much more than an expedient public relations ploy to make the organization look good. This new discipline relates generally to strategic management but specifically to strategic control.

One need only watch the evening news to find abundant evidence of organizational crises. Notable ones in recent years were the near meltdown of the Three Mile Island nuclear power plant in Pennsylvania in 1979, the poisoning of Johnson & Johnson's Tylenol capsules with cyanide in 1982 and 1986, Union Carbide's Bhopal, India, gas leak that killed 3,000 local residents in 1984, and Exxon's Alaskan oil spill in 1989. Regarding these disasters, observers have noted:

In the twentieth century there have been twenty-eight major industrial accidents in fixed facilities, each killing between 50 and 3,000 people. Fifty percent of these accidents occurred in the past decade accounting for nearly 70 percent of people killed in such accidents. Moreover, the scope of destruction caused by corporate disasters is growing exponentially. These disasters not only kill or injure workers, they have wide ranging impacts on health environments, and on economic and social relationships. These impacts transcend national boundaries (as in Chernobyl) and create crises of a global scale. These impacts also transcend time barriers to affect subsequent generations.[38]

Progressive managers can help stem this disastrous tide by incorporating crisis management into their strategic management and control systems.

The tiny zebra mussel is spreading like wildfire. If not checked it is projected to infest all major waterways in the Eastern U.S. in just twenty years. Originally introduced to the Great Lakes by a European cargo ship around 1986, the prolific zebra mussels have become an expensive control problem for boaters, sports anglers, and public utilities. Divers at Detroit Edison are waging a nonstop battle to keep the pests from clogging the cooling system at the utility's Monroe power plant, at a cost so far of $500,000.

A Crisis Typology

Crisis management specialists have taken a needed first step by categorizing and defining kinds of crises in a basic typology (see Figure 16.4). The horizontal axis distinguishes between internal and external crises; the vertical, between technical/economic factors and human factors. Symbolic projection, in the lower-right portion of Figure 16.4, requires some explanation. It refers to situations in which a company's well-being is put at risk because its name has negative associations. For example, Kuwaiti-owned gas stations in Europe bearing the name "Q8" might become the target of terrorists bent on avenging Kuwait's victory over Iraq.[39] Along the same lines, animal rights extremists have vandalized McDonald's restaurants because of the company's extensive use of beef. As bizarre as these situations may seem, they underscore the need for greater managerial preparedness through crisis management.

Technical/Economic

	Internal	External
Technical/Economic	• Product/service defects • Plant defects/industrial accidents • Computer breakdown • Defective, undisclosed information • Bankruptcy	• Widespread environmental destruction/industrial accidents • Large-scale systems failure • Natural disasters • Hostile takeovers • Governmental crises • International crises
People/Social/Organizational	• Failure to adapt/change • Organizational breakdown • Miscommunication • Sabotage • On-site product tampering • Counterfeiting • Rumors, sick jokes, malicious slander • Illegal activities • Sexual harassment • Occupational health diseases	• Symbolic projection • Sabotage • Terrorism • Executive kidnapping • Off-site product tampering • Counterfeiting • Rumors, sick jokes, malicious slander • Labor strikes • Boycotts

People/Social/Organizational

FIGURE 16.4 • A Crisis Typology for Managers

Source: Ian I. Mitroff, Paul Shrivastava, and Firdaus E. Udwadia, "Effective Crisis Management," *Academy of Management Executive,* 1 (November 1987): 287. Reprinted with permission.

Identify the four key elements of a crisis management program.

Developing a Crisis Management Program

As illustrated in Figure 16.5, a crisis management program is made up of four elements. Disasters need to be anticipated, contingency plans need to be formulated, and crisis management teams need to be staffed and trained. Finally, the program needs to be perfected through realistic practice. Let us examine each of these elements.

Conducting a Crisis Audit. A crisis audit is a systematic way of seeking out trouble spots and vulnerabilities. Disaster scenarios become the topic of discussion as managers ask a series of "What if?" questions. Models such as the typology in Figure 16.4 can be useful during this stage. Some crises, such as the untimely death of a key executive, are universal and hence readily identified. Others are industry-specific. For example, crashes are an all-too-real disaster scenario for passenger airline companies.

Formulating Contingency Plans. A contingency plan is a backup plan that can be put into effect when things go wrong.[40] Whenever possible, each contingency plan should specify early warning signals, action to be taken, and expected consequences of those actions.

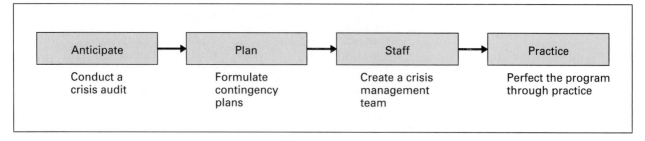

FIGURE 16.5 • Key Elements in a Crisis Management Program

> *Attention to detail is a crucial component of most contingency plans.*
> *Dow has produced a twenty-page program for communicating with the*
> *public during a disaster, right down to such particulars as who is going to*
> *run the copy machines. Many companies designate a single corporate*
> *spokes[person] to field all inquiries from the press. A list may be drawn*
> *up of those executives to be notified in emergency situations, and the*
> *late-night phone numbers of local radio and television stations may be*
> *kept posted on office walls.*[41]

Both crisis audits and related contingency plans need to be updated at least
annually and, if changing conditions dictate, more often.

Creating a Crisis Management Team.   Organizational crisis management teams
have been likened to SWAT teams that police departments use for extraordinary
situations such as hostage takings. Crisis management teams necessarily represent
different specialties, depending on the likely crisis. For example, an electrical
utility company might have a crisis management team made up of a media relations expert, an electrical engineer, a consumer affairs specialist, and a lawyer.
As the case of Dow Chemical Canada illustrates, quick response and effective
communication are the hallmarks of an effective crisis management team:

> *Dow Chemical Canada decided to improve its crisis plans after a railroad*
> *car carrying a Dow chemical derailed near Toronto in 1979, forcing the*
> *evacuation of 250,000 residents. Since then, Dow Canada has prepared*
> *information kits on the hazards of its products and trained executives in*
> *interview techniques.*
> *This paid off in 1982. Another accident spilled toxic chemicals into a*
> *river that supplies water for several towns. Almost immediately, Dow*
> *Canada's emergency-response team arrived at the site and set up a press*
> *center to distribute information about the chemicals. They also recruited*
> *a neutral expert—the regional public health officer—to speak about the*
> *hazards and how to deal with them. The result: Officials praised Dow's*
> *response.*[42]

A 1987 survey of 114 major U.S. companies discovered that 38 percent had a
formal crisis management team.[43]

Perfecting the Program through Practice.   Like athletic teams, crisis management teams can gain the necessary teamwork, effectiveness, and speed of response

only through diligent practice. Simulations, drills, and mock disasters provide this invaluable practice. Top management support of such exercises is essential to provide good role models and create a sense of importance. Moreover, reinforcing employee efforts in this area with an effective reward system should encourage serious practice.[44]

Experts say that management's two biggest mistakes regarding organizational crises are: (1) ignoring early warning signs and (2) denying the existence of a problem when disaster strikes. A good crisis management program effectively eliminates these self-destructive mistakes.

Controlling Employee Theft

The infamous gangster Al Capone once said something to the effect that "one accountant can steal more with his pen than a hundred robbers can with their guns." Little did Capone know how well he was describing modern organizational life. Although estimates vary ($40 to $75 billion annually), experts agree that the amount of company cash, materials, inventory, and services lost each year in the United States to employee pilfering and fraud far exceeds the amount taken through burglary and robbery. The cost of employee theft is approximately ten times that of street crime and is growing 15 percent annually.[45] Losses due to computer fraud, 20 to 50 percent of which go unreported, average more than $500,000 per crime.[46] Whatever the label—"employee theft," "white-collar crime," or "computer crime"—the result is the same: otherwise productive organizational assets are seriously depleted. In some cases, dishonest employees put organizational survival at stake. According to one study, 20 percent of the business failures in the United States each year are caused by the burdensome expense of employee dishonesty.[47]

Why Do Employees Steal? Contrary to what one might initially suspect, more than just a few employees are dishonest. A widely cited study by the U.S. Chamber of Commerce concluded that over half of today's employees engage in some sort of workplace theft, with between 5 and 8 percent stealing large amounts.[48] The first step in controlling this costly problem lies in a better understanding of why employees become thieves.

Although it is tempting to assume that inherent dishonesty is at the heart of this problem, researchers tend to lay the blame on a complex web of individual and situational factors such as:

- An unhealthy organizational climate that alienates employees.
- Personal anger or frustration with management, the organization, or an impersonal "they."
- Ego satisfaction (outsmarting "the system").
- Retaliation (getting even with a boss or coworkers).
- Response to perceived inequity ("they owe it to me").
- Compensation for a feeling of powerlessness.[49]

The complexity of this problem requires a comprehensive feedforward control mechanism.

> • • • • • • • • • • • • • • • •
> Discuss the factors that lead to employee dishonesty and be familiar with a strategy for controlling it.

Three-pronged Prevention. A team of experts has suggested a three-pronged attack on employee fraud: "In short, fraud is reduced by eliminating the pressures and opportunities to commit fraud and by increasing personal integrity."[50] The tips in Table 16.3 can be used for the feedforward control of virtually all forms of employee theft or fraud.

TABLE 16.3 • Tips for Preventing Employee Theft and Fraud

Reducing situational pressures

1. Avoid setting unrealistically high performance expectations.
2. Remove unnecessary obstacles, such as insufficient working capital, excess capacity, and obsolete equipment or inventory, that block effective performance.
3. Offer personal counseling to help employees with financial problems.
4. Establish fair and uniform personnel policies.

Reducing opportunities

1. Monitor the business transactions and interpersonal relationships of suppliers, buyers, purchasing agents, sales representatives, and others who interface in the transactions among financial units.
2. Maintain accurate and complete internal accounting records.
3. Establish a physical security system to secure company assets, including finished goods, cash, equipment, tools, and other items of worth.
4. Do not rely solely on one individual to perform an important function (such as ringing up sales on a cash register as well as tallying the day's receipts).
5. Maintain accurate personnel records regarding employees' previous backgrounds and current financial activities.
6. Develop strong leadership and cohesive work groups.

Strengthening personal integrity

1. Research suggests that teaching, explaining, and modeling are effective techniques for developing moral behavior.
2. Honest and dishonest behavior should be defined.
3. Select honest employees to occupy positions of trust.
4. Build an organizational climate that emphasizes the importance of honesty.
5. The consequences of violating the rules and the punishment of the perpetrators of fraud should be made public.

Source: Adapted from David J. Cherrington, W. Steve Albrecht, and Marshall B. Romney, "The Role of Management in Reducing Fraud," *Financial Executive,* 49 (March 1981): 31–34. Used with permission.

Summary

Planning and control are complementary functions because preventive and corrective actions are usually needed to turn plans into reality. Feedforward control is preventive in nature, whereas feedback control is based on the evaluation of past performance. Managers engage in concurrent control when they monitor and adjust on-going operations to keep them performing to standard. The three basic components of organizational control systems are objectives, standards, and an evaluation-reward system. Benchmarking calls for standards that emulate the best in the business or the world. According to the performance pyramid, strategic control involves the downward translation of objectives and upward translation of performance measures.

Timely identification of control problems is important because things can quickly get out of hand. Executive reality checks, whereby top managers periodically work in lower-level jobs, is a good way of monitoring operations. Internal auditing helps top management objectively determine whether the organization is functioning as intended. If, for some reason, comprehensive internal auditing is not carried out, weak spots in the control system can be detected by monitoring telltale symptoms. Sometimes, especially when management focuses on secondary objectives or fosters a do-or-die environment, the control system itself may breed problems, such as goal displacement, measurementship, and budget games.

Financial control is vital because it monitors the organization's financial health. Both favorable and unfavorable budget variances help management diagnose organizational ills. Managers should focus their feedback control efforts on budget variances that are costly, consistent, controllable, and vital. Feedforward financial control becomes possible when flexible budgets based on standard costs are used. Indexed standard costing has been recommended for adjusting budgets for inflation. Financial ratios enable managers to gauge the financial health of their organizations in terms of liquidity, asset management, debt management, profitability, and market value. When high interest rates prevail, systematic cash management can generate handsome payoffs with relatively little additional expense.

Management experts recommend focusing on eliminating waste, rather than haphazardly cutting costs. Harvard's Robert S. Kaplan criticizes conventional cost accounting techniques for being precise but not accurate. Instead, he recommends activity-based costing (ABC) that gives managers a better idea of what it actually costs to produce a given product. Unprofitable products can then be weeded out.

Two contemporary control problems that require management's attention are crisis management and employee theft. Both are serious threats to organizational survival. The four key elements of a crisis management program are: (1) conduct a crisis audit; (2) formulate contingency plans; (3) create a crisis management team; and (4) perfect the program through practice. A three-pronged program involving reducing pressures, eliminating opportunities, and increasing integrity is recommended for controlling employee theft/fraud.

Terms to Understand

Control
Feedforward control
Concurrent control
Feedback control
Benchmarking
Executive reality check
Internal auditing
Measurementship

Budget
Budget variance
Flexible budget
Indexed standard costing
Financial ratios
Activity-based costing
Crisis management

Questions for Discussion

1. What is the relationship between the planning and control functions?
2. In your opinion, which type of control—feedforward, concurrent, or feedback—is most desirable in an organization?
3. To maintain high-quality service in a fast-food restaurant, what do you believe can be done in terms of the three components of organizational control systems?
4. What can management do to overcome resistance to internal auditing?
5. In observing firsthand an ongoing organization (for example, a factory, a restaurant, a service station, a grocery store, a bookstore, a club, or a fraternity or sorority), what symptoms of inadequate control can you detect?
6. What concerns should be raised by favorable budget variances?
7. Why is cash management especially important today? Are there any personal lessons in the cash management tips provided in this chapter? Explain.
8. In your present or past job, what kinds of waste should be identified and eliminated?
9. What organizations in your locale could use a crisis management team? Specify the nature of the crises and explain how the team probably could handle them.
10. In your experience, how bad is the problem of employee theft? What needs to be done to control it?

Back to the Opening Case

Now that you have read Chapter 16, you should be able to answer the following questions about the Marriott case:

1. Which type of control does Marriott Corporation rely most heavily on? Feedforward? Concurrent? Feedback? Explain with evidence from the case.
2. Why is Marriott's Guest Service Index (GSI) such an important component of the company's control program?
3. How does Marriott Corporation stack up relative to the performance pyramid for strategic control in Figure 16.2?
4. Is there a risk of Marriott's control program becoming misguided? Explain.

CLOSING CASE
FMC Manages the Gulf Crisis

FMC Corporation is a Chicago-based company that does more than $3 billion of business annually, making chemicals, oil-field equipment, food machinery, and military vehicles. Although its major industries have shown little growth over the past decade,

FMC has consistently managed to increase operating profits. The value of a share of FMC stock roughly quadrupled during the 1980s. FMC owes part of its success to clever financial maneuvering, as, for example, when the company bought some of its own shares and avoided possible takeovers. Another key ingredient in FMC's success has been its strategic planning system. It follows an elaborate eleven-step planning process. In this process, planners analyze the situation and target issues; develop competitive strategies and analyze target issues; and, finally, develop, evaluate, and integrate alternative strategies to deal with the key issues. After its stock buyback, FMC used its planning process to shift the emphasis of corporate strategy from increasing shareholder value to "becoming . . . customers' most valued supplier."*

No amount of planning, however, could have prepared FMC and companies like it to deal with the crisis in the Middle East precipitated by Iraq's invasion of Kuwait on August 2, 1990. The company's rapid response to the crisis on a wide variety of fronts demonstrates the values of good planning, control, and companywide preparedness. FMC reacted so quickly that it seemed to have been expecting the unexpected.

One of the company's first reactions was to determine which of its products were headed for the Gulf area. FMC's sweeper division in Pomona, California, discovered to its horror that five new street-sweepers, valued at $400,000, were on a ship just hours away from their Kuwait City destination. The call came just in time for the ship to turn in at Abu Dhabi, the capital of the United Arab Emirates. As one of the top-fifty American exporters, FMC was well aware that it pays to know where your goods are, even in transit.

The street sweepers were not the only FMC product destined for Kuwait. The company also had forty contracts with Kuwait

*Stewart Early, "Issues and Alternatives: Key to FMC's Strategic Planning System," *Planning Review* (May-June 1990): 30.

and $4 million worth of inventory—most of it machines and parts for the oil industry—bound for Kuwait. After three days of hurried research into international business markets, FMC found customers for all but $500,000 of its Kuwaiti inventory. The company also had to decide whether to close its Singapore plant that makes oil equipment for Kuwait. Again, quick decisions allowed FMC to find a silver lining in the cloud of war, and it retooled the plant to make parts that had been back-ordered months before by India and Indonesia.

This decision and many others were made based on an assumption—with oil from Kuwait and Iraq no longer flowing to the rest of the world, other oil-producing countries would want to step up their production. Accordingly, FMC sent extra oil-equipment salespeople to Alaska and Saudi Arabia and hurried a new oil-equipment factory in Malaysia into production.

With offices throughout the Middle East, FMC also had to act quickly just to ensure the safety of its employees. FMC's representative in Kuwait, a Palestinian, couldn't be located for nine days and finally had to borrow a friend's Chevy and drive across the desert to Saudi Arabia. FMC's international business staff dedicated itself to devising evacuation routes for all FMC personnel in the area, and the company instituted a new policy requiring all officials to provide daily itineraries of all their movements.

At the same time, FMC's financial officers were busy trying to make sure that the possible financial repercussions of the crisis weren't too costly. They stopped signing new long-term, fixed-price contracts, afraid that a war and an oil shortage could send inflation out of control. They turned to Iraq's European bankers to try to get payment on debts that the Iraqi government owed FMC. As currency values fluctuated around the world, FMC's foreign exchange manager invested in U.S. dollars and British pounds. During this period, FMC's managers doubled their usual number of phone messages. Many of these activities began in the early morning hours, when officers were first alerted by beepers.

Given its investment in oil field equipment and military vehicles, FMC stood to gain or lose big during a Middle Eastern crisis. If it had waited until the dust settled to make its moves, it almost certainly would have lost. But intensive long-range planning, good corporate communications, and rapid decision making allowed FMC to position itself to turn the crisis into an opportunity.

For Discussion

1. How would you respond to the following statement: "FMC was lucky not to be badly hurt by the Gulf crisis."?
2. From a crisis management perspective, did FMC handle the Gulf crisis well?
3. What does this case have to say about the relationship between planning and control?

References

Opening Quotation. Laurence J. Peter, *Peter's Quotations: Ideas for Our Time* (New York: Bantam, 1977), p. 273.

Opening Case. "How Master Lodger Bill Marriott Prophesied Profit and Prospered," *Fortune* (June 5, 1989): 56–57; John H. Taylor, "Don't Stop Now," *Forbes* (July 9, 1990): 36–37; Ron Zemke, *The Service Edge* (New York: NAL, 1989), 117–120; Dean Foust, "Marriott Is Smoothing out the Lumps in its Bed," *Business Week* (April 1, 1991): 74–75.

Closing Case. Marcia Berss, "Marching to its Own Drummer," *Forbes* (September 17, 1990): 95–98; Stewart Early, "Issues and Alternatives: Key to FMC's Strategic Planning System," *Planning Review* (May-June 1990): 26–33; Robert Johnson, "FMC's Quick Reaction Shows How One Firm Deals with Iraq Crisis," *The Wall Street Journal* (August 16, 1990): A1–A11.

1. Figures extrapolated from data found in Peter Nulty, "Exxon's Problem: Not What You Think," *Fortune* (April 23, 1990): 202–204; "Oil Spill Cleanup: You vs. Exxon," *Fortune* (March 11, 1991): 18; and "Exxon Makes a Deal in the Valdez Case," *Business Week* (March 25, 1991): 36.
2. Harold Koontz and Robert W. Bradspies, "Managing through Feedforward Control," *Business Horizons,* 15 (June 1972): 27.
3. Lucia Mouat, "Crumbling Bridges, Constructive Budgets," *The Christian Science Monitor* (February 26, 1991): 9.
4. See, for example, Michel Lebas and Jane Weigenstein, "Management Control: The Roles of Rules, Markets, and Culture," *Journal of Management Studies,* 23 (May 1986): 259–272; and Jeffrey A. Alexander, "Adaptive Change in Corporate Control Practices," *Academy of Management Journal,* 34 (March 1991): 162–193.
5. See Richard L. Daft and Norman B. Macintosh, "The Nature and Use of Formal Control Systems for Management Control and Strategy Implementation," *Journal of Management,* 10 (Spring 1984): 43–66.
6. Based on Eric Flamholtz, "Organizational Control Systems as a Managerial Tool," *California Management Review,* 22 (Winter 1979): 50–59.
7. Data from James B. Treece and David Woodruff, "Crunch Time Again for Chrysler," *Business Week* (March 25, 1991): 92–94.
8. See Jan Carlzon, *Moments of Truth* (New York: Harper & Row, 1987).
9. See Georg Schreyogg and Horst Steinmann, "Strategic Control: A New Perspective," *Academy of Management Review,* 12 (January 1987): 91–103; and V. Govindarajan and Joseph Fisher, "Strategy, Control Systems, and Resource Sharing: Effects on Business-Unit Performance," *Academy of Management Journal,* 33 (June 1990): 259–285.
10. See Gerald H. B. Ross, "Revolution in Management Control," *Management Accounting,* 72 (November 1990): 23–27; Jonathan B. Schiff and Claire B. May, "What Is Internal Control? Who Owns It?" *Management Accounting,* 72 (November 1990): 37–40; and Robert G. Eccles, "The Peformance Measurement Manifesto," *Harvard Business Review,* 69 (January-February 1991): 131–137.

11. Alan Farnham, "The Trust Gap," *Fortune* (December 4, 1989): 78.

12. Lawrence B. Sawyer, "Internal Auditing: Yesterday, Today, and Tomorrow," *The Internal Auditor,* 36 (December 1979): 26; emphasis added.

13. See Robert Louis Ellis and J. Peter Melrose, "Auditing the Management Process," *The Internal Auditor,* 37 (August 1980): 53–64.

14. This list is based in part on Donald W. Murr, Harry B. Bracey, Jr., and William K. Hill, "How to Improve Your Organization's Management Controls," *Management Review,* 69 (October 1980): 56–63.

15. See Pete Engardio, "Why Cordis' Heart Wasn't in Pacemakers," *Business Week* (March 16, 1987): 80; and Harris Collingwood, "Guilty Plea on Faulty Pacemakers," *Business Week* (September 12, 1988): 44.

16. See Christopher K. Bart, "Budgeting Gamesmanship," *Academy of Management Executive,* 2 (November 1988): 285–294; and Thomas A. Stewart, "Why Budgets Are Bad for Business," *Fortune* (June 4, 1990): 179–190.

17. See Frank Collins, Paul Munter, and Don W. Finn, "The Budgeting Games People Play," *The Accounting Review,* 62 (January 1987): 29–49.

18. Joel G. Siegel and Mathew S. Rubin, "Corporate Planning and Control through Variance Analysis," *Managerial Planning,* 33 (September-October 1984): 35.

19. Ibid., p. 36.

20. For detailed discussion of flexible budgeting, see Lawrence M. Matthews, *Practical Operating Budgeting* (New York: McGraw-Hill, 1977), pp. 30–34. For a good practical example of standard costing, see Dennis M. Boll, "How Dutch Pantry Accounts for Standard Costs," *Management Accounting,* 64 (December 1982): 32–35.

21. See John Dearden, "Facing Facts with Inflation Accounting," *Harvard Business Review,* 59 (July-August 1981): 8–12, 16; and John L. Grant, "Inflation's Full Impact on the Bottom Line," *Business Week* (February 7, 1983): 8.

22. See Ron Scherer, "Brazilians Feel Inflation's Squeeze," *The Christian Science Monitor* (December 14, 1989): 8.

23. Donald Green, "To Predict Failure," *Management Accounting,* 60 (July 1978): 45. See also Avi Rushinek and Sara F. Rushinek, "Using Financial Ratios to Predict Insolvency," *Journal of Business Research,* 15 (February 1987): 93–100.

24. Limitations of the current ratio are discussed in Mary M. K. Fleming, "The Current Ratio Revisited," *Business Horizons,* 29 (May-June 1986): 74–77.

25. Adapted from discussion in J. Fred Weston and Eugene F. Brigham, *Essentials of Managerial Finance,* 8th edition (New York: The Dryden Press, 1987), pp. 240–251.

26. For a discussion of financial ratios applied to hospital administration, see Fred Fitschen, "Look to Ratios to Measure Financial Health," *Hospital Financial Management,* 6 (November 1976): 44–50.

27. Informative background on cash management may be found in Garry W. Caughlin, "The Cash Management Discipline," *CMA,* 62 (March 1988): 49–50; and Henry A. Davis, "Changing Priorities in Corporate Cash Management," *FE,* 3 (January 1987): 18–21.

28. Henry C. Knight, "Making Money from Money Management," *Cost and Management,* 55 (July-August 1981): 45.

29. Leah J. Nathans, "The Money Magician at Philip Morris," *Business Week* (April 10, 1989): 78.

30. An instructive cash management case study may be found in Royce L. Gentzel and Mary Ann Swepston, "The Cardinal Difference in Cash Management," *Management Accounting,* 69 (February 1988): 42–47.

31. This list is adapted from Knight, "Making Money from Money Management" and Leslie N. Masonson, "Cash Is King," *Management Review,* 79 (October 1990): 36–38.

32. Data from James E. Ellis, "United Swallows Hard—and Goes For Growth," *Business Week* (May 15, 1989): 34.

33. C. Jackson Grayson, Jr., ". . . But What Do I Do Monday Morning?" *Academy of Management Executive,* 3 (August 1989): 239. Also see George Gendron and B. Burlingham, "Waste Not, Want Not," *Inc.,* 13 (March 1991): 33–42.

34. Thomas A. Stewart, "Do You Push Your People Too Hard?" *Fortune* (October 22, 1990): 128.

35. Richard J. Schonberger, *Building a Chain of Customers: Linking Business Functions to Create the World-Class Company* (New York: The Free Press, 1990), p. 155.

36. See Robin Cooper and Robert S. Kaplan, "Measure Costs Right: Make the Right Decisions,"

Harvard Business Review, 66 (September-October 1988): 96–103; and Robin Cooper, "You Need a New Cost System When . . ." *Harvard Business Review,* 67 (January-February 1989): 77–82.

37. Based on Norn Raffish, "How Much Does That Product Really Cost?" *Management Accounting,* 72 (March 1991): 36–39.

38. Paul Shrivastava and Ian I. Mitroff, "Strategic Management of Corporate Crises," *Columbia Journal of World Business,* 22 (Spring 1987): 6. Also see Karlene H. Roberts, "Managing High Reliability Organizations," *California Management Review,* 32 (Summer 1990): 101–113.

39. Terrorism is discussed in Steve Kovsky, "Corporate Terrorism: A New Global Threat," *Management Review,* 79 (October 1990): 39–43; and Alan Farnham, "Read This or We'll Cut Off Your Ear," *Fortune* (December 31, 1990): 88–92.

40. See Dale D. McConkey, "Planning for Uncertainty," *Business Horizons,* 30 (January-February 1987): 40–45.

41. Barbara Rudolph, "Coping with Catastrophe," *Time* (February 24, 1986): 53.

42. William C. Symonds, "How Companies Are Learning to Prepare for the Worst," *Business Week* (December 23, 1985): 76.

43. Data from Nancy Jeffrey, "Preparing for the Worst: Firms Set Up Plans to Help Deal with Corporate Crises," *The Wall Street Journal* (December 7, 1987): 23.

44. See Lillian Gorman and Kathryn D. McKee, "Disaster and Its Aftermath," *HRMagazine,* 35 (March 1990): 54–58; and William Briggs, "Taking Control after a Crisis," *HRMagazine,* 35 (March 1990): 60–61, 80.

45. Harry Bacas, "To Stop a Thief," *Nation's Business,* 75 (June 1987): 20. Reprinted by permission, *Nation's Business,* June 1987. Copyright, 1987, U.S. Chamber of Commerce. Robert McGough and Elicia Brown, "Thieves at Work," *Financial World,* 159 (December 11, 1990): 18–21.

46. Data from Katherine M. Hafner, "Is Your Computer Secure?" *Business Week* (August 1, 1988): 64–72.

47. Bacas, "To Stop a Thief."

48. See Chamber of Commerce of the United States, *White Collar Crime* (Washington, D.C.: Chamber of Commerce, 1974).

49. See Donald W. Caudill, "How To Recognize and Deter Employee Theft," *Personnel Administrator,* 33 (July 1988): 86–90; Neil H. Snyder and Karen E. Blair, "Dealing With Employee Theft," *Business Horizons,* 32 (May-June 1989): 27–34; "Preventing Crime on the Job," *Nation's Business,* 78 (July 1990): 36–37; and Jerald Greenberg, "Employee Theft as a Reaction to Underpayment Inequity: The Hidden Cost of Pay Cuts," *Journal of Applied Psychology,* 75 (October 1990): 561–568.

50. David J. Cherrington, W. Steve Albrecht, and Marshall B. Romney, "The Role of Management in Reducing Fraud," *Financial Executive,* 49 (March 1981): 31.

17

Information and Computer Systems Management

CHAPTER OBJECTIVES

When you finish studying this chapter, you should be able to

- Define the term *information* and explain why it is not an ordinary physical resource.

- Identify three factors that dictate the cost of information and discuss how information is organized.

- Specify six basic levels of information processing.

- Distinguish between centralized and distributed computer systems and explain the relative merits of each.

- Explain how personal computers have revolutionized organizational data processing and discuss the significance of computer networks.

- Specify at least four common management information system (MIS) developmental problems.

- Define the term *critical success factors* and explain their role in executive information systems (EIS).

- Discuss how management can reduce personal computer security risks.

Computers Help Mrs. Fields Make Lots of Dough

On the surface, Mrs. Fields Inc. is just what you would expect the world's best-known baker of chocolate chip cookies to be: a big company trying to retain the warmth and feel of a home kitchen. There *is* a real Mrs. Fields—Debbi—and she and husband, Randy, really did start with one store and borrowed money, and they really did give away their first batch of cookies when no one bought them. Debbi Fields still plays a major role in running a company that is approaching $200 million in yearly sales. She likes her stores to serve cookies warm, and she reads hundreds of customer response notes every week.

But beneath this small, homey exterior— in fact, the reason that the company can still *seem* small—is a sophisticated Retail Operations Intelligence (ROI) System and hundreds of laptop computers. Chairman Randy Fields tells people who come into his office without their computer, "I don't think I can talk to you now. Get your laptop."[1]

Fields's ROI includes modules that handle everything from planning daily production to managing inventory to skill testing. The tax and sales analysis features of the system might seem familiar to anyone who'd used a computer in a business, but many features of the ROI are relatively new for the kind of small stores Mrs. Fields operates—they usually employ only ten people.

An interviewing module, for instance, helps the company's six hundred stores standardize their interviewing and ask only legally acceptable questions. Applicants spend 15 minutes answering true-false and multiple-choice questions on the computer. Certain responses from an applicant—those showing an interest in temporary work, for example—lead the computer to ask other questions, such as "How long would you plan to stay?" Headquarters assigns a particular weight to certain answers and sets a minimum score, but the local manager makes the final hiring decision, aided by a computer printout that highlights certain information the manager might find important.

Mrs. Fields's computerized skill-training module can both assess someone's current knowledge about store policies and procedures and help the person learn. Wrong responses are corrected by the computer. The "help text" part of the program can become a tutor, explaining at any point why an answer is right or wrong.

With the labor-scheduling module, a local manager doesn't have to call up every employee to see who can take over a sick employee's shift. In addition, the manager won't be caught shorthanded when the local parade marches by. Computers keep track of everything from individual employee's skills, work preferences, and normal schedules to community events that generate or cut into customer buying. Computers figure out work plans—including breaks—for each person on each shift.

Computer assistance does a lot more than free local managers to devote more of their energies to satisfying customers. It allows Mrs. Fields to have an unusual corporate structure. Because local managers can communicate so well and so quickly with headquarters, Mrs. Fields has virtually no middle management layers. The corporate chart is twenty times as wide as it is high. And the number of people who work at company headquarters—114—is about one-fifth what you would expect for a company the size of Mrs. Fields. Such a structure looks good from the top, allowing Randy and Debbi Fields to keep in close contact with their employees around the country through electronic mail. Employees can expect even the boss herself to respond to a suggestion within forty-eight hours.

The way Debbi and Randy Fields see it, people should spend their time solving problems, not processing information. Computers tell each manager how much batter to mix and when, basing estimates on historical data. In effect, the computers are learning from experience, as they use each day's data to fine tune the next day's forecasts. Computers can look for patterns of errors in such things as the interview module and help managers spot questions that may be poorly worded.

Randy Fields has a lot of ideas about how other businesses should approach computer use—so many that he has developed his own spinoff company, Fields Software Group, to develop software for retail and service companies. He feels strongly that a company's dedication to computer use must start at the top—the CEO must set the example.

It wasn't always that way at Mrs. Fields. Debbi resisted the idea of using a computer but after finally trying Lotus Development Corporation's Agenda management software, she ended up spending half the night typing in her daily planner.

Mrs. Fields eases employees into life with computers by letting them play games on their machines for a couple of hours. Each new employee gets a disk with four games on it. The company also offers regular classes in computer use. Randy Fields created a "guru" department in 1989, and gurus—most of them former hackers—help Fields users solve their computer problems quickly. He also advises Fields executives about their expectations for computers. Some unrealistically expect the computers to bring about miracles without the company's investing time in training its employees to use them. Others buy fancy machines, then use them only for word processing and addressing envelopes. Worst of all, according to Fields, is the situation in which a company's management information systems (MIS) people tell the CEO what computers can do for the company. Instead, the CEO should figure out what the company needs and wants and, only then, get MIS and the computers to deliver.

● ● ● ● ● ● ● ● ● ● ● ● ● ● ● ● ● **W**e are living in the information age. William McGowan, founder and head of MCI Communications Corporation, offered this perspective:

> *Of all the changes that are now transforming the business world, none is more far-reaching than the emergence of the Information Age—that confluence of advances in telecommunications and computer technologies. Already, corporations on the cutting edge of competitive change are using these technologies to move into businesses, to know immediately how each new marketing strategy and product is doing, to reduce inventories, to tie together teams of people working around the world, to produce new levels of efficiency in the way products are designed and manufactured; indeed, to completely reorganize the corporate structure and the way decisions are made.[2]*

Impacts of the information age have become so commonplace that they are easily overlooked or taken for granted. Consider, for example, the apparently simple matter of purchasing something with a credit card. As illustrated in Figure 17.1, credit authorization is obtained or denied via an information network of incredible scope and speed. Managers have a competitive advantage in the information age if they appreciate the power of relevant and timely information and know how to get it.

Skillful information and computer management are essential components of organizational strategy, effectiveness, and control. American Airlines has made strategic use of sophisticated information technology with its SABRE reservation system. This vast network links more than 85,500 video terminals around the world with seven huge IBM mainframe computers secured in a tornado-proof underground bunker near Tulsa, Oklahoma. SABRE is capable of printing tickets, reserving hotel rooms, and tracking luggage through its terminals. It is updated daily with as many as 1.5 million fares from the entire airline industry. "Analysts figure the company earns a higher return on investment by booking tickets than it does by flying airplanes."[3] The way American Airlines manages information gives the firm a strategic competitive advantage.

This chapter focuses on ways to take advantage of information resources and technologies. We begin by developing a clearer perspective of information. A discussion of computers in the workplace follows to demonstrate their power and potential. Next we consider the development of management information systems, with attention devoted to executive information systems (EIS). Finally, information age issues including computer literacy training, computer security risks, telecommuting, and emerging information technologies are explored.

Putting Information into Perspective

information data with relevance and purpose

● ● ● ● ● ● ● ● ● ● ● ● ● ● ● ● ● ●

Define the term *information* and explain why it is not an ordinary physical resource.

Technically, not every message or signal one receives is necessarily information. This distinction has been clarified by Peter Drucker: "**Information** is data endowed with relevance and purpose."[4] Data such as names, numbers, and places need to be organized and interpreted in a timely manner if they are to be useful in decision making. Information should have a "surprise effect," meaning that it should shed light on the unknown.[5] Information that does not surprise or enlighten the individual is probably irrelevant or redundant (as is, for example, last week's weather report).

Because information is the lifeblood of organized endeavor and a strategic tool of increasing importance, you as a manager need to (1) view information as a resource, (2) understand the cost of information, (3) know how to organize and comprehend information, and (4) be familiar with the basics of information processing.

Information Is a Unique Resource

Through the years, managers have generally been preoccupied with specific types of information (for example, market forecasts, production levels, and sales figures) rather than focusing more broadly on the concept of information. One

Total elapsed time: 15 seconds

1. Customer buys diamond earrings for $895 in Detroit. The clerk passes the Visa card through a credit-verification terminal and punches in purchase data

2. The data travel by satellite, land lines, or microwave to National Data Corp.'s computers in Cherry Hill, N.J.

3. From Cherry Hill the credit query goes to NDC headquarters in Atlanta for processing

The transaction tops $50, so it needs a second opinion. The request is turned over to Visa USA minicomputers at NDC.

4. The Visa minis shoot the query to mainframes in McLean, Va., or San Mateo, Calif.

5. The Visa mainframe determines that the card is from a San Francisco bank and sends the transaction to the bank's computer, which checks to see if there is $895 in available credit.

The bank's O.K. retraces the path of the authorization request: from the bank to NDC in Cherry Hill to the merchant in Detroit.

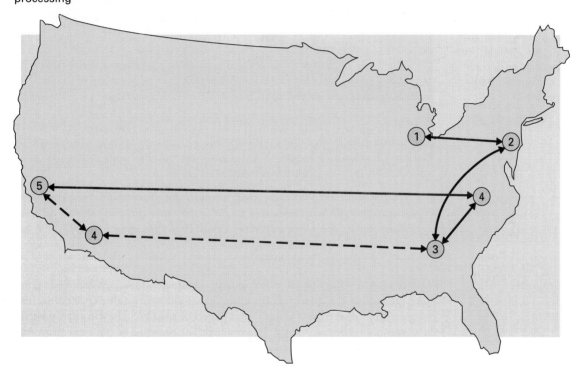

FIGURE 17.1 • The Trail of an Electronic Transaction

Source: Reprinted from October 8, 1990, issue of *Business Week* by special permission, copyright © 1990 by McGraw-Hill, Inc.

unfortunate consequence of this tendency has been the haphazard, bits-and-pieces management of information. Another is the costly inefficiencies that result from the collection of irrelevant or redundant information. In response, information management specialists recommend that information be viewed as a resource.

Although experts agree that information is a valuable resource, they disagree over exactly what kind of resource it is. Is information a physical factor of

This geologist would be between a rock and a hard place if some of his laboriously collected field data were lost. When organized, stored in computer files (with back-up copies), and interpreted within the context of a clear purpose, otherwise meaningless data become a valuable information resource.

production like land, labor, and capital? Or is it something else? According to Harlan Cleveland, a former high government official and university president, information is a very unique resource:

> *Unlike coal, automobiles, food, or clothing, information is* expandable *(it grows with use, enhances its value through dissemination),* diffusive *(it leaks and is therefore harder to hide), and* shareable *(if I give you food or sell you an automobile, you have it and I don't; if I give you a fact or sell you an idea, we both have it).*[6]

The fate of a juicy bit of office gossip illustrates these unique characteristics. Each person in the gossip chain embellishes the story (an expandable resource) when telling others the "secret" (a diffusive resource). They in turn pass it along (a shareable resource). Thus, information is no ordinary physical resource.

The Cost of Information

• • • • • • • • • • • • • • • • • •
Identify three factors that dictate the cost of information and discuss how information is organized.

If information is a resource, it must cost something. But the cost of information, unlike that of a gallon of gasoline or a pound of hamburger, is not easy to specify. Because information comes in many different quantitative and qualitative dimensions, the most productive way to address its cost is in terms of contributing cost factors. The cost of organizational information is dictated by three factors—*accuracy, timeliness,* and *reporting interval.* Managers who demand more accurate, prompt, and frequent information must also pay more in terms of invested time and/or money. American Airlines' SABRE reservation system is very costly because it satisfies all three criteria. Each hour of computer downtime costs American an estimated $34,000 in lost reservation fees.[7]

Organizing and Comprehending Information

While writing his acclaimed book, *Information Anxiety,* Richard Saul Wurman discovered an organizing framework for dealing with information. Regardless of the informational domain in which one is working—from writing a term paper to running a business—the same organizational framework applies, Wurman says. All information is organized following one or more of these criteria:

- *Category* (the topical chapters in this textbook).
- *Time* (an airline schedule).
- *Location* (a map of London).
- *Alphabet* (a dictionary).
- *Continuum* (the *Fortune* 500: U.S. industrial companies, ranked by annual sales).

Wurman offers this example by way of an explanation:

> *If you were preparing a report on the automobile industry, you could organize cars by model (category), year (time), place of manufacture (location), or* Consumer Reports *rating (continuum). Within each, you might list them alphabetically. Your choice would depend on what you wanted to study or convey about the industry.*[8]

As a validity check, try to think of a piece of information that does *not* fit into Wurman's organizing framework. (Remember, numbers taken out of context are data, not information.) An employee's badge number would be numerical information organized by *category*. Monthly sales figures would be numerical information by *time*. One's street address would be numerical information by *location*. A student's grade point average is numerical information by *continuum*.

Wurman also offers good advice on how to comprehend information. First, one must be interested in receiving a particular bit of information. Second, it helps to uncover the organizing structure of the information, as discussed above. Third, it is a good idea to relate new information to what you already know and comprehend. Fourth, test new information against what you know and explore it from different perspectives. "For example: what is an acre? To say that it's 43,560 square feet is an abstraction. To say that it's about the same size as a football field minus the end zones is graspable."[9]

Managers rely heavily on computers today for information processing, but, as Wurman's ideas emphasize, the need for mental discipline when managing information resources is as great as ever.

Types of Information Processing

Every information system has two parts, one tangible, the other intangible.[10] The tangible portion consists of all storage and processing tools and any physical data records. Traditional information processing tools include such familiar objects as pens, paper, typewriters, photocopiers, tape recorders, and telephones. Today, computers supplement or, in many cases, totally replace these traditional tools.

The intangible portion is made up of human beings and their mental and communicative abilities. These two parts are inextricably intertwined, and one cannot realistically be discussed without reference to the other. For example, the seemingly simple act of a production manager reading a quality-control reject report and then telling a quality-control inspector to loosen the specifications is actually a complex bit of information processing using both the tangible and the human components. Objective fact has been merged with subjective judgment in this situation. Organizational information processing can be classified into six levels of sophistication according to how much assistance the user receives from the tangible system.

1. *Manual Storage and Retrieval of Data.* Manual filing systems give managers access to transaction data. Any processing that must be done, such as adding up an employee's vacation days, is done by the user without the aid of a computer.

2. *Selective Data Retrieval.* Data are both stored and screened in an elementary fashion by the information system. A manager may, for example, ask for a list of accounts that are overdue by at least thirty days. Computers are normally used for this level of sophistication and above.

3. *Simple Computation.* Stored data can be aggregated (totaled) for the user. In this case, a manager might use aggregated data to compare this month's total sales with last month's.

4. *Advanced Computation.* More advanced arithmetic computations can be performed on retrievable data. For example, statistical averages, ranges, medians, and standard deviations can provide insight into a set of data.

5. *Mathematical Modeling.* Descriptive models such as PERT and break-even analysis (see Chapter 5) can be used to test the impact of pending decisions. They help answer management's "What if?" questions. Prescriptive models, on the other hand, can be used to select a decision alternative.[11]

artificial intelligence computerized imitation of human thought processes

6. *Artificial Intelligence (Expert Systems).* **Artificial intelligence** (AI) is the general label for attempts to get computers to imitate human thought processes. Expert systems, a subset of AI, are computer programs that mimic the problem-solving capabilities of experts.[12] Expert systems can help relative novices solve complex problems by putting accumulated expertise at their fingertips (see Managers in Action).

Computerized information systems perform clerical, information-provision, decision-support, and programmed decision-making functions[13] (see Figure 17.2). Cost increases significantly with each level of sophistication. Increased sophistication is appropriate as long as benefits outweigh costs.

Computers in the Workplace

computer an automatic data processor capable of arithmetic and logic operations

computer system a collection of components including data, hardware, programs, procedures, and skilled personnel

For our purposes, a **computer** is defined as "a data processor that can perform substantial computation, including numerous arithmetic or logic operations, without intervention by a human operator during the run."[14] A **computer system** is a collection of data-processing components including data, hardware, programs, procedures, and skilled personnel.[15] Remove any one of these components and a functioning system does not exist.

Expert Systems in the Workplace

Science fiction writers have long imagined computers with humanlike intelligence, machines that actually think for themselves. Well, they're here, and they're called expert systems. If you've applied for a loan or a credit card recently, or even had a can of Campbell's soup, you may already have benefited from them.

Like many computer programs, expert systems function primarily by going through hundreds of "if . . . then" routines, doing the kinds of simple "thinking" that we use to run our lives. ("If the clock says 6 a.m. or later, then I'd better get moving.") But expert systems tackle questions more sophisticated than "Should I get up now?" They help American Express decide whether to issue someone a credit card and they enable Hewlett-Packard to find flaws in faulty disk drives in 30 seconds rather than in days. They also help make scores of decisions at Digital Equipment Corp., ranging from how shifts in demand will affect production and inventory, to which accessories a customer will need with a mainframe order.

Computers can do all this because they are programmed with facts about their subject and with rules that human experts use to make decisions based on those facts. These facts and rules make up the system's "knowledge base," which is,

ideally, similar to the headful of experiences and information that a human expert carries around. In fact, that's where knowledge bases come from. A "knowledge engineer" endlessly questions human experts, trying to determine the facts and rules that the human uses to make a decision. The engineer then programs the computer's knowledge base to mimic the human's. If all goes well, the computer becomes the novice employee's best friend, helping the employee make difficult decisions without calling in the boss or waiting until the technician is free.

Expert systems can also reduce the knowledge lost when a human expert retires. Campbell Soup Company created its "Aldo on a Disk" in anticipation of Aldo Cimino's retirement. Cimino was the company's expert on the cookers that kill bacteria in soup. Before he retired in 1987, he spent six weeks telling knowledge engineers everything he knew about the cookers. Now, when a cooker has problems, Campbell can turn to the expert system to make the kind of decision Aldo would have made.

Sources: Jonathan Barker, "Expert Systems Explained," *Management Decision,* 28, No. 3 (1990): 51–54; Andrew Kupfer, "Now, Live Experts on a Floppy Disk," *Fortune* (October 12, 1987): 69–82; Otis Port, "Smart Factories: America's Turn?" *Business Week* (May 8, 1989): 142–148.

Smaller, Faster, and Less Expensive

Experimental computers developed during the 1950s were cumbersome, unreliable, and energy-inefficient. But with the development of the microprocessor (the so-called computer on a chip), today's computers are small, very fast, reliable, and highly energy-efficient. Room-size hardware has shrunk to desktop, laptop, and even hand-held size.[16] As computing power has skyrocketed, prices have plummeted. For instance, computing power that would have cost $15 million in 1966 became available on a quarter-inch-square microprocessor chip for $20 in 1981.[17] And things have not stopped there. By 1990, Intel and Motorola were manufacturing 32-bit microprocessors capable of handling 15 to 20 million instructions per second (MIPS), speeds formerly associated only with mainframes.[18] Supercomputer-speed chips capable of 200 MIPS are said to be just around the corner. Also in 1990, a $42,705 IBM computer workstation outperformed a

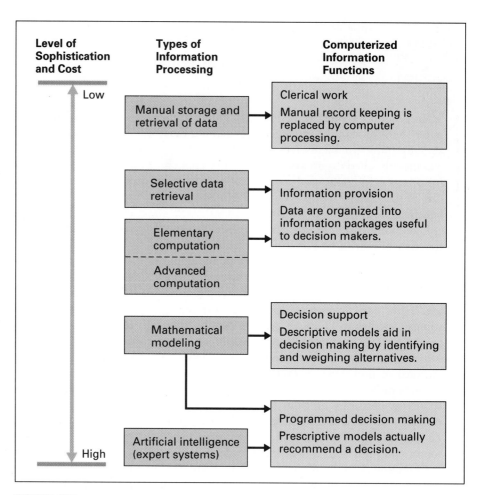

Level of Sophistication and Cost	Types of Information Processing	Computerized Information Functions
Low	Manual storage and retrieval of data	**Clerical work** Manual record keeping is replaced by computer processing.
	Selective data retrieval	**Information provision** Data are organized into information packages useful to decision makers.
	Elementary computation	
	Advanced computation	
	Mathematical modeling	**Decision support** Descriptive models aid in decision making by identifying and weighing alternatives.
		Programmed decision making Prescriptive models actually recommend a decision.
High	Artificial intelligence (expert systems)	

FIGURE 17.2 • Computers Can Help with All Types of Information Processing

$4,000,000 supercomputer in a controlled experiment.[19] Thanks to technological leaps such as this, the price-performance ratio for computers will continue to improve. Smaller, faster, and less expensive computer technology is completely reshaping the field of data processing.

Computer Configurations

Although it is not the purpose of this chapter to probe deeply into computer technology, some background discussion of basic hardware configurations is necessary. Each setup presents different information problems and opportunities.

Centralized Computer Systems. Computer data-processing hardware historically was centralized in one location. Full-fledged departments bearing names like "data processing" or "computer services" took shape around very large and expensive mainframe computers. These mainframe computers were segregated in costly climate-controlled facilities because of their sensitivity to heat and traffic. Although highly centralized, mainframe-based systems such as American Air-

• • • • • • • • • • • • • • • • •
Distinguish between centralized and distributed computer systems and explain the relative merits of each.

People who say they can't or won't use a computer often rely daily on one of the world's most sophisticated computer systems. It is the ultimate in user friendliness—the telephone system. Here, in the command center of AT&T's Worldwide Intelligent Network, traffic managers reroute calls to avoid congestion during peak times. Digital technology, the same as that responsible for the clear, crisp sound on compact disc players, is the backbone of AT&T's incredible computerized information network.

lines' SABRE reservation system still exist, they are rapidly becoming the dinosaurs of the information age.[20] Some companies are reluctant to give up their centralized systems because of multimillion-dollar investments in hardware and software.

In such centralized arrangements, employees at work sites outside the central data-processing department enter data (for example, payments on accounts receivable) through remote "on-line" terminals (see Figure 17.3). After data are processed on the central mainframe computer by computer specialists, statistical summaries and reports are sent back to decision-making managers.

batch processing processing stored data together at the same time

Centralized systems employ batch and/or real-time processing. **Batch processing** means that transactions are stored up, turned into machine-readable form such as magnetic tapes, and processed together at the same time. Time-sheet data for hourly employees, submitted daily from remote sites, could be stored on tape and fed into the central computer every other Friday. In contrast, data files can be updated immediately as each new transaction occurs, as is the case when **real-time processing** is used. Real-time centralized systems, such as those used for airline reservations, provide each remote-site user with up-to-the-minute status reports that take much of the guesswork out of decision making. For example, is a seat available on a certain flight so a ticket can be sold? Real-time processing eliminates the bothersome delays associated with batch processing.

real-time processing processing data as transactions occur

distributed computing system in which some portion of the computer logic function is performed outside a central location

Distributed Computer Systems.

The introduction of personal computers has produced a rapidly growing trend toward more decentralized computing. **Distributed computing** means that at least some portion of the computer logic function is performed outside a central location. Minicomputers (small, multiuser) and microcomputers (personal or laptop) enable people outside the central computer facility to perform computing tasks (see Figure 17.3). Distributed systems contrast sharply with centralized systems, in which remote-site personnel can only "key in" data on terminals that have no computing capability. When connected (on line) to mainframe or minicomputers, microcomputers are called "smart" or "intelligent" terminals.

FIGURE 17.3 • Centralized versus Distributed Computer Systems

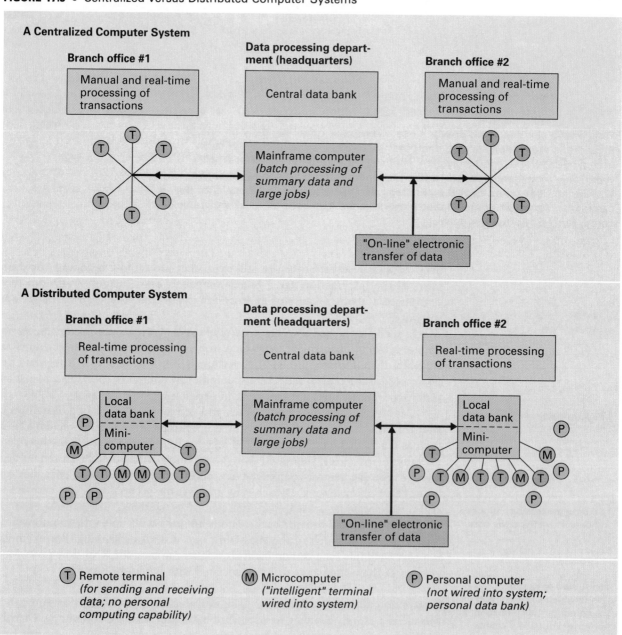

Part V Controlling

Compared with centralized systems, distributed systems offer flexibility, but at a cost—the expense of data security and coordination. Although centralized systems are called electronic dinosaurs, this traditional approach does offer an advantage that distributed systems generally lack: namely, *control*. In fact, one observer called the often uncoordinated influx of personal computers into the workplace "personal computer anarchy." In the final analysis, an organization's structural tradition will probably dictate the appropriateness of centralized versus distributed computer systems. Centralized systems will tend to work better in organizations with a tradition of centralized decision making (recall the discussion of centralization in Chapter 9). In contrast, managers who are used to wielding decentralized decision-making authority will probably demand access to personal computers to enhance their power and autonomy.

personal computer a desktop or smaller computer operated by an individual

●●●●●●●●●●●●●●●●

Explain how personal computers have revolutionized organizational data processing and discuss the significance of computer networks.

Stand-alone Personal Computers. The typical **personal computer** (PC) is a desktop size or smaller computer operated by an individual. It comes complete with its own input devices, central processing and memory unit (CPU), data storage capability, and output devices (see Figure 17.4). In just one decade, personal computers have revolutionized organizational data processing. Managers traditionally have been consumers of computerized information dispensed by programmers with access to large, complex computers. Moreover, managers typically have relied on clerical and technical staff to perform duties such as preparing correspondence, scheduling meetings, collecting decision-support data, and calculating statistical summaries. Now, however, with the rapid dissemination of personal computers in the workplace, many managers have became "producers" of computer-generated information. By 1990, in the United States, there were an estimated 28 million personal computers on the job, 8.2 million in the classroom and 27 million at home.[21] Judging from the proliferation of new models, clones, and size reductions (laptops, for example), the use of personal computers will continue to grow rapidly during the 1990s.

Many managers have already discovered that they can conquer bottlenecks and ask more timely and relevant questions by spending a bit of time at a personal computer. Decisions can be made more confidently and quickly if a manager can

FIGURE 17.4 ● A Typical Personal Computer System

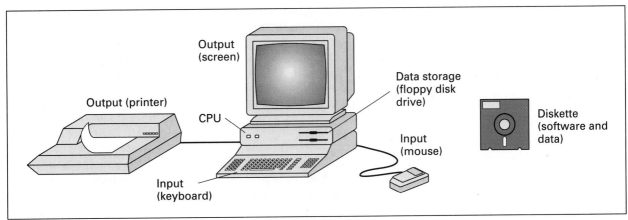

access a data base or spreadsheet program to test a "What-if?" option. Graphical presentations of financial analyses, budgets, sales projections, and so on can be prepared more effectively and quickly than in the past. Word processing often allows an individual to skip the first-draft stage of correspondence or reports in tightly scheduled projects. With electronic mail (E-mail) communications programs, messages can be sent to anyone on the computer network.

This turn of events promises to have two major impacts. First, managerial productivity eventually should rise; a representative group of managers in one study "spent about 25 percent of their time on such unproductive tasks as waiting for meetings or information, expediting assigned tasks, making copies, and arranging reservations."[22] Second, personal computing already shows signs of flattening the organizational pyramid. According to one industry observer:

> *The most far-reaching effect of [personal] computers may be on the power structure of the office—flattening the hierarchy, making it more difficult to hoard authority. Managers with computers quickly notice that they delegate fewer typing chores and less statistical analysis. Secretaries and staff assistants are sometimes eliminated or moved to other positions, but more frequently they are retrained to be designers and keepers of the new computer data bases.*[23]

Layers of middle managers, traditionally serving as conduits for information between the operating and strategic levels, are finding themselves unemployed partly as a result of the personal computer revolution.[24]

Computer Networks. The 1980s brought us a confusing and often incompatible array of computer hardware and software. During the 1990s, the bywords are "standardization" and "connectivity." The challenge for information technologists now is to get all the different makes, models, and sizes of computers to communicate with one another. Significant progress has been made of late.[25]

Computer networking involves connecting computers so that they can communicate with each other, allowing users to share programs, access common data bases, and exchange information electronically. The percentage of workplace personal computers linked by networks is projected to grow from only 15 percent in 1989 to 47 percent by 1992.[26] **Local-area networks,** typically referred to as LANS, involving the wiring together of computers in a single location or a restricted geographic area, have emerged as the most common approach.[27] Larger networks are possible. Texas Instruments (TI), for example, has built a computer network of global proportions, connecting fifty facilities in eighteen countries. All told, "the net includes 23 mainframes, 2,000 minicomputers, 31,000 terminals, and 36,000 desktop computers."[28] TI employees literally have a world of information at their fingertips.

Today's networks have evolved from the distributed systems in Figure 17.3 to ones in which *the network itself is the computer system.*

> *Networks, the experts say, can beat out the mainframe in most applications by assigning tasks to specialized microcomputer servers. Simple work, such as word processing, is best done in workstations and PCs. Complex tasks, such as searching a massive data base, performing lengthy calculations, or routing electronic mail among hundreds of workers, can be assigned to their own servers.*[29]

Computerized Supervision or Snoopervision?

Computers constantly improve our ability to find out what others are doing, or even thinking. Yet that may not always be a good thing. Electronic mail (E-mail) has taken over many of the functions of phone calls and letters. Networks of individual personal computers make efficient use of both people and microchips. Groupware is promising to make teams *the* unit of measure for many businesses of the future. A group of employees can now work on the same text together or use a computer to guide each individual through his or her steps on a group task. A program called Higgins even logs an employee's schedule so that others can check on it and see how the employee is doing.

This last example may give some sense of why critics call groupware and its kin "Naziware." Such programs, critics charge, make it all too easy for a boss to spy on an employee's work, and not all companies are going to resist the temptation. Already E-mail snooping has resulted in at least two lawsuits, one brought by Alana Shoars, an E-mail trainer hired by Epson America. Shoars was fired when she complained that the company had tapped into an E-mail line, giving it access to all E-mail entering or leaving the building.

Some sharing of messages seems ethical and even appropriate. When the head of a project is out sick for a week, for instance, other members of the project may legitimately want to read that person's E-mail to get the latest data. However, employees are likely to feel uncomfortable about the thought that their boss can read anything they write or receive on E-mail, even messages they consider private. The few federal privacy laws on the books are full of loopholes that allow computerized snooping for a variety of purposes. E-mail and groupware are so new that no laws have yet been written to cover them. Until such laws do appear and standards are established, employees should be aware that computers can open up their private lives, and managers need to be sensitive to employees' privacy rights.

Sources: Rich Brandt, " 'Groupware': Big Breakthrough—or Big Brother?" *Business Week* (June 5, 1989): 128–129; Rory J. O'Connor, "Your Computer Mail at Work May Wind up in the Wrong Place," *The Arizona Republic* (February 10, 1991): F3; Evelyn Richards, "Sorting out the Legality of E-Mail E-avesdropping," *The Washington Post National Weekly Edition* (September 17-23, 1990): 21; Jerry Rothfeder and Michele Galen, "Is Your Boss Spying on You?" *Business Week* (January 15, 1990): 74–75; Aaron Bernstein, "How To Motivate Workers: Don't Watch 'Em," *Business Week* (April 29, 1991): 56.

New team-oriented software, called *groupware* is being refined to facilitate the routing of work assignments and the monitoring of job performance via computer networks. Electronic committee meetings and problem-solving sessions also are a feature of groupware.[30] While computer buffs hail the possibilities of networks and groupware, others envision a sinister side, with serious ethical implications (see Management Ethics).

Developing a Management Information System (MIS)

Managers who do not foresee, read, and react to changes in the organization's vital signs cannot do their jobs well, if at all. In today's fast-paced world, it is harder than ever to stay abreast of things. Management information systems are needed to make sure the right manager gets the right information at the right time. A **management information system** (MIS) is a computer-based network that integrates the collection, processing, and transmission of information for an entire organization. An MIS is much more than just a computer network. *Strategic* and *systems* thinking are required if an MIS is to work as intended. IBM, for example, has made a huge commitment to its MIS. According to Terence R. Lautenbach, senior vice president:

> *This is one area where we are not the cobbler's children. Of IBM's top twenty customers, seven are IBM sites. . . .*
>
> *Fully 7 percent of IBM employees are in I/S [information services] functions. They support a worldwide IBM population of over 308,000 who use more than 250,000 intelligent workstations. Virtually every IBM employee around the world has access to the technology we make, sell, and use.*[31]

Practical experience over the last two decades has made it clear that management information systems are easier to conceptualize than to enact. In fact, MIS theory has been roundly criticized for being too idealistic. Accordingly, idealism has been responsible for most MIS failures because managers tend to go too far too fast. Successful MIS implementation is not an all-or-nothing proposition; it is achieved step by step.

We shall now examine key considerations in the MIS development process. They include system design, strategic control, and identifying information needs.

Basic MIS Design

Despite variations among management information systems, they share a number of common design components (see Figure 17.5). First and foremost, an MIS exists to serve the decision-making manager. An MIS's ultimate effectiveness is determined by how well a particular manager's information needs are met. As illustrated in Figure 17.5, an effective MIS responds to a manager's need (demand) for information by determining whether the required data already exist (supply). If sufficient data are available in the system's data bank (or data base), they are then transformed into the type of information requested. For instance, the average age of accounts receivable might be calculated as a basis for reviewing the company's credit-granting policy.

If needed data are not in the system's data bank, the system becomes a data-collecting device. Both auxiliary internal and external data sources are tapped if necessary. Management can gain access to a broad spectrum of general and technical information by subscribing to one or more of the many on-line data bases available today.[32] Newly collected, organized, and filed data are transformed into the information requested. For both existing and new information, the user may have the MIS perform a decision analysis, meaning that additional analytical computations are performed to refine the resulting information. The information is then an effective decision-making aid in the hands of the manager.

Strategic Control of MIS Development

An estimated 35 percent of all organizational computer systems, many costing millions of dollars, qualify as "runaways."[33] In short, these runaway computer

Not only does Ingersoll Milling Machine Company make the world's largest machine tools, it has also been a pioneer in molding itself into a truly computer-integrated business. Beginning in 1979, Ingersoll weaved every single aspect of its business—from product design to production to sales—into one seamless computer network. Engineers, accountants, purchasing and manufacturing managers, executives, and marketers all have access to real-time information because each is "on line." The net results are greater speed and competitiveness.

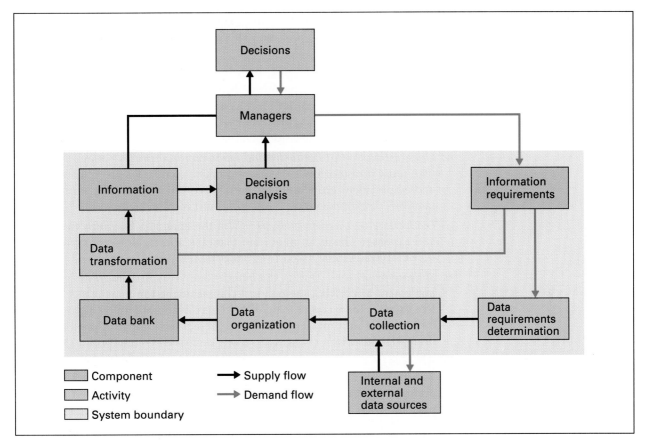

FIGURE 17.5 • Basic MIS Design Components

Source: John C. Carter and Fred N. Silverman, "Establishing a MIS," *Journal of Systems Management,* 31 (January 1980): 16. Reprinted from the *Journal of Systems Management,* Cleveland, OH, with permission.

●●●●●●●●●●●●●●●●●

Specify at least four common management information system (MIS) developmental problems.

systems simply don't work as intended. Angry customers, frustrated employees, and anxious stockholders are by-products of this lapse in good management. This stunning failure rate underscores the need for top-level control of the MIS development process. As with all other organizationwide programs, strategic control is a fundamental part of successful MIS development.[34] An awareness of common MIS development mistakes helps in this regard.

Interviews with MIS executives produced the following instructive list of common developmental problems:

1. *Lack of awareness of company's mission and goals on the part of computer specialists.*   Consequently, a technically marvelous computer information system may be designed and built with inherent practical, maintenance, and cost problems. Top management needs to ask basic questions from the start. "How will it help us to be more competitive?" "How much will it cost to build and maintain?"

2. *Absence of formal implementation plan.*   Incompatibility problems multiply when hardware, software, and network communication systems are

purchased haphazardly. Prior to signing off on a new MIS, top management needs to be convinced that all the pieces fit together.

3. *Failure to identify key information needs.* An effective MIS serves the information *needs* of managers. What kinds of information do specific managers need? When? In what form? Answers to such questions provide a customer-driven foundation for the entire MIS design and development process. (In this context, the term *customer* refers to the managers who will use the MIS as a decision-making tool.)

4. *Underestimation of hardware and labor requirements.* Today's MIS plan must fit tomorrow's organization. The company's projected sales and employment growth figures must be considered when planners calculate MIS development costs. Inflation must also be factored in.

5. *Inadequate cost-benefit analysis.* Will the final MIS be worth the time and expense? This is an important planning and feedforward control question that needs to be asked by strategists.

6. *Shifting priorities.* During the months and years it takes to design and implement a full MIS, the political climate at the top may change. Executive support for a certain type of MIS may evaporate following a change in command or a merger. A degree of design flexibility is a good idea, but dramatic midstream changes are costly and often counterproductive.

7. *Absence of a contingency plan.* What will you do if and when the system "crashes"? If natural disasters or terrorist threats occur? The crisis management program discussed in Chapter 16 can help management anticipate and prepare for the unexpected.[35] Management information systems are complex, and things can and do go wrong.

Identifying Information Needs

Managers require timely information to do five things: generate reports, monitor performance, forecast, plan, and make decisions.[36] The first step in that direction is to systematically identify managers' information needs.

Roadblocks. Systems analysts often run into roadblocks when trying to determine precisely the information that managers need. In spite of expert job knowledge, many people have a difficult time articulating exactly what they do. People also often wrongly assume that systems analysts already know a great deal about the job being studied. Compounding this wrong assumption is the fact that some systems analysts naively think that they know more about a job than the job holder does. And the problems are not all in the analyst's arena: mere mention of the word *computer* often brings up unrealistic expectations or prejudices that can hinder the identification of information needs. In addition, people often mix opinion with fact when discussing their jobs, thus clouding the issue. Systems analysts often have no way of knowing what significant details have been left out. A final roadblock is that job holders often do not have the time or interest for a complete information analysis.[37]

With an eye toward overcoming these obstacles, we now consider two approaches to diagnosing information needs accurately. The first is appropriate for all employees, and the second is best for top-level managers who oversee more than one functional area. Whichever approach is used, the process necessarily starts at the top and works down, ensuring that lower-level suppliers of information act in accordance with the needs of the higher-level users. Otherwise, lower levels would be free to determine the information their superiors see, and top managers could end up getting too much of the wrong kind of information, such as politically safe information that makes subordinates look good.

Conducting an Information Requirements Analysis. "Information requirements analysis refers to the act of identifying the meaningful data that a worker needs in order to perform a job or task."[38] One or more of the following techniques is recommended for those conducting an information requirements analysis:

information requirements analysis identifying the meaningful data that workers need to perform their jobs

- *Interviewing.* Interviews are the most widely used technique for uncovering an employee's information needs. Interviewing can be effective if the interviewer is skilled and the interviewee has had sufficient time to prepare. Questions requiring simple yes or no answers should be avoided.[39]

- *Paper Simulation.* An excellent way to understand information needs is to create documents that simulate the output of a hypothetical information system. This relatively inexpensive diagnostic technique requires the analyst to start at the end rather than at the beginning.

- *Brainstorming.* A rapid-fire exchange of ideas in a nonjudgmental setting can stimulate an employee to think creatively about information needs.

- *Protocol Analysis.* The important details of an employee's information needs can be obtained by having the individual "think out loud" while working through an actual or simulated job. Protocol analysis offers insight into the user's underlying thought processes.

- *Direct Observation.* When the job being studied does not involve a great deal of mental processing (for example, clerical tasks), information requirements can be identified by direct observation.

- *Questionnaires.* Questionnaires are appropriate when large numbers of people or geographically dispersed people need to be questioned. The quality of the findings will generally be a direct reflection of the quality of the survey instrument.[40]

- *Diaries.* This approach asks people to keep track of their daily information transactions for a representative period of time. Although a bit awkward when first attempted and subject to self-report bias, diaries are an efficient way of pinpointing individual information needs.[41]

Time, availability of qualified employees, and cost constraints will determine the particular combination of these diagnostic techniques that is appropriate.

Critical Success Factors. Information systems researchers at MIT have devised a practical method for getting top-level administrators to identify their *own* information needs. They call it the critical success factors (CSF) approach. **Critical success factors** have been defined as "the limited number of areas in which results, if they are satisfactory, will ensure successful competitive performance for the organization."[42] In other words, critical success factors are the strategic vital signs of organizational health[43] (see Table 17.1).

critical success factors key areas or results that determine the success or failure of the organization

TABLE 17.1 • Illustrative Critical Success Factors for a Petroleum Refining Company

Critical success factor	Strategic vital sign
Millions of barrels of proven reserves still in the ground	Supply of key resource
Success rate of drilling program	Drilling efficiency
Total number of producing wells	Pumping capacity
Average number of barrels pumped per well	Pumping efficiency
Unused capacity at refinery	Use of key productive asset
Number of days inventory of refined gasoline will last at low, average, or high levels of demand	Ability to meet demand
Projected demand for next six months, one year, and five years	Demand for product

Define the term *critical success factors* and explain their role in executive information systems (EIS).

Although critical success factors vary according to the situation, they usually are tied to four areas: (1) the nature and structure of the industry, (2) the organization's competitive position and geographic location, (3) environmental factors (for example, political climate, state of the economy, energy shortages), and (4) temporal factors (for example, loss of a key executive, a wildcat strike). Temporal factors include temporary but serious organizational problems. The benefits of the CSF approach are that it:

- Focuses management's attention on key result areas.
- Forces management to measure important factors.
- Differentiates necessary from unnecessary information.
- Draws management's attention to data that are needed but not normally collected.
- Emphasizes that information needs vary as time passes.
- Aids other functions such as planning and communicating.[44]

Advocates of the CSF approach recommend that critical success factors be collected in a series of two or three interviews with each top-level manager. Because there generally is little overlap between traditional financial accounting data and the CSF data requested by top managers, CSF information fills important gaps.

Executive Information Systems (EIS)

When it comes to giving them hands-on access to the computerized information needed, top executives have proven a very difficult group to please. In fact, according to one estimate, a surprisingly small 10 percent of senior executives reportedly use personal computers.[45] What they definitely *don't want* is to have to deal with arcane computer commands, confusing hardware and software specifications, and keyboards. What they *do want* is "transparency," meaning access to organizationwide information on demand.[46] Thanks to recent hardware and software advances, one answer has taken shape in the form of executive information systems.

executive information system
a user-friendly computer system that provides an executive with customized information on critical success factors

Politics Is a Problem. An executive information system (EIS) "is a computerized system that provides executives with easy access to internal and external information relevant to their critical success factors."[47] EIS are sometimes called executive support systems, especially when they include advanced communications options. After studying the implementation of an EIS at a large company, a pair of researchers found organizational politics to be the biggest problem. Middle managers tended to resent losing control over the flow of vital information as the EIS put top executives in direct contact with the farthest reaches of the organization.[48]

EIS Characteristics. Executive information systems have at least three distinguishing characteristics. First, they are tailored to a particular executive's information needs. Thus, virtually no technical training is required to call up information on an EIS. This tailoring, however, makes an EIS more expensive than ordinary information systems. Second, they make extensive use of computer graphics. Bar charts, trend lines, and pie charts are much easier to comprehend than are tedious columns and rows of numbers. Third, they are the ultimate in user friendliness. "Hot spots" on the computer screen, for example, can be touched by finger, pointed to with a mouse, or zapped with an infrared laser light. The desired information display instantly pops up on the colorful screen. Vital information such as budget variances is automatically color coded for easy recognition. Moreover, the executive can drill down from one layer of information to successively more specific layers. Five minutes after arriving at the office, a busy executive with an EIS can get an up-to-date picture of the company's strategic vital signs.[49]

Prospects and Problems in the Electronic Workplace

In this final section, we consider some important challenges that you as a manager will face in the information age. Specifically, we look at computer literacy training, computer security risks, telecommuting, and emerging information technologies.

Computer Literacy Training

Having a personal computer on one's desk and being able to use it skillfully and appropriately are two very different things. Managers who gain on-the-job access to a personal computer simply to boost their status and have something trendy to talk about at parties can wreak havoc with organizational information resources. Novices need systematic computer literacy training to head them in a productive direction. Proper training can also neutralize fear of computers[50] (see Insights & Issues).

This office has everything: a productive person, office furniture, reading material, a telephone, a computer, a watchdog, and a view. Best of all, this office is at home. Thanks to computerized information technologies such as computer modems, fax machines, and telephones, telecommuting is a growing practice today. Although telecommuting is not for everyone, it can save time, reduce traffic congestion, and accommodate people with special restrictions.

Computer literacy training is a lot like a driver training course. Novice drivers are taught to operate a car, not to build cars or tune engines. Similarly, computer literacy training teaches novices to operate personal computers, not to program and repair them. Consider the stated objectives of Allied-Signal Corporation's successful computer literacy training program:

> *At the end of the program we want people to be able to: (1) distinguish between micro, mini, and mainframe computers; (2) describe how a microcomputer could be applied to their own department; (3) use a set of questions and criteria to decide whether a microcomputer is appropriate for their department; and (4) use two popular software packages.*[51]

This program is successful because it gives managers *hands-on* experience that relates to their own jobs.

Some computer specialists criticize computer literacy training for being shallow. They recommend more comprehensive training in computer hardware and progamming to give managers a better understanding of the workings and potential of the organization's MIS. Computer literacy trainers respond by saying that too many managers are intimidated by obscure programming languages. They recommend user-friendly hardware, software, and training. Apple Computer's graphics capabilities and Microsoft's Windows™[52] are significant steps toward user friendliness.

Reducing Personal Computer Security Risks

Movies, such as *War Games,* and widely publicized accounts about computer "hackers" gaining illegal access to corporate, school, and government computer files have made us aware of the problem of computer security. Recent reports

What Is Your Computer Resistance Score?

Instructions: How well do the following statements describe you? Circle one number for each item, total your score, and check the key.

	Not at all like me						Very much like me

1. I have no desire to use a computer. 1–2–3–4–5–6–7

2. I don't trust computers. 1–2–3–4–5–6–7

3. I'm too old to learn how to use a computer. 1–2–3–4–5–6–7

4. I can't think of anything I would use a computer for. 1–2–3–4–5–6–7

5. Computers are too complicated for me. 1–2–3–4–5–6–7

6. The technical terms computer people use tend to intimidate me. 1–2–3–4–5–6–7

7. I'm not good enough with math to be able to program a computer. 1–2–3–4–5–6–7

8. I don't know how to type, so I can't use a computer. 1–2–3–4–5–6–7

9. I'm afraid to buy a computer because new technology will soon make it obsolete. 1–2–3–4–5–6–7

10. Computers are too expensive. 1–2–3–4–5–6–7

Total score = _____

Key

10–29 = Low computer resistance
30–50 = Moderate computer resistance
51–70 = High computer resistance
Note: See interpretations on p. 580.

Source: Robert Kreitner, Barry L. Reece, and James P. O'Grady, *Business,* 2nd edit. (Boston: Houghton Mifflin Company, 1990), p. 486. Used with permission.

●●●●●●●●●●●●●●●●
Discuss how management can reduce personal computer security risks.

about destructive computer "viruses" and "worm" programs secretly implanted within software have heightened that awareness.[53] At stake for the business community are data banks of incalculable value as well as trade secrets and employee and customer privacy. The rapid spread of personal computers has magnified the problem of computer security. According to a leading computer expert, "The back-door personal computers which appeared on middle management's desks without MIS blessing are unwittingly exposing the business community to potential loss of data and various other disasters, including corporate sabotage."[54] It would require a separate chapter to explore this complex topic fully.[55] Consequently, we will settle for outlining the problem here.

Three major types of personal computer security risks deserve management's careful attention.

Computer Hardware Security. This category covers everything from user hazards (such as spilling a soft drink onto the keyboard, damaging diskettes, or burning out the computer's circuits with a spark of static electricity) to physical theft and damage. User-tidiness policies need to be passed along during training. Antistatic mats or rugs and sophisticated locking devices are readily available today.

Information Security. By controlling access to stand-alone personal computers, stored information (on disks), applications software, and supporting documentation, management can maintain the integrity of information resources. Software, back-up disk, and documentation libraries with controlled access can help reduce information-security risks.

Network Security. The integrity of networked computer systems can be ensured by using impossible-to-guess passwords or coding, documenting user identification, and limiting and monitoring telephone access.

A respected computer consultant has summed up the security issue by saying: "Responsibility must reside with the user under policies which will be self-enforced. Central control may work now; it won't when the number of units in existence is so large it may be impossible even to identify all of them."[56] Security policies and risks deserve high-priority attention in computer training programs.[57]

Telecommuting

Alvin Toffler used the term "electronic cottage" to refer to the practice of working at home on a personal computer connected—typically by telephone—to an employer's place of business. More recently, this practice has been labeled **telecommuting** because work is sent to and from the employee's home computer via telephone modem instead of the employee commuting to a central office. The advent of overnight delivery services and low-cost facsimile (fax) machines,[58] combined with traditional telephone communication, has broadened the scope of telecommuting. According to one estimate, "approximately 3.4 million [American] workers have formed work-at-home arrangements with their employers."[59] Given that only about 350 companies engage in telecommuting, the proportion of these work-at-home employees who telecommute is still comparatively small. But this growing practice has produced positive results:

> *Mountain Bell claims that its telecommuters are 35 percent to 40 percent more productive than in-office counterparts. Says William Benham, chairman of the company's telecommuting division: "Employees who work at home develop independent work habits. They learn to set goals." He predicts that by 1995 one-third of the 69,000-member workforce at Mountain Bell's parent company, US West, will be telecommuting.*[60]

Despite some compelling advantages, telecommuting has enough drawbacks to make it unsuitable for many employees as well as employers (see Table 17.2). Still, in line with our discussion of workplace changes in Chapter 3, telecommuting represents a significant accommodation to individual needs and circumstances. Although telecommuting is unlikely to become the prevailing work mode, it is destined to be more than a passing fad.

TABLE 17.2 ● Telecommuting: Promises and Problems

Promises	*Potential problems*
1. Significantly boosts individual productivity.	1. Fear of stagnating at home.
2. Saves commuting time and travel expenses (lessens traffic congestion).	2. Lack of social contact with coworkers can foster sense of isolation.
3. Taps broader labor pool (such as mothers with young children, handicapped and retired persons, and prison inmates).	3. Work may compete or interfere with family duties and produce family conflict.
4. Eliminates office distractions and politics.	4. Can disrupt traditional manager-subordinate relationship.
5. Reduces employer's cost of office space.	5. Fear of being "out of sight, out of mind" at promotion time.

Promising New Information Technologies

Exciting new information technologies are emerging that will put ever-greater information processing capabilities at management's fingertips.[61] Two particularly promising information technologies are multimedia computers and tablet computers.

Multimedia Computers. Tomorrow's personal computers will process pictures and sound in addition to letters and numbers. What was once the stuff of science fiction has become reality with the development of computer chips capable of digitizing video and still pictures. Just as digitized sound can be stored and played on a compact-disc player, so too can digitized pictures be stored, retrieved, and manipulated on a computer. A **multimedia computer** is "a combination PC, television, videocassette recorder, and compact-disc player."[62] The potential for this merging of familiar technologies is immense. For example, using the technology illustrated in Figure 17.6, a marketing manager could put together a stunning presentation made of television segments, graphic data displays, music, and voice. In the near future, it will be standard procedure for students and managers to submit multimedia presentations on videotape or videodisc.

multimedia computer a combination personal computer, television, videocassette recorder, and compact-disc player

Tablet Computers. Someone once described the ideal personal computer as an inexpensive hand-held computer that would recognize voice and handwritten commands. Again, thanks to new microelectronics technology, science fiction is rapidly becoming reality. *Business Week* explains:

> *A new variety of laptops, so-called tablet computers, promises to make computers more accessible than ever by "reading" handwriting entered on the screen with an electronic pen. . . . That should make computers usable by the millions of workers and consumers who have never used a conventional PC. Already, such computers are being tested with traffic cops, delivery people, and utility company meter-readers.*[63]

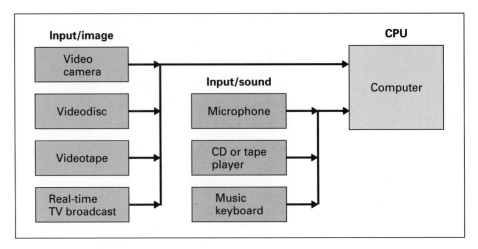

FIGURE 17.6 • Multimedia: Next Generation of Computers

Other names for tablet computers are notepad computers and pen-based computers.[64] Whichever name one prefers, the promise of greater computing convenience is evident. Who knows, maybe even executives who hate computer keyboards will learn to love their pocket-size tablet computers as they scrawl memos at 35,000 feet.

Summary

When properly applied, computerized information technology can give an organization a strategic competitive advantage. Isolated and disorganized data are meaningless because they do not help us achieve some purpose. Accordingly, information is data endowed with relevance and purpose. Information is unlike familiar physical resources because it is expandable, diffusive, and shareable. Since information is a valuable resource, it must cost something. Three factors that determine the cost of organizational information are accuracy, timeliness, and reporting interval.

Wurman observes that information is organized in five ways: category, time, location, alphabet, and continuum. When attempting to comprehend information, one should uncover its organizing structure, relate it to what one already knows, and test and explore it. Ranked by increasing levels of sophistication, six types of information processing are: manual storage and retrieval of data, selective data retrieval, simple computation, advanced computation, mathematical modeling, and artificial intelligence (expert systems).

Computer systems, made up of data, hardware, programs, procedures, and trained operators, are essential to organizational success today. Thanks to technological advancements, computers have become significantly smaller, faster, and less expensive. Traditional centralized computer systems are being replaced by distributed systems, stand-alone personal computers, and computer networks. The large number of personal computers in the workplace has transformed managers from passive consumers of computerized information into active "producers" of computerized information. Networks of microcomputers, often configured as local-area networks, represent the present direction of organizational computing. Accordingly, standardization and connectivity are the bywords for computerized information processing during the 1990s.

A management information system (MIS) is a computer-based network that integrates the collection, processing, and transmission of information for an entire organization. All types of MIS share several common design components. Their ultimate objective is to get the right information to the right manager at the right time. A costly 35 percent of all organizational computer systems fail to work as intended. Researchers have uncovered typical MIS developmental problems involving poor planning, failure to identify key information needs, underestimation of hardware and labor requirements, and inadequate cost-benefit analysis. A number of significant roadblocks can hamper the identification of information needs. Interviews, paper simulations, brainstorming sessions, protocol analysis, direct observation, questionnaires, and diaries can be used separately or in combination by those conducting an information requirements analysis. Researchers recommend that top-level managers identify their own critical success factors (CSFs) to ensure that they receive the information they need. An executive information system (EIS) provides a top-level manager with customized, user-friendly computer displays of critical success factors. Researchers have found organizational politics—stemming from middle-management resentment about losing control over information—to be the biggest problem for EIS.

In the electronic workplace, managers need to face unique challenges related to computer literacy training, computer security risks, telecommuting pros and cons, and new information technologies such as multimedia and tablet computers.

Terms to Understand

Information	Computer networking
Artificial intelligence	Local-area networks
Computer	Management information system
Computer system	Information requirements analysis
Batch processing	Critical success factors
Real-time processing	Executive information system
Distributed computing	Telecommuting
Personal computer	Multimedia computer

Questions for Discussion

1. What makes much of the so-called information that you are exposed to daily qualify as simply data?

2. Do you find Wurman's ideas on organizing and comprehending information useful? Why or why not?

3. What jobs have you had (or observed) that would lend themselves well to expert systems? Explain.

4. Why do you suppose centralized computer systems are destined to become a relic of the past?

5. What sort of experience have you had with personal computers? Summarize the positive and negative aspects of this experience.

6. Why are standardization and connectivity so important today?

7. What critical success factors can you formulate for your present degree-seeking program (or job)?

8. Are executive information systems (EIS) likely to play an important role in organizational computing or will they turn out to be a passing fad? Explain your reasoning.

9. Why is hands-on experience so important in computer literacy training?

10. Have you observed personal computer security problems firsthand? Explain the circumstances and tell what could have been done to prevent it.

Back to the Opening Case

Now that you have read Chapter 17, you should be able to answer the following questions about the Mrs. Fields case:

1. Is information a strategic resource at Mrs. Fields? Explain.

2. What, in your estimation, is the primary reason for the success of Mrs. Fields's computerized ROI system?

3. Has information technology had a positive impact on Mrs. Fields's organizational structure? Explain.

4. What are the advantages of Mrs. Fields's distributed computer system (versus a centralized system)?

5. As a cookie store manager, what critical success factors should you track?

CLOSING CASE

The Dinosaur That Cost Merrill Lynch a Million a Year

In 1987, Joseph Freitas had a radical idea—at least for someone who had always sworn by his mainframe. As director of investment banking systems for Merrill Lynch & Co., Freitas wanted to build a thirteen-city computer network based entirely on microprocessors. "We knew we were getting into uncharted territory," he says.

One of the most difficult parts of his quest involved finding the right software to manage the information flow over the new network. The challenge began when Freitas started phasing out the IBM mainframe that had served as the heart of his information system since 1983. Until this month, when Merrill gave the machine back to IBM, the firm had been paying $1 million per year in maintenance and leasing fees for it. "It became clearer and clearer that the system that was costing us the most money was actually the least useful," says Freitas.

Dealing Out Data

For several years, Merrill had been taking more and more work off the mainframe. By last year, it was doing little processing and was acting more as a central library that served information to 1,100 personal computers. Freitas realized that a computer designed to be a data base server could do that for far less. He bought a $500,000 system, based on multiple Intel microprocessors, from Sequent Computer Systems Inc.

To make the system work, he needed new software, which Saros Corp., a startup in Bellevue, Washington, designed for Merrill and a few other big computer buyers. The package, called Mezzanine, works like a library's card catalog, tracking what information is kept in each computer—no matter where it is on the network. The program also knows how to retrieve all that data.

On Merrill's network, Mezzanine keeps tabs on documents and distributes them. If a banker in London needs a prospectus that the catalog says is stored on a PC in Sydney, for example, he can simply grab it electronically. Without the catalog, "there would be no way of knowing if that document even existed," says Freitas.

Tracking clients also required new types of software. Under the old system, every time a Merrill banker contacted one of the unit's thousands of clients, a secretary would type up a report, which then would be entered into the mainframe by a clerk. That often took days. So bankers began keeping their own data on PCs. But that rendered the central data base useless. "We had no reliable way to tell if someone visited a certain client yesterday," Freitas says.

Under the new system, reports entered on any PC are instantly made available to all the other PCs on the network. That's because a special program from Gupta Technologies Inc. automatically routes the information back to a central data base in New York, where it can be tapped by other computers on the network.

Instant Updates

When he couldn't buy the right networking packages, Freitas rolled his own. Merrill programmers created Cicero, which works with Microsoft's Windows 3.0 graphics software. With Cicero, for example, a banker can ask for current and projected price-earnings ratios for five companies. The system then calls across the network for the latest earnings reports, gets price quotes from another source, and earnings projections from a third. This is done by bankers who don't know where each data base is.

Merrill believes its new network and software give it an edge over many of its competitors. "Our survival depends on fast information and knowing how to analyze it," says Freitas. Indeed, at a time when the financial services business is reeling and Merrill itself is taking drastic cost-cutting measures, a cheaper and more efficient information system can't hurt.

For Discussion

1. Why is it appropriate to say that information is a strategic resource at Merrill Lynch?
2. What roles do centralized and distributed computer systems play in this case?
3. Has Freitas built a true management information system (MIS)? Explain.
4. What critical success factors could Freitas use to assess the effectiveness of Merrill Lynch's computer network?

Interpretations for Insights & Issues

On close inspection, each of these ten items turns out to be an excuse, not a *valid reason,* for not using a computer.

1. A stated desire to not want to use a computer often is an emotional response motivated by fear of failure.

2. Computers don't make mistakes, people do. Because billing mistakes and other administrative problems are often blamed on computers, people have come to mistrust them. Computers do what they are instructed to do. If they are given faulty instructions, they will produce faulty results. "Garbage in—garbage out!"

3. True, computers generally are associated with the young. But that is no reason for older people to shy away from them. James A. Michener, the widely read novelist, did not launch his writing career until he was forty. Age is a state of mind, not a number.

4. A trip to the nearest computer store for some browsing will open up a whole new world of possibilities for using a computer for work and/or play.

5. Technically, computers are complicated. But user-friendly hardware and software are making them accessible for the average individual.

6. Computer users do indeed often engage in terminology overkill. Again, as computer hardware and software become more user friendly, the technical jargon will be pushed aside. Think of the modern telephone. It is a highly complex piece of telecommunications equipment. But it is so user friendly that you do not need a technical vocabulary to make a phone call. All it takes is pushing a few buttons.

7. This item involves two mistaken notions. First, although computers often are used for complex mathematical problems, you do not need to be a math whiz to operate the typical business program. Second, you do not have to be a computer programmer to be able to do work on a computer. All the programming has already been performed for you when you buy an application program for word processing, spreadsheets, and so on. Analogously, you do not have to know how to build and repair an automobile in order to drive one.

8. Though it helps to be a fast touch typist when entering data on a keyboard, many computer users do very nicely with their own version of hunt-and-peck. Moreover, other input devices such as a point-and-push "mouse" eliminate the keyboard altogether.

9. True, computer technology changes rapidly. But the key to buying a computer is finding one that adequately performs the jobs you need to accomplish, for a reasonable price. Even when new computers come on the market, you will still have one that "gets the job done."

10. Personal computers have been around long enough to permit the growth of a used-computer market. Used personal computers, still in good working order, can be purchased for surprisingly little today.

Source: Robert Kreitner, Barry L. Reece, and James P. O'Grady, *Business,* 2nd edit. (Boston: Houghton Mifflin Company, 1990), p. A-2. Used with permission.

References

Opening Quotation. Ruth Simon, "What I Learned in the Eighties," *Forbes* (January 8, 1990): 114.

Opening Case. Richard Brandt and Deidre A. Depke, "The Personal Computer Finds Its Missing Link," *Business Week* (June 5, 1989): 120–129; Dianne E. Kirrane and Peter R. Kirrane, "Managing by Expert Systems," *HRMagazine* (March 1990): 37–39; Stephen D. Solomon, "Use Technology to Manage People," *Inc.* (May 1990): 124–126; Katherine Weisman, "Succeeding by Failing," *Forbes* (June 25, 1990): 160.

Closing Case. Evan I. Schwartz, "The Dinosaur That Cost Merrill Lynch a Million a Year," *Business Week* (November 26, 1990): 122.

1. Quoted in Stephen D. Solomon, "Use Technology to Manage People," *Inc.* (May 1990): 124.

2. "William McGowan," *Management Review*, 75 (July 1986): 26.

3. See Jim Bartimo, "Wanted: Co-Pilots For Reservation Systems," *Business Week* (April 9, 1990): 78–79; Max D. Hopper, "Rattling SABRE—New Ways to Compete on Information," *Harvard Business Review*, 68 (May-June 1990): 118–125; and "The Computer Network That Keeps American Flying," *Fortune* (September 24, 1990): 46.

4. Peter F. Drucker, "The Coming of the New Organization," *Harvard Business Review*, 66 (January-February 1988): 46.

5. See James C. Wetherbe, *Systems Analysis for Computer-based Information Systems* (St. Paul: West, 1979), p. 36.

6. Harlan Cleveland, "King Canute and the Information Resource," *Technology Review*, 87 (January 1984): 12; emphasis added.

7. Data from Katherine M. Hafner, "Is Your Computer Secure?" *Business Week* (August 1, 1988): 64–72.

8. Richard Saul Wurman, *Information Anxiety* (New York: Doubleday, 1989), pp. 59–60.

9. Daniel B. Wood, "Showdown at Information Gap," *The Christian Science Monitor* (February 6, 1989): 14.

10. See R. Clifton "Dick" Young, "A Strategic Overview of Business Information Systems," *Managerial Planning*, 29 (March-April 1981): 28–37.

11. Adapted from John C. Carter and Fred N. Silverman, "Establishing a MIS," *Journal of Systems Management*, 31 (January 1980): 20–21.

12. See Gary Hochron, "Capture That Information on an Expert System," *The Journal of Business Strategy*, 11 (January-February 1990): 11–15; and Marc H. Meyer and Kathleen Foley Curley, "Putting Expert Systems to Work," *Sloan Management Review*, 32 (Winter 1991): 21–31.

13. This list of MIS functions comes from G. W. Dickson and John K. Simmons, "The Behavioral Side of MIS," *Business Horizons*, 13 (August 1970): 59–71.

14. William S. Davis, *Information Processing Systems: An Introduction to Modern, Computer-based Information Systems* (Reading, Mass.: Addison-Wesley, 1978), p. 428.

15. Based on David M. Kroenke and Kathleen A. Dolan, *Business Computer Systems: An Introduction,* 4th ed. (New York: McGraw-Hill, 1990), pp. 24–27.

16. See Deidre A. Depke and Neil Gross, "Laptops Take Off," *Business Week* (March 18, 1991): 118–124.

17. See W. David Gardner and Joseph Kelly, "Technology: A Price/Performance Game," *Dun's Review* (August 1981): 66–68.

18. Data from Emily T. Smith, "The Speediest Chip? Motorola Now Has the Bragging Rights," *Business Week* (January 29, 1990): 71. Also see Andrew S. Grove, "The Future of the Computer Industry," *California Management Review*, 33 (Fall 1990): 148–160; and Robert Neff, "The Costly Race Chipmakers Can't Afford to Lose," *Business Week* (December 10, 1990): 185–188.

19. Data from John Markoff, "Work Station Scares Supercomputers," *The Arizona Republic* (March 25, 1990): E9.

20. See Randall Lichfield. "Mainframes: ZZZapped!" *Canadian Business*, 64 (January 1991): 64–68; and Robert F. Morison, "Beyond Centralized and Decentralized IS: Virtual Centralization," *Information Strategy: The Executive's Journal*, 7 (Spring 1991): 5–11.

21. Data from Deidre A. Depke, "Home Computers," *Business Week* (September 10, 1990): 64–74. Also see Otis Port, "The Best PC Maker? Maybe It's You," *Business Week* (September 18, 1989): 126–127; Keith H. Hammonds, "Booting Up the Used-PC Business," *Business Week* (November 12, 1990): 130–131; and Cary Lu, "Macs or IBMs," *Inc.*, 13 (January 1991): 116–118.

22. "How Computers Remake the Manager's Job," *Business Week* (April 25, 1983): 69.

23. Peter Nulty, "How Personal Computers Change Managers' Lives," *Fortune* (September 3, 1984): 44, 48.

24. See David Kirkpatrick, "The New Executive Unemployed," *Fortune* (April 8, 1991): 36–48.

25. See, for example, Jeremy Main, "Computers of the World, Unite!" *Fortune* (September 24, 1990): 113–122; and John J. Donovan, "Beyond Chief Information Officer to Network Manager," *Harvard Business Review*, 66 (September-October 1988): 134–140.

26. Data from Richard Brandt and Deidre A. Depke, "The Personal Computer Finds Its Missing Link," *Business Week* (June 5, 1989): 120–129.

27. See Ting-Peng Liang, "Local-Area Networks: Implementation of Considerations," *Journal of Systems Management,* 39 (January 1988): 6–12.

28. John W. Verity, Peter Coy, and Jeffrey Rothfeder, "Taming the Wild Network," *Business Week* (October 8, 1990): 145.

29. John W. Verity, "Rethinking the Computer," *Business Week* (November 26, 1990): 118.

30. See Brandt and Depke, "The Personal Computer Finds Its Missing Link"; and Jim Bartimo, "At These Shouting Matches, No One Says a Word," *Business Week* (June 11, 1990): 78.

31. Terence R. Lautenbach, "MIS at IBM: Improving the Business through Better Communication," *Academy of Management Executive,* 3 (February 1989): 26.

32. See Daniel Seligman, "Life Will Be Different When We're All On-Line," *Fortune* (February 4, 1985): 68–72.

33. Data from Jeffrey Rothfeder. "Using the Law to Rein In Computer Runaways," *Business Week* (April 3, 1989): 70–76.

34. See Thomas H. Davenport, Michael Hammer, and Tauno J. Metsisto, "How Executives Can Shape Their Company's Information Systems," *Harvard Business Review,* 67 (March-April 1989): 130–134.

35. Adapted from Albert L. Lederer and Aubrey L. Mendelow, "Information Systems Planning: Top Management Takes Control," *Business Horizons,* 31 (May-June 1988): 73–78.

36. See Carter and Silverman, "Establishing a MIS," pp. 17–18.

37. Based on Albert L. Lederer, "Information Requirements Analysis," *Journal of Systems Management,* 32 (December 1981): 15–19.

38. Ibid., p. 15.

39. For helpful advice, see Paul R. Saunders, "Effective Interviewing Tips for Information Systems Professionals," *Journal of Systems Management,* 42 (March 1991): 28–31.

40. Adapted from Lederer, "Information Requirements Analysis."

41. See Leif O. Jepsen, Lars Mathiassen, and Peter A. Nielsen, "Back to Thinking Mode: Diaries for the Management of Information Systems Development Projects," *Behaviour and Information Technology,* 8 (May-June 1989): 207–217.

42. John F. Rockart, "Chief Executives Define Their Own Data Needs," *Harvard Business Review,* 57 (March-April 1979): 85–88.

43. See James Martin, *Strategic Information Planning Methodologies,* 2nd ed. (Englewood Cliffs, N.J.: Prentice-Hall, 1989), pp. 186–187.

44. Adapted from Rockart, "Chief Executives Define Their Own Data Needs," pp. 85–88. Updates on the CSF technique may be found in "As Information Proliferates, So Does Use of CSF Technique," *Management Review,* 73 (August 1984): 4–5; and Roger Dickinson, Charles Ferguson, and Sumit Sircar, "Setting Priorities with CSFs," *Business,* 35 (April-June 1985): 44–47.

45. Data from Joel Dreyfuss, "Catching the Computer Wave," *Fortune* (September 26, 1988): 78–82.

46. See discussion in Joel Dreyfuss, "Reinventing IBM," *Fortune* (August 14, 1989): 30–39.

47. Hugh J. Watson and R. Kelly Rainer, Jr., "A Manager's Guide to Executive Support Systems," *Business Horizons,* 34 (March-April 1991): 44.

48. See Robert B. Fireworker and William Zirkel, "Designing an EIS in a Multidivisional Environment," *Journal of Systems Management,* 41 (February 1990): 25–31.

49. See, for example, Jeremy Main, "At Last, Software CEOs Can Use," *Fortune* (March 13, 1989): 77–83.

50. See Nick Nykodym, Ian Miners, Jack L. Simoneti, and Joseph C. Christen, "Computer Phobia," *Personnel Administrator,* 34 (August 1989): 54–56; and Steven H. Appelbaum and Brenda Primmer, "An HRx For Computer Anxiety," *Personnel,* 67 (September 1990): 8–11.

51. Dan McElwreath, "Computer Literacy Training," *Personnel Administrator,* 29 (October 1984): 39. Also see Eric Vogt, "PC Education: Which Road to Take?" *Personnel Administrator,* 30 (February 1985): 59–63.

52. See Jon Pepper, "Should You Do Windows? It Depends," *Nation's Business,* 78 (November 1990): 44.

53. See John Schwartz, "The Hacker Dragnet," *Newsweek* (April 30, 1990): 50.

54. "Micros Vulnerable to Data Loss," *Data Management,* 22 (July 1984): 39.

55. See Melvin Schwartz, "Computer Security: Planning to Protect Corporate Assets," *The Journal of Business Strategy,* 11 (January-February 1990): 38–41; David Owen, "Expect the Worst," *Information Strategy: The Executive's Journal,* 6 (Spring 1990): 46–48; and Kenneth P. Weiss, "Controlling the Threat to Computer Security," *Management Review,* 79 (June 1990): 54–57.

56. Peter J. Haigh, "Assuring Security with Distributed Micros," *Small Systems World,* 12 (July 1984): 41.

57. See Rita P. Hull and Louis E. Serio, Jr., "What Managers Should Know about Computer Security," *Business,* 37 (October-December 1987): 3–8.

58. See John Burgess, "The Fax of Life," *The Washington Post National Weekly Edition* (June 25-July 1, 1990): 11–12.

59. Data from Jonathan N. Goodrich, "Telecommuting in America," *Business Horizons,* 33 (July-August 1990): 31–37. Also see "Revising a Forecast," *Training,* 27 (February 1990): 10.

60. Janice Castro, "Staying Home Is Paying Off?" *Time* (October 26, 1987): 112–113. Also see Dori Sera Bailey and Jill Foley, "Pacific Bell Works Long Distance," *HRMagazine,* 35 (August 1990): 50–52.

61. For a good overview, see Jerry Kanter, "New Tools, New Rules," *Information Strategy: The Executive's Journal,* 6 (Winter 1990): 51–54.

62. Otis Port, "Big Blue Plugs in a PC Multimedia Chip," *Business Week* (November 19, 1990): 88. Also see Maria Shao and Richard Brandt, "It's a PC, It's a TV—It's Multimedia," *Business Week* (October 9, 1989): 152–166; and Mark Trumbull, "Mixing Media: Costs Fall for Digitized Video," *The Christian Science Monitor* (February 1, 1991): 8.

63. Depke and Gross, "Laptops Take Off," p. 119.

64. See Brenton R. Schlender, "Hot New PCs That Read Your Writing," *Fortune* (February 11, 1991):113–123.

18

Managing Production and Service Operations

Fortunately, quality and productivity are two sides of the same coin. Everything you do for quality improves your productivity.

LEE IACOCCA

CHAPTER OBJECTIVES

When you finish studying this chapter, you should be able to

- Define the term *product* and explain the relationship between goods and services in today's economy.
- Specify at least three characteristics that distinguish services from goods.
- Discuss the concept of total quality control.
- Identify and discuss three characteristics of the "factory of the future."
- Identify and briefly describe the six criteria of vendor selection.
- Draw a distinction between push and pull systems of inventory control.
- Differentiate between product and process work flow layouts.
- Describe the nature of feedforward quality control.
- Explain how customers judge service quality and how service quality can be improved.

Boeing: A World-class Competitor

Most companies would do anything to get into the position enjoyed by Boeing Company. It is the world's largest aircraft maker and America's number one exporter. It has made about six out of every ten commercial aircraft now flying and has a $91 billion backlog of business that will keep its factories busy until close to the year 2000. The Boeing 747 is so popular that companies from around the world wait five years to get one.

Yet Boeing is undergoing changes and self-scrutiny associated with much less successful companies, and they're not just the result of an industry leader's fear of complacency. The commercial airplane industry is notoriously cyclical. Airlines generally order planes in billion-dollar batches, whereas their customer traffic increases more gradually. A company expanding to meet two or three big orders could find it has too much capacity when those orders are filled. Though Boeing has been on top of its industry since it introduced the first passenger jet, the 707, in the 1950s, it knows about hard times. During a slump in the early sales of the 747, in 1971, it laid off 95,000 of 148,000 workers. Developing a new airplane is so expensive that, in effect, Boeing's management bets the company each time it develops a new model, which helps explain why the 747 is still the firm's only jumbo jet. Economic shifts, fluctuations in oil prices, and world events can send airline ticket prices soaring overnight. When travelers stay home and the airline industry slumps, Boeing runs the risk of cancelled contracts.

Success itself caused Boeing serious problems in the late 1980s. Boeing has always prided itself on delivering planes on time and on offering customers an almost unlimited number of options. But the popularity of Boeing's 747—the aircraft of choice for rapidly expanding airlines of the Pacific Rim—led to overextension. Boeing hired hundreds of inexperienced workers to try to meet a frantic production schedule. Suddenly problems started showing up, especially in the planes' plumbing and wiring. The $120 million 747–400 has one hundred seventy-five miles of wires, seventeen lavatories, and a newly redesigned cockpit. Every 747 customer seems to want a different placement of seats, galleys, and lavatories. Boeing's assembly process was slowed even more because the more than 1,500 suppliers of the 747–400's six million parts weren't prepared for the deluge of orders. By 1989, nearly 60 percent of Boeing's workers had fewer than two years' experience, and for the first time in twenty years, Boeing had slipped behind on its delivery schedule—six months behind. Worse, customers who relied on Boeing quality were furious to find that their planes weren't working properly.

After patching up the 747 problems, Boeing set out to change the way it does business. In the short term, it brought in more experienced workers—transferring some from its military aircraft divisions and hiring others from Lockheed. In the long term, it decided to slow its production increases and invest more heavily in training. And it has radically changed the way it plans to build its next major airplane, the Boeing 777.

Although the company can't hope to produce a 777 until 1995, it already represents a big risk—it will absorb $4 billion in development money. The company needs firm commitments from some big buyers if the 777 is ever to fly, and Boeing's reputation is likely to bring in such orders. Despite glitches in the 747–400 and recent questions about Boeing's quality, its service and customer support cannot be matched. It has two hundred field representatives in fifty-five countries and seven major parts centers with 15 million spare parts in inventory. Boeing can get a part to a grounded plane anywhere in the world in less than twenty-four hours.

Boeing's plans are ambitious—to retain its reputation for service, rebuild its reputation for quality, and use new production and design concepts to simplify designs and make production more efficient. Japanese-style teams will design and build the 777. Representatives from marketing, engineering, manufacturing, finance, and service departments will work together at all stages, rather than waiting for "their turn." The teams will work with three-dimensional computer models that they can assemble and test, thereby reducing the reworking that typically must be done on the factory floor. The 777's unusual support structure will enable cabin design changes to be made more easily and with less cost than that of the 747. If an airline wants all its lavatories up front and its galleys in the rear, the changes won't cause engineering nightmares. By involving eighteen major suppliers in the design, Boeing hopes to dramatically reduce the six hundred requests for custom design changes it gets on most models. The company's goal for the 777 is a maximum of customization at a minimum of cost.

A look at Boeing's assembly facility gives some sense of why the company wants to simplify post-design changes. Boeing's Everett, Washington, plant—the largest building in the world—covers sixty-three acres with one roof. Behind its eleven-story doors, eight thousand people and one robot assemble one 747 and one 767 every seven days. Any design change that could simplify work flow layout is greeted with enthusiasm. One way Boeing keeps from going overboard in new technology is by giving customers the technology they want but letting other manufacturers experiment with technology so new that no one knows if it's needed.

Boeing hopes that the new elements of the 777 production will allow it to become more profitable. Though company revenues are impressive, profit margins are not. Increasingly, and with the approval of the American government, it is looking overseas for its profits. Exports accounted for more than half of Boeing's 1990 revenues. The company's relationships with Japanese customers and suppliers have been good, and some analysts believe the Japanese buy Boeing in part to help offset the Japanese-American trade imbalance. Whether or not politics plays such a major role, Boeing's worldwide reputation, foreign sales, and industry dominance make it a national treasure.

Boeing's international success is the direct result of greater strategic attention to the firm's product and service operations. To keep up with domestic and foreign competition, many large and small companies around the globe can be expected to imitate Boeing's high standards of excellence. This will require you, as a manager, to think creatively and in open-system terms.

Thanks to modern systems thinking, strictly analytical treatments of organizations are being supplemented by more encompassing synthetic approaches.

Anheuser-Busch means beer. Yet as a conglomerate also selling Eagle Snack foods, and family entertainment at Busch Gardens and Sea World parks, Anheuser-Busch is a collection of diverse operations. Skillful operations management placed Anheuser-Busch among the twenty most profitable companies in America during the 1980s, according to *Fortune* magazine.

operations management
designing, operating, and controlling a resource transformation system

• • • • • • • • • • • • • • • • • • •
Define the term *product* and explain the relationship between goods and services in today's economy.

Operations management, which concentrates on the processes involved in producing goods and services, is one such systematic approach. This chapter takes a look at operations management concepts, processes, and techniques that enable management to turn raw materials into marketable goods and services.

What Does Operations Management Involve?

Operations management is the process of designing, operating, and controlling a productive system capable of transforming physical resources and human talent into needed goods and services. Although some prefer the label *production/ operations management,* the more global term *operations management* is used here to emphasize that productive systems generate intangible services as well as tangible goods.

For at least four reasons, it is important that you know something about operations management:

1. Production is a core organizational function.
2. The production function commands the flow of resources through the organization.
3. Society depends heavily on the outputs of productive organizations.
4. The production function is tied closely to many serious societal problems such as resource scarcity, [periodic] inflation, and declining productivity.[1]

These perspectives of operations management, service operations, and the factory of the future are intended to serve as a backdrop for what lies ahead.

A Special Point of View

Operations managers view organizations as productive systems, complete with inputs, a transformation process, and outputs. As illustrated in Figure 18.1, this view conforms to the open-system model of organizations introduced in Chapter 8. The transformation process consists of interrelated parts, each dependent on the others. Among the important parts of productive systems are six activities: product design; production planning, scheduling, and control; purchasing and materials management; inventory control; work flow layout; and quality control. Together, these activities let managers carry out their economic function of transforming resources into useful goods and services.

Goods and Services as Products

Those in the field of operations management use the term *product* as a generic label for the output of a productive system. A product need not be a physical object; it can be anything from health care to an enjoyable meal in a restaurant. By viewing goods, services, and combined goods and services as products, operations management can be generalized to manufacturing and nonmanufacturing operations alike. Today, operations management techniques are used in hospitals, restaurants, stores, government offices, schools and universities, military operations, transportation companies, and a host of other nonfactory organizations.

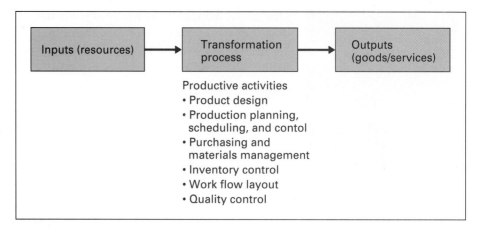

FIGURE 18.1 • Viewing Organizations as a Productive Transformation System

Bundles of Goods and Services. The distinction between goods and services is not so clear-cut as one might believe. In fact, we can envision a continuum, with pure tangible goods at one end and pure intangible services at the other end. Examples of pure tangible goods are televisions, bikes, textbooks, cars, and personal computers. Banking, transportation, telecommunications, realty, education, and insurance qualify as pure intangible services. Midway on the continuum are bundled goods and services.[2] It is important to note that most productive organizations turn out a bundle of tangible goods and intangible services. General Electric's refrigerator business is a good case in point (see Figure 18.2).

A Case in Point. A newly built refrigerator at the end of a GE assembly line is a pure good. Services start to enter the picture as soon as GE ships the refrigerator to an appliance store. A bundled good/service is said to exist at that point. The appliance store, in turn, adds to the service component of the bundle by displaying the refrigerator in an attractive setting, providing knowledgeable salespeople, and making home deliveries. At the pure service end of our continuum is the situation in which an authorized GE repair technician makes a house call to fix a noisy refrigerator fan. If the technician ends up replacing a fan motor, we are back at the middle of the continuum with a bundled good/service (the new motor is the good and the skilled installation is the service). With tough competition and more complex products, service has become ever more important. *Business Week* points out how GE has developed a competitive edge in services: "GE has dazzled dealers with its superfast distribution system. In most cases, major dealers can now get overnight deliveries from GE warehouses. This system, a competing distributor for Frigidaire says, 'had more to do with Frigidaire losing market share than pricing has.' "[3]

General Electric's appliance business is successful because its integrated bundle of goods and services is received well in the marketplace. Throughout the balance of this chapter, the term *product* will refer to both pure goods and pure services, but mostly to *bundles* of goods and services created by productive systems.

Unique Challenges for Service Providers

To a lesser or greater extent, virtually every organization is a service organization. Pure service organizations, such as day-care centers, and manufacturers providing delivery and installation services face similar challenges. Specifically, they need to understand and manage five distinctive service characteristics:

Specify at least three characteristics that distinguish services from goods.

1. *Customers participate directly in the production process.* Although people do not go to the factory to help build their refrigerators, they do need to be present when their hair is cut or a broken bone is set.

2. *Services are consumed immediately and cannot be stored.* Hair stylists cannot store up a supply of haircuts in the way that an electronics manufacturer can build an inventory of videocassette recorders.

3. *Services are provided when and where the customer desires.* McDonald's does more business by building thousands of restaurants in convenient locations than it would if everyone had to travel to its Oak Brook, Illinois, headquarters to get a Big Mac and fries.

4. *Services tend to be labor intensive.* Although skilled labor has been replaced by machines in some service jobs such as automatic bank tellers, most services are still provided by people. A haircut by a scissors-wielding robot is a frightening thought!

5. *Services are intangible.* Objectively measuring an intangible service is more difficult than measuring a tangible good. *Consumer Reports* magazine rates cars and refrigerators, but not trash pickups and cab rides. The U.S. government does, however, publish airline service records.[4]

These unique service characteristics have significant implications for management. Five implications spelled out by Ron Zemke and Dick Schaaf, who identified and profiled 101 respected service companies in the United States, are listed in Table 18.1. First, and most important, service organizations need to be *customer focused.* Customer input must be sought before, during, and after the delivery of service. Service quality is determined by the customer. According to Zemke and Schaaf:

> *Quality control of a service entails watching a process unfold and evaluating it against the consumer's judgment. The only completely valid*

FIGURE 18.2 ● The Goods-Services Continuum

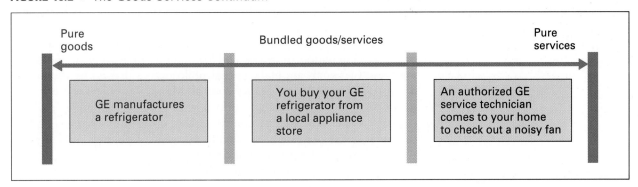

TABLE 18.1 • Secrets of Success from the Best 101 Service Companies in America

> - The Service 101 listen to, understand, and respond—often in unique and creative ways—to the evolving needs and constantly shifting expectations of their customers.
> - They establish a clear vision of what superior service is, communicate that vision to employees at every level, and ensure that service quality is personally and positively important to everyone in the organization.
> - They establish concrete standards of service quality and regularly measure themselves against those standards, not uncommonly guarding against the "acceptable error" mindset by establishing as their goal 100 percent performance.
> - They hire good people, train them carefully and extensively so they have the knowledge and skills to achieve the service standards, then empower them to work on behalf of customers, whether inside or outside the organization.
> - They recognize and reward service accomplishments, sometimes individually, sometimes as a group effort, in particular celebrating the successes of employees who go "one step beyond" for their customers.

Source: From *The Service Edge* by Ron Zemke and Dick Schaaf. Copyright © 1989 by Ron Zemke and Dick Schaaf. Used by permission of New American Library, a division of Penguin Books USA Inc.

standard of comparison is the customer's level of satisfaction. That's a perception—something appreciably more slippery to measure than the physical dimensions of a product.[5]

Later in this chapter we turn our attention to understanding and improving service quality. Also, as Zemke and Schaaf point out, *training* is a key success factor in labor-intensive service operations. This is a particularly important consideration today, in view of the reduced quantity and quality of America's entry-level workforce, as discussed in Chapter 3. Some of today's restaurant employees may require remedial math training to be able to ring up sales and count out change.

Lessons from Japan

As Japan has gained a decisive competitive edge in world automobile and consumer electronics markets, managers from other countries have studied Japanese factories in an effort to discover their "secrets" of success. But observers have found that instead of magic formulas, Japanese manufacturers have only a steadfast devotion to elimination of waste and continuous improvement (*kaizen*).[6] Underlying these two goals are management philosophies that go by the names *just-in-time production* and *total quality control*. Many Westerners confuse just-in-time production and total quality control with specific techniques such as *kanban*, discussed later, and quality control circles, covered in Chapter 12. But these two management philosophies actually are general guiding principles or ideals about producing better products at competitive prices. Just-in-time production and total quality control are introduced here to provide a philosophical base for operations management.

Just-in-time Production. Formally defined, **just-in-time production** (JIT) is "a philosophy that focuses attention on eliminating waste by purchasing or manufacturing just enough of the right items just in time."[7] Observers have called JIT a hand-to-mouth approach to production. In fact, this is what takes place at General Motors' new Saturn auto plant in Spring Hill, Tennessee, where the JIT concept was borrowed from the Japanese:

> *Rather than warehousing weeks' worth of parts, the entire Saturn complex could be called a giant loading dock. Trucks carrying parts from suppliers unload their cargo right where it is needed along the assembly lines.*
>
> *And Saturn uses a sophisticated computer system to tell suppliers what parts are needed each day and when to deliver them. That goes for in-house components, too. There's only a two-hour "float" of transmissions and engines, each for a specific customer's order.*[8]

Thus, JIT attacks the problem of bloated inventories that typically hamper American productivity. However, JIT involves much more. In pursuit of the JIT ideal, managers do varying combinations of the following:

- Purchase and produce goods in smaller but higher-quality lots.
- Design more efficient work flows by eliminating costly bottlenecks.
- Reduce scrap and rework.
- Prevent disruptive machine breakdowns.
- Enhance employee motivation through genuine participation.

Because of JIT, Japanese production operations are lean and flexible. Leanness is achieved by keeping work-in-process inventories to a minimum. Flexibility is achieved by reducing machine setup times so that single units or small batches of different products can be produced in rapid succession. Furthermore, JIT places more emphasis on feedforward control than is typically found in American companies. For instance, preventive maintenance is the *personal* responsibility of machine operators in Japanese factories pursuing the JIT ideal.

Total Quality Control. According to a management scholar who has studied Japanese factories firsthand, **total quality control** (TQC) is a strongly held belief "that errors, if any, should be caught and corrected at the source, i.e., where the work is performed."[9] Under TQC, each employee firmly believes in the idea: "If I don't do it, it won't get done." This belief contrasts sharply with the traditional American production operation, where quality control is something done by others at the end of the line. Not surprisingly, the large quality-control departments one finds in the United States are practically nonexistent in Japan. Under TQC, *every* employee, from the president to the janitor, is a quality control inspector. One observer has offered the following perspective:

> *In many U.S. companies a "we against them" attitude prevails between production workers and quality inspectors. As a result, workers keep potential problems hidden and shunt off defects to be reworked, and the pressure to meet delivery deadlines makes quality inspectors reluctant to delay delivery because of minor quality problems.*
>
> *In Japanese companies "we" is everybody, and "them" are defects.*[10]

The closest thing to a magic formula in Japanese industry today is an unwavering organizational and personal commitment to reducing waste and improving product quality. Fortunately, recent experience demonstrates that these ideals translate readily to other cultures.

> [Nissan's top executives in Japan] questioned whether Americans, especially those who had never worked in the industry before, could turn out trucks approaching the quality of trucks made in Japan.
>
> Nissan's Smyrna [Tennessee] plant has surprised—and somewhat humiliated—the Japanese. Although many managers there are refugees from Detroit—the plant is managed entirely by Americans—80 percent of the workforce had no experience building automobiles. Yet only a year after the plant opened, pickup trucks built in Smyrna are measurably better than their Japanese counterparts, according to customer surveys. Customers in Tennessee now demand Smyrna-made trucks from dealers rather than the imports.[11]

The Factory of the Future Has Arrived

• • • • • • • • • • • • • • • • • • • •
Identify and discuss three characteristics of the "factory of the future."

Stiff foreign competition and sluggish productivity growth are prompting revolutionary changes in the way goods are being manufactured in the United States and Europe. Production setups that would have been categorized as science fiction just fifteen years ago are becoming commonplace in a wide range of industries. The so-called factory of the future has arrived. Consider, for example, the following description of Apple Computer's new Macintosh computer factory just prior to its opening:

> [The $20 million] plant will be able to produce a Macintosh, with its 450 parts, every 27 seconds, or 500,000 a year. All of this will be done by just 300 workers, only 200 of them in production; labor accounts for 1 percent of the cost of making the computer. One of the keys to the increased productivity is cutting the time spent handling materials. Parts arriving at the factory are placed on conveyor belts that carry them to storage. Then, when they are needed for assembly, an operator has only to push a button to transfer them to the workstation, either by moving belts or by vehicles guided by wires embedded in the floor. In some cases, robots attach parts to circuit boards.[12]

Although push-button control and robots are dramatic evidence of the factory of the future, operations managers need a more fundamental understanding of what lies ahead in factory production technology. Three fundamental characteristics of the factory of the future are flexible manufacturing, computerized information and control, and integrated functions and systems.[13]

Flexible Manufacturing. For many years, U.S. manufacturers aimed for long, uninterrupted production runs of highly standardized products—in short, mass production. This approach was epitomized by Henry Ford's often-quoted declaration: "They can have any color they want as long as it's black." Economic theory about economies of scale lent support to this perspective by pointing out that mass production of identical products tends to lower per-unit production costs. For example, the thousandth piece of office furniture is cheaper to produce than the first piece because of such factors as the spreading of fixed costs, quantity discounts on purchased subcomponents, and learning from experience. Traditional mass production made economic sense when people were satisfied with look-alike products. But this form of production is too inflexible and unresponsive in our modern era of diverse and rapidly changing consumer tastes. Adopting a new economic perspective has become a matter of survival in today's global economy.

Thanks to the flexibility of modern automated equipment, economies of scale are giving way to economies of *scope*. **Economies of scope** are achieved when flexible manufacturing makes it economical to produce small batches of a variety of products with the same machines. The term **flexible manufacturing** refers to the ability of computerized machines to perform a variety of programmed functions.[14] Whereas the traditional economies of scale avoided change in an attempt to minimize costly machine changeovers, the newer economies of scope accommodate change. A good example comes from Ford's new engine manufacturing plant in Romeo, Michigan:

> *At Romeo, flexible manufacturing equipment and modular design will permit production of more than a dozen engine sizes and configurations on one line. The engines will share about 350 parts. That will give Ford unprecedented freedom to match the plant's 500,000-engine capacity with customer demand.*
>
> *The new plant will also allow inexpensive, rapid shifts to smaller, lighter engines—crucial if Washington tightens the Corporate Average Fuel Economy (CAFE) standard from the current 27.5 miles per gallon.*[15]

Ford Motor Company has indeed come a long way since its founder's insistence on only black cars.

Computerized Information and Control. As mentioned in Chapter 3, CAD (computer-aided design) and CAM (computer-aided manufacturing) are cornerstones of the factory of the future. (CAD is explored later in this chapter.) CAM involves the computerized control of manufacturing equipment and machines. Here is how one such computer-aided manufacturing program works:

> *A machine-tool operator can select, and combine from a color graphics screen, the geometric shapes that match the shape in which the metal is to be cut, and provide the location and dimensions of the cut. Conventional machine tools, by contrast, require every single machine-tool movement to be specially plotted. By eliminating programming steps, the system makes it easier to get a machine tool to perform new tasks.*[16]

CAM is the heart and soul of flexible manufacturing. Machine setup time, once a costly part of manufacturing, is reduced nearly to zero with CAM.

One of the more exciting developments in operations management in recent years has been the marriage of CAD and CAM to create computer-integrated manufacturing (CIM). This CAD/CAM marriage has been called "closing the loop." According to one CIM specialist:

> *Computer-integrated manufacturing (CIM) is CAD and CAM linked in a system that manages data flow while directing the movement and processing of material. With CIM, all manufacturing tasks and processes*

economies of scope achieved when the same machines are used to produce small batches of different products

flexible manufacturing ability of computerized machines to perform a variety of programmed functions

computer-integrated manufacturing the linkage of computer-aided design (CAD) and computer-aided manufacturing (CAM) within an organization's information and control system

can be put on software. This in turn means that the actual physical production of goods will be integrated with the company's information and control systems. CIM makes manufacturing a system. Manufacturing will no longer be independent: It will be inextricably linked to the operations of the entire organization.[17]

Robots with sensory capabilities promise to extend the scope of CIM even further. They will provide instantaneous feedback to the information system so that programmed adjustments can be made.[18]

One notable consequence of CIM is a higher break-even point. (Recall our discussion of break-even analysis in Chapter 5.) The high cost of designing and installing CIM, usually a three- to five-year process,[19] drives up fixed costs that have to be offset by greater volume. Manufacturing flexibility has it price.

Integrated Functions and Systems. Along with flexibility, *integration* is a key distinguishing characteristic of the factory of the future. "The factory of the future is highly integrated. Production processes are integrated within themselves and with other business operations. Manufacturing is tightly linked with design and marketing to maximize flexibility and responsiveness—the key features a firm uses to compete successfully."[20] This means that interdepartmental competition, conflict, and politics need to be pushed aside in favor of active project-oriented communication and problem solving.[21] Cross-functional teamwork, as discussed in Chapter 13, is required. For example, in factories of the future, engineers design products by working hand in hand with market research and manufacturing specialists.

Product Design

product design process of creating a set of product specifications

Product design is defined as the process of creating a set of product specifications appropriate to the demands of the situation. Generally, a good product increases but does not guarantee the probability of organizational survival. A poorly designed product, on the other hand, virtually guarantees failure. Marketing researchers tell us that each satisfied customer typically tells three others, whereas each dissatisfied customer tells eleven others.[22] Costly product recalls are often rooted in poor design. General Electric learned this lesson the hard way:

> *After GE's appliances unit reworked its large refrigerator, a new compressor began to conk out. Designers hadn't tested the mechanism enough for wear. It was a costly mistake: GE replaced every compressor and took a $297 million aftertax write-off in 1988.*[23]

It would have been considerably less expensive to have validated the design of the compressors in the first place.

Seemingly insignificant product design decisions can have enormous long-term consequences. In fact, about 90 percent of the cost of producing a product is predetermined during the design phase.[24] Fortunately, the area of product design has blossomed with innovations in recent years.[25] Among those innovations are parallel design, design for manufacturability, and design for disassembly (see Insights & Issues).

The Product Design Revolution

Not long ago, almost all new product ideas moved in serial, step-by-step fashion from research and development, to design, manufacturing, and marketing. Each group of experts would complete a step, pass the product "over the wall" to the next group, and turn to another product.

Lately, however, for economic, environmental, and marketing reasons, many companies are turning to parallel product design (or concurrent engineering). Teams composed of experts from every department in the company, from research to finance, work together on a new product idea. With the aid of sophisticated computer programs that can display a product in three dimensions, these teams can create the final design for a product without ever building a prototype. By the time the design is finished, they know how it will be manufactured, how long it will take to assemble, and how much it will cost.

One specific focus of this kind of parallel design is "design for manufacturability and assembly" (DFMA). As the name indicates, this process aims to produce designs that are easy and inexpensive to manufacture and assemble. It has been used by Ford, GM, IBM, and many other American companies. One success of the DFMA process is NCR Corp.'s 2760 electronic cash register, which has 85 percent fewer parts (fifteen altogether) than its predecessor and takes one-quarter as long to

assemble. One of NCR's senior manufacturing engineers can put it together in less than two minutes—blindfolded! The cash register, like most DFMA-process products, has no bolts or screws, which sometimes account for up to 75 percent of total assembly costs. Products designed this way are not only less expensive to produce, they can also reach the market in less time. So DFMA is being called America's answer to Japanese production superiority.

Some companies that have realized the environmental costs of disposable products have taken the process one step further and are designing for ease of *dis*assembly and recycling. That means not only avoiding screws and glue but also using fewer kinds of plastic. BMW has already produced a car designed to be disassembled and recycled—the Z1's plastic skin pops off its metal chassis in 20 minutes. In the future, bundling goods and services may mean that companies design products to sell and later buy back for recycling when they're worn out.

Sources: Bruce Nussbaum, "Built to Last—Until It's Time to Take It Apart," *Business Week* (September 17, 1990): 102–106; Otis Port, "Pssst! Want a Secret for Making Superproducts?" *Business Week* (October 2, 1989): 106–110; Otis Port, "The Best-Engineered Part Is No Part at All," *Business Week* (May 8, 1989): 150; William J. Spencer, "Research to Product: A Major U.S. Challenge," *California Management Review* (Winter 1990): 45–53.

Customer Input and Teamwork Required

Translation of demand into product design specifications requires a great deal of open-system thinking because of the complex combination of individual and societal demands on today's organizations. Meeting society's demands for safer products, a cleaner environment, and safer working conditions necessarily begins at the product design stage. Successful companies respond to the product design challenge in two major ways. First, they involve customers as early as possible. For instance, prior to its very successful launch of the AS/400 minicomputer, IBM made design changes in response to the comments and criticisms of 1,700 potential customers.[26] Second, successful companies rely extensively on cross-functional teamwork. Hewlett-Packard, for example, responded to stiff Asian competition in its computer-terminal business by designing a radically new terminal with 40 percent fewer parts than the model it replaced. The new design, which helped the firm realize a 55 percent savings in materials and a 75 percent savings in labor, resulted from a team effort among engineers and manufacturing and marketing specialists.[27] Good product design is good business.

Computer-aided Design

As discussed earlier, CAD/CAM is helping shape the factory of the future. Computer-aided design permits engineers to develop new designs in much less time than was required by the traditional pencil-and-paper method. Intel Corporation, for example, turned its $250 million investment in CAD to its advantage by designing its 486 microprocessor in less than half the usual time.[28] Design changes can be executed in about one-quarter of the usual time. According to one observer:

> Computers take the drudgery out of design. Instead of laboriously drawing and redrawing blueprints, engineers create designs electronically and alter them at the push of a few buttons. Some computer programs also analyze the designs to see how well they handle stress or changes in temperature. Manufacturers say that encourages experimentation, yields better quality goods, and helps them introduce products more quickly.[29]

One of the ultimate goals of computer-integrated manufacturing, with a CAD component, is to allow customers to phone in their particular product specifications for prompt translation into a design and then into a finished product. In effect, the phone call would trigger appropriate design and production process changes, thanks to computer-integrated manufacturing.

Production Planning, Scheduling, and Control

production planning formulating a resource transformation system to meet forecasted demand

Production planning is the process of formulating a resource transformation system that will effectively and efficiently meet the forecasted demand for goods and services. Productive resources include facilities and space, equipment, skilled and unskilled employees, and purchased parts and raw materials. As illustrated in Figure 18.3, scheduling and control are integral parts of the production-planning process. There is a dynamic relationship between production planning and the productive process. Production planning guides the productive process, which in turn affects future planning.[30] For example, if a vacuum cleaner manufacturer starts getting many complaints of poor quality from dealers and customers, that information is fed back into the production-planning process and translated into the necessary changes in standards, facilities, personnel, and so forth.

Needed: A Stronger Strategic Emphasis

For many years, Wickham Skinner of Harvard University and others urged top managers to pay more attention to the production function when formulating strategic plans. Skinner believed that too many important production decisions

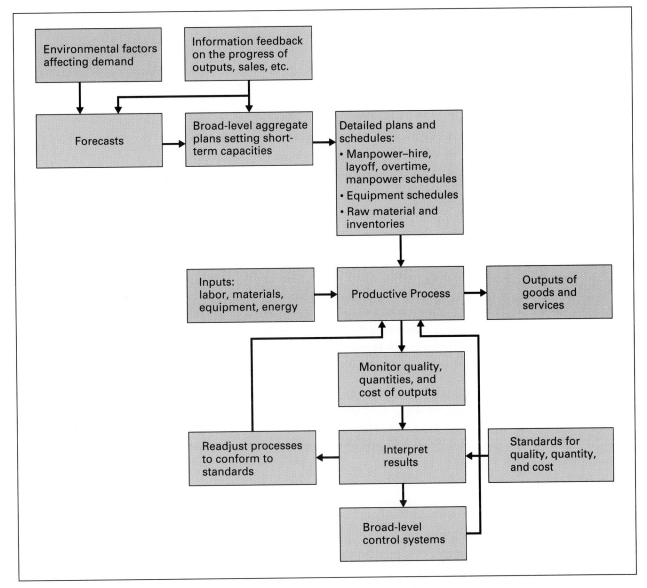

FIGURE 18.3 ● The Production Planning, Scheduling, and Control Process

Source: Elwood S. Buffa, *Elements of Production/Operations Management* (New York: Wiley, 1981), p. 113. Used with permission.

were left to middle and lower-level managers. He believed that production should be managed from the top down, not from the bottom up. According to Skinner:

> *This approach starts with the company and its competitive strategy; its goal is to define manufacturing policy. Its presumption is that only when basic manufacturing policies are defined can the technical experts, industrial and manufacturing engineers, labor relations specialists, and computer experts have the necessary guidance to do their work.*[31]

Belatedly, top managers have begun to heed the call for more strategic attention to production.

At the strategic level, production planning should answer these questions:

- What is our product?
- What shall we make and what shall we buy?
- How much shall we produce?
- Where shall we produce it?
- What technology shall we use to produce it?
- Where shall we get needed material and human resources?
- What core service skills do we need to develop?[32]

The production function tends to be uncoordinated and inefficient when these important questions are ignored by strategic planners.

The Master Production Schedule

master production schedule an authoritative statement of the quantity and timing of output

Coordination of productive activities becomes both more difficult and more important as product lines and facilities are added. This is when the master production schedule comes into play. A **master production schedule** is "an authoritative statement of how many end items are to be produced and when."[33] It includes the procurement of raw materials and subcomponents, fabrication, and subassembly production.[34] In a manner of speaking, operations managers use the master production schedule in the same way that a tour guide uses an itinerary. Because it tells what will take place and when, the master production schedule is the prime source document for activities such as purchasing, inventory control, and quality control. It also provides a rational basis for staffing and training decisions.

Purchasing and Materials Management

purchasing the procurement of needed raw materials, components, equipment, and services

It is not uncommon today for purchased materials to account for more than 50 percent of a product's wholesale price. Take Xerox Corporation's photocopiers, for example. More than half the value added to each photocopy machine during the production process comes from parts manufactured by other companies.[35] General Motors cars roll off the assembly line composed of 60 percent purchased parts.[36] When an organization decides to buy rather than make a portion of its product(s), purchasing becomes an important link in the productive system. In addition to goods, organizations purchase a broad range of services, including insurance coverage, consulting expertise, and housekeeping assistance. As the term is used here, **purchasing** refers to the procurement of raw materials, components, equipment, and services needed to accomplish organizational objectives.

Coordinating the Purchasing Function

Given the magnitude of today's purchasing expenditures, experts recommend the establishment of an adequately staffed purchasing/materials management department and the enforcement of clear-cut purchasing policies:

For a number of years, Stone Container Corporation wrestled with the problem of formulating and manufacturing a recycled paper without the familiar grayish look of recycled paper. Success was achieved in 1990 when the Chicago company introduced its Good News line of paper products. Under pressure to be more environmentally responsible, commercial customers like Burger King eagerly purchased Good News white bags. The look-like-new bags contain 65 percent recycled and de-inked newspapers. All this is good news, not only for Burger King and its customers, but also for paper recyclers who have suffered from an oversupply of raw material and limited demand for recycled products.

- Purchasing should do all the prime buying for every item or service the company purchases.
- Buyers should have the knowledge, willingness, and the authority to challenge engineering specs [design specifications] when, for example, they create unnecessary sourcing problems. [For instance, a purchasing manager may convince a firm's design engineers to use a more economical brand of electric motor readily available from a single, reliable supplier.]
- The organization of the purchasing function—centralized versus various degrees of decentralization—should vary according to the item being bought. [Centralized purchasing is recommended for high-volume and/or high-priced items.]
- All suppliers should deal exclusively with purchasing, or with others under purchasing's supervision.[37]

Variations in product or service quality and periodic inflation make intelligent buying a must.[38]

An organized and disciplined approach to purchasing also is necessary to curb ethical abuses such as payoffs and kickbacks. Purchasing is a particularly sensitive ethical area because purchasers decide who does business with the organization and who doesn't. Purchasers thus wield great power. Organizations must exercise control by establishing strong ethical policies and codes. General Motors has an ethical code for purchasers that conforms to the guidelines discussed in Chapter 4. The GM code identifies specific unethical conduct, covers

General Motors Tells Suppliers: Please, No Tipping

General Motors (GM) purchasing and suppliers are getting the message loud and clear, as spelled out in GM's Guideline for Employee Conduct Handbook: "A corporation's reputation is built by its people. What others think of General Motors is the aggregate of the personal integrity and day-to-day performance of all the people who work or have worked for General Motors."

It goes on to say: "No corporation representative or member of his or her immediate family will give or accept any cash, gifts, special accommodations, favors, or use of property or facilities to or from anyone whom the representative does business or is negotiating business on behalf of the corporation."

The intent of the policy is that giving or accepting anything of value is prohibited. GM's policy is that the monetary value of business gifts should be limited to a total of $25 per year. This includes items such as tickets to cultural or sporting events. Gifts bearing a logo or costing no more than $4 may be excluded from the $25 annual limit.

Giving or accepting the following items is strictly prohibited: alcoholic beverages; gift certificates; services or product discounts which are not available to all employees; jewelry; money. GM policy guidelines also indicate that entertainment should be "infrequent." For GM purchasing people, that is defined as twice a year per supplier.

GM personnel and suppliers at a recent meeting were told by a purchasing executive: "The acceptance of invitations to large corporate parties or banquets must be tempered with good judgment. . . . In all situations the GM employee's ultimate criteria as to the acceptance or refusal of any gift or activity must include the consideration of what unfavorable appearance might be placed on this action by a critical third party who has the advantage of hindsight."

It was stressed that GM and suppliers "must realize that the policy on gifts and gratuities is a major operation policy of GM."

The consequences for violation . . . can range from a reprimand to employment termination. Suppliers face the possible termination of doing business with GM.

To ensure an ethical and professional relationship with GM and its suppliers: Suppliers must stop thinking that entertainment is a prerequisite for doing business; and education within GM must continue, with employees realizing that being entertained is not a perk of their jobs.

Source: "GM Tells Suppliers: Please, No Tipping," *Automotive News* (July 9, 1990): 4i. Reprinted with permission of Crain Communications Inc.

---

all employees, is clearly and widely communicated with top management's full support, and spells out penalties for noncompliance. Moreover, GM makes sure its suppliers fully understand its ethical stand on gifts and entertainment (see Management Ethics).

Vendor Selection

Identify and briefly describe the six criteria of vendor selection.

Purchasing managers typically agree *who* you buy from is just as important as *what* you buy from them. The process of selecting suppliers or vendors should be characterized by systematic analysis, not haphazard guesswork. It is helpful to screen each potential vendor on the basis of the following six criteria:

Price. Shopping around and negotiating for the lowest possible price is nearly always an essential step in deciding on a vendor. Even seemingly insignificant differences deserve careful consideration. For example, a manufacturing firm that purchases 5 tons of copper wire every three months can save $1,200 per year by taking advantage of a 3-cent-per-pound price difference. Also, quantity discounts can offer great savings.

Quality. In accordance with the well-known computer principle "garbage in— garbage out," substandard and shoddy raw materials and subcomponents mean a substandard finished product. Purchasing specialists are constantly challenged to find the best possible product at the lowest possible price. At this point, product design and purchasing come together. Product design specifications are the basis for purchasing specifications. The trend in recent years has been toward closer working relationships with as few vendors as possible. When such a relationship does not exist, all incoming orders should be checked for quality according to purchasing specifications. By refusing to accept a shipment, the purchasing manager sends the vendor a clear signal that substandard performance will not be tolerated.

Reliability. Price and quality mean little if the vendor cannot serve the buyer's needs reliably. Taking time to check a particular vendor's track record with other buyers can pay off handsomely in the long run. Vendors may fail to meet their obligations for a number of reasons, among which are inadequate financing, raw material shortages, strikes and other labor problems, unreliable transportation, and overcommitment.

Service. Vendor follow-up becomes an important criterion in regard to the purchase of complex capital equipment. For example, personal computer and photocopy machine breakdowns can paralyze the flow of work in an office. Similarly, a construction company loses money when heavy equipment stands idle because it cannot be repaired promptly. Purchasers are advised to investigate the vendor's reputation for service and follow-up.

Credit. Does the vendor demand immediate payment, or are liberal credit terms available? By working in concert with financial managers, purchasing personnel can effect measurable savings by negotiating favorable credit terms. It is also possible to save money by taking advantage of cash discounts. For example, a vendor's contract that calls for terms of 2/10 net 30 gives the buyer a 2 percent discount if the account is paid within 10 days. Otherwise, the entire amount is due in 30 days.

Shipping Costs. The cost of getting the purchased goods from the point of manufacture or storage to the point of use is an important, if often overlooked, consideration in vendor selection. Otherwise favorable price and credit economies can be wiped out by shipping costs, especially in today's global economy. When the buyer has to pay shipping costs, it sometimes makes sense to purchase from a higher-priced yet geographically closer vendor. Shipping costs can also be kept in line by placing large orders well enough in advance of use to allow shipment by relatively less expensive forms of transportation (for example, by rail rather than air freight).

Materials Requirements Planning

Piecemeal handling of the various production functions (such as production planning, scheduling, purchasing, and inventory control) results in costly inefficiencies. As a result, a growing number of organizations have turned to a technique called materials requirements planning (MRP). **Materials requirements planning** is a systematic and comprehensive manufacturing planning and control technique designed to increase the efficiency of materials handling and inventory control. A practitioner explains:

> *Say you're making tape recorders and you decide to change to a new speaker. Does your present system tell you what the consequences will be in terms of how many old speakers now in stock must be disposed of? Does it make sure that you don't have machines busily turning out brackets to support that old speaker, that won't fit the new one? And how about the fasteners?*
>
> *A good MRP system answers such questions and greatly reduces the havoc that engineering changes can otherwise create.*[39]

Mature "closed-loop" MRP systems keep the production process on track by sensing and responding to feedback (see Figure 18.4). MRP systems are computerized because of the massive data processing involved.

An extension of MRP is *manufacturing resource planning* (MRP II). The primary distinction between MRP and MRP II is that the latter is organizationwide in scope. According to an expert on the subject:

FIGURE 18.4 • MRP Keeps the Production Process on Track

Source: "The New Game Plan: A Huge Potential Is There to Be Won," *Modern Materials Handling,* 36 (January 6, 1981): 68. Copyright 1981 by Cahners Publishing Company. Division of Reed Holdings, Inc. Used with permission.

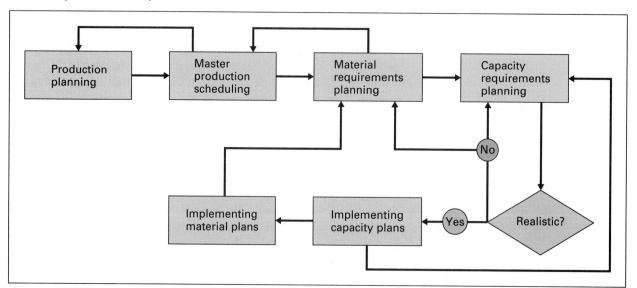

MRP II involves all departments, not just Materials Management. Engineering must maintain bills of material, Sales/Marketing must keep sales plans up to date, Purchasing and the shop floor must meet due dates. . . . MRP II provides a single, common set of reliable resource plans expressed in units, hours, and dollars for everyone in the company to use. . . . MRP II focuses on the fundamental manufacturing question—what are you going to make (production plans and master schedules), what does it take to make it (bills of materials and routings), what do you have (inventory status), and, what do you need to make (planned orders)?[40]

Because MRP is a subset of MRP II, it is good practice to start with the former and grow into the latter. Like other areas of management, experience is a good teacher.

Inventory Control

In regard to raw materials, components, and supplies, purchasing/materials management and inventory control go hand in hand. Except in just-in-time (JIT) operations, these inputs are not used the minute they arrive. They therefore need to be kept on hand for varying periods of time. But inventory control is more than just stockpiling purchased items. Partially completed products and finished goods waiting to be sold enlarge the scope of inventory control. Considering all types of inventory as a whole, manufacturing firms typically tie up one-fourth of their invested capital in inventories. Consequently, **inventory control,** the process of establishing and maintaining appropriate levels of reserve stocks of goods, is an important managerial concern.

inventory control establishing and maintaining needed stocks of goods

Types of Inventory

There are four categories of inventory: (1) raw materials and purchased components, (2) work in process, (3) supplies, and (4) finished goods. The first category, raw materials and components, feeds the productive system. Ideally, it is a steady and reliable source of inputs. Work-in-process inventories are necessary because the transformation process usually consists of a number of consecutive subprocesses requiring different lengths of time to complete. For example, when the JIT philosophy is not being followed, automobile seats are made and stockpiled for eventual mounting during the general assembly process. Supplies such as paper, typewriter ribbons, lubricating oil, and cleansing agents, which are consumed during the transformation process, also require stockpiling for use as needed. Finally, a finished products inventory is necessitated by fluctuating demand.[41]

In spite of subtle differences in the management of these various categories of inventory, all are subject to the same set of conflicting demands. There are reasons both for maintaining large inventories and for keeping inventories as small as possible. These competing demands are outlined in Table 18.2.

The 1980 eruption of the Mount St. Helens volcano in Washington state destroyed thousands of acres of trees. To the Weyerhaeuser Company this was an inventory disaster. To maintain their timber inventory Weyerhaeuser shifted its replanting efforts into high gear following the eruption. Weyerhaeuser has been committed to the concept of sustainable yield forestry since the 1930s. This Douglas fir was planted in a 1986 ceremony marking the completion of the reforestation project. It also marked the planting of Weyerhaeuser's two-billionth tree.

The factors favoring large inventories generally are the product of conservatism and fear of the unknown. Demands for small inventories are based primarily on cost considerations. Neither side is altogether right or wrong; both have merit. The challenge for operations managers is to make sure that inventoried items are available when needed without incurring unreasonable expenses in the process. MRP, MRP II, and a JIT technique called *kanban* (explored later in this chapter) can help managers keep appropriate inventories.

Managing the Inventory Cycle

Part of determining the best inventory size lies in viewing inventory management as a cyclical process (see Figure 18.5). The heart of this process amounts to

TABLE 18.2 • Conflicting Demands in Regard to the Size of Inventories

Factors favoring large inventories	*Factors favoring small inventories*
Fear of running out of stock.	Desire to minimize working capital tied up in inventory.
Anticipation of possible jumps in demand.	Desire to minimize storage costs.
Desire to keep ordering, shipping, and production costs low.	Limitations on storage capacity.
Desire to take advantage of favorable prices and quantity discounts.	Desire to keep insurance and tax expenses down.
Desire to have a hedge against inflation.	Fear of obsolescence.
Fear of unexpected events such as strikes, embargoes, and natural disasters.	Danger of spoilage.

deciding *how much* to order and *when*. Assuming that the usage rate for inventoried goods is relatively predictable, these two decisions are made regularly.

Before exploring the details of the inventory cycle in Figure 18.5 we should insert a qualification. The cycle in Figure 18.5 is somewhat idealized because demand for inventoried items tends to fluctuate. For example, approximately 60 to 70 percent of each year's toy sales are made during the six weeks before Christmas. Consequently, vigorous toy production early in the year requires large raw materials inventories that gradually taper off as Christmas nears and production slows. This type of seasonal fluctuation also affects finished goods inventories. Still, despite seasonal fluctuations, the basic points in Figure 18.5 remain valid.

Note that the inventory cycle has two dimensions, quantity and time. In this example, inventory on hand ranges from zero to 200 units. A safety stock of 40 units exists to reduce the danger of running out. Safety stock levels are based on prior experience and usage patterns and are used as insurance against running out and being unable to meet demand. Of course, proponents of just-in-time production reject the idea of anything more than very small safety stocks. Advocates of safety stock point out that exhaustion of raw materials inventory can bring the entire production process to a halt—for example, a shipment of roller skates cannot leave the factory until the wheels have been mounted. Running out of finished goods can be equally disruptive. "Selling from an empty wagon" means that time-consuming back orders must be processed later or, worse, that dissatisfied customers may be lost to competitors.

FIGURE 18.5 ● The Basic Inventory Cycle

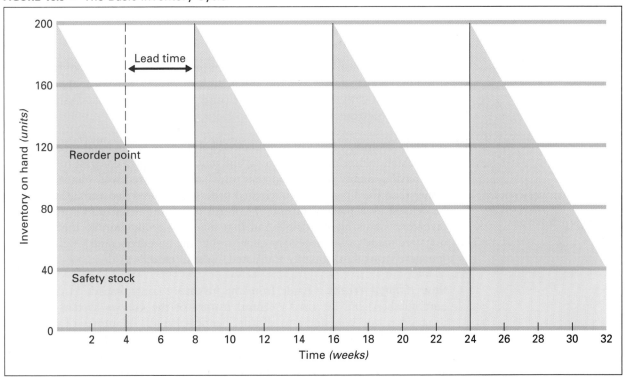

After safety stock levels have been determined, attention turns to ordering the right amount at the right time. Referring once again to Figure 18.5, assume that experience has shown that 160 units are used every eight weeks, or 20 units a week on the average. This average rate of use would fix the order quantity at 160 units. Next, the timing of the order should be determined. Suppose experience has proved that about four weeks elapse between the time the order goes out to the time the goods are received. Orders must therefore be placed at least four weeks before the inventory level reaches the safety threshold of 40 units. This four-week period is referred to as the *lead time.* Consequently, when the inventory level reaches the reorder point of 120 units, which is 40 units of safety stock plus 80 units (four times the weekly average), management knows it is time to reorder. Four weeks later, when the inventory stands at 40 units, 160 units are received, and thus the inventory is back to 200 units. In this saw-tooth fashion, the inventory cycle repeats itself over and over again.

Kanban: A Just-in-Time Inventory Control Technique

••••••••••••••••••
Draw a distinction between push and pull systems of inventory control.

In recent years, U.S. manufacturers have increasingly relied on what experts call *push* systems of inventory control in an attempt to economically balance the cost factors in Table 18.2. The most common inventory push systems are computerized MRP and MRP II. Inventory push systems operate in the following manner:

> *A push system in reality is simply a schedule-based system. That is, a multiperiod schedule of future demands for the company's products (called a master production schedule) is prepared, and the computer breaks that schedule down into detailed schedules for making or buying the component parts. It is a push system in that the schedule pushes the production people into making the required parts and then pushing the parts out and onward.*[42]

In a sense, this push approach is a Western (non-Japanese) version of just-in-time inventory management. All too often, unfortunately, the push approach gets bogged down with excess inventory because of inaccurate demand estimates and work flow bottlenecks.

A "Pull" System. *Kanban* (pronounced kahn bahn) is a manual inventory control technique developed by Toyota, and it stands in sharp contrast to computerized push systems. It relies on the "pull" of orders received (actual demand) rather than the "push" of anticipated orders (estimated demand). *Kanban* may be defined as a manual inventory control procedure "that uses cards to keep inventory status highly visible and that manages production so that necessary units are made in the necessary quantities at the necessary time."[43] *Kanban* is a Japanese word that, roughly translated, means "card."

kanban Japanese word for a manual inventory control system using cards

How *Kanban* Works. Aside from the inventory control cards inscribed with part numbers and lot size, a central feature of the *kanban* system is the use of standardized containers to shuttle identical (small) quantities of parts from workstation to workstation. By switching cards (*kanban*) from containers of unprocessed parts to containers of processed parts and keeping tallies, a workstation operator (such as a milling machine operator) *pulls* inventory through

A fixed-position, work-flow layout gives these McDonnell Douglas employees the capacity to produce twenty-nine C-17 aircraft a year. Because these military transport planes are too cumbersome to move around during construction, everyone involved in the production effort—managers, engineers, technicians, inspectors, and laborers—go to a fixed location. Employees generally find this arrangement more interesting than working on an assembly line.

work flow layout the physical arrangement of a productive system

the production system on a just-in-time basis. An upstream container of parts is not processed until the *kanban* of the downstream container signals the go-ahead.

Managers can fine-tune the flow of work by adding or removing containers of parts with attached *kanban* from the production cycle. Unlike decisions made with computerized push systems such as MRP, these vital decisions are made on the basis of actual, not projected, demand. Despite the apparent primitiveness of manually switching inventory cards in the midst of the computer age, Toyota and other *kanban* users have boosted their productivity significantly by keeping work-in-process inventories to the barest minimum.[44]

A Contingency Approach Compromise.   According to one operations management scholar, the growing argument between proponents of push and pull inventory control systems is pointless. He contends that each approach has its pros and cons, and MRP II and *kanban* can both play valuable roles in a hybrid system. Generally, MRP II is suitable for organizational long-term planning, whereas *kanban* is appropriate for short-term, local control of daily operations. The result is a tandem push-pull inventory system.[45]

Work Flow Layout

Because the transformation of resources into finished goods involves a system, every part of it is important, including the physical movement of work through the production cycle. This aspect of operations management is called **work flow layout,** the process of determining the physical arrangement of the productive system. People, machines, and workstations can be scattered about haphazardly, or they can be arranged in a logical, orderly, and cost-effective manner. This is as true for manufacturing operations as it is for service operations, such as libraries and fast-food restaurants.

Benefits of Good Work Flow Layout

Experts suggest that a good layout of a production operation will accomplish the following:

1. Minimize investment in equipment.
2. Minimize overall production time.
3. Use existing space most effectively.
4. Provide for employee convenience, safety, and comfort.
5. Maintain flexibility of arrangement and operation.
6. Minimize material-handling cost.
7. Minimize variation in types of materal-handling equipment.
8. Facilitate the manufacturing [or service] process.
9. Facilitate the organizational structure.[46]

Balancing these often conflicting considerations is an essential task for operations managers. An understanding of basic layout formats is helpful.

Layout Formats

Although a manager can devise innumerable production layout configurations, all fall into three basic formats: the product layout, the process layout, and the fixed-position layout (see Figure 18.6). Others are simply variations or hybrid combinations of the basic three. The three layouts are defined as follows:

product layout an assembly line arrangement involving progressive steps

- A **product layout** is one in which the components are arranged according to the progressive steps by which the product is made. Conceptually, the flow is an unbroken line from raw material input to finished goods. This type of layout is exemplified in automobile assembly, food processing, and furniture manufacture.

process layout production arrangement in which tools and machines are grouped by function

- A **process layout** (or functional layout) is one in which the components are grouped according to the general function they perform, without re-gard to any particular product. Custom job shops, department stores, and hospitals are generally arranged in this manner.

fixed-position layout product remains in one location

- A **fixed-position layout** is one in which the product, by virtue of its bulk and weight, remains at one location. The equipment required for product manufacture is moved to the product rather than vice versa. Sound stages on a movie lot, aircraft assembly shops, and shipyards typify this mode of layout.[47]

Advantages and Disadvantages of Layout Formats

Each layout format has advantages and disadvantages. In product layouts, one supervisor can oversee the work of many semiskilled workers. But assembly line operations tend to be inflexible and, for employees, monotonous. In contrast, process layouts are more flexible than product layouts, but not as fast. Process layouts also have the advantage of being suitable for the custom processing of diverse products. On the minus side, work scheduling is also much more difficult in process layouts than in product layouts, in which the production sequence is fixed. Care needs to be taken not to overload one department and let others sit idle. Finally, fixed-position layouts are costly because of the duplication of talent and tools when more than one project is in progress at once. But fixed-position layouts tend to be popular among employees, who are able to move about freely rather than being restricted to a single workstation. The fixed-position format is readily adapted to team-oriented service situations:

> *Aetna Life recently reorganized its home office operations into self-managed teams—combining clerks, technical writers, underwriters, and financial analysts—to handle customer requests and complaints. To facilitate teamwork, Aetna is using a new line of "team" furniture designed by Steelcase.*
>
> *The furniture establishes small areas that the folks at Steelcase call neighborhoods. A central work area with a table lets teams meet when they need to, while nearby desks provide privacy.*[48]

Previously, Aetna employees had to run to various locations in the building to get anything done.

Quality Control

As recently as a dozen years ago, American industry was roundly criticized for taking product quality too lightly. Today, things have come full circle, with attention to quality at a fever pitch. Companies such as Ford trumpet their devotion to quality in their advertisements. Now there is even a national trophy for quality that means prestige and lots of free media exposure for the winners. The Malcolm Baldrige National Quality Award, named for a former U.S. Secretary of Commerce, was launched by Congress in 1987 to encourage and reward

FIGURE 18.6 • Basic Production Layout Formats

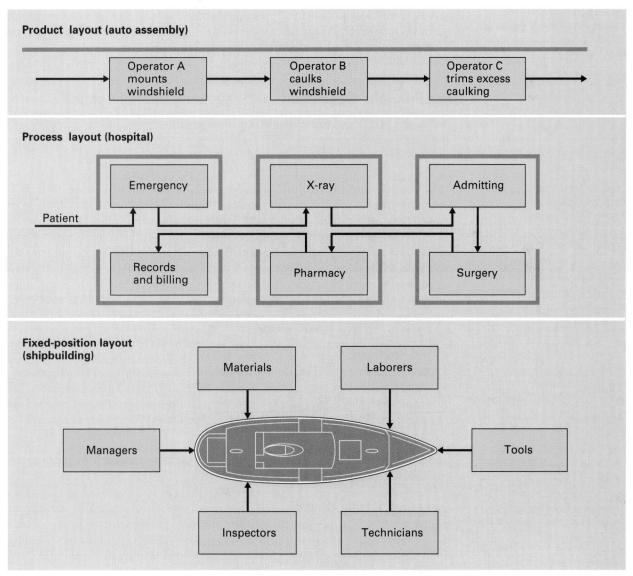

world-class quality.[49] Winners have included Xerox, textile-maker Milliken, IBM, Motorola, and General Motors' Cadillac Division. Even so, American industry still has a long way to go. Detroit's response to intense Japanese competition is an illustrative case in point. In 1990, after a decade of dramatic improvement, the quality of American-made automobiles was said to be somewhat better than the quality of Japan's 1980 models![50] Japanese auto quality, also significantly improved during the 1980s, is not standing still while Detroit tries to catch up.

In addition to stiff international and domestic competition, there is another important stimulus for improving quality. Customers who are injured or sustain a loss because of a faulty product are turning more and more to the courts. Product liability lawsuits remain an ever-present threat, despite recent attempts to legislate liability limits.[51] **Quality control** is the process of ensuring that goods and services closely conform to design specifications.[52] Let us take important steps toward meeting the quality improvement challenge by exploring three types of quality control and focusing on service quality.

quality control ensuring that goods and services closely conform to design specifications

Feedforward, Concurrent, and Feedback Quality Control

In Chapter 16, three types of control were identified: feedforward, concurrent, and feedback. Accordingly, there are three types of *quality* control (see Figure 18.7). Each requires a closer look.

feedforward quality control preventing and screening out substandard parts

Feedforward Quality Control. **Feedforward quality control** is the process of preventing and screening out substandard inputs. This sort of anticipatory approach to quality thrives on the philosophy of total quality control (TQC), where every employee is a quality inspector. Although traditional inspection of purchased raw materials and subcomponents for defects is still important, the primary focus has shifted in recent years to better working relationships with fewer suppliers. As mentioned earlier, the idea is to work closely with a few select vendors to help them achieve higher quality standards. Honda's U.S. motorcycle operation has had significant success with this new approach.

● ● ● ● ● ● ● ● ● ● ● ● ● ● ● ● ●
Describe the nature of feedforward quality control.

> *Two years ago, for example, an Ohio-based supplier struggled to paint the motorcycle parts it had begun selling to Honda. Only one in twenty was deemed fit to ship without reworking. Tom Griffith, senior engineer for Honda's purchasing staff, recruited fifteen Honda volunteers, who spent their week-long Fourth of July vacation coaching the supplier's workers. By the end of the week, four out of five parts were acceptable after the first pass.[53]*

Cooperation and teamwork are the keys to this new approach to feedforward quality control.

concurrent quality control monitoring the quality of work in process

Concurrent Quality Control. After the production process begins, **concurrent quality control** is necessary to monitor the quality of work in process. How should mangement tackle this difficult task? According to W. Edwards Deming, the American father of Japan's post–Second World War quality revolution, sta-

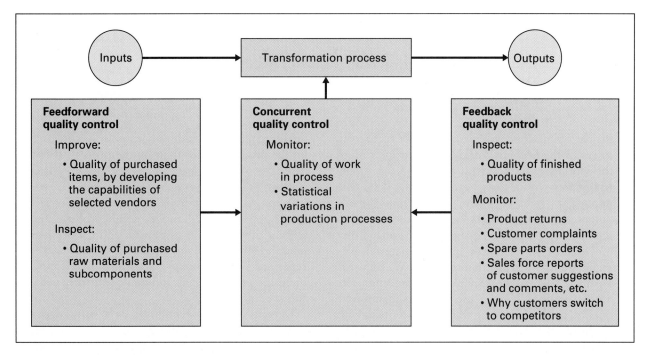

FIGURE 18.7 • Three Types of Quality Control

statistical process control
measuring and managing normal and abnormal variations in production processes

tistical analysis is the answer. Specifically, Deming recommends **statistical process control** (SPC), the process of measuring and managing normal and abnormal variations in production processes[54] (see The World of Management).

In addition to SPC, other prudent steps can be taken during concurrent quality control. Two recognized authorities on operations management have suggested the following rules for inspecting work in process:

1. Inspect *after* operations that are likely to produce faulty items so that no more work will be done on bad items.

2. Inspect *before* costly operations so that these operations will not be performed on items that are already defective.

3. Inspect *before* operations in which faulty products might break or jam the machines.

4. Inspect *before* operations that can cover up defects (such as electroplating, painting, or assembly).

5. Inspect *before* assembly operations that cannot be undone (such as welding parts or mixing paint).

6. On automatic and semiautomatic machines, inspect the first and last pieces, but only occasionally the in-between pieces.

7. Inspect *before* storage (including purchased items).[55]

When Chicago's Schwinn Bicycle Company took over a Hungarian bike maker near Budapest in 1989, managers found flagrant and costly violations of rule number four, above. Quality inspections were being performed only *after*

W. Edwards Deming: The American behind Japan's Quality Revolution

People often wonder how Japan, one of the big losers in the Second World War, became one of the world's most powerful and respected industrial giants within forty years after the war. One important secret was purely American. Japan's desperate business leaders looked to the victors to see what they were doing right. They noticed that the quality of American military material was high, and they learned that one man, W. Edwards Deming, had taught 35,000 American engineers and technicians how to use statistics to improve quality. In 1950, Deming was invited to meet with the heads of Japan's leading companies. The Japanese were so impressed with Deming's ideas—and their results—that in 1951 they created the Deming Prize, still coveted as the ultimate distinction for Japanese companies that put quality first.

It took thirty years and millions of high-quality Japanese imports before American companies felt pinched and began to catch on to Deming's appeal. So for the last decade, Deming, now over 90, has been spreading his message to responsive American companies. The core of his approach is to use statistics to measure the variation in a manufacturing system, then fine-tune the system until the variation is as low as possible. The goal is constant improvement.

According to Deming, traditional American quality control is a failure because it has focused on the product rather than on the process. If few defective products leave its plant, an American company thinks it has achieved high quality, even if it has to pay hundreds of inspectors to reject scores of products. All those rejected products and all that time spent on inspection and rework—as much as 40 percent of a product's total costs—represent wasted money, according to Deming. Build the product right and you don't have to inspect, he insists.

Deming earned a reputation as a curmudgeon in part because he's tough on top executives. He rejects the idea that defects result from workers' sloppiness, asserting that 94 percent of quality failures result from the system itself. Executives don't like hearing that message, but so many of them flock to hear it that Deming's seminars are booked more than a year in advance. And as the quality of American goods rises, a man who was ignored by his own country for most of his professional life should get much of the credit.

Sources: John A. Byrne, "The Prophet of Quality," *Business Week* (January 28, 1991): 14; Lloyd Dobyns, "Ed Deming Wants Big Changes, and He Wants Them Fast," *Smithsonian* (August 1990): 74–82; John Lorinc, "Dr. Deming's Traveling Quality Show," *Canadian Business* (September 1990): 38–42; Jeremy Main, "The Curmudgeon Who Talks Tough on Quality," *Fortune* (June 25, 1984): 119.

the bikes had been assembled, painted, and decorated with decals. Reworked bikes "had to be stripped, repainted, and redecaled."[56] Schwinn revamped the quality inspection program and the former government-run money loser is now turning a profit.

feedback quality control inspecting and testing finished goods for conformance to design specifications

Feedback Quality Control. Feedback quality control occurs when finished goods are inspected and tested to see if they satisfy original design specifications. Items that fail must be reworked, if possible, or recycled. The prudent manager remembers that the organization's reputation is shipped with every product. Bad products or poor service mean dissatisfied customers, and dissatisfied customers are an open door to competitors. In fact, according to a recent U.S. government study, "between 37 percent and 45 percent of people who are unhappy with the service they receive do not complain. They simply go someplace else."[57] Cus-

TABLE 18.3 • Advice from the Field on Handling Customer Complaints

> ***Robert W. Reip, quality assurance specialist, Hercules, Inc.:***
>
> 1. Accept customer complaints. Don't fight them or try to figure out why that sales district is "making up problems."
> 2. Analyze customer complaints for maximum information. Do the detective work—investigate process mistakes, material variations, and even the unlikely things that people do in the field. This investigation is important for those malfunctions that the engineers say are "impossible."
> 3. Eliminate the cause of the defect if possible. Don't allow people to get away with inserting "more inspection" under the "corrective action" heading. Do some engineering, then automate and eliminate.
> 4. Feed complaint information back to the design review people. Complaints, and the results of failure analyses, can provide a bank of information that is valuable for other products.
> 5. Report results of all investigations—and solutions—to everyone involved. Don't forget to inform the original parties when a long, complex problem is solved.

Source: Robert W. Reip, "Make the Most of Customer Complaints," *Quality Progress,* 21 (March 1988): 25. Reprinted by permission.

tomer complaints need to be treated as a valuable information resource, as discussed in Table 18.3, not as an irritant or inconvenience.[58] Other sources of feedback from the field also need to be monitored. For example, orders of spare parts for the company's products, normally viewed only as a source of additional revenue, may pinpoint problems in product design or quality control.

Defining and Improving Service Quality

Services are a rapidly growing and increasingly important part of today's global economy. Pleasing the customer is more important than ever. Experts say it costs five times more to get a new customer than it does to keep a present one.[59] Still, American companies lose an average of about 20 percent of their customers each year.[60] Service quality strategists emphasize that it is no longer enough to simply satisfy the customer. The strategic service challenge today is to *anticipate* and *exceed* the customer's expectations.[61] Consider the following story of exceptional customer service that helps explain why Japanese toolmaking equipment companies have made huge inroads in the United States. A management consultant "tells of a Japanese technician who slept on a bedroll at an American customer's plant for the first ten days after a new machine was delivered, the better to pounce if anything went wrong."[62] If managers are to render exceptional service, they first need to comprehend how customers judge service quality.

●●●●●●●●●●●●●●●●●●
Explain how customers judge service quality and how service quality can be improved.

How Do Customers Judge Service Quality? Researchers at Texas A&M University recently uncovered valuable insights about customer perceptions of service quality.[63] They surveyed hundreds of customers of various types of service organizations. The following five service-quality dimensions emerged: tangibles, reliability, responsiveness, assurance, and empathy. Customers apparently judge the quality of each service transaction in terms of these five dimensions. (To better understand each dimension and to gauge your own service-quality satisfaction, take a moment now to complete the short questionnaire in Table 18.4.) Which of the five dimensions is most important to you? In the Texas A&M study, *reliability* was the most important dimension of service quality, regardless of the type of service involved. Anyone who has waited impatiently for an overdue airplane knows firsthand the importance of service reliability.

Managers who make their living providing services must be familiar with these anchors for customers' expectations. Small increments in customer satisfaction can translate into big dollars. For example, "IBM estimates that if it can improve satisfaction 1 percent for its AS/400 [minicomputer] customers worldwide, it will gain more than $200 million over five years."[64]

TABLE 18.4 ● What Kind of Service Have You Been Getting Lately?

Think of the kind of treatment you have received in service establishments recently. Pick a specific restaurant, hair styling salon, bank, airline, hospital, government agency, auto repair shop, department store, bookstore, or other service organization and rate the kind of customer service you received, using the following five factors. Circle one response for each factor and total them.

1. *Tangibles:* physical facilities, equipment, appearance of personnel.

        Very poor   Very good
        1 2 3 4 5 6 7 8 9 10

2. *Reliability:* ability to perform the desired service dependably, accurately, and consistently.

        Very poor   Very good
        1 2 3 4 5 6 7 8 9 10

3. *Responsiveness:* willingness to provide prompt service and help customers.

        Very poor   Very good
        1 2 3 4 5 6 7 8 9 10

4. *Assurance:* employees' knowledge, courtesy, and ability to convey trust and confidence.

        Very poor   Very good
        1 2 3 4 5 6 7 8 9 10

5. *Empathy:* provision of caring, individualized attention to customers.

        Very poor   Very good
        1 2 3 4 5 6 7 8 9 10

Total score = _____

Scoring Key
  5–10 Cruel and unusual punishment
11–20 You call this service?
21–30 Average, but who wants average service?
31–40 Close only counts in horseshoes
41–50 Service hall-of-fame candidate .

Source: Adapted from discussion in Leonard L. Berry, A. Parasuraman, and Valarie A. Zeithaml, "The Service-Quality Puzzle," *Business Horizons* (September-October 1988), pp. 35–43. From Robert Kreitner, Barry L. Reece, James P. O'Grady, *Business,* 2nd ed. (Boston: Houghton Mifflin Company, 1990). Reprinted by permission.

Improving Service Quality. One workable approach to improving service quality is based on an extension of the manufacturing quality control concept of "zero defects." In the case of services, the goal becomes *zero defections*.[65] In short, don't lose any customers. It is important to note that this approach solves management's common problem regarding the difficulty of measuring customer satisfaction. Under a zero defections program, a departed customer is probably a dissatisfied one, period. Thus, customer defections can be measured and managed. Zero defections programs can be successful only if they are embedded in the organization's mission and culture. Top management support, clear and challenging goals, extensive customer service training, and rewards for outstanding service performance are other essential components.

Summary

Operations management is the design, operation, and control of resource transformation systems. Raw materials and human talent are transformed into needed goods and services. Most resource transformation systems produce bundles of tangible goods and intangible services. The following characteristics make services unique: (1) direct customer participation; (2) immediate consumption; (3) delivery at customer's convenience; (4) labor intensiveness; and (5) intangibility.

Study of highly efficient Japanese factories has revealed lean and flexible just-in-time production (JIT) operations and personal commitment to total quality control, rather than "secret" techniques. Three characteristics of the factory of the future are flexible manufacturing, computerized information and control, and integrated functions and systems. CIM (computer-integrated manufacturing) links CAD and CAM within an organization's information and control system.

Product design, the process of creating a set of product specifications, should be responsive to both individual and societal demands. Cross-functional teamwork and customer input from the very beginning are essential to effective and efficient product design. Poorly designed products can come back to haunt a company through costly rework, scrap, or product recalls. Computer-aided design (CAD) allows engineers to cut new product design time in half.

Production planning is needed to ensure that forecasted demand for goods and services is met effectively and efficiently. Experts recommend that top management devote more attention to the production function. Production tends to be uncoordinated and inefficient when important production decisions are ignored by strategic planners. The master production schedule is a key source document for operations managers because it tells what will be produced and when.

Because purchased materials often account for more than half of a product's wholesale price, systematic purchasing is a fundamental part of effective operations management. Today, an adequately staffed purchasing/materials management department and clear-cut purchasing policies are recommended for most organizations. Purchasing is an ethically sensitive area. Six criteria to be considered when selecting vendors are price, quality, reliability, service, credit, and shipping costs. Computerized material requirements planning (MRP) and manufacturing resource planning (MRP II) help operations managers make data-based decisions regarding the timing and levels of material and inventory transactions. MRP II is organizationwide in scope, whereas MRP is tied more narrowly to the production function.

Organizational success often hinges on how effectively the four categories of inventory—raw materials and purchased components, work in process, supplies, and finished goods—are managed. Successful management of the inventory cycle involves balancing the conflicting demands for large inventories in order to meet unexpected circumstances and for small inventories in order to minimize investment and carrying costs. *Kanban*, a just-in-time inventory control technique developed by Toyota, keeps work-in-process inventory lean by "pulling" containers of parts through the production process with a manual card-switching procedure. A tandem push-pull inventory control system, relying on MRP II for long-term organizational planning and *kanban* for short-term local control, is recommended.

Logical and orderly work flow layouts greatly improve cost-effectiveness. Three basic work flow formats are product layout, process layout, and fixed-position layout. Each has inherent advantages and disadvantages.

A production operation is only as good as its output. Feedforward, concurrent, and feedback quality control are necessary to ensure that goods and services conform to design specifications. Statistical process control (SPC) is appropriate for concurrent quality control. Customers define service quality in terms of tangibles, reliability, responsiveness, assurance, and empathy. Reliability is rated the most important dimension. A zero defections program can improve an organization's service quality.

Terms to Understand

Operations management
Just-in-time production (JIT)
Total quality control (TQC)
Economies of scope
Flexible manufacturing
Computer-integrated manufacturing (CIM)
Product design
Production planning
Master production schedule
Purchasing
Material requirements planning (MRP)

Inventory control
Kanban
Work flow layout
Product layout
Process layout
Fixed-position layout
Quality control
Feedforward quality control
Concurrent quality control
Statistical process control
Feedback quality control

Questions for Discussion

1. How does the idea of production as a resource transformation system help one appreciate the importance of operations management?
2. Why is it safe to say that virtually every organization is a service organization?

3. How could you use the philosophy of total quality control (TQC) to improve your life (your studies, job, and so on)?

4. In your opinion, which fundamental characteristic of the factory of the future is most important? Explain your reasoning.

5. Why is product design getting so much attention today?

6. How might the six criteria of vendor selection help you buy an expensive item (for example, a sound system, car, or bicycle)?

7. Why do operations producing customized products tend to rely on process layouts? Give examples.

8. Which type of quality control—feedforward, concurrent, or feedback—do you think is most important? Why?

9. How do you judge the quality of the services you receive? How does your approach compare to the items in Table 18.4?

10. Do you think the concept of zero defections is a good one? Explain your reasoning.

Back to the Opening Case

Now that you have read Chapter 18, you should be able to answer the following questions about the Boeing case:

1. What is Boeing's "product"?

2. Even though Boeing is a manufacturing company, why is customer service so very important to the firm's success?

3. What sorts of feedforward quality control are evident in this case?

4. Why is Boeing likely to remain a leader in its industry?

CLOSING CASE

SAS Sets the Global Standard in Airline Customer Service

In the two years prior to 1981, when Jan Carlzon took over Scandinavian Airlines System (SAS), the company lost $30 million. SAS's success today—it made almost $200 million in 1989—is a testament to Carlzon's ability to radically alter the way his company views its business and to make his airline perhaps the most service-oriented in the world. After the predicted deregulation of European airlines in 1992, Carlzon believes that large carriers will elbow smaller ones out of business, as happened in the United States in the years following deregulation. Carlzon plans for his airline to be one of the survivors.

When Carlzon became president and chief executive of SAS, he was worried about surviving not into the next century but into the next year. A jump in oil prices had shaken the entire industry, U.S. airlines were in turmoil following deregulation, and SAS's reputation was deteriorating. Because of his airline's high union wages, Carlzon knew it couldn't compete in the fare wars. So he looked to his company's strength—its well-paid workforce and Scandinavia's worldwide reputation for quality. He staked the company's survival on its ability to attract business customers, many of whom are less concerned with a flight's cost than with its amenities.

To turn itself into a business traveler's dream, SAS devoted up to 60 percent of its seats to EuroClass, a business class with wide leather seats and VIP treatment. It also went all out to improve its customers' experiences on the ground. It linked itself to hotels around the world, improved its lounges, and provided more computers and fax machines for business customers who like to work while waiting for a plane.

Most important, Carlzon set out to change the way his employees deal with customers. "We used to fly planes," he says, "now we transport people."[66] Carlzon sees the most important employee-customer interactions—which he calls "moments of truth"—as occurring during check-in, boarding, and any time a problem arises. SAS serves 10 million customers a year, each of whom interacts with an average of five employees. Therefore the company has 50 million interactions, each about 15 seconds long, to prove that it is the best airline. If employees handle such moments well, Carlzon reasons, travelers will feel good about the airline and will return to it.

So SAS gave its employees the power to handle difficult moments themselves, including granting a refund or offering free drinks without cutting through a lot of red tape. Carlzon sees the job of management to be one of supporting its front-line employees, communicating with them, making their jobs easier, and removing the barriers that get in the way of the best possible customer service. "People are not willing to take risks when they feel afraid or threatened," he

says. "But . . . if you show them respect and trust—they start to perform up to their real capabilities."[67]

As an example of the kind of risk a trusted customer-oriented employee will take, Carlzon cites the case of a purser on a snowbound flight who decided to give snacks away free but couldn't get SAS's catering company to give her enough for her planeload. So she took all her cash to a Finnair flight at the next gate and gave it to the Finnair manager, who ordered the extra snacks for her, charged to Finnair. The SAS passengers never knew what the purser had done, but they were no doubt grateful that there were enough snacks to go around. Other companies might see such an action as an extravagance, but Carlzon believes it's much cheaper to keep a satisfied customer than it is to get a dissatisfied customer back.

Carlzon's strategy worked and turned SAS around. But he didn't stop there. To make up for SAS's relatively small size and lack of worldwide bases, he began making cooperative agreements with other airlines. The airlines now work to coordinate such things as their schedules of flights to Eastern Europe, and they hope to win better treatment from airplane manufacturers by cooperating in high-volume purchases. A customer assured of a connecting flight is a happy one.

Ten years after SAS set a new standard for how airlines treat their customers, U.S. airlines are bombarding Americans with ads demonstrating how well *they* treat their business customers. But in doing so, they have missed one of Carlzon's other lessons. His secret for spreading SAS's message, he says, is "show biz." His charismatic high profile, his book (appropriately titled, *Moments of Truth*), and the frequent magazine articles about the company are all calculated to get his message across to customers. But perhaps more important, his message also reaches SAS employees, offering them examples and encouragement to continue giving customers world-class service.

For Discussion

1. What is SAS's "product"?

2. How does Carlzon's concept of "moments of truth" relate to the five distinctive characteristics of services?

3. How well does SAS's approach to service quality stand up to the Service 101 profile in Table 18.1?

4. All things considered, what is the most important step Carlzon took to improve service quality at SAS?

References

Opening Quotation: Lee Iacocca with William Novak, *Iacocca: An Autobiography* (New York: Bantam, 1984), p. 176.

Opening Case: Marc Beauchamp, "No More Weekend Stands," *Forbes* (September 17, 1990): 191–192; Anthony Ramirez, "Boeing's Happy, Harrowing Times," *Fortune* (July 17, 1989): 40–48; Maria Shao, "Trying Times at Boeing," *Business Week* (March 13, 1989): 34–36; Dori Jones Yang and Michael Oneal, "How Boeing Does It," *Business Week* (July 9, 1990): 46–50.

Closing Case: "The Art of Loving," *Inc.* (May 1989): 34–46; Jan Carlzon, *Moments of Truth* (New York: Harper & Row, 1987), 2–3; Kenneth Labich, "An Airline That Soars on Service," *Fortune* (December 31, 1990): 94–96; Kenneth Labich, "Goodbye, Frank, Hello, Jan," *Fortune* (September 10, 1990): 11; Michael Maccoby, "Three Firms That Changed," *Research Technology Management* (January-February, 1990): 44–45.

1. Adapted from Charles G. Andrew and George A. Johnson, "The Crucial Importance of Production and Operations Management," *Academy of Management Review,* 7 (January 1982): 143–147.

2. Excellent discussions of the relationship between goods and services can be found in David E. Bowen and Benjamin Schneider, "Services Marketing and Management: Implication for Organizational Behavior," in Barry M. Staw and L. L. Cummings, eds. *Research in Organizational Behavior,* vol. 10 (Greenwich, Conn.: JAI Press, 1988), pp. 43–80; and Thomas A. Stewart, "There Are No Products—Only Services," *Fortune* (January 14, 1991): 32.

3. Jonathan Kapstein, "The Fast-Spinning Machine That Blew a Gasket," *Business Week* (September 10, 1990): 52.

4. Based on discussion in M. Jill Austin, "Planning in Service Organizations," *SAM Advanced Management Journal,* 55 (Summer 1990): 7–12; and Everett E. Adam, Jr. and Paul M. Swamidass, "Assessing Operations Management from a Strategic Perspective," *Journal of Management,* 15 (June 1989): 181–203.

5. Ron Zemke and Dick Schaaf, *The Service Edge: 101 Companies That Profit from Customer Care* (New York: New American Library, 1989), p. 14.

6. See Andrew Weiss, "Simple Truths of Japanese Manufacturing," *Harvard Business Review,* 62 (July-August 1984): 119–125. The application of Japanese-style frugality in U.S. manufacturing operations is discussed in Richard J. Schonberger, "Frugal Manufacturing," *Harvard Business Review,* 65 (September-October 1987): 95–100. Also see Kim B. Clark and Robert H. Hayes, "Recapturing America's Manufacturing Heritage," *California Management Review,* 30 (Summer 1988): 9–33; and "How to Regain the Productive Edge," *Fortune* (May 22, 1989): 92–104.

7. R. Dave Garwood, "Explaining JIT, MRP II, *Kanban,*" *P & IM Review and APICS News,* 4 (October 1984): 66. Also see Mary Ann Maskery, "Just-in-Time Developer Ohno Revered," *Automotive News* (June 11, 1990): 3, 41; and Paul H. Zipkin, "Does Manufacturing Need a JIT Revolution?" *Harvard Business Review,* 69 (January-February 1991): 40–50.

8. Paul A. Eisenstein, "Saturn Uses New Assembly Process," *The Christian Science Monitor* (October 12, 1990): 8.

9. Richard J. Schonberger, *Japanese Manufacturing Techniques: Nine Hidden Lessons in Simplicity* (New York: Free Press, 1982), p. 35.

10. Robert H. Hayes, "Why Japanese Factories Work," *Harvard Business Review,* 59 (July-August 1981): 62.

11. Gene Bylinsky, "America's Best-Managed Factories," *Fortune* (May 28, 1984): 24.

12. John S. DeMott, "Manufacturing Is in Flower," *Time* (March 26, 1984): 50–51.

13. Adapted in part from Mariann Jelinek and Joel D. Goldhar, "The Strategic Implications of the Factory of the Future," *Sloan Management Review,* 25 (Summer 1984): 29–37. Also see Mark L. Blazey and Karen S. Davison, "Keeping Up with the Factory of the Future," *Training,* 27 (February 1990): 51–55; and P. T. Bolwijn and T. Kumpe, "Manufacturing in the 1990s—Productivity, Flexibility, and Innovation," *Long Range Planning,* 23 (August 1990): 44–57.

14. See Ravi Venkatesan, "Cummins Engine Flexes Its Factory," *Harvard Business Review,* 68 (March-April 1990): 120–127.

15. David Woodruff, "A Dozen Motor Factories—Under One Roof," *Business Week* (November 20, 1989): 90.

16. "IBM's Big Leap onto the Factory Floor," *Business Week* (September 17, 1984): 50.

17. Harry B. Thompson, "CAD/CAM and the Factory of the Future," *Management Review,* 72 (May 1983): 28; emphasis added. CIM is discussed in Robert Bonsack, "Executive Checklist: Are You Ready for CIM?" *CIM Review,* 3 (Summer 1987): 35–38; Bernard Avishai, "A CEO's Common Sense of CIM: An Interview with J. Tracy O'Rourke," *Harvard Business Review,* 67 (January-February 1989): 110–117; Frederick C. Weston, Jr., "Computer-Integrated Manufacturing Systems: Fact or Fantasy," *Business Horizons,* 31 (July-August 1988): 64–68; and Naomi Freundlich, "Japan's Latest Innovation: Computers That Innovate," *Business Week* (March 4, 1991): 57.

18. See Michele J. Gengler and Richard J. Tersine, "Robots—Coming to Work in America," *Business,* 33 (April-June 1983): 3–12; William J. Hampton, "Can Steel-Collar Workers Build Better Cars?" *Business Week* (September 12, 1988): 73; and Gregory L. Miles, "It's a Dirty Job, But Something's Gotta Do It," *Business Week* (August 20, 1990): 92–93, 97.

19. Data from Richard Brandt and Otis Port, "How Automation Could Save the Day," *Business Week* (March 3, 1986): 72–74.

20. Jelinek and Goldhar, "The Strategic Implications of the Factory of the Future," p. 34. Also see Otis Port, "Making Brawn Work with Brains," *Business Week* (April 20, 1987): 56–60; Mohsen Attaran, "The Automated Factory: Justification and Implementation," *Business Horizons,* 32 (May-June 1989): 80–86; and Jeremy Main, "Manufacturing the Right Way," *Fortune* (May 21, 1990): 54–64.

21. See Robert H. Hayes and Ramchandran Jaikumar, "Manufacturing's Crisis: New Technologies, Obsolete Organizations," *Harvard Business Review,* 66 (September-October 1988): 77–85.

22. See "Making Service a Potent Marketing Tool," *Business Week* (June 11, 1984): 164–170; and Robert L. Desatnick, "Service: A CEO's Perspective," *Management Review,* 76 (October 1987): 41–45.

23. Todd Vogel, "Big Changes Are Galvanizing General Electric," *Business Week* (December 18, 1989): 102.

24. Data from Otis Port, "A Smarter Way to Manufacture," *Business Week* (April 30, 1990): 110–117.

25. See Joan O'C. Hamilton, "Rebel with a Cause," *Business Week* (December 3, 1990): 130–135; and Brian Dumaine, "Design That Sells and Sells and . . ." *Fortune* (March 11, 1991): 86–94.

26. Based on Joel Dreyfuss, "Reinventing IBM," *Fortune* (August 14, 1989): 30–39.

27. Adapted from Jonathan B. Levine, "How HP Built a Better Terminal," *Business Week* (March 7, 1988): 114; and Bruce Nussbaum, "Smart Design," *Business Week* (April 11, 1988): 102–106, 108.

28. Data from Carrie Gottlieb, "Intel's Plan for Staying on Top," *Fortune* (March 27, 1989): 98–100.

29. Bob Davis, "Computers Speed the Design of More Workaday Products," *The Wall Street Journal* (January 18, 1985): 19.

30. Case studies of the production planning/control function in six process manufacturing organizations are discussed in Byron J. Finch and James F. Cox, "Process-Oriented Production Planning and Control: Factors That Influence System Design," *Academy of Management Journal,* 31 (March 1988): 123–153.

31. Wickham Skinner, "Manufacturing—Missing Link in Corporate Strategy," *Harvard Business Review,* 47 (May-June 1969): 145: Robert H. Hayes and Steven C. Wheelwright, "Link Manufacturing Process and Product Life Cycles," *Harvard Business Review,* 57 (January-February 1979): 133–140; and Elwood S. Buffa, *Meeting the Competitive Challenge* (Homewood, Ill.: Dow Jones-Irwin, 1984).

32. Core service skills are discussed in James Brian Quinn, Thomas L. Doorley, and Penny C. Paquette, "Beyond Products: Services-Based Strategy," *Harvard Business Review,* 68 (March-April 1990): 58–60, 64–68.

33. Joseph Orlicky, *Material Requirements Planning* (New York: McGraw-Hill, 1975), p. 38.

34. Ibid., p. 235.

35. Data from Port, "A Smarter Way to Manufacture."

36. Data from James B. Treece, "Is Another Smith Headed for the Top at GM?" *Business Week* (March 26, 1990): 78–80.

37. Thomas R. Temin, "Purchasing Audit Helps Uncover Ways to Save," *Purchasing,* 90 (May 28, 1981): 65.

38. For instructive updates on purchasing, see Joseph L. Cavinato, "Purchasing Performance: What Makes the Magic?" *Journal of Purchasing and Materials Management,* 23 (Fall 1987): 10–16; Margaret A. Emmelhainz, "Electronic Data Interchange: Does It Change the Purchasing Process?" *Journal of Purchasing and Materials Management,* 23 (Winter 1987): 2–8; Mohammed I. Al-Mubarak, "Empirical Analysis of the Effects of Environmental Interdependence and Uncertainty on Purchasing Activities: A Cross-Cultural Study," *Industrial Marketing and Purchasing,* 3, No. 1 (1988): 40–51; and John McMillan, "Managing Suppliers: Incentive Systems in Japanese and U.S. Industry," *California Management Review,* 32 (Summer 1990): 38–55.

39. "The New Game Plan: A Huge Potential Is There to Be Won," *Modern Materials Handling,* 36 (January 6, 1981): 68. There is a special series of articles on MRP application in this issue. Also see Sumer C. Aggarwal, "MRP, JIT, OPT, FMS?" *Harvard Business Review,* 63 (September-October 1985): 8–10, 12, 16.

40. Garwood, "Explaining JIT, MRP II, Kanban," pp. 66, 68. Also see Alicia Johnson, "MRP? MRPII? OPT? CIM? FMS? JIT? Is Any System Letter-Perfect?" *Management Review,* 75 (September 1986): 22–27; and Peter Duchessi, Charles M. Schaninger, and Don R. Hobbs, "Implementing a Manufacturing Planning and Control Information System," *California Management Review,* 31 (Spring 1989): 75–90.

41. For instructive discussions of inventory control techniques, see David N. Burt, "Managing Suppliers Up to Speed," *Harvard Business Review,* 67 (July-August 1989): 127–135; and Thomas F. O'Boyle, "Firm's Newfound Skill In Managing Inventory May Soften Downturn," *The Wall Street Journal* (November 19, 1990): A1–A6.

42. Schonberger, *Japanese Manufacturing Techniques,* p. 220.

43. Stephen Moss, "A Systems Approach to Productivity," *National Productivity Review,* 1 (Summer 1982): 277.

44. See Alex Taylor III, "Why Toyota Keeps Getting Better and Better and Better," *Fortune* (November 19, 1990): 66–79.

45. Based on discussion in Uday Karmarker, "Getting Control of Just-in-Time," *Harvard Business Review,* 67 (September-October 1989): 122–131. For empirical evidence of the effectiveness of *kanban,* see Lee J. Krajewski, Barry E. King, Larry P. Ritzman, and Danny S. Wong, "*Kanban,* MRP, and Shaping the Manufacturing Environment," *Management Science,* 33 (January 1987): 39–57.

46. Richard L. Francis and John A. White, *Facility Layout and Location: An Analytical Approach* (Englewood Cliffs, N.J.: Prentice-Hall, 1974), pp. 33–34.

47. Richard B. Chase and Nicholas J. Aquilano, *Production and Operations Management: A Life Cycle Approach,* 3rd ed. (Homewood Ill.: Irwin, 1981): p. 216.

48. Brian Dumaine, "Who Needs a Boss?" *Fortune* (May 7, 1990): 60.

49. See Donald C. Bacon, "How the Baldrige Winners Did It," *Nation's Business* (January 1989): 32–34; Jeremy Main, "How to Win the Baldrige Award," *Fortune* (April 23, 1990): 101–116; and Ron Zemke, "Bashing the Baldrige," *Training,* 28 (February 1991): 29–39.

50. See Annetta Miller, "Japanese Cars: Born in the USA," *Newsweek* (April 9, 1990): 36–37; and Robert Cole, "U.S. Quality Improvement in the Auto Industry: Close But No Cigar," *California Management Review,* 32 (Summer 1990): 71–85.

51. See Marisa Manley, "Product Liability: You're More Exposed Than You Think," *Harvard Business Review,* 65 (September-October 1987): 28–30, 34, 36, 40.

52. See Philip Crosby's definition of quality in James P. Morgan, "Quality is Real: It Isn't Goodness," *Purchasing,* 103 (November 5, 1987): 38–43.

53. David Woodruff, "Ford Has a Better Idea: Let Someone Else Do It," *Business Week* (April 30, 1990): 117.

54. See Larry E. Mainstone and Ariel S. Levi, "Fundamentals of Statistical Process Control," *Journal of Organizational Behavior Management,* 9, No. 1 (1987): 5–21.

55. Condensed from Franklin J. Moore and Thomas E. Hendrick, *Production/Operations Management,* 7th ed. (Homewood, Ill.: Irwin, 1977), p. 676; also see David A. Garvin, "Competing on the Eight Dimensions of Quality," *Harvard Business Review,* 65 (November-December 1987): 101–109.

56. Gregory Miles, "Schwinn's Bike Venture a Model for East Europe," *The Christian Science Monitor* (December 31, 1990): 7.

57. Susan Caminiti, "The New Champs of Retailing," *Fortune* (September 24, 1990): 98.

58. See Jerry Plymire, "Complaints as Opportunities," *Business Horizons,* 34 (March-April 1991): 79–81.

59. Data from Patricia Sellers, "Getting Customers to Love You," *Fortune* (March 13, 1989): 38–49.

60. Data from Patricia Sellers, "What Customers Really Want," *Fortune* (June 4, 1990): 58–68.

61. Based on discussion in William A. Sherden, "Gaining the Service Quality Advantage," *The Journal of Business Strategy,* 9 (March-April 1988): 45–48. Also see Karl Albrecht and Ron Zemke, *Service America! Doing Business in the New Economy* (New York: Warner Books, 1985); and Chip R. Bell and Ron Zemke, "The Performing Arts of Service Management," *Management Review,* 79 (July 1990): 42–45.

62. Edmund Faltermayer, "Is 'Made in U.S.A.' Fading Away?" *Fortune* (September 24, 1990): 68.

63. See Leonard L. Berry, A. Parasuraman, and Valarie A. Zeithaml, "The Service-Quality Puzzle," *Business Horizons,* 31 (September-October 1988): 35–43.

64. Frank Rose, "Now Quality Means Service Too," *Fortune* (April 22, 1991): 97–109.

65. Based on discussion in Frederick F. Reichheld and W. Earl Sasser, Jr., "Zero Defections: Quality Comes to Services," *Harvard Business Review,* 68 (September-October 1990): 105–111. Advice on dealing with difficult customers can be found in Ron Zemke and Kristin Anderson, "Customers from Hell," *Training,* 27 (February 1990): 25–33; and Faye Rice, "How to Deal with Tougher Customers," *Fortune* (December 3, 1990): 38–48. Basic customer service training is covered in George M. Piskurich, "Service Training Made Simple," *Training & Development Journal,* 45 (January 1991): 37–38.

66. Quoted in Michael Maccoby, "Three Firms That Changed," *Research Technology Management* (January-February 1990): 44.

67. Quoted in "The Art of Loving," *Inc.* (May 1989): 35.

Quality: The Big Picture

Learning Objective

To understand the concept of total quality control and know how to implement it.

Link to Textual Material

Productivity, control, operations management, quality control, service quality.

For an organization to compete successfully, customer needs and expectations must be identified, met, and exceeded. An organization's very existence depends upon its ability to satisfy its customers. And it takes world-class quality to satisfy today's customers.

What is total quality? Total quality is a concept—a philosophy—a strategy—it's a way of doing business. *Quality: The Big Picture* introduces the concept of total quality and demonstrates strategies for achieving it in an organization.

Discussion Questions

1. What does the idea of total quality mean to you?
2. Who is responsible for making a total quality program work? Explain.
3. How would you respond to a manager who made the following statement: "Total quality requires nationwide attention because it is one of the keys to global competitiveness"?
4. What steps do you need to take to bring the concept of total quality into your present life and work?

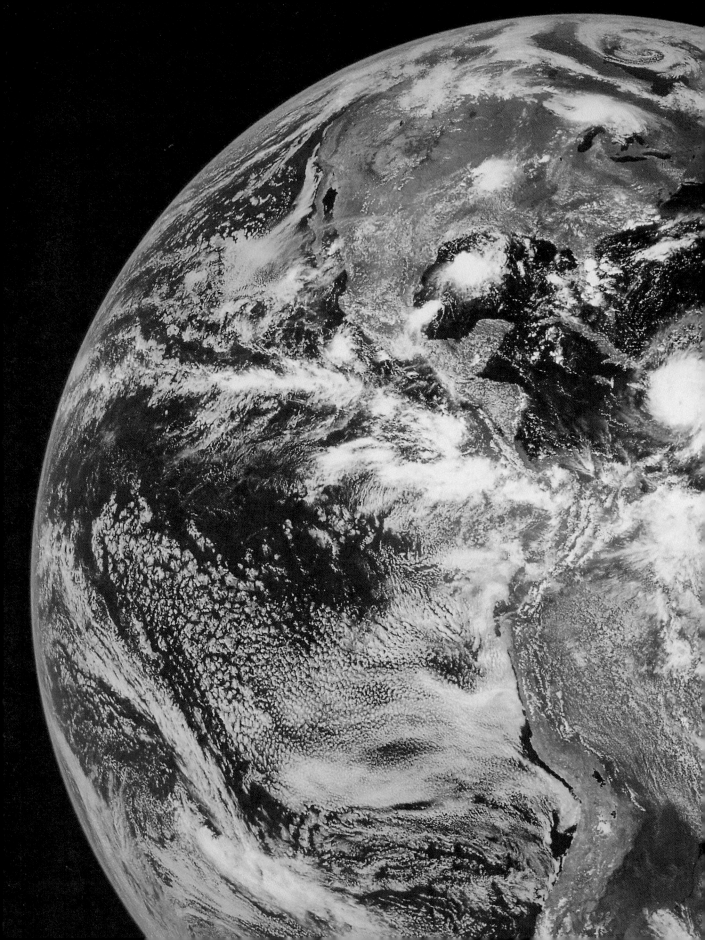

PART VI

Expanding Horizons in Management

Part VI discusses how the managerial agenda has been broadened in recent years by the global economy. Management's growing international responsibilities involve a complex web of problems and opportunities. Chapter 19 distinguishes between multinational companies and global corporations as a backdrop for discussing a six-step internationalization process. Key dimensions of cross-cultural differences are explored along with valuable lessons from international comparative management research. Some problems and issues unique to international operations, including political instability and foreign corruption, are examined. Prompted by the comparatively high expatriate failure rate for American companies, the need for cross-cultural training is discussed.

19

International Management

The boundaries of our countries can no longer be the borders of our minds.

DEAN C. BARNLUND

CHAPTER OBJECTIVES

When you finish studying this chapter, you should be able to

- Distinguish between multinational companies (MNCs) and global corporations.

- Describe the six-step internationalization process.

- Contrast ethnocentric, polycentric, and geocentric attitudes toward foreign operations.

- From a cross-cultural perspective, explain the difference between high-context and low-context cultures and also between monochronic and polychronic time.

- Discuss what Hofstede's research has to say about the applicability of American management theories in foreign cultures.

- Identify important comparative management lessons learned from Ouchi's Theory Z research and international studies of work goals and leadership styles.

- Distinguish between lubrication and whitemail bribes and discuss the U.S. Foreign Corrupt Practices Act.

- Discuss the nature and importance of cross-cultural training in international management.

Asea Brown Boveri, the First *Multidomestic* Organization

Asea Brown Boveri (ABB) is a huge company with an innovative approach to global organization. Its annual revenues top $25 billion, and it employs 240,000 people in 4,500 profit centers spread among 140 countries. It is the world's leading supplier of electric power-generating equipment and a significant force in dozens of other industries, from pollution control to robots. ABB's CEO Percy Barnevik believes that his company is creating the blueprint for the global company of the future—the "multidomestic" organization.

European companies are far ahead of their American counterparts in becoming truly global. Most U.S. top corporations looked for overseas markets and suppliers only after virtually saturating North America with their products. In contrast, European companies learned long ago the growth advantages of ignoring borders and finding buyers and talented people wherever they could. So, although giant multinationals like IBM and Exxon are still clearly American, no national label convincingly sticks to ABB.

ABB grew out of the 1987 merger of two companies that had been industrial leaders in their own countries for a century—Asea was Swedish, Brown Boveri was Swiss. ABB's headquarters are in Zurich, but only about one hundred administrative and technical personnel work there. Barnevik and six of his twelve-member executive committee come from Sweden, but only two of the company's eight-member board of directors are Swedish. (The other members of the executive committee are Swiss, German, and American.) And, although ABB's largest national market is Germany, ABB reports its earnings in American dollars and conducts all high-level meetings in English.

Keeping this diversity organized is a matrix structure, with more or less traditionally organized national companies on one dimension and a global network of business segments on the other. ABB's executive committee sets global strategy and monitors the entire company's performance. Each committee member is responsible for one of the company's eight business segments, into which ABB's fifty "business areas" (BAs) are grouped. For instance, from his office in Stamford, Connecticut, German-born executive committee member Gerhard Schulmeyer looks after the "industry" segment, which includes five business areas that sell products to automate industrial processes.

The leader of each business area uses ABB's resources and personnel around the globe to create an optimal global strategy. BA leaders set cost and quality standards and decide which factory will supply which export markets. They create problem-solving teams with representatives from a number of countries. Leaders move experts from nation to nation to ensure that each factory in the BA takes advantage of the latest technology and management techniques.

With such a global network in place, Barnevik's claim that he believes in strict decentralization might seem suspect. But, in fact, ABB consists of nearly 1,200 companies, each averaging two hundred employees. Those companies are further subdivided into 4,500 profit centers with an average of fifty employees each.

To employees, customers, and suppliers, the ABB profit centers seem very similar to any other small local company. The only difference is in the reporting structure. The head of each subsidiary reports both to the president of the national company and to the head of the business area in which the subsidiary is involved. Hence Barnevik's term, *multidomestic:* ABB is made up of multiple domestic companies, a "federation of national companies." As Barnevik points out, ABB companies can be "superlocal" (one installation business in Stuttgart does business only within a 10-mile radius of that city) or "superglobal" (another part of ABB competes whenever a new electric generating plant is built anywhere in the world).

From his initial two-company merger, Barnevik has built an empire, buying more than sixty companies worth more than $3.6 billion. Barnevik's belief in decentralization applies at all levels, and not everyone is happy to become part of the first "multidomestic." When he buys a company, his first change tends to be a radical reduction in headquarters staff. A German company's staff, for example, was cut from 1,600 to 100. At an American subsidiary, Barnevik sold the lavish corporate headquarters and three corporate jets. He doesn't want more than five layers of management between him and workers on the factory floor.

Does it take multilingual superstars to manage these downsized pieces of the global matrix? According to Barnevik, only 500 of ABB's 15,000 managers need to be "global managers"—people with, as he puts it, "exceptionally open minds," who are able to "sort through the debris of cultural excuses and find opportunities to innovate."[1] These global managers must be fluent in English and have experience in three or four countries. They also need to be patient and generous, especially when dealing with language problems. And, even though the select 500 might feel like royalty, they must be humble when dealing with top brass from the national companies, people who are unexcelled leaders in their own countries.

So what about the rest of ABB's managers? The large majority need to be identified with the country they work in. ABB recognizes that certain cultural differences cannot be overcome and must simply be acknowledged. Even the best global companies still have borders. When Swiss Federal Railways, for example, ordered $420 million worth of locomotives to haul freight through the Alps, ABB knew it had to think Swiss. This meant designing engines strong enough for the terrain, versatile enough to deal with both frigid outdoors and steamy tunnels, and as pollution free as possible to satisfy the tremendous Swiss concern for the environment.

The headaches for top management at a company like ABB are endless. Barnevik and company were so sensitive to the political fallout they expected from the Asea–Brown Boveri merger that they kept all negotiations secret until the merger was announced as a fait accompli. Mergers, acquisitions, and restructuring can raise howls of protest from unions and managers as well as from politicians. So far, with his combination of global strategy, structure, and managers, Barnevik has succeeded in making his multidomestic organization profitable. European executives expect ABB to be the top player at least in the European market as European boundaries come down in the mid 1990s.

• • • • • • • • • • • • • • • • • • **K**ey executives, such as those at Asea Brown Boveri, are moving from country to country as never before, meeting the challenge of international competition. With increasing speed and frequency, air travel and modern information technology are reshaping our world, which seems to be growing smaller. A third global-shrinking force, *corporate globalism,* has also been gaining momentum. By creating a global marketplace, this third force promises to be the main contributor to a smaller world in which similarities prevail.

Striking evidence of the global marketplace is everywhere. Consider the following examples:

- By 1990, Japanese investors were responsible for 25 percent of the New York Stock Exchange's trading volume.
- When American fighter planes shot down Iraqi war planes with Sparrow missiles in the Persian Gulf War, the missiles contained essential parts from Japan, Thailand, and Germany.
- The world's busiest McDonald's restaurant, serving 50,000 customers daily, is located in Moscow.
- In 1990, IBM earned 68 percent of its profits in Europe.[2]

This dizzying array of international commerce is simply business as usual in a global economy. Nevertheless, as indicated in Figure 19.1, this global economy holds some surprises. First, foreigners now own more productive assets in the United States than Americans own in other countries. Second, despite Japan's much-publicized buying spree in the United States, the British are still far and away America's largest foreign investor. Third, the tiny Netherlands holds a huge financial stake in America.

international management
pursuing organizational objectives in international and intercultural settings

Like any other productive enterprise, an international corporation must be effectively and efficiently managed. Consequently, **international management,** the pursuit of organizational objectives in international and intercultural settings, has recently emerged as an important discipline. The purpose of this chapter is to define and discuss multinational and global corporations, stimulate global and cultural awareness, explore comparative management, examine two international management trouble spots, and discuss the need for cross-cultural training.

Global Organizations for a Global Economy

●●●●●●●●●●●●●●●●●●
Distinguish between multinational companies (MNCs) and global corporations.

Many labels have been attached to international businesses over the years. They traditionally have been called *multinational companies.* More recently, the label *global corporations* has been suggested.[3] This section builds a foundation of understanding for the balance of the chapter by defining and contrasting multinational companies and global corporations. Also, evolutionary, financial, and strategic perspectives of international business are discussed.

From Multinationals to Global Corporations

multinational company (MNC)
business that has strategic control over production/marketing facilities in two or more countries

A **multinational company (MNC)** is a business that exercises strategic control over production and/or marketing facilities in two or more countries. Productive facilities include anything from mines and farms to banks, factories, stores, and hotels.[4] Thus, true multinationalism involves more than the export of goods from a producer country to a consumer country.

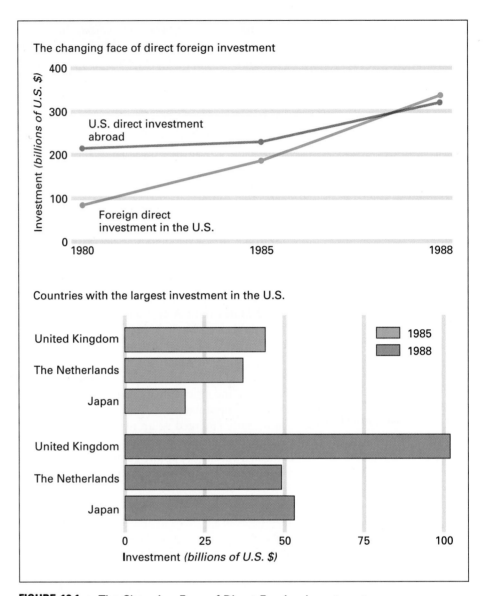

The changing face of direct foreign investment

FIGURE 19.1 ● The Changing Face of Direct Foreign Investment

Source: Data from U.S. Bureau of Census, *Statistical Abstract of the United States: 1990,* pp. 794, 797.

global corporation worldwide network of fully integrated design, production, and marketing operations

In contrast, **global corporations** "have fully integrated operations—product design, process design, manufacturing, and vendor management—in many parts of the world."[5] The few truly global corporations that exist today are very large. But the difference between MNCs and global corporations is more than just a matter of scale. It is a qualitative difference, as *Fortune* explains:

> *Haven't companies like Exxon and GM been global all along? No. They are internationals or multinationals. They happen to do business around the world or are export minded but remain firmly anchored in their home*

Skeptics who say American companies cannot compete in today's global marketplace can learn something from Harley-Davidson, maker of premier motorcycles. Not long ago competitors nearly ran Harley off the road. But Harley, while under a temporary umbrella of government trade protection, accelerated into the passing lane. Thanks to extensive employee retraining, product redesign, inventory discipline, and quality improvement, Harley has cruised back to Number 1 in the U.S. and now exports about one-third of its bikes.

countries with offspring in others. Building a few plants here and there the world over doesn't make you global either.

Running a global company is an order of magnitude more complicated than managing a multinational or international firm. The global corporation . . . looks at the whole world as one market. It manufactures, conducts research, raises capital, and buys supplies wherever it can do the job best. It keeps in touch with technology and market trends all around the world. National boundaries and regulations tend to be irrelevant, or a mere hindrance. Corporate headquarters might be anywhere.[6]

Honda exemplifies the new global corporation. Its Accord coupe and station wagon models have gone from design, to production, to market in the United States. When Honda reaches the point of relying on 75 percent of North American-made parts in its U.S. factories (which will be soon), the cars will be considered "domestic" by the U.S. government. Moreover, Honda plans to export 70,000 American-made Hondas annually to Europe, Asia, and the Middle East by the mid 1990s.[7] By then, the Big Three auto makers in the United States will be General Motors, Ford, and Honda, with Chrysler bumped to fourth place. Global corporations are the wave of the future and they promise to reshape the world's economic landscape.

The Evolution of MNCs and Global Corporations

●●●●●●●●●●●●●●●●●●
Describe the six-step internationalization process.

Multinationalism or globalism do not occur overnight. Instead, they are associated with the final stage of an evolutionary "internationalization" process with six identifiable stages.[8] Companies may skip steps when pursuing foreign markets, so the following sequence therefore needs to be viewed in relative rather than lockstep terms.

Stage 1: Licensing.   Companies in foreign countries are authorized to produce and/or market a given product within a specified territory in return for a fee.

Stage 2: Exporting.   Goods produced in one country are sold for use or resale to one or more companies in foreign countries. Exports amount to a significant slice of the U.S. economy, growing from 12 percent in 1980 to nearly 15 percent in 1990.[9] (See Table 19.1 for America's top ten exporters.)

Stage 3: Local Warehousing and Selling.   Goods produced in one country are shipped to the parent company's storage and marketing facilities located in one or more foreign countries.

Stage 4: Local Assembly and Packaging.   Components, rather than finished products, are shipped to company-owned assembly facilities in one or more foreign countries for final assembly and sales.

Stage 5: Joint Ventures.   A company in one country pools resources with one or more companies in a foreign country to produce, store, transport, and market products with resulting profits/losses shared appropriately. Joint ventures, also known as *strategic alliances*[10] or *strategic partnerships,* have become very popular in recent years. For example, AT&T, formerly a regulated utility with little international experience, has entered global markets by forming joint ventures with companies from Japan, the Netherlands, South Korea, Spain, Italy, and Taiwan. AT&T's strategic goal is to generate 25 percent of the firm's sales from overseas calls and foreign business by 1995.[11] International joint ventures/strategic alliances have tended to be fruitful for Japanese companies but disappointing for American and European partners.

> *Gary Hamel, a professor at the London Business School, regards partnerships as "a race to learn": The partner that learns fastest comes to*

TABLE 19.1 • America's Top Ten Exporters

1989 Rank		Products	Export sales ($ millions)	Exports as percentage of sales
1	Boeing (Seattle)	Commercial and military aircraft	11,021.0	54.4
2	General Motors (Detroit)	Motor vehicles and parts	10,185.1	8.0
3	Ford Motor (Dearborn, Mich.)	Motor vehicles and parts	8,602.0	8.9
4	General Electric (Fairfield, Conn.)	Jet engines, turbines, medical systems	7,268.0	13.2
5	Int'l Business Machines (Armonk, N.Y.)	Computers and related equipment	5,476.0	8.6
6	E.I. Du Pont De Nemours (Wilmington, Del.)	Specialty chemicals	4,844.0	13.8
7	Chrysler (Highland Park, Mich.)	Motor vehicles and parts	4,649.0	12.9
8	United Technologies (Hartford)	Jet engines, helicopters, cooling equipment	3,307.4	16.7
9	Caterpillar (Peoria, Ill.)	Heavy machinery, engines, turbines	3,291.0	29.6
10	McDonnell Douglas (St. Louis)	Commercial and military aircraft	2,896.0	19.3

Source: Jacob Park, "Overseas Sales Take Off at Last," *Fortune* (July 16, 1990): 77. © The Time Inc. Magazine Company. All rights reserved.

dominate the relationship and can then rewrite its terms. Thus, an alliance becomes a new form of competition. The Japanese excel at learning from others, Hamel says, while Americans and Europeans are not so good at it.[12]

Experts offer the following recommendations for successful international joint ventures/strategic alliances. First, exercise *patience* when selecting and building trust with a partner that has compatible (but not directly competitive) products and markets. Second, *learn* as fast and as much as possible without giving away core technologies and secrets. Third, establish firm *ground rules* about rights and responsibilities at the outset.[13]

Stage 6: Direct Foreign Investments. A company in one country produces and markets products through wholly owned subsidiaries in foreign countries. MNCs and global corporations are expressions of this last stage of internationalization. Asea Brown Boveri's multidomestic approach is yet another form of direct foreign investments.

The Financial Performance of MNCs

Multinational companies are more numerous and have been around longer than the emerging global corporations. So our question here is, are MNCs generally a greater or lesser financial risk than domestic companies? Given the explosive growth of international business in recent years, this is a key question for managers and investors alike. According to a comparative study of fifty-eight U.S. MNCs and forty-three wholly domestic U.S. companies, the answer is that MNCs are *less* financially risky. The MNCs had a significantly lower probability of insolvency than the companies without international ties.[14] A more recent study of 304 large British manufacturing companies tipped the scale in favor of MNCs even more. Over a twelve-year period, the companies' profitability tended to increase as their degree of foreign production increased.[15] One possible explanation for these unexpected results is that MNCs are in a better position than domestic firms to respond to shifting global markets, international wage differentials, and currency devaluations.

Strategic Considerations for International Operations

As discussed in Chapter 6, effective strategic planning/implementation/control is the backbone of good management. This is particularly true for MNCs and global corporations because of their geographic dispersion. As with any organization, however, a company with an international presence has three overriding strategic goals: efficiency of operations, management of risks, and adaptation through learning and innovation.[16] Efficiency is made difficult because geographically dispersed operations exaggerate the forces of organizational differentiation and weaken the forces of integration or coordination. Not surprisingly, matrix organization design is common in MNCs.[17] (Recall our discussion of matrix organization design in Chapter 9.) Risk management is more complex for MNCs than for domestic firms as a result of exaggerated cultural variations, unusual economic and political uncertainties, and unpredictable demands from host governments and joint-venture partners.[18]

In this complex environment, pursuing the three strategic goals mentioned above is doubly important. To this end, international strategists need to address six strategic questions about foreign subsidiaries:

1. What technology should the subsidiary employ?
2. How should the subsidiary's product market(s) be defined?
3. What relative emphasis should be placed on the subsidiary's different product lines?
4. What resources should be allocated to the subsidiary?
5. How broadly should the subsidiary be allowed to expand or diversify?
6. How much should each subsidiary participate in a global network of product flows?[19]

In true global corporations, these strategic questions are addressed cooperatively by both headquarters and subsidiary managers.

Toward Greater Global and Cross-cultural Awareness

Americans in general and American business students and managers in particular often are considered too narrowly focused for the global stage. Boris Yavitz, former dean of Columbia University's Graduate School of Business, observed that, "unlike European and Asian managers, who grow up expecting to see international service, U.S. executives are required to prepare only for domestic experience, with English as their only language."[20] This state of affairs must change, in view of the growth of international business and economic globalization. To compete successfully in a dynamic global economy, present and future managers need to develop their international and cultural awareness. In this section, we examine attitudes toward international operations, forces that promote uniformity and diversity among the world's people, and key sources of cultural diversity.

Contrasting Attitudes toward International Operations

Can a firm's degree of internationalization be measured? Some observers believe it can, and they claim a true MNC must have subsidiaries in at least six nations. Others say that, to qualify as a multinational, a firm must have a certain percentage of its capital or operations in foreign countries. However, Howard Perlmutter insists that these measurable guidelines tell only part of the story and suggests it is management's *attitude* toward its foreign operations that really counts.

> *The more one penetrates into the living reality of an international firm, the more one finds it is necessary to give serious weight to the way executives think about doing business around the world. The orientation toward "foreign people, ideas, resources," in headquarters and subsidiaries, and in host and home environments, becomes crucial in estimating the multinationality of a firm.*[21]

C'è un formaggio cremoso che fa sentire un frutto appena colto.

FORMAGGIO FRESCO PHILADELPHIA KRAFT

Philadelphia. Un sapore che rinfresca gli altri.

KRAFT
Cose buone dal mondo

Smile and say "cream cheese!" Better yet, the managers of Kraft's Philadelphia brand cream cheese want Italian consumers to smile and say "Philadelphia brand *formaggio cremoso*." Advertising and marketing in foreign countries require keen cross-cultural awareness to avoid insulting local customers with the wrong message.

• • • • • • • • • • • • • • • • •
Contrast ethnocentric, polycentric, and geocentric attitudes toward foreign operations.

ethnocentric attitude view that assumes home country's personnel and ways of doing things are best

Perlmutter identified three managerial attitudes toward international operations, which he has labeled ethnocentric, polycentric, and geocentric.[22] Each attitude is presented here in its pure form, but all three are likely to be found in a single multinational or global corporation (see Table 19.2). The key question is, "Which attitude predominates?"

Ethnocentric Attitude. Managers with an **ethnocentric attitude** are home-country oriented. Home-country personnel, ideas, and practices are viewed as inherently superior to those from abroad. Foreign nationals are not trusted with key decisions or technology. Home-country procedures and evaluation criteria are applied worldwide without variation. Proponents of ethnocentrism say that it makes for a simpler and more tightly controlled organization. Critics believe this attitude makes for poor planning and ineffective operations because of inadequate feedback, high turnover of subsidiary managers, reduced innovation, inflexibility, and social and political backlash.

In U.S.-Japanese business relations, ethnocentrism cuts both ways. Procter & Gamble failed to do its cultural homework when it ran a series of advertisements for Pampers in Japan. Japanese customers were bewildered by the ads, in which a stork carried a baby, because storks have no cultural connection to birth in Japan.[23] Similarly, Japanese companies operating in the United States seem to be out of touch with the expectations of American managers. In a recent survey of American managers employed by thirty-one such companies, the common complaint was too few promotions and too little responsibility.[24] Ethnocentric attitudes can also cause problems in ethnically diverse countries, such as the United States (see Managers in Action).

Polycentric Attitude. This host-country orientation is based on the assumption that, because cultures are so different, local managers know what is best for their

TABLE 19.2 ● Three Different Attitudes toward International Operations

Organization design	Ethnocentric	Polycentric	Geocentric
Identification	Nationality of owner.	Nationality of host country.	Truly international company but identifying with national interests.
Authority; decision making	High in headquarters.	Relatively low in headquarters.	Aim for a collaborative approach between headquarters and subsidiaries.
Evaluation and control	Home standards applied for persons and performance.	Determined locally.	Find standards which are universal and local.
Communication; information flow	High volume to subsidiaries; orders, commands, advice.	Little to and from headquarters; little between subsidiaries.	Both ways and between subsidiaries; heads of subsidiaries part of management team.
Perpetuation (recruiting, staffing, development)	Recruit and develop people of home country for key positions everywhere in the world.	Develop people of local nationality for key positions in their own country.	Develop best people everywhere in the world for key positions everywhere in the world.

Source: Excerpted from Howard V. Perlmutter, "The Tortuous Evolution of the Multinational Corporation," *Columbia Journal of World Business,* 4 (January-February 1969): 12. Used with permission.

polycentric attitude view that assumes local managers in host countries know best how to run their own operations

operations. A **polycentric attitude** leads to a loose confederation of comparatively independent subsidiaries rather than to a highly integrated structure. Since foreign operations are measured in terms of ends (instead of means), methods, incentives, and training procedures vary widely from location to location.

On the negative side, wasteful duplication of effort occurs at the various units within the confederation precisely because they are independent. Such duplication can erode the efficiency of polycentric organizations. Moreover, global objectives can be undermined by excessive concern for local traditions and success. But there is a positive side: "The main advantages are an intensive exploitation of local markets, better sales since local management is often better informed, more local initiative for new products, more host-government support, and good local managers with high morale."[25]

geocentric attitude world-oriented view that draws upon the best talent from around the globe

Geocentric Attitude. Managers with a **geocentric attitude** are world-oriented. Skill, not nationality, determines who gets promoted or transferred to key positions around the globe. For example, Britain's Imperial Chemical Industries (ICI) has become a more geocentric company in recent years. "Until 1982, ICI's sixteen-person board was all British. Now it includes two Americans, a Canadian, a Japanese, and a German. Among the 180 top people in the company, 35 percent are non-British."[26] In geocentric companies, local and worldwide objectives are balanced in all aspects of operation. Collaboration between headquarters and subsidiaries is high, but an effort is made to maintain a balance between global standards and local discretion. According to Perlmutter, geocentric organizations have the following combination of costs and payoffs:

Advertisers Learn How to Reach America's Rapidly Growing Hispanic Population

When it comes to Hispanic marketing, a little knowledge is a dangerous thing. Remember Braniff's blooper? The airline's ads told Hispanics to fly *en cuero*—or "naked." Tropicana advertised *jugo de china* in Miami. *China* means orange to Puerto Ricans, but Miami's Cubans thought it was juice from the Orient. Jack in the Box goofed with a commercial featuring a band of Mexican mariachis accompanying a Spanish flamenco dancer. "That's like having Willie Nelson sing while Michael Jackson does the moonwalk," says Bert Valencia, a marketing professor at the American Graduate School of International Management in Glendale, Arizona.

Why do companies sometimes end up looking like *idiotas?* Because learning this market takes more than a few lessons at Berlitz. An occasional blunder is forgivable. But many companies are designing advertising for the nation's 19 million Hispanics without understanding the differences among Mexicans, Puerto Ricans, Cubans, and the rich array of other nationalities that make up the U.S. Hispanic population. These misdirected advertisers are shelling out money for prime-time spots and then scrimping on funds to test whether they work. In sum, they're sloughing off a group

of consumers with $130 billion in purchasing power. "And with quick and dirty efforts," says Valenica, "they can't expect big results."

Companies committed to Hispanic marketing, on the other hand, are scoring big. Their secret is often dumping the message they use for Anglos in favor of one with specific Hispanic appeal and picking Spanish media to convey it. Metropolitan Life increased sales of insurance to Hispanics over 150 percent [in 1988] with nationwide Spanish ads. The company chose to use Latin actors rather than Snoopy, the cartoon mainstay of its English ads, but not a big attraction for Hispanics. Adolph Coors Co. has built Hispanic market share in part by sponsoring festivals celebrating such holidays as Columbus Day in Miami and Cinco de Mayo in Los Angeles.

Hispanics are a rapidly growing segment of the population, increasing 34 percent since 1980, four times the overall U.S. growth in that period. Their numbers may exceed 40 million by 2015, surpassing blacks as the nation's largest minority group.

Source: Excerpted from Julia Lieblich, "If You Want a Big, New Market . . ." *Fortune* (November 21, 1988): 181. © 1988 Time Inc. All rights reserved.

Geocentrism's costs are largely related to communication and travel expenses, educational costs at all levels, time spent in decision making because consensus seeking among more people is required, and an international headquarters bureaucracy. Risks include those due to too wide a distribution of power, personnel problems, and those of re-entry of international executives. The payoffs are a more powerful total company throughout, a better quality of products and service, worldwide utilization of best resources, improvement of local company management, a greater sense of commitment to worldwide objectives, and last, but not least, more profit.[27]

Of these three contrasting attitudes, only a geocentric attitude can help management take a long step toward success in today's vigorously competitive global marketplace.

Convergence versus Divergence: Forces for World Uniformity and Diversity

Are the people on this planet becoming more alike? This is a pivotal issue for international managers who work in cross-cultural situations. If so, management techniques would translate readily from country to country in a more uniform world. If not, a more diverse world would require a richer variety of management techniques. According to the idea of **convergence**, the world is becoming more uniform because of forces such as technology, education, and pragmatism.[28] Capitalism and free enterprise, both popular notions today, involve essentially pragmatic pursuits. In opposition, **divergence** is a belief that forces such as cultural inertia, differing stages of economic development, unevenly distributed resources, and regional overpopulation guarantee global diversity. The effects of cultural inertia can be seen in the long-standing and often bitter ethnic and tribal rivalries that threaten to tear apart such countries as the Soviet Union, Canada, Iraq, Yugoslavia, India, and South Africa. The growing gap between rich and poor countries also threatens to become an increasing source of resentment and discord. Figure 19.2 shows convergent forces drawing the peoples of the world together while divergent forces are pulling them apart. It is a dramatic tug-of-war in which a clear victory for either side is not yet in sight.

These opposing forces have immense implications for international management. Those who believe in a convergent world claim that management practices have universal applicability. MBO, for example, will work as well in Paris and Tokyo as it does in Los Angeles. But other managers, who believe in a divergent world, claim that management practices must be adapted culturally if they are to succeed. The challenge for management scholars is to determine, through research, what techniques will work where and with how much cultural adaptation, if any. Comparative management research insights are presented later in this chapter.

convergence belief that the world is becoming more uniform

divergence belief that the world is becoming more diverse

The Cultural Imperative

Culture has a powerful impact on people's behavior. Take the everyday act of a woman driving a car, for example. Women drivers are an ordinary sight in most parts of the world, but not in conservative Islamic Saudi Arabia. In late 1990, when fifty Saudi women broke with cultural tradition and drove automobiles through the capital city of Riyadh, "religious leaders went on the offensive, and the government cracked down hard. All the women involved who had government jobs were fired, and they all lost their passports for two years, as did their husbands."[29] Extreme? Perhaps, depending upon one's cultural assumptions about women. But this incident helps make an important point: people who defy cultural traditions do so at their own risk. In international business, that means the risk of not making the sale or of losing a contract or failing to negotiate a favorable deal. Therefore, a sensitivity to cross-cultural differences is imperative for people who do business in other countries.

In this section, we define the term *culture* and discuss a cultural profile of American managers. Then, drawing primarily from the work of pioneering cultural anthropologist Edward T. Hall, we explore key sources of cross-cultural differences.

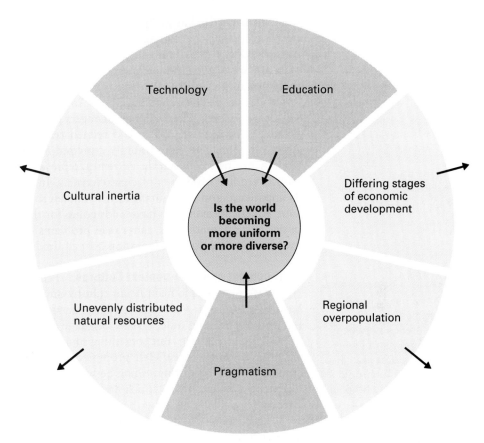

FIGURE 19.2 • Competing Forces of Convergence and Divergence

culture a population's taken-for-granted assumptions, values, beliefs, and symbols that foster patterned behavior

Culture Defined. Culture is the pattern of taken-for-granted assumptions about how a given collection of people should think, act, and feel as they go about their daily affairs.[30] Regarding the taken-for-granted assumptions, Hall noted:

> *Much of culture operates outside our awareness; frequently we don't even know what we know. . . . This applies to all people. The Chinese or the Japanese or the Arabs are as unaware of their assumptions as we are of our own. We each assume that they're part of human nature. What we think of as "mind" is really internalized culture.*[31]

In Chapter 8, we called *organizational* culture the social glue binding members of an organization together. Similarly, at a broader level, societal culture acts as a social glue. That glue is made up of norms, values, attitudes, role expectations, taboos, symbols, heroes, beliefs, morals, customs, and rituals. Cultural lessons are imparted from birth to death via role models, formal education, religious indoctrination, and peer pressure.

A Cultural Profile of American Managers. A good way to become more aware of cross-cultural differences is to look at oneself through the eyes of people from other cultures. One study based on interviews with forty managers from many different countries has given American managers a revealing look in the cultural mirror.[32] All of the managers had professional experience in more than one country. Only three of the interviewees were American. Each manager was asked to characterize the "American style" of management. Results of the study are presented in Table 19.3.

Two sets of characteristics of the American style of managing turned out to be clearly positive. International managers generally like Americans' informality, creativity, open-mindedness, and related traits. At the other end of the scale, American managers were roundly criticized for being educationally and professionally narrow. Between the extremes, representing a mix of positives and negatives, were five other sets of characteristics. In this middle zone, strengths such as impatience and individualism, when taken to extreme, became weaknesses. In sum, American managers have a lot going for themselves. But a number of their basic cultural tendencies can cause problems in cross-cultural dealings. Self-awareness and cultural adaptation are required.

High-context and Low-context Cultures.   People from European-based cultures typically assess people from Asian cultures such as China and Japan as quiet and hard to figure out. Conversely, Asians tend to view Westerners as aggressive, insensitive, and even rude.[33] True, language differences are a significant barrier to mutual understanding. But something more fundamental is involved, something cultural. Anthropologist Hall prompted better understanding of cross-cultural communication by distinguishing between high- and low-context cultures.[34] The difference centers on how much meaning one takes from what is actually said or written versus who the other person is.

● ● ● ● ● ● ● ● ● ● ● ● ● ● ●

From a cross-cultural perspective, explain the difference between high-context and low-context cultures and also between monochronic and polychronic time.

TABLE 19.3 ● How Do International Managers Characterize American Managers? Frequently mentioned features that distinguish the U.S. from other nations.

Positive	*Negative*
Informal, frank, trustworthy	
Innovative, open-minded, objective, pragmatic, flexible	
Work harder than Europeans	But less than many Asians. Often "spinning wheels"
Impatient; get things done; hands-on mentality	Short-term orientation
Materialistic; profit-oriented; business is a valid, worthy profession	Judge persons' worth by their wealth; shun low-pay manufacturing jobs
Individualistic; entrepreneurial	Loyal to division, not firm
Aggressive, hard-nosed, pragmatic	Overlook simpler, diplomatic means
	Not well-rounded educationally; parochial

Source: Ashok Nimgade, "American Management as Viewed by International Professionals," November–December 1989, figure 4, p. 102. Reprinted from *Business Horizons,* November–December 1989. Copyright 1989 by the Foundation for the School of Business at Indiana University. Used with permission.

In **high-context cultures,** people rely heavily on nonverbal and subtle situational messages when communicating with others. The other person's official status, place in society, and reputation say a great deal about the person's rights, obligations, and trustworthiness. In high-context cultures, people do not expect to talk about such "obvious" things. Conversation simply provides general background information about the other person. Thus, in high-context Japan, the ritual of exchanging business cards is a social necessity, and failing to read a card you have been given is a grave insult. The other person's company and position determine what is said and how. Arab, Chinese, and Korean cultures also are high-context.

People from **low-context cultures** convey essential messages and meaning primarily with words. Low-context cultures in Germany, Switzerland, Scandinavia, North America, and Great Britain expect people to communicate their precise intended meaning. While low-context people do read so-called body language, its messages are secondary to spoken and written words (see The World of Management). Legal contracts with precisely worded expectations are important in low-context countries such as the United States. However, according to international communication experts, "in high-context cultures the process of forging a business relationship is as important as, if not more important than, the written details of the actual deal."[35] This helps explain why Americans tend to be frustrated with the apparently slow pace of business dealings in Japan. For the Japanese, the many rounds of meetings and social gatherings are necessary to collect valuable contextual information, as a basis for judging the other party's character. For the schedule-driven American, anything short of actually signing the contract is considered a pointless waste of time. *Patience* is a prime virtue for low-context managers doing business in high-context cultures.

Other Sources of Cultural Diversity. Managers headed for a foreign country need to do their homework on the following cultural variables to avoid awkwardness and problems.[36] There are no rights or wrongs here, only cross-cultural differences.

- *Time.* Hall referred to time as a silent language of culture. He distinguished between monochronic and polychronic time. **Monochronic time** is based on the perception that time is a unidimensional straight line divided into standard units, such as seconds, minutes, hours, and days. In monochronic cultures, including North America and Northern Europe, everyone is assumed to be on the same clock and time is treated as money. The general rule is to do one thing at a time and, above all, to be on time. In contrast, **polychronic time** involves the perception of time as flexible, elastic, and multidimensional. Latin American, Mediterranean, and Arab cultures are polychronic. Managers in polychronic cultures such as Mexico see no problem with loosely scheduled, overlapping office visits. A monochronic American, arriving ten minutes early for an appointment with a Mexican official, resents having to wait another thirty minutes. The American perceives the Mexican official as slow and insensitive. The Mexican believes the American is self-centered and impatient.[37] Different perceptions of time are responsible for this collision of cultures.

Beware of Body Language in Cross-Cultural Situations

As the trade barriers come down in Europe and contact is increased, cross-cultural misunderstandings are bound to rise. As often as not, many of the misunderstandings in communications will arise not from what is said, but from a lack of awareness of the various interpretations different cultures ascribe to nonverbal forms of behavior.

Attaining fluency in a foreign language is often only half the battle when it comes to mastering effective cross-cultural communications. Of equal, and at times, greater importance is the knowledge of nonverbal communication, or body language. This "silent language," or the actions that accompany our words, includes such dimensions as touching, distance between speakers, facial expressions, speech inflection or volume, pauses, as well as hand and arm gestures. Even clothing and colors are symbolic and have different meanings depending on the part of the world.

Very seldom do we speak without an accompanying action in which hands invariably play a crucial role.

The use of gesticulations varies according to culture. The Italians and the French are renowned for relying heavily on hand gestures to replicate or mimic ideas that they are simultaneously communicating in words.

The snag with many hand gestures is that their meanings vary according to where you are. In the United States and many other countries, for example, the rounded, pinched-thumb and index-finger "A-OK" gesture is easily recognized as meaning *fine, perfect,* or simply *okay.* In Japan, the traditional meaning of the gesture is *money.* In Portugal and some other countries, this gesture has an offensive or obscene meaning. . . .

Germans often raise their eyebrows in recognition of a clever idea. The same expression in Britain is a sign of skepticism.

The French have some of the most expressive hand gestures. To symbolize exquisiteness, a Frenchman pinches his fingertips, raises them to his lips, and softly tosses a kiss into the air with his chin held high. On the other hand, if a Frenchman rubs the base of his nose with his forefinger, he's warning "something smells bad," "be cautious," "we can't trust these people."

Very similar is the Italian gesture of tapping the side of the nose with the forefinger. Its meaning: *Take care. There is danger ahead. They are getting crafty.* In the Netherlands, this gesture means *I'm drunk* or *you're drunk.* In England, a forefinger tap on the side of the nose means conspiracy or secrecy.

Source: Excerpted from Robert Moran, "Watch Your Body Language," *International Management,* 45 (May 1990): 84. Reprinted by permission.

- *Interpersonal space.*   People in a number of cultures prefer to stand close when conversing. Both Arabs and Asians fall into this group. An interpersonal distance of only six inches is very disturbing to a Northern European or an American who is accustomed to conversing at arm's length. Cross-cultural gatherings in the Middle East often involve an awkward dance as Arab hosts strive to get closer while their American and European guests shuffle backwards around the room to maintain what they consider to be a proper distance.

- *Agreements.*   A handshake in some cultures is more binding than a legal contract. Contracts in some countries (Greece, for example) signal the start of negotiations, rather than the end.

- *Language.* Foreign language skills are the gateway to true cross-cultural understanding. Translations are not an accurate substitute for conversational ability in the local language.

- *Religion.* Awareness of a business colleague's religious traditions is essential for building a lasting relationship. Those traditions may dictate dietary restrictions, religious holidays, and Sabbath schedules, which are important to the devout and represent cultural minefields for the uninformed.

Comparative Management Insights

comparative management study of how organizational behavior and management practices differ across cultures

Comparative management is the study of how organizational behavior and management practices differ across cultures. In this comparatively new field of inquiry, as in other new fields, there is disagreement about theoretical frameworks and research methodologies.[38] Nevertheless, some useful lessons have been learned. In this section, we focus on (1) the applicability of American management theories in other cultures, (2) Ouchi's Theory Z, which contrasts American and Japanese management practices, (3) a cross-cultural study of work goals, and (4) an international contingency model of leadership.

Applying American Management Theories Abroad

•••••••••••••••••
Discuss what Hofstede's research has to say about the applicability of American management theories in foreign cultures.

The results of a unique study indicate that management theories may not be universally applicable. Geert Hofstede, a Dutch organizational behavior researcher, surveyed 116,000 IBM employees from forty different countries.[39] Hofstede classified each of his forty national samples according to four different cultural dimensions, each of which probed an important question about the prevailing culture:

- *Power distance.* How readily do individuals accept the unequal distribution of power in organizations and institutions?

- *Uncertainty avoidance.* How threatening are uncertain and ambiguous situations, and how important are rules, conformity, and absolute truths?

- *Individualism-collectivism.* Are people responsible for their own welfare within a loosely knit social framework, or does the group look out for individuals in exchange for loyalty?

- *Masculinity-femininity.* How important are masculine attitudes (assertiveness, money and possessions, and performance) versus feminine attitudes (concern for people, the quality of life, and the environment)?

Hofstede scored the forty countries in his sample from low to high on each of the four cultural dimensions. The United States ranked moderately low (15 out of 40) on power distance, low (9 out of 40) on uncertainty avoidance, very high (40 out of 40) on individualism, and moderately high (28 out of 40) on masculinity.

TABLE 19.4 • Top-Ranking Needs Vary from Country to Country

Security	Security and social	Social	Self-actualization
Switzerland	Iran	Singapore	Hong Kong
West Germany*	Thailand	Denmark	Great Britain
Austria	Taiwan	Sweden	India
Italy	Brazil	Norway	United States
Venezuela	Israel	Netherlands	Philippines
Mexico	France	Finland	Canada
Colombia	Spain		New Zealand
Argentina	Turkey		Australia
Belgium	Peru		South Africa
Japan	Chile		Ireland
Greece	Yugoslavia		
Pakistan	Portugal		

Source: Paraphrased with permission from Geert Hofstede, "Motivation, Leadership, and Organization: Do American Theories Apply Abroad?" in *Organizational Dynamics,* 9, no. 1 (Summer 1980): 54–56. This article summarizes Dr. Hofstede's research published in the book *Culture's Consequences: International Differences in Work-related Values* (Beverly Hills, Calif.: Sage Publications, 1980).

*At the time of this study, East and West Germany were separate countries. East Germany was not one of the forty countries surveyed.

The marked cultural differences among the forty countries led Hofstede to recommend that American management theories should be adapted to local cultures rather than imposed on them. Recall that David McClelland, Abraham Maslow, Frederick Herzberg, and Victor Vroom developed their achievement, need, two-factor, and expectancy theories, respectively, within the U.S. cultural context. Hofstede believes that it is therefore naive to expect those theories to apply automatically in significantly different cultures. For example, American-made management theories that reflect Americans' preoccupation with individualism are out of place in countries such as Mexico, Brazil, and Japan, where individualism is discouraged. Moreover, as Hofstede discovered, the need ranked highest differs from culture to culture (see Table 19.4).

Hofstede's research does not attempt to tell international managers *how* to apply various management techniques in different cultures.[40] However, it does provide a useful cultural typology and presents a convincing case for the cultural adaptation of American management theory and practice.[41]

● ● ● ● ● ● ● ● ● ● ● ● ● ● ● ●
Identify important comparative management lessons learned from Ouchi's Theory Z research and international studies of work goals and leadership styles.

Ouchi's Theory Z: The Marriage of American and Japanese Management

The work of UCLA management scholar William Ouchi highlights a type of American company that has successfully melded the American way of managing with some aspects of management in another culture. Ouchi began his study by identifying the contrasting characteristics of Japanese and American companies.[42] During the course of his research, he discovered that certain successful United

States-based companies—including IBM, Intel, Hewlett-Packard, Eastman Kodak, and Eli Lilly—exhibited a style of management that effectively combined the traits of typical American and Japanese companies. He called these hybrid companies *Theory Z* organizations (see Figure 19.3). Interestingly, Ouchi's The-

FIGURE 19.3 • The Evolution of Theory Z Organizations

Source: William G. Ouchi, *Theory Z,* © 1981, Addison-Wesley Publishing Co., Inc. Reprinted with permission of the publisher.

Japanese Organizations	American Organizations	Theory Z Organizations
Lifetime employment	Short-term employment	Long-term employment (Large training investment encourages company to retain personnel through good and bad times.)
Slow evaluation and promotion	Rapid evaluation and promotion	Relatively slow evaluation and promotion (Promotions are tied to skills and contributions rather than to the calendar.)
Nonspecialized career paths	Specialized career paths	Cross-functional career paths (Company wide skills are acquired through varied and nonspecialized experience.)
Implicit control mechanisms (self-control)	Explicit control mechanisms (control through policies and rules)	Balanced explicit and implicit control mechanisms (Bureaucratic control is supplemented by personal judgments and feelings about what is right or wrong, appropriate or inappropriate.)
Collective decision making	Individual decision making	Consensual, participative decision making (Decisions are derived through democratic process involving all affected employees.)
Collective responsibility	Individual responsibility	Individual responsibility (Ultimate responsibility for decisions remains with relevant individuals.)
Holistic concern	Segmented concern	Holistic concern for employees (There is a willingness to deal with the "whole" person rather than fragmented organizational role players.)

ory Z companies did not simply imitate the Japanese. Instead, each firm's Theory Z qualities evolved from a desire to improve upon the typical American way of managing. Each Theory Z company was strictly American in origin, but American and Japanese in conduct and appearance.

The Japanese-like qualities of Theory Z organizations are identified as long-term employment, slower promotions, cross-functional career paths, greater emphasis on self-control, participative decision making, and a concern for the whole employee. Unlike Japanese organizations, Theory Z organizations emphasize *individual* responsibility, a distinctly American trait. Ouchi's work not only gives us a better understanding of Japanese management,[43] it also shows that American organizations can benefit from thoughtful incorporation of the experience of managers in other cultures.

A Cross-cultural Study of Work Goals

What do people want from their work? A survey of 8,192 employees from seven countries found general disagreement about the relative importance of eleven different work goals.[44] Respondents to the survey represented a broad range of professions and all levels of the organizational hierarchy. They were asked to rank eleven work goals. Those work goals are listed in Table 19.5, along with the average rankings for five countries. "Interesting work" got a consistently

TABLE 19.5 • Work Goals Vary from Country to Country

Work goals	Mean rankings (by country)				
	U.S.	Britain	Germany*	Israel	Japan
Interesting work	1	1	3	1	2
Pay	2	2	1	3	5
Job security	3	3	2	10	4
Match between person and job	4	6	5	6	1
Opportunity to learn	5	8	9	5	7
Variety	6	7	6**	11	9
Interpersonal relations	7	4	4	2	6
Autonomy	8	10	8	4	3
Convenient work hours	9	5	6**	7	8
Opportunity for promotion	10	11	10	8	11
Working conditions	11	9	11	9	10

*Formerly West Germany.

**Two goals tied for sixth rank.

Source: Data from Itzhak Harpaz, "The Importance of Work Goals: An International Perspective," *Journal of International Business Studies,* 21 (1st quarter 1990): 81. Reprinted with permission.

high ranking. "Opportunity for promotion" and "working conditions" consistently were at or very near the bottom of each country's rankings. Beyond those few consistencies, general disagreement prevailed.

The main practical implication of these findings is that managers need to adapt their motivational programs to local preferences. Throughout this text, we have consistently stressed the importance of the contingency approach to management. In this case, an international contingency approach to motivation is called for. For instance, pay is relatively less important in Japan than in the other four countries. And job security is much less important to Israelis than it is to American, British, German, and Japanese employees.

An International Contingency Model of Leadership

Like motivational programs, leadership styles must be adapted to the local culture. This conclusion is based on a new international contingency model of leadership, which is the product of two separate but overlapping studies. As indicated in Table 19.6, the four path-goal leadership styles have varying applicability in selected countries. (Refer to our discussion of path-goal leadership theory in Chapter 14 for definitions of the four styles.) Importantly, the model in Table 19.6 is intended to be a general guideline for international managers, not a set of hard-and-fast rules.

TABLE 19.6 ● An International Contingency Model of Leadership: Culturally Appropriate Path-Goal Leadership Styles

Country	Directive	Supportive	Participative	Achievement-oriented
Australia		X	X	X
Brazil	X		X	
Canada		X	X	X
France	X		X	
Germany		X	X	X
Great Britain		X	X	X
Hong Kong	X	X	X	X
India	X		X	X
Italy	X	X	X	
Japan	X	X	X	
Philippines	X	X	X	X
Sweden			X	X
Taiwan	X	X	X	
United States		X	X	X

Source: Adapted in part from Carl A. Rodrigues, "The Situation and National Culture as Contingencies for Leadership Behavior: Two Conceptual Models," in *Advances in International Comparative Management,* 5, ed. S. Benjamin Prasad (Greenwich, Conn.: JAI Press, 1990), pp. 51–68; and Geert Hofstede and Michael Harris Bond, "The Confucius Connection: From Cultural Roots to Economic Growth," *Organizational Dynamics* (Spring 1988): 4–21.

According to the model, participative leadership is the most broadly applicable style. Participative leadership is not necessarily the *best* style; it simply is culturally acceptable in many different countries. Directive leadership is the least appropriate style, relative to the countries listed. Hong Kong and the Philippines, probably because of their rich cultural diversity, are unique in their receptiveness to all four leadership styles. International managers need a full repertoire of leadership styles in a culturally diverse world.

Potential Trouble Spots in International Management

Managers who cross international borders to do business encounter some unique problems. Those who anticipate and prepare for problems such as political instability and foreign corruption are less likely to be caught off guard. Let us examine these two potential trouble spots.

Political Instability

Citizens of established democracies such as the United States take political stability for granted. They do so because the transfer of power from one political party to another occurs in an orderly fashion without general bloodshed or political upheaval. Unfortunately, in most nations political instability is a constant fact of life. Between World War II and early 1991, a period when the United States had nine presidents, Italy went through fifty changes of government![45] Managers of MNCs and globals doing business in politically volatile countries must keep abreast of geopolitical realities and struggles for power.[46] Systematic political risk assessment is a step in the right direction.

political risk assessment systematic assessment of political uncertainties for international business

expropriation forced takeover of a business by a host country's government

Political risk assessment is "the systematic means of assessing and managing the political risks of foreign direct investment or international business."[47] The three major political risks are revolution, expropriation, and government regulation. **Expropriation** occurs when a host government takes over a foreign company. Although these political risks have been a fact of life for MNCs for many years, it took the Iranian revolution to awaken the international management community to the need for some sort of systematic assessment of political risk. The fact that U.S. companies lost more than $1 billion in Iran because of a largely unexpected revolution underscored the importance of knowing what is "really happening" in host countries. Three of the most popular responses to date have been hiring former government foreign relations experts as special consultants, buying political-risk insurance, and employing full-time political analysts.[48] Whichever approach is used, the overriding objective should be geocentric strategies that avoid unreasonable political risks.

Foreign Corruption

Bribery is common in many countries around the globe. However, U.S. law forbids American managers from participating in certain types of activities when doing business in other countries. Let us take a closer look at two types of bribery and the U.S. Foreign Corrupt Practices Act.

Multinational and global companies need to conduct regular political risk assessments for host countries. The idea is to minimize the element of surprise. Political groundswells that may foreshadow a violent revolution can be detected by trained observers. Here, anti-American protestors in Manila vent their anger over U.S. military bases in the Philippines. Although essentially political in nature, this type of instability carries over to the economic sphere.

• • • • • • • • • • • • • • • •

Distinguish between lubrication and whitemail bribes and discuss the U.S. Foreign Corrupt Practices Act.

lubrication bribes small amounts of money paid to low-level bureaucrats

whitemail bribes large sums of money paid to high-level, influential people

Lubrication and Whitemail Bribes.   Two kinds of bribery have been identified, lubrication bribes and whitemail bribes.[49] **Lubrication bribes** involve relatively small amounts of money that grease the wheels of bureaucratic progress. A firm doing business in Italy, for example, may find that a *bustarella* (an envelope stuffed with Italian lire) gets a particular license clerk to do his job. Or *la mordida* ("the bite") passed along to a Mexican building inspector may help ensure that he does *not* do his job particularly well. Although the name varies from country to country, lubrication bribes always have the same purpose: to make sure that things move along smoothly. Lubrication bribery is so deeply entrenched in parts of Asia, Africa, the Middle East, and Latin America that even those who oppose the practice admit it is very difficult to avoid.

Whitemail is an entirely different matter. Rather than going to the little guy, as in the case of lubrication bribes, **whitemail bribes** are large sums of money used to buy influence in high places. Because large amounts of money are involved, whitemail bribery funds must be "laundered"—kept in secret accounts or slush funds and passed through unofficial channels. This practice drew international attention during the mid-1970s, and crackdowns ensued. Two heads of state, a Japanese prime minister in 1974 and an Italian president in 1978, were forced to resign after being accused of receiving payoffs in excess of $1 million from Lockheed, the aerospace giant.[50] Given the huge amounts of money involved, whitemail bribes have been criticized by the U.S. Securities and Exchange Commission because public investors are not informed about them, by the Internal Revenue Service because they are illegal tax deductions, and by others who claim they are immoral and unethical. Proponents of whitemail bribes typically justify them by saying that payoffs and bribes are a necessary part of doing business abroad or that it is inappropriate and arrogant to export one nation's ethical standards to other countries.

The U.S. Foreign Corrupt Practices Act. This act, passed in late 1977 in response to public outcry over abuses such as Lockheed's, made it illegal for U.S. companies to knowingly corrupt a foreign official. (Lubrication bribes are not expressly outlawed.) Guilty companies can be fined up to $1 million, and guilty individuals can be fined up to $100,000 and/or jailed for up to ten years. The act also requires detailed recordkeeping and strict accounting controls.

As one might suspect, the Foreign Corrupt Practices Act is not very popular among corporate leaders.[51] In fact, in one survey of 1,200 high-level U.S. executives, 69 percent gave the Foreign Corrupt Practices Act a negative rating. Sixty-eight percent wanted the recordkeeping requirements reduced. Sixty-four percent wanted the act to draw a more specific distinction between legal and illegal payments. Significantly, however, although 78 percent of the surveyed executives believed the act makes it difficult to compete in countries where bribery is common, only 20 percent said they had lost business as a result of its passage.[52] A more recent study focusing on the Middle East found no convincing evidence that the act had hurt American business interests in the region.[53] As evidenced in the following example, the act can even have a beneficial impact:

> *In a recent contract negotiation in Beijing, for instance, the final agreement was threatened with derailment at the last minute when a Chinese participant in the negotiations demanded a "fee." When representatives from the U.S. company explained that making such a payment could subject the company to criminal prosecution in the United States, the demand was dropped.*[54]

In view of the present law, one observer summed up the foreign payoffs and bribery issue with the following advice: "Improper payments, it therefore appears, are literally a losing game. They may bring short-term benefits, but they involve enormous risks in the form of scandal and even prosecution. To protect itself and its managers, a corporation operating overseas should have a comprehensive, integrated system for preventing questionable payments."[55] In short, MNCs and global corporations need clearly defined ethical standards for foreign business dealings, backed up by strict enforcement (see Management Ethics).

Staffing Foreign Positions

In today's global economy, successful foreign experience is becoming a required steppingstone to top management. Ford Motor Company's past and present chairmen, for example, proved themselves capable during key foreign assignments. Former chairman Donald Petersen was responsible during the late 1970s for Ford's entire international automotive operations. Present chairman Harold Poling spent five years as the head of Ford's European operations.[56] Their first-hand international experience better equipped these executives to run a global enterprise.

Unfortunately, owing largely to the sink-or-swim approach to foreign assignments, Petersen's and Poling's positive experiences are still exceptions in American business. The statistics are grim. Researcher Rosalie L. Tung, after

Dealing with the Issue of Foreign Bribery

To companies that play it superstraight, East Asia can be disheartening. It's the world's fastest-growing region, but business ethics often seem mired in the past. . . .

So what's a clean-behind-the-ears kind of manager to do? While it's always better to forsake a deal than to sacrifice your principles, old hands in the region argue that there are ways to maneuver around corrupt officials without violating either your own standards or the law. You have to think strategically: Pick a partner whose relationships—rather than payoffs—will open doors; find out what makes the bribe seeker tick; and thoroughly master the local laws. . . .

Throughout much of Asia, neither information nor money counts the most in forging business relationships. Rather it is blood and history, the bonds that tie together families and extended families, especially among the Overseas Chinese, whose business networks stretch across Southeast Asia. Westerners who link up with an Asian partner with the right family connections find doors opening that remain closed even to outsiders willing to pay off the doorman. Often the local partner's influence and access are traceable to his indirect relationship with, say, the supervisor of the building-permits bureau, whose uncle happens to be married to the local partner's aunt. Though many Westerners in the [Pacific] Rim may not fully comprehend these extended family trees, making use of them is considerably preferable to paying bribes.

Carefully choosing your business associates won't help much, though, if someone in your own company is on the take. Not only does ITT require newly hired managers to state in writing that they will adhere to the company's code of conduct, it also conducts routine, unannounced audits of operations around the world.

When a manager suspects a problem at his company, he can initiate an investigation. . . . Should the signs point to payoffs, companies may call in outside experts like Dan Grove, the managing director of CTS Group, a Hong Kong-based firm that specializes in investigating commercial skulduggery for such clients as Intel and Louis Vuitton. Though Grove is an American, the company's investigators are mainly Asians, who frequently pose as local businessmen in order to gather evidence. Much of their sleuthing, however, consists of going over paperwork.

While investigating the purchasing department of an electronics company in Malaysia, CTS agents studied past invoices in order to understand buying patterns. Their analysis led to vendors who were offering kickbacks to the company's purchasing agents in exchange for orders. Threatened with exposure, the vendors admitted the arrangement. . . . Eventually the company fired virtually its entire purchasing department.

Source: Excerpted from Ford S. Worthy, "When Somebody Wants a Payoff," *Fortune* (Pacific Rim Special Issue, Fall 1989): 117–122. © The Time Inc. Magazine Company. All rights reserved.

considering her own and other researchers' findings, concluded that "approximately 30 percent of overseas assignments within U.S. multinationals are mistakes."[57] (Comparable figures for European and Japanese companies are significantly lower, typically below 5 percent.) Mistakes, in this context, are foreign-posted employees who perform so poorly that they are either fired or sent home early. The cost of premature returnees has been estimated to range from $50,000 to $150,000 per employee.[58] Included in these surprisingly high figures are the costs of recruitment, employee or family relocation, overseas pay supplements, return and replacement, and inadequate job performance. U.S.

Kate Fickle, pictured here toasting departing friends at a *sayonara* party, is an "expatriate" in the truest sense of the word. Her youth was spent in Thailand and Bangladesh where her father worked on power plant projects. Today, she is an IBM marketing director in Tokyo. Japanese lessons are only part of a whirlwind existence that sees acquaintances come and go all too quickly.

MNCs are challenged not to waste this sort of investment. They need to do a much better job of preparing employees for foreign assignments. Toward that end, let us examine why such a high proportion of American managers fail abroad and what can be done about it. We also will consider the cultural barriers North American women managers face abroad.

Why Is the U.S. Expatriate Failure Rate So High?

Discuss the nature and importance of cross-cultural training in international management.

Although historically a term for banishment or exile to a foreign county, *expatriate* today refers to those who live and work abroad. A survey of eight U.S. MNCs uncovered some important facts about the reasons for corporate expatriate failures (see Table 19.7). *Family and personal adjustment problems* head the list, whereas technical incompetence ranks near the bottom. Expatriate American managers tend to be technically competent, but they and/or their families too often are at a disadvantage in cross-cultural settings. This state of affairs is not surprising in view of the following:

> [Recent research] underscores the woeful lack of preparation many U.S. executives receive for assignments overseas. Of some 100 high-level U.S. executives (average income $172,000) working in Western Europe, 84 percent received no corporate briefing on management practices in their host countries, and 77 percent didn't even get factual information on the new country. Only 15 percent received language training. And over 75 percent of the companies failed to communicate with their employees' spouses about the new assignments and to offer them job assistance overseas.[59]

Twenty percent of the polled executives desired a transfer home, and 9 percent actually went home early.

TABLE 19.7 • Why U.S. Employees Fail in Foreign Assignments (in descending order of importance)

1. Inability of the manager's spouse to adjust to a different physical or cultural environment
2. The manager's inability to adapt to a different physical or cultural environment
3. Other family-related problems
4. The manager's personality or emotional immaturity
5. The manager's inability to cope with the responsibilities posed by overseas work
6. The manager's lack of technical competence
7. The manager's lack of motivation to work overseas

Source: Ranking based on responses to a survey of eighty U.S. MNCs. Rosalie L. Tung, "Expatriate Assignments: Enhancing Success and Minimizing Failure," *Academy of Management Executive,* 1 (May 1987): 117. Reprinted by permission.

Cross-cultural Training

In line with our earlier definition, culture is the unique system of values, beliefs, and symbols that fosters patterned behavior in a given population. It is difficult to distinguish the individual from his or her cultural context. Consequently, people tend to be very protective of their cultural identity. Careless defiance of cultural norms or traditions by outsiders can result in grave personal insult. Cultural sensitivity can be learned, fortunately, through cross-cultural training.

cross-cultural training guided experience that helps people live and work in foreign cultures.

Specific Techniques. Cross-cultural training is defined as any form of guided experience aimed at helping people live and work comfortably in another culture. Five basic cross-cultural training techniques, listed in order of increasing complexity, are:

- *Documentary Programs.* Trainees read about a foreign country's history, culture, institutions, geography, and economics. Videotaped presentations also are often used.

- *Culture Assimilator.* Cultural familiarity is achieved through exposure to a series of simulated intercultural incidents, or typical problem situations. This technique has been used to quickly train those who are given short notice of a foreign assignment.

- *Language Instruction.* Conversational language skills are taught through a variety of methods.[60] Months, sometimes years, of study are required to master difficult languages. But, as a cross-cultural communications professor recently noted, "To speak more than one language is no longer a luxury, it is a necessity."[61]

- *Sensitivity Training.* Experiential exercises teach awareness of the impact of one's actions on others.

- *Field Experience.* Firsthand exposure to ethnic subcultures in one's own country or to foreign cultures heightens awareness.[62]

Is One Technique Better Than Another?   A study of eighty (sixty-three male, seventeen female) managers from a U.S. electronics company attempted to compare the relative effectiveness of different training techniques.[63] A documentary approach was compared with an interpersonal approach. The latter combined sensitivity training and local ethnic field experience. The two techniques were judged equally effective at promoting cultural adjustment, as measured during the managers' three-month stay in South Korea. The researchers recommended a *combination* of documentary and interpersonal training. The importance of language training was diminished in this study because the managers dealt primarily with English-speaking Koreans.

Considering that many American companies have no formal expatriate training programs,[64] the key issue is not which type of training is better, but whether companies have any systematic cross-cultural training at all.

An Integrated Expatriate Staffing System.   Cross-cultural training, in whatever form, should not be an isolated experience. Rather, it should be part of an integrated selection-orientation-repatriation process focused on a distinct career path.[65] The ultimate goal should be a positive and productive overseas experience for the employee and his or her family and a smooth professional and cultural re-entry back home.

During the selection phase, the usual interview should be supplemented with an orientation session for the candidate's family. This session gives everyone an opportunity to "select themselves out" before a great deal of time and money has been invested. Experience has shown that, upon arrival at the foreign assignment, family sponsors or assigned mentors are effective at reducing culture shock. Sponsors and mentors ease the expatriate family through the critical first six months by answering naive but important questions and by serving as cultural translators.

Finally, repatriation should be a forethought rather than an afterthought.[66] Candidates for foreign assignments deserve a firm commitment from their organization that a successful tour of duty will lead to a step up the career ladder upon return. Expatriates who spend their time worrying about being leapfrogged while they are absent from headquarters are less likely to succeed.

Relying on Local Managerial Talent

In recent years, the expensive expatriate failure problem and general trends toward geocentrism and globalism have resulted in a greater reliance on managers from host countries. Foreign nationals already know the language and culture and do not require huge relocation expenditures.[67] In addition, host-country governments tend to look favorably on a greater degree of local control. On the negative side, local managers may have an inadequate knowledge of home-office goals and procedures. The staffing of foreign positions is necessarily a case-by-case proposition.

Understanding the Cultural Barriers to Female Managers

Women have historically had limited opportunities in international business. In one major study, it was discovered that only *3 percent* of a sample of more than 13,000 American and Canadian managers working overseas were women. According to 686 personnel managers questioned, foreigners' prejudice was the number one barrier to North American female managers working overseas. Researcher Nancy Adler interpreted this barrier in the following manner:

> *A wide range of countries (including Japan, Korea, Saudi Arabia, Italy, Greece, Australia, France, etc.) were seen as limiting the role of women in business, considering women as second class citizens, restricting women's mobility, or excluding women altogether from the world of work. . . .*
> *Out of respect for the integrity of the foreign culture and the difficulty in changing fundamental beliefs and values, most companies believed foreigners' prejudice to be a serious, and often insurmountable, barrier confronting North American women's successful pursuit of international careers.*[68]

In spite of limited opportunities, selection bias, and increased cultural risks, the respondents in Adler's study predicted substantial growth in female expatriate managers in the years ahead.[69] Such growth has, in fact, occurred.

Summary

The study of international management has become more important in recent years because of the growing influence of multinational companies (MNCs) and global corporations. MNCs are businesses that exercise strategic control over production and/or marketing facilities in two or more countries. Global corporations go beyond MNCs by designing, making, and selling products anywhere on the planet. Profit potential, rather than international boundaries, determines where and how a global corporation does business. MNCs and global corporations are associated with the final stage of a six-stage internationalization process. The six stages are licensing, exporting, local warehousing and selling, local assembly and packaging, joint venture, and direct foreign investment. Research evidence shows MNCs to be less financially risky than purely domestic firms. Strategic management is especially important in international firms, because geographically dispersed operations strain management processes.

Experts, noting that American managers generally are prepared only for domestic service, recommended that present and future managers begin to think globally and cross-culturally. According to Howard Perlmutter, management may have any of three general attitudes about international operations: an ethnocentric attitude (home-country oriented), a polycentric attitude (host-country oriented), or a geocentric attitude (world oriented). Perlmutter claims that a geocentric attitude will lead to better product quality, improved use of resources, better local management, and more profit than the other attitudes. Disagreement about the universality of management theory and practice derives from differing perspectives of the forces of convergence and divergence. "Convergents" emphasize global similarities and believe management practices apply equally well around the world. "Divergents" emphasize the need to adapt management theory and practice to fit different cultures.

Culture is a social glue binding together given populations of people. It involves shared patterns of taken-for-granted assumptions about all aspects of life. American managers are seen as displaying both positive and negative cultural tendencies. Communications in high-context cultures such as Japan is based more on nonverbal and situational messages than it is in low-context cultures such as the United States. People in monochronic time cultures perceive time to be linear and divided into standard units. In contrast, cultures based on polychronic time consider time to be flexible and multidimensional. International managers need to be aware of cultural differences in interpersonal space, agreements, language, and religion.

Comparative management is a new field of study concerned with how organizational behavior and management practices differ across cultures. A unique study by Geert Hofstede of 116,000 IBM employees in forty nations classified each country by its prevailing attitude toward power distance, uncertainty avoidance, individualism-collectivism, and masculinity-feminity. In view of significant international differences on these cultural dimensions, Hofstede suggests that American management theory and practice be adapted to local cultures rather than imposed on them. Ouchi's Theory Z describes a hybrid type of American company that exhibits a combination of typical American and Japanese characteristics. Theory Z firms rely heavily on Japanese-style consensus and participation during decision making. But Theory Z organizations prefer an American-style emphasis on individual responsibility. Cross-cultural studies of work goals and leadership styles uncovered a great deal of diversity. Thus international contingency approaches to motivation and leadership are recommended.

The task of international management is made difficult by political instability and foreign corruption. Alarmed by the sudden loss of more than $1 billion in property in the Iranian revolution, U.S. companies are increasingly turning to systematic assessment of political risk. Revolution, expropriation, and government regulation are the three major political risks for MNCs and global corporations. The U.S. Foreign Corrupt Practices Act is a strong deterrent to whitemail bribery and payoffs by U.S. managers doing business in other countries.

Compared with European and Japanese companies, U.S. multinationals have a much higher expatriate failure rate. Family and personal adjustment problems to foreign cultures, not lack of technical expertise, are the leading causes of this failure. Systematic cross-cultural training is needed to help solve this costly problem, though use of local managerial talent is also a possible solution, depending on the situation. Despite significant cultural barriers, North American women are gaining greater access to overseas managerial positions.

Terms to Understand

International management
Multinational company (MNC)
Global corporation
Ethnocentric attitude
Polycentric attitude
Geocentric attitude
Convergence

Divergence
Culture
High-context cultures
Low-context cultures
Monochronic time
Polychronic time
Comparative management

Political risk assessment

Expropriation

Lubrication bribes

Whitemail bribes

Cross-cultural training

Questions for Discussion

1. Why would the effective management of a multinational company or global corporation be more difficult than managing a company with only domestic operations?

2. In your opinion, which of the six stages of internationalization is most risky? Explain.

3. What are the advantages of thinking geocentrically even if your company is not a multinational?

4. Which force in the global tug-of-war seems to be winning, convergence or divergence? Which side do you see prevailing in the next five years? What is your evidence?

5. Do you agree with the cultural profile of American managers in Table 19.3? Explain. What, if anything, would you change to make the profile more accurate?

6. What is your personal experience, either internationally or in your home country, with high- and low-context cultures?

7. Should management theories and techniques developed by Americans be applied without modification in foreign cultures? Explain your position.

8. How would you respond to a manager who made the following statement: "Participative leadership will work only in the United States. Everywhere else, you need to rely on a directive style."

9. What is your position on paying off or bribing foreign officials in the course of doing business overseas?

10. Which intercultural training technique (or combination) do you think would be most effective? Explain.

Back to the Opening Case

Now that you have read Chapter 19, you should be able to answer the following questions about the Asea Brown Boveri case:

1. Why is Barnevik's term *multidomestic* an appropriate one for ABB?

2. Which label best fits ABB: ethnocentric, polycentric, or geocentric? Explain your rationale.

3. Using Table 19.3 as a reference point, how well do you think the typical American manager fits Barnevik's vision of a "global manager"?

4. What sort of cross-cultural training program would you recommend for someone slated to become one of ABB's 500 global managers? Explain your rationale.

Anne Benbow Takes Success to the Bank in Tokyo

Living and working in a country that rarely offers women management opportunities, [Anne] Benbow has many stories to tell.

Benbow has been vice president and human resource manager at Chase Manhattan Bank in Tokyo since October 1987. She joined Chase in 1981 as a training specialist. . . .

When it was suggested that Benbow take the Tokyo assignment, the issue of being a woman working in Japan was raised with a "let's try it and see how it works" attitude, she said. . . . "I found after I arrived that people really do tend to see you as a foreigner first" and then as a woman, she said. . . .

The most important advice Benbow offers to Americans doing business in Japan is: "Maintain a positive attitude and be willing to stand up and say what you believe in because that is more important than knowing the social niceties. Most Japanese don't expect you to know the social niceties when you arrive. They hope you'll learn, and they hope you'll learn quickly. But they're very forgiving of new arrivals," she said.

Asking a lot of questions is another management strategy Benbow learned to use quickly. "In the Japanese corporation, the human resource manager is generally perceived as the second most powerful position. As a result, people are extremely deferential and would never dream of insulting you by offering you information that they think you probably already know—or should know," she said. Also, "when you ask a question, and I think this is partly cultural and partly language, you tend to get back only the answer to the question with very limited contextual information," she said.

According to Benbow, there are subtle differences in the Japanese expectations of human resource management. "The HR practitioner is expected to know more about the employees in Japan than they do in the United States," Benbow said. The Japanese company is, in a sense, the individual's family, "so the HR manager is the head of the family in a way. People really do expect you to know about events in their lives—weddings, funerals, births of children. . . ."

Handling the Change

Moving from a headquarters environment to become essentially the on-site person in a small company thousands of miles away has also affected Benbow's role. The great physical distance between her office and the New York headquarters means that she is almost entirely self-reliant.

"The spectrum of issues that I handle directly is much broader than that which I'd handle in my previous jobs," she said. Before, "there were always functional specialists whom I could refer things to for assistance."

In Japan, human resource management is not usually considered a profession. Instead, managers in a company take turns working in the HR field. They may work in human resources soon after they join the company, then rotate into other fields, and later return to HR management when more advanced in their careers.

The most familiar and natural part of Benbow's environment is an American HR network. An informal [dinner] group of American human resource managers from [19] U.S. financial institutions in Japan have provided encouragement and assistance.

The dinner group served as Benbow's introduction to the local network. "People who have been there longer know where the resources are in Tokyo. There was no handbook, and very limited, direct guidance available to me when I got there," she said. . . .

Topping It All

Her own decision to step into the international arena came after a whirlwind of activity on the home front. . . . "After I finished my MBA in June 1987 I promised my husband that we would return to some semblance of a normal life. And we did—for the summer. On our fifth wedding anniversary I was asked to take the position in Japan," Benbow recalled.

"That morning my husband, Andy, had given me an anniversary card that said: 'Five years—four jobs, two houses, two babies, and an MBA. How do you top that?' When I walked in that night, he looked up and . . . I said, 'How much do you like sushi?' So we think we topped it."

The move to Tokyo from New York was accomplished in shifts, with Anne Benbow moving first. . . . "That initial period was a bit disruptive, having the family separated,

but it paid a benefit in that it really allowed me to immerse myself in a very new and strange situation. . . ." Benbow's husband was [also] hired by Chase, first as a consultant and later full time.

For Discussion

1. How could familiarity with the concept of high-context cultures have helped Benbow when she first arrived in Japan?

2. Relative to Ouchi's Theory Z, which characteristics of the typical Japanese organization are evident in this case.

3. What function does the American HR network play in Benbow's career?

4. Why will Anne Benbow's assignment in Japan probably be successful?

References

Opening Quotation. Dean C. Barnlund, "Public and Private Self in Communicating with Japan," *Business Horizons*, 32 (March-April 1989): 40.

Opening Case. Klaus E. Agthe, "Managing the Mixed Marriage," *Business Horizons* (January-February 1990): 37–43; Jonathan Kapstein and Stanley Reed, "The Euro-Gospel According to Percy Barnevik," *Business Week* (July 23, 1990): 64–66; William Taylor, "The Logic of Global Business: An Interview with ABB's Percy Barnevik," *The Harvard Business Review* (March-April 1991): 90–105.

Closing Case. Excerpted from Stephenie Overman, "Different World Brings Challenge," *HRMagazine*, 35 (June 1990): 52–55. Reprinted with the permission of *HRMagazine* (formerly *Personnel Administrator*) published by the Society for Human Resource Management, Alexandria, VA.

1. Quoted in William Taylor, "The Logic of Global Business: An Interview with ABB's Percy Barnevik," *The Harvard Business Review* (March-April 1991): 94.

2. Data for these examples from Brenton R. Schlender, "Are the Japanese Buying Too Much?" *Fortune* (Pacific Rim Special Issue, Fall 1990): 99–101; Paul Magnusson, "American Smart Bombs, Foreign Brains," *Business Week* (March 4, 1991): 18; Linda Feldmann, "Muscovites Have Fallen in Love with a Pair of Golden Arches," *The Christian Science Monitor* (August 24, 1990): 11; Allan T. Demaree, "The New Germany's Glowing Future," *Fortune* (December 3, 1990): 146–154.

3. See Benton Randolph, "When Going Global Isn't Enough," *Training*, 27 (August 1990): 47–51.

4. Based partly on discussion in Arvind V. Phatak, *International Dimensions of Management*, 2nd edition (Boston: PWS-Kent, 1989), p. 4.

5. Patricia A. Galagan, "Executive Development in a Changing World," *Training & Development Journal*, 44 (June 1990): 26.

6. Jeremy Main, "How To Go Global—and Why," *Fortune* (August 28, 1989): 70. Also see William J. Holstein, "The Stateless Corporation," *Business Week* (May 14, 1990): 98–105.

7. See Paul A. Eisenstein, "Honda Reaches for U.S. Identity," *The Christian Science Monitor* (March 25, 1991): 9.

8. The following six-step sequence is based on Alan M. Rugman, "A New Theory of the Multinational Enterprise: Internalization versus Internalization," *Columbia Journal of World*

Business, 15 (Spring 1980): 23–29. Also see Lawrence S. Welch and Reijo Luostarinen, "Internationalization: Evolution of a Concept," *Journal of General Management,* 14 (Winter 1988): 34–55.

9. Data from Michael J. Mandel and Aaron Bernstein, "Dispelling the Myths That Are Holding Us Back," *Business Week* (December 17, 1990): 66–70.

10. See James R. Houghton, "Corning Cultivates Joint Ventures That Endure," *Planning Review,* 18 (September-October 1990): 15–17; Robert J. Brown, "Mixed Marriages," *International Management,* 45 (December 1990): 84; Rose Brady and Rosemarie Boyle, "Combustion Engineering's Dislocated Joint Venture," *Business Week* (October 22, 1990): 49–50.

11. See Dinah Lee and Jonathan Levine, "AT&T Slowly Gets Its Global Wires Uncrossed," *Business Week* (February 11, 1991): 82–83.

12. Jeremy Main, "Making Global Alliances Work," *Fortune* (December 17, 1990): 121–126.

13. Adapted from Ibid. and David Lei and John W. Slocum, Jr., "Global Strategic Alliances: Payoffs and Pitfalls," *Organizational Dynamics,* 19 (Winter 1991): 44–62.

14. For additional details, see Israel Shaked, "Are Multinational Corporations Safer?" *Journal of International Business Studies,* 17 (Spring 1986): 83–106.

15. See Robert M. Grant, "Multinationality and Performance among British Manufacturing Companies," *Journal of International Business Studies,* 18 (Fall 1987): 79–89.

16. Based on discussion in Sumantra Ghoshal, "Global Strategy: An Organizing Framework," *Strategic Management Journal,* 8 (September-October 1987): 425–440. Also see John J. Dyment, "Strategies and Management Controls for Global Corporations," *Journal of Business Strategy,* 7 (Spring 1987): 20–26.

17. For an excellent discussion, see Rodman L. Drake and Lee M. Caudill, "Management of the Large Multinational: Trends and Future Challenges," *Business Horizons,* 24 (May-June 1981): 83–91.

18. See Michael E. Porter, *The Comparative Advantage of Nations* (New York: The Free Press, 1990) and Michael Porter, "Why Nations Triumph," *Fortune* (March 12, 1990): 94–108.

19. This list is derived from C. K. Prahalad and Yves L. Doz, "An Approach to Strategic Control in MNCs," *Sloan Management Review,* 22 (Summer 1981): 5–13.

20. "Amidst Stiffer International Competition, U.S. Managers Need a Broader Perspective," *Management Review,* 69 (March 1980): 34.

21. Howard V. Perlmutter, "The Tortuous Evolution of the Multinational Corporation," *Columbia Journal of World Business,* 4 (January-February 1969): 11.

22. Perlmutter and a colleague later added "regiocentric attitude" to their typology. Such an attitude centers around a regional identification (North America, Europe, and Asia, for example). See David A. Heenan and Howard V. Perlmutter, *Multinational Organization Development* (Reading, Mass.: Addison-Wesley, 1979).

23. Drawn from Brian Dumaine, "The New Turnaround Champs," *Fortune* (July 16, 1990): 36–44.

24. See Amy Borrus, "Can Japan's Giants Cut the Apron Strings?" *Business Week* (May 14, 1990): 105–106.

25. Perlmutter, "The Tortuous Evolution of the Multinational Corporation," p. 16.

26. Main, "How To Go Global—and Why," p. 72.

27. Perlmutter, "The Tortuous Evolution of the Multinational Corporation," p. 16.

28. See Ross A. Webber, "Convergence or Divergence?" *Columbia Journal of World Business,* 4 (May-June 1969): 75–83; George S. Vozikis and Timothy S. Mescon, "Convergence or Divergence? A Vital Managerial Quest Revisited," *Columbia Journal of World Business,* 16 (Summer 1981): 79–87; and Nancy J. Adler, Robert Doktor, and S. Gordon Redding, "From the Atlantic to the Pacific Century: Cross-Cultural Management Reviewed," *Journal of Management,* 12 (Summer 1986): 295–318.

29. Peter Ford, "Saudis Stand Firm under Shadow of War," *The Christian Science Monitor* (January 30, 1991): 4.

30. For more, see Nancy J. Adler, *International Dimensions of Organizational Behavior,* 2nd edition (Boston: PWS-Kent, 1991), pp. 14–33.

31. "How Cultures Collide," *Psychology Today,* 10 (July 1976): 69.

32. Based on Ashok Nimgade, "American Management as Viewed by International Professionals," *Business Horizons,* 32 (November-December 1989): 98–105.

33. See Barnlund, "Public and Private Self in Communicating with Japan," pp. 32–40.

34. See "How Cultures Collide," pp. 66–74, 97; and Edward T. Hall, *The Hidden Dimension* (Garden City, N.Y.: Doubleday, 1966).

35. Ronald E. Dulek, John S. Fielden, and John S. Hill, "International Communication: An Executive Primer," *Business Horizons,* 34 (January-February 1991): 21.

36. This list is based on Edward T. Hall, "The Silent Language in Overseas Business," *Harvard Business Review,* 38 (May-June 1960): 87–96; and Rose Knotts, "Cross-Cultural Management: Transformations and Adaptations," *Business Horizons,* 32 (January-February 1989): 29–33.

37. See Robert W. Moore, "Time, Culture, and Comparative Management: A Review and Future Direction," in *Advances in International Comparative Management,* Vol. 5, ed. S. Benjamin Prasad (Greenwich, Conn.: JAI Press, 1990), pp. 1–20.

38. See Nakiye Avdan Boyacigiller and Nancy J. Adler, "The Parochial Dinosaur: Organizational Science in a Global Context," *Academy of Management Review,* 16 (April 1991): 262–290; and Nancy Adler, "Cross-Cultural Management Research: The Ostrich and the Trend," *Academy of Management Review,* 8 (April 1983): 226–232.

39. See Geert Hofstede, *Culture's Consequences: International Differences in Work-Related Values,* abridged edition (Newbury Park, Calif.: Sage Publications, 1984); and Geert Hofstede, "Motivation, Leadership, and Organization: Do American Theories Apply Abroad?" *Organizational Dynamics,* 9 (Summer 1980): 42–63. Also see Geert Hofstede, "The Cultural Relativity of Organizational Practices and Theories," *Journal of International Business Studies,* 14 (Fall 1983): 75–89; and Geert Hofstede, "The Applicability of McGregor's Theories in Southeast Asia," *Journal of Management Development,* 6, no. 3 (1987): 9–18.

40. For an informative discussion of Hofstede's article, see the articles by Leonard D. Goodstein, John W. Hunt, and Geert Hofstede in *Organizational Dynamics,* 10 (Summer 1981): 49–68.

41. An extension of Hofstede's original work can be found in Geert Hofstede and Michael Harris Bond, "The Confucius Connection: From Cultural Roots to Economic Growth," *Organizational Dynamics,* 16 (Spring 1988): 4–21.

42. See William G. Ouchi, *Theory Z: How American Business Can Meet the Japanese Challenge* (Reading, Mass.: Addison-Wesley, 1981). Also see David M. Hunt and Donald S. Bolon, "A Review of Five Versions of Theory Z: Does Z Have a Future?" in *Advances in International Comparative Management,* Vol. 4, ed. S. Benjamin Prasad (Greenwich, Conn.: JAI Press, 1989), pp. 201–220.

43. See James R. Lincoln, "Employee Work Attitudes and Management Practice in the U.S. and Japan: Evidence From a Large Comparative Survey," *California Management Review,* 32 (Fall 1989): 89–106; Robert H. Doktor, "Asian and American CEOs: A Comparative Study," *Organizational Dynamics,* 18 (Winter 1990): 46–56; Mary E. Lee and Jon P. Alston, "Is Japanese Style Management Exportable: Evidence from the World's Largest Firms," in *Advances in International Comparative Management,* Vol. 5, ed. S. Benjamin Prasad (Greenwich, Conn.: JAI Press, 1990), pp. 197–209; and Carla Rapoport, "The Big Split," *Fortune* (May 6, 1991): 38–48.

44. See Itzhak Harpaz, "The Importance of Work Goals: An International Perspective," *Journal of International Business Studies,* 21 (1st quarter 1990): 75–93.

45. Data from "Italy's 50th Government since WWII Is Already Threatened with Collapse," *The Christian Science Monitor* (April 17, 1991): 3.

46. For an instructive political risk assessment of 86 countries, see William D. Coplin and Michael K. O'Leary, "1990 World Political Risk Forecast," *Planning Review,* 18 (March-April 1990): 41–47.

47. Joseph V. Micallef, "Political Risk Assessment," *Columbia Journal of World Business,* 16 (Summer 1981): 47; Warnock Davies, "Beyond the Earthquake Allegory: Managing Political Risk Vulnerability," *Business Horizons,* 24 (July-August 1981): 39–43; Mark Fitzpatrick, "The Definition and Assessment of Political Risk in International Business: A Review of the Literature," *Academy of Management Review,* 8 (April 1983): 249–254; David A. Schmidt, "Analyzing Political Risk," *Business Horizons,* 29 (July-August 1986): 43–50; and Peter Smith Ring, Stefanie Ann Lenway, and Michele Govekar, "Management of the Political Imperative in International Business," *Strategic Management Journal,* 11 (February 1990): 141–151.

48. Drawn from Louis Kraar, "The Multinationals Get Smarter about Political Risks," *Fortune,* 101 (March 24, 1980): 98. Another good source is Thomas W. Shreeve, "Be Prepared for Political Changes Abroad," *Harvard Business Review,* 62 (July-August 1984): 111–118.

49. See Peter Nehemkis, "Business Payoffs Abroad: Rhetoric and Reality," *California Management Review,* 18 (Winter 1975): 6–7.

50. See Martin C. Schnitzer, Marilyn L. Liebrenz, and Konrad W. Kubin, *International Business* (Cincinnati: South-Western, 1985), chap. 10.

51. See, for example, Jong H. Park, "Time to Remove Self-Imposed Barriers to Export Trade," *The Journal of Business Strategy,* 11 (November-December 1990): 57–60.

52. For more details, see "The Antibribery Act Splits Executives," *Business Week* (September 19, 1983): 16.

53. See Kate Gillespie, "Middle East Response to the U.S. Foreign Corrupt Practices Act," *California Management Review,* 29 (Summer 1987): 9–30.

54. Thomas Peele, "The U.S. Foreign Corrupt Practices Act," *China Business Review,* 15 (January-February 1988): 31.

55. Barry Richman, "Stopping Payments under the Table," *Business Week* (May 22, 1978): 18.

56. See Alex Taylor III, "The U.S.: Team at the Top of No. 2," *Fortune* (November 9, 1987): 82; and "The Corporate Elite," *Business Week* (October 19, 1990): 130.

57. Rosalie L. Tung, "Expatriate Assignments: Enhancing Success and Minimizing Failure," *Academy of Management Executive,* 1 (May 1987): 117.

58. Data from Michael G. Harvey, "The Executive Family: An Overlooked Variable in International Assignments," *Columbia Journal of World Business,* 20 (Spring 1985): 84–92.

59. Gene Koretz, ". . . But It Could Be Cold Comfort for U.S. Companies There," *Business Week* (January 22, 1990): 20. Also see Rosalie L. Tung and Edwin L. Miller, "Managing in the Twenty-First Century: The Need for Global Orientation," *Management International Review,* 30 (First Quarter 1990): 5–18.

60. See Robert McGarvey, "Foreign Language Labs," *Executive Female,* 13 (September-October 1990): 32–34; and Naomi Freundlich, "An English-In, Japanese-Out Computer,"*Business Week* (January 28, 1991): 95.

61. Robert Moran, "Children of Bilingualism," *International Management,* 45 (November 1990): 93.

62. Adapted from Rosalie L. Tung, "Selection and Training of Personnel for Overseas Assignments," *Columbia Journal of World Business,* 16 (Spring 1981): 68–78.

63. See P. Christopher Earley, "Intercultural Training for Managers: A Comparison of Documentary and Interpersonal Methods," *Academy of Management Journal,* 30 (December 1987): 685–698. Also see J. Stewart Black and Mark Mendenhall, "Cross-Cultural Training Effectiveness: A Review and a Theoretical Framework for Future Research," *Academy of Management Review,* 15 (January 1990): 113–136.

64. See F. T. Murray and Alice Haller Murray, "Global Managers for Global Businesses," *Sloan Management Review,* 27 (Winter 1986): 75–80.

65. See Michael A. Conway, "Developing a Unified Selection-Orientation-Repatriation System," *Personnel Administrator,* 29 (July 1984): 31–32, 37–38. Also see Wayne F. Cascio and Manuel G. Serapio, Jr., "Human Resources Systems in an International Alliance: The Undoing of a Done Deal?" *Organizational Dynamics,* 19 (Winter 1991): 63–74.

66. See Michael G. Harvey, "Repatriation of Corporate Executives: An Empirical Study," *Journal of International Business Studies,* 20 (Spring 1989): 131–144.

67. See Paul Lansing and Kathryn Ready, "Hiring Women Managers in Japan: An Alternative for Foreign Employers," *California Management Review,* 30 (Spring 1988): 112–127.

68. Nancy J. Adler, "Expecting International Success: Female Managers Overseas," *Columbia Journal of World Business,* 19 (Fall 1984): 82.

69. See David Nye, "The Female Expat's Promise," *Across the Board,* 25 (February 1988): 38–43; and Mariann Jelinek and Nancy J. Adler, "Women: World-Class Managers for Global Competition," *Academy of Management Executive,* 2 (February 1988): 11–19.

Appendix A
Managing Small Businesses and Public-sector Organizations

Small businesses and government agencies present managers with unique and exciting challenges. A better understanding of what managers can expect in these two areas serves a dual purpose. First, it underscores the point that the practice of management is not restricted to big business. Both the local family-owned pizza parlor and a huge government agency such as the U.S. Department of Health and Human Services need to follow sound management practices. Second, this brief discussion of the special circumstances of small business and public-sector organizations can offer you, as a potential manager, valuable background information that you can use in planning your career. If you yearn to start and manage your own business, the following discussion of small business management will serve as a framework for interpreting the concepts and techniques in this text. If you aspire to a career in government, you will discover some special opportunities and challenges. Even if you eventually take a managerial position in a large corporation, you will gain a richer perspective of management as it is practiced in sectors that profoundly affect large businesses.

Small Business Management

Small businesses are an indispensable part of the U.S. economy, as evidenced by the following facts:

- Small businesses employ nearly half the nongovernment, nonfarm workers in the United States.
- Small businesses generate approximately 38 percent of the U.S. gross national product.
- During the 1980s, small companies with fewer than five hundred employees created nearly 70 percent of the new jobs in the United States.

- Small companies are responsible for nearly 25 percent of all manufactured goods exported from the United States.[1]
- "Firms with under five hundred employees produce 50 percent of all United States-made goods and most of the parts supplied to big companies."[2]

Moreover, small businesses are credited with being responsible for the majority of innovations, so much so that small business has been called the job-creation and innovation "engine" of the economy.

Few would dispute the facts and claims cited above, but agreement on the definition of a small business is not so easily reached. Some of the many yardsticks used to distinguish small from large businesses include the number of employees, level of annual sales, amount of owner's equity, and total assets. For our present purpose, a **small business** is defined as an independently owned and managed profit-seeking enterprise employing fewer than one hundred people. If the small business is incorporated, the owner/manager owns a significant proportion of the firm's stock.

small business an independently owned and managed profit-seeking enterprise with fewer than one hundred employees

To a large extent, the health of every nation's economy depends on how well small businesses are managed. To get a better idea of the challenges small business managers face, we will look at the roles these managers play, including entrepreneurship, and the problems they encounter.

Managerial Roles in Small versus Large Businesses

Does organizational size affect the way management is practiced? There is a general saying that small business managers tend to be generalists, whereas managers in large businesses tend to be specialists. More substantial evidence comes from a study of 178 small companies and 174 large companies. (In this study, three hundred employees was the dividing point between "small" and "large.") Managers employed by each of the firms surveyed "were asked to indicate the importance of each of Mintzberg's ten managerial roles in the effective performance of their present jobs."[3] (Refer to those ten roles, listed in Chapter 1 in Figure 1.4, if necessary.) Analysis of the results showed that role profiles for managers in small businesses differed significantly from those of managers in large businesses (see Figure A.1).

Starting with the most important role—spokesperson versus resource allocator—the small business manager is first and foremost a window to the outside world. This implies that the typical small business manager has valuable outside contacts (such as bankers, suppliers, and customers) and has the ability to influence their behavior. An effective small business manager must not only know the technical aspects of the business but also be attuned to the social, political, and economic environment in which that business operates. In contrast, the typical manager in a large business is generally directing his or her attention *inward*, deciding who should get what resources. This distinction appears to reinforce the axiom of the small business generalist and the large business specialist.

Another important distinction between managers in small and large businesses centers on the entrepreneurial role. In small businesses, managers are

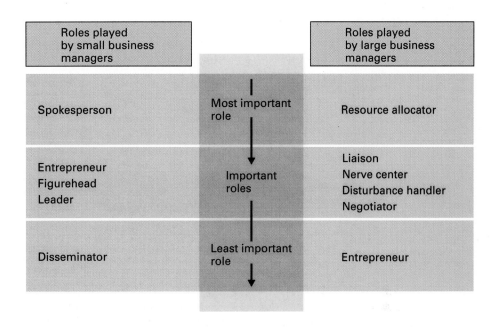

Roles played by small business managers		Roles played by large business managers
Spokesperson	Most important role	Resource allocator
Entrepreneur Figurehead Leader	Important roles	Liaison Nerve center Disturbance handler Negotiator
Disseminator	Least important role	Entrepreneur

FIGURE A.1 ● Managerial Role Profiles for Small versus Large Businesses

Source: Adapted from Joseph G.P. Paolillo, "The Manager's Self-Assessments of Managerial Roles: Small vs. Large Firms," *American Journal of Small Business,* 8 (Jan.-Mar. 1984): 58–64. Reprinted with permission.

expected to be innovative, whereas managers in large businesses generally do not see themselves as entrepreneurs. This finding helps explain why large companies are often criticized for stifling entrepreneurs. According to *Business Week,* for example, "Product ideas for [new companies] are most often formed while the entrepreneurs are still employed by established companies. Frequently, the idea was rejected or sidelined by the bigger company."[4]

In addition, the small business manager's figurehead and leader roles imply a greater degree of power and influence than the large business manager's essentially facilitative roles of liaison, nerve center, disturbance handler, and negotiator. Future managers need to gauge their abilities and preferences when deciding to work for a small or large firm.

Entrepreneurship

The term *entrepreneur* generally is used in conjunction with small business management. Indeed, the role of entrepreneur ranked a strong second for small business managers in the study just discussed. Let us take a closer look at this special breed of manager.

According to experts on the subject, "**entrepreneurship** is the process by which individuals—either on their own or inside organizations—pursue opportunities without regard to the resources they currently control."[5] In effect, entrepreneurs look beyond current resource constraints when they envision new possibilities. Entrepreneurs are preoccupied with "how to," rather than "why

entrepreneurship process of pursuing opportunities without regard to resources currently under one's control

TABLE A.1 • Contrasting Trait Profiles for Entrepreneurs and Administrators

Entrepreneurs tend to	Administrators tend to
Focus on envisioned futures	Focus on the established present
Emphasize external/market dimensions	Emphasize internal/cost dimensions
Display a medium-to-high tolerance for ambiguity	Display a low-to-medium tolerance for ambiguity
Exhibit moderate-to-high risk-taking behavior	Exhibit low-to-moderate risk-taking behavior
Obtain motivation from a need to achieve	Obtain motivation from a need to lead others (i.e., social power)
Possess technical knowledge and experience in the innovative area	Possess managerial knowledge and experience

Source: Philip D. Olson, "Choices for Innovation-Minded Corporations," *The Journal of Business Strategy,* 11 (January-February 1990): Exhibit 1, p. 44. Reprinted from *Journal of Business Strategy* (New York: Warren, Gorham & Lamont) © 1990 Warren, Gorham & Lamont Inc. Used with permission.

not." In Chapter 3, we referred to entrepreneurs in large companies as *intrapreneurs*. Although intrapreneurs are needed to pump new blood into large organizations, our focus here is on entrepreneurs who envision, start, and operate whole new businesses.

A Trait Profile for Entrepreneurs. Exactly how do entrepreneurs differ from general managers or administrators? According to the trait profiles in Table A.1, entrepreneurs tend to be high achievers who focus more on future possibilities, external factors, and technical details. Also, compared with general administrators, entrepreneurs are more comfortable with ambiguity and risk taking. It is important to note that entrepreneurs are not necessarily better or worse than other managers—they are just different.[6]

Entrepreneurship Has Its Limits. Many successful entrepreneurs have tripped over a common stumbling block. Their organizations outgrow the entrepreneur's ability to manage them. Entrepreneurs generally feel stifled by cumbersome and slow-paced bureaucracies. A prime example is Victor Kiam, who became famous with his television advertisements proclaiming that he liked his Remington electric razor so much that he bought the company. In 1991, Kiam admitted, "The company got too big for my entrepreneurial style. . . . A lot of things were falling through the cracks."[7] Remington's costs got out of control and the company lost 25 percent of its U.S. market share for men's electric shavers. Kiam eventually turned the day-to-day management of his company over to David J. Ferrari, a corporate turnaround specialist.[8] Kiam's case is not unique. Entrepreneurs who launch successful and growing companies face a tough dilemma: either grow with the company[9] or have the courage to step aside and turn the reins over to professional managers who possess the administrator traits needed, such as those listed in Table A.1.

Problems Facing Small Business Managers

Managers in small businesses not only have role and trait profiles that differ from their large business counterparts, they also face a unique set of problems. The major threat facing small business managers is business failure. According to recent U.S. Small Business Administration data, about 60 percent of all new businesses fail within six years.[10] Entrepreneurs who put in more than sixty hours a week, emphasize service rather than low prices, and start with more than $50,000 in capital tend to have the greatest chance to survive.[11] And failure seems to have no gender preference: a recent study found women entrepreneurs have the same business survival rate as their male counterparts.[12]

Why do so many small businesses fail? Researchers have uncovered some interesting answers. One study surveyed 1,002 small business owners and managers from across the United States, posing the following question: "What do you think is the primary cause of small business failures in this country?"[13] Twenty-nine percent of the respondents said the major culprit was "lack of management expertise." "High interest rates" came in second, with 16 percent. It is interesting to note that "federal regulations" tallied only 4 percent, in spite of grumbling in the small business community about too much government interference. It appears that small business managers are their own worst enemies when it comes to business failure.

The study, although it points in a general direction, does not reveal specific managerial deficiencies. A thumbnail sketch of some of these deficiencies can be seen in the up-and-down story of one computer entrepreneur:

> [Adam Osborne] chided manufacturers for ignoring the needs of the mass market. When no one listened, he started Osborne Computer Corp. Within just two years it hit $100 million in annual sales of inexpensive portable computers. But the company's smashing success was short-lived. It soon landed in bankruptcy court, with disgruntled investors, who lost $20 million, blaming its flamboyant founder for mismanaged financial controls and marketing tactics.[14]

A team of researchers who analyzed detailed performance reviews of fifty-two small businesses located in the Northeast found a similar pattern. The four major recurring managerial problem areas in this research were marketing, accounting, inventory control, and cash-flow management.[15] The specific managerial shortcomings in each of these four areas are listed in Table A.2. It is easy to see why the successful small business manager is often characterized as a jack-of-all-trades.

The risk of failure is great and the hours are long. Nevertheless, the personal satisfaction and financial rewards can be immense for those willing to try their hand at entrepreneurship and small business management.

Managing in the Public Sector

Like small businesses, public-sector organizations touch our lives each day. An estimated 18 million people work for 80,000 governmental agencies in the United

TABLE A.2 • Persistent Management Problems for Small Business Managers

---

Marketing
Lack of knowledge of target markets
Lack of objectives
Inadequate market research and planning
Poor image and location
Misdirected advertising
Little appreciation for the role of pricing strategy
Lack of promotion and distribution strategies

Accounting
Lack of systematic accounting systems
Antiquated accounting systems
Lack of knowledge of accounting functions (hence, hired accountants are underutilized)
Weak accounts receivable collection procedures
Mismanaged operating expenses

Inventory control
Low inventory turnover (slow-moving or obsolete goods kept in stock)
Stockouts of high-profit items ("selling from an empty wagon")
Failure to detect excessively high inventories due to poor accounting procedures

Cash flow
Weak marketing + inadequate accounting procedures + loose inventory control = poor cash flow
Lack of cash-flow analysis (hence, no early detection of cash shortages)
Lack of knowledge about alternative borrowing arrangements (for example, other than from commercial banks)

Source: Adapted from M. Riaz Khan and Joseph R. Rocha, Jr., "Recurring Managerial Problems in Small Business," *American Journal of Small Business,* 7 (July-Sept. 1982): 50–58. Used with permission.

States.[16] That figure encompasses not only the federal government and the military, but state, county, and municipal governments as well. Sheer size, record budget deficits,[17] and mounting pressure for greater efficiency in government make the need for talented and motivated public-sector managers greater than ever. Managers of tax-funded government organizations face their own unique set of management problems. Public-sector managers must cope with a negative stereotype and constraints generally not found in private, profit-seeking businesses.

A Negative Image

How often have you heard government employees referred to as "bureaucrats"? Recall from Chapter 8 that virtually all large organizations—private or public—are bureaucracies. Nevertheless, the term *bureaucrat,* which carries a strong negative connotation involving inefficiency, waste, and red tape, is rarely applied to managers in large businesses. It is, unfortunately, a well-known label—and a bad one—for those in the public sector.

Trends in public opinion polls indicate that this negative image for government employees is getting worse. For example, whereas 24 percent of those polled in 1958 thought "there are quite a few crooks" in government, that figure jumped to 70 percent in 1980.[18] In a 1990 nationwide poll, 65 percent said the word *honest* did *not* describe government leaders.[19] Worse yet, from a recruiting standpoint, a career as a public servant was recommended by only 13 percent of the government executives in one recent study.[20] Is this negative stereotype justified?

In response to a widely held belief that public-sector employees tend to be less motivated and less creative than their private-sector counterparts, an extensive review of the relevant research evidence led a pair of management scholars to conclude that:

> *The negative stereotype of government employees persists despite the evidence from several recent studies that there are* no *significant differences between managers in the public and private sectors on such critical dimensions as leadership styles, ability, personality, role ambiguity and conflict, motivational orientation, work patterns, time constraints, problem definitions, activities, or job characteristics.*[21]

In spite of sensational news stories about government ineffectiveness, inefficiency, and foul-ups, evidence indicates that public-sector managers are doing a better job than public opinion gives them credit for.[22] The negative image plaguing public-sector employees, however exaggerated or unfounded, hampers the quest for more efficient government. Certainly, some of the talented and highly motivated managers so dearly needed in the public sector are being scared away.

Constraints Facing Public-sector Managers

Not only does public-sector management suffer from a bad press, it also is subject to restrictions that are not found in the private sector. The circumstances in which government managers operate are extremely complex, but it is possible to isolate four major constraints.[23] Each clearly sets public management apart from business management.

Legislated Purposes.   Private businesses can pursue any legal and potentially profitable purposes they desire. In sharp contrast, lawmaking bodies tell government agencies what to do, which seriously limits their options. The U.S. Environmental Protection Agency, for instance, cannot suddenly decide to get out of the air-quality business because it no longer pays. To make matters worse, some government agencies (for example, those in disaster assistance) are mandated to "take a loss." Government managers often must stand and face society's typically vague and often contradictory expectations for performance.

No Competition.   Public-sector organizations do not have to pass the test of the competitive marketplace. Says one government executive: "Without this ultimate discipline of the market, there is no automatic weeding out of bad public management."[24] In place of a market test, public-sector managers must fall back on difficult and time-consuming cost-control programs and program audits to gauge their agencies' effectiveness.

Weak Incentive Systems.   Unlike private businesses, where an impressive array of incentives ranging from cash bonuses to stock options and exotic vacations

Welcome to Government Service: Check *Everything* at the Door

Donald J. Atwood got his phone call just before Christmas, a feeler for the number two job at the Defense Department, that of deputy secretary. Vice chairman of General Motors, Atwood, 65, was looking forward to retirement after twenty-nine years at GM. An interview with John Tower followed, well before Tower's own nomination as Secretary of Defense collapsed. After a few more phone calls, the last from President Bush, Atwood said yes. His reasons for coming to Washington, like those of nearly all the past and present public servants interviewed for this article, were laudable. What government and particularly the Defense Department need, says Atwood, are "people who have an understanding of how a business operates and how it is managed."

Atwood knew that his pay would be only $89,500, versus $625,000 last year at GM, and that he would probably have to sell his GM stock. (He owned or had options on some 140,000 shares last year.) But he was unprepared for the other sacrifices he was asked to make. All his stocks had to go: AT&T, Exxon, Kodak, even Disney. (Companies that do more than $25,000 a year with the Defense Department are off limits.) GM cashed out his stock options and other incen-

tives, normally paid over a period of years, at their present value. All these transactions meant capital gains taxes. Atwood declines to put a figure on his losses, but they easily came to $1 million.

That's not all. The ethics enforcers—full-time, federally paid attorneys working with the General Counsel, at the Office of Government Ethics, and in the Defense Department—were uncomfortable because Atwood would be receiving a GM pension and other normal retirement benefits. The theory, Atwood recalls with an edge to his voice, was that if there were a recession GM might be forced to shore up the pension fund, "and that if the recession were deep enough, I would be in a position to give General Motors contracts to prevent it from going bankrupt so it could fund the pension fund and I could receive my pension." The solution: Atwood had to buy an insurance policy, guaranteeing payment of his pension in the event of GM's insolvency. "The ethics team thought that was such a good idea that I then had to take out a second [policy] to cover my life insurance benefits and a third [policy] to cover my health care benefits."

Source: Excerpted from Robert E. Norton, "Who Wants to Work in Washington?" *Fortune* (August 14, 1989): 78.

can be used to motivate performance, public-sector managers have few "carrots" to dangle in front of their employees. In addition, ethical constraints, aimed at eliminating conflicts of interest, make the transition from business to government difficult (see Management Ethics). Consequently, government agencies have a hard time attracting and retaining first-rate managers and executives.

Organizational Inflexibility. Large governmental bureaucracies such as the U.S. Social Security Administration have to be highly structured to provide standard services to millions of clients nationwide. Unfortunately, reams of procedures and regulations can stifle innovation. Public-sector managers are constantly challenged to find ways to foster creativity and innovation in spite of an overriding emphasis on predictability and uniformity.[25]

These constraints offer a special managerial challenge to those interested in trying to make government more responsive and efficient.

References

1. Data from Gene Koretz, "The Small-Business Job Machine Is Working Overtime," *Business Week* (May 26, 1986): 27; and Brian Bremner, "Hot Growth Companies," *Business Week* (May 21, 1990): 102–104.

2. Jeremy Main, "Manufacturing the Right Way," *Fortune* (May 21, 1990): 60.

3. Joseph G. P. Paolillo, "The Manager's Self-Assessments of Managerial Roles: Small vs. Large Firms," *American Journal of Small Business*, 8 (January-March 1984): 59.

4. "The New Entrepreneurs," *Business Week* (April 18, 1983): 80.

5. Howard H. Stevenson and J. Carlos Jarillo, "A Paradigm of Entrepreneurship: Entrepreneurial Management," *Strategic Management Journal*, 11 (Summer 1990): 23. (Emphasis added.) Also see Robert D. Hisrich, "Entrepreneurship/Intrapreneurship," *American Psychologist*, 45 (February 1990): 209–222.

6. See Jeremy Main, "A Golden Age for Entrepreneurs," *Fortune* (February 12, 1990): 120–125; and Kenneth Labich, "Breaking Away to Go on Your Own," *Fortune* (December 17, 1990): 40–56.

7. Geoffrey Smith and Lisa Driscoll, "Victor Kiam, the Self-Sacking Quarterback," *Business Week* (February 25, 1991): 46.

8. Data from Ibid.

9. For instructive reading, see Eric G. Flamholtz, *How to Make the Transition from an Entrepreneurship to a Professionally Managed Firm* (San Francisco: Jossey-Bass, 1986).

10. Data from Main, "A Golden Age For Entrepreneurs," p. 121.

11. Data from "Good Service, Hard Work Help New Businesses to Survive," *The Christian Science Monitor* (October 19, 1989): 9.

12. See Arne L. Kalleberg and Kevin T. Leicht, "Gender and Organizational Performance: Determinants of Small Business Survival and Success," *Academy of Management Journal*, 34 (March 1991): 136–161. Also see Sharon Nelton, "The Challenge to Women," *Nation's Business*, 78 (July 1990): 16–21.

13. Robert A. Peterson, George Kozmetsky, and Nancy M. Ridgway, "Perceived Causes of Small Business Failures: A Research Note," *American Journal of Small Business*, 8 (July-September 1983): 17.

14. "Adam Osborne Is Back in Computers—With Software," *Business Week* (April 2, 1984): 37.

15. See M. Riaz Khan and Joseph R. Rocha, Jr., "Recurring Managerial Problems in Small Business," *American Journal of Small Business*, 7 (July-September 1982): 50–58. Similar findings are reported in Albert V. Bruno, Joel K. Leidecker, and Joseph W. Harder, "Why Firms Fail," *Business Horizons*, 30 (March-April 1987): 50–58.

16. See Charles T. Goodsell, *The Case for Bureaucracy* (Chatham, N.J.: Chatham House, 1983), pp. 110–111.

17. See Michael J. Mandel and Christopher Farrell, "The Sad State of the States," *Business Week* (April 22, 1991): 24–26.

18. David G. Mathiasen, "Rethinking Public Management," *The Bureaucrat*, 13 (Summer 1984): 11.

19. Data from Everett Carll Ladd, "Officials Have Earned Public's Low Esteem," *The Christian Science Monitor* (February 1, 1991): 18.

20. Data from Susan B. Garland, "Beltway Brain Drain: Why Civil Servants Are Making Tracks," *Business Week* (January 23, 1989): 60–61.

21. Barry Z. Posner and Warren H. Schmidt, "What Kinds of People Enter the Public and Private Sectors? An Updated Comparison of Perceptions, Stereotypes, and Values," *Human Resource Management*, 21 (Summer 1982): 35. Also see J. Norman Baldwin, "Public versus Private: Not That Different, Not That Consequential," *Public Personnel Management*, 16 (Summer 1987): 181–193.

22. Both positive and negative examples can be found in David Kirkpatrick, "It's Simply Not Working," *Fortune* (November 19, 1990): 179–196.

23. This discussion is based on material found in Mathiasen, "Rethinking Public Management," pp. 9–13; Allen H. Barton, "A Diagnosis of Bureaucratic Maladies," *American Behavioral Scientist*, 22 (May-June 1979): 483–492; Laurence E. Lynne, Jr., "Improving Public Sector Management," *California Management Review*, 26 (Winter 1984): 112–124; Elsa A. Porter, Alice G. Sargent, and Ronald J. Stupak, "Managing for Excellence in the Federal Government," *The Bureaucrat*, 16 (Summer 1987): 17–21; and Bernard H. Ross, "Public and Private Sectors: The Underlying Differences," *Management Review*, 77 (May 1988): 28–33.

24. Mathiasen, "Rethinking Public Management," p. 9.

25. See Donald C. Witham and John D. Glover, "Recapturing Commitment," *Training and Development Journal*, 41 (April 1987): 42–45; and Joseph Sensenbrenner, "Quality Comes to City Hall," *Harvard Business Review*, 69 (March-April 1991): 64–75.

Appendix B
Career and
Stress Management

Throughout this book, we have focused on the management of organizational resources. You have been challenged to manage human, material, and financial resources in an effective and efficient manner. Now, realizing that each of us is a valuable resource both as an individual and as an integral part of organized endeavor, we turn to self-management. Two important dimensions of self-management are career management and stress management. Some practical guidelines on effective career and stress management are therefore offered here.

Adopting a Career Perspective

Someone once said that the difference between a job and a career is about twenty extra hours a week. Although it is generally true that a career-oriented person attacks his or her job with above-average vigor, something more fundamental is involved. Specifically, those with a career perspective tend to see their job as a key link in a chain rather than as an isolated experience. As illustrated in Figure B.1, the typical organizational career is made up of identifiable stages.[1] Each stage has its own distinctive combination of challenges. Those who understand this evolutionary process and prepare themselves for each successive stage will do much better than those with a purely here-and-now perspective. The self-doubt that strikes many otherwise successful managers at midcareer, for example, is not as traumatic when one recognizes it as a natural way station in a long career.[2] A career perspective helps one mentally prepare for future stages.[3]

Dual-Career Couples

As more and more women enter the labor force on a full-time basis, the traditional arrangement where the man is the sole breadwinner and the woman is the

dual-career couples both partners have full-time careers

housewife and mother has undergone profound change. **Dual-career couples,** in which both partners pursue professional careers full time, have become commonplace. However, they must often cope with unresolved issues regarding housekeeping and child rearing.[4] Another source of potential conflict is the question of whose career takes precedence relative to relocation and commuting distance. The first step toward resolving these role conflicts is to recognize different kinds of dual-career marriages.

According to researchers, dual-career relationships fall into four categories: traditional, neotraditional, matriarchal, and egalitarian.[5] The roles of husband and wife vary from category to category.

- *Traditional.* In the traditional dual-carrer marriage, the wife both works full time and assumes full responsibility for the home. The husband's career clearly takes precedence over the wife's. Some have referred to this

FIGURE B.1 • The Career Cycle

Source: Edgar H. Schein, *Career Dynamics,* © 1978, Addison-Wesley Publishing Company. Reprinted with permission.

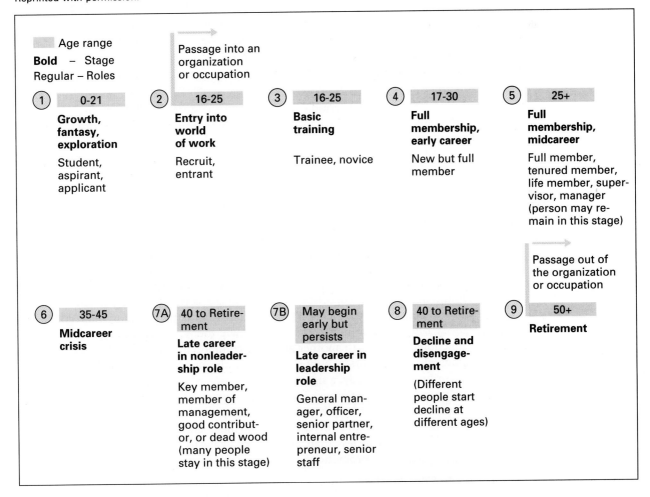

arrangement as the "super mom" or "super wife" syndrome. Not surprisingly, the pressures and stress on the overloaded female partner can strain the marriage.

- *Neotraditional.* In this type of dual-career marriage, the husband recognizes the wife's career as important, perhaps equal in importance to his. Because the husband is supportive of the wife's career, he may assume some of the household chores. "Embodied deeply is the idea of permission to work—the husband is allowing his wife to work and is helping her do this by taking on a few of her duties in the home."[6]

- *Matriarchal.* In a matriarchal relationship, the traditional male-female roles are reversed. Both the couple themselves and their acquaintances fully recognize that the wife's career comes first. Male artists, writers, and others who can conveniently ply their trade at home while assuming housekeeping chores have found the househusband role workable.

- *Egalitarian.* Elimination of traditional gender-specific housekeeping roles is the key to an egalitarian dual-career marriage. Both partners have equally important careers and both contribute equally to keeping house and rearing children. However, sex-role stereotyping and cultural conditioning are formidable barriers to a true egalitarian relationship.

Each of the foregoing arrangements has its own set of advantages and disadvantages. Couples committed to making their marriage work should discuss their mutual expectations frankly, explore alternatives, select a mutually agreeable course of action, and periodically reevaluate the situation. (The conflict resolution techniques discussed in Chapter 15 can be a big help.) Progressive organizational practices—such as flexible work schedules, job sharing, and day-care assistance for children and/or elderly parents—can help dual-career couples balance family and work roles.[7] Because dual-career couples generally enjoy above-average income, hiring a part-time housekeeper can help relieve domestic pressures. As with management, it takes commitment and creative problem solving to keep a dual-career marriage on track.[8]

Basic Career Strategies

Today's managers are climbing a corporate career ladder that only vaguely resembles that of their predecessors. Thanks to the corporate reorganizations of the 1980s that flattened the organizational pyramid, the promotional ladder has fewer rungs. Promotions come more slowly today, and lateral moves from one functional specialty to another are more common than before.[9] Realistic expectations about promotion opportunities are the order of the day. Unfortunately, according to one study, a significant proportion of recent graduates have unrealistic promotion expectations. Twenty-nine percent were willing to spend less than one year in their first job prior to being promoted. Another 69 percent were willing to wait one to two years.[10] Many members of the first group, who expect to be promoted in less than a year, are likely to be disappointed. In the new world of slower promotions, clear and productive career strategies are more important than ever.

There are many ways to get ahead in today's organizations. Career specialists have identified seven basic career strategies:

1. *Competence in current job.* Strive for visibility by becoming very good at your present job.
2. *Extended work involvement.* Make your job the focal point of your life, with investment of considerable energy, time, and emotion.
3. *Skill development.* Build your work-related knowledge and skills through formal education, training, and on-the-job experience.
4. *Opportunity development.* Build a career-development network so that others are aware of you and your abilities, and so that you, in turn, hear about opportunities.
5. *Development of mentor relationships.* Cultivate a career-enhancing relationship with a mentor who can coach you and show you the ropes. (Recall our discussion of mentoring in Chapter 14.)
6. *Image building.* Make sure your appearance is consistent with your career aspirations, such as dressing for success.
7. *Organizational politics.* Associate with powerful people who can help you get ahead. Rely on flattery, cliques, reciprocal favors, and inside information about opportunites.[11] (Refer back to the discussion of organizational politics in Chapter 13.)

These basic career strategies can be used alone or in various combinations. Career aspirations and personal ethics will dictate the strategy that you will emphasize.

Career Tips for New Managers

By being proactive rather than reactive, a new manager can anticipate and overcome adjustment problems.[12] Ross A. Webber, of the University of Pennsylvania's Wharton School, drew up an excellent list of thirteen career tips for young managers (see Table B.1). Webber's list is particularly useful because it deals frankly and realistically with organizational politics and business ethics.

Managing Stress

When our prehistoric ancestors were faced with a charging beast, they had two choices. They could stand and fight, or they could run away from it. Their bodies were mobilized for this fight-or-flight response by a complex change in body chemistry, which helped our prehistoric ancestors survive by fighting harder or running faster than normal. Times have changed, however; instead of charging animals, today's employees face work overload, unreasonable deadlines, angry bosses, financial worries, and family problems. Those who respond to these modern problems as if each was a rampaging animal tend to suffer from headaches, lower back pain, indigestion and ulcers, loss of sleep, nervous tension, heart attack, and stroke. These symptoms are the undesirable side effects of stress. Managers need to learn more about stress and how to deal with it, both in themselves and in their coworkers.

TABLE B.1 • Thirteen Career Tips for Young Managers

1. Remember that good performance that pleases your superiors is the basic foundation of success, but recognize that not all good performance is easily measured. Determine the real criteria by which you are evaluated and be rigorously honest in evaluating your own performance against these criteria.

2. Manage your career; be active in influencing decisions, because pure effort is not necessarily rewarded.

3. Strive for positions that have high visibility and exposure where you can be a hero observed by higher officials. Check to see that the organization has a formal system of keeping track of young people. Remember that high-risk line jobs tend to offer more visibility than staff positions like corporate planning or personnel, but also that visibility can sometimes be achieved by off-job community activities.

4. Develop relations with a mobile senior executive who can be your sponsor. Become a complementary crucial subordinate with different skills than your superior.

5. Learn your job as quickly as possible and train a replacement so you can be available to move and broaden your background in different functions.

6. Nominate yourself for other positions: modesty is not necessarily a virtue. However, change jobs for more power and influence, not primarily for status or pay. The latter could be a substitute for real opportunity to make things happen.

7. Before taking a position, rigorously assess your strengths and weaknesses, what you like and don't like. Don't accept a promotion if it draws on your weaknesses and entails mainly activities that you don't like.

8. Leave at your convenience, but on good terms without parting criticism of the organization. Do not stay under an immobile superior who is not promoted in three to five years.

9. Don't be trapped by formal, narrow job descriptions. Move outside them and probe the limits of your influence.

10. Accept that responsibility will always somewhat exceed authority and that organizational politics are inevitable. Establish alliances and fight necessary battles, minimizing upward ones to very important issues.

11. Get out of management if you can't stand being dependent on others and having them dependent on you.

12. Recognize that you will face ethical dilemmas no matter how moral you try to be. No evidence exists that unethical managers are more successful than ethical ones, but it may well be that those who move faster are less socially conscious. Therefore, from time to time you must examine your personal values and question how much you are willing to sacrifice for the organization.

13. Don't automatically accept all tales of managerial perversity that you hear. Attributing others' success to unethical behavior is often an excuse for one's own personal inadequacies. Most of all, don't commit an act which you know to be wrong in the hope that your supervisor will see it as loyalty and reward you for it. Sometimes [your supervisor] will, but he [or she] may also sacrifice you when the organization is criticized.

Source: © 1976 by the Regents of the University of California. Reprinted from Ross A. Webber, ''Career Problems of Young Managers,'' *California Management Review,* 18 (Summer 1976): 29 by permission of the Regents.

What Does Stress Involve?

stress an adaptive response to external demands on the individual

Stress is "an adaptive response, mediated by individual characteristics and/or psychological processes, that is a consequence of any external action, situation, or event that places special physical and/or psychological demands upon a person."[13] This definition focuses our attention on three major components: situational demands that force us to adapt (called *stressors*); our perception of those demands and our ability to cope with them; and the biochemical stress response. All three elements must be properly interrelated if stress is to be meaningfully discussed.

Although biochemical responses differ from person to person, we will concentrate here on the first two elements of the definition. Regarding the first component, typical organizational stressors include role overload, role conflict, role ambiguity (not knowing what is expected), interpersonal conflict and competition, deadlines, high risk, job dissatisfaction, and unrealized status or career aspirations. Physical work environments, including the tools, machines, and work flow layouts in them, create additional stressors responsible for sore wrists and backs, headaches, and eye strain. **Ergonomics** is the study of the interaction between humans and machines. It has helped identify and correct a whole host of stressors for the large and growing army of employees who spend their workdays at computer terminals.[14]

ergonomics the study of human-machine interactions

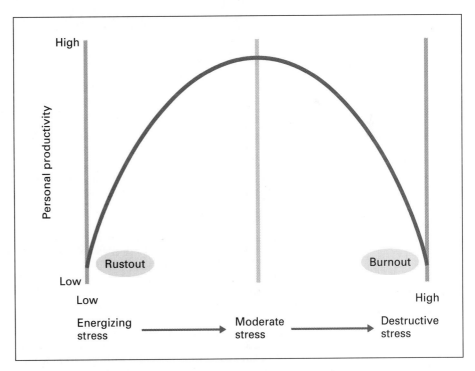

FIGURE B.2 ● The Two Faces of Stress

Source: Adapted From Robert Kreitner, "Personal Wellness: It's Just Good Business," *Business Horizons,* 25 (May/June 1982): 32. Copyright 1982 by the Foundation for the School of Business at Indiana University. Reprinted with permission.

TABLE B.2 • Coping with Stress

Control the situation	Avoid unrealistic deadlines.
	Do your best but know your limits. You cannot be everything to everyone.
	Learn to identify and limit your exposure to stressful situations and people.
Open up to others	Freely discuss your problems, frustrations, and sources of uptightness with those who care about you.
	When faced with a tough situation, smile! A *sincere* smile often can defuse emotion and build a bridge of goodwill.
Pace yourself	Plan your day on a flexible basis.
	Don't try to do two or more things at the same time.
	Counter unproductive haste by forcing yourself to slow down. (Stop to smell the roses along the way.)
	Think before reacting.
	Live on a day-to-day basis rather than on a minute-to-minute basis.
Exercise and relax	Engage in regular noncompetitive physical activity. (e.g., take a ten- to twenty-minute walk each day.) Those who are in good physical condition can stay in shape by jogging; swimming; riding a bike; or playing tennis, handball, or racquetball on a regular basis (three or four times a week).
	See your doctor when in doubt about your physical condition.
	When feeing uptight, relax for a few minutes by following these simple steps:
	1. Sit comfortably with eyes closed in a quiet location.
	2. Slowly repeat a peaceful word or phrase over and over to yourself in your mind. (A mental picture of a peaceful scene also works.)
	3. Avoid distracting thoughts by keeping a passive mental attitude.

The second factor—our perception and coping ability—means that any two people reading this page could react very differently to a given stressor. Accordingly, perceptual screening and coping ability are the keys to effectively managing the two faces of stress.[15]

The Two Faces of Stress

According to Hans Selye, the father of the modern concept of stress, "Complete freedom from stress is death."[16] Stress is inevitable. Fortunately, not all stress is bad. Stress has two faces, an energizing face and a destructive face (see Figure B.2). The challenge, then, is not to totally avoid or eliminate all stress. Rather, it is to take advantage of energizing stress and minimize destructive stress. Too little stress, or understimulation, can lead to "rustout," a condition familiar to anyone who has known the boredom associated with an unchallenging job. At the other end of the stress scale is "burnout," caused by overstimulation.[17]

The trick to managing stress is to experience moderate *energizing* stress that enhances one's personal productivity. Such enhancing stress might occur, when for example, a deadline prompts a student to "burn the midnight oil" to finish a term paper or a new project challenges a manager to create new approaches to a situation. With the onset of destructive stress, however, diminishing returns set in and productivity decreases.[18]

The thin line between energizing and destructive stress is highly personal. In the typical case, symptoms such as unexplained irritability, sleeplessness, excessive alcohol and/or drug use, apathy, and vague but persistent anxiety signal an underlying problem with destructive stress. When the scale tips toward destructive stress, it is time to back off and reevaluate your circumstances.

Coping with Stress

In spite of the recent avalanche of advice on how best to deal with stress, there is no panacea or quick fix. Individual differences are simply too great to make one coping technique useful for all. A comprehensive approach, spelling out the word *cope*, has helped many people deal constructively with stress:

Control the situation.

Open up to others.

Pace yourself.

Exercise and relax.[19]

An expanded version of these coping guidelines is presented in Table B.2. Those who learn to manage stress constructively, rather than depending on alcohol, tobacco, drugs, or other destructive habits, can look forward to a healthier, happier, and more productive career. Company-sponsored employee fitness and wellness programs can play a valuable role in stress management.[20]

References

1. For an instructive compilation of several career-stage models, see Daniel C. Feldman, *Managing Careers in Organizations* (Glenview, Ill.: Scott, Foresman, 1988), pp. 13–15.

2. For useful information on the problem of mid-career crisis, see Joe Thomas, "Mid-Career Crisis and the Organization," *Business Horizons,* 25 (November-December 1982): 73–78.

3. Theory and research in the area of careers may be found in Jeffrey H. Greenhaus, *Career Management* (New York: Dryden Press, 1987); and Daniel C. Feldman, "Careers in Organizations: Recent Trends and Future Directions," *Journal of Management,* 15 (June 1989): 135–136.

4. Interesting and informative results of a survey of 1,700 career-committed mothers are presented in Alma S. Baron, "Working Partners: Career-Committed Mothers and Their Husbands," *Business Horizons,* 30 (September-October 1987): 45–50.

5. For an excellent discussion, see Nancy Lee, "The Dual-Career Couple: Benefits and Pitfalls," *Management Review,* 70 (January 1981): 46–52.

6. Ibid., p. 49

7. See Alan Deutschman, "Pioneers of the New Balance," *Fortune* (May 20, 1991): 60–68.

8. See Douglas T. Hall and Judith Richter, "Balancing Work Life and Home Life: What Can Organizations Do to Help," *The Academy of Management Executive,* 2 (August 1988): 213–223; Douglas T. Hall, "Promoting Work/Family Balance: An Organization-Change Approach," *Organizational Dynamics,* 18 (Winter 1990): 5–18; and Joy A. Schneer and Frieda Reitman, "Effects of Employment Gaps on the Careers of MBA's: More Damaging for Men than for Women?" *Academy of Management Journal,* 33 (June 1990): 391–406.

9. See David Kirkpatrick, "Is Your Career on Track?" *Fortune* (July 2, 1990): 38–48. Also see Zandy B. Leibowitz, Barbara H. Feldman, and Sherry H. Mosley, "Career Development Works Overtime at Corning, Inc.," *Personnel,* 67 (April 1990): 38–45.

10. Data from Ceel Pasternak, "Impatient Grads—Class of '90," *HRMagazine,* 36 (February 1991): 26.

11. Adapted from Greenhaus, *Career Management,* p. 27.

12. See Jack Falvey, "Career Navigation," *Training and Development Journal,* 42 (February 1988): 32–36.

13. John M. Ivancevich and Michael T. Matteson, *Stress and Work: A Managerial Perspective* (Glenview, Ill.: Scott, Foresman, 1980), pp. 8–9.

14. See Robert F. Bettendorf, "Curing the New Ills of Technology," *HRMagazine,* 35 (March 1990): 35–36, 80; and Suzanne Woolley, "Making Your Office Human-Friendly," *Business Week* (August 20, 1990): 100–101.

15. See Emily T. Smith, "Stress: The Test Americans Are Failing," *Business Week* (April 18, 1988): 74–76 and Sana Siwolop, "The Crippling Ills Stress Can Trigger," *Business Week* (April 18, 1987): 77–78.

16. Hans Selye, *Stress without Distress* (Philadelphia: Lippincott, 1974), p. 32.

17. See Hugh F. Stallworth, "Realistic Goals Help Avoid Burnout," *HRMagazine,* 35 (June 1990): 169, 171; and Patti Watts, "Are Your Employees Burnout-Proof?" *Personnel,* 67 (September 1990): 12–14.

18. See Robert W. Eckles, "Stress—Making Friends with the Enemy within," *Business Horizons,* 30 (March-April 1987): 74–78; and Debra L. Nelson and Charlotte Sutton, "Chronic Work Stress and Coping: A Longitudinal Study and Suggested New Directions," *Academy of Management Journal,* 33 (December 1990): 859–869.

19. These guidelines have been adapted from Meyer Friedman and Ray. H. Rosenman, *Type A Behavior and Your Heart* (Greenwich, Conn.: Fawcett, 1974); Herbert Benson, *The Relaxation Response* (New York: William Morrow, 1975); "Executive's Guide to Living with Stress," *Business Week* (August 23, 1976): 75–80; and John W. Farquhar, *The American Way of Life Need Not Be Hazardous to Your Health* (New York: W. W. Norton, 1978).

20. See Deborah L. Gebhardt and Carolyn E. Crump, "Employee Fitness and Wellness Programs in the Workplace," *American Psychologist,* 45 (February 1990): 262–272.

Glossary

Acceptance theory of authority Chester I. Barnard's belief that a leader's authority is determined by his or her subordinates' willingness to comply (Ch. 7)

Accommodative social responsibility strategy assuming additional responsibilities in response to pressure (Ch. 4)

Activity-based costing costing a given product in terms of the chain of activities responsible for its creation (Ch. 16)

Advocacy advertising the controversial practice of promoting a point of view along with a product or service (Ch. 3)

Affirmative action program making up for past discrimination by actively seeking and employing minorities (Ch. 10)

Alcoholism a disease in which an individual's normal social and economic roles are disrupted by the consumption of alcohol (Ch. 10)

Alternative dispute resolution avoiding courtroom battles by settling disputes with less costly methods including arbitration and mediation (Ch. 3)

Altruism an unselfish devotion to the interests of others (Ch. 4)

Amoral managers neither moral nor immoral, but ethically lazy (Ch. 4)

Antecedent an environmental cue that prompts an individual to behave in a given manner (Ch. 14)

Anticipatory changes planned changes based on expected situations (Ch. 15)

Artificial intelligence computerized imitation of human thought processes (Ch. 17)

Authority the right to direct the actions of others (Ch. 8)

Batch processing a data processing procedure whereby transactions are stored up, turned into machine-readable form such as magnetic tapes, and processed all at one time (Ch. 17)

Behavior modification systematic management of the antecedents and consequences of behavior (Ch. 14)

Behaviorally anchored rating scales (BARS) job performance rating scales divided into increments of observable job behavior determined through job analysis (Ch. 10)

Behaviorism a philosophy that holds that observable behavior is more important than hypothetical inner states such as needs, motives, or expectations (Ch. 14)

Benchmarking imitating the standards of the best in the business or world (Ch. 16)

Body language nonverbal communication in the form of facial expressions and body movements (Ch. 11)

Break-even point the level of sales at which the firm neither suffers a loss nor realizes a profit (Ch. 5)

Budget variance the difference between the actual figures and the budgeted ones (Ch. 16)

Budget a formal financial projection (Ch. 16)

Bureaucracy Weber's model of a rationally efficient organization (Ch. 8)

Business cycle the up and down movement of an economy's ability to generate wealth (predictable sequence but variable timing) (Ch. 3)

Cafeteria compensation a plan for allowing each employee to determine the make-up of his or her employee benefit package (Ch. 12)

Capability profile identifying the organization's strengths and weaknesses (Ch. 6)

Causes (of problems) variables that, because of their presence or absence from the situation, are primarily responsible for the difference between actual and desired conditions (Ch. 7)

Centralization top management retains a relatively high degree of decision-making authority (Ch. 9)

Closed system a self-sufficient entity (Ch. 2)

Cluster organization collaborative structure in which teams are the primary unit (Ch. 9)

Coercive power gaining compliance through threats or punishment (Ch. 14)

Cohesiveness the tendency of group members to follow the group and resist outside influences (Ch. 13)

Commonweal organization nonprofit organizations serving all members of a given population (Ch. 8)

Communication the transfer of information and understanding from one person to another person (Ch. 11)

Comparative management the study of how management practices compare across different cultures (Ch. 19)

Computer a data processor that can perform substantial computation, including numerous arithmetic or logic operations, without intervention by a human operator during the run (Ch. 17)

Computer-integrated manufacturing (CIM) computer-aided design (CAD) and computer-aided manufacturing (CAM) linked in a system that manages data flow while directing the movement and processing of material (Ch. 18)

Computer networking connecting computers so they communicate with one another (Ch. 17)

Computer system a collection of components including data, hardware, programs, procedures, and skilled personnel (Ch. 17)

Concurrent control monitoring and adjusting on-going activities and processes (Ch. 16)

Concurrent engineering team approach to product design involving specialists from all functional areas including research, production, and marketing (Ch. 3)

Condition of certainty solid factual basis allows accurate prediction of decision's outcome (Ch. 7)

Concurrent quality control monitoring the quality of work in process (Ch. 18)

Condition of certainty a decision-making situation in which there is no doubt about the factual basis of a particular decision and its outcome can be predicted accurately (Ch. 7)

Condition of risk a decision-making situation in which a decision must be made on the basis of incomplete but reliable factual information (Ch. 7)

Condition of uncertainty a decision-making situation in which there is little or no reliable factual information available (Ch. 7)

Conflict all kinds of opposition or antagonistic interaction; based on scarcity of power, resources, or social position, and differing value structures (Ch. 15)

Conflict trigger a circumstance that increases the chances of intergroup or interpersonal conflict (Ch. 15)

Conformity complying with the role expectations and norms perceived by the majority to be associated with a particular situation (Ch. 13)

Contingency approach an effort to determine through research which managerial practices and techniques are appropriate in specific situations (Ch. 2)

Contingency design fitting the organization to its environment (Ch. 9)

Contingent time off rewarding people with early time off when they get the job done (Ch. 12)

Contingent workers part-timers and other employees who do not have a long-term implicit contract with their ultimate employers (Ch. 3)

Continuous reinforcement reinforcement of every instance of a desired behavior (Ch. 14)

Contribution margin selling price per unit minus variable costs per unit (Ch. 5)

Control taking preventive or corrective actions to keep things on track (Ch. 16)

Convergence the philosophical view that the world is becoming more uniform because of forces such as technology, education, and pragmatism (Ch. 19)

Core competencies areas of expertise that create a competitive advantage (Ch. 6)

Corporate philanthropy the charitable donation of company resources (Ch. 4)

Corporate social responsibility idea that business has social obligations above and beyond making a profit (Ch. 7)

Creativity the reorganization of experience into new configurations (Ch. 7)

Crisis management the systematic anticipation of and preparation for internal and external problems that seriously threaten an organization's reputation, profitability, or survival (Ch. 16)

Critical path the most time-consuming chain of activities and events in a PERT network (Ch. 5)

Critical success factors the limited number of areas in which results, if they are satisfactory, will ensure successful competitive performance for the organization (Ch. 17)

Cross-cultural training guided experience that helps people live and work in foreign cultures (Ch. 19)

Cross-functional team task group staffed with a mix of specialists pursuing a common objective (Ch. 13)

Cross-sectional scenarios describing future situations at a given point in time (Ch. 6)

Culture a population's taken-for-granted assumptions, values, beliefs, and symbols that foster patterned behavior (Ch. 18)

Decentralization an organization design alternative in which top management delegates a relatively high degree of decision-making authority to lower-level managers (Ch. 9)

Decision making the process of identifying and choosing alternative courses of action in a manner appropriate to the demands of the situation (Ch. 7)

Decision rule a statement that identifies the situation in which a decision is required and specifies how the decision will be made (Ch. 7)

Defensive social responsibility strategy resisting additional responsibilities with legal and public relations tactics (Ch. 4)

Delegation the process of assigning various degrees of decision-making authority to subordinates (Ch. 9)

Demographics statistical profiles of population changes (Ch. 3)

Departmentalization the grouping of related jobs, activities, or processes into major organizational subunits (Ch. 8)

Differentiation a structural force involving the tendency among specialists to think and act differently (Chs. 6 & 9)

Distributed computing system in which some portion of the computer logic function is performed outside a central location (Ch. 17)

Divergence a philosophical belief that forces such as cultural inertia, differing stages of economic development, unevenly distributed resources, and regional overpopulation guarantee global diversity (Ch. 19)

Dual career couples a relationship in which both partners pursue professional careers full time (App. B)

Dynamic equilibrium in open systems, the process of maintaining the internal balance necessary for survival by importing needed resources from the environment (Ch. 8)

Economics the study of how scarce resources are used to create wealth and how that wealth is distributed (Ch. 3)

Economies of scope achieved when the same machines are used to produce small batches of different products (Ch. 18)

Effectiveness a central element in the process of management that entails achieving a stated organizational objective (Ch. 1)

Effect uncertainty impacts of environmental changes are unpredictable (Ch. 5)

Efficiency a central element in the process of management that balances the amount of resources used to achieve an objective against what was actually accomplished (Ch. 1)

Egalitarianism a social philosophy that advocates social, political, and economic equality (Ch. 3)

Employment selection test any procedure used as a basis for an employment decision (Ch. 9)

Entrepreneurship the process of pursuing opportunities without regard to resources currently under one's control (App. A)

Ergonomics the study of human-machine interactions (App. B)

Equifinality reaching the same result by different means in open systems (Ch. 8)

Escalation of commitment people get locked into losing courses of action to avoid embarrassment of quitting or admitting error (Ch. 7)

Ethical advocate ethics specialist who plays a role in top-management decision making (Ch. 4)

Ethics the study of moral obligation involving the distinction between right and wrong (Ch. 4)

Ethnocentric attitude an attitude among international managers in which home-country personnel, ideas, and practices are viewed as inherently superior to those from abroad (Ch. 19)

Event outcome forecasts predictions of the outcome of highly probable future events (Ch. 6)

Event timing forecasts predictions of when a given event will occur (Ch. 6)

Executive information system a user-friendly computer system that provides an executive with customized information on critical success factors (Ch. 17)

Executive reality check top managers periodically working at lower-level jobs to become more aware of operations (Ch. 16)

Exit interview brief structured interview with a departing employee (Ch. 11)

Expectancy the subjective probability that one thing will lead to another (Ch. 12)

Expectancy theory a motivation model based on the assumption that motivational strength is determined by perceived probabilities of success (Ch. 12)

Expert power compliance based on ability to dispense valued information (Ch. 14)

Expropriation the takeover or nationalization of a company by the host government (Ch. 19)

Extrinsic rewards payoffs granted to the individual by other people (Ch. 12)

Feedback control the process of gathering information about a completed activity, evaluating that information, and taking steps to improve similar activities in the future (Ch. 16)

Feedback quality control inspecting and testing finished goods for conformance to design specifications (Ch. 18)

Feedforward control the active anticipation of problems and their timely solution, rather than after-the-fact reaction (Ch. 16)

Feedforward quality control preventing and screening out substandard parts (Ch. 18)

Financial ratios measures of an organization's financial status that can be compared with industry standards to gauge the organization's financial health (Ch. 16)

Fixed costs contractual costs that must be paid regardless of the level of output or sales (Ch. 5)

Fixed-position layout a work flow layout in which the product, by virtue of its bulk or weight, remains at one location (Ch. 18)

Flexible budget use of standardized costs to permit concurrent control (Ch. 16)

Flexible manufacturing ability of computerized machines to perform a variety of programmed functions (Ch. 18)

Flextime a work-scheduling plan that allows employees to determine their own arrival and departure times within specified limits (Ch. 12)

Flow chart a graphical device for sequencing significant events and yes-or-no decisions (Ch. 5)

Forecasts predictions, projections, or estimates of future events or conditions in the environment in which the organization operates (Ch. 6)

Formal group a group created for the purpose of doing productive work (Ch. 13)

Formal leadership influencing the appropriate people to pursue official organizational objectives (Ch. 14)

Framing error how information is presented influences one's interpretation of it (Ch. 7)

Functional authority an organic design alternative that gives staff personnel temporary, limited line authority for specified tasks (Ch. 9)

Gantt chart graphic scheduling technique (Ch. 5)

General systems theory an interdisciplinary area of study based on the assumption that everything is part of a larger, interdependent arrangement (Ch. 2)

Geocentric attitude a world-oriented attitude among international managers whereby skill rather than nationality determines who gets promoted or transferred to key positions around the globe (Ch. 19)

Glass ceiling the transparent but strong barrier keeping women and minorities from moving up the management ladder (Ch. 3)

Global corporation worldwide network of fully integrated design, production, and marketing operations (Ch. 19)

Goal setting process of improving performance with objectives, deadlines, or quality standards (Ch. 12)

Grand strategy a general explanation of how the organization's mission is to be accomplished (Ch. 6)

Grapevine the unofficial and informal communication system (Ch. 11)

Group two or more freely interacting individuals who share a common identity and purpose (Ch. 13)

Groupthink Janis's term for blind conformity in cohesive in-groups (Ch. 13).

High-context cultures cultures in which communication is based largely on nonverbal and situational messages (Ch. 19)

Hourglass organization a three-layer structure with a constricted middle layer (Ch. 9)

Human relations movement a concerted effort among theorists and practitioners to make managers more sensitive to their employees' needs (Ch. 2)

Human resource planning the development of a comprehensive staffing strategy for meeting the organization's future human resource needs (Ch. 10)

Idealize changing the nature of a problem's situation (Ch. 7)

Incremental changes subsystem adjustments required to keep the organization on course (Ch. 15)

Indexed standard costing a budgeting procedure whereby standard costs are adjusted for inflation monthly rather than yearly (Ch. 16)

Influence any attempt by an employee to change the behavior of superiors, peers, or subordinates (Ch. 14)

Informal group a group in which the principal reason for belonging is friendship (Ch. 13)

Informal leadership influencing others to pursue unofficial objectives that may or may not serve the organization's interests (Ch. 14)

Information data organized and interpreted within a relevant frame of reference that enhances effective decision making (Ch. 17)

Information requirements analysis the act of identifying the meaningful data that a worker needs in order to perform a job or task (Ch. 17)

Innovation lag the time it takes for a new idea to be translated into satisfied demand for a good or service (Ch. 3)

Innovation process the systematic development and practical application of a new idea (Ch. 3)

Instrumental value an enduring belief that a certain way of behaving is appropriate in all situations (Ch. 4)

Integration a structural force involving the collaboration among specialists that is needed to achieve a common purpose (Ch. 9)

Intercultural training any form of guided experience aimed at helping people live and work comfortably in a foreign culture (Ch. 19)

Intermediate planning the process of determining the contributions that subunits can make with allocated resources (Ch. 5)

Intermittent reinforcement reinforcement of some, rather than all, instances of a desired behavior (Ch. 14)

Internal auditing independent appraisal of organizational operations and systems to assess effectiveness and efficiency (Ch. 16)

International management the pursuit of organizational objectives in an international and intercultural setting (Ch. 19)

Intervention a systematic attempt in organization development (OD) to correct an organizational deficiency uncovered through diagnosis (Ch. 15)

Intrapreneur an employee who takes personal "hands-on responsibility" for pushing any type of innovative idea, product, or process through the organization (Ch. 3)

Intrinsic rewards self-granted and internally experienced payoffs (Ch. 12)

Inventory control the process of establishing and maintaining appropriate levels of reserve stocks of goods (Ch. 18)

Iron law of responsibility the belief that, in the long run, those who do not use power in a way that society considers responsible will tend to lose it (Ch. 4)

Issues management the ongoing organizational process of identifying, evaluating, and responding to relevant and important social and political issues (Ch. 3)

Job analysis the process of determining the fundamental elements of jobs through systematic observation and analysis (Ch. 10)

Job description a clear and concise summary of the duties of a specific job and the qualifications for holding it (Ch. 10)

Job design the delineation of task responsibilities as dictated by organizational strategy, technology, and structure (Ch. 12)

Job enlargement the process of combining two or more specialized tasks in a work flow sequence into a single job (Ch. 12)

Job enrichment redesigning a job to increase its motivating potential (Ch. 12)

Job rotation periodically moving people from one specialized job to another to prevent stagnation (Ch. 12)

Kanban (a Japanese word) a manual inventory control procedure developed by Toyota that uses cards to keep inventory status highly visible and that manages production so that necessary units are made in the necessary quantities at the necessary time (Ch. 18)

Leadership a social influence process in which the leader seeks the voluntary participation of subordinates in an effort to reach organizational objectives (Ch. 14)

Legal audit review of all operations to pinpoint possible legal liabilities or problems (Ch. 3)

Legitimate power compliance based on one's formal position (Ch. 14)

Line and staff organization organization in which line managers make decisions and staff personnel provide advice and support (Ch. 9)

Local-area networks computers wired together in a single location or restricted geographical area (Ch. 17)

Longitudinal scenarios scenarios which describe how the present is expected to evolve into the future (Ch. 6)

Low-context cultures cultures in which words convey primary meaning (Ch. 19)

Lubrication bribes small amounts of money paid to low-level bureaucrats (Ch. 19)

Management the process of working with and through others to achieve organizational objectives in a changing environment. Central to this process is the effective and efficient use of limited resources (Ch. 1)

Management by objectives (MBO) a comprehensive management system based on measurable and participatively set objectives (Ch. 5)

Management information system (MIS) a computer-based network that integrates the collection, processing, and transmission of information (Ch. 17)

Managerial ability the demonstrated capacity to achieve organizational objectives both effectively and efficiently (Ch. 1)

Managerial functions general administrative duties (for example, planning, decision making, organizing, staffing, communicating, motivating, leading, and controlling) caried out by managers in virtually all productive organizations (Ch. 1)

Managerial roles specific categories of managerial behavior (for example, acting as a figurehead, leader, liaison, nerve center, disseminator, spokesperson, entrepreneur, disturbance handler, resource allocator, and negotiator) (Ch. 1)

Managing diversity process of helping all employees, including women and minorities, reach their full potential (Ch. 3)

Master production schedule an authoritative statement of how many end items are to be produced and when (Ch. 18)

Material requirements planning computerized manufacturing planning and control system (Ch. 18)

Matrix an organization structure in which vertical and horizontal lines of authority are combined (Ch. 9)

Measurementship political maneuvering motivated by a desire to "look good," even if it means manipulating reports and control data (Ch. 16)

Mechanistic organizations organizations that are rigid in design and have strong bureaucratic qualities (Ch. 9)

Media richness a media's capacity to convey information and promote learning (Ch. 11)

Mentor an individual who systematically develops a subordinate's abilities through intensive tutoring, coaching, and guidance (Ch. 14)

Motivation the psychological process that gives behavior purpose and direction (Ch. 12)

Motivation to manage desire to succeed in performing managerial functions and roles; one of the three elements of the basic formula for managerial success (Ch. 1)

Multimedia computer a combination personal computer, television, videocassette recorder, and compact-disc player (Ch. 17)

Multinational company (MNC) business that has strategic control over production/marketing facilities in two or more countries (Ch. 19)

Multivariate analysis a research technique used to determine how a combination of variables interacts to cause a particular outcome (Ch. 2)

Network organization only function is coordination of subcontracted production/marketing operations (Ch. 9)

New social contract assumption that employer-employee relationship will be a shorter-term one based on convenience, rather than for life (Ch. 3)

Noise any interference with the normal flow of understanding from one person to another (Ch. 11)

Nonprogrammed decisions those decisions that are made in complex, important, and nonroutine situations, often under circumstances that are new and largely unfamiliar (Ch. 7)

Norms general standards of conduct that help individuals judge what is right or wrong or good or bad in a given social setting (Ch. 13)

Objective a specific commitment to achieve a measurable result within a given time frame (Ch. 5)

Objective probabilities probabilities that are derived mathematically from reliable historical data (Ch. 7)

Open system an entity that depends on the surrounding environment for survival (for example, the human body or an organization) (Ch. 2)

Operational approach a production-oriented area of management dedicated to improving efficiency and cutting waste (Ch. 2)

Operational planning the process of determining how specific tasks can best be accomplished on time with available resources (Ch. 5)

Operations management the process of transforming material and human resources into useful goods and services (Ch. 2)

Optimize systematically identifying the solution with the best combination of benefits (Ch. 7)

Organic organizations organizations that tend to be quite fluid and flexible in structure (Ch. 9)

Organization a system of consciously coordinated activities or forces of two or more persons (Ch. 8)

Organization chart a diagram of an organization's official positions and formal lines of authority (Ch. 8)

Organization development (OD) planned change programs intended to help people and organizations function more effectively (Ch. 15)

Organizational behavior a modern approach to management that attempts to determine the causes of human work behavior and translate the results into effective management techniques (Ch. 2)

Organizational culture shared values, beliefs, and language that create a common identity and sense of community (Ch. 8)

Organizational decline a weakened condition resulting from resource and/or demand restrictions and mismanagement (Ch. 8)

Organizational effectiveness being effective, efficient, satisfying, adaptive and developing, and ultimately surviving (Ch. 8)

Organizational politics the pursuit of self-interest at work in the face of real or imagined opposition (Ch. 13)

Organizational productivity the ratio of an organization's total output to total input, adjusted for inflation, for a specified period of time (Ch. 1)

Organizational socialization the process through which outsiders are transformed into accepted insiders (Ch. 8)

Organizational values shared beliefs about what the organization stands for (Ch. 8)

Organizing the structuring of a coordinated system of authority relationships and task responsibilities (Ch. 9)

Ostracism rejection from the group; figuratively, the capital punishment of group dynamics (Ch. 13)

Outplacement a practice which involves helping displaced employees polish their job-seeking skills to increase their chances of finding suitable employment promptly (Ch. 8)

Participative management empowering employees to assume greater control of the workplace (Ch. 12)

Perception the process by which an individual gives meaning to his environment (Ch. 11)

Perceptual defense the perceptual screening out of environmental stimuli (Ch. 11)

Perceptual organization a perceptual process whereby otherwise meaningless and disorganized stimuli are arranged into meaningful patterns (Ch. 11)

Perceptual set forming a lasting impression from limited information (Ch. 11)

Performance appraisal the process of evaluating individual job performance as a basis for making objective personel decisions (Ch. 10)

Personal computer a desktop or smaller computer operated by an individual (Ch. 17)

PERT an acronym for Program Evaluation and Review Technique; a graphic sequencing and scheduling tool for large, complex, and nonroutine projects (Ch. 5)

PERT event a performance milestone representing the start or finish of some activity (Ch. 5)

PERT time estimated time for the completion of PERT activities (Ch. 5)

Plan a specific, documented intention consisting of an objective and an action statement (Ch. 5)

Planning the process of preparing for change and coping with uncertainty by formulating future courses of action (Ch. 5)

Planning horizon the time that elapses between the formulation and the execution of a planned activity (Ch. 5)

Political risk assessment the systematic means of assessing and managing the political risks of foreign direct investment or international business (Ch. 19)

Polycentric attitude a host-country orientation based on the assumption that local managers know what is best for their operations because cultures are so different (Ch. 19)

Polychronic time a perception of time as flexible, elastic, and multidimensional (Ch. 19)

Positive reinforcement the encouragement of a specific behavior by immediately following it with a consequence that the individual finds pleasing (Ch. 14)

Power the ability to marshal the human, informational, and material resources to get something done (Ch. 14)

Priorities a ranking of goals or objectives in order of importance (Ch. 5)

Proactive social responsibility strategy taking the initiative with new programs that serve as models for the industry (Ch. 4)

Problem the difference between an actual state of affairs and a desired state of affairs (Ch. 7)

Problem solving the conscious process of bringing the actual situation closer to the desired situation (Ch. 7)

Process layout production arrangement in which tools and machines are grouped by function (Ch. 18)

Product design the process of creating a set of product specifications appropriate to the demands of the situation (Ch. 18)

Product layout an assembly line arrangement involving progressive steps (Ch. 18)

Product life cycle a graphic representation of the sequential rise and fall of a product's sales and profit (Ch. 6)

Product technology the development of a working prototype (the second step in the three-step inovation process) (Ch. 3)

Production planning the process of formulating a resource transformation system that will effectively and efficiently meet the forecasted demands for goods and services (Ch. 18)

Production technology the development of a production process that creates a profitable quantity-quality-price relationship (the third step in the three-step innovation process) (Ch. 3)

Programmed decisions those decisions that are repetitive and routine and can be made with decision rules (Ch. 7)

Protectionism fending off foreign competition with import quotas, tariffs, and other trade restrictions (Ch. 3)

Purchasing the procurement of raw materials, subcomponents, equipment, and services required to accomplish organizational objectives (Ch. 18)

Quality control the process of ensuring that goods and services actually conform to the design specifications (Ch. 18)

Quality control circles voluntary problem-solving groups committed to improving quality and reducing costs (Ch. 12)

Reactive changes changes made in response to unexpected situations (Ch. 15)

Reactive social responsibility strategy denying responsibility and resisting change (Ch. 4)

Real-time processing processing data as transactions occur (Ch. 17)

Realistic job preview an honest explanation of what a job actually entails (Ch. 12)

Referent power compliance based on charisma or personal identification (Ch. 14)

Refreezing the process in organization development (OD) of following up on problems, complaints, unanticipated side effects, and any lingering resistance (Ch. 15)

Response uncertainty a type of environmental uncertainty which relates to being able to predict the consequences of a particular decision or organizational response (Ch. 5)

Reward power gaining compliance through rewards (Ch. 14)

Rewards the material and psychological payoffs for doing something (Ch. 12)

Role a socially determined prescription for behavior in a specific position (Ch. 13)

Role analysis the systematic clarification of interdependent modes of behavior in organization development (OD) (Ch. 15)

Satisfice resolving a problem by settling for a solution that is good enough rather than the best possible (Ch. 7)

Scenario analysis the preparation and study of written descriptions of alternative but equally likely future conditions (Ch. 6)

Scientific management developing performance standards on the basis of systematic observation and experimentation (Ch. 2)

Selectivity a sensory screening process that allows one to sort out and mentally process only certain details in one's surroundings (Ch. 11)

Self-managed teams high-performance teams that assume traditional managerial duties such as staffing and planning (Ch. 12)

Sexual harassment unwanted sexual attention that creates an offensive or intimidating work environment (Ch. 10)

Semantics the study of meaning in words (Ch. 11)

Situational analysis finding the organization's niche by performing a SWOT analysis (Ch. 6)

Small business an independently owned and managed profit-seeking enterprise employing fewer than 100 persons (App. A)

Span of control the number of people who report directly to a given manager (Ch. 8)

Staffing human resource planning, acquisition, and development aimed at providing the talent necessary for organizational success (Ch. 9)

Stakeholder audit identifying all parties possibly impacted by the organization (Ch. 4)

State uncertainty unpredictable environment (Ch. 5)

Statistical process control measuring and managing normal and abnormal variations in production processes (Ch. 18)

Strategic business unit (SBU) an organizational subunit that acts like an independent business in all major respects, including the formulation of its own strategic plans (Ch. 9)

Strategic changes altering the overall shape or direction of the organization (Ch. 15)

Strategic management the ongoing process of ensuring a competitively superior fit between the organization and its ever-changing environment (Ch. 6)

Strategic planning the process of determining how to pursue the organization's long-term goals with the resources expected to be available (Ch. 5)

Strategy the pattern of decisions a firm makes (Ch. 6)

Stress an adaptive response, mediated by individual characteristics and/or psychological processes, that is a consequence of any external action, situation or event that places special physical and/or psychological demands upon a person (App. B)

Structured interview a series of job-related questions with predetermined answers that are consistently applied across all interviews for a particular job (Ch. 10)

Synergy the 2 + 2 = 5 effect wherein the whole is greater than the sum of its parts (Ch. 6)

System a collection of parts that operate interdependently to achieve a common purpose (Ch. 2)

Task force multilevel and/or cross-functional team assigned to a specific problem (Ch. 11)

Team building an organization development (OD) process for developing work group maturity and effectiveness (Ch. 15)

Technological displacement the loss of jobs because of automation (Ch. 3)

Technology all the tools and ideas available for extending the natural physical and mental reach of humankind (Ch. 3)

Telecommuting work is sent to the employee's home computer via telephone modem instead of the employee commuting to a central office (Ch. 17)

Terminal value an enduring belief that a certain end-state of existence is worth striving for and attaining (Ch. 14)

Theory Y McGregor's optimistic assumptions about working people (Ch. 2)

Time series forecasts estimates of future values in a statistical sequence (Ch. 6)

Total quality control (TQC) a strongly held belief that errors, if any, should be caught and corrected at the source (where the work is performed) (Ch. 18)

Training the process of changing employee behavior, attitudes, or opinions through some type of guided experience (Ch. 10)

Transformational leaders visionaries who challenge people to do exceptional things (Ch. 14)

Transience Toffler's term for an accelerating rate of change (Ch. 3)

Trend analysis the hypothetical extension of a past pattern of events or time series into the future (Ch. 6)

Trust a belief in the integrity, character, or ability of others that is a key to group effectiveness (Ch. 13)

Unfreezing in organizaton development (OD), the process of preparing the members of a social system for change and neutralizing initial resistance (Ch. 15)

Universal process approach assumes all organizations require the same rational management process (Ch. 2)

Upward communication a process of systematically encouraging subordinates to share with management their feelings and ideas (Ch. 11)

Values abstract ideals that shape an individual's thinking and behavior (Ch. 4)

Variable costs costs that vary directly with the firm's production and sales (Ch. 5)

Whistle blowing the practice of reporting perceived unethical practices to outsiders such as the press, government agencies, or public interest groups (Ch. 4)

Whitemail bribe a large sum of money used to buy influence in high places (Ch. 19)

Work flow layout the process of determining the physical arrangement of the productive system (Ch. 18)

Name Index

Baker, Michael, 377n
Baker, Russell W., 134n
Baker, Timothy L., 345n
Baldor Electric, 398
Baldwin, Norman, A9n
Balkin, David B., 416n
Ball, Ben C., Jr., 201n
Ball-Rokeach, Sandra J., 135n
Ballen, Kate, 102n
Baloff, Nicholas, 417n
Bandrowski, James F., 236n
Barbard, Chester I., 252–253
Barbetta, Frank, 68n
Barkdull, C.W., 308n
Barker, Jonathan, 559
Barnard, Chester I., 55–56, 69n, 235n, 243, 272n
Barnes, A. Keith, 483n
Barnes, Louis B., 449n
Barnevik, Percy, 627–628
Barnlund, Dean C., 659n, 660n
Baron, Alma S., B8n
Barrett, Gerald V., 343n
Barron, Cynthia L., 343n
Barry, Camille, 369
Bart, Christopher K., 549n
Bartimo, Jim, 581n
Bartlett, Christopher A., 308n
Bartol, Kathryn M., 35n
Bartolomé, Fernando, 376n, 442, 449n
Barton, Allen H., A9n
Bass, Bernard M., 470, 471, 483n, 516n
Bassman, Emily S., 342n
Baum, Laurie, 309n
Bavarian Motor Works (BMW), 6, 595
Beatty, Richard W., 326, 343n, 344n
Beauchamp, Marc, 619n
Beaver, Donald L., Jr., 223
Beckhard, Richard, 515n
Bedeian, Arthur G., 308n
Beech-Nut Nutrition Corporation, 110
Beeman, Don R., 448n
Beer, Michael, 328, 344n, 515n, 516n
Begley, Sharon, 13, 104n
Behling, Orlando C., 482n
Behn Prescot, 417n
Bell, Chip R., 622n
Belohlav, James A., 345n
Beltramini, Richard F., 135n
Ben & Jerry's Homemade, Inc., 119, 129, 403
Ben-Shakhar, Gershon, 343n

Benbow, Anne, 658–659
Benfari, Robert C., 483n
Benham, William, 574
Benke, Ralph L., Jr., 534
Bennis, Warren G., 272n, 309n, 448n, 481n
Benson, Herbert, B9n
Benson, Philip G., 309n
Berenbeim, Ronald E., 136n
Bergmann, Thomas J., 516n
Bergsman, Steve, 345n
Berkowitz, Eric N., 135n
Bernardin, H. John, 326, 343n, 344n
Bernstein, Aaron, 50, 102n, 255, 273n, 565, 660n
Bernstein, Peter L., 104n
Berry, Leonard L., 614, 622n
Berry, Waldron, 201n
Berryman-Fink, Cynthia, 377n
Berss, Marcia, 548n
Bertalanffy, Ludwig von, 69n
Bettendorf, Robert F., B9n
Betti, John A., 531
Betz, Ellen L., 415n
Beyer, Janice M., 266
Billard, Mary, 23, 103n
Bird, Frederick B., 135n
Black, J. Stewart, 662n
Blackwell, Kate, 136n
Blair, Edward, 342n
Blair, Karen, 550n
Blake, Robert R., 462, 464, 482n, 504, 515n
Blanchard, Kenneth, 483n
Blank, Sally J., 272n
Blau, Peter M., 272n
Blazey, Mark L., 620n
Blinder, Alan S., 27, 36n
Block, Barbara, 234n
Blocklyn, Paul L., 320, 376n
Blondell, Michael, 123
Bluedorn, Allen C., 68n
Bluestone, Mimi, 104n, 200n
The Body Shop, 132–133
Boeing Company, 260–261, 406, 439–440, 441, 585–586
Boesky, Ivan, 87, 107
Bohl, Marilyn, 171n
Boll, Dennis M., 549n
Bologna, Jack, 171n
Bolon, Donald S., 661n
Bolwijn, P.T., 620n
Bond, Michael Harris, 647, 661n
Bonsach, Robert, 620n
Booth, William, 35n
Borrus, Amy, 660n
Bowen, David E., 619n

Bowman, James S., 135n, 417n
Boyacigiller, Nakiye Avdan, 661n
Boyce, T.A., 202n
Boyle, Rosemarie, 660n
Bracey, Harry, B., Jr., 549n
Bracker, Jeffrey, 105n, 273n
Braddock, Richard, 199
Bradford, David L., 481n
Bradspies, Robert W., 548n
Brady, Rose, 660n
Brainerd, Paul, 281
Brandt, Richard, 105n, 481n, 565, 580n, 581n, 582n, 583n, 620n
Breaugh, James A., 416n
Brecher, John, 345n
Bremner, Brian, 170n, A9n
Brennan, Bernard F., 396
Brenner, Steven N., 135n
Bridwell, Lawrence G., 415n
Brigham, Eugene F., 549n
Brightman, Harvey J., 234n
Brinkerhoff, Robert O., 29 (fig.)
British Airways, 443
British Petroleum (BP), 276–277
Brookmire, David A., 342n
Broughton, James, 170n
Brown, Abby, 345n
Brown, Courtney C., 134n
Brown, David S., 376n
Brown, Elicia, 550n
Brown, Robert J., 660n
Brownell, Judy, 378n
Bruno, Albert V., A9n
Buchholz, Rogene A., 135n
Buchholz, Steve, 449n
Budhraja, Vikram, 195
Buehler, William F., 67
Buell, Barbara, 234n, 307n
Buffa, Elwood S., 597, 620n
Buller, Paul F., 342n
Burck, Charles G., 417n
Burger King, 173
Burgess, Charles, 103n
Burgess, John, 583n
Burke, James, 117
Burke, Jeffrey W., 69n
Burke, R.J., 483n
Burke, W. Warner, 496, 502, 515n
Burlingham, Bo, 133n, 549n
Burnett, C. Don, 170n
Burns, James McGregor, 469–470, 483n
Burns, Tom, 279, 280, 307n
Burt, David N., 621n
Burton, Amy A., 342n
Busch, Michael C., 342n
Bush, George, 220, 319, 457, A8
Busquet, Ann M., 23

Kapstein, Jonathan, 104n, 414n, 619n, 659n
Karmarker, Uday, 621n
Karp, H.B., 515n
Karren, Ronald J., 415n
Kast, Fremont E., 69n, 255, 272n
Katz, Daniel, 272n, 307n
Katz, Jennifer, 235n
Katz, Michael, 101n, 102n, 447n
Katzell, Raymond A., 414n
Kaul, James D., 69n
Keating, David E., 417n
Keeley, Michael, 273n
Keenan, A., 377n
Keidel, Robert W., 308n
Keim, Gerald D., 134n
Kelleher, Herb, 347–348
Keller, John J., 68n, 308n, 514n
Keller, Robert T., 482n
Kellinghusen, Georg, 201n
Kelly, H.H., 376n
Kelly, Joseph, 581n
Kelly, Kevin, 376n
Kennedy, Allan A., 273n, 274n
Kenney, Robert I., 207
Kent, Cilla Duff, 133n
Kentucky Fried Chicken, 486
Keon, Thomas L., 415n
Kernan, Mary C., 343n
Keys, Bernard, 481n
Khan, M. Riaz, A6, A9n
Kiam, Victor, A4
Kidder, Rushworth M., 102n
Kiechel, Walter, III, 103n, 377n, 516n
Kiefer, Charles, 515n
Kikoski, John F., 378n
Kilman, Ralph H., 515n
Kim, Myung U., 261, 273n
Kimball, Ranch, 92
Kimberly-Clark, 336
Kindel, Stephen, 234n
King, Barry E., 621n
King, Paula J., 113 (fig.), 134n
King, William R., 200n
Kinicki, Angelo, 105n, 273n
Kipnis, David, 481n
Kirkland, Richard I., 272n
Kirkland, Richard I., Jr., 447n
Kirkpatrick, David, 103n, 416n, 581n, A9n, B9n
Kirrane, Diane, 345n
Kirrane, Peter R., 580n
Kizilos, Peter, 483n
Klein, Deborah P., 416n
Kleiner, Brian H., 378n
Knickerbocker, Brad, 104n
Knight, Henry C., 549n

Knocke, Alison A., 367
Knotts, Rose, 661n
Knowlton, Christopher, 234n
Koenig, Richard, 417n
Koestler, Arthur, 235n
Kolton, Ellen, 308n
Konrad, Alison M., 344n
Konrad, Walecia, 103n, 170n, 272n
Koontz, Harold, 548n
Koopman, Cheryl, 502
Koretz, Gene, 28 (fig.), 36n, 103n, 662n, A9n
Korman, Abraham K., 482n
Koslowsky, Meni, 308n
Kotter, John P., 481n, 496, 515n
Kouzes, James M., 35n, 460, 482n
Kovach, Kenneth A., 35n
Kovsky, Steve, 550n
Kowalska, Dorota, 331
Koys, Daniel J., 342n
Kozmetsky, George, 135n, A9n
Kraar, Louis, 661n
Krainik, Ardis, 480
Krajewski, Lee J., 621n
Kram, Kathy E., 473, 483n
Kramlinger, Tom, 483n
Kraut, Allen I., 35n
Kravetz, Dennis J., 342n
Kreitner, Robert, 105n, 273n, 416n, 484n, 572, 580n, 614, B6
Kroc, Ray, 173–174, 264
Kroenke, David M., 581n
Kubin, Konrad W., 661n
Kumpe, T., 620n
Kupfer, Andrew, 272n, 559

Labich, Kenneth, 50, 201n, 255, 378n, 619n, A9n
Ladd, Everett Carll, A9n
Lancaster, Lisa L., 273n
Landler, Mark, 210
Landon, Lucia, 418n
Langley, Monica, 68n
Lansing, Paul, 662n
Larsen, Janet K., 349, 376n
Larson, Erik W., 308n
Larson, James S., 377n
Latack, Janina C., 415n
Latham, Gary P., 171n, 344n, 415n
Laurent, André, 376n
Lautenbach, Terence R., 566, 582n
Lawler, Edward E., III, 301, 309n, 415n, 417n
Lawrence, Barbara S., 68n
Lawrence, Paul R., 282, 307n
Lawrence, Robert, 92
Lawrence, Stephanie, 342n
Lawrence, William, 146

Leana, Carrie R., 308n, 448n, 481n
Leathers, Dale G., 377n
Lebas, Michel, 548n
Lechner, Anita, 136n
Lederer, Albert L., 582n
Ledford, Gerald E., Jr., 417n
Lee, Charles, 343n
Lee, Chris, 344n, 417n
Lee, Cynthia, 415n
Lee, Dinah, 660n
Lee, Mary E., 661n
Lee, Robert E., 398
Lei, David, 660n
Leibowitz, Zandy B., B9n
Leidecker, Joel K., A9n
Leigh, David R., 342n
Lemak, David, 105n, 273n
Lengel, Robert H., 352, 353, 376n
Lenway, Stefanie Ann, 661n
Leonard, Bill, 377n
Levering, Robert, 101n, 102n, 307n, 447n
Levi, Ariel S., 621n
Levi, Michael, 87
Levi Strauss & Company, 311–312 470
Levin, Irwin P., 234n
Levine, David I., 417n
Levine, Dennis B., 107, 125, 133n
Levine, John M., 447n
Levine, Jonathan, 660n
Levine, Jonathan B., 34n, 620n
Levine, Mel, 200n
Levinson, Marc, 104n
Lewin, Kurt, 482n
Lewis, Geoff, 68n, 170n
Lewis, Phillip V., 135n
Lewis Galoob Toys Inc., 303
Liang, Ting-Peng, 582n
Lieberman, David, 200n
Lieblich, Julia, 637
Liebrenz, Marilyn L., 661n
Lincoln, James R., 661n
Lincoln Electric, 383–384
Linden, Eugene, 35n
Lippitt, Ronald, 482n
Litchfield, Randall, 581n
Litterer, Joseph A., 272n, 447n
Lituchy, Terri R., 415n
Litzinger, William D., 135n
Liz Claiborne, Inc., 190, 313
L.L. Bean, 527
Locke, Edwin A., 69n, 171n, 391, 415n
Lockheed, 294
Lockwood, Chris, 105n, 273n
Lockwood, Diane L., 416n
Lombardo, Michael M., 35n

Subject Index